Two year olds of 2012

28TH EDITION

Two year olds of 2012

28TH EDITION

STEVE TAPLIN

Raceform

FRONT COVER: Johnny Murtagh on Lightening Pearl
wins the 2011 Cheveley Park Stakes, Newmarket.
© Cranhamphoto.com

BACK COVER: The author with Andrew Balding at Tattersalls

Published in 2012 by Raceform
High Street, Compton, Newbury, Berkshire, RG20 6NL

A catalogue record for this book is available from the British Library.

ISBN 978-1-908216-34-2

Designed by Fiona Pike

Printed and bound in the UK by the MPG Books Group.

Contents

Foreword

Steve Taplin's excellent 'Two Year Olds' publication has become part of the flat racing season. It is designed to be an informative guide to what might happen in any particular year, but has become just as illuminating when used for retrospective purposes!

It is always fun to look back on what various trainers thought of their horses well before they really knew! Michael Bell was fairly certain that Motivator was a decent horse, Richard Hannon was damned sure Canford Cliffs was a star in the making and whilst a little more reserved in his assessment, one feels that John Oxx had more than an inkling over Sea The Stars.

As a result of its retrospective qualities I would imagine that most purchasers of this book will resist the temptation to throw it away when the current subjects of this edition have finished their juvenile campaign. In fact, it would not surprise me if the book still had a place on the bookshelf in ten or even 20 years time!

At this very early stage of a two-year-old's career it is almost impossible to predict how each and every horse will turn out, but at the same time it is highly unlikely that a really good one will have escaped their trainer's notice and that is what makes this book valuable to punters and racing enthusiasts alike.

The other thing worth noting about this publication is the willingness of almost every trainer in the land to talk openly about their horses to its author. The reason for this is that everyone who knows him recognises Steve Taplin to be a genuine lover of horseracing. This book is a well-researched labour of love that has developed into an institution.

I hope that *Two Year Olds of 2012* will not only prove to be a valuable guide to the year ahead, but will stay on your bookshelf for many years to come.

Andrew Balding

Introduction

Welcome to the 28th edition of *Two-Year-Olds*, a book that aims to provide punters, racing fans and breeding enthusiasts with information they are likely to find interesting, informative and hopefully valuable throughout the year.

It is very nice indeed for me to have Andrew Balding endorsing the book this year. I've been visiting Park House Stables in Kingsclere for a good few years now and I've always been given a warm welcome there, both by Andrew and his father Ian before him. The great trainer John Porter was at Kingsclere for almost 40 years before his retirement in 1905. However you may be surprised to hear that I never met him!

One of Racing's 'feel good' stories in 2012 came when champion jockey Paul Hanagan became first jockey to Sheikh Hamdan al Maktoum. Paul gets to ride some of the best horses in the UK and in return the Sheikh is getting a top jockey and one of the nicest men in the sport. I hope their partnership turns out to be very successful.

My racing partnership had four horses in 2011 and two of them managed to win three races between them. Not a bad effort at all from a small outfit like ours, if I do say so myself. If anyone reading this is interested in having a small share in a racehorse, do please bear us in mind.

Those trainers who are either new to the book this year, or haven't been in for a while, are Hans Adielsson, Alan Bailey, Keith Dalgleish, Simon Dow, Ron Harris, Dan Kubler, David O'Meara, Tim Pitt, Hugo Palmer, Derek Shaw, James Tate, Richard Whitaker and Mahmood Al Zarooni. In terms of the number of trainer interviews I conduct for the book, things have gone from strength to strength over the last few years. So much so that this year you'll find comments from 87 trainers – seven more than last year. Gleaning information from so many trainers in a little over three weeks takes some doing, as I'm sure you can imagine! I do appreciate the help of each and every one of them and it's nice to be accepted back by the trainers each year, be it at the yards, in their homes or on the phone.

Last year the 'Bloodstock Experts' section of the book was once again a very good source of winners. Out of the 69 selections that actually ran, 35 of them won (a shade over 50%), representing a slight improvement on the previous year (32 from 70).

In the main body of the book you will notice a 'star rating' for each of the two-year-olds. Those with three stars or more warrant particular inspection. Please note there is no star rating for those two-year-olds that don't have a comment from the trainer. I think to give them a rating just based on the pedigree is too speculative.

The following is a rough guide to my description of the ability of family members mentioned in the pedigree assessment of every two-year-old, based upon professional ratings. Please note that these descriptions are standard throughout the book in the vast majority of cases, but there are instances where I rely upon my own judgement of each horse's rating.

Below 60 = moderate
60 – 69 = modest
70 – 79 = fair
80 – 89 = quite useful
90 – 99 = fairly useful
100 – 107 = useful
108 – 112 = very useful
113 – 117 = smart
118 – 122 = very smart
123 – 127 = high-class
128 – 134 = top-class
135 and above = outstanding

The two-year-olds in this book are listed under their trainers and my aim has been to choose those horses most likely to be winners. There are several horses to follow lists, such as the sections 'Fifty To Follow' and 'Star Two-Year-Olds'. These are always useful for those who want to follow a select number of horses. The 'Bloodstock Experts Mark Your Card', is a particularly fruitful section for pinpointing winners and note also that many trainers suggest their 'Bargain Buy'. My only stipulation is that the horse cannot have cost more than 25,000 guineas at the yearling sales. It's always a bit of a problem as to what price I should set. Many trainers won't have a single horse costing that amount, whilst others don't have any below it!

To make it easier to find a specific horse the book is comprehensively indexed. So you'll find an index of the horses, their dams and their sires.

The book is divided into the following sections:

- Fifty To Follow.
- Ten to Follow in Ireland.
- Star Two-Year-Olds. This system gives an instant appraisal of the regard in which a horse is held. Those horses awarded the maximum of five stars are listed here.
- The Bloodstock Experts Mark Your Card. Bloodstock agents and stud managers suggest potentially smart two-year-olds bought or raised by them.
- Bargain Buys. A list of relatively cheaply bought two-year-olds the trainers feel will turn out to be good deals.
- Two-Year-Olds of 2012. The main section of the book, with each two-year-old listed under the trainer. *Trainers' comments (when given) are in italics after the pedigree assessments.* Readers should bear in mind that all the trainers' comments come from my interviews, which took part in late March and early April.
- Stallion Reference, detailing the racing and stud careers of sires with two-year-old representatives in the book.
- Stallion Index.
- Racing Trends. An analysis of some juvenile events that regularly highlight the stars of the future. It includes a list of three-year-olds to follow this season.
- Index of Two-Year-Olds.
- Index of Dams.

There are inevitably some unnamed horses in the book, but please access my website www.stevetaplin.co.uk throughout the season for updates on those horses named after the book was published.

I must say a big 'Thank You' to the racing and stud secretaries for their assistance and, as I mentioned earlier in this Introduction, to the trainers for being so helpful during my interviews with them.

In particular, I must also thank my friend Hilda Marshall for her sterling efforts in helping me get the book published on time.

Researched and compiled by
Steve Taplin BA (Hons).

Fifty to Follow

The trainers have spoken highly about this choice selection of two-year-olds.

AGERZAM
br.c. Holy Roman Emperor – Epiphany (Zafonic). "He's in fast work and he's a strong, quite precocious colt. Definitely a sharp, early type, he goes along OK and I could see him being out before the end of May. He's got a bit of speed and I'm sure he'll win races this year". **Jeremy Noseda.**

ARBEEL
b.f. Royal Applause – Waafiah (Anabaa). "She's very nice ... a big, leggy filly, seven furlongs in August time should suit her. She'd be one of my picks from the whole stable and she could have a bit of class". **Peter Chapple-Hyam.**

ASSEMBLY
ch.c. Kyllachy – Constitute (Gone West). "This is a nice horse, he's tall ... but he's a nice mover. A classy colt for the second half of the season". **William Haggas.**

BIT OF A GIFT (FR)
b.c. Dark Angel – Dilag (Almutawakel). "A nice type of horse ... he's a strong 2-y-o that moves nicely ... I like him. With his size and pedigree you'd have to hope he could go a bit". **Roger Varian.**

BORNEAN (IRE)
ch.c. Street Cry – Calando (Storm Cat). "This is a strong two-year-old type who is loving his work at the moment and he should be one of our earlier runners. He has a very good temperament, which will help him too". **Mahmood Al Zarooni.**

CANON LAW (IRE)
b.c. Holy Roman Emperor – Delisha (Salse). "I like him a lot, he's very well put-together and he'll be working in May with the idea of racing him in June. He's very likeable and looks like being speedy as well". **Luca Cumani.**

CODEBREAKER
"A really nice horse, he looks very much like the sire and reflects all the nice things about him ... I'm looking forward to him". **Hughie Morrison.**

COUNT PALATINE (IRE)
b.c. Holy Roman Emperor – Blue Iris (Petong). "He's from a fast family, he goes well and he already looks like he's got an engine. A neat, level, strong-quartered five furlong 2-y-o type". **Andrew Balding.**

DREAM ALLY (IRE)
b.c. Oasis Dream – Alexander Alliance (Danetime). "A lovely colt ... I'm very taken with him and he's coping very easily with all the work we're giving him ... and we like him a lot. **Jedd O'Keeffe.**

DUST WHIRL
b.c. Bahamian Bounty – Dust (Green Desert). "Right now he's one of our nicest 2-y-o's, he goes well and he'll be out in April. Five furlongs is his trip and he might make the Supersprint". **Richard Hannon.**

ESTIFZAAZ (IRE)
b.c. Invincible Spirit – Lulua (Bahri). "They paid quite a bit for him at the sales and I'm not surprised because he's an attractive looking colt. We'll start him at six furlongs in May and it would be nice to think he could be one for Royal Ascot". **Charles Hills.**

EXCELERATION
b.c. Exceed And Excel – Saabiq (Grand Slam). "He works extremely well ... and we wouldn't be afraid to take him somewhere nice like the Dante meeting at York in May. Very impressive in his homework, he's a big, strong colt and a fabulous mover. Everything comes easy to him". **James Tate.**

EXCELLENT HIT
b.c. Exceed And Excel – Broadway Hit (Sadler's Wells). "He's a lovely horse. A scopey, seven furlong type 2-y-o with a lovely action, a great brain and a smashing attitude. One of those types of horses that never seems to get tired. Very likeable". **David Simcock.**

FIRST SECRETARY

b.f. Nayef – Spinning Queen (Spinning World). "A very attractive filly, she moves well and surprises me because she looks more precocious than I expected ... I like her and she's done very well since she came here". **Roger Charlton.**

FUNK SOUL BROTHER

b.c. Cockney Rebel – Sweet Afton (Mujadil). "He's an attractive colt and we've always liked him ... the more work he's done the better he's become and he's taken it all well". **Charles Hills.**

GOLD HUNTER (IRE)

b.c. Invincible Spirit – Goldthroat (Zafonic). "This colt is coming together nicely and is showing pleasing speed. He is strong with a good attitude and all being well should make his debut in May". **Saeed bin Suroor.**

GRAPHIC GUEST

ch.f. Dutch Art – Makara (Lion Cavern). "A very nice filly by Dutch Art. She's certainly sharp and I think she's pretty good. Strong, mature and ready to go". **Mick Channon.**

GRASPED

ch.f. Zamindar – Imroz (Nureyev). "This is a nice filly and a good mover that should make a 2-y-o later on". **Sir Henry Cecil.**

HASBAH (IRE)

b.f. Cape Cross – Gimasha (by Cadeaux Genereux). "A real nice filly, she does everything well ... for a Cape Cross she's very sharp and she goes real well". **Peter Chapple-Hyam.**

HENRIETTA ROSE (USA)

b.f. Henrythenavigator – Shermeen (Desert Style). "In fast work now, she's a neat filly and definitely a 2-y-o. She goes about her job and will definitely be winning this year. Very much a sprinter type". **Jeremy Noseda.**

JAMMY GUEST

b.c. Duke Of Marmalade – Ardbrae Lady (Overbury). "He's the apple of my eye at the moment. A serious horse and his aim will be the Chesham Stakes at Royal Ascot ... He does everything effortlessly, he's very straightforward and mentally he's grown up already". **George Margarson.**

JILLNEXTDOOR (IRE)

b.f. Henrythenavigator – Royal Shyness (Royal Academy). "She's very nice indeed and she's in the top group of our early 2-y-o's. Very mature, she's not over-big and she's just a smashing-looking filly with a lot of quality". **Mick Channon.**

KIMBERELLA

b.c. Kyllachy – Gleam Of Light (Danehill). "He looks like having the speed to win over five furlongs, he has a good temperament and he's a real model 2-y-o type". **Michael Bell**

LA DANZA

b.f. Country Reel – Freedom Song (Singspiel). "I think she's real good filly – probably the best I've got ... six or seven furlongs should suit her from the mid-season onwards". **Alan Bailey.**

MAJEED

b.c. Mount Nelson – Clever Millie (Cape Canaveral). "He's probably the most attractive 2-y-o in the yard – an absolute belter to look at. He has a very fluent, very natural action ... I'm very pleased with him, he's a lovely horse". **David Simcock.**

MAKAFEH

b.c. Elusive Quality – Demisemiquaver (Singspiel). "A very nice horse, he goes well, he seems to have speed and I'm very pleased with him. He's very forward ... everything's good about him". **Luca Cumani.**

MIRLO BLANCO

gr.c. Dark Angel – Danzolin (Danzero). "A lovely horse and a good mover, he'll make a 2-y-o over six and seven furlongs". **Richard Fahey.**

MORAWIJ

ch.c. Exceed And Excel – Sister Moonshine (FR) (Piccolo). "He really is a very mature horse for his age – a very strong, thick-bodied colt. He'd be one of the most forward in the yard and he ought to be racing in May". **Roger Varian.**

MUJADORA

b.f. Mujadil – Golden Ora (Nordance). "She's a nice 2-y-o, she's quite sharp, goes well and I hope to go to the Supersprint with her". **William Haggas.**

MYSTERY BET
b.f. Kheleyf – Dancing Prize (Sadler's Wells). "She'll be a nice filly over six and seven furlongs this year. A good mover, we like her and she's done everything asked of her". **Richard Fahey.**

NARDIN
b.f. Royal Applause – Third Party (Terimon). "She's very nice. A strong, powerful filly and a beautiful mover, she'll be an early 2-y-o". **Ed Dunlop.**

NO JET LAG (IRE)
b.c. Johar – Desert Sky (Green Desert). "A nice horse ... he's done very well and I think he's a horse we can have some fun with from June onwards. He does everything nicely and even though he's a big horse he carries himself well, so he's a nice type". **David Lanigan.**

OVATORY
b.c. Acclamation – Millsini (Rossini). "He'd be one of the most forward that we've got and he'd have enough speed to run over five furlongs before moving up to six. He's a nice individual and although he cost a pretty penny he'll hopefully prove well worth it. Possibly a Royal Ascot 2-y-o if all goes well". **Amanda Perrett.**

PEARL BOUNTY (IRE)
ch.c. Bahamian Bounty – Roslea Lady (Alhaarth). "He's very nice, very forward, he has plenty of speed and we're hopeful of him being a decent 2-y-o. Small and sharp-looking, he's just a thoroughly nice 2-y-o type". **Andrew Balding.**

PEDRO SERRANO
b.c. Footstepsinthesand – Shaiyadima (Zamindar). "A very strong, big horse and an excellent mover ... he'll be out around July time over six furlongs. He looks a classy horse". **Henry Candy.**

RASKOVA (USA)
b.f. Henrythenavigator – Diamond Necklace (Unbridled's Song). "If we've only got one good 2-y-o this will be the one ... she's done everything right so far, she's a good-sized 2-y-o with good conformation". **William Jarvis.**

REQAABA
b.f. Exceed And Excel – Something Blue (Petong). "A speedy little thing, she's got a bit of 'zip' about her, she's been settled in everything she's been doing and she has a quick, low action". **John Gosden.**

RIOJA DAY (IRE)
b.c. Red Clubs – Dai E Dai (Seattle Dancer). "He's been working and he'll be on the racecourse in April. He's well-balanced and has a great temperament –so much so that you could do anything you want with him. A horse with natural speed, he looks all over a winner". **John Hills.**

ROYAL BAR
b.c. Royal Applause – Our Faye (College Chapel). "A nice horse out of a filly I trained to win seven races. This colt is sharp and early and I'll try to get a run into him in May, just to see if he's good enough to get to Royal Ascot". **Sylvester Kirk.**

SAGESSE
ch.f. Smart Strike – Summer Night (Nashwan). "I've had nearly all the foals out of the mare –they're good and the sire is good as well". **Sir Mark Prescott.**

SAVED BY THE BELL (IRE)
b.c. Teofilo – Eyrecourt (Efisio). "A lovely colt, he shows plenty of speed and he seems to have a lot of ability...I'd say he'll be running by early June". **Brian Meehan.**

SECRET SESSION (USA)
b.c. Mizzen Mast – Lynnwood Chase (Horse Chestnut). "At this stage I would say he's one of the nicest we have this year. He's strong, very straightforward and has the speed for six furlongs although he'll probably get a mile in time. A gorgeous horse, he's strong and compact – everything is there". **Marco Botti.**

SENATOR BONG
ch.c. Dutch Art – Sunley Gift (Cadeaux Genereux). "A bonny little colt that shouldn't take long before he's ready ... No 2-y-o I've got has done better, physically, than he has. Dutch Art is a prolific sire of 2-y-o winners and this is

a damn nice horse. He'll start off at five or six furlongs". **David Elsworth.**

SIR PRANCEALOT
b.c. Tamayuz – Mona Em (Catrail). "A lovely horse. Very sharp ... he goes well and you ought to see him a fair bit over five furlongs in the first few months of the season. A very nice colt". **Richard Hannon.**

SMOOTH HANDLE
ch.c. Dutch Art – Naomi Wildman (Kingmambo). "Dutch Art is such a good sire. This colt will probably be out in May, he's a five/six furlong sort and a proper 2-y-o". **Tom Dascombe.**

SWEEPING ROCK (IRE)
b.c. Rock Of Gibraltar – Sweeping Story (End Sweep). "This is a nice-looking horse, I think he was a good buy and I'm particularly keen on him ... this horse is coming along great and he's a good mover". **Marcus Tregoning.**

TALENT
ch.f. New Approach – Prowess (Peintre Celebre). "I'm a real fan of this filly, she's very attractive, has a good way about her ... and she's a neat filly with a bit of strength about her". **Ralph Beckett.**

THE MANX MISSILE
ch.c. Sakhee's Secret – Careless Freedom (Bertolini). "A very sharp colt from a speedy family, he's a well-muscled 2-y-o type. He's definitely got the speed for five furlongs and it's a question if he'll stay six. He's quick and was a January foal to boot". **Michael Bell.**

TOAST OF THE TOWN (IRE)
b.f. Duke Of Marmalade – Boast (Most Welcome). "She's gone through a growing stage but she's an attractive filly and a good mover that's showing a bit of class". **John Gosden.**

WENTWORTH (IRE)
b.c. Acclamation – Miss Corinne (Mark Of Esteem). "A very big, gorgeous-looking colt ... we're very excited about him". **Richard Hannon.**

Ten to Follow in Ireland

In 2011, six of the ten selections ran and four of them were winners. Let's hope a few more of them get to the racecourse this time.

ANTRIM (IRE)
b.c. *Iffraaj – Causeway Song (Giant's Causeway)*. "He's a nice, well-balanced colt that looks a real 2-y-o ... we like him, he has a good attitude and he goes well. A nice, straightforward, very professional horse". **Michael Halford.**

CALISSA (IRE)
b.f. *Danehill Dancer – Mauralakana (Muhtathir)*. A very nice filly, she's very well-bred and so far she's going really well ... fairly compact ... she looks the part and she has the pedigree to go with it". **Jessica Harrington.**

CLANCY AVENUE
b.c. *Henrythenavigator – Saintly Speech (Southern Halo)*. "A fine, big, strong horse. He looks like a horse that won't be short of speed and he goes well, so look out for him". **Tommy Stack.**

DAYMOOMA
ch.f. *Pivotal – Adaala (Sahm)*. "I like her an awful lot ... I trained the dam and all three of her foals and they've all won. I think this could be the best of them so far". **Kevin Prendergast.**

FLASHY APPROACH
ch.c. *New Approach – Flashy Wings (Zafonic)*. "A nice horse, he's very agile and has a very fluent action ... he'll certainly be out in the second half of the year. A nice colt". **John Oxx.**

HARASIYA (IRE)
br.f. *Pivotal – Hazariya (Xaar)*. "A very well-made, strong and mature filly. A good sort, it looks like she'll make a 2-y-o and she should show ability at two. She's a good looker and you'd be very happy with her". **John Oxx.**

MIDNIGHT THOUGHTS (USA)
b.f. *Henrythenavigator – Irresistible Jewel (Danehill)*. "A big, scopey filly, she's very nice and should be racing in July or August over seven furlongs". **Dermot Weld.**

PEARL TURN (USA)
b.f. *Bernardini – Turn Me Loose (Kris S)*. "A lovely filly with a lot of quality ... she'll be racing by the middle of the season over six/ seven furlongs and we like her a lot. **Ger Lyons.**

RASMEYAA (IRE)
ch.f. *New Approach – Posterity (Indian Ridge)*. "A very nice filly, she's big and has a lot of quality ... she looks like being a very nice 2-y-o". **Dermot Weld.**

ROCKABILLY RIOT (IRE)
b.c. *Footstepsinthesand – Zawariq (Marju)*. "A very straightforward colt, I love him to death and he'd be ready to go any time I wanted. He's typical of the sire and we've been very lucky with him ... we like him a lot". **Ger Lyons.**

Star Two-year-olds

The stars placed alongside each two-year-old in the main section of the book give the reader an instant appraisal of the regard in which they are held. The highest rating a horse can attain is five stars.

Bear in mind that some of the "Five Star" horses will be at their peak as three-year-olds, so keep an eye on them next year as well. Two excellent examples of this from last year's book are the William Haggas trained Sentaril and the Sir Henry Cecil trained Noble Mission (Frankel's full-brother). Both won impressively at Newbury in April 2012.

The five-star two-year-olds of 2012 are listed below for quick reference. As you can see, two of them were still unnamed at the time of publication, so don't forget to access my website www.stevetaplin.co.uk for updates of names.

ABSOLUTELY SO	Andrew Balding
A LADIES MAN	Richard Hannon
BIG BREAK	Dermot Weld
GOLDEN CAUSEWAY	Charles Hills
HERE COMES WHEN	Andrew Balding
HIGHEST PRAISE	Dermot Weld
INVINCIBLE CARA	John Dunlop
MAKAFEH	Luca Cumani
MORPHEUS	Sir Henry Cecil
MUNDAHESH	William Haggas
MYSTERIAL	Richard Hannon
NEW PEARL	David Brown
NOOR AL WATAN	John Oxx
PASSING PARADE	Sir Henry Cecil
STRICTLY SILCA	Mick Channon
WOODY BAY	James Given
B.F. GALILEO – OUIJA BOARD (CAPE CROSS)	Ed Dunlop
B.C. SHAMARDAL – PRIMA LUCE (GALILEO)	David Lanigan

The Bloodstock Experts Mark your Card

Last year this section highlighted 35 individual winners of 46 races, compared with 33 of 43 in 2010 and 23 of 28 in 2009. We're getting better and better!

Who got the top tipster award for last year? Let's look at the contenders. Most of the experts managed to pick at least one winner and those who selected two were David Redvers, Peter Doyle, Tom Goff, Johnny McKeever and Ross Doyle. Ross must surely be 'mentioned in despatches' for selecting the Group winner and ultra-consistent Lilbourne Lad.

Will Edmeades, David McGreavy and Ed Sackville did really well with three winners each – and Will recently pointed out to me that he missed out on mentioning the good filly Best Terms. But there again so did I – she wasn't in the book at all I'm afraid!

On the podium with a smashing four winners each are Angus Gold and Robin O'Ryan – a terrific effort! But when a guy picks out the Group 1 Cheveley Park Stakes winner about ten weeks before she makes her debut he's surely got to take top spot, so well done Mr Redvers!

Thank you to all the experts who have had a go at selecting potential winners once again. Remember that most of the two-year-olds selected here can be found in the main section of the book listed under their trainers and highlighted by the symbol ♠

JAMES DELAHOOKE
SORN
ch.c. Galileo – Dame Again. This robust, well-grown Galileo colt bred on the rocket cross came up early in Tattersalls Part One sale and failed to catch anyone's eye. I liked his athleticism and was undiscouraged by his plain head and flashy colouring. I bought him privately for a new client and I will not be surprised if he turns out to be a proper horse. Trained by **J Fanshawe.**

UNNAMED
b.f. Hard Spun – Jena Jena. I bought her privately for Malcolm Bastard in USA last autumn. She is going brilliantly and is entered for the Tattersalls Craven 2-y-o's breeze up sale. *n.b. This filly was bought at the breeze-up sale for 50,000 Gns by William Haggas.*

UNNAMED
b.c. Manduro – Tamalain. n.b. This colt was bought at the breeze-up sale for 75,000 Gns. He was bred by my good friends Bob and Pauline Scott. He was quite backward last autumn so we decided to give him some time to find himself. He has turned inside out over winter and could be anything. Coincidentally he is also in Malcolm Bastard's draft at the Craven sale and I am sure he will not lack for admirers. He goes well.

ALASTAIR DONALD
DARING DRAGON
gr.c. Intikhab – The Manx Touch. A very similar type to his useful brother Frog Hollow who I bought for 20,000gns. The mare has been very good so I had to dig deep but he does everything right and he has a better temperament than many in the family. Expect to see him over 7 furlongs in August/September. **Ed Walker.**

ELNA DANCER
b.c. Elnadim – Freedom. The mare has had two black-type horses from her first three runners. This colt has some speed should be ready by mid-April. By a solid stallion, he looked a runner at the Sales. **Alan Swinbank.**

GLORIOUS PROTECTOR
b.c. Azamour – Hasaiyda. A quality athlete, I was amazed to get him for 55,000gns. From an Aga Khan family, he's a great mover and should be on the track by August time over 7f furlongs or a mile. **Ed Walker.**

GLORIOUS STAR

ch.c. Soviet Star – Caerlonore. The first lot in the ring at Tattersalls October Book 2 and was a lovely, scopey, solid individual. Looks very cheap for his purchase price, he's bred for 1m and should be out in August over 7 furlongs. **Ed Walker.**

PETER DOYLE

OVATORY

b.c. Acclamation – Millsini. This is a good sort by an outstanding sire and comes from a pedigree that the Doyle family has had a lot of good luck with. Trained by **Amanda Perrett.**

ROYAL BAR

b.c. Royal Applause – Our Faye. He has the looks and is bred to fly, hopefully he will. Trained by **Sylvester Kirk.**

TAMAYUZ STAR

ch.c Tamayuz – Magical Peace. He is a very strong, sharp sort that has progressed well since the yearling sales. Trained by **Richard Hannon.**

WENTWORTH

b.c. Acclamation – Miss Corinne. This is a lovely horse that has thrived in his work to date and could be the real deal. Trained by **Richard Hannon.**

ROSS DOYLE

BROADWAY DUCHESS

ch.f. New Approach – Annee Lumiere. A 120,000gns yearling from Book 1 of the Tattersalls Yearling Sales. She is a beautiful filly and the reason we liked her so much was she looked mature for a New Approach with the added bonus that her mother is a black type mare by Giant's Causeway, bringing some toughness to the table. She looks like a filly that could be anything long term but I could she her appearing mid-season all being well in a good fillies maiden and going on to bigger and better things from there. In training with **Team Hannon.**

CARRY ON CLAPPING

b.f. Acclamation – Embassy Belle. A €65,000 yearling from Goffs Orby Sale. She is a filly with lots of class and typical of her stallion, a great mover, well-balanced and a great temperament. She is out of a black type mare and looks the type to come to hand sooner rather than later. In training with **Team Hannon.**

DUST WHIRL

b.c. Bahamian Bounty – Dust. A £42,000 DBS Premier Sale yearling, he is a very smart looking colt with great muscle definition for such a young horse which would lead you to believe that he is mature and forward. He looks like he could be an early type but also has a bit of size to last out the season and is by a very solid stallion in Bahamian Bounty out of a Green Desert mare also a positive and in training with **Team Hannon.**

MISTER MARC

b.c. Acclamation – Fathoming. A £70,000 DBS Premier Sale yearling, we just had to buy this fella. He had everything we would want in a horse, good looking, well balanced, strong and a great temperament by a stallion that we have been very lucky with from day one. He just looks so professional in everything he does and he has a lucky owner who got very lucky with Lilbourne Lad last year by the same stallion. Hopefully lightning will strike twice. In training with **Team Hannon.**

WILL EDMEADES

CARLARAJAH

ch.c. Sleeping Indian – Carla. This colt was not originally on my inspection list at Doncaster Sales, but his action and presence really caught my eye on several occasions. He is half brother to two stakes winners by unfashionable stallions. He was bought for Thurloe Thoroughbreds and Michael seems very happy with him. **Michael Bell.**

DAY IN DAY OUT

b.c. Notnowcato – Cockatrice. A nice foal who turned into a cracking yearling, but a disappointing pinhook as he was catalogued during the first hour of the Sale. All credit to the trainer, who had seen the colt at Fair Winter Farm, for buying him without an owner at the time. He is from a good family and has a lovely attitude. **Ralph Beckett.**

FOXY DANCER

*b.f. Jeremy – Date Mate.*I loved this filly and, when she failed to make her breeder's valuation in the ring, she was bought privately for Richard Hannon's shop window. A little bit 'Danehill' in front, this is a racey filly with a good outlook, who is half sister to 2 two year old stakes winners. **Richard Hannon.**

MISS DIVA

b.f. Acclamation – Mina. Not the biggest, but a sweet filly who was bought for Bunny Roberts. She is from the family of Owington by a very successful sire of two year olds, as her trainer knows only too well. She is going well at Everleigh and should be quite early. **Richard Hannon.**

TOM GOFF
DIVERGENCE (IRE)

b.f. Teofilo – Min Alhawa. A sweet and quite sharp Teofilo filly out a Riverman half sister to Harayir sold for €120,000 by Lodge Park Stud, Ireland in Goffs. She seems to travel up Warren Hill nicely enough at this early stage. We bought her half sister by Nayef the previous year and she goes well, so I hope this filly can be a useful performer for Michael and her owner Mr Lawrie Inman. **Michael Bell.**

DODINA

b.f. Acclamation – Etica. A very pretty and attractive filly by Acclamation who I hope was value at £20,000 from Rathbarry Stud at DBS Premier Sale compared with the price of some of the yearlings by this stallion last year. I went to see her at Dukes Stud in late October and she didn't look out of place next to some much more expensive animals. She moves well and Pete seems to like her, so fingers crossed she's got an engine when she is stepped up to faster work. **Peter Chapple-Hyam.**

TOAST OF THE TOWN (IRE)

b.f. Duke of Marmalade – Boast. A lovely filly sold by John Troy in Tattersalls October Book 1 last year. She's a half sister to Strut, who was a fast filly trained by Roger Charlton for Lady Rothschild. We got a bit stuck in to Duke of Marmalade's first crop yearlings buying. I think we bought five in all, so I sincerely hope we didn't get a bit too carried away. Simon Marsh

also liked her very much so she is owned by Lady Lloyd-Webber and Rachel Hood. She has loads of quality and we are all rather enamoured with her, so are living in hope at this stage. **John Gosden.**

UNNAMED

b.c. Authorized – Zam Zoom. Richard Brown (my business partner) and John Gosden bought this colt together out of Tattersalls Book 3 from Charlie Vigors' Hillwood Stud for 48,000gns while I was on a plane to Kentucky to watch a few runners across the pond. After plenty of banter between us all about what had occurred in my absence, I went to see the colt the other day and had to grudgingly admit that I was particularly taken with him. He is very much a staying three-year-old in the making, out of a Dalakhani mare, so won't be early by any means but he has lots of quality and class. **John Gosden.**

ANGUS GOLD
ESTIFZAAZ (IRE)

b.c. Invincible Spirit – Lulua. He is a well balanced colt who looks a two year old as a type and Paul Hanagan had a sit on him recently and liked the way he goes. He was bought for 280,000 Gns at Tattersalls October Book One. **Charlie Hills.**

JARYAL

b.c. Dubawi – Strings. Although I can't believe this horse will be very early from his pedigree, the Hannon team very much like the way he goes and he could be one for the second part of the season. He was bought for 190,000 Gns at Tattersalls October Book One. **Richard Hannon.**

LANANSAAK (IRE)

b.f. Zamindar – Bunood. For later on in the season I suggest this homebred filly who was a beautiful yearling and Roger describes her as a natural athlete, and hopefully she will make a nice filly in the second half of the year. **Roger Varian.**

MAYAASEM

b.c. Royal Applause – Rolexa. He looks a two year old type and Charles Hills says he has a beautiful action and he likes the horse very much so far. He was bought for 90,000 Gns at Tattersalls October Book Two. **Charles Hills.**

MOORTAHAN
b.c. Dutch Art – Rotunda. Richard Hannon Jnr loved this horse as a yearling and he said he looked sharp and hopefully will be. He was bought for 75,000 Gns at Tattersalls October Book Two. **Richard Hannon.**

REQAABA
b.f. Exceed and Excel – Something Blue. This was a small, sharp filly when she was bought. She's by a good sire of two year olds and, although she is keen at home, John Gosden says she does it all very easily and hopefully should be one to follow early. She was bought for 130,000 Gns at Tattersalls October Book One. **John Gosden.**

CHARLIE GORDON-WATSON
BEDOUIN INVADER (IRE)
b.c. Oasis Dream – Hovering. A well-balanced, powerful horse, he's athletic and has size and scope. One maybe for later on but an exciting prospect all the same. Out of In The Wings mare, so it's the same cross as Sri Putra. **Sir Michael Stoute.**

BIT OF A GIFT (FR)
b.c. Dark Angel – Dilag. An Arqana purchase by a proper two-year-old sire, he's the first horse Roger has trained for Saeed Suhail. Looks the right type and showing all the right signs. **Roger Varian.**

PASSING PARADE
b.f. Cape Cross – Model Queen. Looks the part and has the pedigree to match. All seems to be going well with her. **Sir Henry Cecil.**

PIRA PALACE
b.f. Acclamation – Takrice. A very speedy looking type with an excellent attitude, she's bred for speed and I hope she'll be out around June or earlier. **Sir Michael Stoute.**

SHADES OF SILVER
b.c. Dansili – Silver Pivotal. A big, athletic horse with a lot of presence and a nice pedigree. He's the first foal out of a listed winner and is a very good-moving horse. **Sir Michael Stoute.**

SOARING SPIRITS (IRE)
ch.c. Tamayuz – Follow My Lead. By a stallion who I think has a good chance, he had very nice speedy looking yearlings and some sold very well. This is one of the cheaper ones but he's a real two-year-old type, from a very tough and hardy family. **Roger Varian.**

HARRY HERBERT
ASSEMBLY
ch.c. Kyllachy – Constitute. A son of Kyllachy who appears to have plenty of natural ability. He has grown a lot since we bought him but he has retained his shape and I would think that he could be a July/early August starter. A special colt to look at and the trainer seems keen too! **William Haggas.**

CONSERVE (IRE)
b.f. Duke of Marmalade – Minor Point. I love this filly who is strong and a great mover. To my eye she could make up into a July starter. We loved the Duke Of Marmalades at the sales and were delighted to be able to take this one home. **Sir Henry Cecil.**

MYSTERIAL
b.c. Invincible Spirit – Diamond Dilemma. He too is very strong and precocious and has just received his first entry, so he may even be seen out sooner than Tassel. He is not over big but is one of those who seems to look bigger when under tack! **Richard Hannon.**

PERSEPOLIS (IRE)
b.br.c. Dansili – La Persiana. He too is very well bred and I think very well bought by John Warren for only 50,000 Gns. He is a very forward going colt who really wants to run and he looks competitive. He won't be early either but he is one for the notebook later on in the season. **Sir Michael Stoute.**

RESPONSE
ch.c. New Approach – Spotlight (Dr Fong). This son of New Approach is coming to hand way quicker than anticipated and he does find it all very easy so far. He could be the type to be running over seven furlongs in June so the Chesham could come into the reckoning if he is good enough. I certainly like what I see of

him going up Warren Hill and there seems to be some good chat about his sire's first crop. **William Haggas.**

SABRE

br.c. Kheleyf – Spiritual Air. He was a stunning yearling that we bought from Doncaster and he too looks to be a summer two-year-old in the making. He has a great action and, although not quite as precocious as the above two, he still should make up into a June starter. **Michael Bell.**

TASSEL

b.f. Kyllachy – Xtrasensory. This is a very precocious filly who could be our first two-year-old runner. She seems to find it all very easy and has the physique of a Queen Mary filly if good enough. Richard Hughes loves her and says that she can be released any time! **Richard Hannon.**

TELESCOPE (IRE)

b.c. Galileo – Velouette. This beautifully bred son of Galileo could be anything and at 225,000 Gns was our most expensive yearling last sales season. He is simply stunning and moves like a panther but of course he won't be early. I suspect that Sir Michael will give him a couple of runs this year towards the back-end but if this horse is no good then there will be a lot of hat eating! **Sir Michael Stoute.**

LUKE LILLINGSTON

BARRACUDA BOY

b.c. Bahamian Bounty – Madame Boulangere. A real Doncaster 2-y-o type. By a Group 1 winning 2-y-o out of a winner of the Watership Down sales race. He's quite a big colt and you wouldn't expect him to be early but he should make a good sprinter in time. **Tom Dascombe.**

HOT SECRET

b.f. Sakhee's Secret – Harryanna. Sam Hoskins and I have recently founded the Hot To Trot Racing Club. This filly is a half brother to Temple Meads, a very fast 2-y-o of a couple of years ago. Her trainer says she is well forward and we hope she might even be our first winner. **Andrew Balding.**

INSOMNIA (IRE)

b.f. Sleeping Indian – Spree. A relatively inexpensive, fast looking filly. The dam won as a 2-y-o and both her first two foals have also won. Her trainer seems very happy so far. **Ian Wood.**

MINISTER OF MAYHEM

ch.c. Sakhee's Secret – First Fantasy. I persuaded his breeders to keep a half interest when he was sold as a yearling as I felt he could increase his value on the racecourse. He is a scopey horse but the trainer suggests we will not have to wait too long. **Ger Lyons.**

RESILIENT

b.c. Shamardal – Zither. A big, strong colt who is unlikely to be early, but with a great action and wonderful disposition. I have rarely sold a yearling that displayed such confidence and willingness to please. **William Haggas.**

ZERO GAME (IRE)

b.f. High Chaparral – Freezing Love. A beautiful filly who we felt rather slipped through the cracks at Tattersalls Book 1. By a sire we have been lucky with (Wigmore Hall) her trainer has spoken positively about her already. **Michael Bell.**

DAVID MCGREAVY

MRS PEEL

b.f. Sixties Icon – Jollyhockeysticks. A racey filly who is very genuine and is pleasing her capable trainer. **Desmond Donovan.**

TOBACCO ROAD

b.c. Westerner – Virginia's Best. A smashing colt who is a real athlete and although he is by a sire who is excelling with his NH stock, it will not stop this fellow from performing this season. **Richard Hannon.**

UNNAMED

b.f. Marju – Kazatzka. A sweet filly I bought as a foal. I believe she is going to the Tattersalls Craven Breeze Up. As she is a three-quarter sister to the five-time Group 1 winner Soviet Song she has all the credentials. *n.b. She was bought at the breeze-up sale by Denis Coakley for 42,000 Gns.*

JOHNNY MCKEEVER
COUNT PALATINE
b.c. *Holy Roman Emperor – Blue Iris*. Cost €140,000 at Goffs Orby. A real sprinting model, I purchased him for Dr Philip Brown who was looking for a two-year-old performer. He certainly looks the part. **Andrew Balding.**

ROCKY GROUND
b.c. *Acclamation – Keriyka*. Bought for £105,000 at Doncaster Premier. One of my favourite yearlings of last year, I bought him for Steve Parkin for whom I have been very lucky at this sale notably with Beyond Desire. He's been impressing in pre-training and has now gone to be trained by **Roger Varian.**

ZAMOYSKI
ch.c. *Dutch Art – Speech*. A 10,500 Gns foal originally bought for a syndicate managed by my assistant Charlie Budgett. He was subsequently bought by Jane Allison on behalf of Paul Roy for 55,000 Gns at Tattersalls Book 2, representing a nice profit! He is trained by **Jeremy Noseda** and I hear on the grapevine he's going well!

UNNAMED
ch.c. *Exceed And Excel – Psychic*. Cost 80,000 Gns at Tattersalls October 1. A typical example by this sire who seems to be so consistent. He goes very nicely at Manton. Trained by **Brian Meehan.**

ROBIN O'RYAN
FLYMAN
b.c. *Pastoral Pursuits – Satin Bell*. A nice, big horse by a sire we've been lucky with. He'll be a nice mid-season type 2-y-o. All these are in training with **Richard Fahey.**

MIRLO BLANCO
gr.c. *Dark Angel – Danzolin*. He'll be a nice horse when he goes over six and seven furlongs. A very sound horse, he's big and scopey.

MYSTERY BET
b.f. *Kheleyf – Dancing Prize*. A half-sister to Firebet, she's doing everything asked of her and I like her a lot.

WYLDFIRE
ch.c. *Raven's Pass – Miss Sally*. A grand, scopey horse from the first crop of Raven's Pass. I like him, he's a good mover and I'd be disappointed if he wasn't a good horse in the second half of the season.

KIRSTEN RAUSING
ALCAEUS
b.c. *Hernando – Alvarita*. Bred at Lanwades and sold at the October Sales (Book 2) for 40,000 Gns from Staffordstown Stud to Sir Mark Prescott. A strapping, big but elegant colt who moves exceptionally well, he has an air of class about him. He is a half-brother to last year's useful two-year-old filly Alla Speranza (Jim Bolger) and a full brother to the decent winner Albert Bridge. His grandam is the dual Champion Stakes winner Alborada. Expect this colt to show from the second half of September. **Sir Mark Prescott.**

ALPINIST
gr.c. *New Approach – Alouette*. Lanwades-bred, he is the last foal of our marvellous mare Alouette, a Listed winner herself and dam of multiple Group 1 winners Alborada and Albanova, as well as the French Listed winner Alma Mater and five other winners. His trainer, who trained this both the parents of this colt, seems to like him. **Jim Bolger.**

GRANULE
br.f. *Hernando – Grain Only (Machiavellian)*. A Lanwades home-bred, she is an own-sister to Caravan Rolls On (4 wins at 2 and 3) and Gabrial's Star (a winner in his only start at two in 2011) but is perhaps a slightly earlier type than either of them. She already pleases in her work and we hope to see her out during the second half of the season. **Peter Chapple-Hyam.**

SAVANNA-LA-MAR
ch.f. *Curlin – Soft Morning (Pivotal)*. A member of the first crop of world champion Curlin, this filly is a first foal of Deauville Listed winner Soft Morning. The filly herself is a fifth-generation homebred Lanwades' produce, from the family of Petoski and Starlit Sands. She looks useful at home and could be seen out by the end of June. **Sir Mark Prescott.**

UNNAMED

b.br.c. Vita Rosa (JPN) – Pat or Else (Alzao). A very impressive-looking colt, he is a member of the first crop of Vita Rosa (himself a multiple Group 2 winner and also Group 1 placed in his homeland, Japan) – the only son of Sunday Silence to stand in the UK. This colt is an outstandingly good mover and is showing impressive pace in his early-season work. His dam has bred 6 winners already and she is a half-sister to the dual Group 1 winners My Emma (Yorkshire Oaks & Prix Vermeille) and Classic Cliche (Ascot Gold Cup & St Leger). Bred by Lanwades Stud. (Lot 91; Doncaster Breeze-Up Sales, 22-23 April).

BRUCE RAYMOND

FANTASTIC MOON

ch.c. Dalakhani – Rhadegunda. The first foal of the dam, he's quite precocious for the pedigree and should be seen out around June time. **Jeremy Noseda.**

TAHAF

b.c. Authorised – Lady Zonda. A half brother to Hibaayeb and a quality colt, he'll be out early. **Clive Brittain.**

DAVID REDVERS

PEARL BOUNTY

b.c. Bahamian Bounty – Roslea Lady. The most expensive by his sire at the yearling sales and a very precocious colt showing up well at Kingsclere. **Andrew Balding.**

NEW PEARL

gr.c. Acclamation – New Deal. Relatively cheap for this exceptional sire at £75k and bought to replace Frederick Engels who did so well for David last year. **David Brown.**

LIBER

b.c. Ishiguru – Startori. Bred at Tweenhills and a full brother to last year's selection Guru Girl who won a RPYB maiden. Sir Mark admitted this was the first time he has worked a 2-y-o in March for years as he is so precocious. Hopefully he will be as good as Coeus whom he replaces. **Sir Mark Prescott.**

PEARL TURN

b.f. Bernardini – Turn Me Loose. An expensive filly at $225k but an absolute beauty and gave JP Murtagh a lovely feel at Ger's at the end of March, but don't expect to see her out until July. **Ger Lyons.**

CHRIS RICHARDSON

BUTTERFLY DREAM

ch.f. Kyllachy – Dream Again. A sharp looking filly who is perhaps not bred to be that early. However she is from the family tracing back to Iceman, who proved to be a leading two year-old of his generation. **William Haggas.**

CAPE ELIZABETH

b.f. Invincible Spirit – Maine Lobster. A half sister to the Group 2 winner, Group 1 placed Major Cadeaux, who was placed second in the Coventry Stakes. This filly looks an interesting prospect. **John Gosden.**

FANTASY IN BLUE

b.f. Galileo – Blue Symphony. A beautifully bred three parts sister to Fantasia (by Sadler's Wells) who proved herself a useful two year-old when winning the Group 3 Prestige Stakes, Goodwood. She looks sharp. **Sir Michael Stoute.**

INFATUATE

b.f. Dalakhani – Fantasize. Fantasize is a half sister to the dam of Champion two year-old Hooray, and the Cherry Hinton winner Dazzle. This filly has always caught the imagination since birth and potentially looks the one to follow this year. **Sir Michael Stoute.**

RED BATON

b.f. Exceed And Excel – Ruby Rocket. A lovely daughter of Exceed and Excel whose dam did nothing but improve with racing. Certainly not expected to be that early, however she looks a class act in the making. **Jeremy Noseda.**

ED SACKVILLE

IAN'S DREAM

ch.c. Speightstown – She's Loaded. I loved everything about this horse. Let's hope he is as good as he is good-looking! **Jeremy Noseda.**

SKY LANTERN
gr.f. Red Clubs – Shawanni. A great walker and correct. She came from Goffs and we had to dig deep to get her. **Richard Hannon.**

THIS IS NICE
ch.f. Exceed and Excel – Spanish Quest. I bought this filly for my best friend so the pressure is on. Nevertheless, she's attractive and racey and will hopefully be early. **Tom Dascombe.**

UNNAMED
b.f. Mount Nelson – Statua. A good-looking filly with a nice page, she has a touch of class about her. I would expect her to be a mid-summer prospect who will get better with age. **Tom Dascombe.**

ROBIN SHARP
MYSTICAL MOMENT
ch.f. Dutch Art – Tinnarinka. Very attractive filly with a good stride on her with the top man in **Richard Hannon.**

PIPPY
b.c. Exceed and Excel – Gandini. A very sharp close coupled colt that we bred. Bought by a good judge in Richard Brown. **Tom Dascombe.**

SALLY BRUCE
b.f. Byron – Show Trial. A small, sharp, cheap filly will give her owners a bit of fun. There is a nice story to her name, so I hope she does the friends and family of Sally Bruce proud. **Olivia Maylam.**

UNNAMED
b.f. Sakhee's Secret – Sabrina Brown. Full of quality, she should be a back-end of the season filly. **Tom Tate.**

AMANDA SKIFFINGTON
EQUITANIA
b.f. Pastoral Pursuits – Clarice Orsini. A lovely filly, bought at Doncaster, who I gather looks above average. **Richard Hannon.**

TORONADO
b.c. High Chaparral – Wana Doo. I will eat my proverbial hat if this is not a decent horse. He is absolutely gorgeous, and I told Richard when I bought him that this was a 'top hat and tails' horse. Hopefully I will be right. **Richard Hannon.**

UNNAMED
b.f. Oasis Dream – Politesse. She looks a real two-year-old and let's hope she is good, because she wasn't cheap! **William Haggas.**

UNNAMED
b.f. Acclamation – Superstar Leo. A homebred filly belonging to Lael Stable, who has always looked attractive and who is certainly bred to be useful. **William Haggas.**

PETER STANLEY
OF COURSE DARLING
ch.f. Dalakhani – Whazzis. A forward-looking 2-y-o, despite the breeding, going nicely. **Ed Dunlop.**

RED BATON
b.f. Exceed and Excel – Ruby Rocket. Sharp and racey, owned by Cheveley Park. **Jeremy Noseda.**

UNNAMED
b.f. Galileo – Ouija Board. A late maturing type but maybe with enough class to achieve something at the back end of this year. **Ed Dunlop.**

LARRY STRATTON
DREAM SCENARIO
b.f. Araafa – Notjustaprettyface. A foal purchase, she would have made a lot more by any other sire, as she is such a nice individual. A half-sister to a good stakes winner in Tropical Treat from the family of Sri Pekan, if she can overcome her sire she should win races. **Mel Brittain.**

DR FUNKENSTEIN
ch.c. Excellent Art – Romancing. A half-brother to three winners, he is very closely related to and bred on the same cross as, a very good Cheveley Park Stud filly of a couple of seasons back called Infallible. If he is half as good as she was, he will do. **Ger Lyons.**

NARDIN

b.f. Royal Applause – Third Party. A foal purchase, she turned into a 90,000 Gns yearling purchase by Shadwell Estates. A half-sister to a very useful 7 furlong Listed horse in Party Boss and also to this year's Triumph Hurdle winner Countrywide Flame, she has a lot of class. **Ed Dunlop.**

REVEILLE

ch.f. Sakhee's Secret – Up At Dawn. Bred by me, she's a half-sister to Up In Time who, after winning a Newmarket maiden at two, progressed into a high-class grass filly in California as a 3-y-o last year when winning a Grade 2 and a Grade 3. She races for a partnership that includes the Harpers who stand her sire Sakhee's Secret who was trained, like this filly, by **Hughie Morrison.**

ANTHONY STROUD

GLANELY

b.c. Exceed & Excel – Bon Ton Roulet. A big, powerful colt who is the first foal out of a half sister to Lowther Stakes winner Infamous Angel. **James Fanshawe.**

ROYAL STEPS

b.c. Royal Applause – Ask Carol. A precocious filly who has been showing plenty of zip in her early work and should hopefully feature prominently early in the season, although she is thought to have a preference for fast ground. **James Tate.**

VINO COLLAPSO

b.c. Jeremy – Compradore. A half-brother to the Listed winning and Group placed sprinting filly Beyond Desire who has been showing up well on the gallops and should be on the track fairly soon. **James Given.**

WOODY BAY

b.c. New Approach – Dublino. By a Group 1 winner out a Group 1 winner. A horse for the second half of the year but the trainer is very keen on him. **James Given.**

Trainers' Bargain Buys

When interviewing trainers in the Spring, the last question I ask is usually: 'Which do you think was your bargain buy at the yearling sales, for 25,000gns or less?' The following are their recommendations. If your favourite trainer isn't on this page, it's probably because I forgot to ask, or perhaps that trainer doesn't tend to deal with horses at this end of the market!

As you can see, some of them are real cheapies and in fact Ingleby Royale, who cost only 800gns, won just over a week after I spoke to his trainer Richard Fahey.

CATCH THE CIDER	£15,000	Hans Adielsson
BADDILINI	£14,000gns	Alan Bailey
TRANSLUCENT	€8,500	Andrew Balding
INKA SURPRISE	€7,500	Ralph Beckett
THE MANX MISSILE	25,000gns	Michael Bell
CH.F. DUTCH ART – BREAK OF DAWN	16,000gns	John Best
STARBOTTON	11,000gns	James Bethell
JET ACCLAIM	3,500gns	Marco Botti
UNCOMPLICATED	16,000gns	Jim Boyle
B.C. RED CLUBS – OSSIANA	£13,500	David Brown
BENONI	£1,000	Henry Candy
JONTLEMAN	£5,500	Mick Channon
TOMMY'S SECRET	£1,000	Jane Chapple-Hyam
DODINA	£20,000	Peter Chapple-Hyam
PERCY'S GIFT	22,000gns	Denis Coakley
MISS LEGAL EAGLE	€23,000	Jo Crowley
B.C. STRATEGIC PRINCE – SILK MEADOW	25,000gns	Keith Dalgleish
PREMIER STEPS	£24,000	Tom Dascombe
FIDUCIA	£14,000	Simon Dow
MYANNE	£8,500	Ann Duffield
PAIRUMANI PRINCE	€1,500	Ed Dunlop
BURLESQUE STAR	18,000gns	Harry Dunlop
INGLEBY ROYALE	800gns	Richard Fahey
GIRL AT THE SANDS	£8,000	James Given
ROSIE FUTURE	£25,000	Rae Guest
MUJADORA	23,000gns	William Haggas
BRIGADE	€20,000	Richard Hannon
GOWERTONIAN	£400	Ron Harris
B.C. BYRON – BALWARAH	£5,000	Ben Haslam
DALI'S LOVE	18,000gns	Charles Hills
RIOJA DAY	17,500gns	John Hills
B.F. SAKHEE'S SECRET – BOLSENA	16,000gns	William Jarvis
VESTIBULE	£5,000	Eve Johnson Houghton
B.F. INDESATCHEL – FOUR LEGS GOOD	5,500gns	Sylvester Kirk
KEEP THE SECRET	19,000gns	William Knight
LIGHTNIN HOPKINS	20,000gns	Ger Lyons
B.F. DUBAI DESTINATION – BLINDING MISSION	800gns	Alan McCabe
SMOOTHTALKINRASCAL	£21,000	Brian Meehan
BLACKDOWN SPIRIT	15,000gns	Rod Millman
MOSSTANG	€6,000	Robert Mills
OUR THREE GRACES	19,000gns	Gary Moore

THE BLACK JACOBIN	£1,000	*Stan Moore*
COUNTRYMAN	22,000gns	*Hughie Morrison*
B.F. JEREMY – STACEYMAC	£10,000	*Willie Muir*
INFINITE MAGIC	$7,000	*Jeremy Noseda*
BRONTE BELLE	20,000gns	*Jedd O'Keeffe*
DEVOUT	£12,000	*Jamie Osborne*
TIPPING OVER	€8,500	*Hugo Palmer*
PASAKA BOY	£1,000	*Jon Portman*
B.C. MANDURO – RAKATA	£800	*Derek Shaw*
AL EMIRATI	£19,000	*David Simcock*
PUSSYCAT LIPS	£6,000	*Tommy Stack*
MIDNIGHT DREAM	€9,000	*Linda Stubbs*
B.F. MOTIVATOR – ELA'S GIANT	1,000gns	*James Toller*
LIKEITLIKEIELKEIT	2,000gns	*Mark Tompkins*
CH.F. SIR PERCY – SIRENA	€3,000	*Marcus Tregoning*
TUSCAN FUN	22,000gns	*Roger Varian*
GLORIOUS STAR	21,000gns	*Ed Walker*
SMART ALICE	10,000gns	*Chris Wall*
THREEPENCE	£10,000	*Richard Whitaker*

Two year olds of 2012

HANS ADIELSSON

Hans was the last of the trainers I visited in the Spring, but thanks to the alphabet he becomes No.1 in the book, although he did question whether I ought to put the Queen's horses first! Hans was a very successful harness racing trainer in Sweden and was approached by his countryman, the owner-breeder Erik Penser, to train racehorses for him in England. So eighteen months ago he and his predominantly Swedish staff found themselves at Kingston Lisle, near Lambourn.

1. BEAUCHAMP ASTRA ★★

b.f. Observatory – Ashford Castle (Bates Motel). April 13. Half-sister to the fair 2012 3-y-o 1m winner Beauchamp Castle (by Motivator), to the quite useful 12f winner Aspasias Tizzy (by Tiznow) and the modest 8.6f winner Kiyari (by Key Of Luck). The dam, a minor stakes winner of 6 races from 6f to 8.5f, was Grade 3 placed twice and is a half-sister to 8 winners including the US dual Grade 1 winner Strategic Maneuver. The second dam, Prayer Wheel (by Conquistador Cielo), a listed-placed winner in Canada, is a half-sister to 7 winners. (Mr Erik Penser). *"A medium-sized filly that's showing promise, she's very correct and has a good temperament. Her x-rays show that she's physically mature enough to make a 2-y-o".*

2. CATCH THE CIDER ★★

b.c. Medicean – Zanna (Soviet Star). March 16. Fourth foal. £15,000Y. Doncaster Premier. Compton Beauchamp. The dam was placed 4 times in France at 2 and 3 yrs including at Longchamp and is a half-sister to 5 winners including the French listed winner Zandiyka (dam of the French 1,000 Guineas winner Zalaiyka). The second dam, Zanata (by African Sky), a winner of 3 races at 3 yrs, is a half-sister to 4 winners. (P & D Bronsman AB). *"I like him very much, he's a scopey colt, his hocks aren't the best but he's shown promise in his early work and he shows good balance. He's a good-looker and he has a grand head on him. From an Aga Khan family, he has a very good temperament and he'll make a 2-y-o from mid-season onwards. The owner has a big brewing* company in Sweden that specialises in cider, so he uses the name 'Cider' for all his horses". TRAINERS' BARGAIN BUY

3. COMPTON SILVER ★★★

ch.c. Haafhd – Anna Oleanda (Old Vic). March 21. Sixth living foal. £36,000Y. Doncaster Premier. Compton Beauchamp. Half-brother to the Group 3 Prix d'Astarte winner and Group 2 Oaks d'Italia second Middle Club (by Fantastic Light), to the French dual 10.5f winner and Group 3 Prix de Royaumont third Anna Mona (by Monsun) and the German winner and listed-placed Anna Royal (by Royal Dragon). The dam won twice at 3 yrs in Germany and is a sister to the German Group 3 winner Anno Luce and a half-sister to the dams of the Group winners Annus Mirabilis, Anna of Saxony, Annaba and Pozarica. The second dam, Anna Paola (by Prince Ippi), won the Group 2 German Oaks and is a half-sister to 7 winners. (Mr Erik Penser). *"His conformation and his x-rays show us that he won't be a late 2-y-o, he's pleasing us in his work and I like him a lot. Had he been by a more fashionable stallion he would have cost a lot more at the sales because his breeding is very good. He's well put-together and he looks the right size for a 2-y-o".*

ERIC ALSTON

4. CANTARA ★★

b.f. Piccolo – Damalis (Mukaddamah). February 22. Fourth foal. Half-sister to the modest 5f winner Dalarossie (by Kyllachy) and to the moderate 1m winner Saving Grace (by Lend A Hand). The dam, a useful sprint winner of 7 races from 2 to 5 yrs, is a half-sister to 4 winners. The second dam, Art Age (by Artaius), is an unraced half-sister to 9 winners. (Liam & Tony Ferguson). *"She's probably the 2-y-o I'm most looking forward to because I know the family quite well, but we won't see her out until the back-end of the season as she's got quite a bit of growing to do".*

5. COLOURS OF NATURE ★★★

b.g. Lucky Story – Sweetly Sharp (Daggers Drawn). April 13. Second foal. The dam was a moderate 2-y-o 5f seller winner. The second dam, Pecan Pie (by Sri Pekan), is an unraced half-sister to several winners out of a half-sister to the dual Group 2 winner Docksider. (Gordon Edwards). *"He's very forward and will be racing in April. His mother was a sprinter and he'll be the same I should think, especially as the sire can put some speed into a pedigree. He's showing up quite well".*

6. LITTLE ELI ★★

b.g. Green Desert – Princess Ellis (Compton Place). March 29. First foal. The dam, a quite useful 5f winner of 5 races, was listed-placed twice and is a half-sister to 2 winners. The second dam, Star Cast (by In The Wings), a minor 11f and 12f winner, is a half-sister to 7 winners. (J E Jackson). *"He's very tall so he just needs plenty of time and we won't see him until the back-end of the season. I trained the dam and she barely got five furlongs, so you'd expect this horse to be a sprinter as well".*

7. MY BOY WALTER ★★★

b.g. Multiplex – Springtime Parkes (Medicean). February 13. First foal. The ran three times unplaced and is a half-sister to numerous winners including the useful 2-y-o 5f and 6f winner Ace Of Parkes, the useful dual 5f winner and Moyglare, Lowther and Queen Mary Stakes placed My Melody Parkes, the listed 6f winner Summerhill Parkes and the useful winner of 13 races over 5f Lucky Parkes. The second dam, Summerhill Spruce (by Windjammer), a fair 3-y-o 6f seller winner, is a half-sister to 6 winners including the German Group 2 winner Jimmy Barnie. (Mr Nigel Leadbetter & Mrs Val Leadbetter). *"A nice, big horse, he'll make a 2-y-o and I should think he'd want seven furlongs from June or July onwards".*

ALAN BAILEY

8. BADDILINI ★★★★

b.c. Bertolini – Baddi Heights (Shirley Heights). February 17. Eighth foal. £14,000Y. Doncaster Premier. Ken Ivory. Brother to the fairly useful 2-y-o 1m winner and Group 2 12f Ribblesdale Stakes third Uvinza and half-brother to the minor French 11f and 12f winner Eklektos (by Bahhare), the fair 11f winner Ugalla (by Where Or When) and the modest 1m winner Anthill (by Slickly). The dam, a minor French 2-y-o winner, also won over 11f and was listed-placed over 12f and is a half-sister to 5 winners. The second dam, Baddi Baddi (by Sharpen Up), won at 2 yrs in France and is a half-sister to 7 winners. (Mrs A Shone & Mrs V Hubbard). *"A real nice horse and although he's sharp enough to start off in April he has the scope to continue throughout the year. He'll end up getting seven furlongs and I think he's a good horse. Hopefully we can win the Lily Agnes Stakes at Chester in May, because that's a race I've always wanted to win".*

9. BUBBLY BAILEY ★★

b.c. Byron – Night Gypsy (Mind Games). April 9. Eighth foal. 34,000Y. Tattersalls October Book 1. AB Racing. Half-brother to the useful 2-y-o 6f and listed 7f winner and Group 3 Oh So Sharp Stakes second Electric Feel (by Firebreak), to the fairly useful 2-y-o 6f winner and listed placed Aunt Nicola, the quite useful 5f and 6f winner Mymumsysimthebest (both by Reel Buddy) and the quite useful 5f winner of 6 races from 3 to 5 yrs Safari Mischief (by Primo Valentino). The dam, a fair 2-y-o 5f winner, is a sister to the listed 2-y-o winner On The Brink and a half-sister to 4 winners including the listed winner and Group 2 placed Eastern Romance and the useful 2-y-o triple 6f winner Blue Tomato. The second dam, Ocean Grove (by Fairy King), a quite useful 2-y-o 6f winner, is a half-sister to 5 winners here and abroad. (The Champagne Club). *"He'll make a 2-y-o but he's had a setback that'll keep him out a bit. He should be out around June time and he's a big, well-made horse that looks like a sprinter".* TRAINERS' BARGAIN BUY

10. LA DANZA ★★★

b.f. Country Reel – Freedom Song (Singspiel). January 22. First foal. 7,000Y. Tattersalls October Book 3. AB Racing. The dam, a fair 2-y-o 7f placed maiden, is a half-sister to 2 winners including the 2-y-o Group 2 7f Rockfel Stakes winner Luvah Girl. The second dam, Girl Of My Dreams (by Marju), a poor dual 7f winner at 4 and 5 yrs, is a half-sister to one winner abroad. *"I think she's real good filly – probably the best I've got. We've been held up through several niggling issues but she's fine now. Six or seven furlongs should suit her from the mid-season onwards".*

11. SERAPHIMA ★★★

b.f. Fusaichi Pegasus – Millestan (Invincible Spirit). February 8. First foal. The dam, a quite useful 2-y-o 8.3f and subsequent US winner, is a half-sister to 4 winners including the useful French 9.5f (at 2 yrs) to 15f winner and listed-placed Grey Mystique. The second dam, Atnab (by Riverman), a modest 12f winner, is a half-sister to 6 winners including the listed winner Dansili Dancer. *"A real nice filly, she works well and I'm hoping to send her to a five furlong fillies' maiden at Chester in May. She's forward, does everything right and just wants to please you".*

GEORGE BAKER

12. BOOMSHACKERLACKER (IRE) ★★★

gr.c. Dark Angel – Allegrina (Barathea). March 16. Fourth foal. 65,000Y. Tattersalls October Book 2. Angie Loder. Half-brother to the fair 2-y-o 6f winner Baronovici (by Namid). The dam, a fair 7f winner, is out of the 10f winner, on her only start, Pianola (by Diesis) – herself a half-sister to two stakes winners in the USA. (PJL Racing). *"A big, strong sort, we'll probably start him over six furlongs before stepping him up to seven furlongs and a mile. He's done really well over the winter and I think plenty of him".*

13. BOUNTYBEAMADAM ★★★

b.f. Bahamian Bounty – Madamoiselle Jones (Emperor Jones). March 25. Fifth foal. 12,000Y. Tattersalls October Book 2. Angie Loder. Half-sister to the fair 2011 2-y-o 7f winner Maroosh (by Kyllachy) and to the fair triple 1m winner Abidhabidubai (by Dubai Destination). The dam, a fair winner of 3 races at around 1m, is a half-sister to 4 winners including the useful Group 3 7f Dubai Duty Free (Fred Darling Stakes) and 2-y-o 7f listed winner and Irish 1,000 Guineas second Penkenna Princess. The second dam, Tiriana (by Common Grounds), is a placed half-sister to 4 winners including the 2-y-o listed 5.2f winner Head Over Heels. (The Whitsbury Hopefuls). *"As the name would suggest she has a bit of attitude about her, but I don't mind that at all as long as it's channelled in the right direction. She'll be out in late April and she's speedy, a beautiful mover and very athletic".*

14. NENGE MBOKO ★★★

b.c. Compton Place – Floppie (Law Society). April 25. Thirteenth foal. 21,000Y. Tattersalls October Book 2. Angie Loder. Half-brother to the dual Group 3 5f winner Ringmoor Down (by Pivotal), to the fairly useful Irish 7f, 12f and hurdles winner and Group 3 placed Still Going On (by Prince Sabo), the fairly useful 6f (at 2 yrs) and 7f winner Lindoro (by Marju), the quite useful dual 6f winner (including at 2 yrs) Bailey Gate (by Mister Baileys), the quite useful 2-y-o 5f winner Floppie Disk (by Magic Ring), the modest 6f winner Hireath (by Petong) and the 1m seller winner On Porpoise (by Dolphin Street). The dam won over 1m in France and is a half-sister to 2 minor winners. The second dam, Enfant d'Amour (by Lyphard), was an unraced half-sister to 7 winners. (Russell, Wheeler, Vail, Conrad). *"The name is that of a character in the film 'Trading Places'. This is a strong, sturdy, compact colt that carries plenty of condition and he'll need plenty of graft and work. We haven't rushed him and he was a little bit mentally immature but we're stepping up his work now. One for late June or July over five furlongs".*

15. PETITE GEORGIA ★★★

b.f. Camacho – Petite Maxine (Sharpo). April 21. Thirteenth foal. 37,000Y. Tattersalls October Book 2. Angie Loder. Sister to the fair 7f and 1m winner of 5 races George Baker and half-sister to the useful 2011 2-y-o 6f winner and Group 3 6f Prix de Cabourg second B Fifty Two (by Dark Angel), to the fairly useful 5f and 6f winner of 8 races from 2 to 4 yrs and listed-placed Pipadash, a minor winner in Sweden (both by Pips Pride), the fairly useful 2-y-o 7f winner of 3 races Under My Thumb, the fair 1m to 10f winner of 4 races Luck Will Come (both by Desert Style), the quite useful 2-y-o 6f winner Moonlight Affair (by Distant Music), the fair 12f winner of 3 races Pont Neuf (by Revoque) and a hurdles winner by Definite Article. The dam, a modest 6f and 7f placed maiden, is a full or half-sister to 11 winners. The second dam, Penny Blessing (by So Blessed), won twice at 2 yrs, was fourth in the Cheveley Park Stakes and is a half-sister to 8 winners. (George Baker & Partners). *"I liked her from the moment she walked into the sales ring, she's not an overly precocious sort so we're taking our time with* her but I would imagine she'll be ready to run by mid-June over six furlongs. She's a well put-together filly with a decent pedigree and being a full-sister to George Baker she has a lot to live up to!"

16. SECRET BEAU ★★★

b.c. Sakhee's Secret – Belle Reine (King Of Kings). February 13. 25,000Y. Ascot December. Not sold. Half-brother to the fairly useful 2-y-o 5f and 6f winner Ishbelle (by Invincible Spirit), to the fairly useful 1m (including at 2 yrs) to 12f winner Layline (by King's Best) and the quite useful 6f (at 2 yrs) and 7f winner Belle Des Airs (by Dr Fong). The dam is a half-sister to the very useful 1m winner of 4 races and subsequent Scandinavian listed winner Smart Enough and to the useful listed 6f winner Oasis Dancer. The second dam, Good Enough (by Mukaddamah), won once at 3 yrs in the USA and was third in the Group 1 Prix Saint-Alary and is a half-sister to 5 winners including the Group 3 Molecomb Stakes winner Classic Ruler. (Mrs H I Slade). "Obviously everyone around here at Whitsbury is very interested to see how the sire does because he stands here. People at the sales seemed to love his yearlings and I like this colt a lot. He's very forward-going, not that sharp but certainly a very uncomplicated horse with a great attitude. He does have something about him".

17. SUTTON SID ★★★★

ch.c. Dutch Art – Drastic Measure (Pivotal). March 7. Second foal. €60,000Y. Arqana Deauville August. Angie Loder. The dam, a modest 5f placed 2-y-o, is a half-sister to 3 winners including the dam of the US listed winner and Grade 3 placed Driving Snow. The second dam, Drastic Measure (by Pivotal), an Irish listed-placed 7f winner, is a half-sister to 5 winners including the high-class Irish Oaks, Yorkshire Oaks and Prix de l'Opera winner Petrushka. (Paul Bowden). "This colt is precocious and has shown plenty. He's been 'on the go' for a while now so I'll be looking for a five furlong maiden for him at the end of April or early May. He's always given us plenty of hope and he's amongst the best of our early 2-y-o's, so hopefully he can win a maiden before going on to better things".

18. UNNAMED ★★★

gr.f. Sakhee's Secret – Fluttering Rose (Compton Place). May 11. Second foal. The dam, a fair 2-y-o 5f winner, is a half-sister to 3 winners including the smart Group 2 5f King George Stakes winner Masamah. The second dam, Bethesda (by Distant Relative), a fairly useful 5.7f and 6f winner at 4 yrs, is a half-sister to 4 winners including the Group 1 6f Middle Park Stakes winner Fard. (Lady Cobham & Mr Giles Irwin). "My first impression of her as that she's a little bit backward, but she's done nothing but please. I had considered giving her a break but we're pressing on and with a fair wind we'll be running her towards the end of May".

19. UNNAMED ★★★

b.c. Invincible Spirit – Mascara (Mtoto). April 16. Second foal. 42,000Y. Tattersalls October Book 2. Five Star Bloodstock. 50,000 2-y-o. Tattersalls Craven Breeze-up. Angie Loder. Half-brother to the unplaced 2011 2-y-o Lady Jane Grace (by Amadeus Wolf). The dam is an unraced half-sister to 4 winners including the Group 3 10.5f Rose Of Lancaster Stakes winner of 6 races Mulaqat. The second dam, Atamana (by Lahib), a quite useful 1m winner, is a half-sister to 7 winners including the Irish 2-y-o 6f winner and Group 3 7f Killavullen Stakes third Dance Clear – subsequently a winner of 4 races and Grade 3 placed in the USA. "He's just arrived from the recent breeze-up sale where he was a standout for me. I was very pleased to buy him and I hope he'll prove to be good value because he looks very nice. He's an athletic, strong, well put-together colt with beautiful conformation. Just an all-round lovely horse".

ANDREW BALDING

20. ABSOLUTELY SO (IRE) ★★★★★

b.c. Acclamation –Week End (Selkirk). January 14. Third foal. 230,000Y. Tattersalls October Book 2. John Warren. The dam is an unraced half-sister to one winner abroad. The second dam, Tarfshi (by Mtoto), won 5 races including the Group 2 Pretty Polly Stakes and is a half-sister to 6 winners including the Group 1 Cheveley Park Stakes winner Embassy. (Jackie & George Smith). "A lovely horse, the sire was all the rage at the sales by the time he came along and hence the price tag, but he's a fabulous physical specimen. He looks every inch a nice horse, he's quite big and scopey and he's already shown a bit of ability at home. Six furlongs in June should be fine for him to start with".

21. BLUE TWISTER ★★★★
ch.c. Pivotal – Blue Siren (Bluebird). February 21. Half-brother to the useful 2-y-o listed 5.2f winner and Group 2 Flying Childers Stakes third Speed Cop, to the fairly useful dual 5f winner (including at 2 yrs) Siren's Gift (both by Cadeaux Genereux), the fair 2-y-o 7f winner King's Siren (by King's Best) and the fair 6f winner Indiana Blues (by Indian Ridge). The dam, a very useful winner of three races from 5f to 7f, was disqualified from first place in two more, notably the Group 1 5f Nunthorpe Stakes (the winner on merit) and is a half-sister to several winners including the quite useful 9f winner Northern Habit. The second dam, Manx Millenium (by Habitat), was placed over 1m and is a half-sister to several winners. (Mr J C Smith). "We know the family very well and this colt is quite a typical Pivotal, meaning he's going to be a nice horse but he won't be that early. One for the latter part of June and he's a really nice type".

22. BUONA FORTUNA ★★★
b.f. Oasis Dream – Sadie Thompson (King's Best). March 18. Third foal. 55,000Y. Tattersalls October Book 1. Andrew Balding. Half-brother to the fair 2011 2-y-o 10f winner Daneking (by Dylan Thomas) and to a 3-y-o winner in Italy by Halling. The dam, a fair 2-y-o 7f winner, is a half-sister to one winner. The second dam, Femme Fatale (by Fairy King), a useful dual 6f winner of 2 races (including a listed event at 2 yrs), was second in the Group 2 Sun Chariot Stakes and is a half-sister to 3 winners including the smart dual listed 10f winner Foodbroker Fancy (herself the dam of two stakes winners). (Mick & Janice Mariscotti). "A filly we bought from Catridge Farm who we've had a lot of luck with. She looks a 2-y-o type and she's nice. Probably one for six/seven furlongs from June onwards".

23. COUNT PALATINE (IRE) ★★★★ ♠
b.c. Holy Roman Emperor – Blue Iris (Petong). April 8. Eleventh foal. €140,000Y. Goffs Orby. McKeever Bloodstock. Brother to the fair Irish

2011 2-y-o 5f winner Nero Emperor and half-brother to the dual listed 5f winner (including at 2 yrs) Swiss Lake (by Indian Ridge and herself dam of the Group 3 winner Swiss Diva), the 5f (including at 2 yrs) and 6f winner and listed-placed Dubai Princess (by Dubai Destination) and the fairly useful 6f and 7f winner of 5 races Hajoum (by Exceed And Excel). The dam, a useful winner of 5 races over 5f and 6f including the Weatherbys Super Sprint and the Redcar Two-Year-Old Trophy, is a half-sister to 10 winners including the quite useful triple 6f winner Abbajabba. The second dam, Bo' Babbity (by Strong Gale), a fair 2-y-o 5f winner, is a half-sister to 6 winners including the high-class Group 3 5f King George Stakes winner Anita's Prince. (Dr P Brown). "He's from a fast family, he goes well and he already looks like he's got an engine. A neat, level, strong-quartered five furlong 2-y-o type".

24. CUISINE (IRE) ★★★
b.c. Holy Roman Emperor – Samorra (In The Wings). April 1. First foal. £42,000Y. Doncaster Premier. Badger Bloodstock. The dam, a fair 2-y-o 6f winner, is a half-sister to 4 winners including the Group 1 10f Nassau Stakes and Group 10.4f Musidora Stakes winner Zahrat Dubai. The second dam, Walesiana (by Star Appeal), won the German 1,000 Guineas and is a half-sister to 8 winners. (Brook Farm Bloodstock). "A nice type, he looks a good, solid 2-y-o type and he should be one of our earlier 2-y-o's. He has the same sort of make and shape as a nice 2-y-o we had last year called Charles The Great". Won 1l5 9f mdn Bath by a nk.

25. DAYLIGHT ★★★★
ch.c. Firebreak – Dayville (Dayjur). February 10. Twelfth foal. 70,000Y. Tattersalls October Book 1. G Howson. Half-brother to the moderate 2011 5f and 6f placed 2-y-o Yearbook (by Byron), to the 5f and 6f winner and listed-placed Day By Day (by Kyllachy), the Irish 3-y-o 5f winner Alexander Ballet (by Mind Games and herself dam of the Group 1 Gran Criterium winner Hearts Of Fire), the 2-y-o 1m winner Musical Day (by Singspiel), the 10f and 12f winner My Daisychain (by Hector Protector) – all quite useful – and the fair 2-y-o 6f winner Tedsmore Game (by Indesatchel). The dam, a quite useful triple 6f winner, is a half-sister to

4 winners including the Grade 1 Yellow Ribbon Handicap winner Spanish Fern and to the unraced dams of the Group/Grade 1 winners Lord Shanakill and Heatseeker. The second dam, Chain Fern (by Blushing Groom), is an unraced sister to the Irish 1,000 Guineas and Coronation Stakes winner Al Bahathri (herself dam of the 2,000 Guineas and Champion Stakes winner Haafhd) and a half-sister to the US Grade 2 winner Geraldine's Store. (Kennet Valley Thoroughbreds V). *"Very precocious, he looks every inch a 2-y-o type and he looks just like his sire did at that age. He's closely related to a 2-y-o Group 1 winner in Hearts of Fire and we have high hopes for him. He'll be our first 2-y-o runner I would have thought".*

26. DESERT COMMAND ★★★

b.c. *Oasis Dream – Speed Cop (Cadeaux Genereux).* February 17. Third foal. Brother to the dual 6f winner (including at 2 yrs) Desert Law (by Oasis Dream) and half-brother to the 2011 2-y-o 6f winner Top Cop (by Acclamation) – both fairly useful. The dam, a useful 2-y-o listed 5.2f winner and third in the Group 2 Flying Childers Stakes, is a sister to the fairly useful triple 5f winner (including at 2 yrs) and listed-placed Siren's Gift and a half-sister to the fair 6f winner Indiana Blues. The second dam, Blue Siren (by Bluebird), a very useful winner of three races from 5f to 7f, was disqualified from first place in two more, notably the Group 1 5f Nunthorpe Stakes (the winner on merit) and is a half-sister to several winners including the quite useful 9f winner Northern Habit. (J C Smith). *"A big, backward Oasis Dream, he's a bit unfurnished at the moment and his full-brother Desert Law came together at the latter end of his 2-y-o career, so he'll be fine I'm sure".*

27. DESERT DONKEY ★★★

b.c. *Acclamation – Honky Tonk Sally (Dansili).* January 25. First foal. €42,000Y. Tattersalls Ireland. Andrew Balding. The dam, a quite useful 2-y-o 7f winner, is a half-sister to 7 winners including the very useful Group 3 1m Prix Saint-Roman winner and Group 2 9.8f Prix Dollar third Eco Friendly. The second dam, Flower Girl (by Pharly), a very useful winner of 5 races including the Group 3 6f Goldene Peitsche and the listed 6f Sandy Lane Stakes, is a sister to the useful listed 9.4f winner

Farmost and a half-sister to 3 winners. (GAD Partnership). *"He had a setback but he's OK now and he's very much a 2-y-o type so we'll get cracking with him now".*

28. HAVANA BEAT (IRE) ★★★

b.c. *Teofilo – Sweet Home Alabama (Desert Prince).* March 2. Fourth foal. 65,000Y. Tattersalls October Book 1. Andrew Balding. Half-brother to the modest 1m and hurdles winner King's Realm (by King's Best) and to the minor Italian 3-y-o winner Keyluck (by Key Of Luck). The dam, placed fourth over 7f and 1m, is a half-sister to the Group 1 1m Sussex Stakes winner Proclamation and to the German dual listed winner and smart hurdler No Refuge. The second dam, Shamarra (by Zayyani), is an unraced half-sister to the smart middle-distance performer Shantaroun and to the dams of the Group 3 Meld Stakes and subsequent US Grade 2 winner Sardaniya and the Group 3 Prix du Lutece winner Shaiybara. (Mick & Janice Mariscotti). *"A nice horse, he's a big, long-striding type that won't be early but he looks like he'll make a 2-y-o from mid-summer onwards".*

29. HAVANA MOON (IRE) ★★★

b.f. *Teofilo – Island Destiny (Kris).* April 9. Seventh foal. 22,000Y. Tattersalls December. Norris/Huntingdon. Half-sister to the Italian winner of 4 races at 2 and 3 yrs Federica Vegas (by Desert Prince), to the modest 1m seller winner Divine Rule (by Cacique) and a winner in Denmark by Red Ransom. The dam, a fair 6f placed 2-y-o, is a sister to the Group 1 Coronation Stakes winner Balisada and a half-sister to 3 winners. The second dam, Balnaha (by Lomond), a modest 3-y-o 1m winner, is a sister to Inchmurrin (winner of the Child Stakes and herself dam of the very smart and tough colt Inchinor) and a half-sister to 6 winners including the Mill Reef Stakes winner Welney. (CHF Partnership). *"She's done very well since the sale – she's grown a lot and filled out. So she won't be an obviously early one but she's a nice type".*

30. HERE COMES WHEN (IRE) ★★★★★

b.c. *Danehill Dancer – Quad's Melody (Spinning World).* April 29. Fifth foal. €170,000Y. Goffs Orby. Hugo Merry. Half-sister to Morant Bay (by Montjeu), placed fourth over 1m on her only start at 2 yrs in 2011 and to the Hong Kong winner of 5 races California Moon (by Malibu Moon). The dam won the Group 3 Prix d'Aumale at 2 yrs and is a half-sister to 3 winners including Bonapartiste (Grade 2 Del Mar Handicap). The second dam, Fab's Melody (by Devil's Bag), is a placed half-sister to 2 winners. (Mrs F H Hay). *"A very nice horse indeed. He's done everything we've asked him of so far easily and impressed. We're looking forward to him and he'll be a seven furlong type to begin with I should think. A nice, rangy, athletic horse".*

[handwritten: Slowly away and won. Nice 7f mdn Salisbury on debut]

31. HOT SECRET ★★★★ ♣

br.f. Sakhee's Secret – Harryana (Efisio). April 29. Eighth foal. £23,000Y. Doncaster Premier. Whitsbury Manor Stud. Half-sister to the quite useful 2011 2-y-o 5f winner O'Gorman (by Sleeping Indian), to the 2-y-o Group 2 6f Mill Reef Stakes winner Temple Meads (by Avonbridge), the useful 2-y-o 6f winner and Group 3 Firth of Clyde Stakes second Sneak Preview (by Monsieur Bond) and the moderate French 10f winner Flaxby (by Mister Baileys). The dam, a fair 2-y-o dual 5f winner, is out of the quite useful 3-y-o 5f winner Allyanna (by Thatching), herself a half-sister to 8 winners. (Hot to Trot Racing Club). *"She should be in our first rank of runners, she's shown good speed already as you'd expect from the family. She looks every inch a nice 2-y-o type".*

[handwritten: Won 5f nursery c1.5]

32. INTERNATIONAL LOVE (IRE) ★★ *[handwritten: F. 6(c)]*

ch.f. Manduro – Marika (Marju). April 3. Seventh foal. 50,000Y. Tattersalls October Book 1. Not sold. Half-sister to the quite useful 7f (including at 2 yrs) and 1m winner Folly Lodge (by Grand Lodge), to the minor French 6f winner of 3 races at 2 and 3 yrs Sabratah (by Oasis Dream) and the minor Italian winner of 2 races at 3 and 4 yrs La Sibilla (by Fantastic Light). The dam, a useful 6f listed and 1m winner, is a half-sister to 8 winners including the very useful Group 3 7.3f Fred Darling Stakes winner and Group 2 10f Nassau Stakes third Sueboog (herself dam of the Group 1 Prix d'Ispahan winner Best Of The Bests). The second dam, Nordica (by Northfields), a useful 6f and 1m winner, is a half-sister to 2 winners. (Mr & Mrs R Gorell / Mr & Mrs P Pausewang).

"A nice Manduro from a family we know well. She looks like being an autumn type filly over seven furlongs or a mile".

33. KING MURO ★★★★

b.c. Halling – Ushindi (Montjeu). March 27. Third living foal. 35,000Y. Tattersalls October Book 2. Norris/Huntingdon. Half-brother to the useful 2-y-o dual 6f winner and triple listed-placed Mon Cadeaux (by Cadeaux Genereux). The dam, a modest 12f winner, is a half-sister to 8 winners including the smart broodmare Frond. The second dam, Fern (by Shirley Heights), a fairly useful 12f winner and third in the listed 10f Lupe Stakes, is a half-sister to 6 winners including the Group 1 Fillies Mile winner and Oaks second Shamshir. (Mr P Brend & Mr J Dwyer). *"A very nice colt, we had the half-brother Mon Cadeaux and this is probably a more appropriate mating. I'm a big fan of the sire and this colt looks a really nice type, he's athletic, has plenty of scope and should be a mid-summer 2-y-o".*

34. LIGHT CATCHER ★★★

b.f. Sakhee – Exorcet (Selkirk). February 11. Sister to the fairly useful dual 1m winner Breakheart and half-sister to the very useful 6f winner of 4 races and Group 2 6f Diadem Stakes second Dark Missile, the fair 2-y-o 6f winner Guided Missile and the fair dual 6f winner Night Rocket (all by Night Shift). The dam, a fair 3-y-o 6f winner, is a half-sister to 2 winners including the useful UAE 7f and 1m winner Rock Music. The second dam, Stack Rock (by Ballad Rock), was a very useful winner of 9 races from 5f to 1m including the listed Hopeful Stakes and was second in the Group 1 Prix de l'Abbaye. (J C Smith). *"She's been coughing so I haven't done much with her, but she's a good make and shape and it's a family we've done well with. As a physical specimen she's probably better than either Braveheart or Dark Missile, so that's got to be encouraging".*

35. LIZZIE TUDOR ★★★

ch.f. Tamayuz – Silca Destination (Dubai Destination). March 16. First foal. 30,000Y. Tattersalls October Book 2. Norris/Huntingdon. The dam, a modest 7f and 1m winner, is a half-sister to one winner. The second dam, Golden Silca (by Inchinor), a smart Group 2 6f Mill

Reef Stakes and German Group 2 winner, was second in the Group 1 Coronation Stakes and the Group 1 Irish 1,000 Guineas and is a half-sister to 6 winners including the smart 2-y-o Group 1 6f Prix Morny winner Silca's Sister and the very useful 5f and 6f winner of 12 races (including at 2 yrs) Green Manalishi. (Ms K Gough). *"She's nice, she's done very well since the sale and I like her. A neat, attractive 2-y-o type that should be out soon".*

36. MARISHI TEN (IRE) ★★★
b.f. Invincible Spirit – Scripture (Sadler's Wells). March 11. Fifth foal. €70,000Y. Goffs Orby. McKeever Bloodstock. Half-sister to the listed 12f Swedish Derby winner Moe Green (by Xaar). The dam is an unraced sister to the Group 3 Gordon Richards Stakes winner Scribe and the German listed winner Northern Hal. The second dam, Northern Script (by Arts And Letters), a fairly useful 1m winner, is a half-sister to 10 winners including the Melbourne Cup and Grand Prix de Paris winner At Talaq and Annoconnor (winner of four Grade 1 events in the USA). (Dr P Brown). *"A lovely filly, she goes very well and should be racing by June or July. A nice type of filly".*

37. MARTIAL ART (IRE) ★★★
ch.c. Compton Place – Brush Strokes (Cadeaux Genereux). April 9. Ninth foal. 26,000Y. Tattersalls October Book 2. Not sold. Half-brother to the quite useful 12f winner Kassiopeia (by Galileo), to the French 10.5f winner and listed-placed Craft Fair (by Danehill), the fair 2-y-o 7f winner Kalleidoscope (by Pivotal), the fair dual 1m winner Shesells Seashells (by Tiger Hill), the modest 10f winner My Girl Jode (by Haafhd) and the moderate 5f to 7f winner Tenancy (by Rock Of Gibraltar). The dam is an unraced sister to one winner and a half-sister to 6 winners including the very useful 2-y-o dual 7f winner and Group 1 Racing Post Trophy second Mudeer. The second dam, Colorvista (by Shirley Heights), is an unraced half-sister to 9 winners including Colorspin (winner of the Irish Oaks and dam of the Group 1 winners Zee Zee Top, Opera House and Kayf Tara), Bella Colora (winner of the Prix de l'Opera and dam of the very smart colt Stagecraft) and the Irish Champion Stakes winner Cezanne. (Jackie & George Smith). *"A home-bred by the owners, he*

looks reasonably forward so I'd say he'll make a 2-y-o type by the end of May".

38. MELVIN THE GRATE (IRE) ★★★
b.c. Danehill Dancer – Hawala (Warning). April 20. Ninth foal. 200,000Y. Tattersalls October Book 1. Stephen Hillen. Brother to the useful 2011 2-y-o 6f winner and Group 2 Mill Reef Stakes fourth Foxtrot Romeo, to the smart Group 3 7f Minstrel Stakes winner and Group 1 6f Phoenix Stakes second Air Chief Marshal, the listed 6f (at 2 yrs) and listed 7f winner and Group 3 placed Misu Bond and the fair 7f winner Hunza Dancer and half-brother to the dual sprint listed winner and Group 3 placed Slip Dance (by Celtic Swing), the fairly useful 2-y-o 7f and 1m winner Numen (by Fath), the quite useful 6f winner Winged Harriet (by Hawk Wing) and the minor French 3-y-o winner Hawazi (by Ashkalani). The dam, a useful 8.3f winner, is a half-sister to 4 winners including the French Group 3 winner Afaf. The second dam, the minor French 3-y-o winner Halawa (by Dancing Brave), won once at 3 yrs in France and is a half-sister to 7 winners. (Mrs F H Hay). *"A big horse, he's nice but he'll take a bit of time. He's a good type and is out of a Warning mare which I think is encouraging, but I don't think we'll see him until the autumn".*

39. MUSIKHANI ★★★
b.f. Dalakhani – Musicanna (Cape Cross). February 15. Third foal. 72,000Y. Tattersalls October Book 1. Pitchall Farm Stud. Half-sister to a minor winner abroad by Pivotal. The dam, a smart listed 1m winner of 4 races, was third in the Group 1 Falmouth Stakes and the Group 1 Sun Chariot Stakes and is a half-sister to 8 winners and to the dam of the Group 2 and Group 3 winning sprinter Overdose. The second dam, Upend (by Main Reef), a smart winner of 3 races from 10f to 12f including the Group 3 St Simon Stakes and the listed Galtres Stakes, was second in the Group 3 Princess Royal Stakes and is a half-sister to 6 winners including the dam of the high-class stayer and champion hurdler Royal Gait. (Mrs K Holmes). *"Her owners stand the sire Passing Glance and they bought this filly from the sales, she looks very nice and a bit more forward than you'd expect for a Dalakhani. She'll be a mid-summer 2-y-o".*

40. MR FITZROY (IRE) ★★★

ch.c. Kyllachy – Reputable (Medicean). March 22. Third foal. €72,000Y. Goffs Orby. McKeever Bloodstock. The dam is an unraced half-sister to 14 winners including the US Grade 1 Oaklawn Handicap winner Jovial, the US Grade 3 winner Brave Note and the minor US stakes winner Never Force. The second dam, Rensaler (by Stop The Music), won at around 1m in the USA at 4 yrs and is a half-sister to 10 winners including the US Grade 3 winner Rose Bouquet and the good broodmare Green Rosy (dam of the French Group 2 winners Majorien and America). (Dr P Brown). "A nice, big, tall, scopey colt – very Pivotal-looking. He won't be ready until the late summer at the earliest, but he's a good mover, a nice colt and he's done everything right so far".

41. NEAR TIME ★★

ch.f. New Approach – Time Away (Darshaan). March 27. Seventh foal. 100,000Y. Tattersalls October Book 1. Not sold. Half-sister to the Group 2 Prix de Malleret and listed Cheshire Oaks winner Time On, to the quite useful 10f winner Time Control (both by Sadler's Wells) and the French 3-y-o winner Time Pressure (by Montjeu). The dam won the Group 3 10.4f Musidora Stakes, was third in the Group 1 Prix de Diane and the Group 1 Nassau Stakes and is a half-sister to 6 winners including the 10f winner and Prix de Diane second Time Ahead. The second dam, Not Before Time (by Polish Precedent), is an unraced half-sister to 7 winners including the Group 2 winners Zinaad and Time Allowed. (R Barnett). "A nice filly by first season sire New Approach. She represents that good Sadler's Wells – Darshaan cross and although she'll take time it is a lovely family. We won't be in any hurry with her".

42. NELLIE FORBUSH ★★★★

b.f. Phoenix Reach – Santa Isobel (Nashwan). January 28. Sister to the fairly useful 1m (at 2 yrs) and 12f winner Whiplash Willie and half-sister to the fair 15f and 2m winner Isabelonabicycle (by Helissio) and a hurdles winner by Diktat. The dam, a fairly useful listed 10f winner, is a half-sister to 3 winners. The second dam, Atlantic Record (by Slip Anchor), is an unraced half-sister to 4 winners including the useful 2-y-o 8.2f winner Fascinating Rhythm and the

useful 10f and 10.3f winner Migwar. (J C & S R Hitchins). "A very nice filly, she's got plenty of quality, she won't be early but I like her very much. One for later on this season".

43. NEW FFOREST ★★★★

b.f. Oasis Dream – Ffestiniog (Efisio). April 3. Closely related to the quite useful 5f and 6f winner Oceans Apart (by Desert Prince) and half-sister to the Group 3 1m Solonaway Stakes winner of 4 races Border Patrol (by Selkirk), to the smart sprint winner of 11 races (including the Group 3 Prix de Meautry) Eisteddfod (by Cadeaux Genereux), the useful 2-y-o 5f to 7f winner Brecon Beacon (by Spectrum), the useful dual 7f (at 2 yrs) and UAE Group 3 1m winner Boston Lodge (by Grand Lodge), the fairly useful 2-y-o 6f winner Harlech Castle (by Royal Applause) and the quite useful 2-y-o dual 7f winner Tredegar (by Inchinor). The dam, a fairly useful 2-y-o listed 7.3f and 3-y-o 1m winner, is a half-sister to several winners. The second dam, Penny Fan (by Nomination), was placed once over 5f at 3 yrs, is closely related to the listed 5f Scarborough Stakes winner Rivers Rhapsody and a half-sister to the Group 3 5f Prix d'Arenburg winner Regal Scintilla. (Elite Racing Club). "She's a good make and shape – a very typical Oasis Dream. The dam was useful and this filly looks a 2-y-o type for sure. Six furlongs should be her trip".

44. NOT RIGG (USA) ★★★

b.c. Henrythenavigator – St Helens Shadow (Septieme Ciel). January 23. Ninth foal. 95,000Y. Tattersalls October Book 1. Stephen Hillen. Half-brother to 3 winners including the US Grade 1 Champagne Stakes winner Officer. The dam, a minor US stakes winner, is a half-sister to 9 winners including 2 US stakes winners. (Mrs F H Hay). "He's had a high testicle removed and that delayed us a bit but he's alright and he should make a mid-summer 2-y-o".

45. OPERATION CHARIOT ★★

b.c. Refuse To Bend – Dona Royale (Darshaan). April 27. Tenth foal. €23,000Y. Tattersalls Ireland. Andrew Balding. Brother to the quite useful dual 1m winner Negotiation and half-brother to the quite useful 8.6f and 9.5f winner Bazelle, to the quite useful 2-y-o dual 7f winner Old Malt (both by Ashkalani), the minor French

3-y-o winner Dream West (by Zafonic) and a winner in Scandinavia by Captain Rio. The dam was placed over 1m and 10f and is a half-sister to 7 winners including the Grade 2 9f San Gorgonio Handicap and Group 2 8.5f Grosser Preis von Dusseldorf winner Royal Touch, the Group 2 12f Blandford Stakes winner Foresee, the listed 2-y-o Stardom Stakes winner Bonarelli and the US Grade 2-placed winner Aventino. The second dam, Sovereign Dona (by Sovereign Path), won 4 races including the Group 3 10f Prix de Psyche and is a half-sister to the St James's Palace Stakes winner Don and the French dual Group 3 winner American Prince. (Mr P Brend & Mr J Dwyer). *"He's a nice horse and he's another one that represents that good Sadler's Wells – Darshaan cross. He looks more precocious than I imagined he would do, so we'll get him out when the seven furlong races start".*

46. PEARL BOUNTY (IRE) ★★★★ ♠

ch.c. Bahamian Bounty – Roslea Lady (Alhaarth). February 14. Third foal. 120,000Y. Tattersalls October Book 2. David Redvers. Half-brother to the quite useful 2-y-o 6f winner Hoot (by Invincible Spirit). The dam, placed fourth once over 1m, is a half-sister to the Group 2 Gimcrack Stakes winner Conquest. The second dam, Aguinaga (by Machiavellian), won over 12.5f in Ireland and is a half-sister to 7 winners including the Group 1 Haydock Park Sprint Cup winner Iktamal and the Group 2 winners First Magnitude and Rockamundo. (Pearl Bloodstock Ltd). *"He's very nice, very forward, has plenty of speed and we're hopeful of him being a decent 2-y-o. Small and sharp-looking, he's just a thoroughly nice 2-y-o type".*

47. PEARL CASTLE (IRE) ★★★★

b.c. Montjeu – Ghurra (War Chant). January 14. Second foal. 150,000Y. Tattersalls December. David Redvers. The dam, a quite useful 2-y-o 6f winner, subsequently won in the USA and was third in the Grade 3 Wilshire Handicap. She is a sister to the winner and US Grade 2 third Zifzaf and a half-sister to 7 winners including the smart 2-y-o Group 1 6f Middle Park Stakes winner Hayil and the useful 2-y-o winners Mizhar, Farqad and Elnahaar. The second dam, Futuh (by Diesis), a fairly useful 2-y-o 6f winner, is a half-sister to 7 winners including

the Canadian stakes winner Rose Park (herself the dam of the smart US Grade 2 winner Wild Rush). (Pearl Bloodstock Ltd). *"A very nice, athletic colt and a great mover. He's very well put-together and for a Montjeu I'm hopeful he'll be quite early, so in mid-season we should see him out. Hopefully he'll turn into a nice horse".*

48. PRAIRIE PRINCE (IRE) ★★★

b.c. High Chaparral – Palatine Dancer (Namid). April 24. Third foal. 45,000Y. Tattersalls December. Will Edmeades. Half-brother to the quite useful 2-y-o 6f winner Blaze Of Thunder (by Ad Valorem). The dam is an unplaced half-sister to 3 winners including the useful 6f to 8.2f and subsequent US stakes winner Wixoe Express. The second dam, Esquiline (by Gone West), is an unplaced half-sister to 5 minor winners in France. (Thurloe Thoroughbreds). *"He's had sore shins, but he's nice and looks more like his damsire Namid than High Chaparral in many ways. We won't be in a hurry with him and I'd like to think he'll be out in July or August".*

49. PURCELL (IRE) ★★★★

b.c. Acclamation – Lyca Ballerina (Marju). April 24. Fourth foal. £115,000Y. Doncaster Premier. John Warren. Brother to the fair dual 6f winner Pose. The dam, a fair 7f winner at 3 yrs, is a half-sister to 6 winners. The second dam, Lovely Lyca (by Night Shift), a fair 1m and 11.8f winner, is a sister to the listed 1m winners Barboukh (herself dam of the Group 3 10f Prix Exbury winner Barbola) and a half-sister to 7 winners. (Highclere Thoroughbred Racing – John Porter). *"A cracking type – a lovely, athletic colt with a good attitude. He's done a fair bit of growing since he came in so and he's still quite backward in his coat, but I think he'll make giant strides in the few weeks and we hope to get him out around June time".*

50. RACE AND STATUS (IRE) ★★★

b.c. Raven's Pass – Love Excelling (Polish Precedent). February 3. Fifth foal. 240,000Y. Tattersalls October Book 1. John Warren. Half-brother to the smart Group 3 6f Anglesey Stakes and Group 3 1m Irish 2,000 Guineas Trial winner Dunboyne Express (by Shamardal), to the fairly useful Irish dual 10f winner Angels Story (by Galileo) and a minor winner abroad by

Rock Of Gibraltar. The dam ran once unplaced and is a half-sister to 7 winners including the high-class Group 1 12f Oaks and listed Lupe Stakes winner Love Divine (herself dam of the St Leger winner Sixties Icon) and the listed 12f winner Floreeda. The second dam, La Sky (by Law Society), a useful 10f winner and second in the Group 3 Lancashire Oaks, is closely related to the Champion Stakes winner Legal Case and a half-sister to 4 winners. (Jackie & George Smith). *"A lovely horse, he was expensive and he looks to me like a middle distance horse in the making. A fine, great big horse, he's a very easy mover with a good attitude – a nice horse".*

51. REFECTORY (IRE) ★★

b.c. Danehill Dancer – Akuna Bay (Mr Prospector). May 23. Eighth foal. €75,000Y. Goffs Orby. Badgers Bloodstock. Brother to the fairly useful 2011 2-y-o 1m winner Secretary Of State and to the useful 2-y-o 5f and 6f winner and Group 3 Solario Stakes third Gaspar Van Wittel, closely related to the useful 10f and 12f winner and Group 3 Cumberland Lodge Stakes second Sugar Ray (by Danehill) and half-brother to the fair Scandinavian listed 12f winner Demeanour (by Giant's Causeway) and a minor winner abroad by King Of Kings and half-brother to the minor US winner of 3 races at 3 yrs Princess Eliza (by Johannesburg). The dam, a 2-y-o 7f winner, is a half-sister to 3 winners including the Ribblesdale Stakes second Gothic Dream (herself the dam of two listed winners). The second dam, Dark Lomond (by Lomond), won the Irish St Leger and is a half-sister to 5 winners including the Irish Group winners South Atlantic and Forlene. (Brook Farm Bloodstock). *"He was a late May foal but he's done well since he came in. He was a rig and has had the high testicle removed, but he'll be alright. We're not in a hurry with him".*

52. ROYAL WHISPER ★★

b.f. Royal Applause – Never A Doubt (Night Shift). January 26. Fifth foal. 260,000Y. Tattersalls October Book 1. John Warren. Sister to the useful 5f (at 2 yrs) and listed 7f winner and Group 2 7f Rockfel Stakes third Royal Confidence and half-sister to the quite useful 1m winner Rougette (by Red Ransom). The dam, a very useful 2-y-o winner of the Group 2 5.5f Prix Robert Papin, is a half-sister to 3 winners. The second dam, Waypoint (by Cadeaux Genereux), a fairly useful 6f and 7f winner, is a half-sister to 5 winners including the Group 2 6f Diadem Stakes winner and sire Acclamation. (Jackie & George Smith). *"She had a small setback so we're just going to have to be cautious with her. She's a lovely type, but we probably won't get her onto the track until the autumn".*

53. SOVIET ROCK (IRE) ★★★★

b.c. Rock Of Gibraltar – Anna Karenina (USA) (Atticus). March 25. Sixth foal. 180,000Y. Tattersalls October Book 1. John Warren. Brother to the useful Irish 7f (at 2 yrs) and listed 7.5f winner Anna's Rock (by Rock Of Gibraltar) and half-brother to the unplaced 2011 2-y-o (in one start) Precious Stone (by Galileo) and the useful 1m winner and listed-placed Sugar Mint (by High Chaparral). The dam is an unraced half-sister to 10 winners including the Group 3 Prix de Psyche winner and French 1,000 Guineas and French Oaks placed Agathe (herself dam of the Grade/Group 1 winners Artiste Royale and Aquarelliste), to the Breeders Cup Classic winner Arcangues and the dams of the Group/Grade 1 winners Cape Verdi and Angara. The second dam, Albertine (by Irish River), a smart winner of two races at up to 10f, was third in the Group 2 Prix de l'Opera and is a half-sister to 8 winners including the high-class middle-distance stayer Ashmore and the smart middle-distance filly Acoma. (Jackie & George Smith). *"A lovely horse, he's really coming together now. It's a wonderful family and he's a good mover and a nice type with plenty of scope, so I'm looking forward to him".*

54. STORMING (IRE) ★★★★

b.c. Stormy Atlantic – French Lady (Entrepreneur). May 5. Third foal. €35,000Y. Goffs Orby. Badgers Bloodstock. Half-brother to the US 2-y-o winner Philosopher Queen (by Empire Maker). The dam, a 3-y-o winner in New Zealand and Grade 1 placed, is a half-sister to 2 winners. The second dam, La Tebaldi (by Cure The Blues), won 3 minor races at 3 yrs in Italy and is a half-sister to 7 winners. (CJJR Partnership). *"His progress has been delayed by a persistent cough unfortunately, but he's a really nice type of horse, strong, straight forward and certainly a mid-summer 2-y-o".*

55. SUBTLE DIFFERENCE ★★★

b.f. *Vita Rosa – Sulitelma (The Minstrel)*. March 19. Half-sister to the quite useful 2-y-o 5f winner Ice Mountain (by Kyllachy), to the quite useful 10f to 12f winner Tromp, the fair 7f and 1m winner Robinzal (both by Zilzal), the fair 2-y-o 1m winner Min Mirri, the modest 6f and 1m winner Border Glen (both by Selkirk), the fair Irish 5f winner Neeze (by Cadeaux Genereux), the fair 2-y-o 7f winner Song Of The Siren (by With Approval), the modest 2-y-o 6f winner Seta Pura (by Domedriver) and the modest 9.4f winner Semiramis (by Darshaan). The dam, a modest 2-y-o 5f all-weather winner, is a half-sister to 3 winners including the German listed winner El Supremo. The second dam, Sharmila (by Blakeney), ran once unplaced and is a half-sister to the King George VI and Queen Elizabeth Diamond Stakes winner Petoski. (Kirsten Rausing). *"We've had plenty from the family and this a really nice type of filly, I'm very happy with her. She'll make a 2-y-o from mid-season onwards and she's an attractive, good-moving filly".*

56. TOO DIFFICULT (IRE) ★★★★

ch.f. *Rock Of Gibraltar – Etizaan (Unfuwain)*. March 20. Third foal. €20,000Y. Goffs Orby. Hugo Merry. Half-sister to the fairly useful dual 1m winner Etizaan (by Dalakhani). The dam is an unplaced half-sister to 8 winners including the Group 3 10f Gallinule Stakes winner Grand Ducal and the useful 2-y-o 6f winner and Group 2 6f Gimcrack Stakes fourth Hurricane Floyd. The second dam, Mood Swings (Shirley Heights), a fair 2-y-o 6f winner, is a sister to the listed 2-y-o Sweet Solera Stakes winner Catwalk and a half-sister to 5 winners. (Mrs F H Hay). *"A lovely filly, I can't believe she only cost 20 Grand. She's a good mover with plenty of scope and I see her as a mid-summer 2-y-o".*

57. TRANSLUCENT ★★★

b.c. *Trans Island – Little Miss Diva (Diktat)*. April 14. First foal. €8,500Y. Tattersalls Ireland. Andrew Balding. The dam, a modest Irish 1m (at 2 yrs) and 9f placed maiden, is a half-sister to 8 winners and to the placed dam of the Group winners Sayif and Hunter Street. The second dam, Anchorage (by Slip Anchor), a quite useful dual 12f winner, is a half-sister to 6 winners including the Group 3 Ormonde Sakes winner Brunico. *"He looks very much like his damsire, Diktat and for what he cost I think he was a snip".* TRAINERS' BARGAIN BUY

58. VAN PERCY ★★★

b.c. *Sir Percy – Enforce (Kalanisi)*. April 24. Second foal. 27,000Y. Tattersalls October Book 2. BBA (Ire). The dam, a smart listed 1m winner, was in third in the Group 3 8.5f Princess Elizabeth Stakes and is a half-sister to 2 winners. The second dam, Kinetic Force (by Holy Bull), was placed over 6f at 2 yrs in France and is a half-sister to 7 winners including the US Grade 1 7f winner Mizzen Mast. (Mrs L E Ramsden & Richard Morecombe). *"A smashing type, not the biggest horse in the world but he looks very active, he's a good mover and I'd be disappointed if he's not ready for when the seven furlong races start".*

59. VICKSBURG ★★★

b.f. *Cape Cross – Totality (Dancing Brave)*. April 3. Ninth foal. 50,000Y. Tattersalls October Book 1. Huntingdon/Norris. Half-sister to the 10f winner Total Devotion (by Desert Prince) and to the 12f winner Total Care (by Caerleon) – both quite useful. The dam, a quite useful 14f winner from just two outings, is a sister to the Epsom and Irish Derby winner Commander in Chief and a half-sister to 8 winners including the champion 2-y-o and miler Warning, the Irish Derby second Deploy, the Great Voltigeur Stakes winner Dushyantor and the Flower Bowl Handicap and Ribblesdale Stakes winner Yashmak. The second dam, Slightly Dangerous (by Roberto), winner of the 7.3f Fred Darling Stakes, was second in the Oaks and is a half-sister to the dams of the Arc winner and top class sire Rainbow Quest and the Dewhurst Stakes dead-heater Scenic. (Mr R J C Wilmot-Smith). *"She's going to take a bit of time but it's a wonderful family and she's a really nice filly that was well-bought. I'm very happy with her".*

60. WALTER WHITE (IRE) ★★★

b.c. *Dark Angel – Fun Time (Fraam)*. April 11. Third foal. £32,000Y. Doncaster Premier. Emma Balding. The dam, a modest 2-y-o 7f winner, is a half-sister to 2 winners. The second dam, Kissing Time (by Lugana Beach), a quite useful

5f winner of 5 races (including at 2 yrs), is a sister to a winner in Germany and a half-sister to 3 winners including the Group 2 6f Diadem Stakes winner and sire Acclamation and the dam of the Group 2 Prix Robert Papin winner Never A Doubt. (GAD Partnership). *"He should be one of our earlier types, he's done plenty and he'll be racing in May over five furlongs but I'm sure he'll stay six. He's got a bit more scope than I was thinking he'd have, he's tall and athletic".*

61. YOU DA ONE (IRE) ★★★★

br.c. *Footstepsinthesand – Shenkara (Night Shift).* March 2. Fifth foal. 45,000Y. Tattersalls October Book 2. Andrew Balding. Half-brother to the fair 5f (at 2 yrs) to 1m winner of 7 races and listed-placed Crocodile Bay (by Spectrum), to the 2-y-o 5f winner (on his only start) Metal Soldier (by Antonius Pius) and a winner in Greece by Invincible Spirit. The dam, placed fourth once over 1m at 2 yrs in Ireland, is a half-sister to 3 minor winners. The second dam, Sheriyna (by Darshaan), a listed winner in France at 3 yrs, is a half-sister to 5 winners including the Prix de Diane winner Shemaka (herself the dam of 3 stakes winners in France). (Mr & Mrs R Gorell / Mr & Mrs P Pausewang). *"He's done well since the sale, he's a nice colt, he goes well and he'll be an early June 2-y-o I have reasonably high hopes for".*

62. ZANETTO ★★★

b.c. *Medicean – Play Bouzouki (Halling).* February 9. Fourth living foal. 40,000Y. Tattersalls October Book 1. Andrew Balding. Half-brother to Dream Tune (by Oasis Dream), unplaced in one start at 2 yrs in 2011. The dam, a modest 1m placed 3-y-o, is a half-sister to 4 winners including the UAE Group 2 and Group 3 Select Stakes winner Alkaadhem. The second dam, Balalaika (by Sadler's Wells), won the listed Dahlia Stakes and is a sister to the high-class Group 2 10f Prince of Wales's Stakes and dual US Grade 2 winner Stagecraft and a half-sister to 5 winners including the Group 3 winner Mullins Bay. (Mick & Janice Mariscotti). *"He's done plenty, he'll probably just have the speed for six but he'll be better over seven furlongs and a mile in time. I expect he'll be ready at the end of May or the beginning of June".*

Stayed on well made all to early win cl 4 mbn Newmnt

RALPH BECKETT
63. ALDBOROUGH (IRE) ★★

b.c. *Danehill Dancer – Kitty O'Shea (Sadler's Wells).* April 14. Fourth foal. Brother to the smart Irish 2-y-o 7f winner and Group 1 Moyglare Stud Stakes third Kissable and to the quite useful 2-y-o 7f winner and listed placed Kingdom Of Munster. The dam ran twice and won both races over 1m (including at 2 yrs and a listed event at 3 yrs). She is a sister to the Group 1 Racing Post Trophy and Group 1 St Leger winner Brian Boru and a half-sister to the Group winners Sea Moon and Moon Search and to the dam of the Derby winner Workforce. The second dam, Eva Luna (by Alleged), won the Group 3 14.6f Park Hill Stakes and is a half-sister to 5 winners including the US listed winner Rougeur (herself dam of the US Grade 1 winner Flute). (Mr & Mrs David Aykroyd). *"It's a family that takes time, so he's not going to be appearing in the near future. One for the back-end, he has a good temperament and he's a big horse in every way. Much more of a 3-y-o type".*

64. ANNA'S PEARL ★★★

ch.c. *Pivotal – Mi Anna (Lake Coniston).* April 18. Ninth foal. 80,000Y. Tattersalls October Book 1. David Redvers. Half-brother to the German dual Group 2 1m winner Mi Emma (by Silvano), to the German winner and listed-placed Mi Rubina (by Rock Of Gibraltar) and 5 minor winners in Germany by Azamour, Soviet Star, Sholokov, Lavirco and Grand Lodge. The dam a German 2-y-o listed winner, is a half-sister to 3 winners. The second dam, Medicenal (by Robellino), won 4 races in Germany and is a half-sister to 3 winners. (Pearl Bloodstock Ltd). *"I expected him to be more backward than he now appears to be. He was a bit of a lad, so we got on with him and he responded for work. He's a good-moving horse and he has a good way of going, so I think he'll be racing from mid-summer onwards and he looks a nice prospect".*

65. ARE YOU MINE ★★★

b.f. *Nayef – Celtic Slipper (Anabaa).* March 10. First foal. 32,000Y. Tattersalls October Book 2. Not sold. The dam, a very useful 7f (at 2 yrs) and Group 3 1m Premio Dormello winner, was third in the Group 2 May Hill Stakes and is a half-sister to 2 winners. The second dam,

Celtic Silhouette (by Celtic Swing), was placed four times at 4 and 5 yrs in France and is a sister to the listed winner and Group 2 Dante Stakes second Celtic Silence and a half-sister to the dual Group 3 winner Royal And Regal. (P D Savill). *"She'll need a bit of time, but her mother was a decent 2-y-o for us and she's not dissimilar to her. We like her and hopefully she'll be appearing by July/August time and go on from there".*

66. BIRDLOVER ★★★

ch.f. *Byron – Bird Over (Bold Edge).* March 5. Half-sister to the fair 2-y-o 7f winner Birdolini (by Bertolini). The dam was a fairly useful 7f (including at 2 yrs) and 6f winner of 6 races. The second dam, High Bird (by Polar Falcon), was an unraced half-sister to several winners. *"I trained the mother who won six races for us. This filly is more attractive than Bird Over who was as plain as a pikestaff and I wouldn't be against the sire either because he gets plenty of winners. She was suffering from a cold but she's healthy now and we'll crack on with her because she won't take forever to get ready. I think she'll start at six furlongs".*

67. CITY GIRL (IRE) ★★★★

b.f. *Elusive City – Lochridge (Indian Ridge).* February 26. Half-sister to the fair 2-y-o 6f winner Echo Ridge (by Oratorio). The dam, a smart listed 6f winner of 5 races, is a half-sister to 3 winners including the useful listed 5f winner Loch Verdi. The second dam, Lochsong (by Song), a champion sprinter and winner of the Prix de l'Abbaye (twice), the Kings Stand Stakes and the Nunthorpe Stakes, is a half-sister to the Nunthorpe Stakes winner Lochangel. (J C Smith). *"It's a very fast family, I trained her half-sister Echo Ridge who won as a 2-y-o but didn't have very good knees. This filly has more bone about her and I would think she'll make a 2-y-o. I'll start working her around the end of April and we'll see where we go from there. I'm a fan of the sire and this is a strong filly that seems to have a good attitude".*

2nd list 2 racer won bf mtn Lingfield

68. DAY IN DAY OUT ★★★ ♠

b.c. *Notnowcato – Cockatrice (Petong).* March 14. Seventh foal. 31,000Y. Tattersalls October Book 2. David Redvers. Half-brother to the Italian listed 5f winner Cocktail (by Most

Welcome), to the modest Irish 11f and hurdles winner Coffee, Tea Or Me (by Vettori) and the poor 2m winner Tiffin Brown (by Erhaab). The dam is an unplaced half-sister to 7 winners including the very useful 6f (at 2 yrs) and triple listed winner Dubai's Touch, the very useful 8.5f and 9f winner and Group 3 Diomed Stakes third Wannabe Around, the useful triple 6f winner (including at 2 yrs) and subsequent Abu Dhabi listed winner Grantley Adams and the useful 7.5f to 10f winner and French Group 3 1m third Nobelist. The second dam, Noble Peregrine (by Lomond), an Italian 10f winner, is closely related to the French 2-y-o listed 10f winner Noble Ballerina and a half-sister to 6 winners. (P Hickey). *"He was a horse we bought in the first hour of the sale at Newmarket and I think everyone was being cagey and watching rather than bidding, so I hope he was well-bought. I like him very much for his attitude as much as anything – he's got a very good way about him. I thought the sire did well last year but you'd expect them to need time, so he's a horse you'd expect would improve from 2 to 3. We should be able to have a campaign with him this year from seven furlongs onwards".*

69. EXOTIC ISLE ★★★

ch.f. *Exceed And Excel – Paradise Isle (Bahamian Bounty).* March 21. Second foal. 80,000Y. Tattersalls October Book 2. David Redvers. Half-sister to the modest 2011 2-y-o 5f winner Princess Banu (by Oasis Dream). The dam, a useful 5f (at 2 yrs) and 6f winner of 8 races including two listed events, was third in the Group 3 6f Summer Stakes and is a full or half-sister to 9 winners. The second dam, Merry Rous (by Rousillon), a moderate 2-y-o 6f winner, is a half-sister to 5 winners including the dual Group 3 winning sprinter Tina's Pet. (Pearl Bloodstock & Nicholas Wrigley). *"She's very forward – an early sort of filly that's done a bit on the grass and she'll be racing in May. She's a neat filly, Chris Wall trained the mother and he tells me none of the family are big".*

70. HIPSTER ★★★

b.c. *Kingsalsa – Hip (Pivotal).* March 25. First foal. 20,000Y. Tattersalls October Book 2. Ralph Beckett. The dam, a quite useful 2-y-o 6f winner, is a half-sister to 4 winners including the 2-y-o Group 1 6f Cheveley Park Stakes and

Group 2 6f Lowther Stakes winner Hooray and the useful 2-y-o listed 8.3f winner of 7 races Hypnotic. The second dam, Hypnotize (by Machiavellian), a useful 2-y-o dual 7f winner, is closely related to 2 winners including the Group 3 6f Cherry Hinton Stakes winner Dazzle and a half-sister to 5 winners including the useful 7f (at 2 yrs) and 1m listed winner Fantasize and to the placed dam of the Group 2 winning sprinter Danehurst. (Mr R J Roberts). *"She has a good pedigree on the dam's side although the sire isn't fashionable. He was a very correct yearling, which is what attracted me to him, he has a good step to him but he's grown quite a lot over the winter so he's not quite as forward as I'd expected. He's doing plenty at the moment though and I could see him being out in June/ July time. I like him and I see him as being one for auction races".*

71. HOLD ON TIGHT ★★★

ch.f. Hernando – Wait It Out (Swain). January 25. Second foal. The dam won two races at 2 and 4 yrs in the USA and was stakes placed and is a half-sister to 5 winners. The second dam, As Long As Ittakes (by Sky Classic), is an unraced half-sister to 7 winners. (Eclipse Partnership). *"It's the same Hernando – Blushing Groom cross as the good filly we had called Look Here. I'm not sure this filly will be as good as her, but she's nice and she's done very well in the last six to eight weeks. One for the second half of the season and we like her".*

72. INGOT OF GOLD ★★★

b.f. Dubawi – Cresta Gold (Halling). January 29. Second foal. 270,000foal. Tattersalls December. R Frisby. Half-sister to the fair 2011 2-y-o 7f winner Rhagori (by Exceed And Excel). The dam, a useful 11f and 12f winner, was listed-placed and is a half-sister to the Group 3 Lingfield Classic Trial and Group 3 Dee Stakes winner African Dream and the listed-placed winners Fenella's Link and Lone Wolfe. The second dam, Fleet Hill (by Warrshan), winner of the listed Superlative Stakes and third in the Group 3 Rockfel Stakes, is a half-sister to 6 winners including the useful listed 6f Sandy Lane Stakes winner Lee Artiste. (Landmark Bloodstock & GB Partnership). *"A very attractive filly, she was very expensive and it was a great compliment that we were sent her. Her half-sister Rhagori needed* a bit of time and has done very well from two to three. I expect this filly will improve throughout the year, she has plenty of bone, she's strong but she isn't forward. So she'll need a bit of time and she'll definitely want seven furlongs".*

73. INKA SURPRISE ★★★

b.c. Intikhab – Sweet Surprise (Danetime). March 7. First foal. €7,500Y. Tattersalls Ireland. David Redvers. The dam was placed once over 5f at 2 yrs in Ireland. The second dam, Last Rolo (by Mark Of Esteem), is an unplaced half-sister to 10 winner Samsaam (Group 3 Prix Berteux). (McDonagh, Murphy & Dixon). *"He'll have run by the time of publication, he's doing well and I like him. So he's a sharp 2-y-o, but like a lot by his sire he should progress and get further than five furlongs. Definitely one for the list, he's a nice horse. He was cheap because of the lack of winners in the pedigree but I'm glad we have him".* TRAINERS' BARGAIN BUY

74. LADY VERMEER ★★★

b.f. Dutch Art – Classic Vision (Classic Cliché). March 1. Fourth living foal. 32,000Y. Tattersalls October Book 2. R Frisby. Half-sister to the fair 2-y-o 7f winner Farsighted (by Where Or When) and to the moderate 9f winner Excellent Vision (by Exceed And Excel). The dam, a modest 6f and 1m winner, is a half-sister to 5 winners including the dual Group 3 winner Orientor, to the Royal Hunt Cup winner Yeast and the dam of the Irish Group 3 winner Montecastillo. The second dam, Orient (by Bay Express), a useful sprint winner of 3 races, was third in the Group 1 Kings Stand Stakes. (W.E.A Fox). *"She had a small problem with a foot but it looks like we'll be getting on with her this year. It's a fast family even though the dam is by Classic Cliché and who could help being a fan of Dutch Art? So she'll make a 2-y-o alright".*

75. LA SURAMA ★★★

ch.f. Sakhee – La Dangeville (Danehill). April 3. Third foal. €50,000Y. Arqana Deauville August. Not sold. Half-sister to the French 2-y-o 6f and 1m winner Manhaj (by Medicean). The dam is a placed half-sister to 5 winners including the Group 1 German Derby winner Lavirco, the Group 2 German St Leger winner Laveron and the Group 3 German winner Lyonels Glory. The second dam, La Virginia (by Surumu), won twice and is a half-sister to 6 winners including the dam of the triple Group 1 winner and sire Lomitas. (Newsells Park Stud Ltd). *"A strong filly, she's quite heavy-topped and she's had a few issues this spring so she needs to go home for some spring grass this week. We'll see her later on though, she's a good-mover and has a good way about her, tall but not backward. One for seven furlongs and a mile later in the year".*

76. LEMON PEARL ★★

ch.f. Singspiel – Basemah (Lemon Drop Kid). April 12. Third foal. 55,000Y. Tattersalls October Book 1. David Redvers. The dam, a 1m (at 2 yrs), 9f and listed 10f winner, is a half-sister to one winner. The second dam, Attractive Crown (by Chief's Crown), a useful Irish 6f (at 2 yrs) and 1m winner, was second in the Group 2 10f Pretty Polly Stakes and is a half-sister to 5 winners. (Pearl Bloodstock Ltd). *"A tall, long filly, she's done very well physically over the winter. She has her own ideas but she's been training well, she'll have a spring break now and we'll see her in the autumn".*

77. MME SAND GENE ★★★

gr.f. Verglas – Diablerette (Green Desert). February 11. Third foal. Half-sister to Rainbow Gold, unplaced in one start at 2 yrs in 2011 and to the fair 1m winner Ecossaise (both by Selkirk). The dam, a fair 2-y-o dual 6f winner, is a sister to one winner and a half-sister to the German Group 1 10f winner Lady Jane Digby, the very smart Group 3 7f and 9f winner and Group 1 placed Gateman and the smart 1m Royal Hunt Cup winner Surprise Encounter. The second dam, Scandalette (by Niniski), is an unraced half-sister to 9 winners including the Group 1 July Cup winner Polish Patriot and the Italian listed winner Grand Cayman. (Miss K Rausing). *"A burly, robust sort of filly, I'm just starting to step up her work now. It looks like she'll need a bit of dig in the ground but she's by a speed horse and she's an early foal, so we'll get on with her soon with a view towards getting her out in May or June over six furlongs".*

78. PEARL BRIDGE ★★★★

b.c. Avonbridge – Our Little Secret (Rossini). March 21. Third foal. £28,000Y. Doncaster Premier. David Redvers. Half-brother to the promising 2011 2-y-o 5f winner Pearl Secret (by Compton Place). The dam, a useful listed 5f winner of 6 races, is a half-sister to 3 winners. The second dam, Sports Post Lady (by M Double M), a fair 5f winner of 4 races, is a half-sister to 5 winners including the useful sprinter Palacegate Episode (a winner of 11 races here and abroad including a Group 3 race in Italy and numerous listed events). (Pearl Bloodstock Ltd). *"His half-brother looked very good on his only run at York. I bought this colt on spec and David decided he was one for Pearl Bloodstock so I hope it works out! It's a very speedy pedigree but he's not that forward and although he's shown us a bit I haven't pressed on with him. He'll be appearing in the second half of the summer, he has a good attitude, he puts everything in and he's a good-moving sort of horse. At the moment he doesn't look to be all-speed, as his pedigree would suggest. I'm looking forward to him".*

79. PERFECT HAVEN ★★

gr.f. Singspiel – Night Haven (Night Shift). February 14. Eighth foal. £16,000Y. Doncaster Premier. Ralph Beckett. Half-sister to the useful 2-y-o 7f and listed 10f winner and US dual Grade 2 placed Rosa Grace (by Lomitas), to the fairly useful 5f and 6f winner and listed-placed Secret Night (by Dansili), the moderate 5f winner of 5 races, including at 2 yrs, Duke Of Rainford (by Bahamian Bounty) and a winner in Denmark by Observatory. The dam, a fairly useful 5f (at 2 yrs) and 6f winner and 6f listed-placed, is a sister to 3 winners including the French 2-y-o listed 5f winner Shoalhaven. The second dam, Noble Haven (by Indian King), won once at 2 yrs and is a half-sister to 6 winners. *"It's not a pedigree you'd normally find in the Doncaster catalogue, so perhaps she slipped under the radar a bit. It's more of a Tattersalls Book 2 pedigree really. She's going to need some time but she's a February foal and she's not backward, so she might be sharper than her pedigree".*

80. POMPEIA ★★

ch.f. Singspiel – Caesarea (Generous). April 22. Ninth foal. Sister to the fairly useful listed 14f placed and bumpers winner Caesar's Song and half-sister to the useful 10f and 12f winner Corriolanus (by Zamindar), the quite useful 11f and 14f winner Ashbrittle (by Rainbow Quest), three minor winners abroad by Monsun, Daylami and Tiger Hill and a winner over hurdles by Spectrum. The dam is a half-sister to the German Group 1 12f winner Catella and a half-sister to 4 winners. The second dam, Crystal Ring (by Kris), a quite useful 1m winner, is a half-sister to 7 winners including the top-class middle-distance colts Diamond Shoal and Glint Of Gold. (J L Rowsell). *"I trained the half-brother Ashbrittle who I think only ran once at two and I think this filly will be similar. She's a slightly different type in that she's closer coupled and not as tall, she'll need seven furlongs to begin with, she has a good way of going and I like her".*

81. PROSPERA (IRE) ★★★

b.f. Cape Cross – Opera (Forzando). March 20. Half-sister to the very useful 9f to 12f winner (including a Breeders Cup listed event over 11f) Muhannak (by Chester House) and to 2 winners in the USA by Gold Case including the minor stakes winner Gold Taker. The dam, a fair 7f and 1m 2-y-o winner, subsequently won and was stakes-placed in the USA and is a half-sister to 2 winners. The second dam, Flattering (by Nodouble), won over 6f at 2 yrs in Ireland and is a half-sister to 2 winners. (The Millennium Madness Partnership). *"She hasn't got the quirks that her half-brother Muhannak had, thankfully! She's not a tall filly, she looks like making a 2-y-o and I would think we'd see her out in June or July. A filly with a good attitude".*

82. RATHNAREE ★★

b.g. Intikhab – United Passion (Emarati). February 7. Fifth foal. 23,000Y. Tattersalls October Book 2. David Redvers. Half-brother to the modest 2011 2-y-o 5f winner Bookiesindexdotnet, to the fair 5f winner of 5 races Bookiesindex Boy (both by Piccolo) and the fair 5f winner of 4 races Fair Passion (by Trade Fair). The dam, a fair 5f winner of 3 races, is a half-sister to 5 winners. The second dam, Miriam (by Forzando), a modest dual 5f winner, is a half-sister to 7 winners. *"A very big horse, but he was a very big yearling as well. Fortunately he hasn't grown over the winter, I gelded him to help him because I didn't want him getting too heavy and too boisterous. He might not take that long but given his size I'll*

give him plenty of time. One for late summer, he'll be a six furlong horse".*

83. RIO'S PEARL ★★★

b.f. Captain Rio – Agony Aunt (Formidable). March 14. Ninth foal. £50,000Y. Doncaster Premier. David Redvers. Sister to the listed 1m winner Agony And Ecstasy and half-sister to the fairly useful 6f winner of 6 races here and in the UAE winner Doctor Hilary (by Mujahid), the quite useful 6f and subsequent Hong Kong winner Cool Tune (by Piccolo), the modest 5f to 7f winner of 7 races Only If I Laugh (by Piccolo), the moderate 1m winner Disabuse (by Fleetwood) and the moderate 10f and 11f winner Miss Havisham (by Josr Algharoud). The dam, a quite useful 10f winner, is a half-sister to 2 winners. The second dam, Loch Clair (by Lomond), is an unplaced half-sister to 6 winners including the Group 1 winner Wind In Her Hair (herself the dam of four stakes winners including the champion Japanese horse Deep Impact). (Pearl Bloodstock Ltd). *"A full-sister to one of ours, Agony And Ecstasy, she's done a bit of work on the grass and it won't be long before she appears. She's quite big but not backward and she'll need some give in the ground or polytrack. She might appear in May, probably over six furlongs".*

84. ROYAL PRIZE ★★★

ch.c. Nayef – Spot Prize (Seattle Dancer). March 12. Half-brother to the useful 7f (at 2 yrs) and listed 10f winner Premier Prize (by Selkirk), to the Group 2 15f Prix Kergorlay winner Gold Medallist (by Zilzal), the fairly useful 12f winner Stage Right (by In The Wings), the quite useful 1m and 12f winner Western Prize (by High Chaparral), the quite useful 14f winner Prize Dancer (by Suave Dancer) and the modest 12f and hurdles winner Prize Ring (by Bering). The dam, a useful filly, won over 5f at 2 yrs and was fourth in the Oaks. The second dam, Lucky Break (by What Luck), won 4 races in the USA. (J C Smith). *"A half-brother to Western Prize, who we train, he's a lot more forward than he was and not as tall. A good-moving horse – he doesn't have that big action that some Nayef's have, he'll need seven furlongs this year, but he might not take forever and it may be worth noting that Western Prize needs faster ground".*

85. SECRET GESTURE ★★★

b.f. Galileo – Shastye (Danehill). January 22. Third foal. 230,000Y. Tattersalls October Book 1. Not sold. The dam, a useful 12f and 13f winner, was listed-placed and is a half-sister to 7 winners including the Prix de l'Arc de Triomphe winner Sagamix, the Group 1 Criterium de Saint-Cloud winner Sagacity and the Group 2 Prix de Malleret winner Sage Et Jolie (herself dam of the Group 1 winner Sageburg). The second dam, Saganeca (by Sagace), a very smart winner of the Group 3 12.5f Prix de Royallieu and second in the Group 1 Gran Premio di Milano, is a half-sister to 2 winners. (Newsells Park Stud Ltd). "A very nice filly. We've only trained one Galileo before so it's very nice to have her, she was an early foal and she's not a big, robust 2-y-o but you wouldn't say she was light-framed either. She's sweet, straightforward and a pleasure to deal with, we'll be minding her for the time being but getting on with her in June or July – then we'll see how we go".

Easily won gl 1m f m1a Newbury

86. SILVER RIDGE (IRE) ★★★

gr.c. Verglas – Jacaranda Ridge (Indian Ridge). February 26. Second foal. £22,000Y. Doncaster Festival. David Redvers. Half-brother to La Pampita (by Intikhab), placed third over 7f on her only start at 2 yrs in 2011. The dam, a quite useful 7f winner, is a half-sister to the very smart Group 1 12f Gran Premio del Jockey Club and listed 10f winner Rainbow Peak and the smart 7f (at 2 yrs) and 1m listed winner Celtic Heroine. The second dam, Celtic Fling (by Lion Cavern), a fair 3-y-o 8.3f winner, is a half-sister to the outstanding champion 2-y-o Celtic Swing, winner of the French Derby and the Racing Post Trophy. (The Pickford Hill Partnership). "I've done a bit with him but he got sore shins so we're just giving him some time to come back. He'll need some give in the ground and as regards what sort of trip he'll be best suited to there are mixed messages from the family, but he does look like a 2-y-o. We'll start him at six furlongs I should think".

Won sf cl5 mdn Windsor by 5l

87. SIZZLER ★★★

ch.c. Hernando – Gino's Spirits (Perugino). March 18. Seventh foal. 60,000Y. Tattersalls October Book 1. Not sold. Brother to the 9f (at 2 yrs) and subsequent US Grade 1 9f winner Gitano Hernando (by Hernando) and half-brother to the minor Italian 2-y-o winner India Spirit (by Dr Fong), a hurdles winner by Lomitas and two minor winners abroad by Dubai Destination and Rainbow Quest. The dam won 9 races here and in the USA including the Grade 3 Noble Damsel Handicap and was second in the Group 2 Sun Chariot Stakes and is a half-sister to 5 winners. The second dam, Rising Spirits (by Cure The Blues), a fair 2-y-o 7f winner, later won in the USA and is a half-sister to 6 winners including the dual Group 3 winner Citidancer. (Heseltine, Henley & Jones). "A big, tall, long horse that's going to take plenty of time and plenty of work, but he's attractive and I think he'll start at the back-end much like his full-brother".

88. TALENT ★★★★

Won cl3 7f rnds Kempton

ch.f. New Approach – Prowess (Peintre Celebre). February 25. Second foal. Half-sister to the useful dual 1m winner Skilful (by Selkirk). The dam, a fairly useful 12f winner, was listed-placed and is a half-sister to the fairly useful 11.5f winner and listed placed Genoa and the useful 2-y-o 1m winner and listed-placed Clipper. The second dam, Yawl (by Rainbow Quest), winner of the Group 3 7f Rockfel Stakes, was second in the 10f Lupe Stakes and is a half-sister to 7 winners. (James Rowsell & Mark Dixon). "I'm a real fan of this filly, she's very attractive, has a good way about her and she shouldn't take forever. She'll need six furlongs to start off with and probably seven by the end of the year. I like her, she's by no means backward and she's a neat filly with a bit of strength about her".

89. THORPE (IRE) ★★★

b.c. Danehill Dancer – Minkova (Sadler's Wells). April 8. Third foal. Closely related to the fairly useful Irish 2-y-o 7f winner and listed-placed East Meets West (by Dansili). The dam is an unraced daughter of the Irish listed winner and Irish Oaks and Breeders Cup Filly & Mare Turf second L'Ancresse (by Darshaan), herself a sister to the Group 1 Prix Saint-Alary winner Cerulean Sky and a half-sister to the Irish Oaks winner Moonstone. (Mr & Mrs David Aykroyd). "Much like our other Danehill Dancer 2-y-o he'll need plenty of time because he's pretty backward and weak at the moment, but I expect him to improve significantly over the next 3 months. He's a long way off any fast work, but with a pedigree like his of course I'm looking forward to him".

90. UNNAMED ★★★

b.c. Ishiguru – Tharwa (Last Tycoon). February 18. Eighth foal. 25,000Y. Tattersalls December. R Frisby. Half-brother to the useful 5f and 6f winner of 5 races Enchantment (by Compton Place), to the quite useful 6f and 7f winner Nisr (by Grand Lodge), the modest dual 5f winner Minnow (by Averti), the modest 7f and 1m winner Taiyo (by Tagula) and the moderate 7f winner Riczar (by Intikhab). The dam, a modest 5.2f and 6f winner, is a half-sister to 8 winners including the French listed winner Blushing All Over and good broodmare Come On Rosi (the dam of four stakes winners). The second dam, Victory Kingdom (by Vice Regal), was a stakes-placed winner of 5 races in the USA. (The Quick Fill Partnership). "He's forward and I hope he's as quick as the half-sister Enchantment. He'll be one for auction races initially but he has a good way of going and he looks sharp. He gashed his leg as a yearling which set him back a bit, so I haven't been able to do any fast work with him just yet, but he'll be fine".

MICHAEL BELL

91. ALGORITHMIC (IRE) ★★

b.c. Danehill Dancer – Tanami Desert (Lycius). April 17. Fifth foal. 340,000Y. Tattersalls October Book 1. Blandford Bloodstock. Brother to the Group 2 Prix Daniel Wildenstein and Group 3 Prix de la Grotte winner and dual Group 1 second Tamazirte. The dam is an unplaced half-sister to 4 winners including the 2-y-o Group 2 7f Rockfel Stakes winner Cairns. The second dam, Tanami (by Green Desert), a very useful 5f and 6f winner and second in the Group 1 Cheveley Park Stakes, is a half-sister to 3 winners including the dam of the Cheveley Park Stakes winner Wannabe Grand. (Mr L J Inman). "A well-bred horse, he'll hopefully continue to thrive but he won't be early".

92. BILL OF RIGHTS ★★★

b.f. Kyllachy – Bijou A Moi (Rainbow Quest). April 20. Fourth foal. 52,000Y. Tattersalls October Book 2. Not sold. The dam is an unraced half-sister to 4 winners including the Irish 2-y-o 7f winner and listed placed Pietra Dura (herself dam of the US Grade 3 winner and Grade 1 second Turning Top). The second dam, Bianca Nera (by Salse), a smart 2-y-o winner of the Group 1 7f Moyglare Stud Stakes and the Group 2 6f Lowther Stakes, is half-sister to 4 winners including the very useful Group 1 Moyglare Stud Stakes second Hotelgenie Dot Com (herself dam of the dual Group 1 winner Simply Perfect). (R Frisby). "She hasn't been in long but she's a nice, straightforward, easy-moving filly that hasn't been asked any questions yet. She'll make a 2-y-o in the second half of the season".

93. BLACK TRUFFLE ★★★

b.c. Kyllachy – Some Diva (Dr Fong). April 22. Third foal. €60,000Y. Goffs Orby. Jane Allison. Half-brother to the fair 2011 2-y-o 1m winner Shannon Spree (by Royal Applause). The dam, a modest 9f winner, is a half-sister to 3 winners including the Group 1 Middle Park Stakes winner Primo Valentino and the Group 2 6f Cherry Hinton Stakes winner and Group 1 6f Phoenix Stakes third Dora Carrington. The second dam, Dorothea Brooke (by Dancing Brave), won over 9f and is a half-sister to 6 winners. (Mrs S M Roy). "He's taking time to come to hand but the penny is just beginning to drop and I view him as a second half of the season 2-y-o".

94. CAPELLA'S SONG (IRE) ★★★

b.f. Oratorio – Bright Bank (Sadler's Wells). February 14. Fourth foal. €42,000Y. Goffs Orby. R Frisby. Half-sister to the fairly useful 2011 2-y-o 7f winner Devotion (by Dylan Thomas). The dam is an unraced half-sister to 6 winners including the very useful listed 6f and 7f winner and dual Group 1 placed My Branch (herself the dam of the Group 1 Sprint Cup winner Tante Rose). The second dam, Pay The Bank (by High Top), a quite useful 2-y-o 1m winner, stayed 10f and is a half-sister to 4 winners. (P.A Phillipps & C.E.L Phillipps). "She's pleasing me and she looks quite sharp. She wasn't expensive considering her family and although the sire hasn't set the world on fire this filly's sister by Dylan Thomas was pretty useful, so I'm happy with her so far".

95. CARLARAJAH ★★★ ♠

ch.c. Sleeping Indian – Carla (Cardoun). March 5. Tenth foal. £52,000Y. Doncaster Premier. Will Edmeades. Half-brother to the Group 3 1m Prix Edmond Blanc winner Svedov (by Exit To Nowhere), to the listed Oaks Trial winner Zain Al Boldan (by Poliglote) and 2 minor winners in France by Goldneyev and Zieten. The dam, a dual listed winner in France over 7f and 1m, is a half-sister to 5 winners including Golani (Prix Edmond Blanc). The second dam, El Quahirah (by Cadoudal), a winner of 4 races and Group 3 placed, is a half-sister to 6 winners. *"A well-bred horse, he has a good temperament and is a very well-made colt. We're just ticking along with him at the moment but I like what I see. I'd say he'd be a seven furlong 2-y-o".*

96. CHARTER (IRE) ★★

b.c. Elusive City – Lucky Norwegian (Almutawakel). April 26. Fourth foal. €64,000Y. Goffs Orby. John Warren. Half-brother to the quite useful 2-y-o dual 7f winner Astonishment (by Desert Style) and a winner of the dam won one race in Norway at 3 yrs and is a half-sister to 3 other minor winners and to the dams of Elusive Wave (Group 1 French 2,000 Guineas) and Langs Lash (Group 2 Queen Mary Stakes). The second dam, Echoes (by Niniski), won the Group 3 Prix Corrida and is a half-sister to 5 winners. (Royal Ascot Racing Club). *"He's a horse that's changed shape physically since he was bought. He's beginning to come to hand but he's a late April foal and I'm taking my time with him".*

97. DEFICIT (IRE) ★★★★

gr.c. Dalakhani – Venturi (Danehill Dancer). April 24. Fifth foal. 140,000Y. Tattersalls October Book 1. Blandford Bloodstock. Half-brother to the fairly useful 10f winner and dual listed fourth Stella Point, to the quite useful 1m winner Call To Reason (both by Pivotal) and the quite useful Irish 1m and 11f winner and listed-placed Cilium (by War Chant). The dam, winner of the Group 3 7f C L Weld Park Stakes, was subsequently second in two US Grade 3 events and is a sister to the French listed winner and Group 1 Criterium de Saint-Cloud third Feels All Right. The second dam, Zagreb Flyer (by Old Vic), is an unraced half-sister to 8 winners including the listed winner and Group 1 Italian Oaks second Flying Girl. (Mr J L Inman). *"A nice*

colt, I loved him as a yearling and considering he's by Dalakhani he's showing plenty at this stage, so although he's very much a 3-y-o prospect I could see him being a high-class autumn 2-y-o".

98. DIVERGENCE (IRE) ★★★ ♠

b.f. Teofilo – Min Alhawa (Riverman). April 19. Tenth foal. €140,000Y. Goffs Orby. Blandford Bloodstock. Half-sister to the fair 2011 7f placed 2-y-o Buzkashi (by Nayef), to the smart 10f, 12f and UAE listed winner Mutasallil (by Gone West), the useful 10f and 12f winner Nuzooa (by A P Indy), the useful 10f and 11f winner and Group 3 Cumberland Lodge Stakes third Ajhar (by Diesis), the fairly useful 10f winner Matraash (by Elusive Quality) and the fairly useful 12.3f winner Tasneef (by Gulch). The dam, a useful 7f (at 2 yrs) to 10f winner, is a sister to the very smart 1,000 Guineas and Celebration Mile winner Harayir and a half-sister to 3 winners. The second dam, Saffaanh (by Shareef Dancer), a quite useful 12.2f winner, is a half-sister to 4 winners including the Group 2 Falmouth Stakes winner Alshakr. (Mr L J Inman). *"She's a bit more precocious than I imagined when we bought her, we're not trying to do too much too soon with her, but I like what I see".*

99. FILS ANGES (IRE) ★★★★

gr.c. Dark Angel – La Piaf (Fabulous Dancer). February 16. Thirteenth foal. £35,000Y. Doncaster Premier. Sackville/Donald. Half-brother to the fairly useful 5f and 6f winner of 7 races Merlin's Dancer (by Magic Ring), to the quite useful 7f and 1m winner Gilded Dancer (by Bishop Of Cashel), the fair 2-y-o 8.6f winner Bridegroom, the fair 9f winner Show No Fear (both by Groom Dancer), the fair 9f and 10f winner Mick's Dancer (by Pivotal) and a winner of 9 races in Turkey by Primo Dominie. The dam, a 2-y-o French 7.5f winner, later won a minor stakes in the USA and was Grade 3 placed and is a full or half-sister to 6 winners including the Grade 1 Del Mar Oaks winner Golden Apples and the Group 3 Park Hill Stakes winner Alexander Three D. The second dam, Loon (by Kaldoun), was a French listed winner of 4 races. (Mr D Hanafin). *"He'll be racing in April, I like the sire's progeny and this colt seems quite sharp. The dam has produced plenty of* winners, although nothing of any class, but I think this colt looks an above average 2-y-o type". *Bolted up when well backed for in ord 6 runner*

100. GAMBLE ★★★ *c1 5 mdn Nottingham*

ch.f. *Galileo – Pretty Face (Rainbow Quest)*. March 19. Second foal. The dam is an unraced sister to the Group 2 14f Yorkshire Cup winner Manifest and a half-sister to 9 winners including Reams of Verse (Epsom Oaks and the Group 1 Fillies Mile) and Elmaamul (Group 1 10f Coral Eclipse Stakes and the Group 1 10f Phoenix Champion Stakes). The second dam, Modena (by Roberto), is an unraced half-sister to the smart 2-y-o 7f winner and Queen Elizabeth II Stakes third Zaizafon (herself the dam of Zafonic). (The Queen). *"A big, scopey filly, she's very rangy and probably won't do too much until the autumn. A classy filly, she has a good temperament, she moves well and won't be rushed".*

101. GEORGE CINQ ★★★

b.c. *Pastoral Pursuits – Fairnilee (Selkirk)*. January 24. Second foal. 42,000Y. Tattersalls October Book 2. Kern/Lillingston. Half-brother to the unplaced 2011 2-y-o Sweet Fernando (by Hernando). The dam, a modest 6f winner, is a half-sister to 2 winners including the fairly useful triple 6f winner (including at 2 yrs) Fantaisiste. The second dam, Fantastic Belle (by Night Shift), a quite useful 6f winner, is a sister to the Canadian Grade 2 winner Moon Solitaire and a half-sister to 9 winners including the Group 3 10f Gordon Richards Stakes winner Germano. (Tamdown Group Ltd). *"A good-looking horse that's grown significantly since we bought him. I'm just taking my time with him because he's very much a second half of the season 2-y-o".*

102. HISPANIA (IRE) ★★★

b.f. *Teofilo – Badalona (Cape Cross)*. April 17. First foal. The dam, a quite useful 2-y-o 1m winner, is a sister to one winner and a half-sister to numerous winners including the very useful 2-y-o 6f winner and Group 1 Cheveley Park Stakes third Badminton, the useful 2-y-o 7f winner and Group 3 7f Vintage Stakes third Fox and the useful 6f and 7f winner and Group 3 Nell Gwyn Stakes second Cala. The second dam, Badawi (by Diesis), was a useful 1m and 9f

winner of 4 races. (Marwan Al Maktoum). *"She's a nice filly, very straightforward and a good mover. All those that ride her seem to like her".*

103. HOT MUSTARD ★★★

b.c. *Pastoral Pursuits – Lihou Island (Beveled)*. February 20. Fifth foal. 55,000Y. Tattersalls October Book 2. Michael Bell. Half-brother to the useful 7f (including at 2 yrs) and 6f winner of 6 races Horseradish (by Kyllachy). The dam, a quite useful 2-y-o 6f winner, is a half-sister to 6 winners. The second dam, Foreign Mistress (by Darshaan), was placed 12 times in Italy and is a half-sister to 3 winners. (Mrs G Rowland-Clark). *"He hasn't been in that long but we did well with his brother Horseradish and this horse is a better physical specimen. So I'd be hopeful of him being quite nice".*

104. HUNTSMANS CLOSE ★★★★

b.c. *Elusive Quality – Badminton (Zieten)*. April 20. Half-brother to the quite useful 7f winner Burghley (by Shamardal). The dam, a very useful 2-y-o 6f winner and third in the Group 1 Cheveley Park Stakes, is a half-sister to numerous winners including the useful 2-y-o 7f winner and Group 3 7f Vintage Stakes third Fox, the useful 6f and 7f winner and Group 3 Nell Gwyn Stakes second Cala and the useful 7f winner Rafferty. The second dam, Badawi (by Diesis), was a useful 1m and 9f winner of 4 races. (Marwan Al Maktoum). *"A good-looking horse and a very good mover, he looks like one for the second half of the season. Given the way he moves I'd be disappointed if he's not good".*

105. JADESNUMBERONE (IRE) ★★★

b.f. *Authorized – Gabriella (Cape Cross)*. February 23. Second foal. €42,000Y. Goffs Orby. John Warren. Half-sister to the fair 7f and 1m winner The Guru Of Gloom (by Dubai Destination). The dam is an unraced half-sister to 4 winners including the Group 1 Golden Jubilee Stakes and Australian Group 1 winner Cape Of Good Hope, the promising 2011 Group 3 winning 2-y-o Nephrite and the useful 2-y-o 6f winner and Group 1 Coronation Stakes fourth Cape Columbine. The second dam, Cape Merino (by Clantime), a useful winner of 4 races over 5f and 6f, is a full or half-sister to 4 winners. (Sir Alex Ferguson & Mr Mike Dawson). *"Despite this filly being by*

Authorized it's quite a fast family and she was a February foal, so I very much hope she'll be able to do something in the Autumn. She looks a classy, good-moving filly".

106. KENSINGTON GARDENS ★★★★

b.f. Oasis Dream – Wendylina (In The Wings). February 28. Sister to the very smart 2-y-o Group 3 Solario Stakes and 3-y-o Group 2 10f Prix Guillaume d'Ornano winner Sri Putra and half-sister to the fairly useful 11f and hurdles winner Duty (by Rainbow Quest). The dam is an unraced half-sister to 9 winners including the Group 1 10.5f Prix de Diane winner Caerlina. The second dam, Dinalina (by Top Ville), a French 2-y-o 10f winner, is a half-sister to 8 winners including the Doncaster Cup winner Karadar and the dams of the Group 1 winners Kartajana and Khariyda. (Mrs Julia Scott & Mr James Dean). *"I like this filly a lot. She gets up Warren Hill very well and she should be one to watch out for".*

107. KIMBERELLA ★★★★

b.c. Kyllachy – Gleam Of Light (Danehill). April 15. Twelfth living foal. £85,000Y. Doncaster Premier. Richard Frisby. Brother to the very smart dual Group 2 7f Park Stakes and Group 2 7f Challenge Stakes winner Arabian Gleam and half-brother to the fairly useful 12f winner and listed-placed Bumptious (by Mister Baileys), the fairly useful 2-y-o 7f winners Gleaming Blade (by Diesis) and Opening Ceremony, the French winner of 3 races Light Quest (both by Quest For Fame) and the modest 6f and 7f winner Blue Noodles (by Reset). The dam, a quite useful dual 7.5f winner at 3 yrs, is a half-sister to 4 minor winners. The second dam, Gold Runner (by Runnett), is a placed half-sister to 6 winners including the dual Guineas winner Don't Forget Me. (Mr K.J.P Gundlach). *"He looks like having the speed to win over five furlongs, he has a good temperament and he's a real model 2-y-o type".*

Won g¹ by m dn Dunc pron g¹

108. MOVES LIKE JAGGER ★★ dead

b.c. Danehill Dancer – Lucky Spin (Pivotal). April 15. Third foal. 100,000Y. Tattersalls October Book 1. Kern/Lillingston. The dam, a winner of 5 races including the Group 3 7f Chartwell Stakes and the Group 3 6f Summer Stakes, is a half-sister to 4 winners. The second dam, Perioscope (by Legend Of France), placed over 6f in Scandinavia, is a half-sister to 4 minor winners. (Mr K.J.P Gundlach). *"By a very good stallion, he's quite a scopey colt so I haven't done much with him yet because I'm giving him time to fill his frame".*

109. OILINDA ★★★

b.f. Nayef – Loyal Love (Danzig). February 23. Second foal. 50,000Y. Tattersalls October Book 2. John Warren. Half-sister to the minor French 3-y-o winner Infidelite (by Diktat). The dam, a quite useful 2-y-o 6f winner, is a half-sister to 3 winners. The second dam, Always Loyal (Zilzal), won 3 races including the French 1,000 Guineas and the Group 3 1m Prix de la Grotte and is a half-sister to the top-class sprinter Anabaa, the Group 3 Prix d'Arenburg winner Key Of Luck and the listed winner Country Belle (dam of the Group 2 Gimcrack Stakes winner Country Reel). (Karmaa Racing Ltd). *"She's a nice filly with a very decent pedigree, the dam bolted up on her only outing as a 2-y-o. Being by Nayef we're not rushing her but she should turn into a decent filly".*

110. POINT OF CONTROL ★★★

b.f. Pivotal – Finlaggan (Be My Chief). January 29. Eleventh foal. 250,000Y. Tattersalls October Book 1. Blandford Bloodstock. Sister to the smart Group 3 5f Palace House Stakes and subsequent US Grade 3 9f winner Needwood Blade and to the quite useful 1m winner Summers Lease and half-sister to the quite useful 6f to 7.5f and subsequent US Grade 3 winner Islay Mist (by Distant Relative), the German listed winner Australian Dreams (by Magic Ring), the useful 1m (at 2 yrs) to 2m and hurdles winner Merveilles (by Vettori), the fair 1m winner Feolin (by Dr Fong) and the fair 4-y-o 8.2f winner Flashing Blade (by Inchinor). The dam, a quite useful 11f to 2m winner, is a half-sister to 7 winners. The second dam, Misty Halo (by High Top), a fairly useful winner of 22 races (including in the Isle Of Man) from 1m to 2m 2f, is a half-sister to 4 winners. (Mr L J Inman). *"The sire isn't renowned for early 2-y-o types but this filly is a real beauty to look at. We'll step up the pace in the second half of the season and see what we've got".*

111. RISKIT FOR A BISKIT (IRE) ★★★

b.f. Kodiac – Miss Brief (Brief Truce). April 9. Fifth foal. £60,000Y. Doncaster Premier. Richard Frisby. Half-sister to the smart 2011 2-y-o dual 6f winner and dual Group 2 placed Crown Prosecutor (by Exceed And Excel) and a hurdles winner by Revoque. The dam, a fair 5f placed maiden, is a half-sister to 6 winners including the Group 3 winner and Group 1 placed Dhanyata. The second dam, Preponderance (by Cyrano de Bergerac), a quite useful 2-y-o dual 5f winner, is a half-sister to 6 winners. (Mr C Wright & The Hon Mrs J M Corbett). *"She had a minor setback after looking like she'd be a sharp 2-y-o. She did look quite useful and hopefully she'll be back with me soon".*

112. SABRE (IRE) ★★★★ ♠

br.c. Kheleyf – Spiritual Air (Royal Applause). February 16. Fourth foal. £70,000Y. Doncaster Premier. John Warren. Half-brother to the fair 2-y-o 7f winner Andean Margin (by Giant's Causeway) and to the moderate 7f and 1m winner Emeralds Spirit (by Rock Of Gibraltar). The dam, a fairly useful 2-y-o 6f winner, subsequently won at 4 yrs in the USA and is a half-sister to 3 winners including the very useful 2-y-o 5f winner and Group 2 6f Mill Reef Stakes second Mystical Land. The second dam, Samsung Spirit (by Statoblest), a fair dual 6f winner (including at 2 yrs), is a half-sister to 7 winners and to the placed dam of the Group 2 6f Mill Reef Stakes winner Indian Rocket. (Highclere Thoroughbred Racing – Herbert Jones). *"A big, strong horse and one of our earlier types. The dam was a decent 2-y-o, it's a good, fast family and he's a very strong, well-made horse that looks like being a nice summer 2-y-o".*

113. SEEMENOMORE ★★★

b.c. Bahamian Bounty – Rise (Polar Falcon). February 27. Fourth foal. 95,000Y. Tattersalls October Book 2. Half-brother to the moderate 1m and 9f winner of 5 races Join Up and to a minor winner in Greece (both by Green Desert). The dam won 3 races from 6f to 7f at 2 and 3 yrs and is a half-sister to 5 winners including the smart 6f winner Feet So Fast and the Group 2 Lowther Stakes winner Soar. The second dam, Splice (by Sharpo), a smart winner of 7 races including the listed 6f Abernant Stakes, is a full

or half-sister to 7 winners. (Mr K.J.P Gundlach). *"I like him. He had a minor hold-up which stopped me doing much more with him, but he's a very good-looking, well-made 2-y-o type".*

114. SOUVENIR ★★★

b.f. Cape Cross – Trianon (Nayef). February 1. First foal. The dam, a fair 2-y-o 1m winner, is a half-sister to the smart Group 2 12f Ribblesdale Stakes and Group 2 13.3f Geoffrey Freer Stakes winner Phantom Gold (herself dam of the Oaks second Flight Of Fancy) and the useful 10f listed winner Fictitious. The second dam, Trying For Gold (Northern Baby), was a useful 12f and 12.5f winner at 3 yrs. (The Queen). *"A nice filly from a staying family, she'll take a little time and is an Autumn type 2-y-o".*

115. STAR OF ROHM ★★★★

ch.c. Exceed And Excel – Noble Desert (Green Desert). February 13. Fourth foal. 32,000Y. Tattersalls October Book 2. Stephen Hillen. Half-brother to the quite useful 5f (including at 2 yrs) and 6f winner Mr Optimistic (by Kyllachy), to the fair 6f (including at 2 yrs) and 7f winner The Human League (by Tobougg) and the modest 2-y-o 1m winner Noble Dictator (by Diktat). The dam is an unplaced half-sister to 9 winners. The second dam, Sporades (by Vaguely Noble), won 3 races in France including the Group 3 10.5f Prix de Flore and is a half-sister to 9 winners including the high-class colts Mill Native (Grade 1 10f Arlington Million) and French Stress (three Group 3 1m wins in France) and the 2-y-o Group 3 5f Prix du Bois winner American Stress. (Mrs Louise Whitehead and Mr Chris Lomas). *"A sharp 2-y-o type by a sire we like, he's definitely got the speed for six furlongs and possibly five. I hope he'll be above average".*

116. THE MANX MISSILE ★★★★

ch.c. Sakhee's Secret – Careless Freedom (Bertolini). January 25. First foal. 25,000Y. Tattersalls October Book 2. Charlie Gordon-Watson. The dam ran once unplaced and is a half-sister to 6 winners including the Group 3 5f Premio Omenoni winner and Group 2 Diadem Stakes second Leap For Joy (herself dam of a Japanese Group 3 winner) and the listed-placed Waffle On (the dam of three stakes winners) and to the unraced Lower

Chapel (dam of the New Zealand champion and multiple Group 1 winner King's Chapel). The second dam, Humble Pie (by Known Fact), a fairly useful 2-y-o 6f winner, was listed-placed and is a half-sister to 4 winners including the high-class sprinter College Chapel and the dam of the Group 2 winners Barrow Creek and Last Resort. (P J Ransley). *"A very sharp colt from a speedy family, he's a well-muscled 2-y-o type. He's definitely got the speed for five furlongs and it's a question if he'll stay six. He's quick and was a January foal to boot".* TRAINERS' BARGAIN BUY

117. WE ARE CITY ★★★

b.f. *Elusive City – Musique Magique (Mozart).* March 3. Third foal. 22,000Y. Tattersalls October Book 2. Kern/Lillingston. Half-sister to Dinvar Diva (by Dalakhani), placed fourth over 1m on her only start at 2 yrs in 2011. The dam, a quite useful Irish 2-y-o 7f winner on her only start, is a half-sister to 2 winners including the Group 3 12f Prix d'Hedouville winner Magadan. The second dam, Molasses (by Machiavellian), is an unraced half-sister to 8 winners including the Oaks winner Light Shift, the champion older mare and Group 1 10.5f Tattersalls Gold Cup winner Shiva and the Group 2 12f Prix Jean de Chaudenay winner Limnos. (Middleham Park Racing VI & Partner). *"She's been slightly held-up with a sore shin but the dam was useful at two and this filly looks a 2-y-o type. Five/six furlongs in May/June should suit her – and the dam was quick".*

118. WILDCRAFTING ★★★

ch.f. *Exceed And Excel – Local Spirit (Lion Cavern).* February 9. Third foal. Half-sister to the quite useful 2011 2-y-o 7f winner Al Saham (by Authorized). The dam, a useful 10f winner, was second in the Group 2 12f Lancashire Oaks and is a sister to the high-class Irish 1,000 Guineas, Coronation Stakes and Nassau Stakes winner Crimplene and a half-sister to 7 winners including the smart Group 3 12.3f Chester Vase winner Dutch Gold. The second dam, Crimson Conquest (by Diesis), a quite useful 2-y-o 6f winner, is a half-sister to the US stakes winner at around 1m Sword Blade. (Marwan Al Maktoum). *"Sore shins is stopping us getting on with her for now, but she's a very good mover and she'll certainly be a summer 2-y-o".*

119. ZERO GAME (IRE) ★★★★ ♠

b.f. *High Chaparral – Freezing Love (Danzig).* April 17. Fifth foal. 40,000Y. Tattersalls October Book 1. Kern/Lillingston. Half-sister to the French 3-y-o dual 1m winner Frozen Ardour (by Dr Fong). The dam won once at 2 yrs in France and is a sister to the US stakes winner and Grade 1 San Carlos Handicap second Alyzig and a half-sister to 3 winners. The second dam, Touch Of Love (by Alydar), a winner of two stakes events in the USA and Grade 3 placed, is a half-sister to 8 winners. (E J Ware). *"She was well-bought for 40,000 at the Sales – you could hardly buy a sandwich at Tattersalls that week for that sort of money! She looks nice, we've done well with the sire and he's probably still underrated. A very good-moving, athletic filly, she'll be one for seven furlongs and a mile later this season and she looks well bought".*

120. UNNAMED ★★★

b.c. *Kheleyf – Blue Echo (Kyllachy).* March 1. Second foal. 220,000Y. Tattersalls October Book 1. A O Nerses. The dam won 3 races including two listed events over 6f is a half-sister to 6 winners including the smart dual 2-y-o 6f winner and subsequent US Grade 2 9f winner Sapphire Ring and the smart dual listed winner Putra Pekan. The second dam, Mazarine Blue (by Bellypha), a modest sprint winner at 3 yrs, is a half-sister to 7 winners including Rich Charlie (Group 2 6f Richmond Stakes). (Saleh Al Homaizi & Imad Al Sagar). *"He's a very strong, well-made horse and a summer type 2-y-o".*

121. UNNAMED ★★★

b.f. *Duke Of Marmalade – Crystal Curling (Peintre Celebre).* April 18. Fourth foal. €40,000Y. Goffs Orby. Frank Barry. Closely related to the fair 1m winner Sparkling Crystal (by Danehill Dancer) and to a minor winner abroad by Oratorio. The dam, a fairly useful 2-y-o 7f winner, is a half-sister to 5 winners including the dam of the Group 3 Minstrel Stakes winner Three Rocks. The second dam, State Crystal (by High Estate), won the Group 3 12f Lancashire Oaks and was placed in the Yorkshire Oaks and the Prix Vermeille. She is a half-sister to 6 winners including the Group 1 Fillies' Mile winner Crystal Music, the Group 3 winners Dubai Success and Solar Crystal and the Irish Derby third Tchaikovsky. (Magnier,

Tabor, Smith). *"She's not that sharp on pedigree but I'm very pleased with the way she goes, given that her pedigree suggests she shouldn't be going so well at this stage. I think she could be quite nice, she looks quite sharp and I'm encouraged".*

122. UNNAMED ★★★★ AZRUR
b.c. *Sir Percy – Tiger Spice (Royal Applause).* March 15. First foal. 110,000Y. Tattersalls October Book 2. A O Nerses. The dam, a modest 2-y-o 9f winner, is a half-sister to 4 winners including the dam of the Group 3 Oak Tree Stakes winner Summer Fete and the unplaced dam of the US Grade 2 and Grade 3 winner Up In Time. The second dam, Up And About (by Barathea), a fair 14.8f winner, is a half-sister to 8 winners including the listed winner and Group 1 placed Musicanna and the dam of the champion European 3-y-o sprinter Overdose. (Saleh Al Homaizi & Imad Al Sagar). *"A very nice colt, a beautiful-looking horse and very strong. He comes from a good, solid family and he'll be a late summer 2-y-o".*

JOHN BEST
123. ELOUNTA ★★★
b.f. *Dubawi – Santiburi Girl (Casteddu).* March 27. Half-sister to the 7f (including at 2 yrs) and 1m winner Mr Willis (by Desert Style), to the 7f winner of 8 races Resplendent Nova (by Pivotal), the 7f to 12f and hurdles winner Samsons Son (by Primo Valentino) – all quite useful – and the modest 11f winner Mister Bit (by Tobougg). The dam, a fair 7f (including at 2 yrs) to 11f winner, is a half-sister to 2 winners. The second dam, Lake Mistassiu (by Tina's Pet), a quite useful triple 5f winner including at 2 yrs, is a full or half-sister to numerous winners. (Laura Malcolm and Bob Malt). *"I bred her myself, she's not over-big but she's stocky and strong. Her sire Dubawi, along with Pivotal, would be the best the mare has been to and this filly surprises us in that she shows a lot more speed than you'd expect from the pedigree. You would think she'd be a seven furlong/mile type but she's actually quite sharp at home and likely to be out in April or early May. Although she does appear to be sharp I'm not really sure, because I try to take them at face value on what I see, rather than what the pedigree tells me".*

124. FEARLESS LAD (IRE) ★★
b.c. *Excellent Art – Souffle (Zafonic).* April 17. Ninth foal. €19,000Y. Goffs Orby. David Goulding. Half-brother to the fair 10f and 12f winner of 4 races Country Road (by Montjeu) and to the minor US dual winner at 3 and 4 yrs El Damien (by El Prado). The dam, a very useful 10f and 10.5f winner, was fourth in the Group 2 Park Hill Stakes and is a half-sister to 10 winners including the very smart Group 1 10f Grand Prix de Paris winner Grape Tree Road, the smart Group 2 13.3f Geoffrey Freer Stakes winner Red Route and the smart Queens Vase and Northumberland Plate winner Windsor Castle. The second dam, One Way Street (by Habitat), a winner of 4 races including the Group 3 12f Princess Royal Stakes, is a sister to the dual 7f winner Shorthouse (dam of the Hungerford Stakes and May Hill Stakes winner Ever Genial) and a half-sister to the dam of the Group 2 Pretty Polly Stakes winner Polaire. (Mrs J O Jones). *"A big, backward sort of horse that's going to take a bit of time, but he does everything nicely, he has a great temperament and I can see him being on the track in mid-summer. Once he grows into himself I can see him being a really nice-looking horse and hopefully he'll have the ability to go with it. Whatever he does this year will be a bonus because he's more of a 3-y-o type".*

125. FIT FOR A KING ★★★
b.c. *Royal Applause – Sancia (Docksider).* March 24. Fourth foal. €23,000Y. Goffs Orby. David Goulding. Half-brother to a minor 3-y-o winner in France by Azamour. The dam, a fair 7f and 1m placed maiden, is a half-sister to 6 winners including the German listed winner and Group 3 third Silk Petal (herself dam of the listed winner Star Tulip) and the dam of the Group 2 winners Tashawak and Fairy Queen. The second dam, Salabella (by Sallust), is a placed half-sister to 7 winners including the Irish St Leger and the Grosser Preis von Baden winner M-Lolshan. (Malt, Howland, Sharp & Partners). *"He's done well since the sales and has grown quite a lot, but he's gone leggy as a result and although I don't think he's going to be late, if I get him out in May I'll be happy. He can be a little bit 'buzzy' so we just have to keep the lid on him a bit, but he's doing everything fine and it looks as if he's got a bit of speed".*

126. HABESHIA ★★
ch.c. Muhtathir – Lumiere Rouge (Indian Ridge). March 31. Fifth living foal. €68,000Y. Arqana Deauville October. C B Goodyear. Half-brother to the French listed 1m winner Desert Blanc (by Desert Style), to the German listed 7f winner Lumiere Noire (by Dashing Blade) and the French listed-placed winner Lumiere Astrale (by Trempolino). The dam is a placed half-sister to 5 winners including the Group 2 Criterium de Maisons-Laffitte winner Signe Divin. The second dam, Lumen Dei (by Raise A Native), a French listed placed maiden, is a half-sister to 6 winners. (C. B Goodyear). *"Another one we bought in France but he'll probably need plenty of time because he looks the type that will want ten furlongs plus next year. He was my most expensive yearling purchase last year and plenty of good judges seemed to like him at the sales".*

127. HATS OFF ★★★★
b.c. Royal Applause – Miriam (Forzando). March 10. Eleventh foal. £33,000Y. Doncaster Premier. John Best. Half-brother to the fairly useful triple 6f winner Para Siemple (by Mujahid), to the quite useful 5f to 7f winner of 13 races Ivory Lace (by Atraf), the fair 5f (including at 2 yrs) and 6f winner of 6 races Park Star (by Gothenberg), the modest 5f and 6f winner of 10 races Viewforth, the fair 5f winner of 3 races United Passion (both by Emarati) and a 2-y-o winner in Italy by Distant Relative. The dam, a modest dual 5f winner, is a half-sister to 7 winners. The second dam, Song Of Hope (by Chief Singer), a useful 2-y-o 5f winner, was second in the listed Firth of Clyde Stakes and is a half-sister to 10 winners. (Malt, Longman and Goulding). *"He'll almost certainly be our first 2-y-o runner and he's a decent sized, strong and mature colt with a very good temperament. He'll want a bit further in time but he's an obvious 2-y-o type and he'll be able to hold his own in the early five furlong races. This is a really nice 2-y-o, he represents a decent chance for me getting a 2-y-o to Royal Ascot and he was recommended to me by Richard Tucker who sold us our dual 2-y-o winner Gung Ho Jack last year".*

128. LE DELUGE (FR) ★★
b.c. Oratorio – Princess Sofia (Pennekamp). February 16. Second foal. €42,000Y. Arqana Deauville August. David Goulding. The dam, a 9f winner in France at 5 yrs, is a half-sister to 4 winners including the useful 2-y-o 7f winner and Group 3 1m May Hill Stakes third Gretel and the useful French 2-y-o and 3-y-o 1m winner Queen Catherine. The second dam, Russian Royal (by Nureyev), a useful winner over 6f at 2 yrs and 7f at 3 yrs and placed in the Jersey Stakes, the Fred Darling Stakes, the Supreme Stakes and the Beeswing Stakes, is a half-sister to numerous winners here and in the USA. (Malt, Longman and Goulding). *"He was bought in France and we'll probably aim him at a maiden race there to begin with, partly because of the better prize money but also because of the French-bred bonuses that go with it. He'll hopefully be out in June, he's bred to want a bit of a trip and he looks that way on the gallops too".*

129. MAD ABOUT HARRY ★★
b.c. Mujadil – Caro Mio (Danehill Dancer). February 17. Second foal. £13,000Y. Doncaster Premier. John Best. Half-brother to Catherine Laboure (by Kheleyf), unplaced in one start at 2 yrs in 2011. The dam ran once unplaced and is a half-sister to 5 winners including the fairly useful Irish 2-y-o 7f and 9f winner and listed placed Derivative and the fairly useful Irish 10f winner and listed-placed Harrington. The second dam, Our Hope (by Dancing Brave), is an unraced half-sister to 5 winners including the Irish listed winner Golden Temple. (H J Jarvis). *"Very backward mentally, he's a nice sort of horse but he's going to take time because the penny hasn't dropped yet. I think when it does he'll be fine because he moves well and he looks a powerful horse. In fact his shape reminds me of Kingsgate Native – but of course he was already showing he was a very good horse at this stage".*

130. MOSSGO ★★★
b.c. Moss Vale – Perovskia (Stravinsky). April 6. Fourth foal. £15,000Y. Doncaster Premier. Half-brother to the quite useful 1m winner African Art (by Johannesburg). The dam is an unraced half-sister to 3 minor winners. The second dam, Lignify (by Confidential Lady), won a Grade 1

event in Argentina and is a half-sister to the Argentine Grade 1 winner Litigado. (Hucking Horses V). *"He looks very much like Gung Ho Jack (one of our 2011 2-y-o's) did at this time last year. He's doing everything very well, he's quite relaxed in everything he does and he'll be one of the earlier types. I would expect him to be running in April, he's pretty sharp and quite mature both mentally and physically".*

131. OTTO THE FIRST ★★★
b.c. Holy Roman Emperor – Paquita (Sadler's Wells). January 26. Fifth living foal. €15,000Y. Goffs Orby. David Goulding. Closely related to 2 minor winners in the USA and Germany by Danehill and Danehill Dancer and half-brother to a minor winner abroad by Tiger Hill. The dam won over 7f in Ireland at 3 yrs and is a sister to the 2,000 Guineas winner King Of Kings, to the Group 3 Athasi Stakes winner Lucky and the Leopardstown 1,000 Guineas Trial winner and Irish 1,000 Guineas second Amethyst and a half-sister to the Group 2 5.5f Prix Robert Papin winner General Monash. The second dam, Zummerudd (by Habitat), is an unplaced sister to the triple Group 3 winner Ancestral and to the dam of the smart colt Batshoof. (Longman, Goulding, Malt & Fuller). *"He's small, strong and stocky and looks an obvious 2-y-o type. He's doing everything fine and was the first of our two-year-olds to get a perfect score in terms of how mature his knees are, so he should be an earlyish 2-y-o. It's a proper pedigree on the dam's side and we've had some luck with the sire who tends to get them a little bit on small side so that doesn't bother me".*

132. SABRE ROCK ★★
b.c. Dubawi – Retainage (Polish Numbers). March 17. Second foal. Half-brother to the fair 2-y-o 7f winner Charles Fosterkane (by Three Wonders). The dam won 2 races at 3 and 4 yrs in the USA and is a half-sister to 3 minor US winners. The second dam, Seventeen Below (by Smarten), a minor winner of 2 races in the USA at 3 and 4 yrs, is a half-sister to 2 winners. (J H Maine). *"A tall, leggy Dubawi colt and completely different to the Dubawi filly we've got! He moves pretty well and given time I think he'll be a nice horse".*

133. UNNAMED ★★★
ch.f. Dutch Art – Break Of Dawn (Mt Livermore). April 30. Fifth foal. 16,000Y. Tattersalls October Book 3. J R Best. The dam is an unraced half-sister to one winner. The second dam, Atelier (by Warning), is an unraced half-sister to 3 winners. (Mr S Malcolm & Mr J Foulger). *"She was recommended to me by the breeder David Botterill, who we got Stone Of Folca from. We've had a couple from the family before but this is the first time the mare has been to a really good sire. I think she was well-bought, she's very correct, a decent size and she has a great attitude. We x-ray all their knees and hers haven't fully closed yet, so we're waiting for that before we push on with her. I'd hope to get a run into her before the end of May".* TRAINERS' BARGAIN BUY

134. UNNAMED ★★★
b.c. Azamour – Brixa (Linamix). March 31. Fourth foal. €26,000Y. Arqana Deauville October. John Best. The dam, a minor winner in France at 3 yrs, is a half-sister to 2 winners. The second dam, Broad And High (by Broad Brush), a stakes-placed winner of 7 races in the USA, is a half-sister to four US stakes winners. *"I think he was the last lot through the Arqana sales, I really liked him there and he's done everything great at home since. He's probably one that will be heading off to France for his early races and one that will need a bit of a trip. A decent looking horse and very much like another of my 2-y-o's Le Deluge. The under bidder to me for this colt was Willie Browne, who I respect enormously – it makes me think that we bought him at the right price".*

JAMES BETHELL
135. FAB LOLLY (IRE) ★★★★
b.f. Rock Of Gibraltar – Violet Ballerina (Namid). April 28. Third foal. 24,000Y. Tattersalls October Book 2. J Bethell. The dam, a fair 7f (at 2 yrs) and 6f winner, is a half-sister to the very useful 2-y-o Group 2 6f Richmond Stakes winner Carizzo Creek. The second dam, Violet Spring (by Exactly Sharp), a 5-y-o 2m winner in Ireland, is a half-sister to 3 other minor winners and to the placed dam of the US Grade 3 winner Doc Holliday. *"A filly for July/August time and she'll be a seven furlong/miler. A lovely mover and a very nice filly".*

136. JACKADDOCK ★★★★

b.g. Motivator – Selkirk Sky (Selkirk). February 20. Second foal. 10,000Y. Tattersalls October Book 3. J Bethell. Half-brother to Mr Fong (by Dr Fong), placed fourth over 9f from 2 starts at 2 yrs in 2011. The dam, a moderate 7f winner, is a half-sister to 2 winners including the triple listed winner and Group 2 6f Gimcrack Stakes second Andronikos. The second dam, Arctic Air (by Polar Falcon), a quite useful 2-y-o 7f winner, is a sister to the useful listed 7f winner Arctic Char and a half-sister to 6 winners including the Group 2 winners Barrow Creek and Last Resort and the dam of the Group 2 winner Trans Island. (John Carrick). *"A very nice horse and a beautiful mover, he could easily be a stakes horse at some point I would have thought. A seven furlong/mile 2-y-o for August onwards".*

137. RICH FOREVER (IRE) ★★★

b.g. Camacho – Sixfields Flyer (Desert Style). March 13. Second foal. £26,000Y. Doncaster Premier. James Bethell. Brother to the fair 2011 5f to 7f placed Flambard House. The dam, a moderate 1m placed maiden, is a half-sister to 6 winners including Rich Ground (Group 3 July Stakes) and the Group 3 Princess Margaret Stakes third Bandanna. The second dam, Gratclo (by Belfort), a modest winner of 5 races from 2 to 4 yrs, is a half-sister to 3 winners. (R T Vickers). *"I can see him being out in May over six furlongs, he's grown quite a bit since the sales but he's still quite well put-together".*

138. STARBOTTON ★★★★

b.f. Kyllachy – Bonne Etoile (Diesis). March 22. Tenth foal. 11,000Y. Tattersalls October Book 2. James Bethell. Sister to the fair 5f (at 2 yrs) to 9f winner of 5 races Handsome Falcon (by Kyllachy) and half-sister to the quite useful 7f and 1m winner Soviet Secret (by Soviet Star) and the minor French middle-distance winners Coming Home (by Vettori) and Xanthus (by Hector Protector). The dam, a fairly useful winner of 3 races at 3 yrs including a listed event over 10f, is a half-sister to 5 winners. The second dam, Bonne Ile (by Ile de Bourbon), won 7 races here and in the USA including the Grade 1 Yellow Ribbon Invitational Handicap and is a sister to the Group 3 winner Ile de Nisky and a half-sister to the Group 3 winner Hi Lass. (Clarendon Thoroughbred Racing). *"A very nice, sharp-looking filly and I think she was well bought. She's the sharpest of my bunch I'd say and hopefully she'll start her career at Beverley in mid-April. She's not very big but she's well put-together and goes very nicely".* TRAINERS' BARGAIN BUY

139. STEELRIVER ★★★

b.c. Iffraaj – Numerus Clausus (Numerous). March 30. Second foal. 22,000Y. Tattersalls October Book 2. J Bethell. The dam, placed once at 3 yrs in France, is a half-sister to 8 winners including the US Grade 2 placed Garden In The Rain and Embraceable You. The second dam, Marcotte (by Nebos), won 5 races in Belgium and is a half-sister to 10 winners including the multiple German Group 1 winner Mondrian. *"He's quite leggy and has grown quite a lot since I bought him. A very good mover, he looks very much like a top of the ground 2-y-o that should start off in May or June. He looks quite sharpish and I would have thought he'd start off at six furlongs before graduating to seven later in the season. He's showing us a fair bit and he's quite a nice horse".*

JIM BOLGER

140. ALPINIST ♠

gr.c. New Approach – Alouett (Darshaan). April 25. Twelfth foal. Half-brother to the dual Champion Stakes winner Alborada, to the triple German Group 1 winner Albanova (both by Alzao), the very useful dual 12f winner and listed placed Albinus (by Selkirk), the fairly useful 1m (at 2 yrs) to 2m winner Alanbrooke, the fairly useful dual middle-distance winner and useful broodmare Alakananda (both by Hernando), the fairly useful 12f and French listed 12.5f winner Alma Mater (by Sadler's Wells), the fairly useful dual 12f winner Alba Stella (by Nashwan) and the fair 12f winner Altitude (by Green Desert). The dam, a useful 1m (at 2 yrs) and listed 12f winner, is a sister to the listed winner and Irish Oaks third Arrikala and a half-sister to the Nassau Stakes and Sun Chariot Stakes winner Last Second (dam of the French 2,000 Guineas winner Aussie Rules) and the Doncaster Cup winner Alleluia (dam of the Prix Royal-Oak winner Allegretto). The second dam, Alruccaba (by Crystal Palace), was a quite useful 2-y-o 6f winner. (Mrs J Bolger).

141. EINSTEINS FOLLY (IRE)
b.c. Whipper – Azra (Danehill). May 8. Brother to the Irish 2-y-o 6f and 1m winner and Group 2 7f Rockfel Stakes second Atasari and half-brother to the Irish 2-y-o 7.5f winner Basra, to the fair 2-y-o 5f winner Russian General (both by Soviet Star), the fair Irish 7f and 10f winner Asafa (by King's Best) and the Irish 3-y-o dual 1m winner Spectacular (by Spectrum). The dam, a useful Irish dual 6f listed winner (at 2 yrs), was third in both the Group 1 Moyglare Stud Stakes and the Group 1 National Stakes and is a half-sister to 3 minor winners. The second dam, Easy To Please (by What A Guest), a useful Irish 2-y-o 1m winner, trained on to win the Queen Alexandra Stakes and is a half-sister to 4 winners including the Group 3 Concorde Stakes winner Pernilla. (Mrs J Bolger).

Won 4th start 7f mdn Leop

142. GLOBAL REACH (IRE)
ch.f. Galileo – Luminaria (Danehill). March 20. Third foal. The dam is an unraced half-sister to 6 winners including the very useful 2-y-o listed 6f winner and dual Group 1 placed Luminata and the very useful dual 6f winner (including at 2 yrs) and Group 3 placed Aretha. The second dam, Smaoineamh (by Tap On Wood), an Irish 6f winner at 2 yrs and useful at up to 14f, is a half-sister to the champion sprinter Double Form and the Lupe Stakes winner Scimitarra. (Mrs J S Bolger).

143. LEITIR MOR (IRE)
b.c. Holy Roman Emperor – Christinas Letter (Galileo). January 27. First foal. The dam is an unraced half-sister to 3 winners including the useful 5f winner and listed-placed Whip Hand. The second dam, Danemarque (by Danehill), ran unplaced in Australia and is a half-sister to 7 winners including the listed winners Lady Shipley and Ellie Ardensky and to the unraced dam of the Group 3 Solario Stakes and US Grade 3 winner Brave Act. (Mrs J Bolger).

144. LOCH GARMAN (IRE)
b.c. Teofilo – Irish Question (Giant's Causeway). January 27. Fourth foal. Brother to the fair 2011 1m placed 2-y-o Amhrasach and half-brother to the quite useful Irish 2-y-o 5f winner Eireannach (by Rock Of Gibraltar). The dam, a fair Irish 1m winner, is a half-sister to 2 winners. The second dam, Key To Coolcullen

(Royal Academy), is an unraced half-sister to numerous winners including the Group 1 6f Phoenix Stakes winner Eva Luna and the Group 3 1m Futurity Stakes winner Cois Na Tine. (Mrs J S Bolger).

145. MONT FERRAT (IRE)
b.c. Invincible Spirit – Alessandria (by Sunday Silence). May 1. Third foal. The dam, a fairly useful 1m (at 2 yrs) and 12f winner, is a half-sister to 4 winners including the useful 2-y-o 7f and UAE 10f and 11f winner Kriskova. The second dam, Tereshkova (by Mr Prospector), a winner of 6 races including the Group 3 6f Prix de Cabourg, was second in the Group 1 7f Moyglare Stud Stakes and third in the Group 1 6f Prix Morny. She is a sister to the Group 1 6f Middle Park Stakes and multiple Group 1 placed Lycius and a half-sister to the US dual Grade 2 winner Akabir. (Sheikh Mohammed).

146. NEW REGALIA (IRE)
b.f. New Approach – Simonetta (Lil's Boy). February 15. First foal. The dam, a fairly useful Irish 2-y-o 1m winner, was listed-placed and is a half-sister to numerous winners including the Group 3 12f Noblesse Stakes winner Danelissima. The second dam, by Zavaleta (Kahyasi), a useful dual listed 7f winner, is a half-sister to numerous winners including the 2-y-o Group 1 1m Gran Criterium winner Sholokov and the 2-y-o listed 7f winner Affianced (herself dam of the Irish Derby winner Soldier Of Fortune). (Mrs J S Bolger).

147. PACK THE PUNCH (IRE)
b.c. Teofilo – Zavaleta (Kahyasi). Brother to the quite useful 2011 Irish 7f and 1m placed 2-y-o Rigoletta, closely related to the fair 12f winner Alessandro (by Galileo) and half-brother to the Group 3 12f Noblesse Stakes winner Danelissima, to the Irish 2-y-o 7f winner and listed placed Daneleta (both by Danehill), the fairly useful Irish 2-y-o 1m winner and listed placed Simonetta (by Lil's Boy), the Irish 3-y-o 6.5f winner and listed-placed Benicio (by Spectrum) and a winner in Japan by Caerleon. The dam a useful dual listed 7f winner, is a half-sister to numerous winners including the 2-y-o Group 1 1m Gran Criterium winner Sholokov and the 2-y-o listed 7f winner Affianced (herself dam of the Irish Derby winner Soldier

Of Fortune). The second dam, La Meilleure (by Lord Gayle), a listed winner in Ireland, was Group 3 placed. (Mrs J S Bolger).

148. RAPID APPROACH (IRE)
b.c. New Approach – Blas Ceoil (Mr Greeley). May 2. First foal. The dam, a useful Irish 2-y-o 5f and 6f winner, is a half-sister to the Irish dual Group 3 winner Radharcnafarraige out of Extraterrestral (by Storm Bird). (Mrs J S Bolger).

149. SCINTILLULA (IRE)
b.f. Galileo – Scribonia (Danehill). May 15. Fifth foal. Sister to the smart Irish 2-y-o 7f winner and Coronation Stakes second Gile Na Greine, to the smart 2-y-o dual Group 3 6f winner and 1,000 Guineas second Cuis Ghaire and the very useful Irish 1m winner and dual Group 3 placed Claiomh Solais. The dam is an unraced half-sister to 6 winners including the very useful 2-y-o listed 6f winner and dual Group 1 placed Luminata and the very useful dual 6f winner (including at 2 yrs) and Group 3 placed Aretha. The second dam, Smaoineamh (by Tap On Wood), an Irish 6f winner at 2 yrs and useful at up to 14f, is a half-sister to the champion sprinter Double Form and the Lupe Stakes winner Scimitarra. (Kirsten Rausing).

150. STARLAND (IRE)
b.f. Galileo – Key To Coolcullen (Royal Academy). March 25. Sister to the fairly useful Irish 2-y-o 7f winner Solas Na Greine and half-sister to the fairly useful Irish 1m to 11f winner Coolcullen Times (by Rock Of Gibraltar) and the fair Irish 1m winner Irish Question (by Giant's Causeway). The dam is an unraced half-sister to numerous winners including the Group 1 6f Phoenix Stakes winner Eva Luna and the Group 3 1m Futurity Stakes winner Cois Na Tine. The second dam, Guess Again (by Stradavinsky), won over 1m at 3 yrs and is out of the Molecomb Stakes third Galka (by Deep Diver), herself a half-sister to the high-class sprinter Double Form and the Lupe Stakes winner Scimitarra. (Mrs J S Bolger).

151. THE VISITOR (IRE)
b.c. Invincible Spirit – Aeraiocht (Tenby). April 5. Half-brother to the fairly useful 2-y-o triple 7f winner Bunsen Burner (by Lil's Boy), to the quite useful Irish 2-y-o 7f winner Chennai (by Mozart) and the fair Irish 7f winner Webcast (by Verglas). The dam, a dual Irish 2-y-o 7f winner, is a half-sister to one winner. The second dam, Direct Lady (by Fools Holme), a winner of three races at 3 yrs over 11f and 12f and also three races over hurdles, is a half-sister to the Group 1 Heinz "57" Phoenix Stakes winner Eva Luna and the Group 3 Futurity Stakes winner Cois Na Tine. (Mrs J Bolger).

152. TOBANN (IRE)
b.f. Teofilo – Precipitous (Indian Ridge). May 8. Half-sister to the quite useful 2011 2-y-o 6f winner Cardigan (by Barathea). The dam, a quite useful Irish 7f and 1m winner, is a half-sister to several winners. The second dam, Dathuil (by Royal Academy), a fairly useful 1m winner, was subsequently Grade 3 placed in the USA and is a half-sister to numerous winners including the 2-y-o listed 6f winner and Group 1 placed Luminata. (Mrs J Bolger).

153. TOQUETTE (IRE)
b.f. Acclamation – Tariysha (Daylami). March 13. Fourth foal. Half-sister to the 2-y-o Group 1 6f Prix Morny and Group 2 6f July Stakes winner Arcano (by Oasis Dream) and half-sister to the quite useful 9f winner El Muqbil (by Medicean). The dam is an unraced half-sister to 2 winners and to the dam of the Group 1 Prix de l'Abbaye winner Gilt Edge Girl and the Group 2 Flying Childers Stakes winner Godfrey Street. The second dam, The second dam, Tarwiya (by Dominion), won the Group 3 7f C L Weld Park Stakes, was third in the Irish 1,000 Guineas and is a half-sister to 5 winners including the Group 3 Norfolk Stakes winner Blue Dakota. (John Corcoran).

MARCO BOTTI
154. ADMIRABLE ART (IRE) ★★★★
b.c. Excellent Art – Demi Voix (Halling). April 13. Third foal. Half-brother to the fair 2011 2-y-o 7f winner Operettist (by Singspiel) and to the quite useful 2-y-o 6f winner Admirable Spirit (by Invincible Spirit). The dam, a minor winner at 2 yrs in France, is a half-sister to 3 winners. The second dam, Quarter Note (by Danehill), won the Group 3 Prix de la Grotte and is a half-sister to 7 winners including Quito (seven listed wins). (Longview Stud & Bloodstock Ltd). "A precocious colt, he's quite strong and his

pedigree suggests he should be an early type but he hasn't done any fast work as yet. We like him a lot and I'm aiming to run him over six furlongs before the end of May".

155. ALGA REH (IRE) ★★★★

b.c. Invincible Spirit – Mosaique Beauty (Sadler's Wells). April 3. Third foal. £48,000Y. Doncaster Premier. Blandford Bloodstock. The dam, a minor Irish 13f winner, is a full or half-sister to 7 winners including the US Grade 1 Gulfstream Park Breeders Cup Handicap and Group 2 King Edward VII Stakes winner Subtle Power. The second dam, Mosaique Bleue (by Shirley Heights), is an unraced half-sister to the Prix Royal-Oak winner Mersey and to the 10f Prix Saint-Alary winner Muncie. (S Ali). *"A good-looking horse, he's quite strong, in fast work and he's going to be an early type. He probably won't be a five furlong horse but we'd be happy to run him from the middle of May onwards. He's definitely shown the ability to win a maiden".*

156. AVATAR STAR (IRE) ★★★

b.c. Peintre Celebre – Homegrown (Mujadil). February 8. Second foal. €50,000Y. Tattersalls Ireland. Armando Duarte. The dam, a fairly useful 5f to 1m winner in Ireland, was listed placed and is a half-sister to 2 minor winners. The second dam, Don't Wary (by Lomond), won 7 minor races in France from 3 to 5 yrs is a half-sister to 5 winners including New Target (Group 3 Prix Exbury). (Mr K.J.P Gundlach). *"A good-looking horse and good mover, we haven't done a lot with him because he came in from pre-training with ringworm, so we just had to turn him out again. He's changing and growing, but he's compact and should make a 2-y-o from the mid-summer onwards".*

157. FATHER AND SON (IRE) ★★★

b.c. Duke Of Marmalade – Slap Shot (Lycius). April 6. Fifth foal. 30,000Y. Tattersalls October Book 1. Marco Botti. Closely related to the Italian Group 3 7f winner Sandslash (by Holy Roman Emperor) and half-brother to the quite useful 2-y-o 7f and subsequent German winner and 1m listed-placed Samara Valley (by Dalakhani) and a minor winner in Italy by Shamardal. The dam won 6 races in Italy including the Group 3 Gran Premio Citta di Napoli and was second in the Group 1 5f Prix de l'Abbaye and is a half-sister to 2 winners in Turkey. The second dam, Katanning (by Green Desert), is a placed half-sister to 4 winners abroad. *"A colt out of a speedy dam, we trained the half-sister last year and this is quite a good-looking, strong, compact colt and I think he'll make a 2-y-o. We're not rushing him, but perhaps seven furlongs in June/July will be right for him".*

158. FORWARD ★★

b.c. Danehill Dancer – Drifting (by Sadler's Wells). February 6. Second foal. Closely related to the quite useful 2011 2-y-o 1m winner Devdas (by Dylan Thomas). The dam, a fair Irish 3-y-o 6f winner, is a half-sister to 2 winners including the fair 2-y-o 7f winner Glinting Desert (herself dam of the Group 1 Phoenix Stakes winner Alfred Nobel). The second dam, Dazzling Park (by Warning), a very smart winner of the Group 3 1m Matron Stakes and a listed 9f event, was placed in the Group 1 Irish Champion Stakes and the Irish 1,000 Guineas and is a half-sister to 7 winners including New Approach. (HE Sheikh Sultan Bin Khalifa Al Nahyan). *"A colt with plenty of scope, he's nice and he's very straightforward, but he's backward and will take plenty of time. He's growing and has gone 'up behind', so I think he's one for the back-end of the season".*

159. GLORY CITY ★★★

b.c. Azamour – Zara's Birthday (Waajib). May 6. Twelfth foal. 88,000Y. Tattersalls October Book 2. Dwayne Woods. Half-brother to the smart listed 7f winner of 8 races Dohasa, to the fair 5f (at 2 yrs) to 1m winner of 11 races Bold Marc (both by Bold Fact), the useful 2-y-o triple 1m winner and listed-placed Star Inside, the poor 7f winner Beginners Luck (both by Key Of Luck), the fair 12f winner Maunsell's Road (by Desert Style), the fair Irish 12f winner Pigeon Top (by Paris House), the moderate 14f and 2m winner Blair (by Persian Bold) and a hurdles winner by Victory Note. The dam, placed from 7f (at 2 yrs) to 2m, is a half-sister to 4 winners. The second dam, David's Star (by Welsh Saint), is an unplaced half-sister to 9 winners. *"A nice, well-bred colt that's doing well. He'll probably need seven furlongs or a mile but he's quite a smart colt".*

160. JET ACCLAIM ★★★

b.f. Acclamation – Jellett (Green Desert). March 18. Fourth foal. 3,500Y. Tattersalls December. Not sold. Half-sister to the moderate 2011 1m and 9f placed maiden Artistic Thread (by Barathea) and to the fairly useful Irish dual 7f winner Smart Striking (by Smart Strike). The dam is an unraced sister to the Irish 2,000 Guineas, Prix du Moulin and Queen Elizabeth II Stakes winner Desert Prince and a half-sister to 6 winners including the 2-y-o Group 3 6.5f Anglesey Stakes winner Ontario. The second dam, Flying Fairy (by Bustino), placed twice at up to 12f, is a half-sister to 6 winners including the Group 3 Prix Penelope third Fleet Fairy. (Rathbarry Stud). "A filly that's doing quite well, she didn't make her reserve as a yearling because she was a bit small and had slack pasterns, but she's showing up well and being by Acclamation she has a lot of speed. We're aiming to run her in May and from what we've seen she's got ability". TRAINERS' BARGAIN BUY

161. LETTERS (FR) ★★★

b.f. Raven's Pass – Lady Elgar (Sadler's Wells). March 14. Eighth foal. €300,000Y. Arqana Deauville August. Blandford Bloodstock. Half-brother to the US Grade 1 12f Sword Dancer Handicap and Grade 1 Turf Classic Invitational winner Grand Couturier (by Grand Lodge), to the smart 10f and listed 12f winner of 5 races Alainmaar (by Johar), the very useful 7f and listed 10f winner Yaqeen (by Green Desert) and the quite useful 10f winner Sir Edward Elgar (by King's Best). The dam, unplaced in one start in France, is a sister to the Sha Tin Trophy winner and Irish Derby third Desert Fox and a half-sister to the US Grade 3 winners Poolesta and Home Of The Free. The second dam, Radiant (by Foolish Pleasure), won at 3 yrs and is a half-sister to the multiple German Group 1 and Group 2 Royal Lodge Stakes winner Gold And Ivory. (HE Sheikh Sultan Bin Khalifa Al Nahyan). "A gorgeous filly, she's quite big, we like her a lot and she's a good mover. She's not in fast work yet, but we'll probably end up running her from the mid-summer onwards".

162. MAGICAL KINGDOM (IRE) ★★★★

b.c. Danehill Dancer – Al Saqiya (Woodman). March 18. Eighth foal. Closely related to the quite useful Irish 6f winner Rock Of Veio, to the Japanese winner Rock Balloon (by Rock Of Gibraltar) and half-brother to the French 10f winner Cashel Blue (by Aljabr). The dam was placed at 2 yrs and is a half-sister to 5 winners including the Grade 2 Sorrento Stakes winner Buffythecenterfold. The second dam, Augusta Springs (by Nijinsky), a US stakes-placed winner, is a half-sister to 4 winners including Grade 1 Starlet Stakes winner Cuddles. "He's a big, strong colt and obviously well-bred, it looks like he might run as a 2-y-o but he'll need time. He's done nothing wrong, he has a very good temperament and he's straightforward".

163. MESMERIZED (IRE) ★★

b.f. Duke Of Marmalade – Margot (Sadler's Wells). March 3. Sixth foal. £30,000Y. Doncaster Premier. Marco Botti. Half-sister to the modest 2m and hurdles winner Strolling Home (by Medicean) and a winner in Japan by Rock Of Gibraltar. The dam ran twice unplaced and is a half-sister to 3 winners including the 2,000 Guineas winner and sire Footstepsinthesand and the dam of the Group 2 Ribblesdale Stakes winner Thakafaat. The second dam, Glatisant (by Rainbow Quest), winner of the Group 3 7f Prestige Stakes, is a half-sister to 8 winners and to the placed dam of the very smart 2-y-o Superstar Leo. "A nice filly, she moves well and I like her a lot. Duke Of Marmalade is a first-season sire, we have three of his two-year-olds and I like them all. A first foal from a decent family, she's quite strong but the pedigree suggests she'll need at least a mile, so we're taking our time with her".

164. OPEN CACTUS (USA) ★★

b.f. Johannesburg – Momix (Selkirk). January 20. Second foal. €60,000Y. Arqana Deauville August. Not sold. Half-sister to Summer Fall (by Mizzen Mast), placed at 2 yrs in Italy in 2011. The dam, a listed winner of 3 races at 3 and 4 yrs in Italy, is a half-sister to one winner. The second dam, Savignano (by Polish Precedent), a French 3-y-o winner, is a half-sister to 7 winners including the Group 1 Prix de la Foret winner Field Of Hope. (Scuderia Vittadini Srl). "A good-looking filly, she's not the easiest filly to train because she's just a bit hot – maybe Johannesburg is the reason for that. She's just having a break to let her chill out and we'll bring her back into training by the end of

May. She moves well and she's good-looking, but she'll take a bit of time".

165. SALFORD EXCEL ★★★

b.f. Exceed And Excel – Steeple (Selkirk). April 21. Ninth foal. 30,000Y. Tattersalls October Book 2. Marco Botti. Half-sister to the useful 9.3f to 12.2f winner Arturius (by Anabaa), to the quite useful dual 10f winner Hunting Country (by Cape Cross), the quite useful 2-y-o 6f winner Carillon (by Desert Prince) and the French 1m and 9f winner Royal Puck'r (by Bering). The dam won twice at 3 yrs in France over 9f and is a half-sister to 10 winners including the Group 3 8.5f Diomed Stakes winner Enharmonic and the listed 1m Atalanta Stakes winner Soprano. The second dam, Contralto (by Busted), a useful 2-y-o 6f and 7f winner, is a half-sister 4 winners including the Group 1 placed Noalto. (A J Thompson). *"A nice, leggy filly, I like her a lot and she's showing speed, but the experience I've had with the sire tells me to hang on with her for a bit, until June or July. She's still growing but she's a very nice filly".*

166. SECRET SESSION (USA) ★★★★

b.c. Mizzen Mast – Lynnwood Chase (Horse Chestnut). March 19. Third foal. 55,000Y. Tattersalls October Book 1. Armando Duarte. Half-brother to the very smart Group 2 10f Prix Eugene Adam and Group 3 10f Tercentenary Stakes Pisco Sour and to the jumps winner Ultravox (both by Lemon Drop Kid). The dam is a placed half-sister to 3 winners including the UAE Group 2 and Irish Group 3 Ballycorus Stakes winner Lord Admiral. The second dam, Lady Ilsley (by Trempolino), a winner in France and listed-placed twice, is a half-sister to 6 winners including the dam of the Grade 1 Breeders Cup Juvenile winner Action This Day. (Mr K.J.P Gundlach). *"At this stage I would say he's one of the nicest we have this year. He's strong, very straightforward and has the speed for six furlongs although he'll probably get a mile in time. A gorgeous horse, he's strong and compact – everything is there".*

167. SENAFE ★★★

b.f. Byron – Kiruna (Northern Park). April 5. Fifth living foal. 3,000Y. Tattersalls October Book 3. Mubarak Al Nuami. Half-brother to the minor French winner at 2 and 5 yrs Treto (by Numerous) and a bumpers winner by Domedriver. The dam was placed fourth twice over 13f and 2m and is a half-sister to the German listed winner Kiswahili and two winners over hurdles. The second dam, Kiliniski (by Niniski), won the Group 3 Lingfield Oaks Trial and was second in the Group 1 Yorkshire Oaks and is a half-sister to 5 winners. (Mubarak Al Naemi). *"This filly is doing really well. She's quite forward and has plenty of physique, so we've started working her and she's responding well. She's coming to hand quite quickly and she should be one of our first runners, probably in May over five furlongs. We like her and she's got a great attitude".*

168. SUMMER DREAM (IRE) ★★★

b.f. Oasis Dream – Star On Stage (Sadler's Wells). February 16. Fourth foal. €100,000Y. Arqana Deauville August. Not sold. Half-sister to the quite useful UAE 7f winner Air Of Grace (by Dalakhani) and to the minor Italian 3-y-o winner Place In The Sun (by Dubai Destination). The dam, a minor winner at 3 yrs in France, is a full or half-sister to 4 winners including the 2,000 Guineas third Olympian Odyssey. The second dam, Field Of Hope (by Selkirk), won 6 races including the Group 1 7f Prix de la Foret and the Group 2 1m Prix d'Astarte and is a half-sister to 6 winners. (Niarchos Family). *"A smart filly, she was a bit small when she came to us from the Sales but she's grown a lot and has done really well. The family probably need at least a mile, so June or July would be the time to start her campaign".*

169. TEOPHILIP (IRE) ★★★

b.c. Teofilo – Triomphale (Nureyev). April 23. Eighth foal. £26,000Y. Doncaster Premier. Marco Botti. Half-brother to the very useful 6f listed winner of 4 races (including at 2 yrs) One Putra (by Indian Ridge), to the quite useful 2-y-o 5f winner Maggie Lou (by Red Ransom), the quite useful 10f winner Rondelet (by Bering), the fair 1m winner Brave Hawk (by Hawk Wing) and the moderate 6f winner Lambency (by Daylami). The dam, a French 2-y-o 6f winner, is a half-sister to 4 winners including the dual stakes winner Tresoriere. The second dam, Time Deposit (by Halo), is an unraced half-sister to 4 winners including the Group 2 Richmond Stakes winner Gallant

Special. (G Manfredini). *"We've just given him a break after a slight setback, but once he's back in I don't think it'll take too long to get him to the track because it's quite a speedy family. He's already shown us speed, so it wouldn't surprise me to see him come to hand quite soon and be a six furlong type 2-y-o".*

170. WAKEUP LITTLE SUZY (IRE) ★★

ch.f. Peintre Celebre – Maramba (USA) (Hussonet). February 27. First foal. The dam, a fairly useful 2-y-o listed-placed 6f winner, is a half-sister to 3 winners. The second dam, Coco (by Storm Bird), a fairly useful listed-placed 1m winner of 2 races, is a half-sister to the US stakes winner and Grade 1 placed Last Romance. (P Newton). *"A neat filly that's done nothing wrong, but she's a bit light-boned and she's a first foal. She's cantering at the moment, she's shown us some ability but will want seven furlongs plus".*

171. YELLOW MOUNTAIN (IRE) ★★★★

b.c. Danehill Dancer – Singing Diva (Royal Academy). April 29. Sixth foal. Brother to the fairly useful 2011 Irish 2-y-o 6f winner Choir and to the fair 1m and 10f winner Lucky Legs and half-brother to the modest 10f, 11f and hurdles winner Rising Force (by Selkirk). The dam is an unraced half-sister to 8 winners including the Group 2 12f King Edward VII Stakes winner Amfortas and the Group 3 10.5f Prix de Royaumont winner Legend Maker (herself dam of the 1,000 Guineas winner Virginia Water). The second dam, High Spirited (by Shirley Heights), was quite useful and won two of her seven races over 14f and 2m at 3 yrs. She is a sister to the Premio Roma, Ribblesdale Stakes and Park Hill Stakes winner High Hawk (herself dam of the Breeders Cup Turf winner In the Wings) and a half-sister to the dams of the Derby winner High Rise and the Rothmans International winner Infamy. *"A gorgeous horse and very athletic, he's doing well and mentally he's quite forward. But as he's by Danehill Dancer I think we need to wait for the six/seven furlong races. We like him a lot".*

172. UNNAMED ★★★

b.c. Cape Cross – Eternity Ring (Alzao). March 27. Fourth foal. 80,000Y. Tattersalls October Book 2. Marco Botti. The dam is an unraced half-sister to 7 winners including the Group 3 winners Baron Ferdinand and Love Everlasting. The second dam, In Perpetuity (by Great Nephew), a fairly useful 10f winner, is a half-sister to 6 winners including the Derby winner and high-class sire Shirley Heights and to the placed Bempton (herself dam of the Group winners Gull Nook, Mr Pintips and Banket). (Scuderia Rencati Srl). *"I like him a lot, he's a good mover that's growing and changing at present, but he'll turn into a good-looking horse. He's bred to be a mile and a quarter horse, so he's one for later in the year".*

173. UNNAMED ★★★

b.c. Exceed And Excel – Mango Lady (Dalakhani). April 22. First foal. 40,000Y. Tattersalls October Book 2. Marco Botti. The dam, a fair 12f winner, is a half-sister to 4 winners including the Group 2 12f King Edward VII Stakes and dual Group 3 winner High Accolade and the dual listed-placed Oasis Knight. The second dam, Generous Lady (by Generous), a middle-distance winner of 4 races in Ireland including a listed event, is a half-sister to 6 winners including the Group 2 Premio Guido Beradelli and Group 3 St Leger Italiano winner Jape. (Scuderia Rencati Srl). *"When we bought him he was a very weak yearling and didn't really have any shape at all, but he'd done really well. He's grown, I like him and he's a very good mover, but he's out of a Dalakhani mare so I think he'll take a bit of time".*

174. UNNAMED ★★★

b.f. Dutch Art – Smart Ass (Shinko Forest). April 10. Third foal. £11,000Y. Doncaster Festival. Marco Botti. The dam, a quite useful 7f and 1m winner of 5 races, is a half-sister to 2 winners. The second dam, Jayess Elle (by Sabrehill), is an unplaced half-sister to 4 winners including the very useful listed 7f winner Supercal. (Mr A N Mubarak). *"She was quite small at the Sales but she's done well physically and is now quite stocky and strong. She's shown us speed and is one of our earlier types, so she might start over five furlongs in May".*

175. UNNAMED ★★

ch.f. Kyllachy – Triple Sharp (Selkirk). April 2. Seventh foal. 210,000Y. Tattersalls October Book 1. A O Nerses. Sister to the useful 2-y-o dual 6f winner and triple listed-placed Nasri and half-sister to the useful 6f (at 2 yrs) to 11f winner and 2-y-o Group 2 7f Superlative Stakes third Ellmau (by Dr Fong), the listed-placed Laureldean Express (by Inchinor) and a winner in Spain by Vettori. The dam, a quite useful 10f and hurdles winner, is a half-sister to 5 winners including the US stakes winner and Grade 2 placed Pina Colada and to the unraced dam of the top-class miler Canford Cliffs. The second dam, Drei (by Lyphard), placed fourth over 1m at 3 yrs on her only outing, is a half-sister to 3 winners. (Saleh Al Homaizi & Imad Al Sagar). *"She had a bit of a setback and she's a big filly so although she's by Kyllachy she'll take a bit of time. One for much later in the season".*

JIM BOYLE

176. PERSIAN MARVEL ★★★★

b.c. Captain Marvelous – Jezyah (Chief's Crown). March 30. Eleventh foal. £24,000Y. Doncaster Premier. Peter & Ross Doyle. Half-brother to the French 6f to 9f and subsequent US winner Royal Guard (by Hector Protector), the moderate 12f and hurdles winner Plemont Bay (by Robellino), a winner in Italy by Arakan and a hurdles winner by Mark Of Esteem. The dam, a quite useful 2-y-o 7f winner, is a half-sister to several winners including the listed winner Tajannub and the dam of the Flying Childers winner Chateau Istana. The second dam, Empress Jackie (by Mount Hagen), a US stakes winner of 8 races, is a half-sister to the Grade 3 winners Star Of Gdansk and W D Jacks. (The "In Recovery" Partnership). *"A bloody nice horse and he'll be my first 2-y-o runner all being well. A good-looking, correct horse that moves very nicely and at this stage he does appear to be above average. He might well get further than five furlongs a bit later on but he's got plenty of speed as well".*

177. SONNETATION ★★

b.f. Dylan Thomas – Southern Migration (Kingmambo). February 28. Fourth foal. €26,000Y. Goffs Orby. Peter & Ross Doyle. The dam, placed in the USA, is a half-sister to 8 winners including the US Grade 3 winner Surprising Fact. The second dam, Seattle Summer (by Seattle Slew), is an unraced half-sister to 5 winners including the Grade 1

winner and smart broodmare Lovlier Linda. (The "In Recovery" Partnership). *"A second half of the year filly, she's a good-moving type with a lovely attitude. Everything she's done so far has pleased me, although we're not pressing any buttons with her just yet. One for seven furlongs plus and she'll turn into a good-sized individual".*

178. UNCOMPLICATED ★★★★

b.f. Bahamian Bounty – Complication (Compton Place). March 9. Fourth foal. €16,000Y. Tattersalls Ireland. Peter & Ross Doyle. Half-sister to the fair dual 1m winner Maunsells Duke (by Bachelor Duke). The dam, a fair dual 6f winner at 3 and 4 yrs, is a half-sister to 4 winners including the useful 1m and 9f winner and Group 3 10f Sandown Classic Trial third Gryffindor. The second dam, Hard Task (by Formidable), a quite useful 12.3f winner, is a half-sister to 7 winners including the smart middle-distance colt Midnight Legend. (The "In Recovery" Partnership). *"A really nice filly, she's sharp and has a fabulous temperament and lovely conformation. She'll be an early runner for the yard, I like her a lot and she's showing up promisingly in her early gallops. I'd like to think she'd be above average".* TRAINERS' BARGAIN BUY

179. UNNAMED ★★★

br.f. Sleeping Indian – Spring Clean (Danehill). February 19. Fifth foal. £12,000Y. Doncaster Premier. Sylvester Kirk. Sister to the 6f winner Hoover (by Sleeping Indian) and half-sister to the fair 2011 2-y-o dual 5f winner Amis Reunis (by Bahamian Bounty) and the quite useful 6f and 7f winner Duster (by Pastoral Pursuits). The dam, a quite useful 2-y-o 6f winner, is a half-sister to 2 winners in France. The second dam, Spring Haven (by Lear Fan), is a placed half-sister to 7 winners including the German Group 3 winner Tahreeb. (The Paddocks Base Partnership). *"She's from our mare Spring Clean who has been quite successful so far. Not over-big, this filly is just a nice-sized, athletic type and I haven't rushed her so I'd expect her out in mid-summer. I like her – she's an uncomplicated filly, she looks pretty bomb proof and hopefully she'll follow in the family's footsteps".*

180. UNNAMED ★★★

b.f. Sakhee – Sweet Pickle (Piccolo). March 8. Second foal. Half-sister to the modest 2011 5f placed 2-y-o Look At Me Now (by Choisir). The dam, a fair 6f (including at 2 yrs) and 7f winner of 12 races, is a half-sister to several winners. The second dam, Sweet Wilhelmina (by Indian Ridge), was a fair 7f (including at 2 yrs) and 1m winner of 8 races. (M Khan x2). *"A big, imposing, leggy filly who isn't going to be out before the second half of the year but she's a nice filly and I know the family well because the dam won plenty of races for us. The half-brother has been placed and is rated about 60-65 but this filly would seem to be a bit classier than him. She'll need at least six furlongs this year".*

181. UNNAMED ★★★

ch.f. Sleeping Indian – Desert Cristal (Desert King). March 17. Third foal. Half-sister to the fair 2011 2-y-o 7f winner Cristal Gem (by Cadeaux Genereux). The dam, a fairly useful 7f to 10f winner, is a half-sister to the Group 2 7f Challenge Stakes winner Stimulation. The second dam, Damiana (by Thatching), was placed 5 times in France at 2 and 3 yrs and is a half-sister to 5 winners including the listed Prix Coronation winner and US Grade 2 placed Dirca. *"A smallish filly that should make a 2-y-o and she's the spitting image of her mother who was a useful horse for us and very consistent. A sharp, tough, racey filly that should be out in early summer".*

CLIVE BRITTAIN

182. SINAADI (IRE)

b.f. Kyllachy – Quantum (Alhaarth). March 5. Third foal. 65,000Y. Tattersalls October Book 3. Rabbah Bloodstock. The dam, a fairly useful 10f winner, is a half-sister to 3 winners including the 2-y-o Group 1 7f National Stakes winner Power and the Group 2 12f Ribblesdale Stakes winner Thakafaat. The second dam, Frappe (by Inchinor), a fairly useful 2-y-o 6f winner, is a half-sister to 2 winners including the 2,000 Guineas winner Footstepsinthesand. (S Manana).

183. TAHAF ♣

b.c. Authorized – Lady Zonda (Lion Cavern). March 25. Seventh foal. Half-brother to the 2-y-o Group 1 Fillies' Mile, US Grade 1 10f Yellow Ribbon Stakes and Group 2 12f Ribblesdale Stakes winner Hibaayeb (by Singspiel), to the Irish 2-y-o 6f winner and listed 6f second (from only two starts) May Meeting (by Diktat) and the quite useful dual 12f winner Halifax (by Halling). The dam, a quite useful 7f and 1m winner, is a half-sister to 8 winners. The second dam, Zonda (by Fabulous Dancer), a useful 5f to 8.5f winner and listed-placed here, subsequently won twice in the USA. (M Al Nabouda).

184. TUFFAN (IRE)

b.c. Bernardini – Love Of Dubai (More Than Ready). May 1. First foal. The dam won over 7f here at 2 yrs and the Group 3 1m Premio Regina Elena at 3 yrs in Italy. The second dam, Diamond Kris (by Prospect Bay), is an unraced sister to the US Grade 2 winner Square Cut. (Mr M Al Shafar).

185. UNNAMED

b.f. Green Desert – Amalie (Fasliyev). March 4. Fourth foal. 48,000Y. Tattersalls October Book 1. Not sold. Half-sister to the useful dual 7f listed placed maiden Elshabakiya (by Diktat). The dam, a quite useful 2-y-o 6f winner, is a half-sister to 2 winners. The second dam, Princess Amalie (by Rahy), is an unplaced half-sister to 10 winners (including 5 stakes winners) notably the Group 1 1m William Hill Futurity Stakes winner Al Hareb. (S Manana).

186. UNNAMED

b.f. Cape Cross – Fragrancy (Singspiel). February 19. First foal. The dam, a useful 1m (including at 2 yrs) and 10f winner, was listed-placed and is a half-sister to 3 winners. The second dam, Zibet (by Kris), a fairly useful 7f winner, is a half-sister to numerous winners including the smart 2-y-o 6f and 7f winner and 2,000 Guineas fourth Zoning and the French 1m winner and listed-placed Zambezi. (M Al Nabouda).

187. UNNAMED

b.f. Medicean – Regal Riband (Fantastic Light). March 19. Third foal. 36,000Y. Tattersalls October Book 3. Rabbah Bloodstock. Sister to the 2011 2-y-o Group 3 7f Prestige Stakes winner and Group 3 6f Princess Margaret Stakes second Regal Realm and half-sister to a winner in the Czech Republic by Kyllachy. The dam, a modest 7f winner at 2 yrs from three starts, is a half-sister to 2 winners by Medicean including the fairly useful 2-y-o 6f winner Regal Royale. The second dam, Regal Rose (by Danehill), won both her starts including the Group 1 6f Cheveley Park Stakes and is a sister to the Japanese 10f stakes winner Generalist and a half-sister to 8 winners. (S Manana).

188. UNNAMED
b.f. Singspiel – Zibet (Kris). February 19. Sister to the useful 1m (including at 2 yrs) and 10f winner and listed-placed Fragrancy and half-sister to the fair 2011 2-y-o 7f winner Daghash (by Tiger Hill), the quite useful 5f (at 2 yrs) and jumps winner Categorical (by Diktat) and the modest 6f winner Deal Flipper (by Xaar). The dam, a fairly useful 7f winner, is a half-sister to numerous winners including the smart 2-y-o 6f and 7f winner and 2,000 Guineas fourth Zoning and the French 1m winner and listed-placed Zambezi. The second dam, Zonda (by Fabulous Dancer), a useful 5f to 8.5f winner, was listed-placed.

DAVID BROWN
189. BOTANIC GARDEN ★★★
b.c. Royal Applause – Rock Lily (Rock Of Gibraltar). March 29. Second foal. £35,000Y. Doncaster Premier. John Fretwell. Half-brother to the fair 2011 6f and 7f placed 2-y-o Rockme Cockney (by Cockney Rebel). The dam, a quite useful Irish 2-y-o 1m winner, is a half-sister to 8 winners including the Group 2 6f Cherry Hinton Stakes winner Please Sing, the very useful 7f (at 2 yrs) to 10f winner and Group 1 National Stakes third Mountain Song and the fairly useful 2-y-o 6f winner and Group 3 6f Princess Margaret Stakes third Raindancing. The second dam, Persian Song (by Persian Bold), is an unplaced sister to the Solario Stakes winner Bold Arrangement (placed in seven Group/Grade 1 races including the Kentucky Derby). (J C Fretwell).

190. FIDGET ★★★
ch.f. Bertolini – Record Time (Clantime). March 29. Seventh foal. Sister to the smart dual Group 3 5f winner Moorhouse Lad and half-sister to the useful 5f (including at 2 yrs) and 6f winner of 5 races Off The Record (by Desert Style) and the modest 2-y-o 5f winner Pro Tempore (by Fraam). The dam, a fair 5f winner at 3 and 4 yrs,

is a sister to the listed winning sprinter Lago Di Varano and a half-sister to 3 winners. The second dam, On The Record (by Record Token), a fair dual sprint winner at 2 and 4 yrs, is a half-sister to 3 winners. (Peter Onslow). *"A lovely filly, she's very active and sharp. She's sure to be decent and I'd say her job will be over five furlongs from the end of May onwards. Her brother Moorhouse Lad was the first horse I ever bought".*

191. HOLLOWINA ★★
ch.f. Beat Hollow – Trick Or Treat (Lomitas). March 9. Second foal. The dam, a winner of 7 races including the Group 3 12f Princess Royal Stakes and the listed Pinnacle Stakes, was third in the Group 1 Yorkshire Oaks and is a half-sister to 2 winners. The second dam, Trick Of Ace (by Clever Trick), a stakes-placed winner of 4 races in the USA over 1m or more, is a half-sister to 5 winners including the US Grade 2 La Prevoyante Handicap winner Prospectress. (Peter Onslow). *"A nice filly, a lighter-type altogether than Fidget and more of a back-end type filly because she'll want seven furlongs or maybe more".*

192. NEW PEARL (IRE) ★★★★★ ♠
br.c. Acclamation – New Deal (Rainbow Quest). March 28. Fourth foal. £75,000Y. Doncaster Premier. David Redvers. Brother to the useful 6f (at 2 yrs) and 12f winner Alrasm. The dam, a minor 3-y-o 1m winner in France, is a half-sister to 6 winners including the Group 2 Lowther Stakes third Dunloskin. The second dam, Dalinda (by Nureyev), a winner at 4 yrs in France, is a half-sister to 4 winners. (Pearl Bloodstock). *"He's a very nice colt and at this stage he looks like being a nice horse in the making. I might start him at five furlongs but I think he'll be more suited to six".* David Redvers was pleased to highlight this colt to me as being one of the stars of the Pearl Bloodstock string this year.

193. NEWSTEAD ABBEY ★★★
b.c. Byron – Oatcake (Selkirk). February 11. Third foal. 37,000Y. Tattersalls October Book 2. J C Fretwell. Closely related to the fairly useful Irish 3-y-o 6f and 1m winner Coprah (by Bertolini) and half-brother to the moderate 7f winner Motty's Gift (by Lucky Story). The dam,

placed over 6f (including at 2 yrs) and 1m, is a half-sister to 6 winners including the Group 3 5f Premio Omenoni winner and Group 2 Diadem Stakes second Leap For Joy and the listed-placed Waffle On (dam of the Group 3 Supreme Stakes winner Express Wish and the listed winners Desert Alchemy and Madid) and to the unraced dam of the New Zealand dual Group 1 winner King's Chapel. The second dam, Humble Pie (by Known Fact), a fairly useful 2-y-o listed 6f winner, is a half-sister to 4 winners including the high-class sprinter College Chapel and the dam of the Group 2 winners Barrow Creek and Last Resort. (J C Fretwell). *"He's going to be a 2-y-o but not until the middle of the season because he's a big colt. He's a lovely mover and at this stage he looks very nice".*

194. PEARL SEA (IRE) ★★★★

b.f. Elusive City – Catch The Sea (Barathea). March 26. Second foal. €40,000Y. Goffs Orby. David Redvers. Half-sister to the 2011 French 2-y-o listed 6f winner Vladimir (by Kheleyf). The dam, a modest 10f placed maiden, is a half-sister to 3 winners. The second dam, Catch The Blues (by Bluebird), a smart 5f to 7f winner of 3 races including the Group 3 5f Ballyogan Stakes, was third in the Group 1 Haydock Park Sprint Cup and is a half-sister to 6 winners. (Pearl Bloodstock). *"Very much a quality filly, the pedigree looks nice and although she's more of a long-term filly she will make a 2-y-o from the mid-summer onwards".*

195. SATSUMA ★★★

b.f. Compton Place – Jodrell Bank (Observatory). January 29. Second foal. £12,000Y. Doncaster Festival. John Kilbride. The dam, a modest 6f placed 3-y-o, is a sister to the winner and subsequent Grade 1 Hollywood Derby second Sebastian Flyte and a half-sister to the dual 5f (at 2 yrs) and Group 3 6f Ballyogan Stakes winner Age Of Chivalry (by Invincible Spirit). The second dam, Aravonian (by Night Shift), won once over 1m at 3 yrs. (Kilbride, Watson, Hughes). *"This filly will be an early 2-y-o, she shows us lots of speed and I can see her being a proper five furlong type".*

196. UNNAMED ★★★ Beach Club

b.c. Footstepsinthesand – Dunya (Unfuwain).

March 29. Third foal. 30,000Y. Tattersalls October Book 2. J C Fretwell. Half-brother to the fairly useful 2-y-o 5f winner Glas Burn (by Avonbridge). The dam is an unraced half-sister to 3 winners including the Group 3 Ballycorus Stakes winner Al Tadh. The second dam, Tithcar (by Cadeaux Genereux), is a placed half-sister to 6 winners including the dual Group 2 winner Zindabad. (J C Fretwell). *"A nice colt, he'll make a 2-y-o alright and he's one I can see running in mid-season over six or seven furlongs".*

197. UNNAMED ★★★ Green but won bf cl 4mls Thirsk

b.c. Red Clubs – Ossiana (Polish Precedent). May 10. Third foal. £13,500Y. Doncaster November. David Brown. The dam, a modest 12f and hurdles winner, is a sister to the US stakes winner of 7 races Polish Spring and a half-sister to 7 winners including the French listed 11f winner Go Boldly and the dam of the US Grade 1 winner Ashkal Way. The second dam, Diavolina (by Lear Fan), a French 10f winner at 3 yrs, is a half-sister to 7 winners. (Mr D H Brown & Partners). *"He's built to be a 2-y-o, he's doing well and should win, so considering how well the sire did last year I don't think he cost too much".* TRAINERS' BARGAIN BUY

198. UNNAMED ★★★

br.f. Street Boss – Strike Hard (Green Desert). March 6. Eighth living foal. £32,000Y. Doncaster Premier. John Fretwell. Half-sister to the useful 2-y-o 7f winner of 5 races and Group 3 6f Sirenia Stakes third Red Alert Day (by Diktat), to the French 3-y-o winner Emily Blackwell (by Dr Fong) and the Japanese winner at 2 and 3 yrs Chorus Master (by Singspiel). The dam won 3 races at 2 and 3 yrs including the Group 3 6f Greenlands Stakes and is a half-sister to 4 winners. The second dam, Chinese Justice (by Diesis), an Irish listed 6f winner, is a half-sister to 4 winners including the dam of the Australian Grade 1 winner Isolda. (J C Fretwell).

199. UNNAMED ★★★

b.c. Elusive City – Vanitycase (Editor's Note). March 19. Fourth foal. £38,000Y. Doncaster Premier. John Fretwell. Half-brother to the fair dual 6f (at 2 yrs) and 7f winner Angel Of Fashion (by Invincible Spirit) and to a minor winner in France and Spain by One Cool Cat. The dam is an unplaced half-sister to a winner in Japan.

The second dam, Like My Style (by Alzao), is an unraced half-sister to 6 winners including the triple Group 1 winner Scorpion and the US Grade 2 winner Memories. (J C Fretwell).

HENRY CANDY

200. BENONI ★★★

b.c. Bertolini – Ladykirk (Slip Anchor). March 19. Eighth foal. £1,000 foal. Tattersalls December. £10,000Y. Doncaster St Leger Festival. Not sold. Half-brother to the fair 1m to 13f winner of 7 races Lennel (by Presidium), the fair 1m winner Lyford Lass (by Bahamian Bounty) and a minor 10f winner in France by Ishiguru. The dam, a fair 2-y-o 1m winner, is a half-sister to 5 winners. The second dam, Lady Day (by Lightning), a dual French listed winner, is a half-sister to 8 winners. *"After buying him for £1,000 as a foal I took him to Doncaster Yearling Sales but ended up buying him back. He's a big, very strong colt, but he finds everything easy and we're just starting to do a bit of work with him. He'll be a six/seven furlong type 2-y-o".* TRAINERS' BARGAIN BUY

201. CODE OF HONOR ★★★

b.c. Zafeen – Verbal Intrigue (Dahar). April 25. Ninth foal. 60,000Y. Tattersalls October Book 2. Not sold. Half-brother to the US Grade 2 winner Monkey Puzzle (by Country Pine), to the very useful listed 7f winner and Group 3 Jersey Stakes second Codemaster (by Choisir), the fair 10f winner Sainglend (by Galileo), four minor winners in the USA by Dr Caton, Bates Motel, Saint Ballado and Pleasant Tap and a winner in Spain by Bahri. The dam, a minor US 3-y-o winner, is a half-sister to 6 winners including the US Grade 1 placed Verbasle (herself dam of the US Grade 1 winner High Fly and the dual UAE Group 3 winner Estimraar). The second dam, Verbality (by Verbatim), a stakes winner and Grade 2 placed in the USA, is a half-sister to 2 winners. (Clark/Byrne). *"A half-brother to a good horse we had called Codemaster, this colt had the most immature knees of all our 2-y-o's and had to be kept in his box for six weeks in the wintertime. He's OK again now and he's a big, scopey horse that'll take a bit of time. I would say he'd make a 2-y-o by July time over six furlongs. He's an interesting proposition".*

Won for Newbury (1 in min 7f 2.1 run at 50/1

202. DALGIG ★★★★

b.c. New Approach – Bright Halo (Bigstone). February 16. Ninth foal. 70,000Y. Tattersalls October Book 1. H Candy. Half-brother to the useful 6f (at 2 yrs) and listed 1m winner and Group 2 6f Mill Reef Stakes third Nantyglo (by Mark Of Esteem), to the fairly useful 1m (at 2 yrs) and 12f winner Resplendent Light (by Fantastic Light), the minor French 3-y-o winner Halo de Lune (by Halling) and the moderate 2m 1f winner Arabian Sun (by Singspiel). The dam, a minor French 3-y-o 9f winner, is a half-sister to 8 winners including the Group 1 Irish Oaks winner Moonstone, the Breeders Cup second L'Ancresse and the Group 1 10f Prix Saint-Alary winner Cerulean Sky (herself dam of the Group 2 Doncaster Cup winner Honolulu). The second dam, Solo de Lune (by Law Society), a French 11f winner, was listed-placed in Germany and is a half-sister to 7 winners including the Grade 2 E P Taylor Stakes winner Truly A Dream and the French Group 2 winner Wareed. (T Barr). *"He's grown a lot and is slightly 'on the leg' at the moment, but he's a classy individual that goes along nicely. Hopefully he'll be ready to do something by July or August over seven furlongs. I like the look of him".*

203. GREY'S ELEGY ★★★

gr.g. Ishiguru – Christmas Rose (Absalom). March 25. Eighth foal. 16,000Y. Tattersalls October Book 3. Henry Candy. Half-brother to the quite useful 6f winner Snow Wolf (by Wolfhound), to the French winner of 3 races at 2 and 3 yrs Olga Luck (by Inchinor), the modest 1m winner Snow Bounty (by Bahamian Bounty) and the Italian 2-y-o winner Nurdole (by Sleeping Indian). The dam is an unplaced half-sister to 6 winners including the Group 2 Gimcrack Stakes winner Bannister. The second dam, Shall We Run (by Hotfoot), placed once over 5f at 2 yrs, is a full or half-sister to 8 winners including the Group 1 6f Cheveley Park Stakes winner Dead Certain. (Simon Broke & Partners III). *"A good, strong, easy-going horse. He's grown and lengthened and I think he'll be out in June or July. A very easy-goer and a nice looking horse".*

204. HERBALIST ★★★

ch.g. Haafhd – Puya (Kris). March 27. Half-brother to the fair 2-y-o 7f winner Pandorea (by Diktat). The dam, a quite useful dual 7f winner, is a half-sister to several winners including the multiple Group 3 6f winner Gorse. The second dam, Pervenche (by Latest Model), is an unplaced half-sister to the smart 2-y-o Cut Throat. (Girsonfield Ltd). *"He seems to be finding everything easy at the moment, he was one of the first ones to do a bit of upsides work and he might conceivably be running in the second half of May. A strong sort of horse and we like him".*

205. JUST CHARLIE ★★★

b.g. Piccolo – Siryena (Oasis Dream). March 1. First foal. 18,000Y. Tattersalls October 2. Not sold. The dam, a moderate 10f winner, is a half-sister to several winners. The second dam, is an unraced half-sister to 9 winners including the champion sprinter Marwell (herself dam of the high-class Coronation Stakes and Sussex Stakes winner Marling and the good 5f to 1m colt Caerwent) and the Group 2 Mill Reef Stakes winner Lord Seymour. (Mrs A D Bourne/H Candy). *"He's very strong and pretty mature, so he'll be working shortly and I see him as one of our earlier runners. A tough horse for five and six furlongs".*

206. PEARL STREET (USA) ★★★★

b.f. Street Sense – Pretty Meadow (Meadowlake). February 12. Fourth foal. $290,000Y. Keeneland September. David Redvers. Half-sister to the minor US 3-y-o winner Resume (by Songandaprayer). The dam, a stakes winner and Grade 3 placed in Canada, is a sister to the stakes-placed winner Que Bonita and a half-sister to 3 stakes winners and to the dam of the US Grade 3 winner Seattle Borders. The second dam, Why So Much (by Northern Baby), won at 2 yrs in the USA and is a half-sister to 2 winners. (Pearl Bloodstock). *"Very tall and rather 'on the leg', she needs to strengthen up a bit behind, but she's very mature and finds things very easy. I think she'll be on the racecourse by July time and she looks to have a bit of class".*

207. PEDRO SERRANO ★★★★

b.c. Footstepsinthesand – Shaiyadima (Zamindar). March 28. Second foal. 42,000Y. Tattersalls October Book 2. H Candy. The dam is an unplaced half-sister to 3 winners including the Group 1 10f Prix de l'Opera winner and

Grade 1 E P Taylor Stakes third Shalanaya. The second dam, Shalamantika (by Nashwan), a useful 10f winner, was listed placed over 12f and is a half-sister to 3 winners. (Six Too Many). *"A very strong, big horse and an excellent mover. He's been quite hard to handle so far but he's settling down now and I would think he'll be out around July time over six furlongs. He looks a classy horse".*

208. SECRETLY ★★★

ch.f. Sakhee's Secret – The Cat's Whiskers (Tale Of The Cat). February 28. Third foal. 54,000foal. Tattersalls December. Neil Jenkinson. Half-sister to the 2011 2-y-o 6f winner (on her only start) Pussycat Dream (by Oasis Dream) and to the fairly useful 2-y-o dual 6f winner Walk On Water (by Exceed And Excel). The dam, a winner over 7f and 1m in New Zealand, is a half-sister to 2 winners including the Australian Group 3 winner and Group 1 placed Tully Dane. The second dam, Good Faith (by Straight Strike), a champion 2-y-o filly and a Group 1 winner in New Zealand, is a half-sister to 6 winners. (Henrietta, Duchess of Bedford). *"Not very tall but very strong, she's just learning to settle down now after being a bit over-zealous in her work. She looks a nice filly and she'll definitely be a 2-y-o".*

209. SILK ROUTE ★★

ch.f. Dubai Destination – Crinolette (Sadler's Wells). April 11. Tenth foal. Sister to the fairly useful 2011 2-y-o 5f and 7f winner Cravat and half-sister to the useful 2-y-o 6f winner and Group 2 6f Richmond Stakes third Cedarberg (by Cape Cross) and to the fair dual 7f winner Materialism (by Librettist). The dam, unplaced over 8.2f on her only start at 2 yrs, is a half-sister to the very smart Group 3 7f Tetrarch Stakes and Group 3 7f Ballycorus Stakes winner Desert Style. The second dam, Organza (by High Top), a useful 3-y-o 10f winner, is a half-sister to the Group 1 Prix de la Foret winner Brocade – herself the dam of Barathea and Gossamer. (Mr D Clark). *"She's only just come in and been broken, so she'll take time because she's weak at the moment. She's very athletic and I would think she'll probably change quite quickly, but she definitely won't be racing until the autumn".*

SIR HENRY CECIL

210. ALEGRA ★★★

gr.f. Galileo – Altitude (Green Desert). February 28. First foal. €300,000Y. Goffs Orby. Sir Robert Ogden. The dam, a fair 12f winner, is a half-sister to 7 winners including the dual Champion Stakes winner Alborada, the triple German Group 1 winner Albanova and the fairly useful dual middle-distance winner and useful broodmare Alakananda. The second dam, Alouette (by Darshaan), a useful 1m (at 2 yrs) and listed 12f winner, is a sister to the listed winner and Irish Oaks third Arrikala and a half-sister to the Nassau Stakes and Sun Chariot Stakes winner Last Second (dam of the French 2,000 Guineas winner Aussie Rules) and the Doncaster Cup winner Alleluia (dam of the Prix Royal-Oak winner Allegretto). (Sir Robert Ogden). *"A nice filly, she's not over-big but she's furnishing nicely and could make up into a two-year-old later on".*

211. AL GUWAIR (IRE) ★★★

b.c. Shirocco – Katariya (Barathea). March 24. Fourth foal. €35,000Y. Tattersalls Ireland. Mubarak Al Naimi. Half-brother to the fair 2-y-o 6f winner Katehari (by Noverre). The dam ran twice unplaced and is a half-sister to 4 winners including the Group 2 Blandford Stakes winner and Oaks third Katiyra. The second dam, Katiykha (by Darshaan), a smart Irish listed 12f and 14f winner, is a half-sister to 6 winners. (Mr A N Mubarak). *"A nice colt, but he will need time".*

212. AMELIORATE (IRE) ★★★

b.f. Galileo – Arkadina (Danehill). March 16. First foal. The dam, a fairly useful Irish 9f winner, was third in the Group 3 12f Give Thanks Stakes and is closely related to the 2-y-o Group 1 Moyglare Stud Stakes and Irish 1,000 Guineas winner Again and to the Irish winner and listed-placed Aris. The second dam, Cumbres (by Kahyasi), is an unraced half-sister to Montjeu. (Merry Fox Stud Ltd). *"A very nice filly, she has plenty of scope and will need plenty of time".*

213. ATARAXIS (FR) ★★★

b.c. Nayef – Seven Magicians (Silver Hawk). January 27. Half-brother to the quite useful 3-y-o 7f winner Magician's Cape (by Montjeu). The dam, a useful 10f winner, was listed-placed over 11.5f and is a half-sister to the smart listed Lupe Stakes winner and Group 1 Yorkshire Oaks second Ocean Silk. The second dam, Mambo Jambo (by Kingmambo), a minor winner at 3 yrs in France, is a sister to the multiple Group 1 winner Divine Proportions and a half-sister to the dual Group 1 winner Whipper. (Niarchos Family). *"A good-looking colt, he was an early foal but his pedigree tells you he'll still need time to develop".*

214. BEJEWELED (IRE) ★★★

br.f. Rock Of Gibraltar – Gems Of Araby (Zafonic). April 23. Third foal. 65,000Y. Tattersalls October Book 2. Henry Cecil. Half-sister to the fair 2011 6f and 7f placed 2-y-o Symphony Time (by Cape Cross) and to the fairly useful 2-y-o 1m winner Il Boro (by Oratorio). The dam, a fair 10f placed maiden, is a half-sister to 5 winners including the Group 1 Falmouth Stakes winner Timepiece, the Group 1 10f Criterium de Saint-Cloud winner Passage Of Time and the Group 2 King Edward VII Stakes winner Father Time. The second dam, Clepsydra (by Sadler's Wells), a quite useful 12f winner, is a half-sister to 6 winners including the useful listed 10.5f winner Double Crossed (herself dam of the multiple Group 1 winner Twice Over). (Mr V I Araci). *"This is an active filly that should make a 2-y-o".*

215. BLIGHTY (IRE) ★★★

ch.c. Beat Hollow – Brisk Breeze (Monsun). April 3. Second foal. Half-brother to Bon Allumage (by Nayef), unplaced in one start at 2 yrs in 2011. The dam, a very useful listed 12f winner, was third in the Group 2 Park Hill Stakes and is a sister to one winner and a half-sister to 2 winners including the German listed 11f winner Belle Syrienne. The second dam, Bela-M (by Ela-Mana-Mou), a German listed winner and Group 3 placed twice, is a half-sister to 4 winners. (Ennismore Racing I). *"Not over-big, he's a compact 2-y-o that moves nicely".*

216. BUCHANAN ★★★★

b.c. Dansili – Because (Sadler's Wells). January 26. Fifth foal. 50,000Y. Tattersalls October Book 1. Not sold. Half-brother to the unplaced 2011 2-y-o Perfect Paradise (by Giant's Causeway) and to the useful 1m (at 2 yrs) and 12f winner Anhar (by Kingmambo). The dam is an unraced sister to 4 winners including the Irish 1,000

Guineas winner Yesterday and the Group 1 7f Moyglare Stud Stakes winner and Irish 1,000 Guineas, Oaks and Irish Oaks placed Quarter Moon. The second dam, Jude (by Darshaan), a moderate 10f placed maiden, is a sister to the very useful Irish listed 14f winner and Irish Oaks third Arrikala and to the useful Irish 12f listed winner Alouette (herself dam of the multiple Group 1 winners Albanova and Alborada) and a half-sister to the Group 2 10f Nassau Stakes and Sun Chariot Stakes winner Last Second (dam of the French 2,000 Guineas winner Aussie Rules) and the Group 3 Doncaster Cup winner Alleluia (dam of the Group 1 Prix Royal-Oak winner Allegretto). (T Barr). *"A lovely-moving colt, he has a staying pedigree and so is more of a 3-y-o/4-y-o type, but I like him a lot".*

217. CONSERVE (IRE) ★★★

b.c. Duke Of Marmalade – Minor Point (Selkirk). March 14. Second foal. 80,000Y. Tattersalls October Book 1. John Warren. The dam is an unraced half-sister to 2 winners including the 2-y-o Group 1 Prix Marcel Boussac winner Proportional. The second dam, Minority (by Generous), won over 11f, was Group 3 placed twice and is a half-sister to 6 winners including the 2-y-o listed 7f winner Innocent Air and the French listed and US stakes winner and US Grade 1 placed Skipping. (Highclere Thoroughbred Racing – Lord Mayor). *"He needs a little time, but he's a good mover and an attractive individual".*

218. CRYOSPHERE (USA) ★★★

b.f. Candy Ride – Polar Circle (Royal Academy). March 12. First foal. $190,000Y. Keeneland September. Course Investment Co. The dam, a useful 2-y-o listed 6f winner, is a sister to the smart 2-y-o listed 7f winner and Group 2 6f Gimcrack Stakes second Fokine and a half-sister to several winners including the Group 2 6f Prix Robert Papin winner and Group 1 1m Coronation Stakes second Ocean Ridge. The second dam, Polar Bird (by Thatching), a very useful winner of 6 races here and in the USA including 2-y-o Group 3 5f Debutante Stakes, is a half-sister to 6 winners. (Niarchos Racing). *"Still slightly weak and needs time, but she's an attractive, workmanlike filly".*

219. DISCLAIMER ★★★★

b.c. Dansili – Novellara (Sadler's Wells). January 23. Half-brother to the fair 10f winner Word Power (by Oasis Dream). The dam, a fairly useful 10f and listed 14f winner, is a sister to the listed 14f winner Modesta, closely related to the Oaks and Fillies Mile winner Reams Of Verse and a half-sister to numerous winners including the Eclipse Stakes and Phoenix Champion Stakes winner Elmaamul. The second dam, Modena (by Roberto), is an unraced half-sister to the smart 2-y-o 7f winner and Queen Elizabeth II Stakes third Zaizafon – herself dam of Zafonic. (Khalid Abdulla). *"A medium-sized colt, a good mover and a tough horse that could be seen out around May time".*

220. EMPERICAL ★★★

b.c. Oasis Dream – Kalima (Kahyasi). May 14. Closely related to the smart 9f and 10f winner and listed-placed Jet Away (by Cape Cross). The dam is an unraced sister to the listed 14f winner Arrive and to the 2-y-o 5f winner and outstanding broodmare Hasili (dam of the top-class performers Banks Hill, Heat Haze, Intercontinental, Cacique, Champs Elysees and Dansili) and a half-sister to several winners. The second dam, Kerali (by High Line), a quite useful 3-y-o 7f winner, is a half-sister to numerous winners including the Group 3 6f July Stakes winner Bold Fact, the Group 1 Nunthorpe Stakes winner So Factual and the very useful Irish 7f to 1m winner Field Dancer. (Khalid Abdulla). *"A late foal that needs time, but he'll be nice later on".*

221. FAFA O O (IRE) ★★★★

b.f. Galileo – Witch Of Fife (Lear Fan). January 31. Ninth living foal. 850,000Y. Tattersalls October Book 1. Sir Robert Ogden. Sister to the very useful 2-y-o Group 3 7f Silver Flash Stakes winner Cabaret and half-sister to the 2-y-o Group 3 7f Solario Stakes and subsequent dual 10f winner Drumfire (by Danehill Dancer), the useful 2-y-o 6f winner, Group 2 6f Gimcrack Stakes second and subsequent Hong Kong stakes winner Ho Choi (by Pivotal) and the moderate 1m winner Witchcraft (by Zilzal). The dam, a fairly useful 2-y-o 6f and 7f winner and third in the listed 7f Sweet Solera Stakes, is a half-sister to 5 winners out of the fairly useful 1m winner Fife (by Lomond), herself a half-sister to 5 winners including the dam of the US Grade 1 winner Frenchpark and the Prix Vermeille winner Pearly Shells. (Sir Robert Ogden). *"A big filly, she's slightly unfurnished at present but is very likeable".*

222. FLOW (USA) ★★★

b.c. Medaglia d'Oro – Enthused (Seeking The Gold). Seventh foal. Half-brother to the quite useful 2011 Irish 6f placed 2-y-o Gush (by Empire Maker), to the very useful 2-y-o Group 3 6f Round Tower Stakes winner and Group 2 6f Criterium de Maisons-Laffitte second Norman Invasion (by War Chant), the useful 1m winner and subsequent US Grade 3 turf 8.5f second Ea (by Dynaformer) and the quite useful 2-y-o dual 6f winner Erytheis (by Theatrical). The dam won the Group 2 6f Lowther Stakes and the Group 3 6f Princess Margaret Stakes and is a half-sister to the listed 12f Prix Vulcain winner From Beyond. The second dam, Magic Of Life (by Seattle Slew), won the Group 1 1m Coronation Stakes and the Group 2 Mill Reef Stakes and is a half-sister to 4 winners. (Niarchos Family). *"This colt has a good action and he should make a 2-y-o a little later on".*

223. GHOST RUNNER (IRE) ★★★

b.c. Tagula – Ball Cat (Cricket). April 23. Tenth foal. 55,000Y. Tattersalls October Book 1. Peter & Ross Doyle. Brother to the 2-y-o listed 5f winner Drawnfromthepast and to a minor winner in Greece and half-brother to the minor winner of 8 races here and in France Aldiruos (by Bigstone). The dam won once in Belgium and is a half-sister to 7 winners including the Irish Group 3 winner Leading Time. The second dam, Copy Cat (by King Of Macedon), a listed-placed winner in France, is a half-sister to 9 winners including Rich And Famous (Group 3 Prix du Bois). (Middleham Park Racing L). *"A nice mover, he's going through a growing stage at present but he should make a 2-y-o".*

224. GRASPED ★★★★

ch.f. Zamindar – Imroz (Nureyev). March 12. Sister to the quite useful 2011 2-y-o 7f winner Elbe and half-sister to the fairly useful listed 10f winner Posteritas (by Lear Fan), the useful 2-y-o dual 7f winner Apex Star (by Diesis) and the fair 10f winner Mainland (by Empire Maker). The dam, a useful 6f (at 2 yrs) and 7f

winner, was listed-placed and is a half-sister to 5 winners including the useful 3-y-o listed 1m winner Insinuate. The second dam, All At Sea (by Riverman), a high-class winner of 5 races from 1m to 10.4f including the Group 1 Prix du Moulin, is a half-sister to the Free Handicap winner Over the Ocean, the listed 10f winner Quandary and the US stakes winner Full Virtue. (Khalid Abdulla). *"This is a nice filly and a good mover that should make a 2-y-o later on".*

225. HALUL ★★★

b.c. Dutch Art – Bella Bertolini (Bertolini). March 26. Third foal. £28,000Y. Doncaster Premier. Mubarak Said Al Naemi. The dam is a placed half-sister to one winner. The second dam, Fly Like The Wind (by Cyrano de Bergerac), a fair 3-y-o 5f winner, is a half-sister to 6 other minor winners. (Mr A N Mubarak). *"A nice colt that should make a 2-y-o later on".*

226. KELVINGROVE (IRE) ★★★

b.c. Hurricane Run – Silversword (Highest Honor). April 28. Ninth living foal. 180,000Y. Tattersalls October Book 1. C de Moubray. Half-brother to the Group 1 Grand Prix de Paris and Group 2 Prix Niel winner Cavalryman (by Halling), to the useful 2-y-o 7f winner and Group 3 7f C L Weld Park Stakes third Finity (by Diesis), the modest 6f winner Jahanara (by Exceed And Excel), the modest UAE 9f winner Dramatic Edge (by Theatrical) and a minor 12f winner in France by Jade Robbery. The dam, a winner at 3 yrs in France and second in the Group 3 Prix de Royaumont, is a sister to 2 winners including the German listed winner and Group 2 Goodwood Cup second Double Honour and a half-sister to 4 winners. The second dam, Silver Cobra (by Silver Hawk), won twice at 2 yrs in France and is a sister to the US Grade 1 and Grade 2 winner Silver Ending. (T Barr). *"A nice colt, he's a bit backward mentally at this stage but he moves nicely and just needs to mature and develop".*

227. KYLLACHY RISE ★★★

b.c. Kyllachy – Up And About (Barathea). April 10. Tenth foal. 100,000Y. Tattersalls October Book 2. C de Moubray. Half-brother to the unplaced 2011 2-y-o Isolde's Return (by Avonbridge), to the fairly useful 6f, 10f (both at 2 yrs) and 1m winner of 6 races and listed-placed Take It To The Max (by Bahamian Bounty), the fairly useful 2-y-o 8.3f and UAE 3-y-o winner Tamarillo (by Daylami and herself dam of the Group 3 Oak Tree Stakes winner Summer Fete), the fairly useful 6f (at 2 yrs) and 7f winner of 4 races and listed-placed Wake Up Call (by Noverre), the modest 2-y-o 9f winner Tiger Spice (by Royal Applause) and the moderate 12f and hurdles winner Park's Prodigy (by Desert Prince). The dam, a fair 14.8f winner, is a half-sister to 8 winners including the listed winner and Group 1 placed Musicanna. The second dam, Upend (by Main Reef), a smart winner of 3 races from 10f to 12f including the Group 3 St Simon Stakes and the listed Galtres Stakes, is a half-sister to 6 winners including the dam of the Group 1 Prix du Cadran and champion hurdler Royal Gait. (Mr Arjun Waney). *"This colt is doing well, he's nicely made and should make a 2-y-o alright".*

228. MAJESTY (IRE) ★★★

gr.c. Shamardal – Princess Serena (Unbridled's Song). February 13. Fourth foal. 110,000Y. Tattersalls October Book 1. John Warren. Half-brother to the fair 2011 2-y-o 7f winner Serene Oasis (by Oratorio) and to the quite useful 2-y-o 7f winner Serena's Storm (by Statue Of Liberty). The dam, a minor US 4-y-o winner, is a half-sister to 4 winners including the US Grade 2 American Turf Stakes winner Doubles Partner and the minor US stakes winner Stormy Venus. The second dam, Serena's Sister (Rahy), is an unplaced sister to the outstanding US winner of eleven Grade 1 events Serena's Song (herself dam of the Coronation Stakes winner Sophisticat and the US Grade 2 winners Harlington and Grand Reward) and a half-sister to the US Grade 3 Golden Rod Stakes winner Vivid Imagination. (Highclere Thoroughbred Racing – Archer). *"A nice colt and a good mover that needs time".*

229. MIGHTY YAR (IRE) ★★★

gr.c. Teofilo – Karaliyfa (Kahyasi). April 5. Sixth foal. 45,000Y. Tattersalls October Book 2. C de Moubray. Half-brother to the fairly useful Irish 1m and 10f winner Karawana (by King's Best), to the moderate 12f winner Ocean Bluff (by Dalakhani) and the hurdles winner Karashar (by Kalanisi). The dam, a quite useful 9f winner, is a half-sister to 7 winners including Karasta (2-y-o

Group 3 1m May Hill Stakes), Kasthari (Group 2 2m 2f Doncaster Cup in a dead-heat) and Kargali (Group 3 Gladness Stakes). The second dam, Karliyka (by Last Tycoon), a French 3-y-o winner of 4 races, was listed placed over 1m and 10f and is a half-sister to 4 winners. (R.A.H Evans). *"A lovely mover, but he's a very big colt that will need time".*

230. MORPHEUS ★★★★★

b.c. Oasis Dream – Kind (Danehill). March 13. Fourth foal. Half-brother to the champion 2-y-o and champion 3-y-o, Group 1 7f Dewhurst Stakes and Group 2 1m Royal Lodge Stakes winner Frankel (by Galileo) and to the very useful Group 3 11.5f Derby Trial winner Bullet Train (by Sadler's Wells). The dam, a dual listed winner over 5f and 6f, was Group 3 placed and is a half-sister to the Arlington Million and Tattersalls Rogers Gold Cup winner Powerscourt (by Sadler's Wells) and to the smart 14f winner of 3 races Brimming. The second dam, Rainbow Lake (by Rainbow Quest), a smart winner of 3 races including the Group 3 12f Lancashire Oaks and the listed 10f Ballymacoll Stud Stakes, is a half-sister to several winners including the useful middle-distance winner Vertex. (Khalid Abdulla). *"A nice colt with a good temperament, he'll obviously need time because physically he's got to strengthen and mature, but he's very nice".*

231. ORIGINATE ★★★

b.f. Oasis Dream – Sandglass (by Zafonic). February 4. Third foal. The dam, a fairly useful 10f winner, is a half-sister to the Group 1 10f Criterium de Saint-Cloud (at 2 yrs) and Group 3 10.3f Musidora Stakes winner Passage Of Time and to the Group 2 10f King Edward VII Stakes winner Father Time. The second dam, Clepsydra (Sadler's Wells), a quite useful 12f winner, is a half-sister to several winners including the useful listed 10.5f winner Double Crossed (herself dam of the multiple Group 1 10f winner Twice Over). (Niarchos Family). *"A nice-moving filly, but she's a big 2-y-o that will need time".*

232. PARALLAX (IRE) ★★★

b.c. Galileo – Moonlight's Box (Nureyev). May 11. Eighth living foal. 200,000Y. Tattersalls October Book 1. Not sold. Half-brother to Bago (by Nashwan), a winner of five Group 1 events from 1m to 12f including the Prix de l'Arc de Triomphe, to the Group 3 1m Prix Thomas Bryon winner Maxios (by Monsun), the French 2-y-o listed 5f winner and Group 3 placed Beta (by Selkirk), the French 7f (at 2 yrs) and 1m winner Makani (by A P Indy) and the French 2-y-o 6f and 7f winner Million Wishes (by Darshaan). The dam is an unraced half-sister to the Group 1 Prix Marcel Boussac winner Denebola and to the Group 3 winners Snake Mountain and Loving Kindness. The second dam, Coup de Genie (by Mr Prospector), won the Group 1 6f Prix Morny and the Group 1 7f Prix de la Salamandre and is a sister to the champion 2-y-o and top-class sire Machiavellian and the Group 3 winner Ocean Of Wisdom and a half-sister to the high-class miler Exit To Nowhere and the Group 2 winner Hydro Calido. (Niarchos Family). *"A nice colt and a good mover, but he's backward at the moment".*

233. PASS AND GO ★★★

b.c. Exceed And Excel – Monnavanna (Machiavellian). April 21. Fourth foal. 70,000Y. Tattersalls October Book 1. C de Moubray. Closely related to a winner in Norway by Green Desert and half-brother to the fairly useful 6f (at 2 yrs) to 1m winner of 4 races Manassas (by Cape Cross). The dam, a smart 6f and 7f listed winner, is a half-sister to the Group 2 Blandford Stakes winner Monturani. The second dam, Mezzogiorno (by Unfuwain), a very useful 7f (at 2 yrs) and 10f listed winner, was third in the Oaks is a half-sister to 3 winners. (The Johnson & Ives Families). *"It's difficult to tell at this early stage, but he'll be a much better horse in mid-summer".*

234. PASSING PARADE ★★★★★

b.f. Cape Cross – Model Queen (Kingmambo). March 30. Eighth foal. 500,000Y. Tattersalls October Book 1. Charlie Gordon-Watson. Half-sister to the smart 2011 2-y-o Group 3 7f Acomb Stakes winner and Group 2 7f Champagne Stakes third Entifaadha (by Dansili), to the Group 1 6f Haydock Sprint Cup and Group 3 Hackwood Stakes winner Regal Parade (by Pivotal), the useful 1m (at 2 yrs) and 10f winner and Group 3 Derby Trial third Hot Prospect (by Motivator), the useful

French 11f and 12f winner and Group 2 Prix Noailles fourth Mount Helicon (by Montjeu) and the minor French 10f winner Sister Sylvia (by Fantastic Light). The dam, a fair 3-y-o 7f winner, is a half-sister to 5 winners including the French listed 1m winner Arabride. The second dam, Model Bride (by Blushing Groom), is an unraced half-sister to 6 winners including the smart Queen Elizabeth II Stakes third Zaizafon (herself the dam of Zafonic and Zamindar) and to the unraced Modena (the dam of Elmaamul and Reams Of Verse). (Merry Fox Stud Ltd). *"A very nice filly that will hopefully make a 2-y-o in the second half of the season".*

235. PERPETUAL GLORY ★★★

b.f. Dansili – Grail (Quest For Fame). March 4. Eighth foal. 50,000Y. Tattersalls October Book 2. C de Moubray. Closely related to the quite useful 4-y-o 7f winner Aliceinwonderland (by Danehill) and half-sister to the fairly useful 2-y-o 6f winner Divine Right (by Observatory) and the fair 6f winner Opus Dei (by Oasis Dream). The dam won once over 12f in France and is a half-sister to 5 winners including the Group 3 Coventry Stakes winner and subsequent US Grade 2 winner Three Valleys. The second dam, Skiable (by Niniski), won four times at up to 9f in France and the USA and is a half-sister to the outstanding broodmare Hasili (dam of the Group/Grade 1 winners Banks Hill, Cacique, Champs Elysses, Intercontinental and Heat Haze and the Group 2 winner and top-class sire Dansili). (Mr Mehernosh H Deboo & Mrs C Glenn). *"This is an active colt and although he needs a bit of time he could be fine".*

236. PHAENOMENA (IRE) ★★★

ch.f. Galileo – Caumshinaun (Indian Ridge). April 1. Eighth foal. 700,000Y. Tattersalls October Book 1. Course Investment Corp. Sister to the Group 1 Irish 1,000 Guineas winner Nightime, closely related to the 2011 1m placed 2-y-o (on only start) Tajriba (by Teofilo) and half-sister to the Irish 2-y-o 1m winner and listed-placed Mermaid Island (by Mujadil) and the fairly useful dual 7f winner Gunga Din (by Green Desert). The dam won 5 races from 6f to 1m in Ireland at 3 and 4 yrs including a listed event, was Group 3 placed and is a half-sister to one winner. The second dam, Ridge Pool (by Bluebird), was an Irish 2-y-o 6f winner and a half-sister to one winner. (Niarchos Family). *"A nice filly, but she'll obviously need time".*

237. PHOSPHORESCENCE (IRE) ★★

b.c. *Sakhee – Eccentricity (Kingmambo).* April 18. Third foal. The dam, placed once over 1m at 3 yrs from 2 starts, is a half-sister to one winner. The second dam, Shiva (by Hector Protector), a high-class winner of the Group 2 10.5f Tattersalls Gold Cup and the Group 3 10f Brigadier Gerard Stakes, is a sister to the high-class Group 2 12f Prix Jean de Chaudenay and Group 3 12f Prix Foy winner Limnos and a half-sister to the useful 7f and listed 1m winner Burning Sunset. (Niarchos Family). *"A backward 2-y-o at present, but he's a good-looking colt".*

238. RAJARATNA (IRE) ★★★★

b.f. *Galileo – Coup de Genie (Mr Prospector).* June 4. Half-sister to the Group 1 Prix Marcel Boussac winner and Group 1 7f Prix de la Foret second Denebola (by Storm Cat), to the listed Prix Imprudence and minor US stakes winner and Grade 2/Group 2 second Glia, the US triple Grade 3 winner Snake Mountain (both by A P Indy), the Group 3 Prix de Cabourg winner Loving Kindness (by Seattle Slew) and to the dam of the 'Arc' winner Bago. The dam was a smart winner of the Group 1 6f Prix Morny and the Group 1 7f Prix de la Salamandre and was third in the 1,000 Guineas. She is a sister to the champion 2-y-o Machiavellian and a half-sister to the high-class miler Exit To Nowhere, the smart miler Hydro Calido and the unraced dam of the Grand Criterium winner Way Of Light. The second dam, Coup de Folie (by Halo), won the Group 3 1m Prix d'Aumale at 2 yrs and is out of an unraced half-sister to Northern Dancer. (Niarchos Family). *"A very late foal, she's immature in her joints and needs to strengthen. But although she'll need some time she's a nice filly with a touch of class".*

239. REASON TO SMILE ★★★

b.c. *Teofilo – Easy To Love (Diesis).* April 5. Ninth foal. 22,000Y. Tattersalls December. Henry Cecil. Half-brother to the fairly useful 2-y-o 7f and 1m winner and listed-placed Easy Lover (by Pivotal), to the fair 2-y-o 7f winner Pezula Bay (by Oasis Dream) and the modest 13f winner Blinka Me (by Tiger Hill). The dam, a quite useful 4-y-o 11.5f winner, is a sister to the

Oaks winner Love Divine (herself dam of the St Leger winner Sixties Icon) and a half-sister to 5 winners including the listed winner Floreeda and Dark Promise. The second dam, La Sky (by Law Society), a useful 10f winner and second in the Group 3 Lancashire Oaks, is closely related to the Champion Stakes winner Legal Case and a half-sister to 4 winners. (Maze Rattan Ltd) *"He's a lovely mover and a nice colt, but he'll need some time".*

240. REMINISCE (IRE) ★★

b.c. *Oasis Dream – Sedna (Priolo).* March 15. First foal. 100,000Y. Tattersalls October Book 1. Brian Grassick Bloodstock. The dam, a quite useful Irish 6f and 7f winner at 5 yrs, is a half-sister to 4 winners including the dual Group 3 winning sprinter Captain Gerrard and the Hong Kong stakes winner Saturn. The second dam, Delphinus (by Soviet Star), won once at 3 yrs in France and is a half-sister to 3 minor winners. (Miss Y.M.G. Jacques). *"A nice colt that will need time to strengthen and develop".*

241. RETIREMENT PLAN ★★★★

b.br.c. *Monsun – Passage Of Time (Dansili).* February 6. First foal. The dam, a very smart winner of the Group 1 10f Criterium de Saint-Cloud (at 2 yrs) and the Group 3 10.3f Musidora Stakes, is a sister to the 6f (at 2 yrs) and Group 2 12f King Edward VI Stakes winner Father Time and a half-sister to 3 winners including the smart triple listed 1m and 10f winner Timepiece. The second dam, Clepsydra (by Sadler's Wells), a quite useful 12f winner, is a half-sister to several winners including the useful listed 10.5f winner Double Crossed. (Khalid Abdulla). *"Being by Monsun you would naturally expect him to need some time, but nonetheless he's a very nice colt".*

242. RIDGEWAY STORM (IRE) ★★★

b.c. *Hurricane Run – Hesperia (Slip Anchor).* March 22. Eleventh foal. 37,000Y. Tattersalls October Book 2. Highflyer Bloodstock. Half-brother to the fairly useful 2-y-o 7f winner and listed-placed Lucky Date (by Halling), to the fairly useful 1m winner Namroc (by Indian Ridge), the fair dual 14f winner and very smart hurdler Hollow Tree (by Beat Hollow), the modest 11f and 12f winner Western Point (by Pivotal) and a minor 3-y-o winner in Germany by Acatenango. The dam, a winner over 11f and 12f including a listed event in Italy, is a half-sister to 4 winners including the French listed winners Wavey and Rebuff . The second dam, Throw Away Line (by Assert), won once in the USA at 4 yrs and is a half-sister to 9 winners including Go For Wand (a winner of seven Grade 1 events in the USA) and the US Grade 2 winners Dance Spell and Discorama. (Henry Ponsonby). *"A very big colt and a good mover"*.

243. RIPOSTE ★★★

b.f. Dansili – Rainbow Lake (Rainbow Quest). February 25. Sister to the quite useful 10f winner Arizona Jewel, closely related the listed 5f and listed 6f winner Kind (by Danehill and herself the dam of Frankel) and half-sister to the high-class 7f (at 2 yrs) and Group 2 12f Great Voltigeur Stakes winner Powerscourt, to the useful Irish 10f and 12f winner Westlake (both by Sadler's Wells), the smart 14f winner of 3 races Brimming (by Generous) and the fairly useful 2-y-o 1m winner Unaware (by Unfuwain). The dam, a smart winner of 3 races including the Group 3 12f Lancashire Oaks and the listed 10f Ballymacoll Stud Stakes, is a half-sister to several winners including the useful middle-distance winner Vertex. The second dam, Rockfest (by Stage Door Johnny), a useful 2-y-o 7f and 1m winner, was second in the Lingfield Oaks Trial and is a half-sister to the very smart 5f to 7f winner Glen Strae. (Khalid Abdulla). *"This is a likeable filly but she'll need time"*.

244. ROME ★★★

b.c. Holy Roman Emperor – Magical Cliché (Affirmed). March 23. Ninth foal. 40,000Y. Tattersalls October Book 1. C de Moubray. Closely related to the Irish 3-y-o 6f winner Clever Myth (by Green Desert) and half-brother to the Irish 9f to 12f winner Legend Has It (by Sadler's Wells). The dam was placed 4 times at up to 1m and is a sister to four stakes winners including the Group 2 Premio Legnano winner Easy To Copy (herself the dam of 3 stakes winners) and the Irish 1,000 Guineas winner Trusted Partner (dam of the high-class filly Dress To Thrill). The second dam, Talking Picture (by Speak John), a champion American 2-y-o filly, won the Grade 1 Matron Stakes and the Grade 1 Spinaway Stakes. (John Penny).

"This colt has had a colic operation and so is behind the main bunch of my 2-y-o's, but all is fine with him now. He's tough, a good mover and hopefully he'll make a 2-y-o later on".

245. SAGUE LA GRANDE (IRE) ★★★

b.c. Teofilo – Water Fountain (Mark Of Esteem). April 16. Second foal. 70,000Y. Tattersalls October Book 2. BBA (Ire). The dam is an unraced sister to the Group 3 Prix Cleopatre winner Spring Oak and a half-sister to 8 winners including the 10f Lupe Stakes winner Fragrant Hill (herself the dam of five Group winners including the French Group 1 winners Fragrant Mix and Alpine Rose). The second dam, English Spring (by Grey Dawn II), won 7 races from 1m to 10f including the Group 2 Prince of Wales's Stakes and is a half-sister to 4 winners including the US Grade 1 winner Dance of Life. (Lady Cecil). *"A tall colt and a good mover"*.

246. SEA MEETS SKY (FR) ★★★

b.f. Dansili – Sacred Song (Diesis). March 4. Closely related to the Group 2 10f Prix Guillaume d'Ornano and Group 3 10.5f Rose Of Lancaster Stakes winner Multidimensional (by Danehill). The dam won 4 races from 6f (at 2 yrs) to 12f including the Group 3 Princess Royal Stakes and the Group 3 Lancashire Oaks and is a half-sister to the dual Canadian Grade 2 winner Strut The Stage. The second dam, Ruby Ransom (by Red Ransom), won over 1m in Canada and is a half-sister to the Grade 1 Breeders Cup Turf winner Chief Bearheart. (The Niarchos Family). *"A nice filly and a good mover"*.

247. SLEEK ★★★

b.f. Oasis Dream – Slink (Selkirk). January 29. Second foal. 120,000foal. Tattersalls December. Brian Grassick Bloodstock. The dam is an unraced half-sister to 5 winners including the Group 1 10f Hong Kong Cup, Group 2 1m Beresford Stakes and Group 2 10f Royal Whip Stakes winner Eagle Mountain, the 2-y-o Group 1 1m Prix Marcel Boussac winner and triple Group 1 placed Sulk and the listed 1m winner Wallace. The second dam, Masskana (by Darshaan), a minor 9f and 10f winner in France, is a half-sister to 3 winners including the Group 2 Gallinule Stakes winner Massyar and the US Grade 3 Arcadia Handicap winner

Madjaristan. (Miss Y.M.G Jacques). *"An early foal, she's nice but backward at present".*

248. SQUIRE OSBALDESTON (IRE) ★★★
b.c. Mr Greeley – Kushnarenkovo (Sadler's Wells). March 10. Third foal. 100,000Y. Tattersalls October Book 2. BBA (Ire). The dam, a fairly useful 12f winner, was second in the Group 3 12f Noblesse Stakes and is a sister to the Group 1 Racing Post Trophy and St Leger winner Brian Boru and the listed Park Express Stakes winner Kitty O'Shea and a half-sister to the Group 2 Prix de Royallieu winner Moon Search and to the unraced dam of the Derby and Prix de l'Arc de Triomphe winner Workforce. The second dam, Eva Luna (by Alleged), won the Group 3 14.6f Park Hill Stakes and is a half-sister to 5 winners including the dam of the US Grade 1 winner Flute. (Paul Hickman). *"A good-looking colt that needs time".*

249. TOMINTOUL MAGIC (IRE) ★★★
b.f. Holy Roman Emperor – Trois Graces (Alysheba). May 2. Tenth foal. 52,000Y. Tattersalls October Book 2. C de Moubray. Closely related to the 2-y-o listed 5f Prix Yacowlef winner and Group 3 Prix de Cabourg second Abbeyside (by Danehill Dancer) and half-sister to the unplaced 2011 2-y-o Surrey Dream (by Oasis Dream), the smart 7f (at 2 yrs) and listed 1m winner Flat Spin (by Spinning World), the fairly useful 2-y-o 7f winner Goodness Gracious (by Green Desert) and the quite useful 10f and 12f winner Tartan Tie (by Grand Lodge). The dam won once over 1m at 3 yrs in France and is a half-sister to 5 winners including Rami (Group 3 Concorde Stakes), Crack Regiment (Group 3 Prix Eclipse) and La Grand Epoque (second in the Group 1 Prix de l'Abbaye). The second dam, Ancient Regime (by Olden Times), won the Group 1 Prix Morny and is a full or half-sister to 5 winners including the Prix Maurice de Gheest winner Cricket Ball. (Angus Dundee Distillers plc). *"An active filly, I can see her making a 2-y-o later on".*

250. UNNAMED ★★★★
b.c. Jeremy – Collada (Desert Prince). April 13. Fifth foal. £60,000Y. Tattersalls October Book 1. Mubarak Al Naimi. Half-brother to the fair 2011 9f placed 2-y-o Dynamic Duo, to the fairly useful 2-y-o 7f and 1m winner Cai Shen (by Iffraaj) and a winner in Greece by Celtic Swing. The dam is an unplaced half-sister to 3 winners including the very smart 2-y-o Group 3 7f Horris Hill Stakes winner and French 2,000 Guineas second Clearing. The second dam, Bright Spells (by Alleged), a French 12f winner, is a sister to 3 winners including the Group 2 German winner Non Partisan and the Grade 3 Canadian stakes winner Jalaajel and a half-sister to 7 winners including the useful dual 2-y-o 7f winner and Group 3 Prix d'Aumale third Suntrap (herself dam of the Grade/Group 1 winners Raintrap and Sunshack). (Mr A N Mubarak). *"This is a likeable, active colt and a very good mover".*

251. UNNAMED ★★★
b.c. Invincible Spirit – Ghazal (Gone West). March 6. Seventh foal. 240,000Y. Tattersalls October Book 1. Not sold. Closely related to the quite useful 5f to 1m winner Muftarres (by Green Desert) and half-sister to the quite useful triple 1m winner from 3 to 5 yrs Hassaad (by Danehill). The dam, a useful dual 6f winner (including at 2 yrs), is a sister to the US dual Grade 3 winner and good sire Elusive Quality and a half-sister to 5 winners including the 2-y-o Group 2 5.5f Prix Robert Papin winner Rossini. The second dam, Touch Of Greatness (by Hero's Honor), is an unraced half-sister to 5 winners including the German Group 1 and Royal Lodge Stakes winner Gold And Ivory and to the dam of the Group 1 National Stakes winner Heart Of Darkness. (Ms A Quinn). *"A backward colt at this stage, but he should start improving in the next few months".*

252. UNNAMED ★★★
b.f. Authorized – Incoming Call (Red Ransom). February 28. Second foal. 75,000Y. Tattersalls October Book 1. C de Moubray. Half-sister to the quite useful 2011 7f placed 2-y-o Protanto (by Lawman). The dam, placed third over 7f at 3 yrs on her only start, is a half-sister to 4 winners including the French Group 3 10.5f winner Dance Dress (herself dam of the US Grade 2 winner Costume). The second dam, Private Line (by Private Account), a useful 7f (at 2 yrs) and listed 1m winner, is a half-sister to 8 winners including the 2-y-o listed 1m winner and Group 1 placed Most Precious (the dam of four stakes winners including the French 1,000

Guineas winner Matiara). (M C Denmark). *"A nice filly, she's active and should make a 2-y-o later on".*

253. UNNAMED ★★★
b.f. *Cape Cross – Kissing (Grand Lodge)*. March 25. Second foal. The dam, a fair 9.5f winner, is a half-sister to several winners including the Group 1 St Leger, Group 2 Jockey Club Cup and Group 3 Gordon Stakes winner Sixties Icon and the Group 2 second Native Ruler. The second dam, Love Divine (by Diesis), winner of the Group 1 12f Oaks and the listed Lupe Stakes, is a half-sister to 4 winners including the listed 12f winner Floreeda. (Lordship Stud). *"A big filly that will need time, but she's very likeable".*

254. UNNAMED ★★★
b.c. *Cape Cross – Love Divine (Diesis)*. March 31. Brother to the useful 10f winner and Group 2 12f Jockey Club Stakes second Native Ruler and half-brother to the Group 1 St Leger, Group 2 Jockey Club Cup and Group 3 Gordon Stakes winner Sixties Icon (by Galileo) and the fair 9.5f winner Kissing (by Grand Lodge). The dam, winner of the Group 1 12f Oaks and the listed Lupe Stakes, is a half-sister to 4 winners including the listed 12f winner Floreeda. The second dam, La Sky (by Law Society), a useful 10f winner and second in the Lancashire Oaks, is closely related to the Champion Stakes winner Legal Case and a half-sister to 4 winners. (Lordship Stud). *"A nice sort of colt and a good mover, in time he should make up into a nice horse".*

255. UNNAMED ★★★
ch.f. *Pivotal – Midsummer (Kingmambo)*. March 29. Third foal. Half-sister to the high-class filly Midday (by Oasis Dream), winner of the Group 1 Breeders Cup Filly & Mare Turf, Prix Vermeille, Yorkshire Oaks and Nassau Stakes (three times) and to the fairly useful 10f and 12f winner Midsummer Sun (by Monsun). The dam, a quite useful 11f winner and listed-placed over 12f, is a half-sister to numerous winners including the Oaks and Fillies Mile winner Reams of Verse, the Eclipse Stakes and Phoenix Champion Stakes winner Elmaamul. The second dam, Modena (by Roberto), is an unraced half-sister to the smart 2-y-o 7f winner

and Queen Elizabeth II Stakes third Zaizafon – herself the dam of Zafonic. (Khalid Abdulla). *"This filly is going through a growing stage at the moment, but she's a very nice mover".*

256. UNNAMED ★★★
b.c. *Galileo – Miss Beatrix (Danehill Dancer)*. February 10. Second foal. €260,000foal. Goffs. Mertoun Paddocks. Brother to the quite useful Oh So Lucy, placed over 7f on all three of her outings at 2 yrs in 2011. The dam won 3 races at 2 yrs including the Group 1 7f Moyglare Stud Stakes and was third in the Group 1 Phoenix Stakes. The second dam, Miss Beabea (by Catrail), an Irish 2-y-o listed 6f winner and second in the Group 1 6f Phoenix Stakes, is a half-sister to 8 winners including the very useful 5f winner Ellen's Lad. (Mr V I Araci). *"A nice colt, he'll need a bit of time but he moves well".*

257. UNNAMED ★★★
b.f. *Dansili – Modesta (Sadler's Wells)*. March 9. Fourth foal. Sister to the fairly useful 7f (at 2 yrs) and 1m winner Intense and half-sister to Model Pupil (by Sinndar), placed third over 7f on his only start at 2 yrs in 2011. The dam, a useful 11.5f and listed 14f winner, is closely related to the Oaks, Fillies Mile, Musidora Stakes and May Hill Stakes winner Reams of Verse and to the smart 2-y-o 1m winner and Group-placed High Walden and a half-sister to the high-class Group 1 10f Coral Eclipse Stakes and Group 1 10f Phoenix Champion Stakes winner Elmaamul. The second dam, Modena (by Roberto), is an unraced half-sister to the smart 2-y-o 7f winner and Queen Elizabeth II Stakes third Zaizafon – herself the dam of Zafonic. (Khalid Abdulla). *"Hasn't been in training very long, but she's a nice filly that moves well".*

258. UNNAMED ★★★★ Autun
b.c. *Empire Maker – Sense Of Joy (Dansili)*. February 19. First foal. The dam, winner of the 2-y-o Group 3 7f Prestige Stakes, is a half-sister to the multiple Group 3 middle-distance winner and French Derby fourth Day Flight and the very useful 2-y-o 7f winner Bionic. The second dam, Bonash (by Rainbow Quest), a very useful filly, won 4 races in France from 1m to 12f including the Prix d'Aumale, the Prix

Vanteaux and the Prix de Malleret and is a full or half-sister to 4 winners. (Khalid Abdulla). *"A big colt and a good mover – he's very likeable".*

MICK CHANNON

[handwritten: Won fair ... 1m rl 5mln ... Notts]

259. AMRALAH ★★★
b.c. *Teofilo – Sharp Mode (Diesis)*. March 11. Fourth foal. 50,000Y. Tattersalls October Book 1. Hugo Merry. Half-brother to the modest 2-y-o 5f winner Midget (by Invincible Spirit). The dam is an unraced half-sister to 2 minor winners. The second dam, A La Mode (by Known Fact), placed at 2 yrs and subsequently a minor winner at 5 yrs in the USA, is a sister to the US Grade 3 winner Modernise and a half-sister to 9 winners including the Group 1 winners Elmaamul and Reams Of Verse and the Group winners Manifest, Modernise and Modern Day. (Prince A A Faisal). *"A colt for later in the year but he's a nice horse and a good-sized 2-y-o".*

260. AYAAR (IRE) ★★★
br.c. *Rock Of Gibraltar – Teide Lady (Nashwan)*. March 15. Third foal. 48,000Y. Tattersalls October Book 2. Gill Richardson. Half-brother to the modest 2011 1m placed 2-y-o Teide Peak (by Cape Cross) and to the quite useful 5f (including at 2 yrs) and 6f winner of 4 races Albany Rose (by Noverre). The dam, a modest 9f winner, is a half-sister to the 2-y-o Group 2 7f Superlative Stakes and US Grade 3 7f winner Hatta Fort. The second dam, Oshiponga (by Barathea), a fair 9f winner, is a half-sister to 8 winners including the Group 2 second Kotsi and the Group 3 second Sir George Turner. *"A backward colt, he'll be more of a mile type 2-y-o from the summer onwards but he's a nice colt".*

261. BUNGLEINTHEJUNGLE ★★★★
b.c. *Exceed And Excel – Licence To Thrill (Wolfhound)*. April 27. Eighth foal. 40,000Y. Tattersalls October Book 1. Not sold. Brother to the fairly useful 5f (at 2 yrs) and listed 6f winner of 4 races Waveband and half-brother to the useful 2-y-o dual 5f winner and Group 2 5f King George Stakes second Group Therapy (by Choisir), the fairly useful dual 5f winner (including at 2 yrs) and Group 3 5f Norfolk Stakes third Classic Encounter (by Lujain), the fairly useful 2-y-o 5f winner and listed placed

The Thrill Is Gone (by Bahamian Bounty), the fair 6f and 7f winner Cheap Thrills (by Bertolini) and the modest 6f winner Gimme Some Lovin (by Desert Style). The dam, a quite useful dual 5f winner, is a half-sister to 4 winners including the useful 2-y-o 5f winner Master Of Passion. The second dam, Crime Of Passion (by Dragonara Palace), winner of the Group 3 Cherry Hinton Stakes and third in the Group 1 Prix Robert Papin, is a half-sister to 4 winners including the Ayr Gold Cup winner Primula Boy. (Mr C Wright and Miss E Asprey). *"Very sharp, he'll be ready to go soon and he looks a nice type. A big, strong horse, he'll be a sprinter like most of the family and he knows his job".*

[handwritten: Won Cornwallis]

262. CAPPADOCIA (IRE) ★★★
b.c. *Mujadil – Green Vision (Green Desert)*. March 14. First foal. 16,000Y. Doncaster Premier. Emerald Bloodstock. The dam, a minor winner at 4 yrs in France, is a half-sister to one winner. The second dam, Mighty Isis (by Pleasant Colony), a listed-placed winner at 3 yrs in France, is a half-sister to 4 winners out of the 1,000 Guineas and Champion Stakes winner Hatoof. *"He shows a bit of dash, we're pleased with him, he's going the right way and he's as tough as old boots. He's a nice horse and he'll be racing in May".*

263. CAY VERDE ★★★★
b.c. *Bahamian Bounty – All Quiet (Piccolo)*. February 17. Second foal. £27,000Y. Doncaster Premier. Gill Richardson. The dam, a fair 7f and 1m winner of 3 races, is a half-sister to 5 winners. The second dam, War Shanty (by Warrshan), is an unplaced half-sister to 4 winners including the Group 1 Prix Maurice de Gheest winner Bold Edge and the listed winner Brave Edge. (Box 41). *"He's a nice horse and he'll get better with time even though he'll make a 2-y-o. He's sharp and he'll win early, but he'll improve throughout the year".*

[handwritten: Won Ascot, Won listed 5f Curragh]

264. CHILWORTH ICON ★★★
b.c. *Sixties Icon – Tamara Moon (Acclamation)*. May 8. First foal. The dam, a fair winner of 2 races over 7f and 1m at 2 yrs, is a half-sister to one winner. The second dam, Non Ultra (by Peintre Celebre), a moderate 1m winner, is a half-sister to 4 winners. *"A good, early sort, he's had one run and he'll improve for that. He'll*

[handwritten: Won 5f mdn Salisbury, Won gd 5f cndn Beverley]

win races alright and he'll definitely stay further than five furlongs". Wur Woodcote 2cb?ly

265. DUKE OF ORANGE (IRE) ★★★★
br.c. Duke Of Marmalade – High Society (Key Of Luck). March 15. Fifth foal. 42,000Y. Tattersalls October Book 1. Gill Richardson. Closely related to the modest 2011 7f placed 2-y-o Byron Blue (by Dylan Thomas), to the Group 1 Golden Jubilee Stakes and listed 6f winner Society Rock (by Rock Of Gibraltar) and a winner in Greece by One Cool Cat and half-brother to the minor German 2-y-o 6f winner Johannesburg Cat (by Johannesburg). The dam, an Irish 2-y-o listed 6f and subsequent US stakes winner, was Grade 2 placed and is a half-sister to 4 winners. The second dam, Ela's Gold (by Ela-Mana-Mou), a moderate 6f placed maiden, is a full or half-sister to 6 winners. "He's a real nice horse and I couldn't be happier with him. I don't think we'll see him until May or June time, but he's really pleased me in everything he's done and he looks the type to start at six furlongs".

266. ELIDOR ★★★
b.c. Cape Cross – Honorine (Mark Of Esteem). April 16. Third foal. 120,000foal. Tattersalls December. Gill Richardson. Half-brother to the very smart 7f (at 2 yrs) and Group 1 12f Irish Derby winner and 2-y-o Group 2 1m Royal Lodge Stakes third Treasure Beach (by Galileo). The dam, a quite useful 1m and 10f winner of 3 races, is a half-sister to the Group 2 Hardwicke Stakes and Group 3 Earl Of Sefton Stakes winner and triple Group 1 placed Indian Creek. The second dam, Blue Water (by Bering), won 5 races in France including the listed 12f Prix des Tourelles, was third in the Group 3 10.5f Prix de Flore and is a half-sister to 3 winners including the French winner and Group 3 placed Norton Sound. (Jon & Julia Aisbitt). "He's a lovely horse, we won't get him out until August onwards, but he's nice and I'm very pleased with him. He's made up into a real nice horse".

267. ENAITCH (IRE) ★★★★
gr.f. New Approach – Hotelgenie Dot Com (Selkirk). February 22. Eighth foal. 250,000Y. Tattersalls October Book 1. Gill Richardson. Half-sister to the Group 1 Fillies' Mile and Group 1 Falmouth Stakes winner Simply Perfect (by Danehill) and to the minor Irish 12f winner

Allied Answer (by Danehill Dancer). The dam, a 7f winner at 2 yrs, was second in the Group 1 7f Moyglare Stud Stakes and third in the Group 1 Fillies' Mile and is a half-sister to 4 winners including the Moyglare Stud Stakes and the Group 2 6f Lowther Stakes winner Bianca Nera. The second dam, Birch Creek (by Carwhite), was placed five times including when third in the Group 3 1m Premio Royal Mares and is a half-sister to 7 winners including the useful Group 3 winning sprinter Great Deeds. (Derek & Jean Clee). "I trained the dam and this is a nice filly for later in the year, just like the other New Approach filly we have called Orpha. I like her, she's very nice, but I haven't done an awful lot with her. Whatever she has done I'm happy with and I would have thought we'd wait for seven furlongs with her".

268. GRAPHIC GUEST ★★★★
ch.f. Dutch Art – Makara (Lion Cavern). April 10. Fifth foal. 80,000Y. Tattersalls October Book 1. Gill Richardson. Half-sister to the Irish 5f (at 2 yrs) and dual listed winner (over 7f and 1m) Fourpenny Lane (by Efisio), to the French dual 7f winner of 3 races at 2 and 3 yrs Asque and the fair 7f winner Copper Penny (both by Dansili). The dam is an unraced half-sister to 7 winners including the useful 5f (at 2 yrs) and listed 7f winner Kalindi. The second dam, Rohita (by Waajib), a fairly useful 2-y-o 5f and 6f winner, was third in the Group 3 6f Cherry Hinton Stakes and is a half-sister to 5 winners. (John Guest Racing). "A very nice filly by Dutch Art. She's certainly sharp, she'll be running over five furlongs in the next month and I think she's pretty good. Strong, mature and ready to go".

Bt Lairy rocuet in 3 runner Wnlr

269. HAYYONA ★★★ cl 2 roods 6f
b.f. Multiplex – Shemriyna (King Of Kings). February 22. Third foal. 145,000Y. Tattersalls October Book 1. Gill Richardson. Half-sister to the 2011 1m placed 2-y-o (on his only start) Frasers Hill (by Selkirk) and to the Group 2 10f Prix Eugene Adam winner Shimraan (by Rainbow Quest). The dam won once at 3 yrs in France and is a half-sister to the dual 1m winner and listed-placed Shendaya. The second dam, Shemaya (by Darshaan), won 2 races at 3 yrs in France including a listed 9f event and is a half-sister to 4 winners including the dual Group 3 winner Shemima. (Prince A A Faisal). "She's a

strong filly and she was going well but then just had a little setback. But she'd already showed me enough to say she'll be alright when we get her going again".

270. INDIAN COMMANDO (IRE) ★★★
ch.c. Indian Haven – Kadooment (Desert Prince). March 30. First foal. 10,000Y. Tattersalls December. Gill Richardson. The dam is an unraced half-sister to 7 winners including the smart 1m winner and Irish 2,000 Guineas second Fa-Eq and the listed 7.3f and 1m winner Corinium. The second dam, Searching Star (by Rainbow Quest), a modest 6f (at 2 yrs) to 11.3f placed maiden, is a half-sister to 8 winners including the smart listed Blue Riband Trial winner Beldale Star and the listed winner and useful broodmare Moon Drop. (Jaber Abdullah). *"We won't see him until June time but he's a nice horse that's going the right way. He was quite backward when we bought him, but now he's a good, strong colt with a bit of quality".*

Won 5m 5f rd. 6.Clas

271. JILLNEXTDOOR (IRE) ★★★★
b.f. Henrythenavigator – Royal Shyness (Royal Academy). April 23. Seventh foal. 40,000Y. Tattersalls October Book 1. Gill Richardson. Half-sister to the 2011 7f and 1m placed 2-y-o Van Rooney (by Van Nistelrooy), to the useful 7f and 1m winner and listed-placed Commander Cave (by Tale Of The Cat) and the fair 7f to 10f winner Shy Glance (by Red Ransom). The dam, a useful 2-y-o 6f winner, was third in the Group 1 6f Cheveley Park Stakes and subsequently won a listed stakes race in the USA and is a half-sister to 8 winners. The second dam, Miss Demure (by Shy Groom), won the Group 2 6f Lowther Stakes. (Nick & Olga Dhandsa/ John & Zoe Webster). *"She's very nice indeed and she's in the top group of our early 2-y-o's. Very mature, she's not over-big and she's just a smashing-looking filly with a lot of quality".*

2nd 6f 2 clr 3f nd. cup

272. JONTLEMAN (IRE) ★★★
b.c. Whipper – Gandia (Danehill). April 2. Fourth foal. £5,500Y. Doncaster Premier. Gill Richardson. The dam won over 15f in France, is a half-sister to 3 winners. The second dam, Al Galop (by Affirmed), won at 3 yrs in France and is a half-sister to 10 winners including the US dual Grade 1 winner Both Ends Burning. *"He*

was cheap, but he's one that should pay his way this year". TRAINERS' BARGAIN BUY

273. JULLUNDAR (IRE) ★★★
b.c. Refuse To Bend – Announcing Peace (Danehill). February 9. Eighth foal. £40,000Y. Doncaster Premier. Gill Richardson. Half-brother to the smart winner of 6 races from 6f (at 2 yrs) to 12f (dual listed) and Group 3 placed Crosspeace, to the fairly useful 2-y-o dual 7f winner So Sweet (both by Cape Cross), the Irish 2-y-o 1m winner Desert Eagle (by Hawk Wing), the fair 1m winner Tatbeeq (by Invincible Spirit), the Italian 5f (at 2 yrs) and 7.5f winner Carburatore (by College Chapel) and the minor Irish 2-y-o 1m winner Desert Eagle (by Hawk Wing). The dam is an unplaced full or half-sister to 5 minor winners. The second dam, Remoosh (by Glint Of Gold), is an unplaced half-sister to 5 winners including Nomination (Group 2 Richmond Stakes). (Nick & Olga Dhandsa/John & Zoe Webster). *"A nice, big horse for later in the year over seven furlongs. I like him".*

274. LADY MARMELO (IRE) ★★★
b.f. Duke Of Marmalade – Mooretown Lady (Montjeu). March 15. First foal. €44,000Y. Goffs Orby. Gill Richardson. The dam, a fairly useful Irish 8.5f winner, was second in the Group 3 Ridgewood Pearl Stakes and is a half-sister to 4 winners. The second dam, Chaturanga (by Night Shift), is an unraced half-sister to 6 winners including the Group 2 Prix Eugene Adam winner Sobieski. *"She's a nice little filly that had a setback with a pulled muscle, but I like her and she'll be OK when we get going with her again".*

275. LIGHTNING LAUNCH (IRE) ★★★
b.c. Kheleyf – Launch Time (Relaunch). May 1. Twelfth foal. 65,000Y. Tattersalls October Book 2. Gill Richardson. Closely related to the smart 2-y-o Group 2 7f Superlative Stakes and Group 2 12f Bosphorus Cup winner of 10 races Halicarnassus (by Cape Cross) and half-brother to the fair 8.3f winner Follow My Lead (by Night Shift), the Canadian stakes-placed winner My Lucky Strike (by Smart Strike) and two minor winners in the USA by Hennessy and Two Punch. The dam is a US placed half-sister to 4 winners including the US Grade 2 winner

Palace March, the US Grade 1 second Executive Pride and the dam of the 2,000 Guineas second Rebel Rebel. The second dam, Pride's Palace (by Majestic Palace), won once at 2 yrs and is a half-sister to 5 winners including the US Grade 1 winner Winds Of Thought and the Group 3 Princess Elizabeth Stakes winner and smart broodmare Elegant Tern. (Jaber Abdullah). *"We probably won't see him until the seven furlong/ mile races later on. He was a late foal but he's a nice colt".*

276. LUHAIF ★★★
b.c. Cape Cross – Hot And Spicy (Grand Lodge). January 23. Third foal. 50,000Y. Tattersalls October Book 2. Gill Richardson. The dam, placed third over 7f at 2 yrs in Ireland, is a half-sister to 3 winners including the Group 1 11f Italian Oaks winner Zanzibar (herself dam of the US Grade 2 winner Spice Route) and the listed winner New Guinea. The second dam, Isle Of Spice (by Diesis), a fair 3-y-o 9.7f winner, is a half-sister to 5 winners including the minor US 2-y-o stakes winner Crown Silver. (Sheikh Mohammed). *"He's not going to be too long before he's out and it wouldn't matter if it was five or six furlongs with him. He's got a bit of speed, he's a nice horse and shows enough to say we ought to be looking out for him".*

277. MICHAEL'S SONG (IRE) ★★★
b.f. Refuse To Bend – Raindancing (Tirol). April 25. Eleventh foal. 20,000Y. Tattersalls October Book 2. Gill Richardson. Half-sister to the fairly useful triple 5f winner and listed-placed Jack Spratt (by So Factual), to the fair 7f and hurdles winner Dash For Cover (by Sesaro), the fair 7f winner Areeda (by Refuse To Bend), the fair 12f winner Yossi (by Montjeu), the modest 10f winner Paco Belle (by Whipper), the moderate 1m and 9f winner Ballare (by Barathea) and a winner in Hungary by King's Best. The dam, a fairly useful 2-y-o 6f winner, was third in the Group 3 6f Princess Margaret Stakes and is a sister to the smart 7f (at 2 yrs) to 10f winner and Group 1 National Stakes third Mountain Song and a half-sister to 7 winners including the Group 2 Cherry Hinton Stakes winner Please Sing. The second dam, Persian Song (by Persian Bold), is an unplaced sister to the Kentucky Derby second Bold Arrangement. *"A lovely filly that's just going the right way at the*

moment. One for six furlongs I'd say, possibly around May time when she gets a bit of sun on her back".

278. MISS YOU TOO ★★★
b.f. Montjeu – Portrait Of A Lady (Peintre Celebre). March 29. Fifth foal. 28,000Y. Tattersalls October Book 1. Gill Richardson. Half-sister to Marshall Art (by Lawman), unplaced in two starts at 2 yrs in 2011 and to the useful Irish 2-y-o 7f winner and Group 3 7f Killavullan Stakes second Vitruvian Man (by Montjeu). The dam was a fairly useful listed-placed 12f winner of 3 races and a half-sister to 3 winners. The second dam, Starlight Smile (Green Dancer), is an unraced half-sister to 4 winners including the dam of the Irish Derby winner Grey Swallow. *"She's not bad at all and she shows a lot more speed than I thought she would. So we'll have a look at starting her in May over six furlongs".* Won 7f cl 3 mdn York

279. NELSON'S ROCK ★★
b.c. Mount Nelson – Really Ransom (Red Ransom). February 1. First foal. £44,000Y. Doncaster Premier. Gill Richardson. The dam, a quite useful Irish 2-y-o 7f and 1m winner, is a half-sister to 4 winners. The second dam, Really Polish (by Polish Numbers), a winner of 9 races in the USA including the Grade 3 Dogwood Stakes, was third in the Grade 1 Kentucky Oaks and is a half-sister to 3 winners. (Mr Paddy Bowles). *"A lovely, big horse but a backward type for later in the year over seven furlongs or a mile".*

280. NINE IRON (IRE) ★★★
gr.c. Verglas – Sevi's Choice (Sir Ivor). April 30. Tenth foal. €36,000Y. Goffs Orby. Gill Richardson. Half-brother to the very useful Group 3 10f Kilternan Stakes winner Galileo's Choice (by Galileo), to the useful Irish listed 11f winner Celebrity Sevi (by Peintre Celebre), the fairly useful listed 10f placed Almendrados (by Desert Prince), the fair 2-y-o 5f winner Dontstopthemusic (by Night Shift), the fair Irish 7f winner Indicative (by Azamour) and the fair 2m and hurdles winner Tharawaat (by Alhaarth). The dam, a minor 10f winner at 3 yrs in Germany, is a sister to the winner and listed Canadian Oaks second Ivory Dance and a half-sister to 5 winners. The second dam,

Dance Call (by Nijinsky), a minor winner in the USA, is a half-sister to 8 winners including the US Grade 1 winner Miss Toshiba and the dam of the champion sprinter Committed and the US Grade 1 winner Pharma. (Mr C Wright & Mr J Corbett). *"He wasn't expensive but he's going the right way. I can't say a lot about him yet, except that he's a nice horse that's pleased me. I wouldn't have thought you'd see him before June, over seven furlongs".*

281. OLLIE OLGA ★★★

b.f. Stormy Atlantic – Card Shop (Chester House). January 11. First foal. 42,000Y. Tattersalls October Book 1. Gill Richardson. The dam, placed at 2 and 3yrs in France, is a half-sister to the Group 2 Hardwicke Stakes winner and Group 1 Juddmonte International Stakes third Await The Dawn and to the French listed winner and Group 1 Criterium de Saint-Cloud third Putney Bridge (by Mizzen Mast). The second dam, Valentine Band (by Dixieland Band), a listed-placed 3-y-o winner, is a half-sister to 8 winners including the Group 3 winners Memorise and Multiplex. (Nick & Olga Dhandsa/John & Zoe Webster). *"I haven't done a lot with her yet because she's grown and is a big filly now. She's lovely".*

282. ORPHA ★★★★

b.f. New Approach – Garah (Ajdal). March 13. Half-sister to the Group 1 9f Prix Jean Prat winner Olden Times (by Darshaan), to the useful 1m (at 2 yrs) and listed 6f winner and Group 1 Cheveley Park Stakes third Festoso (by Diesis), the quite useful 10f and 12f winner And Again (by In The Wings), the modest 12f winner All Good Things (by Marju) and the minor US 6f winner Idma (by Midyan). The dam was a very useful winner of 4 races over 6f, was second in the Group 3 5f Duke Of York Stakes and is a half-sister to 3 winners. The second dam, Abha (by Thatching), a very smart 5f and 6f winner of 4 races, was fourth in the Group 1 5f Kings Stand Stakes and is a half-sister to the listed Princess Margaret Stakes winner Sarissa. (Prince A A Faisal). *"A lovely filly for later in the year over seven furlongs. The way she's shaping I'd say she's capable of getting to Goodwood, she's a big filly with plenty of scope".*

283. OUZINKIE (IRE) ★★★

b.c. Kodiac – Sleeponit (Marju). April 21. Fifth living foal. 20,000Y. Tattersalls October Book 2. Gill Richardson. Half-brother to the quite useful 5f to 1m winner Leeside Champ (by Soviet Star). The dam, placed fourth once over 7f, is a half-sister to 5 winners including the Group 1 St James's Palace Stakes third Sorbie Tower. The second dam, Nozet (by Nishapour), won once at 3 yrs in France and is a half-sister to 3 winners. (Box 41). *"An early 2-y-o we can be getting on with, but he's not just a whiz-bang, I think he'll get a mile later on".*

284. PAY FREEZE (IRE) ★★

b.c. Baltic King – Banco Solo (Distant Relative). April 2. €7,500Y. Goffs Orby. Gill Richardson. Brother to the modest 2011 3-y-o 5f winner Bella Ophelia, closely related to the Italian listed winner of 20 races Golden Danetime and to the fair 1m (including at 2 yrs) to 10f winner of 6 races Bridge Of Fermoy (both by Danetime) and half-brother to the useful 8.2f to 10f winner Internationalguest (by Petardia), the fairly useful 8.3f winner Bold Act (by Brave Act) and the quite useful 12f to 2m winner The Last Don (by Redback). The dam is an unraced sister to the dual listed winner and Irish 1,000 Guineas third My Branch (herself dam of the Group 1 Haydock Park Sprint Cup winner Tante Rose) and a half-sister to 5 winners. The second dam, Pay The Bank (by High Top), a quite useful 2-y-o 1m winner, stayed 10f and is a half-sister to 4 winners. (Lord Ilsley Racing – Hern Syndicate). *"A nice, rangy type of horse, he does everything nicely, he'll run soon and we'll have a bit of fun with him".*

Won d 3 6f mdr York by 5l

285. QIBTEE (IRE) ★★★

b.c. Antonius Pius – Embers Of Fame (Sadler's Wells). March 21. Seventh foal. £36,000Y. Doncaster Premier. Gill Richardson. Half-brother to the quite useful 6f (at 2 yrs) and 1m winner of 4 races and dual 2-y-o listed placed Rainbow Mirage (by Rainbow Quest). The dam ran twice unplaced and is a half-sister to 4 winners including Free To Speak, a winner of 3 listed events over 1m in Ireland. The second dam, Love For Poetry (by Lord Gayle), won 3 races at 3 yrs and is a half-sister to 5 winners. (Sheikh Mohammed). *"A very good-looking horse and a nice, big type. He was going the right way until he got a haematoma on his backside, but he'll be OK when we get him sorted. It won't matter when he's ready because he's a nice horse".*

286. RATED ★★★★

b.c. Sixties Icon – Arasong (Aragon). April 3. Half-brother to the 2011 2-y-o winner Majestic Zafeen (by Zafeen), to the quite useful triple 2-y-o 5f and 3-y-o 6f winner Gone Hunting, the fair dual 5f winner Ronnie Howe (both by Hunting Lion), the modest dual 7f winner (including at 2 yrs) Annie's Song (by Farfelu) and the modest 1m and 9f winner La Viola (by Fraam). The dam, a fair dual 5f winner (including at 2 yrs), is a half-sister to 8 minor winners. The second dam, Songstead (by Song), a fairly useful 6f winner of 4 races at 2 and 3 yrs, is a half-sister to 3 winners. *"He'll be better over six furlongs but he'll win over five. He's not over-big, but after all he is out of a sprint-bred mare. He has a lot of quality".*

287. SANDREAMER ★★★★

b.f. Oasis Dream – Alsharq (Machiavellian). April 5. Fourth foal. £85,000Y. Doncaster Premier. Gill Richardson. Half-sister to the modest 2011 2-y-o 7f winner Lolita Lebron (by Royal Applause), to the fair dual 5f winner, including at 2 yrs, Commanche Raider (by Tale Of The Cat) and the fair 1m winner Eastern Breeze (by Red Ransom). The dam, a modest 7f winner, is a sister to one winner and a half-sister to 5 winners including the Group 2 7f Rockfel Stakes winner Sayedah. The second dam, Balaabel (by Sadler's Wells), a quite useful 1m winner, is a half-sister to 6 winners including the US Grade 2 7f winner Kayrawan and the good broodmare Sayedat Alhadh (dam of the Group winners Haatef and Walayef). (Jon & Julia Aisbitt). *"A lovely filly, she's quite sharp and she'll make a 2-y-o in May over five furlongs. A solid, compact filly that lacks a bit of scope if anything, but she looks a sharp 2-y-o".*

288. SHORE STEP ★★★

br.c. Footstepsinthesand – Chatham Islands (Elusive Quality). April 1. Second foal. €75,000Y. Goffs Orby. Gill Richardson. Half-brother to the smart 2011 2-y-o 6f winner and Group 1 Middle Park Stakes fourth Balty Boys (by Cape Cross). The dam, a fair 2-y-o 6f winner, is a half-

sister to 5 winners including the French Group 3 winner Time Prisoner and the 2-y-o listed 6f winner and Group 2 6f Cherry Hinton Stakes second Pearl Grey. The second dam, Zelanda (by Night Shift), a very useful winner of 4 races over 5f and 6f including a listed event, is a half-sister to 6 winners including the Group 3 1m Prix des Reservoirs winner Emily Bronte. (Jon & Julia Aisbitt). *"A lovely big colt, he's a had a few niggling issues but nothing serious. I think he'll be a nice horse as the year goes on, but I haven't had a clean run with him yet".*

289. SHRIMPTON ★★★★

b.f. Cadeaux Genereux – Feather Boa (Sri Pekan). February 23. Fifth foal. 40,000Y. Tattersalls October Book 2. Gill Richardson. Half-sister to the fair 1m (at 2 yrs) and 1m winner White Dart (by Rakti), to the quite useful 2-y-o 5f winner Mazzanti (by Pivotal) and the modest 9f winner Vamos (by Royal Applause). The dam, a quite useful 2-y-o dual 6f winner, is a half-sister to 6 winners including the listed winner Wagtail. The second dam, Dancing Feather (by Suave Dancer), a quite useful 1m winner, is a half-sister to 8 winners including the good broodmare Fragrant Hill (dam of the Group 1 winners Fragrant Mix and Alpine Rose). *"A beautiful filly, a real smasher. She's shown a bit of speed and I've laid off her because she's big, so I'm in no rush with her but she goes very well".*

290. SILCA'S DREAM ★★★★

b.c. Oasis Dream – Silca-Cisa (Hallgate). May 3. Eleventh foal. Closely related to the useful sprint winner of 14 races (including at 2 yrs) Green Manalishi (by Green Desert) and half-brother to the smart 2-y-o Group 1 6f Prix Morny winner Silca's Sister, to the smart Group 2 6f Mill Reef Stakes and German Group 2 winner and Group 1 placed Golden Silca (both by Inchinor), the smart 2-y-o 6f winner and dual Group 1 placed Silca Chiave (by Pivotal), the quite useful 2-y-o dual 6f winner Silca Legend (by Efisio), the quite useful 6.8f winner King Silca (by Emarati) and the Italian 2-y-o 5f winner Muso Corto (by Reprimand). The dam, a fairly useful dual 5f winner, was listed placed over 5f at 4 yrs and is a half-sister to the Group 3 placed sprint winner Azizzi. The second dam, Princess Silca-Key (by Grundy), was a modest 7f winner and a half-sister to 3 winners. (Aldridge Racing). *"He's the last of the Silca-Cisa foals, he's nice and he goes well. A real professional, he looks a 2-y-o type despite the fact that he's a May foal. He's lovely".*

291. STRICTLY SILCA ★★★★★
ch.f. Danehill Dancer – Silca Chiave (Pivotal). January 18. First foal. 100,000Y. Tattersalls October Book 1. Not sold. The dam, a smart 2-y-o 6f winner, was placed in the Group 1 Moyglare Stud Stakes and the Group 1 Cheveley Park Stakes and is a half-sister to 6 winners including the 2-y-o Group 1 6f Prix Morny winner Silca's Sister, the Group 2 6f Mill Reef Stakes and German Group 2 winner and Group 1 placed Golden Silca and the useful triple listed winning sprinter Green Manalishi. The second dam, Silca-Cisa (by Hallgate), a fairly useful dual 5f winner, was listed placed and is a half-sister to the Group 3 placed sprint winner Azizzi. (Aldridge Racing). *"She's gorgeous. A smashing big, chestnut filly and typical of the family, I don't think she'll be early, so I'd say she's one for later on this year over seven furlongs. She's a big, strong filly and I like her a lot".*

292. SYMBOLINE ★★★
b.f. Royal Applause – Ashes (General Monash). March 2. First living foal. 30,000Y. Tattersalls October Book 2. Gill Richardson. The dam, a modest 5f winner of 7 races (including at 2 yrs), is a half-sister to 5 winners including the smart listed 7f winner Royal Storm. The second dam, Wakayi (by Persian Bold), a quite useful 2-y-o 5f winner, was fourth in the Group 3 Queen Mary Stakes and is a half-sister to 4 winners including the Group 3 sprint winners Reesh and Tadwin (herself the dam of two Group 3 winners) and to the dam of the Group 3 winning sprinter and sire Averti. (Insignia Racing – Ensign Syndicate). *"This filly goes well, she's one of the sharper ones, so look out for her early in the season over five and six furlongs".*

293. TALQAA ★★★
b.f. Exceed And Excel – Poppo's Song (Polish Navy). February 27. Third foal. £70,000Y. Doncaster Premier. Gill Richardson. Half-sister to a 3-y-o winner in Italy by Johannesburg. The dam, a Canadian listed stakes winner of 2 races

at 3 and 4 yrs, is a half-sister to 2 winners. The second dam, Bridled Song (by Seattle Slew), is a placed half-sister to 4 winners. (Sheikh Mohammed). *"A nice filly, she's just growing a bit at the moment so we're taking our time with her, but she showed a bit of dash early on so that's good".*

294. UNIDEXTER (IRE) ★★★
br.c. Footstepsinthesand – Run To Jane (Doyoun). April 6. Eighth living foal. £20,000Y. Doncaster Premier. Gill Richardson. Half-brother to the fair 2011 2-y-o 6f winner Taro Tywod (by Footstepsinthesand), to the quite useful 10f to 14f and hurdles winner Beyond (by Galileo), the quite useful 9f winner Tarzan (by Spinning World), the fair 2-y-o 7f winner Emerald Penang (by Alzao), a 4-y-o winner in Greece by Fasliyev and a winner in the Czech Republic by Montjeu. The dam is an unplaced half-sister to 6 winners including the Irish listed winners Mora and Broadway Rosie (herself dam of the dual Group 3 winner Eastern Purple). The second dam, Broadway Royal (by Royal Match), is an unraced half-sister to the Kings Stand Stakes winner African Song. *"He's not sharp but he's a nice, big horse that'll come to himself by mid-season, starting over six furlongs. He'll probably get a mile later on".*

295. VALLARTA (IRE) ★★★
b.c. Footstepsinthesand – Mexican Miss (Tagula). April 7. Third foal. 17,000Y. Tattersalls October Book 2. Gill Richardson. The dam, a modest Irish 12f winner at 5 yrs, is a half-sister to 5 winners here and abroad. The second dam, Hear Me (by Simply Great), a listed-placed winner of 2 races at 3 yrs in Ireland, is a half-sister to 8 winners. *"He's done enough to show he's got some ability, but he's one for a bit later on so we're not pushing any buttons with him yet. I like him a lot".* Won at l,.../ at Newbury

296. WHISKEYMACK ★★
b.c. Mount Nelson – Dream Day (Oasis Dream). January 12. First foal. 40,000Y. Tattersalls October Book 1. Gill Richardson. The dam, a fairly useful 2-y-o 6f winner and second in the Group 3 Nell Gwyn Stakes, is a sister to one winner and a half-sister to 2 winners including the useful 6f (at 2 yrs) to 1m winner and Group 3 Supreme Stakes third Sabbeeh. The second

dam, Capistrano Day (by Diesis), a smart listed 7f winner, was third in the Group 3 Fred Darling Stakes, fourth in the 1,000 Guineas and is a full or half-sister to 5 winners. *"The Mount Nelson's I have are just needing a bit of time, so although he's an early foal he'll not be out before mid-season".*

297. UNNAMED ★★★

b.f. Sixties Icon – Fading Away (Fraam). January 31. Half-sister to the modest 10f and hurdles winner Brilliant Barca (by Imperial Dancer) and to the modest 2-y-o 7f winner Alphacino (by Hunting Lion). The dam is an unraced half-sister to the useful Dayglow Dancer. The second dam, Fading (by Pharly), was unraced. *"A very nice filly and similar to the Sixties Icon 2-y-o out of Funny Girl in that she'll just take a bit of time".*

298. UNNAMED ★★★

b.f. Sixties Icon – Funny Girl ((Darshaan). April 8. Eighth foal. Half-sister to the 2012 3-y-o dual 1m winner Laugh Out Loud (by Clodovil), to the useful 6f (at 2 yrs), 10f and listed 12f winner Suzi's Decision (by Act One), the fairly useful 10f and 12f winner of 4 races Pippa Greene (by Galileo), the fair 5 winner of 3 races Brynfa Boy (by Namid) and the modest 6f winner Nadinska (by Doyen). The dam was placed from 7f to 9f and is a daughter of the minor German winner Just For Fun (by Lead On Time), herself a sister to the listed Prix Herbager winner Judge Decision. *"Because the sire didn't win as a 2-y-o no-one believes he can get 2-y-o winners, which is a load of old rubbish. The 2-y-o's I have by him have got quality. This a beautiful filly and a half-sister to a black-type horse. She's one for later in the year".*

299. UNNAMED ★★★

b.c. Sir Percy – Night Over Day (Most Welcome). February 12. Ninth foal. 26,000Y. Tattersalls October Book 1. Gill Richardson. Half-brother to the quite useful 2-y-o 6f winner As One Does (by Lujain), to the Italian winner and listed placed Mrs Seek (by Unfuwain) and a winner in Norway by Bertolini. The dam was an unplaced daughter of the fairly useful dual 7f winner Etosha (by Green Desert), herself a half-sister to 12 winners including Sasuru (Group 1 Prix d'Ispahan) and Sally Rous (Group 2 Challenge Stakes) and the dams of the US Grade 1 winner Tuscan Evening and the French 1,000 Guineas winner Rose Gypsy. *"Yes, this colt goes alright, he's a nice horse. In fact both of my Sir Percy 2-y-o's are similar sorts. You'll see them in July/August time".*

300. UNNAMED ★★★

gr.f. Kyllachy – Park Acclaim (Clodovil). Second foal. The dam is an unraced half-sister to the Group 3 7f Jersey Stakes winner Rainfall. The second dam, Molomo (Barathea), an Irish 12f winner and second in both the Group 2 10f Pretty Polly Stakes and the Group 2 10f Royal Whip Stakes, is a sister to the Irish 1m and 9f winner and listed-placed Pepperwood and a half-sister to 2 winners. (Andrew Black). *"Quite a strong filly that shows a bit of speed. I've only just started on her, so I could tell you a lot more in a month's time, but she's going the right way and has just started doing nice work. A nice filly".*

301. UNNAMED ★★★

b.f. Bahamian Bounty – Perfect Partner (Be My Chief). January 14. Sister to the modest 9f winner Bountiful Guest (by Bahamian Bounty) and half-sister to the fair 5f (at 2 yrs) and 6f winner Hot Pursuits (by Pastoral Pursuits) to the modest 2-y-o 6f winner Molly Dancer (by Emarati) and a winner in Saudi Arabia by Medicean. The dam is an unraced half-sister to 6 winners including the 6f Ayr Gold Cup and Washington Singer Stakes winner Funfair Wane and the Italian listed 7.5f winner Cabcharge Striker. The second dam, Ivory Bride (by Domynsky), won the listed 6f Rose Bowl Stakes and is a half-sister to 7 winners including the useful listed 8.5f and listed 10f winner Putuna and the useful sprinter Lochonica. *"She's a nice filly, she's big and just growing at the moment, but she'll be alright later on".*

302. UNNAMED ★★★★

ch.c. Raven's Pass – Sadinga (Sadler's Wells). March 13. Seventh foal. €60,000Y. Goffs Orby. Gill Richardson. Half-brother to the fairly useful 9f (at 2 yrs) and 10f winner and listed-placed Cool Judgement (by Peintre Celebre) and to the fair 6f winner Showboating (by Shamardal). The dam, a quite useful Irish 12f winner, is a half-sister to 7 winners including the Group

1 Moyglare Stud Stakes winner Priory Belle and the Group 1 Premio Lydia Tesio winner Eva's Request. The second dam, Ingabelle (by Taufan), won the Group 3 Phoenix Sprint Stakes and is a half-sister to 4 winners. (Mrs Theresa Burns). *"This is a lovely horse. He shows ability, but he's such a big horse I haven't done a lot with him, so I'm giving him plenty of time but I like him a lot. He'll be a proper horse come Goodwood time".*

303. UNNAMED ★★★

b.f. *Sixties Icon – Solmorin (Fraam).* February 13. Fifth foal. Half-sister to the fair 2011 2-y-o 5f winner Majestic Rose (by Imperial Dancer), to the fairly useful dual 5f winner (including at 2 yrs) Lucky Leigh, the modest 2-y-o 6f winner Saxonette (both by Piccolo) and the modest dual 1m winner (including at 2 yrs) Alfredtheordinary (by Hunting Lion). The dam is an unplaced half-sister to 2 winners. *"They all win out of the dam but this one is bigger than most of them and he'll need a trip, probably seven furlongs to start with".*

304. UNNAMED ★★★

ch.f. *Sixties Icon – Straight Sets (Pivotal).* February 17. First foal. 13,000Y. Tattersalls October Book 3. Gill Richardson. The dam, a fair 7f winner, is a half-sister to 4 winners including the very smart Group 3 10.3f Huxley Stakes and 2-y-o listed 7f winner Championship Point. The second dam, Flying Squaw (by Be My Chief), winner of the Group 2 6f Moet and Chandon Rennen at 2 yrs, is a half-sister to 7 winners including the quite useful 5f and 6f winner Cauda Equina. *"She's sweet and I've given her plenty of time. Like most of the Sixties Icon 2-y-o's she's got a bit of quality, but whereas I've been able to press on with some of them, this filly needs a bit more patience".*

305. UNNAMED ★★

ch.c. *Johannesburg – Whiletheiron'shot (Smart Strike).* March 21. Fourth foal. 20,000Y. Tattersalls October Book 2. Gill Richardson. Half-brother to the German 3-y-o winner and listed-placed Moscow Ballet (by El Prado). The dam, a US stakes-placed winner of 4 races at 3 and 4 yrs, is a half-sister to 8 winners including two US stakes winners. The second dam, No More Ironing (by Slew O'Gold), a minor 2-y-o

winner in the USA, is a half-sister to 5 winners including Zanzibar (Group 1 Italian Oaks). *"He goes alright, I quite like him but he's had a few minor setbacks which means he's a bit behind some of the others".*

306. UNNAMED ★★★

b.c. *Sir Percy – Zooming (Indian Ridge).* April 16. Seventh foal. 28,000Y. Tattersalls October Book 3. Gill Richardson. Half-brother to Speeding (by Selkirk), unplaced in one start at 2 yrs in 2011, to the Irish 2-y-o 6f winner Gripping and to the 5f (at 2 yrs) and 6f winner Tribute (both by Green Desert) – both quite useful. The dam is an unplaced half-sister to the very smart 2-y-o Group 2 5.5f Prix Robert Papin winner Zipping and to the Group 3 winners Nipping and Zelding (herself dam of the Group 2 winner Beauty Is Truth). The second dam, Zelda (by Caerleon), won once over 6.5f and is a half-sister to 10 winners including the top-class sprinter/miler Last Tycoon, the Group 3 winners Astronef and The Perfect Life and the dam of the French 1,000 Guineas winner Valentine Waltz. *"He's nice, just like the other Sir Percy 2-y-o we have he needs a bit of time, but he'll come".*

JANE CHAPPLE-HYAM

307. MISTY SECRET (IRE) ★★

b.f. *Clodovil – Villafranca (In The Wings).* March 20. Tenth foal. 11,000Y. Tattersalls December. Jane Chapple-Hyam. Half-sister to the 2-y-o listed 7.5f winner Villa Sciarra (by Elnadim), to the fair 2-y-o 1m winner Eternal Ruler (by Aussie Rules), the modest 1m winner Sweet Potato (by Monashee Mountain), the modest 12f and 2m winner Okafranca (by Okawango) and a winner in Scandinavia by Desert Style. The dam, a dual 10f winner at 3 and 4 yrs in France, is a half-sister to 4 winners abroad. The second dam, Villa Eternelle (by Slew O'Gold), won 3 races in France and is a half-sister to 9 winners including Mill Native (Arlington Million) and the Group 3 winners French Stress, Sporades and American Stress. (Mr & Mrs S Pierpoint and Mr P Salisbury). *"She arrives here tomorrow! So I don't know a lot about her, but in pre-training she's done everything asked of her. I'd hope she'd be able to start off in mid-season over six furlongs".*

308. SKATING OVER (USA) ★★★
ch.f. *Giant's Causeway – Annie Skates (Mr Greeley)*. March 24. First foal. 32,000Y. Tattersalls October Book 1. Not sold. The dam, a fairly useful 2-y-o 7f winner, was third in the Group 3 Oh So Sharp Stakes and second in two listed events including the Breeders Cup Juvenile Fillies at Monmouth Park. She is a half-sister to 5 minor winners of the unraced Vivalita (by Deputy Minister), herself a full or half-sister to 8 winners including the dam of the US dual Grade 1 winner and sire Vicar. (Mr R Morecombe and Mrs L E Ramsden). *"I absolutely love her. I trained her dam and she was second in the Juvenile Fillies' race at Monmouth Park. She's the absolute clone of her mother in terms of how she looks in her head, but she has the legs of Giant's Causeway. She's a quick learner but just needs time before I get her on the track".*

309. TOMMY'S SECRET ★★
gr.g. *Sakhee's Secret – La Gessa (Largesse)*. April 25. Second foal. £1,000Y. Ascot December. Not sold. The dam, a moderate 10f and 13f winner at 3 and 4 yrs, is a half-sister to one winner. The second dam, En Grisaille (by Mystiko), a moderate 6f (at 2 yrs) and 10f winner, is a half-sister to 5 winners including the multiple listed winner Angus Newz. *"I bought him for just £500, so he was certainly cheap – but I can't fault the horse. I part own him with a friend of mine in Argentina (called Tommy!), he's qualified for the £25,000 Ascot race and that's his goal!"* TRAINERS' BARGAIN BUY

Win of il s aucmda fdul

310. UNNAMED ★★
b.f. *Mount Nelson – Cruinn A Bhord (Inchinor)*. March 17. 5,000Y. Tattersalls December. Not sold. Half-sister to the fairly useful 1m and 10f winner of 3 races (including a listed event) Viva Vettori and to the modest 12f and hurdles winner Chess Board (both by Vettori). The dam, a fairly useful 7f winner, is a half-sister to 6 winners including the top-class filly Ouija Board. The second dam, Selection Board (by Welsh Pageant), was placed over 7f at 2 yrs and is a sister to the top class Queen Elizabeth II Stakes and Budweiser Arlington Million winner Teleprompter. *"A tall, leggy filly that wants time. She has character and I'll start her off at seven furlongs".*

PETER CHAPPLE-HYAM

311. AL MUDAFAA ★★★
b.c. *Elnadim – Popolo (Fasliyev)*. March 20. Second foal. Brother to the fairly useful 2011 2-y-o 6f winner Al Khan. The dam, a modest maiden, was placed six times over 5f and 6f and is a half-sister to 4 winners including the very smart Group 3 6f Phoenix Sprint Stakes winner Al Qasi (by Elnadim). The second dam, Delisha (by Salse), won once at 3 yrs in Germany and is a half-sister to 5 winners including the Group 1 Hong Kong Mile winner Ecclesiastical. (Ziad A Galadari). *"He's a full-brother to a 3-y-o of mine called Al Khan, he goes really nicely and he's a bit the same as him. Six furlongs in July or August should be his starting point, he has a good attitude and he does go well. Quite a big colt, but not bulky as his brother".*

312. AL MUKHDAM ★★★★
b.c. *Exceed And Excel – Sakhya (Barathea)*. February 26. Fourth foal. Half-brother to the fair 7f winner Falakee (by Sakhee). The dam, unplaced in one start, is a half-sister to 4 winners including the useful 2-y-o 6f winner Mr Sandancer and the useful 2-y-o 7f winner Fantasy Island. The second dam, Um Lardaff (by Mill Reef), a winner over 11f and 12f at 3 yrs in France, is a sister to the Derby winner and high-class sire Shirley Heights and a half-sister to the good mare Bempton – dam of the Group 3 winners Mr Pintips and Banket and of the Group 2 winner Gull Nook (herself dam of the smart filly Spring). (Ziad A Galadari). *"He had a touch of sore shins and some ringworm so we left him alone for a bit. He's a big, strong colt that looked like he'd be one for the end of the season, but he's changed a lot now and he'd probably be my bulkiest colt. I'm getting back onto him now and he should be ready by July time. One of my picks of the two-year-olds, he's quite laid-back which isn't what you'd expect from the sire, so I don't know if that's good or bad!"*

313. ARBEEL ★★★★
b.f. *Royal Applause – Waafiah (Anabaa)*. March 19. Half-sister to the useful 2011 2-y-o 6f winner and listed-placed Telwaar (by Haafhd) and to the fairly useful triple 1m winner Jaser and the modest 6f and subsequent UAE 7f winner Ragad (both by Alhaarth). The dam,

second over 7f at 3 yrs on her only start, is a half-sister to several winners including the very useful 1m and hurdles winner Atlantic Rhapsody. The second dam, First Waltz (by Green Dancer), winner of the Group 1 6f Prix Morny and second in the Cheveley Park Stakes, is a half-sister to the dam of the Prix Lupin second Angel Falls. (Ziad A Galadari). *"She's very nice and very similar to the half-sisters that I've had, Jaser and Telwaar, in that she has a bit of an attitude, but she's getting better all the time the more work she does. A big, leggy filly, seven furlongs in August time should suit her. She'd be one of my picks from the whole stable and she could have a bit of class".*

314. BOITE ★★

b.c. *Authorized – Albiatra (Dixieland Band).* Half-brother to the Italian listed 11f winner Ansiei, to the French middle distance winner of 4 races and listed-placed Santa Biatra (both by Highest Honor) and the minor French 5.5f (at 2 yrs) to 11f and hurdles winner Nike Walker (by Bering). The dam was placed twice in France and is out of Jon's Singer (by Caro), a winner of 4 races in the USA. (Eledy). *"He's going to want time because he's one for seven furlongs in August, but he does everything right and he moves really well. It's nice for me to have an Authorized colt of course!"*

315. CAPE OF HOPE (IRE) ★★★

b.c. *Cape Cross – Bright Hope (Danehill).* March 27. Sixth foal. 75,000Y. Tattersalls December. Eledy. Half-brother to the 2-y-o 1m winner Wintercast, to the 10f to 14f winner of 15 races (by Spinning World), the 7f winner Brief Candle (by Diktat) – all quite useful – and the modest 12f winner Bright Abbey (by Halling). The dam, a fair 10f winner, is a half-sister to 3 other minor winners including the dam of the Group 3 winners Above Average and Sent From Heaven. The second dam, Crystal Cross (by Roberto), a quite useful winner of 4 races at up to 14f, is a half-sister to 7 winners including the Group 1 Haydock Park Sprint Cup winner Iktamal, the French Group 2 winner First Magnitude, the Grade 2 Arkansas Derby winner Rockamundo and the dam of the Group 2 Gimcrack Stakes winner Conquest. (Eledy Srl). *"He was quite expensive but he does everything right and he'll be a seven furlong type this year. He's done a*

bit upsides, like all of them, and I like what I see so far".

316. DODINA (IRE) ★★★★ ♠

b.f. *Acclamation – Etica (Barathea).* March 30. Fifth foal. £20,000Y. Doncaster Premier. Blandford Bloodstock. Sister to two 2-y-o winners in Italy and half-sister to a minor winner abroad by Shinko Forest. The dam won two races at 2 yrs in Italy and is a half-sister to 6 winners. The second dam, Minodora (by Marju), was listed-placed in Italy and a half-sister to 4 winners. (Eledy Srl). *"A very nice filly and one of our sharper ones but she'll be better at six furlongs than five. I see her starting off in May, she goes really well and has a great attitude. A filly that does everything just spot on".* TRAINERS' BARGAIN BUY

317. GRANULE ★★ ♠

b.f. *Hernando – Grain Only (Machiavellian).* February 26. Second foal. Sister to the quite useful 2011 2-y-o 1m winner (from one start) Gabrial's Star and to the quite useful 10f and 12f winner Caravan Rolls On. The dam is an unraced half-sister to one winner. The second dam, All Grain (by Polish Precedent), a useful 12.6f winner, was third in the Group 3 Lancashire Oaks and is a sister to the Irish Oaks and Yorkshire Oaks winner Pure Grain and a half-sister to 6 winners. (Miss K Rausing). *"She's going to take a bit of time but she's coming together well and has pulled her act together a lot. She's one for next year really, but she'll be out towards the end of this season".*

318. HASBAH (IRE) ★★★★

b.f. *Cape Cross – Gimasha (by Cadeaux Genereux).* January 24. Third foal. Half-sister to the fairly useful 2011 2-y-o 6f winner Samminder (by Red Ransom). The dam, a useful 5f and 6f winner of 5 races, is a half-sister to 5 winners including the very useful triple 1m and hurdles winner Atlantic Rhapsody and the useful French winner of 3 races and Group 3 Prix Thomas Bryon third Gaitero. The second dam, First Waltz (by Green Dancer), winner of the Group 1 6f Prix Morny and second in the Cheveley Park Stakes, is a half-sister to the dam of the Prix Lupin second Angel Falls. (Ziad A Galadari). *"A real nice filly, she's one for six furlongs in May and does everything well. I can* see her being better over seven furlongs in time, but for a Cape Cross she's very sharp and she goes real well".

319. HOT DIGGITY (FR) ★★★

b.c. Librettist – Como (Cozzene). April 1. €35,000Y. Arqana Deauville October. J Brummitt. Half-brother to the Irish 2-y-o listed 5f winner Pencil Hill (by Acclamation) and to the modest 6f winner Arzaag (by Bertolini). The dam, a fairly useful 3-y-o dual 6f winner, is a half-sister to several winners and to the dam of the Group 1 Nunthorpe Stakes winner Sole Power. The second dam, Merida (by Warning), a 1m winner in France and the USA, is a full or half-sister to 8 winners including the dual US Grade 2 1m winner Tychonic. (The Horse Players 2). "He's likely to run at the end of April over five furlongs before we step him up to six. He does everything nice, he's a strong-bodied colt and he should be good enough to win races".

320. MARIELLA ★★★

ch.f. Piccolo – Viva Maria (Hernando). March 28. Half-sister to the fair 10f and 12f winner Maria de Scozia (by Selkirk). The dam is an unraced half-sister to 9 winners including the Group 1 July Cup winner Polish Patriot and the Italian listed winner Grand Cayman. The second dam, Maria Waleska (by Filiberto), won 6 races including the Group 1 Gran Premio d'Italia and the Group 1 Oaks d'Italia. (Miss K Rausing). "I trained her half-sister Maria de Scozia who took quite a while before she won her maiden. This is a different model altogether, she's a lot smaller and she'll be out over six furlongs in May or June. She tries her hardest and she's quite nice, so she'll be alright".

321. MAXENTIUS ★★★

b.c. Holy Roman Emperor – Guantanamera (Sadler's Wells). February 7. Third foal. £8,000Y. Doncaster Premier. Not sold. Brother to the fair 7f (at 2 yrs) and 1m placed maiden Lord Jim. The dam is an unraced half-sister to 5 winners. The second dam, Bluffing (by Darshaan), a 2-y-o 1m winner at the Curragh, was listed-placed over 9f (at 2 yrs) and 12f and is a half-sister to 6 winners. (Tony Elliott). "For a Holy Roman Emperor he's quite big, but his colts in general

seem to be bigger than the fillies. He's doing everything right and I'm just moving along with him now. I'll try and get him out over six furlongs in May or June but he'll be better over seven I think. I like him a lot – he does come along real good and there are no problems with him at all. He's turning into a nice horse".

Hacked up wn m3r of folk

322. ST ELMO'S FIRE ★★★★

b.c. Bahamian Bounty – Firebelly (Nicolotte). March 17. Fourth foal. Half-brother to the useful 6f and dual 7f winner Firebeam (by Cadeaux Genereux) and to the fair dual 1m winner (including at 2 yrs) Bombina (by Lomitas). The dam, a fairly useful 2-y-o dual 6f and Italian listed 1m winner, is a half-sister to 3 winners including the South African listed winner L'Passionata. The second dam, Desert Delight (by Green Desert), is an unraced half-sister to 9 winners including the Group 3 May Hill Stakes winner Intimate Guest and the dams of the Grade 1 winners Luas Line and Prince Arch. (Saints and Sinners Partnership). "He was sold for 32,000gns at Tattersalls but failed the wind test and ended up here, he goes well and he doesn't seem to have a problem with his wind at all. He's got stronger over the winter, six furlongs in May time should suit him for starters and whether he's one for Royal Ascot or not I don't know yet, but he'd be one of my hopes for there".

323. UNNAMED ★★★

b.f. Holy Roman Emperor – Casablanca Jewel (Kalanisi). March 3. Second foal. £10,000Y. Doncaster Premier. Global Equine Group. Half-sister to the 2011 Italian 2-y-o winner Super Alessandro (by Oratorio). The dam, a 2-y-o winner, is a half-sister to 5 winners including the Group 3 July Stakes winner Fallow and the listed Hong Kong winner Lucky Six. The second dam, Cartier Bijoux (by Ahonoora), a fairly useful 2-y-o 5f winner, is a half-sister to 7 winners including the Group 3 Jersey Stakes winner Miss Silca Key (herself the dam of the Group 3 winner Central City). (Joey Barton & Partners). "She hasn't been here long but she does everything just right. Quite a narrow filly, she just needs to fill out a bit more but I'm really pleased with her. She looks sharp and should be racing in May or June time".

324. UNNAMED ★★★★

br.f. Kheleyf – Elegant Times (Dansili). February 3. Third foal. Half-sister to the fairly useful 2011 2-y-o 5f winner Tioman Legend (by Kyllachy). The dam, a modest 6f winner, is a half-sister to 6 winners including the Group 2 7f Hungerford Stakes and Group 3 6f Bentinck Stakes winner Welsh Emperor, the very useful listed 5f winner Majestic Times and the useful 6f and 7f winner and Group 3 6f third Brave Prospector. The second dam, Simply Times (by Dodge), ran twice unplaced at 2 yrs and is a half-sister to 5 winners including the US 2-y-o stakes winner Bucky's Baby. (Allan Belshaw). *"She was late coming in and so was a bit behind the others, but she's caught up now and she does go well. A filly that's bred to be sharp, she looks that way too and although I'd like to think she'd be out in May but I think it'll be more like June. She's done really well and got really strong. I like her a lot".*

325. UNNAMED ★★★ Agent All: 500

b.f. Dutch Art – Loquacity (Diktat). April 10. Third foal. £22,000Y. Doncaster Premier. Blandford Bloodstock. The dam is an unraced half-sister to 2 minor winners. The second dam, Cybinka (by Selkirk), a fairly useful listed 7f winner, is a half-sister to 2 minor winners. (Mrs F H Hay). *"She goes really well, just has a bit of a dirty nose at the moment, but was doing everything spot on beforehand and I can see her being out in May time over six furlongs. She's grown a lot and become quite strong".*

ab hacked up cl 5f mdn Poole

326. UNNAMED ★★★

b.f. Holy Roman Emperor – Parvenue (Ezzoud). April 14. Seventh foal. £5,000Y. Doncaster Premier. Not sold. Half-sister to the useful Irish 2-y-o 1m winner Vivaldi, the minor South African 4-y-o winner Monaco Dream (both by Montjeu), the fairly useful 2-y-o 1m winner Luxurious (by Galileo), the quite useful 2-y-o 6f winner Three Decades (by Invincible Spirit) and a winner at 2 yrs in Italy by Fasliyev. The dam, a quite useful 2-y-o 6f winner, is a half-sister to 4 winners including the useful 8.3f winner Pedrillo. The second dam, Patria (by Mr Prospector), a fair 2-y-o 7.6f winner, is a sister to Lycius (winner of the Group 1 6f Middle Park Stakes and placed in numerous Group 1

events) and to the Group 3 6f Prix de Cabourg winner Tereshkova and a half-sister to the US dual Grade 2 winner Akabir. (Mr M Tabor). *"She wouldn't be the biggest filly in the world but she's getting there now. She's coming along really well, has a good attitude and I can see her being out in May".*

327. UNNAMED ★★★

b.f. Sir Percy – Seal Indigo (Glenstal). April 14. Fourteenth living foal. £11,000Y. Tattersalls October Book 2. J Brummitt. Half-brother to the very useful listed 6f Rockingham Stakes winner Prism (by Spectrum), to the fairly useful 10f and smart hurdles winner Deep Purple (by Halling), the quite useful 11f, 12f and hurdles winner Conquisto (by Hernando), the fair 3-y-o 6f winner Cielito Lindo (by Pursuit Of Love), the fair 2-y-o 6f winner Bhutan Prince (by Robellino), the 12f winner Neptune (by Dolphin Street), a winner in Germany by Inchinor and a hurdles winner by Dubai Destination. The dam, a fairly useful winner of 5 races over middle distances, is a half-sister to 3 winners including the listed Oaks Trial fourth Gorgeous Dancer (herself dam of the dual Group 1 Premio Roma winner Imperial Dancer). The second dam, Simply Gorgeous, (by Hello Gorgeous), is an unraced half-sister to 4 winners including the Irish Oaks winner Give Thanks. *"She's very nice and probably a seven furlong type in July/August time. She's grown a hell of a lot since she's been here and I'm very pleased with her. She should be quite useful".*

328. UNNAMED ★★★

b.c. Lawman – Stella Del Mattino (Golden Gear). March 26. Third foal. £18,000Y. Doncaster Premier. Blandford Bloodstock. Brother to the moderate 2-y-o 5f seller winner Seven Year Itch. The dam, a 2-y-o winner in Italy, is a half-sister to 4 winners including the Group 3 second Hasanat. The second dam, Eye Witness (by Don't Forget Me), is a placed sister to the listed winner Well Beyond and a half-sister to 3 winners. (Mrs F H Hay). *"He's quite a nice horse and although he's taken some time he's coming now, but he'll be a better horse over seven furlongs. He could be real nice and he's quite a big, strong, bay colt that does everything spot on".*

329. UNNAMED ★★★★

b.c. Invincible Spirit – Tiger's Gene (Perugino). March 19. Third foal. 40,000Y. Tattersalls October Book 1. Global Equine Group. The dam is an unraced half-sister to 5 winners including the triple Group 1 winner and sire Tiger Hill. The second dam, The Filly (by Appiani II), won 4 races in Germany and is a half-sister to 3 winners. (Joey Barton & Partners). *"He's very sharp and will be out in May time. I think he'll win over five furlongs, but he'll be better over six. I really like him".*

ROGER CHARLTON

330. ABATED ★★★

b.f. Dansili – Tantina (Distant View). March 11. Sixth foal. Sister to the high-class Group 1 9f Dubai Duty Free and triple Group 3 1m winner Cityscape (by Selkirk), to the very smart listed 6f winner of 5 races and triple Group 1 placed Bated Breath and half-sister and the useful triple 1m winner and listed-placed Scuffle (by Daylami). The dam, a smart winner of 4 races including two listed events over 7f, was Group 3 placed and is a half-sister to 2 winners. The second dam, Didina (by Nashwan), a winner over 6f at 2 yrs here, subsequently won the Grade 2 8.5f Dahlia Handicap in the USA and is a sister to one winner and a half-sister to 4 winners including the French listed 10f winner Espionage. (Khalid Abdulla). *"She hasn't been here very long and she's a nice, neat and slightly smaller filly than either Bated Breath or Cityscape were at this stage. She has a lovely pedigree, I don't know much about her yet but she seems a nice filly".*

331. ALERTED (USA) ★★★

b.f. First Defence – Alvernia (Alydar). February 24. Half-sister to the useful 9f and 10f winner and subsequent US Grade 2 placed Exterior (by Distant View), to the useful 10.5f listed winner of 5 races Acrobatic (by Storm Boot), the fairly useful listed-placed 1m winner Verbose (by Storm Bird) and the French 10f and 12f winner Safari Journey (by Johannesburg). The dam, a winner over 8.5f and 9f in the USA, is a half-sister to 5 winners and to the dam of the French 1,000 Guineas and US Grade 1 winner Matiara. The second dam, Miss Summer (by Luthier), won the listed 1m Prix de Saint-

Cyr and is a half-sister to the Group 2 Prix Hocquart winner Mot d'Or, the Group 1 Gran Premio de Milano winner Lydian, the Group 2 Ribblesdale Stakes winner Ballinderry (herself the dam of Sanglamore) and the French 2,000 Guineas second Sharpman. (Khalid Abdulla). *"We wait with interest to see how the sire does, but this filly looks attractive, she seems to be fairly together and I would guess she'll be one for seven furlongs from mid-summer onwards. She doesn't look that backward and she's a nice filly".*

332. CANDOLUMINESCENCE ★★★

b.br.f Dansili – Flash Of Gold (Darshaan). March 11. Fifth foal. Half-sister to the fair 2011 2-y-o 1m winner Moidore (by Galileo), to the fairly useful triple 7f winner (including at 2 yrs) Firestreak (by Green Desert), the quite useful 10f winner Audacious (by Motivator) and the fair 12f winner Going For Gold (by Barathea). The dam, a fair 12f placed maiden, is a half-sister to 5 winners including the smart Group 2 12f Ribblesdale Stakes and Group 2 13.3f Geoffrey Freer Stakes winner Phantom Gold. The second dam, Trying For Gold (by Northern Baby), was a useful 12f and 12.5f winner at 3 yrs. (The Queen). *"She's a rangy, attractive filly that moves well. She had a setback when she came into training so she hasn't done very much yet but she's a rangy, nice-natured filly. It's a staying pedigree, so you'd expect her to want a mile this year".*

333. DEFIANT SPIRIT ★★★

ch.c. Compton Place – Muffled (Mizaaya). April 26. Seventh foal. 40,000Y. Tattersalls October Book 2. Roger Charlton. Half-brother to the quite useful 2011 2-y-o dual 5f winner Rafeeej (by Iffraaj), to the fairly useful 2-y-o 5f winner and listed-placed Excello (by Exceed And Excel), the French 2-y-o 7f winner Hushed (by Cape Cross), the modest dual 10f winner Benbrook (by Royal Applause) and the modest 2-y-o 6f winner Chandrayaan (by Bertolini). The dam, a modest 3-y-o 7f winner, is a half-sister to 3 other minor winners. The second dam, Sound It (by Believe It), is a placed half-sister to 7 winners including the Cheveley Park Stakes winner Pas de Reponse and the French 2,000 Guineas winner Green Tune. (Mr D Carter & Mr

P Inglett). *"He's grown a lot since I bought him. He looked like her might be sharp and early but he isn't. One for the middle of the year, he's got a nice pedigree and he's a nice horse that moves well. He's bred to be a sprinter".*

334. DON MARCO ★★★
b.c. Choisir – Dolma (Marchand de Sable). February 11. Half-brother to the fairly useful dual 1m winner Thistle Bird (by Selkirk). The dam won 6 races over 6f and 7f (including at 2 yrs), notably three listed events at 3 yrs. The second dam, Young Manila (by Manila), was listed placed over 10f and is a half-sister to Fabulous Hostess, a winner of three Group 3 events from 11f to 13f. (Lady Rothschild). *"A small, neat, strong horse that looks like a sprinter. He ought to be out in June or July over five or six furlongs".*

335. FIRST SECRETARY ★★★★
b.f. Nayef – Spinning Queen (Spinning World). February 7. Third foal. Half-sister to Gallipot (by Galileo), unplaced in one start at 2 yrs in 2011. The dam, winner of the Group 1 1m Sun Chariot Stakes and the Group 3 7f Brownstown Stakes and third in the Group 2 Cherry Hinton Stakes, is a half-sister to 4 winners including the useful 10f and 12f winner and 2-y-o 7f listed-placed Shannon Springs. The second dam, Our Queen Of Kings (by Arazi), is an unraced half-sister to 7 winners including the Grade 1 9f Hollywood Derby winner Labeeb, the Grade 2 Arlington Handicap winner Fanmore and the Group 2 9f Budweiser International Stakes winner Alrassaam. (Lady Rothschild). *"A very attractive filly, she moves well and surprises me because she looks more precocious than I expected. A nice filly, she's attractive, I like her and she's done very well since she came here".*

w;ll
improve

336. MAGOG ★★ Lingfield easy rider
No chance from poor draw 7f f a Jh
br.c. Dansili – Margarula (Doyoun). March 21. Half-brother to Rosslyn Castle, fourth over 1m on his only start at 2 yrs in 2011, to the quite useful 11f winner Marywell (both by Selkirk) and the fair 12f winner Set The Scene (by Sadler's Wells). The dam, a 1m (at 2 yrs) and Group 1 12f Irish Oaks winner, is a half-sister to 4 winners including the Irish 2-y-o listed 9f winner Wild Heaven. The second dam, Mild

golds

Intrigue (by Sir Ivor), a fairly useful 10f winner, is a half-sister to the useful listed 10f winner Grimesgill, the US stakes winner Determined Bidder and the dam of the South African Grade 1 winner Milleverof. (Lady Rothschild). *"A nice, big, rangy, attractive horse. He's bigger and has more scope than his half-brother Rosslyn Castle. One for the back-end of the season, he's a nice horse".* on debut

won cl 4 mh Salisbury 1m

337. PYTHAGOREAN ★★★ 15 runs
b.c. Oasis Dream – Hypoteneuse (Sadler's Wells). March 12. First foal. The dam, a fair 12f winner, is a sister to the smart 2-y-o 6f winner and Group 1 12f Oaks second Flight Of Fancy and the dual listed 7f winner and dual Group 3 placed Golden Stream and a half-sister to several winners. The second dam, Phantom Gold (by Machiavellian), a very useful winner from 1m (at 2 yrs) to 12f including the Group 2 Ribblesdale Stakes and the Group 3 St Simon Stakes, is a sister to the listed 10f winner Fictitious and a half-sister to the 1m winner and dual listed-placed Tempting Prospect. (Khalid Abdulla). *"He's an attractive horse, strong and deep. It looks like a good mating to Oasis Dream and he's probably a 2-y-o for July over seven furlongs. A nice horse that looks OK".*

338. ROCKPOOL ★★★
b.f. Rock Of Gibraltar – Waterfall One (Nashwan). February 6. Fifth foal. Half-sister to Waterclock (by Notnowcato), a 1m winner on his only start at 2 yrs in 2011 and to the fair 2-y-o 7f winner Water Biscuit (by Bertolini). The dam is an unplaced half-sister to 4 winners. The second dam, Spout (by Salse), was a very smart winner of the Group 3 12f John Porter Stakes and the Group 3 Lancashire Oaks and is a half-sister to numerous winners including the French listed winner Mon Domino. (Lady Rothschild). *"She looks a bit like her half-brother Waterclock, there's a lot of stamina on her dam's side and she looks like a filly for seven furlongs plus as a 2-y-o, from the middle of the summer onwards. A good-moving filly".*

339. SPIRAEA ★★
ch.f. Bahamian Bounty – Salvia (Pivotal). March 16. Second foal. Half-sister to the moderate 1m 2-y-o winner Salvationist (by Invincible Spirit).

The dam, unplaced in one start, is a half-sister to 3 winners including the very useful 6f (at 2 yrs) and 9f winner Zabaglione. The second dam, Satin Bell (by Midyan), a useful 7f winner, is a half-sister to several winners including the useful listed 6f winner Star Tulip. (Mr Nicholas Jones). *"She looks quite early, but she hasn't been in long and she's been coughing so I don't know anything about her. Probably a six furlong 2-y-o in mid-summer".*

340. TARTARY (IRE) ★★★

b.c. Oasis Dream – Tamso (Seeking The Gold). April 10. Sixth foal. The dam is an unraced half-sister to the French 1,000 Guineas and US Grade 1 winner Matiara, to the French listed winner and US Grade 2 placed Precious Ring, the 2-y-o Group 2 6f Richmond Stakes winner Pyrus and the Group 2 Prix du Muguet winner Marathon. The second dam, Most Precious (by Nureyev), won the listed Prix de Lieurey, was placed in the Group 1 Prix de la Salamandre and Group 1 Grand Criterium and is a half-sister to 8 winners including the listed Atalanta Stakes winner Private Line. (Lady Rothschild). *"A nice horse, the mare has been disappointing so far but this is the best prospect she's had because he's an attractive horse with a good temperament. Six furlongs in June or July should be his starting point".*

341. TELAMON (IRE) ★★★

b.c. Rock Of Gibraltar – Laureldean Express (Inchinor). March 30. Second foal. 45,000Y. Tattersalls October Book 2. Amanda Skiffington. The dam, a fairly useful 7f and 9f placed maiden here, was listed-placed over 1m in France and is a half-sister to 3 winners including the Group 2 third Ellmau. The second dam, Triple Sharp (by Selkirk), a quite useful 10f and hurdles winner, is a half-sister to 5 winners including the US stakes winner and Grade 2 placed Pina Colada and to the unraced dam of the top-class miler Canford Cliffs. (M Pescod). *"He's been coughing more than most, but he's a strong, deep horse that was bought to make a 2-y-o. Hopefully he'll start off at six furlongs in mid-summer and he looks a sprinter type".*

342. WORLDWIDE ★★

b.c. Oasis Dream – Global Trend (Bluebird). April 20. Fourth foal. Half-brother to the quite useful 7f and 9f winner of 6 races from 3 to 6 yrs Bawaardi (by Acclamation) and to the fair 5f winner of 5 races at 3 and 4 yrs Estonia (by Exceed And Excel). The dam is an unraced half-sister to 3 winners including the French and US stakes winners Night Chapter. The second dam, Context (by Zafonic), is a placed half-sister to 5 winners including the US Grade 2 winner Bon Point. (Khalid Abdulla). *"A neat, strong horse, I haven't got going with him yet but he looks the type to be fairly early. I know nothing about him yet".*

343. UNNAMED ★★

b.f. Empire Maker – Didina (Nashwan). February 4. Seventh foal. Half-sister to the smart dual listed 7f winner Tantina (by Distant View), to the quite useful 10f winner Trekking (by Gone West) and the quite useful 2-y-o 1m winner Auction Room (by Auction House). The dam, a winner over 6f at 2 yrs here, subsequently won the Grade 2 8.5f Dahlia Handicap in the USA and is a sister to one winner and a half-sister to 4 winners including the French listed 10f winner Espionage. The second dam, Didicoy (by Danzig), a useful winner of 3 races over 6f, is closely related to the Group 3 1m Prix Quincey winner Masterclass and a half-sister to the champion 2-y-o Xaar. (Khalid Abdulla). *"She has a nice pedigree, she looks attractive and she's a big, rangy filly that will need time. One for the end of the year".*

344. UNNAMED ★★ Dundonell

b.c. First Defence – Family (Danzig). January 30. Seventh foal. The dam is an unraced sister to the top-class sprinter and sire Danehill, the US Grade 2 9f winner Eagle Eyed, the very smart Group 3 Criterion Stakes winner Shibboleth, the US Grade 3 winner Harpia and the listed 7f winner Euphonic. The second dam, Razyana (by His Majesty), was placed over 7f at 2 yrs and 10f at 3 yrs. (Khalid Abdulla). *"The mare's been very disappointing so far considering she's a sister to Danehill, but this is a nice colt. He's attractive, big, rangy and a good mover. Because he's one of our biggest 2-y-o's I'd say we won't see him until later in the year".*

Won Acomb 7f York Gp 3

345. UNNAMED ★★★

b.c. Dark Angel – Knapton Hill (Zamindar). March 27. Second foal. £26,000Y. Doncaster

Premier. Amanda Skiffington. Half-brother to the fairly useful 2011 Irish 2-y-o 6f winner Pitlochry (by Chineur). The dam, a quite useful 7f winner at 3 yrs, is a half-sister to one winner in Germany. The second dam, Torgau (by Zieten), a Group 2 6f Cherry Hinton Stakes winner, was second in the Group 1 Cheveley Park Stakes and the Group 1 7f Moyglare Stud Stakes and is a half-sister to 9 winners. (Mr P Inglett & Mr D Carter). *"He was bought to be early but he's not as mature as we'd hoped. He's been coughing so he'll need a bit of time, he'll be a sprinter and we'll run him when we can, but that won't be before June or July".*

346. UNNAMED ★★★

b.c. Mizzen Mast – Skiable (Niniski). April 4. Half-brother to the 2-y-o Group 3 6f Coventry Stakes and disqualified Group 1 6f Middle Park Stakes winner Three Valleys (by Diesis), to the quite useful triple 10f winner Ski Jump (by El Prado), the quite useful 2-y-o 6f winner Morzine (by Miswaki), the fair 1m winner Lahberhorn (by Affirmed), the modest 12f winner Back Pass and to the French 12f winner Grail (both by Quest For Fame). The dam won four times at up to 9f in France and the USA and is out of a half-sister to the smart sprinter So Factual. (Khalid Abdulla). *"A very strong colt but not at all similar to Three Valleys, his half-brother. He ought to be a 2-y-o though and he shows promise, so in the middle of the year he should be out over six furlongs. Mizzen Mast can often inject speed".*

347. UNNAMED ★★★

b.br.f. Exchange Rate – Trekking (Gone West). March 15. Fifth foal. Half-sister to the quite useful 10f winner Deck Walk (by Mizzen Mast). The dam, a quite useful 10f winner, is a half-sister to 4 winners including the smart dual listed 7f winner Tantina (herself the dam of the Group winners Bated Breath and Cityscape). The second dam, Didina (by Nashwan), a winner over 6f at 2 yrs here, subsequently won the Grade 2 8.5f Dahlia Handicap in the USA and is a sister to one winner and a half-sister to 4 winners including the French listed 10f winner Espionage. (Khalid Abdulla). *"The sire had a very good year in America last year and he's an influence for speed. This filly has just had*

an operation so I don't know anything about her, but she's a neat, 2-y-o type".

348. UNNAMED ★★★ So Beloved

b.c. Dansili – Valencia (Kenmare). April 30. Brother to the useful 2-y-o 6f winner and Group 3 7f placed Cantabria (by Dansili) and half-brother to the useful 2-y-o 5f and listed 6f winner Deportivo (by Night Shift), the useful 2-y-o listed 5f winner Irish Vale (by Wolfhound), the fairly useful 2-y-o 7f and 7.6f winner La Coruna (by Deploy), the quite useful dual 5f (including at 2 yrs) Affluent (by Oasis Dream) and the fair 7f winner Subadar (by Zamindar). The dam, placed over 1m at 2 yrs on her only start, is a half-sister to numerous winners including the dual US Grade 1 winner Wandesta, the Group 2 12f winner De Quest and the smart 10f to 15f winner Turners Hill. The second dam, De Stael (by Nijinsky), a fairly useful dual 7f winner at 2 yrs, is a sister to the high-class middle-distance colts Peacetime and Quiet Fling. (Khalid Abdulla). *"He's a very big, tall horse and completely different to both Deportivo and Irish Vale. They were strong, sprinter-types whereas he's a lovely, big, rangy type for somewhere like Newmarket or Newbury in October".*

Won cl 4 mdn 1m Salisbury

DENIS COAKLEY   15 runners

349. INDIGO MOON ★★

b.f. Sleeping Indian – Ewenny (Warrshan). March 11. Ninth foal. 9,000Y. Tattersalls October Book 3. Denis Coakley. Half-sister to the fairly useful 6f and 7f winner Johnny The Fish (by Most Welcome), to the quite useful triple 6f winner Elusive Prince (by Storming Home), the fair 6f winner of 4 races (including at 2 yrs) Bazguy (by Josr Algarhoud), the moderate 7.5f seller winner Hymns And Arias (by Mtoto) and a hurdles winner by Reset. The dam, a fair 2-y-o 5f winner, is a half-sister to 5 winners. The second dam, Laleston (by Junius), won two races at 2 and 3 yrs. (Count Calypso Racing). *"A medium-sized, well-made filly and one for the middle of the season onwards, over six furlongs plus. She's a bit backward at present so she won't be as early as we'd have liked".*

350. KASTINI ★★

b.c. Halling – Toucantini (Inchinor). April 6. Second foal. 10,000Y. Tattersalls October Book

3. Denis Coakley. Half-brother to the modest 2011 2-y-o 5f seller winner First Bid (by Kyllachy). The dam, a modest 7f placed 2-y-o, is a half-sister to 3 minor winners. The second dam, French Quartet (by Lycius), is an unplaced half-sister to 8 winners including the high-class broodmare Lucayan Princess (dam of the Group 1 winners Warrsan and Luso). (West Ilsley Racing). *"One for August onwards, he's a nice colt for when the seven furlongs and mile races start. A good-looking, laid-back horse that seems to be doing everything right at the moment".*

351. PERCY'S GIFT (IRE) ★★★

b.c. Hurricane Run – Bysshe (Linamix). April 1. Fifth foal. 22,000Y. Tattersalls December. Denis Coakley. Half-brother to 4 minor winners in Italy by Mark Of Esteem, Monashee Mountain (both at 2 yrs), Hawk Wing and Spinning World. The dam, a minor French winner of 2 races at 3 yrs, is a half-sister to 4 other minor winners here and abroad. The second dam, Percy's Girl (by Blakeney), a useful 10f and 10.3f winner, is a sister to the Group 3 September Stakes winner Percy's Lass (herself dam of the Derby winner Sir Percy) and a half-sister to 5 winners including the very smart Grade 1 E P Taylor Stakes and Group 2 Sun Chariot Stakes winner Braiswick. (Count Calypso Racing). *"A nice, compact horse and hopefully he'll be out in May, starting off at six furlongs. He's bred to go further than that but he seems sharp enough".* TRAINERS' BARGAIN BUY

352. STUPENDA ★★★

b.f. Misu Bond – Opera Babe (Kahyasi). January 24. 6,000Y. Tattersalls October Book 3. Denis Coakley. Half-sister to the moderate 2-y-o 6f seller winner All Angel (by Lend A Hand). The dam, a fair maiden, was placed fourth once over 6f at 2 yrs and is a half-sister to 4 winners here and abroad. The second dam, Fairybird (by Pampabird), a modest 2-y-o 5f winner, is a half-sister to 5 winners including the US dual Grade 2 winner Gothland. (Finders Keepers Partnership). *"A lovely, compact, well-made filly that won't take too long. She probably won't run in April but she'll be away by May time. An early foal, she looks that way too and seems pretty speedy, so five and six furlongs should be fine for her this year".*

PAUL COLE

353. ANOTHER NAME

b.c. Red Clubs – Pure Gold (Dilum). April 1. Seventh foal. 40,000Y. Tattersalls October Book 2. Paul Cole. Half-brother to the useful 6f (at 2 yrs), 1m listed and UAE 9f listed winner and Group 2 placed Royal Alchemist (by Kingsinger), the fair 1m and 10f winner Swift Alchemist (by Fleetwood) and two hurdles winners by Slickly and Woodborough. The dam, a quite useful 7f winner, is a half-sister to 4 winners including the dam of the Group 2 Challenge Stakes winner Arabian Gleam. The second dam, Gold Runner (by Runnett), is a placed half-sister to 6 winners including the English and Irish 2,000 Guineas winner Don't Forget Me.

354. BLUEGRASS BLUES (IRE)

br.c. Dark Angel – Dear Catch (Bluebird). April 19. Seventh foal. £38,000Y. Doncaster Premier. Oliver Cole. Half-brother to the fairly useful 5f and 6f winner and Group 3 second Golden Destiny (by Captain Rio), to the modest 5f to 7f winner Choc 'a' Moca and the modest dual 1m winner Quite A Catch (both by Camacho). The dam, a 9f winner in Ireland, is a sister to the Group 3 5f Ballyogan Stakes winner and Group 1 Haydock Park Sprint Cup third Catch The Blues and a half-sister to 5 winners. The second dam, Dear Lorraine (by Nonoalco), won over 10f in France and is a half-sister to 4 winners.

355. COMPOSED

b.c. Sakhee's Secret – Cheeky Girl (College Chapel). February 16. Second living foal. 30,000Y. Tattersalls October Book 2. Oliver Cole. Half-brother to the fair 2011 2-y-o 7f winner Bountiful Girl (by Bahamian Bounty). The dam, a modest 12f winner of 4 races, is a half-sister to 9 winners including the dual listed winner Paradise Isle. The second dam, Merry Rous (by Rousillon), won once at 2 yrs and is a half-sister to 5 winners including the dual Group 3 winning sprinter Tina's Pet.

356. CUT NO ICE (IRE)

gr.f. Verglas – Limpopo (Green Desert). April 29. Seventeenth foal. €210,000Y. Goffs Orby. Oliver Cole. Half-sister to 12 winners including the fair 2012 2-y-o 5f winner Lesotho (by Excellent Art), the Group 1 6f Haydock Park Sprint Cup and Group 3 5f Palace House Stakes winner

Pipalong (by Pips Pride), the useful 2-y-o 5f winner and Group 2 5f Flying Childers Stakes second China Eyes (by Fasliyev), the fairly useful 7f winner and Group 3 6f placed 2-y-o Silver Shoon (by Fasliyev), the fairly useful 2-y-o 6f listed winner Out Of Africa, the minor US winner of 2 races Henry Kitchener (both by Common Grounds), the fairly useful French 6f winner of 4 races at 2 and 3 yrs Raja (by Pivotal) and the quite useful 2-y-o winners Walvis Bay (by Footstepsinthesand) and Corton (by Definite Article). The dam, a poor 5f placed 2-y-o, is a half-sister to 7 winners here and abroad. The second dam, Grey Goddess (by Godswalk), was a smart winner of 5 races in Ireland from 7f to 8.5f including the Group 3 Gladness Stakes and the Group 3 Matron Stakes. (Denford Stud Ltd).

357. DANCE WITH DRAGONS (IRE)

b.c. Namid – Duck Over (Warning). April 9. Eighth foal. €20,000Y. Goffs Orby. Oliver Cole. Brother to the useful Hong Kong 6f and 7f winner Pocket Money and half-brother to the fairly useful 5f winner of 4 races (including at 2 yrs) Colorus (by Night Shift) and the fair 2-y-o 7f winner Confucius Fortune (by Verglas). The dam, a fair 1m placed maiden, is a half-sister to 5 winners including the useful 10f listed winner Maid Of Camelot. The second dam, Waterfowl Creek (by Be My Guest), a quite useful 3-y-o dual 1m winner, is a sister to the Group 1 Coronation Stakes third Guest Artiste, closely related to the Group 2 Child Stakes winner Inchmurrin (herself dam of the very smart colt Inchinor) and a half-sister to 6 winners including the 2-y-o Group 2 6f Mill Reef Stakes winner Welney.

358. FALUKA (IRE)

ch.f. Iffraaj – Tortue (Turtle Island). April 14. Fourth foal. 55,000Y. Tattersalls October Book 2. Oliver Cole. Half-sister to the useful 2-y-o listed 5f winner and Group 1 Nunthorpe Stakes third Piccadilly Filly (by Exceed And Excel). The dam, a quite useful Irish 1m and 9f winner, is a half-sister to 5 winners including Tiraaz (Group 1 Prix Royal-Oak). The second dam, Tarikhana (by Mouktar), a listed winner over 13f, is a half-sister to 8 winners including the Group 3 winners Tassmoun, Tashkourgan and Tashtiya. (Denford Stud Ltd).

359. LOOK AT LULU

ch.f. Kyllachy – Sari (Faustus). March 13. Half-sister to the fairly useful 2011 2-y-o 1m winner Commissar, to the quite useful dual 7f winner of 4 races Pravda Street (both by Soviet Star), the 2-y-o listed 7f winner Lily Again (by American Post), the fairly useful 2-y-o 6f and 1m winner Genari (by Generous) and the fairly useful dual 5f (at 2 yrs) and dual 6f winner Saristar (by Starborough). The dam, a quite useful 7f winner of 2 races (including at 2 yrs), is a half-sister to one winner. The second dam, Fire Lily (by Unfuwain), is a placed half-sister to one winner.

360. SECRET SUCCESS

b.c. Exceed And Excel – Magic Music (Magic Ring). April 20. Fifth foal. 67,000Y. Tattersalls October Book 2. Charlie Gordon-Watson. Half-brother to the fair 2011 6f and 7f placed 2-y-o Magic Destiny (by Dubai Destination) and to the useful 5f listed (at 2 yrs), 6f and 1m winner Magic Cat (by One Cool Cat). The dam, a fair 6f winner of 3 races, is a half-sister to 5 winners here and abroad. The second dam, Chiming Melody (by Cure The Blues), a moderate 1m winner, is a half-sister to 12 winners. (A D Spence).

361. SOVEREIGN POWER

b.c. Royal Applause – Tafiya (Bahri). April 30. Second foal. 31,000Y. Tattersalls October Book 2. Paul Cole. Half-brother to the fairly useful 2011 2-y-o 6f and 7f winner Overpowered (by Choisir). The dam, a fair 7f (at 2 yrs) to 11f placed maiden, is a half-sister to the useful Group 3 Dahlia Stakes and listed Rosemary Stakes winner Tarfah. The second dam, Fickle (by Danehill), a fairly useful 1m and listed 10f winner, is a half-sister to 7 winners including the useful 11.5f listed winner Birdie and the French middle-distance winner of four listed events Faru.

362. ST PAUL DE VENCE

b.c. Oratorio – Ring The Relatives (Bering). February 17. Sixth foal. €80,000Y. Goffs Orby. Paul Cole. Brother to the quite useful Irish 1m winner Betrothed and half-brother to the quite useful 2-y-o 6f winner Newsround (by Cadeaux Genereux) and the fair Irish 2-y-o 7f winner Footprint (by Footstepsinthesand). The dam, a fair 7f and 10f placed 3-y-o (from 2 starts), is a half-sister to the Irish listed winner and French Group 2 placed Just Special and the listed winner Blue Gold. The second dam, Relatively Special (by Alzao), won the Group 3 7f Rockfel Stakes at 2 yrs and was placed in the Irish 1,000 Guineas, the Nassau Stakes and the Sun Chariot Stakes. She is a half-sister to 8 winners including the Dante Stakes winner Alnasr Alwasheek and the Juddmonte International winner One So Wonderful.

363. UNNAMED
b.c. *Strategic Prince – Starfish (Galileo).* April 30. Third foal. 150,000Y. Tattersalls October Book 2. Charlie Gordon-Watson. Brother to the 2011 2-y-o Group 1 6f Phoenix Stakes winner and Group 1 7f Moyglare Stud Stakes third La Collina and half-brother to the quite useful 2-y-o 7f winner Next Edition (by Antonius Pius). The dam is an unraced half-sister to 2 winners including the Group 3 placed Icon Dream. The second dam, Silver Skates (by Slip Anchor), is a placed half-sister to 8 winners including the Group 2 Derrinstown Derby Trial winner Fracas.

JO CROWLEY
364. CAPTAIN STARLIGHT (IRE) ★★
b.c. *Captain Marvelous – Jewell In The Sky (Sinndar).* March 28. Third foal. €10,000Y. Goffs Orby. Kilstone Ltd. Half-brother to the moderate 2011 5f placed 2-y-o Rhianna Brianna (by Bertolini) and to the modest 7f, 9f (both at 2 yrs) and dual 1m winner Sky Diamond (by Diamond Green). The dam is an unraced half-sister to several winners including the very useful 2-y-o 7f winner and Group 3 Horris Hill Stakes third Aahaykid. Closely related to the 2004 2-y-o Tiny Petal (by Grand Lodge) and half-sister to the Irish dual 10f winner Out Of Thanks (by Sadler's Wells), the minor Irish 3-y-o 10f winner Trusted Instinct (by Polish Precedent) and the Irish 2-y-o 6f winner Whistle Down (by Danehill). The second dam, Trust In Luck (by Nashwan), an Irish 7f winner, is a half-sister to numerous winners including the US Grade 1 winner Dress To Thrill. (Kilstone Ltd). *"He's done really well since the sales, he's grown and looks handsome now. He's coming along really nicely, but he won't be early and I should think he'll want seven furlongs to start with because he's not about speed".*

365. MADAME SCARLETT (IRE) ★★
br.f. *Red Clubs – Shining Desert (Green Desert).* January 27. Ninth foal. €7,000Y. Goffs Orby. Kilstone Ltd. Half-sister to the useful 9f, 10f and 11f winner of 6 races and multiple Group 3 placed Mid Mon Lady (Danetime), to the Italian winner of 19 races from 2 to 9 yrs Bryan Gold (by Bahhare), the modest 6f winner of 4 races Maison Dieu (by King Charlemagne) and the Italian winner (including at 2 yrs) Compton Flowers (by Compton Place). The dam, a quite useful 2-y-o 5f winner, is a half-sister to 2 winners including the listed winner Wing Collar. The second dam, Riyoom (by Vaguely Noble), won over 1m in Ireland at 2 yrs and is a half-sister to 5 winners including the US triple Grade 3 winner Lt Lao. (Mrs E.A.M Nelson). *"She's tiny and I need to crack on with her because by May the other two-year-olds will be towering above her. She's like a little tank, she knows her job and she's all about speed".*

366. MISS LEGAL EAGLE (IRE) ★★★
b.f. *Authorized – Pride Of My Heart (Lion Cavern).* April 20. Seventh foal. €23,000Y. Goffs Orby. Liz Nelson. Half-sister to the quite useful 2011 2-y-o 7f winner Tidy Affair (by Amadeus Wolf), to the Group 2 5f Temple Stakes winner of 8 races Night Prospector (by Night Shift), the fairly useful 2-y-o 6f and 7f winner Memen (by Verglas), the fair 2-y-o 6f winner Soliniki (by Danzero), the minor Italian 2-y-o winner Pazzo Pazzini (by Tiger Hill) and a winner in Russia by Spectrum. The dam, a fair 3-y-o 7f winner, is a half-sister to 7 winners including the Group 3 Phoenix Sprint Stakes winner Northern Goddess (herself dam of the US Grade 2 winner Northern Quest). The second dam, Hearten (by Hittite Glory), is an unraced half-sister to 7 winners. (Mrs E.A.M Nelson). *"I think we did really well with our purchases at the yearling sales and got value for money. I'm pleased with all of them but especially this filly – she's my favourite of all them but we'll have to wait until September time with her. A big, beautiful, graceful filly that moves really well".* TRAINERS' BARGAIN BUY

367. MUSIC MAN (IRE) ★★
b.g. *Oratorio – Chanter (Lomitas).* February 22. Second foal. €26,000Y. Goffs Orby. Kilstone Ltd. The dam is an unraced half-sister to 8 winners

including King George VI and Queen Elizabeth Diamond Stakes winner Belmez and the dam of the Grade 1 Arlington Million winner Debussy. The second dam, Grace Note (by Top Ville), a fairly useful 10f winner and second in the Group 3 12f Lingfield Oaks Trial, is a half-sister to 7 winners including the dams of the Prix de Diane winner Lypharita and the Group 3 winners Arousal and River Test. (Kilbride Ltd). *"He'll be racing in May but he's not a speedy type and he'll probably want seven furlongs. A lovely, chunky two-year-old, he's 'all there' in that he's not got much growing to do and he has plenty of bone. A workmanlike sort that'll do a job for us even if it's not at Royal Ascot!"*

368. SWEET MARWELL (IRE) ★★

b.f. Excellent Art – Bee Eater (Green Desert). April 5. Second foal. €23,000Y. Goffs Orby. Liz Nelson. The dam, a 6f winner of 4 races and listed-placed, is a half-sister to several winners. The second dam, Littlefeather (by Indian Ridge), a very useful 5f (at 2 yrs) and 6f winner, was third in the Group 1 7f Moyglare Stakes and is a half-sister to several winners including the high class Cheveley Park Stakes, Irish 1,000 Guineas, Coronation Stakes and Sussex Stakes winner Marling and the good 5f to 1m colt Caerwent, a winner of 4 races and placed in the Prix de l'Abbaye, Irish 2,000 Guineas, St James's Palace Stakes and Vernons Sprint Cup. (Mrs E.A.M Nelson). *"A lovely filly, but she's ever so big and will need time. I can't see her making a 2-y-o until the end of the season but having said that she's not as weak as you might think, given her size. A nice filly for seven furlongs plus".*

LUCA CUMANI

369. AJMAN BRIDGE ★★★

ch.c. Dubawi – Rice Mother (Indian Ridge). April 7. Third foal. 125,000Y. Tattersalls October Book 1. Charlie Gordon-Watson. The dam, a modest 10f winner, is a half-sister to 6 winners including the Group 3 6f Prix de Meautry winner Do The Honours and the 2-y-o listed 7f Chesham Stakes winner Seba. The second dam, Persian Secret (by Persian Heights), a fairly useful 2-y-o 6f winner here, subsequently won a listed race in France and is a half-sister to 8 winners including the dual Group 2 winning

sprinter Cassandra Go (dam of the triple Group 1 winner Halfway To Heaven) and the Group 3 6f Coventry Stakes winner and sire Verglas. (Sheikh Mohammed Obaid Al Maktoum). *"He had a setback but he'll be fine and beforehand he was going OK, cantering well and doing everything OK. I was happy with him but now we won't see him out before September over seven furlongs or a mile. He's a very good-looking horse, nice, compact and correct. This bunch of two-year-olds appear to be the best I've ever had. Physically they're more developed than they have been in the past".*

370. AJMANY (IRE) ★★★

b.c. Kheleyf – Passarelle (In The Wings). February 9. Second foal. €65,000Y. Goffs Orby. John Warren. The dam, a fair 12f winner, is a half-sister to 2 winners including the very useful listed 8.5f winner of 3 races Fort Dignity. The second dam, Kitza (by Danehill), won 3 races including the listed Irish 1,000 Guineas Trial and was second in the Irish Oaks and the Irish 1,000 Guineas. She is a half-sister to 5 winners including the fairly useful Irish sprinter Hi Bettina (dam of the Group 2 winner Fred Bongusto) and the Group 3 Norfolk Stakes winner Marouble. (Sheikh Mohammed Obaid Al Maktoum). *"He's a good-looking horse, he's quite big and his breeding is a bit of a mixture because he's by a sprinter and out of an In The Wings mare. So we'll have to see which way it pans out, whether he'll be quick or whether he'll be a stayer. He's well put-together and strong, so he should be out around July time".*

371. BARTACK (IRE) ★★★

b.c. Acclamation – Bentley's Bush (Barathea). March 16. Third foal. 78,000Y. Tattersalls October Book 2. Charlie Gordon-Watson. The dam, a quite useful 2-y-o 6f winner, was listed-placed and is a half-sister to 3 minor winners. The second dam, Veiled Threat (by Be My Guest), a French 10f winner and third in the Group 3 Prix de Sandringham, is a half-sister to 5 winners including the Group 2 6f Moet & Chandon Rennen third Prime Glade. (B Corman). *"A nice horse that should make a July type 2-y-o. He's already shown me a bit of ability, he'll start off at six furlongs and get a mile".*

372. BLACK ROLLER ★★★

b.c. Kavafi – Vallota (Polish Precedent). March 31. Half-brother to the Group 3 5f and listed 5f winner Ialysios (by So Factual). The dam is an unraced half-sister to several winners including the useful 6f (at 2 yrs) and 7f listed winner Epagris. The second dam, Trikymia (by Final Straw), was placed third over 5f at 2 yrs on her only outing and is a half-sister to the Irish Derby winner Tyrnavos, the champion 2-y-o Tromos, the Coronation Stakes winner Tolmi and the Middle Park Stakes winner Tachypous. (Mrs L Marinopoulos). "The sire, a son of Zafonic, won the Group 3 1m Prix Quincey and he now stands in Greece. This colt is a very, very good-looking horse, big, strong, well put-together with a marvellous temperament. I haven't tested him for ability yet but I should think he'll be out around July time".

373. CANON LAW (IRE) ★★★★

b.c. Holy Roman Emperor – Delisha (Salse). April 6. Tenth foal. 98,000Y. Tattersalls October Book 2. Rachel Boffey. Half-brother to the very smart Group 3 6f Phoenix Sprint Stakes winner Al Qasi (by Elnadim), to the quite useful 10f winner of 5 races Ivan Vasilevich (by Ivan Denisovich), the modest 12f, 2m and hurdles winner Frameit (by Antonius Pius), the moderate 1m and 9f winner Margot Mine (by Choisir) and two multiple winners in Italy by Be My Guest and Victory Note. The dam won once at 3 yrs in Germany and is a half-sister to 6 winners including the Group 1 Hong Kong Mile winner Ecclesiastical. The second dam, Rachael Tennessee (by Matsadoon), was placed once in the USA and is a half-sister to 7 winners including the top-class miler Lear Fan. (Mr S A Stuckey). "I like him a lot, he's very well put-together and he'll be working in May with the idea of racing him in June. He's very likeable and looks like being speedy as well".

374. DESERTED ★★★

b.f. Oasis Dream – Tentpole (Rainbow Quest). February 2. Half-sister to the useful 1m (at 2 yrs) and 12f winner Too Much Trouble (both by Barathea) and the fair 11f winner Loden (both by Barathea) and the fair 1m to 14f and hurdles winner Bivouac (by Jade Robbery). The dam, an Irish 14f winner, is a half-sister to 3 winners. The second dam, Polent (by Polish Precedent), a minor

French 13f and 15.5f winner, is a half-sister to 6 winners including the Oaks winner Snow Bride (herself dam of the Derby, King George and 'Arc' winner Lammtarra). (Fittocks Stud Ltd). "A lovely filly, very good-looking, strong and well put-together. She's got scope, so maybe she takes after Rainbow Quest rather than Oasis Dream. I expect her to get a mile if not further later on, but having said that she's well-forward and she could be a Newmarket July meeting type 2-y-o".

375. DUKE OF PERTH ★★★

b.c. Danehill Dancer – Frangy (Sadler's Wells). May 4. Ninth foal. Half-brother to the very useful 12f and listed 14f winner Savarain (by Rainbow Quest), to the useful 9f and 10f winner of 5 races and Group 3 placed Forte Dei Marmi (by Selkirk), the quite useful 1m to 12f winner Franciscan (by Medicean) and the quite useful 6f and 1m and subsequent US stakes winner Wallis (by King's Best). The dam, a fair dual 12f winner, is a full or half-sister to 8 winners including the German 1m to 9.5f winner of 7 races and listed-placed Flying Heights. The second dam, Fern (by Shirley Heights), a useful 12f winner and third in the listed 10f Lupe Stakes, is a half-sister to 6 winners including the Group 1 Fillies Mile winner and Oaks second Shamshir. (Fittocks Stud). "A very nice horse and Frangy is doing rather well as a broodmare. He's a bit smaller than some members of the family, but he's well put-together and very athletic. The family take a bit of time to learn their job – they're always better at 3 or 4, but there's a chance that this colt may be a bit different and win as a 2-y-o in August or September".

376. ELHAAME (IRE) ★★★★

b.c. Acclamation – Gold Hush (Seeking The Gold). March 17. Second foal. 160,000Y. Tattersalls October Book 2. Charlie Gordon-Watson. The dam, a quite useful 1m and 10f winner, is a half-sister to 3 winners including the useful 2-y-o 1m winner and Group 3 1m Autumn Stakes second Menokee. The second dam, Meniatarra (by Zilzal), unplaced in one run at 2 yrs, is a sister to the smart 1m to 10f winner Kammtarra and the useful 10f winner Haltarra and a half-sister to 4 winners including the top-class colt Lammtarra, winner of the Derby, the King George and the Prix de l'Arc de Triomphe. (Sheikh Mohammed Obaid Al Maktoum). *"A very nice horse, he was expensive but he's very well put-together. A lovely type that's going well, he should be out by June/July time starting off at six furlongs".*

377. GREATWOOD ★★

b.c. Manduro – Gaze (Galileo). March 1. Second foal. 85,000Y. Tattersalls October Book 1. John Warren. The dam, placed over 10f and 12f here, won twice in Germany and is a half-sister to 7 winners including the Irish Derby, Coronation Cup and Tattersalls Gold Cup winner Fame And Glory and the listed-placed Guaranda (dam of the Group 3 winner Gravitation). The second dam, Gryada (by Shirley Heights), a fairly useful 2-y-o 7f and 8.3f winner, was third in the Group 3 1m Premio Dormello and is a full or half-sister to 4 winners. (Highclere Thoroughbred Racing – Archer). *"A back-end 2-y-o and a middle-distance type next year. He's a good sort, biggish and very nice to look out. He moves well but he'll be trained very much with next year in mind".*

378. JAZZ MASTER ★★

b.c. Singspiel – Turn Of A Century (Halling). April 30. Sixth foal. 28,000Y. Tattersalls October Book 1. Not sold. Half-brother to the quite useful Irish 1m winner Time 'N' Talent (by Act One), to the fair 2-y-o 1m winner Sin City (by Sinndar) and a winner in Greece by Green Desert. The dam, a quite useful 12f winner, is a half-sister to 5 winners including the top-class King George VI and Queen Elizabeth Stakes winner Opera House, the Ascot Gold Cup and Irish St Leger winner Kayf Tara and the Prix de l'Opera winner Zee Zee Top and to the dam of the Group 1 Moyglare Stud Stakes winner Necklace. The second dam, Colorspin (by High Top), won the Irish Oaks and is a half-sister to 8 winners including the Irish Champion Stakes winner Cezanne and the Group 2 Prix de l'Opera winner and high-class broodmare Bella Colora. (Castle Down Racing). *"I'm pleased with him because when he arrived he wasn't much to look at. He looked a bit feminine and wasn't well developed, but since then he's done well physically. It isn't a speedy family, so we'll give him some time and then see if he's able to do something as a 2-y-o".*

379. KIKONGA ★★★

b.f. Danehill Dancer – Kibara (Sadler's Wells). April 16. Fourth foal. Half-sister to the unplaced 2011 2-y-o Kiwayu (by Medicean). The dam, a fair 11f winner, is a sister to 4 winners including the St Leger and Great Voltigeur Stakes winner Milan and half-sister to the Irish 2-y-o 7f winner and Group 2 Great Voltigeur Stakes third Go For Gold. The second dam, Kithanga (by Darshaan), was a smart winner of 3 races including the Group 3 12f St Simon Stakes and the listed 12f Galtres Stakes. (Fittocks Stud Ltd). *"A very nice filly and, for the family, much more forward than you'd expect. She uses herself well, good-looking and is doing really well. I would say she'd be starting off at seven furlongs in July or August. Eventually she'll get at least a mile and a quarter".*

380. KRAKEN (IRE) ★★

br.c. Notnowcato – Madame Claude (Paris House). February 15. Eighth foal. 42,000Y. Tattersalls October Book 2. Charlie Gordon-Watson. Half-brother to the Irish 2-y-o 7f and subsequent US listed stakes winner Insan Mala, to a minor winner abroad over 11.5f (both by Bahhare), the quite useful 2-y-o 5f winner Takoda (by Namid) and the French 6f and 7f winner Ballinapark (by Captain Rio). The dam, a fair 2-y-o 6f winner, is a half-sister to 4 winners including the Irish and German listed winning sprinter Nashcash. The second dam, Six Penny Express (by Bay Express), is a placed half-sister to 4 winners including Charlie Bubbles (Group 2 Hardwicke Stakes). (L Marinopoulos & Partners). *"He's a very good-looking horse but he doesn't give me great vibes at the moment, maybe it's just that he's very laid-back. Physically he's done very well but we'll have to wait and see what he can produce when push comes to shove".*

381. LIONHEART ★★★

ch.c. Zamindar – Victoire Celebre (Peintre Celebre). April 5. First foal. The dam ran twice unplaced and is a half-sister to the Group 2 Prix du Muguet winner Vetheuil, the Group 3 Prix de l'Opera winner Verveine (herself dam of the Grade 1 winners Vallee Enchantee and Volga) and the dams of the Group 1 Coronation Stakes winner Maid's Causeway and the Group 1 Grand Prix de Paris winner Vespone.

The second dam, Venise (by Nureyev), is an unraced three-parts sister to the Mill Reef Stakes and Richmond Stakes winner Vacarme and a half-sister to the Prix Jacques le Marois winner Vin de France. (Fittocks Stud & Andrew Bengough). *"A colt from a good family, he's not going to be a speedy horse but he goes well and is very good-looking. Going the right way, he's strong and I think that seven furlongs in August will be his cup of tea".*

382. MAKAFEH ★★★★★

b.c. Elusive Quality – Demisemiquaver (Singspiel). January 29. First foal. 190,000Y. Tattersalls October Book 1. John Warren. The dam, a dual winner in the USA and stakes-placed, is a half-sister to 5 winners including the US Grade 3 Cardinal Handicap winner Miss Caerleona (herself dam of the Graded stakes winners Karen's Caper and Miss Coronado) and the dam of the Group 3 Musidora Stakes winner Joviality. The second dam, Miss d'Ouilly (by Bikala), won a listed event over 9f in France and is a half-sister to 6 winners including the Prix Jacques le Marois winner Miss Satamixa and the Group 3 placed Mrs Annie (the dam of four stakes winners). (Sheikh Mohammed Obaid Al Maktoum). *"A very nice horse, he's medium-sized, goes well and he should be out by July time. He seems to have speed and I'm very pleased with him. He's very forward, he's got a good brain – everything's good about him".*

383. MALLORY HEIGHTS (IRE) ★★

b.c. Dalakhani – My Dark Rosaleen (Sadler's Wells). February 27. First foal. The dam is a placed sister to one winner and a half-sister to the 2-y-o Group 2 7f Debutante Stakes winner Silk And Scarlet and the Group 3 6f Prix de Seine-et-Oise winner Danger Over. The second dam, Danilova (by Lyphard), is an unraced half-sister to the high-class middle-distance colt Sanglamore – winner of the French Derby and the 9.3f Prix d'Ispahan – and the very useful listed 10f winner Opera Score. (Merry Fox Stud). *"He'll hopefully have a run or two at the back-end but you can see by his breeding that he's a 3-y-o type. We'll try and get him out in the autumn and if we're lucky he might win, but he's bred to be a mile and a half horse next year".*

384. MONAWER ★★★

b.c. Teofilo – Israar (Machiavellian). March 10. Third foal. 115,000Y. Tattersalls October Book 2. John Warren. Half-brother to the fair 2-y-o 7f winner Rutland Boy (by Bertolini) and to the moderate 3-y-o 5f winner Exceed Power (by Exceed And Excel). The dam is an unraced half-sister to 3 minor winners. The second dam, El Opera (by Sadler's Wells), a useful dual 7f winner, is a half-sister to 8 winners including the very useful Group 1 6f Phoenix Stakes winner Pharaoh's Delight. (Sheikh Mohammed Obaid Al Maktoum). *"Quite tall and leggy, he's a good-sort but I think he's grown a lot and he's a bit weak at this stage. One for September time I should think, he's likeable but not the type you push on with now".*

385. MOUNT MACEDON ★★★

b.c. Hernando – White Palace (Shirley Heights). April 18. Eleventh living foal. 38,000Y. Tattersalls October Book 2. Rachel Boffey. Brother to the useful 7f (at 2 yrs) and listed 10f winner Portal and half-brother to the useful 1m and listed 10f winner Ice Palace (by Polar Falcon), the useful 7f winner of 4 races (including at 2 yrs) Palatial (by Green Desert and herself dam of the dual Group 2 winner Spacious), the quite useful 14f winner Palazzo Bianco (by Shirocco), the quite useful 10f winner Holyrood (by Falbrav) and the quite useful 11f winner Pediment (by Desert Prince). The dam, a quite useful 3-y-o 8.2f winner, is a half-sister to one winner. The second dam, Blonde Prospect (by Mr Prospector), is an unplaced half-sister to 6 winners including the dam of the US Grade 1 winner Link River. (Mr S A Stuckey). *"A lovely horse that goes well and he has natural ability, but his pedigree tells you he'll be a much better horse next year and beyond. In fact we've already dubbed him the Melbourne Cup winner of 2016! He's not the sort of horse you'd want to push now, but having said all that I wouldn't be surprised if he wins as a 2-y-o at the back-end".*

386. MARGYS (IRE) ★★★★

b.f. Lawman – Spesialta (Indian Ridge). March 3. Second foal. €125,000Y. Goffs Orby. John Warren. The dam, a quite useful Irish 7f winner, is a half-sister to 2 winners. The second dam, Just Special (by Cadeaux Genereux), winner of the listed 7f Knockaire Stakes in Ireland and second in the Group 2 Prix d'Astarte, is a half-sister to the listed winner Blue Gold. (Sheikh Mohammed Obaid Al Maktoum). *"A good, strong filly, she's very likeable and I'd say she'll be one for seven furlongs around July/August time. She goes well and I like her".*

387. PARADISE WATCH ★★★

b.c. *Royal Applause – Ocean View (Gone West).* April 18. Tenth foal. 70,000Y. Tattersalls October Book 2. Charlie Gordon-Watson. Half-brother to the US Grade 3 winner Officer Rocket (by Officer), to the fair 2-y-o 8.3f winner and US stakes-placed Desert View (by Sadler's Wells), the fair 6f winner of 3 races Main Beach (by Starcraft) and the modest 14f winner Montage (by Montjeu). The dam won 2 races in the USA, was second in the Grade 1 Oak Leaf Stakes and third in the Grade 1 Hollywood Oaks. She is a half-sister to 10 winners including the Grade 2 winner Westerly Breeze and the US stakes winner and Grade 2 placed Jacksonport. The second dam, On The Brink (by Cox's Ridge), won twice in the USA at 3 yrs and is a half-sister to 2 winners. (L Marinopoulos & Partners). *"He's a strange one in that he's extremely good-looking, quite big and quite strong but not the Royal Applause type you'd expect – they tend to be small, muscular and sharp types. So he won't be a speedy Royal Applause but he moves well, he'll be racing by July and as I say he's particularly good-looking".*

388. PLEASURE BENT ★★★

b.c. *Dansili – Nitya (Indian Ridge).* February 21. First foal. 150,000Y. Tattersalls October Book 1. Charlie Gordon-Watson. The dam is an unraced sister to the Grade 1 Breeders Cup Mile winner Domedriver and a half-sister to 5 winners including the French Group 3 winner Tau Ceti and the dam of the Group 2 winner Freedonia. The second dam, Napoli (by Baillamont), a winner of 3 listed races in France and Group 3 placed, is a sister to the French Group 3 winner D'Arros and a half-sister to 2 winners. (C Bennett). *"A very good-looking horse, he's one for August or September, he goes well, has a good temperament and is very likeable".*

389. NELSON'S HILL ★★★★

b.c. *Mount Nelson – Regal Step (Royal Applause).* February 8. First foal. 55,000Y.

Tattersalls October Book 2. John Warren. The dam, a quite useful 2-y-o 5f winner, is a half-sister to 6 winners. The second dam, Two Step (by Mujtahid), a modest 5f and 7f winner at 4 and 5 yrs, is a half-sister to 3 winners. (L Marinopoulos & Partners). *"I don't know if I've got all this wrong or not because this is another one that I like! He's a very determined horse that does everything right in that he loves to lead and yet he also loves to come from behind. I've done a bit of work with him but he's big and still a little bit weak, so I won't push on with him mid-summer and we should see him out in July. The dam was speedy but she was a sort of 'jump and go' type and we don't do that here!"*

390. ROMANOFF (IRE) ★★★★

b.c. *Holy Roman Emperor – Alexander Anapolis (Spectrum).* March 6. Fifth foal. 50,000Y. Tattersalls October Book 2. Charlie Gordon-Watson. Closely related to the quite useful dual 5f (at 2 yrs) and 7f winner Cut The Cackle and to the fairly useful dual 6f winner Film Maker (both by Danetime) and half-brother to the quite useful 2011 dual 6f winner Jessie's Spirit (by Clodovil) and the fair 6f winner Vanilla Loan (by Invincible Spirit). The dam, a quite useful 12f winner, is a full or half-sister to 3 winners. The second dam, Pirouette (by Sadler's Wells), winner of the listed 7f Athasi Stakes and the listed 7f Boland Stakes in Ireland and Group 3 placed, is a half-sister to 8 winners including the Irish listed 6f Greenlands Stakes winner and very useful sire Ballad Rock. (Mrs A Silver & Partners). *"A likable horse, he's strong-bodied and he moves well. A six furlong type in June or July to start with, he does everything right at the moment so I'm very pleased with him".*

391. ROYAL BALLET ★★★

ch.c. *Pivotal – Dance A Dream (Sadler's Wells).* April 2. Tenth foal. 85,000Y. Tattersalls October Book 1. John Warren. Half-brother to the useful German listed 2m winner and smart hurdler Elusive Dream (by Rainbow Quest), to the modest 10f winner Dance A Daydream (by Daylami), a hurdles winner by Exit To Nowhere and the placed dam of the dual Group 2 winner Pipedreamer. The dam, a smart winner of the Cheshire Oaks and second in the Epsom Oaks, is a sister to the 2,000 Guineas winner Entrepreneur and to the very useful middle-distance listed winner Sadler's Image and a half-sister to numerous winners including the Coronation Stakes winner Exclusive (herself dam of the Group 1 Matron Stakes winner Echelon). The second dam, Exclusive Order (by Exclusive Native), won 4 races in France including the Group 2 6.5f Prix Maurice de Gheest and the Group 3 7f Prix de la Porte Maillot. (Highclere Thoroughbred Racing – Lord Mayor). *"A very nice horse. Pivotal's can lose their shape physically as 2-y-o's and go into bits and pieces before they come back together again, but this colt has kept a marvellous shape and is really good-looking. He moves well, but as he's out of a Sadler's Wells mare from a family that isn't particularly speedy his future will be over at least ten furlongs. But the way he's shaping up I would say that he should win as a 2-y-o".*

392. SHARAREH ★★

b.f. Sir Percy – You Too (Monsun). February 23. Third foal. 40,000Y. Tattersalls October Book 1. Charlie Gordon-Watson. Half-sister to the minor French 2-y-o winner and 1m placed 3-y-o Your So High (by High Chaparral). The dam, a fair 14f winner, is a half-sister to one winner. The second dam, the quite useful 1m winner You Are The One (by Unfuwain), is a half-sister to 8 winners including One So Wonderful (Group 1 10.4f Juddmonte International Stakes), Alnasr Alwasheek (Group 2 10.4f Dante Stakes) and Relatively Special (Rockfel Stakes). (Sheikh Mohammed Obaid Al Maktoum). *"She'll take a bit of time because there's quite a bit of staying blood in the family, but she's likeable and she goes well enough. An autumn filly".*

393. SHARQAWIYAH ★★★★

b.f. Dubawi – Pompey Girl (Rainbow Quest). April 25. Third foal. 50,000Y. Tattersalls October Book 2. Charlie Gordon-Watson. Half-sister to the fairly useful 2011 2-y-o 7f winner and listed 1m second Ptolomaic (by Excellent Art). The dam is an unraced half-sister to 4 winners including the quite useful dual 10f and subsequent South African Group 3 winner Hawk's Eye. The second dam, Inchiri (by Sadler's Wells), a very useful 12f listed winner, is a half-sister to 3 winners. (Sheikh Mohammed Obaid Al Maktoum). *"She's lovely. She goes well and*

should be out by July time, probably over seven furlongs rather than six. I like her".

394. SICUR ★★

b.c. Dylan Thomas – Dubious (Darshaan). May 2. Sixth foal. 87,000Y. Tattersalls October Book 2. Charlie Gordon-Watson. Half-brother to the modest 2-y-o 1m winner Number One Guy (by Rock Of Gibraltar) and to the moderate 12f winner Linby (by Dr Fong). The dam ran once unplaced in the USA and is a half-sister to 7 winners including Shady Heights, winner of the Group 1 International Stakes (on disqualification) and second in both the Eclipse Stakes and the Phoenix Champion Stakes. The second dam, Vaguely (by Bold Lad, Ire), was a fairly useful 1m (at 2 yrs) and 10f winner. (Scuderia Rencarti Srl). *"He had a problem and has only just come in, so although he's a good-looking colt I don't know about his level of ability at this stage".*

395. SORYAH (IRE) ★★★

b.f. Shamardal – Dirtybirdie (Diktat). April 6. First foal. 110,000Y. Tattersalls October Book 1. Charlie Gordon-Watson. The dam, a moderate Irish 11f winner, is a half-sister to 4 winners including Predappio (Group 2 12f Hardwicke Stakes and Group 2 12f Blandford Stakes) and Khamseh (the dam of three stakes winners). The second dam, Khalafiya (by Darshaan), won the Group 3 12f Meld Stakes and is a half-sister to 4 winners. (Sheikh Mohammed Obaid Al Maktoum). *"She's nice, she goes well and shows a bit of speed, so she could start at six furlongs, but more likely seven, in mid-summer".*

396. VELOX ★★

b.c. Zamindar – Victoire Finale (Peintre Celebre). April 29. Fourth foal. Brother to the fairly useful 2011 2-y-o 1m winner Validus. The dam, a useful French 1m winner, was fourth in a listed event and is a half-sister to numerous winners including the French Group 2 winner Vertical Speed. The second dam, Victoire Bleue (by Legend Of France), won the Group 1 Prix du Cadran. (Mr S A Stuckey). *"He's a different type than his year-older half brother Validus. I'm not sure if he's heavier or stronger – maybe a bit of both! He'll be alright, I was pleasantly surprised by Validus and this is a likeable colt but one for later on".*

397. UNNAMED ★★

b.f. Giant's Causeway – Measure (Seeking The Gold). April 15. Sixth foal. Sister to the quite useful Irish 1m winner Animal Kingdom and to the fair Irish dual 12f winner Quaintly. The dam, placed over 7.5f at Saint-Cloud, is a sister to the useful 2-y-o 6f winner Inkling, closely related to the Group 1 Grand Criterium winner Jade Robbery and the US Grade 3 winners Chequer and Numerous and a half-sister to 5 winners. The second dam, Number (by Nijinsky), won the Grade 2 Firenze Handicap and the Grade 2 Hempstead Handicap and is closely related to Nureyev and a half-sister to the dam of Sadler's Wells. *"She's growing at the moment. When I first saw her I thought she'd make a 2-y-o but in the last few weeks she's gone well 'up behind' and she's lengthening now. So she's changing shape and we'll have to see what we end up with. She's nice and my guess is that we'll end up with a good-looking filly but not a precocious one".*

398. UNNAMED ★★★

br.c. Red Clubs – Rejuvenation (Singspiel). January 20. Second foal. 45,000Y. Tattersalls October Book 2. Charlie Gordon-Watson. Half-brother to the 2011 Italian placed 2-y-o Fotogenica (by Footstepsinthesand). The dam, a fair 1m placed maiden, is a half-sister to 5 winners including the Grade 1 Breeders Cup Mile and Grade 1 Santa Anita Derby winner Castledale. The second dam, Louju (by Silver Hawk), is an unraced half-sister to 10 winners and to the unraced dam of the US Grade 1 winner Keeper. (L Marinopoulos & Partners). *"A nice, good-looking horse. He shouldn't be too long in coming to hand, he seems to be going well and I'm happy with him. Probably a six furlong horse around July time".*

399. UNNAMED ★★★

b.br.f. Footstepsinthesand – Zee Zee Gee (Galileo). February 4. First foal. 65,000Y. Tattersalls October Book 1. G Howson. The dam is an unraced half-sister to 2 winners including the Group 3 10.5f Prix de Flore winner and Oaks third Izzi Top. The second dam, Zee Zee Top (by Zafonic), won the Group 1 Prix de l'Opera and was third in the Group 1 Nassau Stakes and is a half-sister to 5 winners including the Group 1 winners Kayf Tara and Opera House. (Helena

Springfield Ltd). *"A bonny little filly, she came in very late after breaking so she's behind the others and I don't know her level of ability yet. But she's strong and good-looking".*

KEITH DALGLEISH

400. CORTON LAD ★★

b.c. Refuse To Bend – Kelucia (Grand Lodge). March 11. Third foal. £25,000Y. Doncaster Premier. Not sold. Half-brother to the modest dual 6f winner Monel (by Cadeaux Genereux). The dam, a useful 2-y-o dual 1m winner and third in the Group 2 7f Rockfel Stakes, is a half-sister to 3 winners. The second dam, Karachi (by Zino), a listed-placed winner of 6 races in Spain, is a half-sister to 7 other minor winners. *"A nice horse, he's working OK and I hope to start him off when the six furlong races start".*

401. FRANCESCADARIMINI ★★★

b.f. Bertolini – Cal Norma's Lady (Lyphard's Special). March 8. Twelfth foal. Sister to the 2-y-o Group 1 6f Cheveley Park Stakes and Group 2 6f Cherry Hinton Stakes winner Donna Blini and half-sister to the quite useful 10f winner Lion Mountain (by Tiger Hill), the quite useful 2-y-o 6f winner and subsequent US Grade 3 8.5f Will Rogers Handicap winner Magical, the fair 7f winner Dundonald (both by Magic Ring), the quite useful 2-y-o 5f winner Sabre Lady (by Sabrehill), the fair all-weather 7f and 9f winner Bijou Dan (by Bijou d'Inde), the fair 8.5f and 9f winner Jordan's Elect (by Fleetwood) and the modest 2-y-o 5f winner Under Pressure (by Keen). The dam, a quite useful 2-y-o 6f and 7f winner, is out of the unraced June Darling (by Junius), herself a half-sister to 8 winners. *"She's got a great attitude and she goes well but she's slightly weak at the moment so we're thinking of the mid-summer with her. She'll have plenty of speed for five furlongs".*

402. SECRET ADVICE ★★★

ch.f. Sakhee's Secret – Flylowflylong (Danetime). April 13. Second foal. Half-sister to the quite useful 2011 2-y-o 7f winner and 1m listed placed Sound Advice (by Echo Of Light). The dam, a fair 6f (at 2 yrs), 7f and 1m winner, is a sister to the fair 5f to 1m winner of 10 races Goodbye Cash. The second dam, Jellybean (by Petardia), a modest 2-y-o 9f winner, is a half-sister to 2 winners. (GLS Partnership). *"A nice,* strong filly, she's well-made and has a good attitude. We'll be looking to run her in July over six furlongs to start with".

403. UNNAMED ★★

b.c. Strategic Prince – Silk Meadow (Barathea). February 17. First foal. 25,000Y. Tattersalls October Book 2. Jill Lamb. The dam is an unplaced sister to the Irish listed 1m winner Hymn Of Love and a half-sister to 5 winners. The second dam, Perils Of Joy (by Rainbow Quest), a 3-y-o 1m winner in Ireland, is a half-sister to 5 winners including the Italian Group 3 winner Sweetened Offer. (Mrs Janice MacPherson). "He's grown a lot and he's a big horse now so he's more than likely one for the back-end of the season and anything he does this year will be a bonus. More of a 3-y-o type, but he'll be fine". TRAINERS' BARGAIN BUY

404. UNNAMED ★★

b.c. Jeremy – Twilight Belle (Fasliyev). February 26. First foal. 12,000Y. Tattersalls October Book 3. Jill Lamb. The dam, a modest 6f placed 2-y-o, is a half-sister to the Group 2 5f Duke Of York Stakes winner Twilight Blues and to the quite useful 2-y-o winners Sharp As A Tack, Incise and Mobsir. The second dam, Pretty Sharp (Interrex), a modest 7f placed 2-y-o, is a half-sister to 6 winners including the quite useful 6f (at 2 yrs) to 10f winner Kings Assembly. (Mrs Janice MacPherson). "He's not over-big but he's strong and well put-together. We'll be looking towards running him early on over five furlongs before stepping him up in trip in the summer. He's laid-back at home so he's probably one that will switch on when he gets to the track".

TOM DASCOMBE

405. ARCHIE STEVENS ★★★

b.c. Pastoral Pursuits – Miss Wells (Sadler's Wells). February 14. First foal. £40,000Y. Doncaster Premier. Sackville/Donald. The dam is an unraced sister to the winner and Group 3 placed Temple Place and a half-sister to 3 winners. The second dam, Puzzled Look (by Gulch), a stakes winner in the USA, is a half-sister to 8 winners. (The Black House Boys). "A nice-looking horse, he'll probably start over six furlongs in May".

406. ATTENSHUN (IRE) ★★

ch.c. Salute The Sarge – Southern House (Paris House). March 15. Fourth foal. €32,000Y. Goffs Orby. Sackville/Donald. Half-brother to the Japanese Group 3 winner Cosmo Phantom (by Stephen Got Even) and to a minor winner in the USA by Smart Strike. The dam, a listed winner in Italy, was second in the Group 2 Italian 1,000 Guineas and is a half-sister to 5 winners including the Italian listed winner Rio Napo. The second dam, My Southern Love (by Southern Arrow), won 5 minor races in Italy and is a half-sister to 5 other minor winners. (The Folly Racers). "He's just been gelded. He'd gone a little bit backward so we thought we'd cut him now, give him a month's break and then see if he just comes forward again. He was showing plenty of speed early doors and he should be a five furlong type when we get him going again".

407. BACK IN THE FRAME ★★★

b.f. Dutch Art – Ile Deserte (Green Desert). February 9. Second foal. £40,000Y. Doncaster Premier. Sackville/Donald. Half-sister to the very useful 2011 2-y-o 6f winner and Group 2 6f Coventry Stakes third St Barths (by Cadeaux Genereux). The dam is an unraced half-sister to one winner. The second dam, Audacieuse (by Rainbow Quest), winner of the Group 3 Prix de Flore, is a half-sister to 5 winners including Waiter's Dream (Group 3 Acomb Stakes) and the Irish listed 14f winner Lord Jim. (M Owen & M Williams). "A perfectly nice filly, she'll be racing in late April or early May. We need to give her two or three more gallops beforehand because she's a bit chubby, but she'll be a nice, early 2-y-o".

408. BARRACUDA BOY (IRE) ★★★★ ♠

b.c. Bahamian Bounty – Madame Boulangere (Royal Applause). February 13. Fifth living foal. £68,000Y. Doncaster Premier. Sackville/Donald. Half-brother to the fairly useful 2-y-o dual 7f winner Lamh Albasser (by Mr Greeley) and to the fair Irish 12f winner Jazz Girl (by Johar). The dam, a useful dual 6f winner (including at 2 yrs), was listed-placed and is a half-sister to one winner. The second dam, Jazz (by Sharrood), a fair 7f (at 2 yrs) and 10f placed maiden, is a half-sister to 12 winners including the US Grade 2 winner Sign Of Hope and the Group 2 placed

Finian's Rainbow and Carmot. (L A Bellman). *"He's improving all the time physically and he's really growing into a nice-looking horse. He'll probably start over five furlongs in May but I don't think that's necessarily going to be his trip. He'll want further than that and he's not an out-and-out early 2-y-o, so my policy with a horse like that is to give him a run, win if he can, but improve".*

409. BONNE AMIE (FR) ★★★★
b.f. Elusive City – Sintra (Kris). March 6. Third foal. €35,000Y. Arqana Deauville August. Sackville/Donald. The dam, a minor French 1m winner, is a half-sister to 7 winners including US stakes winner Aliena and the US Grade 2 placed Brianda and Bedmar. The second dam, Gracious Line (by Fabulous Dancer), a minor French 3-y-o winner, is a half-sister to the Group 3 winners Gay Minstrel and Greenway. (L A Bellman). *"A very nice filly, she's done nothing but grow, but she's absolutely gorgeous to look at and we won't be in a rush with her. The plan is to send her to France in August (where she can race for the breeder's premiums), after having had a run under her belt here. She has to prove she's good enough first of course, but she's a nice filly".*

410. BRAVE ACCLAIM (IRE) ★★★
b.c. Acclamation – Indienne (Indian Ridge). April 30. Fourth foal. €70,000Y. Goffs Orby. Sackville/Donald. Brother to the moderate 5f winner Brown Lentic. The dam, placed once over 7f in Ireland, is a sister to the 2-y-o Group 3 7f Curragh Futurity Stakes winner St Clair Ridge (herself dam of the Grade 2 winner Cat By The Tail) and a half-sister to 8 winners. The second dam, St Clair Star (by Sallust), a winner in Canada, is a half-sister to 7 winners including the Flying Childers Stakes winner Superlative. (Mr G Lowe & Mrs A Whiteside). *"He's one for the middle of the season so he's just doing two canters a day at the moment. He hasn't been asked any questions yet, but he does look a nice type of horse".*

411. CANADIAN RED ★★
b.c. Sleeping Indian – Pontressina (St Jovite). March 4. Seventh foal. £8,000Y. Doncaster Premier. Sackville Donald. Brother to the fair 3-y-o 5f and 6f winner Hills Of Dakota and half-brother to the quite useful 6f (at 2 yrs) to 11f winner of 5 races Robustian (by Rebellino). The dam won 3 minor races at 3 yrs in Germany and is a half-sister to 6 winners including the listed-placed Etenia, the US stakes winner Spark Of Dubai and the US 2-y-o winner and Grade 1 Matron Stakes third Carrielle. The second dam, Eternelle (by Green Desert), is an unraced half-sister to 6 winners including the Group 1 Premio Roma winner Fire Of Life. (The MHS 4x10 Partnership). *"A big, backward horse and since we bought him his full-brother has won both his starts. Hopefully we'll get a couple of runs out of him later this year, but he's much more of a 3-y-o type".*

412. CAPE ROSSO (IRE) ★★★
b.c. Red Clubs – Satin Cape (Cape Cross). April 20. Fourth foal. €14,000Y. Tattersalls Ireland. Sackville/Donald. Half-brother to the fair 2011 2-y-o 5f winner Molamento and to the quite useful Irish 2-y-o 5f winner Jolly Snake (both by Elusive City). The dam, placed once over 5f at 2 yrs from 2 starts, is a half-sister to 6 winners. The second dam, Marylou Whitney (by Fappiano), was placed in the USA and is a half-sister to 3 winners. (Deva Racing Red Clubs Partnership). *"A very nice horse, he'll be racing in late April and although he was a bit weak a month ago he's not any more. Improving all the time, he looks quite useful and he could be one for the Lily Agnes at Chester".*

413. CEILING KITTY ★★★★
b.f. Red Clubs – Baldovina (Tale Of The Cat). February 4. Second foal. 16,000Y. Tattersalls October 2. Not sold. Half-sister to the fair 2011 2-y-o triple 5f winner Van Go Go (by Dutch Art). The dam is a placed half-sister to the Japanese dual Group 3 winner One Carat. The second dam, Baldwina (by Pistolet Bleu), won the Group 3 Prix Penelope and is a half-sister to 5 winners. (A W Black). *"She ran well on her debut despite missing the break and she learned a lot. She'll be out again before your book is out and she'll stay at five furlongs for the foreseeable future. A better quality animal than her half-brother Van Go Go".*

Wor turn, Wor Q. Mary
414. COOL RUNNINGS (IRE) ★★
gr.c. Dalakhani – Aguinaga (Machiavellian). March 15. Fifth foal. 40,000Y. Tattersalls

December. Sackville/Donald. Half-brother to the 2-y-o Group 2 6f Gimcrack Stakes winner of 5 races Conquest, to the minor French 4-y-o 1m winner Nymfia (both by Invincible Spirit) and the quite useful 2-y-o dual 7f winner Storm Force (by Cape Cross). The dam, an Irish 12.5f winner, is a half-sister to 7 winners including the Group 1 6f Haydock Park Sprint Cup winner Iktamal, the Grade 2 9f Arkansas Derby winner Rockamundo and the French dual Group 2 winner First Magnitude. The second dam, Crystal Cup (by Nijinsky), is an unplaced half-sister to 8 winners including the Gladness Stakes winner Rose Reef and the Lupe Stakes winner Golden Bowl. (Siwan & David Ward Jnr). *"A big, backward type of horse, he won't be in any rush. If he runs this year, great, if not it won't be the end of the world".*

415. CUBAN TASH ★★★
b.c. Exceed And Excel – Crinkle (Distant Relative). April 3. Seventh foal. €65,000Y. Goffs Orby. Sackville/Donald. Half-brother to the fair 2011 2-y-o 6f winner Sardanapalus (by Byron), to the useful 2-y-o 1m winner and listed-placed Wave Aside (by Reset), the fairly useful dual 6f winner Mr Sandicliffe (by Mujahid), the quite useful 7f and 1m winner Froissee (by Polish Precedent) and the quite useful 6f to 1m winner of 6 races Steed (by Mujahid). The dam is an unraced half-sister to 4 winners including the useful 2-y-o 6f winner and Group 2 6f Richmond Stakes third Cedarberg. The second dam, Crinolette (by Sadler's Wells), unplaced on her only start at 2 yrs, is a half-sister to the very smart Group 3 7f Tetrarch Stakes and Group 3 7f Ballycorus Stakes winner Desert Style. (The Cuban Partnership). *"He's just had a few issues so we haven't really been able to push on with him, but he's going the right way and we'll wait until he tells us he's ready. I guess he'll be pretty quick and going off his pedigree you would hope he'd have a bit of speed".*

416. DOUBLE DISCOUNT (IRE) ★★
b.c. Invincible Spirit – Bryanstown Girl (Kalanisi). January 26. Second foal. €70,000Y. Goffs Orby. Sackville/Donald. The dam is an unraced half-sister to 3 minor winners. The second dam, Stiletta (by Dancing Brave), is an unraced sister to the Epsom and Irish Derby winner Commander In Chief and a half-sister to the champion 2-y-o and miler Warning, the US Grade 1 winner Yashmak, the Irish Derby second Deploy and the Great Voltigeur Stakes winner Dushyantor. (L A Bellman). *"I haven't done a lot with him because he's a big colt and, for us, he was expensive. We'll be aiming him towards his three-year-old career and it depends how he improves from now on as to whether he has a couple of runs this season or not. He's a beautiful horse to look at. Big, imposing and powerful, mentally he's backward at the moment, but that's fine".*

417. DREAM MAKER (IRE) ★★
ch.f. Bahamian Bounty – Pointed Arch (Rock Of Gibraltar). March 4. First foal. £10,000Y. Doncaster Premier. Not sold. The dam, a modest 12f winner, is closely related to the listed 12f winner Chartres and a half-sister to 6 winners including the listed 10f and listed 14f winner Pugin and the dam of the 2-y-o Group 2 Railway Stakes winner Lilbourne Lad. The second dam, Gothic Dream (by Nashwan), won over 7f in Ireland at 2 yrs, was third in the Irish Oaks and is a half-sister to 3 winners. (Hot to Trot Racing). *"We haven't had her long, but she looks a perfectly nice, racey, early season 2-y-o filly. We'll need to learn a bit more about her before I could comment further".*

418. ELUSIVE BLEU (IRE) ★★★
b.c. Elusive City – Jamrah (Danehill). March 15. Third foal. €16,500Y. Tattersalls Ireland. Sackville/Donald. Half-brother to the fairly useful 2011 2-y-o 7f winner Raphael Santi (by Excellent Art). The unraced dam is closely related to the Group 3 Anglesey Stakes winner Walk On Bye. The second dam, Pipalong (by Pips Pride), won 10 races including the Group 1 6f Haydock Park Sprint Cup, the Group 3 Duke Of York Stakes and the Group 3 Palace House Stakes and is a half-sister to 10 winners including the fairly useful 2-y-o 6f listed winner Out Of Africa. (Manor House Stables LLP). *"He's grown and grown, and yet he's still three inches up behind. He should be a sprinter and he's bred to be one, so when he eventually stops growing I think he'll be one of those that will win a five furlong maiden".*

419. FAT GARY ★★★

ch.c. Dutch Art – Suzuki (Barathea). February 5. Second foal. €34,000Y. Goffs Orby. Sackville/Donald. The dam is an unplaced sister to the Irish 12f winner and Group 2 10f Pretty Polly Stakes and Group 2 10f Royal Whip Stakes second Molomo and to the listed-placed winner Pepperwood and a half-sister to 3 winners. The second dam, Nishan (by Nashwan), is a placed half-sister to 3 winners including the Group 3 Prix de Sandringham winner and good broodmare Orford Ness. (Fat Gary Sports). "A nice colt – and his name is very apt! He's just a big horse in terms of width, but he's done hard gallops and he's ready to run. I think he's quite a nice horse and he'll be a five/six furlong 2-y-o".

420. GOLDEN PURSUIT ★★

ch.c. Pastoral Pursuits – Rainy Day Song (Persian Bold). February 25. Eleventh foal. 6,500Y. Tattersalls October Book 3. Sackville/Donald. Half-brother to the modest 5f and 6f winner Rainy Night (by Kyllachy), to the modest 6f and 1m winner Broughtons Day (by Mujahid), the moderate 1m and 10f winner Broughton Spirit (by Bishop Of Cashel) and two minor winners abroad by Pivotal and Colonel Collins. The dam is an unplaced half-sister to 4 winners and to the unraced dam of the 1,000 Guineas second Princess Ellen. The second dam, Sawaki (by Song), a fair 7f winner, is a half-sister to 6 winners. (The MHS 2012 Olympic Partnership). "He had a niggling problem, so although he was ready to run he's had a couple of easy weeks. But as soon as he's had a couple of gallops he'll be on the racecourse. He was inexpensive, he'll initially be aimed at a maiden auction race over five furlongs and he'll probably end up getting seven".

421. LEA VALLEY BLACK ★★

b.c. Three Valleys – Sambarina (Victory Note). January 31. Third foal. €11,000Y. Tattersalls Ireland. Sackville/Donald. Half-brother to the dual Italian winner Zafeen Plus (by Zafeen). The dam, a modest 6f placed 2-y-o, is a half-sister to 3 winners including the Italian listed winner Meanya and the fairly useful winner of 8 races at around 7f Santisima Trinidad and to the unplaced dam of the Group 2 July Stakes winner Classic Blade. The second dam, Brazilia

(by Forzando), a modest 6f placed 2-y-o, is a half-sister to 4 winners including the Group 2 5f Kings Stand Stakes winner Dominica. (London Market Racing Club). "He'll be racing in April, but he's always in an awful hurry in that he wants to do everything as fast as he can, so if he can settle down it'll help him. He's not over-big but he's a well-muscled sprinter".

422. LORD ASHLEY (IRE) ★★★★

ch.c. Iffraaj – Mrs Dalloway (Key Of Luck). March 20. Second foal. €36,000Y. Tattersalls Ireland. Sackville/Donald. The dam is an unplaced half-sister to 5 winners including the useful 9f and 10f winner La De Two. The second dam, Firecrest (by Darshaan), won 5 races at around 12f including the listed Galtres Stakes and is a half-sister to 4 minor winners. (Mr D R Passant). "He's a very nice horse and although initially I thought he'd be a miler, he's showing an awful lot more speed than I expected and he'll be racing in April. He's close-coupled and short in his back and a good-looking, bright chestnut. I sold him to the owner thinking that he'd improve with time but he's ready now, so if he does improve he'll be useful".

423. MAJESTIC JESS (IRE) ★★★

b.c. Majestic Missile – Ginger Not Blonde (Atticus). April 6. Third foal. €20,000Y. Tattersalls Ireland. Sackville/Donald. The dam is an unplaced half-sister to 7 winners including the US dual Grade 2 placed Brittons Hill. The second dam, Quick To Quibble (by Fit To Fight), a minor winner at 3 yrs in the USA, is a half-sister to 6 winners. (The MHS 2012 Olympic Partnership). "He starts his career in April, he wasn't showing an awful lot until we took him for a gallop at Wolverhampton and it's improved him massively. If he proves good enough he'll be considered for Chester in May and he'll definitely get six furlongs later on".

424. NORTHERN STAR (IRE) ★★

b.f. Montjeu – Slow Sand (Dixieland Band). February 6. First foal. €50,000Y. Goffs Orby. Sackville/Donald. The dam ran twice unplaced and is a half-sister to 3 winners including the French listed winner Slow Pace. The second dam, Slow Down (by Seattle Slew), a winner in France and a listed winner in the USA, is a half-sister to 6 winners including the US dual Grade

3 winner Olmodavor. (Mr D Ward). *"A nice filly, but considering her middle distance pedigree we haven't done a lot with her yet and she's just going through the motions, cantering away. She's got a great attitude, I'm very happy with her and she's one for seven furlongs plus in the second half of the season".*

425. OUT OF THE BLOCKS ★★

b.c. *Firebreak – Suzie Fong (Dr Fong).* April 20. Third foal. 2,500Y. Tattersalls October Book 2. Sackville/Donald. The dam ran once unplaced and is a half-sister to 4 minor winners. The second dam, Limuru (by Salse), is an unraced sister to the Italian Group 1 and US Grade 1 winner Timboroa. (The MHS 2012 Olympic Partnership). *"He's had a run already but he missed the break and got bashed about a lot. When he finally got some daylight he ran on well. He definitely needs six furlongs now, but there aren't any such races for him, so he'll be out again in April over five".*

426. PIPPY ★★★ ♠

b.c. *Exceed And Excel – Gandini (Night Shift).* April 9. Sixth foal. 26,000Y. Tattersalls October Book 3. Blandford Bloodstock. £60,000 2-y-o. Goffs Kempton Breeze-up. Sackville/Donald. Half-brother to the modest 2011 2-y-o dual 5f and 2012 3-y-o 6f winner Russian Bullet (by Royal Applause), to the Italian winner of 5 races and listed-placed Powerful Speed (by Compton Place) and two minor winners in Italy and Spain by Diktat and Tagula. The dam, a minor winner at 3 yrs in Italy, is a full or half-sister to 8 winners. The second dam, Actress (by Arctic Tern), is a placed half-sister to 2 winners. *"I don't know a lot about him because we only bought him the other day, but I liked the way he breezed at the sales and he looked a quality two-year-old".*

427. PREMIER STEPS (IRE) ★★★

b.f. *Footstepsinthesand – Primissima (Second Set).* March 19. Second foal. £24,000Y. Doncaster Premier. Sackville Donald. The dam won at 3 yrs in Germany and is a half-sister to 5 winners there. The second dam, Princess Taufan (by Taufan), won the listed National Stakes and was third in the Group 2 Lowther stakes and is a half-sister to the dam of the stakes winners Gracefully and Lady Grace. (Attenborough,

Bellman, Ingram, Lowe). *"A very nice filly who has two gears – stood still or flat out! We've just got to get her to settle and if she does she'll be fine. First time out she'll be trying to win obviously, but she'll get a good education from it as well".* TRAINERS' BARGAIN BUY

3rd Albany

428. SAGA LOUT ★★

b.c. *Assertive – Intellibet One (Compton Place).* April 2. Fifth foal. £16,000Y. Doncaster Premier. Sackville/Donald. Half-brother to the quite useful 2011 2-y-o 6f winner Decision By One (by Bahamian Bounty) and to the quite useful 5f and 6f winner of 6 races Taurus Twins (by Deportivo). The dam, a fair 5f (including at 2 yrs) and 6f winner of 3 races, is a half-sister to 8 winners. The second dam, Safe House (by Lyphard), a winner at 3 yrs, is a half-sister to 4 other minor winners. (L A Bellman). *"We've got his full-brother Decision By One and he's an almost identical racehorse. We thought that horse would be racing in April last year but he went wrong and in the end he took until September. This horse could be exactly the same, because he was looking like an early type and now he isn't. But I bet that by September he'll be winning a five furlong maiden".*

429. SMOOTH HANDLE ★★★

ch.c. *Dutch Art – Naomi Wildman (Kingmambo).* April 5. Sixth foal. £45,000Y. Doncaster Premier. Sackville/Donald. Half-brother to the quite useful 11f to 14f winner Sherman McCoy (by Reset), to the fair 7f (at 2 yrs) to 12f winner Exceedthewildman (by Exceed And Excel) and a winner over jumps in France by Red Ransom. The dam is an unplaced half-sister to 4 winners in France including the listed winner Mondovino. The second dam, Divinite (by Alleged), won twice at 3 yrs in France and is a half-sister to 5 winners. (The Oddfellows Partnership). *"Dutch Art is such a good sire. This colt will probably be out in May, he's a five/six furlong sort and a proper 2-y-o".*

430. SPIRIT OF PARKES ★★★

gr.g. *Fair Mix – Lucky Parkes (Full Extent).* April 9. Half-brother to the fairly useful triple 5f winner Charlie Parkes (by Pursuit Of Love), to the quite useful 5f and 6f winner of 5 races Doctor Parkes (by Diktat), the quite useful 2-y-o 5f and 6f winner Robinia Parkes (by Robellino) and the fair dual 5f winner (including at 2 yrs) Johnny Parkes (by Wolfhound). The dam, a useful winner of 13 races, is a half-sister to 6 winners including the useful dual 5f winner and Moyglare, Lowther and Queen Mary Stakes placed My Melody Parkes. The second dam, Summerhill Spruce (by Windjammer), was a fair winner of a 6f seller at 3 yrs and a half-sister to 6 winners. (J Heler). *"It's lovely having a horse for Mr Heler – he brightens up my day when he comes in! We've already gelded this horse as he was a little bit fruity! The pedigree is a bit of a mix in that he's by a jumps sire out of a five furlong sprinter, but he'll probably start over six furlongs and I'm pretty sure he'll win, because now he's been gelded he's quite a nice horse. He's tall, lean and long, he's going the right way and enjoying his work".*

431. SPYMISTRESS ★★★★

ch.f. Sakhee's Secret – Martha (Alhaarth). March 4. First foal. €85,000Y. Goffs Orby. Sackville/Donald. The dam, placed once over 5f at 3 yrs, is a sister to the Group 2 5f Kings Stand Stakes and Group 3 5f Cornwallis Stakes Dominica and a half-sister to 3 winners including the dam of the Group 3 winner Rimth. The second dam, Dominio (by Dominion), a 2-y-o listed 5f winner, was second in the Group 2 5f Temple Stakes and is a half-sister to 6 winners including the very smart Group 1 5f Nunthorpe Stakes winner Ya Malak. (Mr P A Deal & Mr A Black). *"She's a very nice type of filly who probably hasn't grown as much as I'd hoped. It won't be long before she runs and she's a good-looking, five furlong type".*

432. STRIPPED BEAR ★★★

b.f. Kodiac – Triple Zero (Raise A Grand). February 9. Third foal. £18,000Y. Doncaster Premier. Sackville/Donald. Half-sister to the modest 2011 2-y-o 7f winner Galilee Chapel (by Baltic King). The dam, the modest dual 1m (including at 2 yrs) and 6f winner, is a full or half-sister to the very useful Irish 7f winner and subsequent US Grade 2 third Good Day Too. The second dam, Locorotondo (by Broken Hearted), a fair 10f to 11f winner of 5 races, is a half-sister to 6 winners. (The MHS 4x10 Partnership). *"She'll start her career in April, I love the sire and this is just a straightforward, honest filly. If you had ten horses like her you'd*

be laughing because her attitude is just lovely. She's seems an out-and-out five furlong type that might struggle to get six".*

Won 5f at nursery Kempton

433. SWITCHAROONEY (IRE) ★★★

b.c. Bahamian Bounty – Amazon Beauty (Wolfhound). March 5. Third foal. 60,000Y. Tattersalls October Book 1. Sackville/Donald. The dam won twice at 2 and 3 yrs in France, was third in the Group 3 Prix de Seine-et-Oise and is a half-sister to the US stakes winner and Group 1 Prix Saint-Alary second Asti. The second dam, Astorg (by Lear Fan), won the listed 1m Prix de la Calonne and is a half-sister to 8 winners including the Group 3 winners Android and Article Rare. (Mr & Mrs W Rooney). *"He's just cantering at present, so he's not going to be an early 2-y-o but I see no reason to suggest that he won't be running by the end of May. He canters nicely, he hasn't worked yet because we haven't pushed him and he's had no setbacks or problems as yet. A good-looking colt, he looks like he could turn out to be a nice animal".*

434. TAMALETTA (IRE) ★★

ch.f. Tamayuz – Annaletta (Belmez). March 6. Eighth foal. €22,000Y. Goffs Orby. Sackville/Donald. Half-sister to the useful 1m and listed 15f winner Anousa (by Intikhab), to the useful 7f (at 2 yrs) and 11f winner Prince Nureyev (by Desert King) and the fairly useful Irish 2-y-o 7f winner and listed-placed Excelente (by Exceed And Excel). The dam, a minor 12f winner at 3 yrs in France and listed-placed in Germany, is a half-sister to 7 winners including two listed winners in Germany and the dam of the Grade 1 E P Taylor Stakes winner Fraulein. The second dam, A Priori (by Prince Ippi), is a placed sister to the Group 2 German Oaks winner Anna Paola. (L A Bellman). *"She's weak and backward at present. One for the middle of the summer, probably over seven furlongs to start with".*

435. THIS IS NICE ★★★★ ♠

ch.f. Exceed And Excel – Spanish Quest (Rainbow Quest). March 10. Sixth foal. £32,000Y. Doncaster Premier. Sackville Donald. Half-sister to the quite useful 2011 6f placed 2-y-o Supreme Quest (by Exceed And Excel) and to the fair 2-y-o 7f winner Hey Up Dad (by Fantastic Light). The dam is an unraced half-sister to 2 winners including the listed winner

Spanish Don. The second dam, Spanish Wells (by Sadler's Wells), won at 3 yrs in France and is a full or half-sister to 6 winners including the Irish Oaks winner Wemyss Bight (dam of the Group 1 winner Beat Hollow) and the dams of the Group 1 winners Oasis Dream, Zenda and Reefscape. (L A Bellman). *"She'll probably find herself starting off in April. She's very quick and might struggle to see out five furlongs! But I have it in my head that she's perfect for the York listed race for fillies in May, so that's what we'll be aiming at. I like her".*

436. UNKNOWN VILLAIN (IRE) ★★
gr.c. Verglas – Ragtime Blues (Grand Lodge). March 9. Third foal. €16,000Y. Goffs Orby. Sackville/Donald. Half-brother to the modest 4-y-o 1m and 9f winner Mount Abora (by Rock Of Gibraltar). The dam, a fair dual 12f placed Irish maiden, is a half-sister to 5 winners including the Peruvian stakes winner and multiple Grade 1 placed Zamba Canuta. The second dam, Ragtime Rumble (by Dixieland Band), is an unraced half-sister to 4 winners including the US Grade 3 winner and Irish 1,000 Guineas second Julie La Rousse (herself dam of the Grade 2 winners Mariensky and Julie Jalouse). (Panarea Racing). *"A big, strong, backward type of horse. He doesn't have a great pedigree but he's just a really nice-looking individual, which is why I bought him. He won't be in a hurry to start and he'll need at least six furlongs this year".*

437. UPWARD SPIRAL ★★★★
ch.f. Teofilo – Welsh Cake (Fantastic Light). February 27. First living foal. 60,000Y. Tattersalls October Book 1. Sackville/Donald. The dam, a fair 7f winner, is a half-sister to 8 winners including the Group 2 1m Prix du Rond-Point and Group 3 8.5f Diomed Stakes winner Trans Island and the Italian Group 3 winner Welsh Diva. The second dam, Khubza (by Green Desert), a quite useful 3-y-o 7f winner, is a half-sister to 7 winners including the Group 2 winners Barrow Creek and Last Resort (herself dam of the US Grade 2 winner Rebellion) and the listed winners Arctic Char and Heard A Whisper. *"Unfortunately she had a bit of a setback and needed some time off, but she should be back soon and she was already fit and ready to run, so I think she'll be racing by*

the beginning of May. She's showing plenty of speed and she's a nice type of horse".

Won cls 9f mdn Sandown

438. ZARLA ★★★★
b.f. Zamindar – Ikhteyaar (Mr Prospector). May 2. Fourth foal. 40,000Y. Tattersalls October Book 1. Sackville/Donald. Half-sister to the minor US winner of 3 races at 2 and 3 yrs Jovial Joshua (by Bahri) and to the minor French 3-y-o winner Monyaar (by Montjeu). The dam, a useful 2-y-o 6f listed Doncaster Stakes winner, is a half-sister to 4 winners including the US Grade 2 placed Albaha and the very useful 7f and 1m winner Mur Taasha. The second dam, Linda's Magic (by Far North), was a smart winner of the Group 3 7f Criterion Stakes and the listed 7f John Of Gaunt Stakes and is a half-sister to 2 winners. (K P Trowbridge). *"She's a gorgeous filly to look at and has been bought specifically to go for the Tattersalls Sales race towards the back-end of the season. In the meantime she'll probably have a race or two from July onwards".*

439. UNNAMED ★★★
ch.c. Mount Nelson – Alexia Reveuse (Dr Devious). April 29. Seventh foal. £55,000 2-y-o. Doncaster Premier. Sackville/Donald. Half-brother to the modest 2011 6f placed 2-y-o Lollina Paulina (by Holy Roman Emperor), to the useful listed 1m winner of 5 races and Group placed Deauville Vision (by Danehill Dancer) and the fair 10f winner Aspro Mavro (by Spartacus). The dam is an unraced half-sister to 3 minor winners. The second dam, Marienthal (by Top Ville), is a placed sister to the Group 1 Prix Royal Oak winner Top Sunrise and a half-sister to 6 winners. (Fat Gary Sports). *"Not an early two-year-old, he's just cantering away and he'll be a mid-season horse that we're not rushing. He's done nothing wrong, he moves well and he's a nice animal".*

440. UNNAMED ★★★
b.c. Elusive City – Beal Ban (Daggers Drawn). April 5. First foal. £30,000 2-y-o. Goffs Kempton Breeze-Up. Sackville/Donald. The dam is an unraced half-sister to 6 minor winners here and abroad. The second dam, Easy Romance (by Northern Jove), won two minor races at 3 yrs in the USA and is a half-sister to 3 other minor winners there. *"I liked the way he breezed at the sale the other day and he's one we might*

target at Chester, perhaps in the five furlong maiden there".

441. UNNAMED ★★★

br.c. Footstepsinthesand – Birthday (Singspiel). February 4. Seventh foal. £30,000 2-y-o. Goffs Kempton Breeze-Up. Sackville/Donald. Half-brother to the fair 2011 Irish 1m placed 2-y-o Lady Geronimo (by Hawk Wing), to the fairly useful 1m (at 2 yrs) to 11f winner Charles Camoin (by Peintre Celebre), the fair triple 5f winner Stratton Banker (by One Cool Cat), the winner of 5 races over 5f Liberty Island (by Statue Of Liberty) and the fair 2-y-o 7f winner Midnight In May (by Mull Of Kintyre). The dam is an unraced half-sister to 2 winners. The second dam, Kindergarten (by Trempolino), won the Group 3 Prix d'Aumale and was second in the Group 1 Prix Marcel Boussac and is a half-sister to 2 minor winners. *"He breezed well at the Kempton breeze-up sale the other day. I don't like going there and seeing horses that aren't as good as the ones I've already got, so I try to buy ones with a bit of size and scope. If they're ready to run that's great and if not they can have a couple of months off. I thought this was a nice, big, strong-looking horse".*

442. UNNAMED ★★★

b.c. Kodiac – Gouache (Key Of Luck). April 22. Fifth foal. £30,000 2-y-o. Goffs Kempton Breeze-Up. Sackville/Donald. Half-brother to the modest 2011 6f fourth placed 2-y-o Mr Cooper (by Red Clubs). The dam, a fair Irish 2-y-o 6f winner, is a half-sister to 2 winners including the fairly useful 2-y-o 5f winner and triple listed-placed Mizillablack. The second dam, Sketch Pad (by Warning), was placed over 5f at 2 yrs. *"I bought him because I like the sire. He looks like a real 2-y-o and he puts his head down and gallops".*

443. UNNAMED ★★

b.f. Refuse To Bend – Munaawashat (Marju). March 15. Second foal. 8,500Y. Tattersalls October Book 3. Not sold. The dam, a quite useful 6f (at 2 yrs) and 1m winner of 5 races, is a half-sister to 7 winners including the useful 3-y-o dual 7f winner and Group 3 5f Queen Mary Stakes second Al Ihsas and the listed winner

Anna Karenina. The second dam, Simaat (by Mr Prospector), a fair 1m winner, is a half-sister to 2 winners. (Mr J A Duffy). *"A good-moving filly, she probably won't be out that early but she wasn't broken-in until the New Year. She's progressing well".*

444. UNNAMED ★★★

b.c. Holy Roman Emperor – Queen Of Deauville (Diableneyev). February 13. First foal. £30,000 2-y-o. Goffs Kempton Breeze-Up. Sackville/Donald. The dam is an unraced half-sister to 6 winners including the German Group 3 10f and multiple listed winner Lady Deauville and the Japanese dual stakes winner and Group 1 Japan Cup second Fabulous La Fouine. The second dam, Mercalle (by Kaldoun), won 8 races including the Group 1 Prix du Cadran and is a half-sister to 2 winners. *"To get a French-bred at the breeze-up sale that can motor for just 30 grand is for nothing. If he shows enough ability he can run in France for the premiums, he's a really nice, good-looking horse with a big, strong physique – and I like the sire".*

445. UNNAMED ★★ ♠

b.f. Mount Nelson – Statua (Statoblest). April 4. Eighth foal. €60,000Y. Goffs Orby. Sackville/Donald. Half-sister to the fair 2011 1m placed 2-y-o Fort Sam Houston (by Dylan Thomas), to the dual listed 1m winner and Group 3 Diomed Stakes second St Moritz (by Medicean), the fairly useful 6f to 1m winner of 4 races Annemasse (by Anabaa), the fair 7f (at 2 yrs) and 2m winner Dream Mountain (by Mozart) and the fair 2-y-o 5f winner Dance Anthem (by Royal Academy). The dam was placed four times at 2 yrs including in the Group 3 Rockfel Stakes and subsequently won 3 minor races in the USA. She is a half-sister to 8 winners including the Group 3 Diomed Stakes and US Grade 3 winner Bluegrass Prince. The second dam, Amata (by Nodouble), won 3 races in France and the USA over middle distances, was Grade 3 placed and is a half-sister to the Group 3 Princess Royal Stakes winner Trillionaire. (Manor House Stables LLP). *"A big filly that's going to take a bit of time. She's probably a seven furlong filly to start off with and we'll see the best of her next year I should imagine".*

446. UNNAMED ★★

b.c. Manduro – Treble Heights (Unfuwain). March 28. Fifth foal. Closely related to the 7f (at 2 yrs) and triple 12f winner and Group 1 St Leger second Brown Panther (by Shirocco) and half-brother to the fair 2011 2-y-o 7f winner Third Half (by Haafhd), the moderate 15f and jumps winner Holoko Heights and the hurdles winner Paddy Partridge (both by Pivotal). The dam, a listed 12f winner, was Group 2 placed over 14f in France and is a half-sister to numerous winners including the very useful winner of 5 races and Group 1 Ascot Gold Cup third Warm Feeling, the useful Group 1 Italian Derby third Precede and the useful 7.6f (at 2 yrs) and 10f winner Rainbow Heights. The second dam, Height Of Passion (by Shirley Heights), is an unplaced half-sister to 8 winners. (Owen Promotions Ltd). *"A very nice-looking horse who is the spitting image of Brown Panther. But at the moment he's lanky, weak and just a shell of a horse really. He'll just have a run or two towards the back-end and we'll see the best of him next year and beyond".*

447. UNNAMED ★★★★

b.c. Acclamation – Vintage Tipple (Entrepreneur). April 25. Sixth foal. €58,000Y. Tattersalls Ireland. Sackville/Donald. Half-brother to the promising 2011 1m placed 2-y-o Venegazzu (by Dubawi), to the quite useful Irish dual 7f winner Cape Vintage (by Cape Cross), the quite useful 11f winner King's Vintage (by King's Best) and a minor French winner at 3 yrs by Dubai Destination. The dam, a 7f, 1m (at 2 yrs) and Group 1 Irish Oaks winner, is a half-sister to 4 winners including the useful 2-y-o 7f and 1m winner and Group 1 1m Gran Criterium third Spettro. The second dam, Overruled (by Last Tycoon), a quite useful 1m (at 2 yrs) and 10.2f winner, is a half-sister to 6 winners including the Grade 2 American Derby winner Overbury. (Lowe Silver Deal). *"He looks great and he's doing well, but he's just cantering away at present and we won't be asking him any questions until May. If he comes to hand he'll be running at the end of May/early June and he's a good shape, which I don't think a lot of Acclamation's are. I thought he was a bargain considering he's out of a Group One winner and yet his price at the yearling sales was about half the average for the sire. He's a really nice horse".*

448. UNNAMED ★★

b.f. Montjeu – Wing Stealth (Hawk Wing). February 12. First foal. 30,000Y. Tattersalls December. Sackville/Donald. The dam, a fair 7f (at 2 yrs) and 12f placed maiden, is a half-sister to 4 winners. The second dam, Starlight Smile (by Green Dancer), is an unraced half-sister to 4 winners including the multiple Irish listed winner Seasonal Pickup and the dam of the Irish Derby winner Grey Swallow. (The Tipperary Partners). *"Exactly the same as our other Montjeu filly in that she has a nice shape to her and she's a good filly to deal with, but we haven't done enough with her yet to suggest how much ability she'll have. She'll start off at seven furlongs in mid-summer".*

SIMON DOW

449. FIDUCIA ★★★

b.f. Lawman – Silca Key (Inchinor). March 31. Second foal. 14,000Y. Tattersalls October Book 2. Simon Dow. Half-sister to the 2011 7f placed 2-y-o (from 2 starts) Shotley Music (by Amadeus Wolf). The dam, a fairly useful 9f and 10f winner of 3 races, is a half-sister to 5 winners including the fairly useful triple 1m winner Cross The Line. The second dam, Baalbek (by Barathea), a fair 3-y-o 1m winner, is a half-sister to 4 winners. (P. G Jacobs). *"Quite precocious, she has plenty of speed and all being well she'll be running in April over five furlongs".* TRAINERS' BARGAIN BUY

450. MARJONG ★★

b.f. Mount Nelson – Vermilliann (Mujadil). January 22. Third foal. 27,000Y. Tattersalls October Book 2. S Dow. Half-sister to the fair 2011 dual 5f placed maiden Royal Red (by Holy Roman Emperor) and to a minor winner abroad by One Cool Cat. The dam, fairly useful 2-y-o dual 5f winner, is a sister to the Group 2 6f Mill Reef Stakes winner and Group 1 placed Galeota and a half-sister to 4 winners including the 11f and listed 13f winner Loulwa and the fairly useful 2-y-o 5f Weatherbys Supersprint winner Lady Livius. The second dam, Refined (by Statoblest), a fairly useful dual 5f winner, is a half-sister to 6 winners including the very smart Group 3 7f Criterion Stakes winner Pipe Major. (Mr J L Marsden). *"A big, well-grown filly that might make the track around May time over six furlongs but I see her getting a mile in time. Mount Nelson is a first season sire so we don't know for sure, but I expect his 2-y-o's will be quite racey".*

451. PRESUMIDO (IRE) ★★★

b.c. Iffraaj – Miss Megs (Croco Rouge). April 13. Fourth foal. 19,000Y. Tattersalls October 2. S Dow. Half-brother to the quite useful 2-y-o 6f winner Chips O'Toole (by Fasliyev) and to a winner in Norway by Danetime. The dam, a fair 9f and 11f winner in Ireland, is a half-sister to 3 winners including the listed winner Santa Isobel. The second dam, Atlantic Record (by Slip Anchor), is an unraced full or half-sister to 4 winners. (R Moss & J Page). *"A tall, well-grown colt that looks like a 2-y-o type. He's had a slight hold up but he'll be precocious enough. Six furlongs should be his trip".*

452. UNNAMED ★★★

b.f. Rock Of Gibraltar – Ommadawn (Montjeu). March 6. First foal. 26,000Y. Tattersalls October Book 2. S Dow. The dam, a fair 12f winner, is a half-sister to 3 winners including the Group 3 Irish 1,000 Guineas Trial and Group 3 Desmond Stakes winner and US Grade 1 placed Carriban Sunset. The second dam, Bonheur (by Royal Academy), won over 6f at 3 yrs in Ireland and is a half-sister to 7 winners including the German 1,000 Guineas winner Quebrada and to the placed dam of the Group 1 German Oaks winner Silvester Lady. (Malcolm & Alice Aldis). *"She's slightly backward at the moment but she's a strong, compact, 2-y-o type that's well-made and likely to make her debut in the summer rather than earlier".*

453. UNNAMED ★★

b.c. Anabaa – Sourire (Domedriver). February 12. First foal. 25,000Y. Tattersalls October Book 2. S Dow. The dam, a dual 2-y-o 7f winner, later won a listed event over 1m in Sweden and is a half-sister to 5 winners including the 2-y-o Group 3 1m Prix des Reservoirs winner Songerie, the German listed winner and Group 1 Italian Oaks third Souvenance and the French listed winner and Group 3 placed Soft Morning. The second dam, Summer Night (by Nashwan), a fairly useful 3-y-o 6f winner, is a half-sister to 7 winners including the Group 3 Prix d'Arenburg winner Starlit Sands. (Mr M McAllister). *"A slightly backward, very strong and quite heavy-*

topped colt that needs a bit of time. One for the middle of the season onwards".

ANN DUFFIELD

454. BY A WISKA ★★★

b.c. Kheleyf – Tropical Breeze (Kris). February 2. Fifth foal. 13,000Y. Tattersalls October Book 2. Sun Hill Racing. Half-brother to the fair 11f and 12f winner Dubai Storming (by Storming Home) and to the modest 14f and hurdles winner Head Hunted (by Dubai Destination). The dam is an unraced half-sister to the fairly useful 6f (at 2 yrs) and 1m winner of 4 races and listed placed Rainbow Mirage. The second dam, Embers Of Fame (by Sadler's Wells), ran twice unplaced and is a half-sister to 4 winners including Free To Speak, a winner of 3 listed events over 1m in Ireland. *"A very strong, good-looking, scopey horse that we like. A 2-y-o for the mid-summer onwards".*

455. CHANT (IRE) ★★

b.g. Oratorio – Akarita (Akarad). March 1. Eighth foal. £12,500Y. Doncaster November. T Adams. Half-brother to the quite useful Irish 6f winner Scarsdale (by Polar Falcon), the moderate 6f seller winner Tahitian Princess (by One Cool Cat) and the moderate Irish 7f winner Soviet Trooper (by Soviet Lad). The dam won over 7.5f at 3 yrs and was listed placed twice. She is a half-sister to 9 winners including the useful 2-y-o 5f winner and Group 3 third Safka (herself dam of the listed winner Speedfit Too), the Group 2 7f Lockinge Stakes winner Safawan and the dam of the Group 2 12f Prix Hocquart winner Sayarshan. The second dam, Safita (by Habitat), won the listed 1m Prix de la Calonne and was second in the French 1,000 Guineas and the Prix Saint-Alary. (Mrs A Starkie). *"A good-looking horse and a good mover, but he'll be one for later in the season over seven furlongs and a mile".*

456. CHLOE'S DREAM (IRE) ★★★

gr.f. Clodovil – Extravagance (King's Best). April 12. Second foal. 6,000Y. Tattersalls October Book 2. Sun Hill Racing. Half-sister to the quite useful 2011 2-y-o dual 5f winner Signifer (by Titus Livius). The dam, a fair 6f (at 2 yrs) and 7f placed maiden, is a half-sister to 2 winners. The second dam, Meritxell (by Thatching), won once at 3 yrs in France and is a half-sister to 10 winners including the Group 2 winner Almushtarak. (Mr P. A Bowles). *"She's a nice filly, a quality mover, has a lot of scope and she goes well. Capable of winning".*

457. LADY MOONLIGHT (IRE) ★★★

gr.f. *Jeremy – Lady Georgina (Linamix).* February 2. €6,000Y. Tattersalls Ireland. Ann Duffield. Half-sister to the quite useful 2-y-o 5f winner King's Approach (by Fasliyev). The dam, a fair dual 7f winner at 3 yrs, is a half-sister to one winner abroad out of the fair 14f and 2m winner Georgia Venture (by Shirley Heights), herself a half-sister to 10 winners. *"A strong filly, scopey and a good mover, she's an early runner that has speed. Five and six furlongs will suit her".*

458. MYANNE ★★★

b.f. *Indesatchel – Mookhlesa (Marju).* February 4. First foal. £8,500. Doncaster Premier. Ann Duffield. The dam, a quite useful 2-y-o 5f winner, is a half-sister to one winner. The second dam, Ikhlas (by Lahib), is an unraced sister to the Group 3 Horris Hill Stakes winner La-Faah and a half-sister to 6 winners. (Jimmy Kay & Lovely Bubbly Racing). *"A nice, sharp, early filly that shows ability. We like her, she shows a great attitude and she'll be ideally suited to five and six furlongs".* TRAINERS' BARGAIN BUY

459. RANGOONED ★★★

gr.f. *Bahamian Bounty – Dansa Queen (Dansili).* February 18. Second foal. £20,000Y. Doncaster Premier. Ann Duffield. The dam, a quite useful 7f and 1m winner of 3 races, is a half-sister to 4 winners including Halicardia (listed Lupe Stakes). The second dam, Pericardia (by Petong), is an unplaced half-sister to 4 winners including Prince Ferdinand, winner of the Group 3 7f Jersey Stakes. (Morecool Racing & David Redvers). *"She's ready to go and she's a nice filly with a great attitude. A lovely mover, she's very light on her feet, very athletic and shows ability. Five and six furlongs will suit her nicely".*

460. RED CHARMER (IRE) ★★

b.g. *Red Clubs – Golden Charm (Common Grounds).* April 29. Ninth foal. €21,000Y. Tattersalls Ireland. Ann Duffield. Half-brother to the 5f and 6f winner of 11 races (including at 2 yrs), to the 1m winner English Rocket (by Indian Rocket), the 2-y-o 5f winner Golden Dane (by Danetime) and the 2-y-o 6f winner Upthedowns (by Beckett) – all modest. The dam, a modest 2-y-o 6f winner, is a half-sister to 5 winners. The second dam, Credit Crunch (by Caerleon), is an unplaced half-sister to one winner. (Mr I Farrington & Mr R Chapman). *"A nice, big gelding, he's a bit backward and very scopey. One for the mid-summer onwards".*

461. RED HIGHLITES (IRE) ★★★

br.f. *Red Clubs – High Lite (Observatory).* February 21. First foal. £14,000Y. Doncaster Premier. Middleham Park Racing. The dam is an unplaced half-sister to 6 winners including the 2-y-o Group 2 Gimcrack Stakes winner Bannister. The second dam, Shall We Run (by Hotfoot), is a placed full or half-sister to 8 winners including Dead Certain (Group 1 Cheveley Park Stakes). (Middleham Park Racing XL). *"Sharp and early, she'll run soon and will be happy over five or six furlongs. A good mover and ready to go".*

462. RUST (IRE) ★★★★

b.c. *Elnadim – Reddening (Blushing Flame).* February 13. Sixth foal. €30,000Y. Goffs Orby. Ann Duffield. Half-brother to the very useful 2-y-o 6f and 7f winner and Group 1 Nunthorpe Stakes third Pivotal Flame (by Pivotal) and the fairly useful 5f (at 2 yrs) and 6f winner of 4 races Olynard (by Exceed And Excel). The dam, a fairly useful 2m winner, is a sister to the Italian winner and Group 3 placed Musical Score and a half-sister to 5 winners. The second dam, Music In My Life (by Law Society), a modest 7.5f and 1m placed 3-y-o, is a half-sister to 4 winners. (Evelyn, Duchess of Sutherland). *"A quality individual, he's a fantastic mover and has plenty of scope. One for the mid-summer onwards, he's very laid back and we like him".*

463. SCENTPASTPARADISE ★★★

b.f. *Pastoral Pursuits – Centenerola (Century City).* May 13. First foal. £10,000Y. Doncaster Festival. Ann Duffield. The dam, a fair 7f winner, is a half-sister to 3 winners including the Group 3 7f Nell Gwyn Stakes winner Barefoot Lady. The second dam, Lady Angharad (by Tenby), a winner of 5 races from 6f to 10f including the 2-y-o listed Woodcote Stakes, is a half-sister to

5 minor winners here and in Italy. (Mr M Curtis). *"A May foal from a good family, she's a great mover but she's still growing so we're in no rush with her. She's a very nice filly and we like her".*

464. SWAYING GRACE ★★★

b.f. Celtic Swing – Saying Grace (Brief Truce). March 20. Fourth foal. €7,000Y. Tattersalls Ireland. Ann Duffield. Sister to the quite useful Irish 9f and 10f winner of 4 races Ghetto Gospel. The dam, a very useful 6f and 7f winner in Ireland at 2 yrs, was third in the Group 2 1m Prix d'Astarte. The second dam, Adamparis (by Robellino), won twice at 3 yrs and is a half-sister to 3 winners. (David & Carol McMahon). *"Nicely-bred out of a mare rated 107 and full-sister to a horse that's now in Hong Kong. She's one for six/seven furlongs, she won't be early but she'll be out from June time onwards. A nice, quality, genuine filly".*

465. YORKSHIRE ICON ★★★

b.c. Sixties Icon – Evanesce (Lujain). April 1. Fourth foal. £5,500Y. Doncaster November. Ann Duffield. Half-brother to the modest 2011 2-y-o dual 5f seller winner Selinda (by Piccolo) and the fair dual 7f winner (including at 2 yrs) and hurdles winner Alfraamsay (by Fraam). The dam, a fair 2-y-o 6f winner, is a half-sister to one winner. The second dam, Search Party (Rainbow Quest), a fair 8.3f and 10f placed maiden, is a half-sister to the 6f (at 2 yrs) and subsequent Grade 1 10f Santa Barbara Handicap winner Bequest and to the useful 2-y-o 7f winner Fitzcarraldo. (Middleham Park Racing XXIX). *"He goes well, he's not very big and lacks a bit of scope, but he's got ability. He'll run earlier than you might expect for a Sixties Icon and he's a nice boy".*

466. UNNAMED ★★★

b.c. Sleeping Indian – Desert Gold (Desert Prince). April 5. €8,000Y. Tattersalls Ireland. Ann Duffield/J Cullinan. Half-brother to the fair 6f (at 2 yrs) to 10f and hurdles winner Royal Opera (by Acclamation). The dam, a fairly useful Irish dual 7f winner, is a half-sister to one winner. The second dam, Brief Sentiment (by Brief Truce), an Irish 2-y-o winner and second in the listed Irish 1,000 Guineas Trial, is a half-sister to 2 winners. *"A nice colt, he's a little heavy*

topped, strong bodied and has a good attitude. There's no reason why he can't do well, he's doing everything right and he'll be fairly early. I'm still looking for someone to buy a share in him, if anyone is interested in joining us".*

467. UNNAMED ★★

b.f. Tobougg – Prairie Sun (Law Society). March 10. Second foal. The dam, a modest 10f to 2m and hurdles winner of 9 races, is a sister to a winner over 11f in Germany. The second dam, Prairie Flame (by Marju), was placed twice over 1m at 2 yrs in Ireland. (Mrs A Duffield). *"I need an owner for her and she's bred to get a trip or be a dual-purpose horse. We trained the dam who won nine races including five on the bounce. In fourteen days she won four flat races between 13f and 2m – so she was very tough! She also got black-type over hurdles, this is her daughter and she's lovely. She's strong and scopey, one for the middle of the summer onwards".*

ED DUNLOP

468. ABRAQ ★★★

b.c. Danehill Dancer – Nordhock (Luhuk). February 20. First foal. 130,000Y. Tattersalls October Book 1. Not sold. The dam, a 2-y-o 6f seller winner, is a half-sister to 4 winners including the multiple Group 1 winner (Phoenix Stakes, National Stakes, Irish 1,000 Guineas and St James's Palace Stakes) Mastercraftsman, the Irish 2-y-o 7f winner and Group 1 7f Moyglare Stud Stakes second Famous and the US Grade 3 winner Genuine Devotion. The second dam, Starlight Dreams (by Black Tie Affair), won twice at 3 yrs in the USA and is a half-sister to 5 winners including the listed Zetland Stakes winner Matahif and the dams of the dual Group 1 winner Pressing and the Group 3 Princess Royal Stakes winner Mazuna. (Royal Cavalry Oman). *"A strong, powerful, seven furlong horse that goes OK".*

469. AMAZONAS (IRE) ★★★

b.f. Cape Cross – Francesca d'Gorgio (Proud Citizen). February 24. First foal. The dam, a fairly useful 2-y-o 6f winner, was listed placed at 3 yrs and is a half-sister to 2 winners. The second dam, Betty's Solutions (by Eltish), a minor US dual 3-y-o 6f to 1m winner, is a half-sister to the dam of the US Grade 1 winner My Trusty Cat. (Sir Robert Ogden). *"A strong, powerful filly that moves well. She's goes alright".*

470. AUCTION (IRE) ★★★
b.f. Mr Greeley – Exhibit One (Silver Hawk). February 23. Second foal. €80,000Y. Arqana Deauville August. John Warren. The dam, a smart Italian Group 3 10f and 12f winner, was third in the Group1 Gran Premio di Milano and is a half-sister to 3 winners. The second dam, Tsar's Pride (by Sadler's Wells), won over 12f in France and was listed-placed over 10f. (Highclere Thoroughbred Racing – Coventry). *"A strong, good-looking filly that moves well. She's just come back in after a break at the stud and she could be a nice filly".*

471. CONCISE ★★★
b.f. Lemon Drop Kid – Cut Short (Diesis). April 15. Fourth foal. 155,000Y. Tattersalls October Book 1. David Simcock. Half-sister to the useful 2-y-o listed 6f winner Brevity (by Street Cry) and to the fair 5f winner Special Quality (by Elusive Quality). The dam, a quite useful 1m winner, is a sister to the smart Daggers Drawn (winner of the Group 2 6f Richmond Stakes and the Group 2 7f Laurent Perrier Rose Champagne Stakes) and a half-sister to the very useful 2-y-o dual 6f winner Enemy Action (herself dam of the 1,000 Guineas third Super Sleuth). The second dam, Sun And Shade (by Ajdal), a useful 2-y-o 6f winner here and a stakes-placed winner in the USA, is a half-sister to the very smart dual Group 2 winner Madame Dubois (herself dam the Irish 2,000 Guineas winner Indian Haven and the Group 1 Gran Criterium winner Count Dubois). (Cliveden Stud/St Albans Bloodstock). *"A nice filly, she's strong and powerful. Being by Lemon Drop Kid she won't be that early, but she moves well".*

472. EGHNAA ★★★
b.br.f. Cape Cross – Alzaroof (Kingmambo). January 30. First foal. The dam is an unplaced half-sister to the smart 7f (at 2 yrs) to 11f winner of 3 races and dual listed-placed Anmar (by Rahy). The second dam, Ranin (by Unfuwain), a smart Group 2 14.6f Park Hill Stakes winner, is a half-sister to 6 winners including the very useful 7f and 1m winner Ghalib, the useful 2-y-o 1m and listed 9f placed Wahchi and the

useful 6.5f (at 2 yrs) to 7f winner Qhazeenah. (Hamdan Al Maktoum). *"She shows some speed and goes well".*

473. GWORN ★★★★
b.c. Aussie Rules – Crochet (Mark Of Esteem). March 3. Fourth foal. The dam is an unraced sister to the Group 3 Prix Chloe and Group 3 Premio Sergio Cumani winner Needlecraft and a half-sister to 4 winners. The second dam, Sharp Point (by Royal Academy), a useful Irish listed 5f winner at 3 yrs, was second in the Group 1 Phoenix Stakes and is a half-sister to 3 winners including the listed Hong Kong winner High Target. (N Martin). *"I quite like him, he's a strong, powerful horse that goes quite well".*

474. HANZADA (USA) ★★
b.br.f. Arch – Chocolate Mauk (Cozzene). March 17. Fourth foal. 225,000Y. Tattersalls October Book 1. Charlie Gordon-Watson. Half-sister to 2 minor winners in the USA by Posse and Purge. The dam is an unplaced half-sister to 8 winners including the US stakes winners Total Bull and Seattle Pattern. The second dam, Pattern Step (by Nureyev), won the Grade 1 Hollywood Oaks and is a half-sister to the Grade 2 winner Motley. (N Bizakov). *"A big filly that will need some time".*

475. JEERAAN (USA) ★★★
b.c. Distorted Humor – Jaish (Seeking The Gold). March 12. Third foal. Half-brother to Eshaab (by Dynaformer), placed fourth once over 1m from two runs at 2 yrs in 2011. The dam, a useful 2-y-o 6f winner, was listed-placed over 1m and 10f and is a half-sister to 4 winners. The second dam, Khazayin (by Bahri), was placed over 10f and is a sister to the high-class Prix de l'Arc de Triomphe and Juddmonte International winner Sakhee and closely related to the useful 7f (at 2 yrs) and 10f winner Nasheed. (Hamdan Al Maktoum). *"He's just come from Dubai so we don't know a lot about him but he's a good-looking colt that moves well, so he could be OK".*

476. JABHAAT (USA) ★★
b.f. Hard Spun – Ishraak (Sahm). February 5. Second foal. Half-sister to the 2011 Italian 1m listed-placed 2-y-o Motheeba (by Mustanfar). The dam is an unraced half-sister to 6 winners including the US Grade 2 7f winner Kayrawan.

The second dam, Muhbubh (by Blushing Groom), won the Group 3 6f Princess Margaret Stakes, was second in the Group 2 6f Lowther Stakes and is a half-sister to Mathkurh (dam of the Group winners Asfurah and Istintaj). (Hamdan Al Maktoum). *"Just arrived from Dubai".*

477. LAMUSAWAMA ★★★★

b.c. Acclamation – Intrepid Queen (Theatrical). February 25. Fourth foal. 180,000Y. Tattersalls October Book 2. Shadwell Estate Co. The dam won one race at 3 yrs in the USA and is a half-sister to 10 winners including the US listed winners Bravo Bull and Russian Tango (herself dam of the US Grade 2 winner Eurosilver) and the dam of the US Grade 2 winner Muntej. The second dam, Brave Raj (by Rajab), won the Grade 1 Breeders Cup Juvenile Fillies and is a half-sister to 2 winners. (Hamdan Al Maktoum). *"I like this horse but he's not a mature Acclamation, he'll be one for later in the season. A good-moving colt".*

478. MAHAAFEL (USA) ★★★

b.br.c. Street Cry – Henderson Band (Chimes Band). March 14. Eighth foal. $300,000Y. Keeneland September. Shadwell Estate Co. Half-brother to the US Grade 1 Oak Leaf Stakes winner and Grade 1 Santa Anita Oaks third Cash Included (by Include). The dam is an unraced half-sister to 5 winners including the French Group 2 winner and French Derby second Lord Flasheart. The second dam, Miss Henderson Co (by Silver Hawk), a minor winner of 2 races in the USA, is a sister to the Delaware Oaks winner Like A Hawk and a half-sister to 6 winners including the US dual Grade 1 winner By Land By Sea (herself dam of the Group 3 Rose Of Lancaster Stakes winner Fahal). (Hamdan Al Maktoum). *"I like him, he's just come from Dubai and he's a strong, powerful horse that seems to move well. Looks a nice horse".*

479. MISTRAL WIND (IRE) ★★★

b.f. Hurricane Run – Grable (Sadler's Wells). January 25. Fourth foal. 32,000Y. Tattersalls December. Charlie Gordon-Watson. Half-sister to 2 minor winners abroad by Holy Roman Emperor and Rock Of Gibraltar. The dam, a fair 10f and 11f placed maiden, is a sister to two

listed-placed winners. The second dam, Movie Legend (by Affirmed), is an unraced sister to 4 stakes winners including the Irish 1,000 Guineas winner Trusted Partner (dam of the US Grade 1 winner Dress To Thrill) and the Group 2 winner Easy To Copy (herself the dam of 3 stakes winners). (A Partnership). *"Her pedigree tells you she'll need time, but she's a very good-moving, good-bodied filly that goes OK".*

480. NABAT SEIF (USA) ★★★

b.f. Street Sense – Sierra Madre (Baillamont). February 11. Half-sister to the high-class Group 1 7f Prix de la Salamandre and Group 1 1m Sussex Stakes winner Aljabr (by Storm Cat), to the useful 10f winner Jabaar (by Silver Hawk) and the useful French 2-y-o winner Makaarem (by Danzig). The dam, a very smart winner of the Group 1 1m Prix Marcel Boussac and Group 1 12f Prix Vermeille, is a half-sister to several minor winners. The second dam, Marie d'Irlande (by Kalamoun), a modest French 1m winner, is a sister to the very smart French 9f and 10f winner Dom Racine. (Hamdan Al Maktoum). *"A good-topped filly, she's the nicest the mare has had since Aljabr. A big, scopey filly and the sire is doing very well".*

481. NARDIN ★★★★ ♠

b.f. Royal Applause – Third Party (Terimon). April 25. Ninth foal. 90,000Y. Tattersalls October Book 2. Shadwell Estate Co. Half-sister to the very useful listed 7f and listed 1m winner Party Boss (by Silver Patriarch), to the fair 7f and 1m winner Best In Class (by Best Of The Bests), the modest 7f winner Party Turn (by Pivotal) and the modest 1m (at 2 yrs) to 14f and hurdles winner Countrywide Flame (by Haafhd). The dam, a modest 3-y-o 6f winner, is a half-sister to 6 winners including the German Group 3 winning sprinter Passion For Life and the fairly useful sprint winner of 13 races Very Dicey. The second dam, Party Game (by Red Alert), a fair 6f winner at 3 yrs, is a half-sister to 5 minor winners. (Hamdan Al Maktoum). *"She's very nice. A strong, powerful filly and a beautiful mover, she'll be an early 2-y-o".*

482. OF COURSE DARLING ★★★ ♠

ch.f. Dalakhani – Whazzis (Desert Prince). February 25. Second foal. 65,000Y. Tattersalls October Book 1. Not sold. The dam won 3 races here and in Italy including the Group 3 1m Premio Sergio Cumani and the listed Valiant Stakes and is a half-sister to 5 winners including the listed Chesham Stakes winner Whazzat. The second dam, Wosaita (by Generous), a fair 12.3f placed maiden, is a half-sister to 10 winners including the very smart Group 1 10.5f Prix de Diane winner Rafha (herself the dam of 4 stakes winners including the Haydock Sprint Cup winner Invincible Spirit) and the Group 3 12f Blandford Stakes winner Chiang Mai (dam of the Group 1 Pretty Polly Stakes winner Chinese White). (A Partnership). *"It's a slightly strange pedigree because the dam was a Group winner over a mile but Dalakhani suggests 3-y-o. She's strong, mature and goes well".*

483. PAIRUMANI PRINCE (IRE) ★★★★

b.c. Choisir – Pairumani Princess (Pairumani Star). February 19. First foal. €1,500Y. Tattersalls Ireland November. Not sold. The dam, a modest 2-y-o 1m winner, is a half-sister to 3 winners including the very useful listed 1m to 12f winner Persian Lightning and the fairly useful 14f and 2m winner Height Of Fantasy and to the unplaced dam of the Group 3 winner Big Bad Bob. The second dam, Persian Fantasy (by Persian Bold), a fairly useful dual 12f winner, is a half-sister to numerous winners including the Group 2 winner Lucky Guest and the dam of the Group 3 winners Elusive Pimpernel and Palavicini. *"He'll be out early and he's a strong, powerful, six furlong horse that'll win races. He wouldn't want fast ground".* TRAINERS' BARGAIN BUY

484. SAXON SOLDIER ★★

br.c. Kyllachy – Gwyneth (Zafonic). April 11. Fourth foal. 26,000Y. Tattersalls October Book 2. Ed Dunlop. Half-brother to the unplaced 2011 2-y-o Isobella (by Royal Applause). The dam is an unplaced sister to the Italian Group 3 winner Guest Connections and a half-sister to 5 winners including the dam of the Group 1 Irish St Leger winner Sans Frontieres. The second dam, Llyn Gwynant (by Persian Bold), won the Group 3 1m Desmond Stakes and the Group 3 1m Matron Stakes and is a half-sister to 2 winners. (H Channon). *"A good-looking horse, he's actually not that mature but he's OK".*

485. SHARAARAH (IRE) ★★★

b.f. Oasis Dream – Nidhaal (Observatory). February 26. Third foal. Sister to the quite useful 2-y-o 5f and 6f winner Sadafiya and half-sister to the useful 2011 2-y-o 5f winner and dual Group 2 placed Burwaaz (by Exceed And Excel). The dam, a very useful 2-y-o listed 6f winner and second in the Group 3 6f Princess Margaret Stakes, is a half-sister to 2 winners. The second dam, Jeed (by Mujtahid), a quite useful 2-y-o 6f winner, is a half-sister to 2 winners. (Hamdan Al Maktoum). *"A half-sister to Burwaaz who was a good 2-y-o last year. She's small and racey and will win early".*

Won 6f cls f mdn Kempton

486. SINGERSONGWRITER ★★★

ch.f. Raven's Pass – Independence (Selkirk). February 23. Seventh foal. Half-sister to the Group 1 1m Criterium International and Group 1 Eclipse Stakes winner Mount Nelson (by Rock Of Gibraltar), to the 1m (at 2 yrs) and Group 2 12f Great Voltigeur Stakes winner Monitor Closely (by Oasis Dream), the fairly useful 1m and 10f winner Stone Of Scone (by Pivotal), the quite useful 9.5f winner Off Message (by In The Wings) and the modest 12f winner Apparel (by Cape Cross). The dam won four races at 3 yrs from 7f to 1m including the Group 2 Sun Chariot Stakes and the Group 3 Matron Stakes and is a half-sister to one winner. The second dam, Yukon Hope (by Forty Niner), a fair maiden, is out of a half-sister to Reference Point. (Cliveden Stud Ltd). *"She's a very nice filly but she's very big, the good ones out of the mare have been the same – including Mount Nelson".*

Won early fair 7f mdn Donc

487. SPECKLED HILL ★★★

b.c. Oasis Dream – World's Heroine (Spinning World). March 25. Second foal. 75,000Y. Tattersalls October Book 2. R Frisby. Half-brother to the fair 2011 2-y-o 7f winner Always Et Toujours (by Notnowcato). The dam, a quite useful 2-y-o 7f winner, is a half-sister to 2 winners. The second dam, Metaphor (by Woodman), a minor 2-y-o winner in France, was listed-placed and is a half-sister to 5 winners including the Group 3 Craven Stakes and US Grade 3 winner and Grade 1 second King Of Happiness. (H Channon). *"A solid, powerful sort that probably wants six/seven furlongs this year".*

488. PRINCESS LOULOU (IRE) ★★★
ch.f. Pivotal – Aiming (Highest Honor). March 27. Fourth foal. 310,000Y. Tattersalls October Book 1. A O Nerses. Half-sister to the useful 6f (at 2 yrs) to 9f winner of 5 races and listed-placed Easy Option (by Danehill Dancer), to the quite useful 2-y-o 7f winner La Adelita (by Anabaa) and the fair 2-y-o 7f winner Conducting (by Oratorio). The dam was placed over 7f (at 2 yrs) and 1m and is a half-sister to 4 winners including the very smart dual listed 5f winner Watching. The second dam, Sweeping (by Indian King), a useful 2-y-o 6f winner, is a half-sister to 10 winners. (Saleh Al Homaizi & Imad Al Sagar). *"A good-looking filly, she's by Pivotal so she won't be early, but she's nice".*

489. UNNAMED ★★★
b.f. Invincible Spirit – Needles And Pins (Fasliyev). March 1. Fourth foal. 120,000Y. Tattersalls October Book 2. A O Nerses. Half-sister to the useful 2011 2-y-o Group 3 7f Oh So Sharp Stakes winner Alsindi (by Acclamation), to the fairly useful UAE 7f winner and listed-placed I Am The Best (by King's Best) and the fair 7f winner Seamster (by Pivotal). The dam, a useful 2-y-o listed 5.2f winner and second in the Group 3 5.5f Prix d'Arenburg, is a half-sister to 2 winners. The second dam, Fairy Contessa (by Fairy King), is a 6f placed half-sister to 5 winners including River Falls (Group 2, 6f Gimcrack Stakes). (Saleh Al Homaizi & Imad Al Sagar). *"She was broken in and sent home for a break but she comes back in today. It's a precocious family".*

490. UNNAMED ★★★★★ ♠
b.f. Galileo – Ouija Board (Cape Cross). February 20. Third foal. Half-sister to the quite useful 1m winner Voodoo Prince (by Kingmambo). The dam was a top-class winner of 10 races from 7f (at 2 yrs) to 12f including seven Group/Grade 1 races and is a half-sister to 6 winners. The second dam, Selection Board (by Welsh Pageant), was placed over 7f at 2 yrs and is a sister to the top-class Queen Elizabeth II Stakes and Budweiser Arlington Million winner Teleprompter. (The Earl of Derby). *"The nicest the mare's had so far, she's big and beautiful and if this was a 3-y-o's to follow book she'd be on top of the list. She's the nicest filly I've ever seen, but I suppose everything's relative!"*

491. UNNAMED ★★★
b.c. Exceed And Excel – Prayer (Rainbow Quest). March 3. Fifth foal. £67,000Y. Doncaster Premier. Jane Allison. Half-brother to the smart listed 1m and 10f winner and Group 3 Acomb Stakes third Without A Prayer (by Intikhab). The dam ran twice unplaced and is a half-sister to 3 winners. The second dam, Shunaire (by Woodman), won over 6f 3 yrs in Ireland and is a half-sister to 9 winners. (Mrs S M Roy). *"We thought he might be early, but of course he's out of a Rainbow Quest mare so he's going to need a bit of time. He shows a lot of speed and looks nice".*

492. IHTIKAR (USA) ★★★
b.c. Invasor – Ranin (Unfuwain). April 21. Sixth foal. Half-brother to the smart 7f (at 2 yrs) to 11f winner of 3 races and dual listed-placed Anmar (by Rahy). The dam, a smart Group 2 14.6f Park Hill Stakes winner, is a half-sister to 6 winners including the very useful 7f and 1m winner Ghalib, the useful 2-y-o 1m and listed 9f placed Wahchi and the useful 6.5f (at 2 yrs) to 7f winner Qhazeenah. The second dam, Nafhaat (by Roberto), a fairly useful 12f winner, stayed 15f. (Hamdan Al Maktoum). *"We know the family well, he's just arrived from Dubai and he moves well but is probably more of a seven furlong 2-y-o I would think".*

493. SUMMER ISLES ★★★
b.f. Exceed And Excel – Summers Lease (Pivotal). April 20. First foal. 50,000Y. Tattersalls October Book 1. Ed Dunlop. The dam, a quite useful 1m winner, is a sister to the smart Group 3 5f Palace House Stakes and subsequent US Grade 3 9f winner Needwood Blade and a half-sister to 5 winners including the US Grade 3 winner Islay Mist. The second dam, Finlaggan (by Be My Chief), a quite useful 11f to 2m winner, is a half-sister to 7 winners. *"A racey filly, she'll be early and she shows speed".*

494. UNNAMED ★★★
ch.c. Mount Nelson – Wild Clover (Lomitas). April 12. Fourth foal. €30,000Y. Goffs Orby. John Hassett. £20,000 2-y-o. Kempton Breeze-Up. Jane Allison. Half-brother to the modest 1m winner Pacific Bay (by Diktat) and to a minor winner at 3 yrs in Italy by Azamour. The dam, a French 2-y-o 9f winner, is a half-sister

to 5 winners including the very useful 7f and 1m winner Three Graces and the French 12f listed winner Trefula. The second dam, Trefoil (by Kris), a very useful listed winner over 10.5f in France, is a full or half-sister to 12 winners including the smart middle-distance winners Maysoon, Richard of York, Three Tails (dam of the high-class middle-distance colts Sea Wave and Tamure) and Third Watch. *"Just bought at the breeze-up sales, he's not a backward Mount Nelson, he looks very racey and he's out of a Lomitas mare, which we like. He'll be OK"*.

HARRY DUNLOP

495. BAY LAUREL (IRE) ★★★
b.f. *Baltic King – Bayleaf (Efisio)*. April 28. Ninth living foal. 18,500Y. Tattersalls October Book 2. McKeever Bloodstock. Half-sister to the fairly useful 2-y-o 5f and listed 6f winner Bathwick Bear (by Kodiac), to the useful 5f, 6f (at 2 yrs) and 10f winner of 9 races and Group 3 5f Molecomb Stakes third Folio (by Perugino) and the quite useful triple 6f winner (including at 2 yrs) Aroundthebay (by Diktat). The dam, a useful 2-y-o 5f winner, was listed-placed and is a sister to the 2-y-o 5f winner, Group 3 Molecomb Stakes third and subsequent US winner of 3 races at up to 6f Baize (herself dam of the US Grade 1 Del Mar Oaks winner Singhalese). The second dam, Bayonne (by Bay Express), a dual 5f winner at 3 yrs, is a half-sister to 7 winners. (Susan Abbott Racing). *"A filly that comes from a decent family, she's nice, not the most correct but she looks a 2-y-o type and I should imagine she'll be out in mid-summer over six/seven furlongs. There's plenty of speed in the pedigree"*.

496. BURLESQUE STAR ★★★
b.f. *Thousand Words – Es Que (Inchinor)*. April 18. Third foal. 18,000Y. Tattersalls October Book 2. Sackville/Donald. Half-brother to the quite useful 2011 2-y-o 5f winner Es Que Love (by Clodovil) and to the very useful 7f (at 2 yrs) and 10f winner, Group 2 10.5f York Stakes third and subsequent Hong Kong Group 1 third Dominant (by Cacique). The dam, a minor winner at 3 yrs in France, is a half-sister to one winner abroad. The second dam, Bellona (by Bering), a listed 11f winner in France, is a half-sister to 7 winners including the Group 2 Prix de Flore winner In Clover. (The Wigwam

Partnership). *"A filly that's well-bred, she looked a bit weak and backward at the sales so I think we got some value. Thousand Words is a first season sire so he's an unknown, but this filly will make a 2-y-o in mid-summer, she just needs a bit of time to grow into herself first"*. TRAINERS' BARGAIN BUY

497. CRYSTAL MIST ★★
gr.f. *Dalakhani – Snow Crystal (Kingmambo)*. April 15. Third foal. 40,000Y. Tattersalls October Book 1. Not sold. Half-sister to the fair 12f winner Sky Crystal (by Galileo). The dam, a quite useful 2-y-o 7f winner, is a half-sister to 6 winners including the Group 1 Fillies' mile winner Crystal Music and the Group 3 winners Solar Crystal, Dubai Success and State Crystal and to the unraced dam of the US Grade 2 winner Grande Melody. The second dam, Crystal Spray (by Beldale Flutter), a minor Irish 4-y-o 14f winner, is a half-sister to 8 winners including the Group 2 winner Crystal Hearted. (Kieron Drake & Simon Withers). *"We've turned her out at the moment because it's a backward family and she's by a sire that doesn't get early 2-y-o's too often, but what we've seen of her she's done nicely"*.

498. ROZ ★★★
b.f. *Teofilo – Debonnaire (Anabaa)*. April 23. First foal. 16,000Y. Tattersalls October Book 3. Crimbourne Stud. The dam, a fair 7f (at 2 yrs) and 1m winner, is a half-sister to 4 winners including the useful 2-y-o 6f winner and listed placed Proceed With Care and the useful 6f and 7f winner and listed-placed Dramatic Quest. The second dam, Ultra Finesse (by Rahy), a useful French 8.5f and 10f winner, was second in the Group 2 12f Prix de Malleret and is a half-sister to 6 winners including the top-class colt Suave Dancer (winner of the Prix de l'Arc de Triomphe, the Prix du Jockey Club and the Phoenix Champion Stakes) and the dual Group 1 second Suave Tern. (Mrs Mary-Ann Parker). *"I like her, she's done some faster work already and she's a big-bodied filly. Possibly not the biggest, but we should see her out in June over six furlongs"*. Won Kempton and 1f listed fillies Sandown

499. SIR PATRICK MOORE (FR) ★★★
gr.c. *Astronomer Royal – America Nova (Verglas)*. March 18. First foal. €16,000Y. Arqana

Deauville October. MAB Agency. The dam, a French 2-y-o listed 1m winner, is a half-sister to 3 winners including the French listed 13f winner Cat Nova. The second dam, Las Americas (by Linamix), won 5 minor races in France from 3 to 5 yrs and is a half-sister to 2 winners. (A Partnership). *"He's a horse that we bought in France, he's well-bred and I like him. The plan is to have a run here and then send him over to France to race for the breeder's premiums. He goes nicely and I would think six furlongs would be his game, moving up to seven".*

500. TRISARA ★★★

b.f. Exceed And Excel – Hiddendale *(Indian Ridge).* May 23. The dam, a useful 6f winner at 2 yrs, was third in the Group 3 7f Nell Gwyn Stakes and is a half-sister to several winners including the Italian Group 3 second That's The Way. The second dam, That'll Be The Day (by Thatching), won over 5f (at 2 yrs) and 7.5f including an Italian listed event and is a half-sister to numerous winners including the Group 1 Gran Criterium winner Candy Glen and the Group 3 Irish Derby Trial winner Ashley Park. (Mr Paul Roy). *"She's only just come in to us so it's very early days. An athletic filly with a good action, she was a late foal so she'll take a bit of time, but she's a nice model by a very good sire in Exceed And Excel".*

501. VECTIS ★★★

b.c. Pastoral Pursuits – Eishin Eleuthera *(Sadler's Wells).* April 1. Sixth foal. Half-brother to the quite useful 2-y-o dual 7f winner Seven Samurai (by Mark Of Esteem), to the modest 1m winner Courageously (by Aljabr), the Japanese winner Eishin Runrun (by Mayano Top Gun) and a winner in Norway by Dubai Destination. The dam won once at 3 yrs in Japan and is a half-sister to 2 minor winners in the USA. The second dam, Riverbride (by Riverman), won four races in France and was third in the Group 1 Prix Marcel Boussac and is a half-sister to 4 winners. (The Bow Wave Partnership). *"A bonny little colt that looks a 2-y-o, I can imagine him starting over five furlongs and progressing to six. I like him for what he's done at this stage and he should be racing in May or June".*

JOHN DUNLOP

John pointed out to me that ten of his two-year-olds arrived from Dubai in early April and at this stage it's very difficult for him to give a useful description of them. But they're all nice, quality horses and, to date, look very good movers without any obvious problems. They are ADEEM, ALNAWIYAH, ARBAAH, DAIRAM, JALASAAT, KAWAAKIB, RASHFA, SHABEBEEK, SHEBEBI and WASEELH.

502. ADEEM ★★★

b.c. Invasor – Thawakib *(Sadler's Wells).* April 29. Half-brother to the Prix de l'Arc de Triomphe and Juddmonte International winner Sakhee (by Bahri), to the useful 7f (at 2 yrs) and 10f winner Nasheed (by Riverman), the fairly useful 2-y-o 7f winner Alharir (by Zafonic), the quite useful 10.2f winner Weqaar (by Red Ransom), the fair 4-y-o 7f winner Haasem (by Seeking The Gold) and the fair 1m winner Yathreb (by Kingmambo). The dam, a useful filly, won twice over 7f (at 2 yrs) and the Group 2 12f Ribblesdale Stakes. She is a half-sister to numerous winners including the top-class middle-distance colt Celestial Storm (winner of the Group 2 Princess of Wales's Stakes) and to the placed dam of the Group 1 Rothmans International winner River Memories. The second dam, Tobira Celeste (by Ribot), won twice at up to 9f in France and was third in the Group 3 12f Prix de Minerve. (Hamdan Al Maktoum).

503. ALNAWIYAH ★★

b.f. Dalakhani – Mokaraba *(Unfuwain).* April 22. Fourth foal. Sister to the quite useful 2011 1m placed 2-y-o Mubaraza and half-sister to the quite useful 7f (at 2 yrs) and 10f winner Qaraaba (by Shamardal). The dam, a quite useful 12f winner, is a half-sister to the fairly useful triple 10f winner Kaateb. The second dam, Muhaba (Mr Prospector), a fairly useful 2-y-o 1m winner, is a sister to the very useful 2-y-o 6f and 7f winner Sahm and a half-sister to the very useful 6f to 10f winner Bint Salsabil. (Hamdan Al Maktoum).

504. ALPINE MYSTERIES (IRE) ★★★

b.f. Elusive City – Alpine Gold *(Montjeu).* April 17. Half-sister to the fair 7f winner Bobskier (by Big Bad Bob). The dam, a quite useful 2-y-o

1m winner, is closely related to the quite useful 2-y-o 1m winner Ski For Me and a half-sister to 3 winners. The second dam, Ski For Gold (by Shirley Heights), a fair 2-y-o 7f winner, stayed 2m and is a half-sister to the very useful 6f (at 2 yrs) and subsequent Grade 1 10f Santa Barbara Handicap winner Bequest and the useful 2-y-o 7f winner Fitzcarraldo. (Windflower Overseas Holdings Inc). *"Appears to take after the dam and is relatively immature".*

505. ANNINA (IRE) ★★

b.f. Singspiel – Lysandra (Danehill). February 2. Second foal. 16,000Y. Tattersalls October Book 2. J Dunlop. The dam, a quite useful 1m to 10f winner of 4 races, is a half-sister to 5 winners including the Irish 1m winner and Group 2 12f King Edward VII Stakes third Barati. The second dam, Oriane (by Nashwan), won over 1m, was listed-placed in Ireland and is a half-sister to the smart 8.2f winner Killer Instinct and to the very useful 2-y-o 7f winner and Group 1 Hoover Fillies Mile second Pick of the Pops. (The Earl Cadogan). *"Has suffered a minor skeletal injury but is bred to be a second half of season 2-y-o at the earliest".*

506. ARBAAH (USA) ★★★

b.f. Invasor – Alshadiyah (Danzig). May 2. Half-sister to the 2011 2-y-o 7f and 1m winner Farhaan (by Jazil), to the 7f to 9f winner and listed-placed Haatheq (by Seeking The Gold), the 2-y-o dual 6f winner and dual listed-placed Wid (by Elusive Quality) – all 3 useful – and the fair 6f and 7f winner Badweia (by Kingmambo). The dam, a useful 2-y-o 6f winner, is a half-sister to 7 winners including the smart 7f (at 2 yrs) and 10f listed winner Imtiyaz and the very useful Bint Shadayid, winner of the Group 3 7f Prestige Stakes and placed in the 1,000 Guineas and the Fillies Mile. The second dam, Shadayid (by Shadeed), a very smart filly, won the 1,000 Guineas and the Prix Marcel Boussac. (Hamdan Al Maktoum).

507. DAIRAM (USA) ★★★

b.c. Jazil – Tarteel (Bahri). March 12. First foal. The dam was a fairly useful 1m (including at 2 yrs) and 7f winner. The second dam, Elrehaan (by Sadler's Wells), a fairly useful 2-y-o 7f winner, was third in the listed Cheshire Oaks and is a half-sister to 4 winners including the

useful 2-y-o 7f winner Wahsheeq and the US Grade 2 placed Dover Dere. (Hamdan Al Maktoum).

508. GOODWOOD MIRAGE (IRE) ★★★

b.c. Jeremy – Phantom Waters (Pharly). March 22. Eighth foal. 27,000Y. Tattersalls October Book 2. R Frisby. Half-brother to the quite useful 5f winner Diman Waters (by Namid), to the fair 1m winner Tina's Best (by King's Best), the fair 9f and hurdles winner Phantom Lad (by Desert Prince) and the modest dual 1m winner Tina's Ridge (by Indian Ridge). The dam, a quite useful dual 12f winner, is a full or half-sister to 9 winners including the top-class broodmare Shining Water (dam of numerous winners including the high-class Group 1 1m Ciga Grand Criterium winner Tenby and the Group 1 placed Bude and Bright And Clear). The second dam, Idle Waters (by Mill Reef), won the Group 2 Park Hill Stakes. (Goodwood Racehorse Owners Group (Nineteen) Ltd). *"A good-looking colt but not particularly precocious in appearance and another second half of season prospect".* Staged on well to win
Cl 4 nh Nwmkt

509. INVINCIBLE CARA (IRE) ★★★★★

b.f. Invincible Spirit – Cara Fantasy (Sadler's Wells). April 2. Fifth foal. Half-sister to the very smart 2-y-o Group 3 7f Acomb Stakes and Group 3 1m Craven Stakes winner and Group 1 Racing Post Trophy second Elusive Pimpernel (by Elusive Quality), to the smart 1m (at 2 yrs), Group 3 10f Strensall Stakes and listed 9f winner Palavicini (by Giant's Causeway), the fair 10f and 12f winner Miss Topsy Turvy (by Mr Greeley) and the moderate 2011 2-y-o 10f winner Better Be Mine (by Big Bad Bob). The dam, a quite useful dual 12f winner, is closely related to the Group 2 winner Lucky Guest and a half-sister to numerous winners. (Windflower Overseas Holdings Inc). *"A very good looking filly who could prove a very interesting prospect by mid-summer".*

510. JALASA'AT (USA) ★★★

b.f. Lemon Drop Kid – Itnab (Green Desert). March 5. Sixth foal. Half-sister to the useful 7f (at 2 yrs), 10f and subsequent UAE 6f winner and Group 3 6f second Alazeyab (by El Prado) and to the fair 2-y-o 1m winner Istishaara (by Kingmambo). The dam won the Group 3 12f

Princess Royal Stakes and is a sister to the very useful 6f winner of 4 races Haafiz and the useful 7f and 1m winner and Irish 1,000 Guineas third Umniyatee and a half-sister to numerous winners including the Group 1 Epsom Oaks winner Eswarah. The second dam, Midway Lady (by Alleged), won the Prix Marcel Boussac, the 1,000 Guineas and the Oaks and is a half-sister to 5 winners including the very useful 11.8f listed winner Capias. (Hamdan Al Maktoum).

511. KAWAAKIB ★★★
b.f. Nayef – Muthabara (Red Ransom). April 6. First foal. The dam, a very useful listed 7f Star Stakes (at 2 yrs) and Group 3 7f Nell Gwyn Stakes winner, is a half-sister to 3 winners. The second dam, Hureya (by Woodman), a quite useful 3-y-o 1m winner, is a half-sister to several winners including the very smart listed 7f (at 2 yrs) and listed 10f winner Muqbil. (Hamdan Al Maktoum).

512. MOMBASA ★★★
b.c. Dubawi – Limuru (Salse). April 15. Half-brother to the quite useful 10f (at 2 yrs) to 12f winner Shimoni (by Mark Of Esteem), to the fair dual 1m winner Shanzu, the modest 10f and 12f winner Shianda (both by Kyllachy) and the moderate 12f and 13f winner Abulharith (by Medicean). The dam is an unraced sister to the US Grade 1 and Italian Group 1 winner Timboroa. The second dam, Kisumu (by Damister), is an unraced half-sister to 5 winners including the Group 1 winners Efisio and Mountain Bear. (Wis Green Partners). "A big, relatively backward colt but a good mover with an interesting pedigree".

Won on 1m cls mdn Newbury

513. MUTHAFAR ★★
b.c. Tamayuz – Etizaaz (Diesis). April 9. Eighth foal. Half-brother to the smart 6f (including at 2 yrs) and listed 7f winner of 6 races Munaddam (by Aljabr), to the useful 1m (at 2 yrs), 10f and UAE 11f winner Almiqdaad (by Haafhd), the quite useful 1m winner Mashaaref (by Cape Cross), the quite useful 1m to 10f winner of 6 races Munsarim (by Shamardal) and the fair UAE 7f winner Alwaabel (by Green Desert). The dam, a listed 1m winner and second in the Group 1 12f Prix Vermeille, is a half-sister to the listed 6f Sirenia Stakes winner Santolina and the

US Grade 3 7f Lafayette Stakes winner Trafalger. The second dam, Alamosa (by Alydar), is an unraced half-sister to the King George VI and Queen Elizabeth Diamond Stakes winner Swain out of the US Grade 1 winner Love Smitten. (Hamdan Al Maktoum). "An attractive but immature colt and mid-summer at the earliest by current appearances".

514. OLYMPIC JULE ★★★
b.f. Shamardal – Jules (Danehill). April 3. Seventh foal. Half-sister to the useful 6f and 7f winner of 7 races from 2 to 5 yrs Golden Desert (by Desert Prince), to the quite useful dual 7f winner (including at 2 yrs) Romantic Wish (by Hawk Wing), the modest 1m and 12f winner The Blue Dog (by High Chaparral) and a winner in Hungary by Fasliyev. The dam, a fair 3-y-o 7f winner, is a half-sister to 10 winners including the dam of the Australian Group 1 winner Prowl. The second dam, Before Dawn (by Raise A Cup), a champion US 2-y-o filly, won two Grade 1 events and is a half-sister to 6 winners. (Mr M Stewkesbury). "An attractive, good-moving filly. Hopefully she'll be seen on the track by late Spring".

515. OMOOR (IRE) ★★
b.f. Tamayuz – Miracolia (Montjeu). February 16. Second foal. 130,000Y. Tattersalls October Book 1. Shadwell Estate Co. The dam is an unraced sister to 2 winners including the UAE Group 3 winner Stagelight and a half-sister to 7 winners including the smart Group 2 12f Premio Ellington winner Ivan Luis, the listed 1m Masaka Stakes winner and 1,000 Guineas third Hathrah and the French/German listed winners Amathia and Zero Problemo. The second dam, Zivania (by Shernazar), a useful Irish winner of 4 races from 1m to 9.5f, is a half-sister to 7 winners including the Group 3 Prix Gontaut Biron winner Muroto. (Hamdan Al Maktoum). "A backward filly who looks to have taken after her dam rather than the unproven Tamayuz".

516. POLHEM ★★
b.c. Dansili – Mondschein (Rainbow Quest). March 15. Half-brother to the Group 3 9f Prix Chloe winner Beatrice Aurore (by Danehill Dancer) and to the Swedish listed 1m winner Vigelegere (by Be My Chief). The dam, a French listed 12f winner, is a sister to the Group 3 12f

winner Jahafil and a half-sister to numerous winners. The second dam, River Spey (by Mill Reef), a fairly useful 2-y-o 7f winner, stayed 12f and is closely related to the listed Glorious Stakes winner Spinning. (B Andersson). *"A very big colt and I suspect a non-runner until the Autumn".*

517. RASHFA ★★

b.f. Cape Cross – Ayun (Swain). March 3. Fifth foal. Half-sister to the promising 2011 2-y-o 9f winner Aazif (by Nayef), to the very useful Group 2 2m and Group 3 2m winner of 8 races Akmal (by Selkirk), the fair 13f winner Elrasheed (by Red Ransom) and the fair 14f winner Albeed (by Tiger Hill). The dam, a useful 1m and 10f winner, is a half-sister to 4 winners including the smart 7f (at 2 yrs) and Group 3 1m Desmond Stakes winner Haami. The second dam, Oumaldaaya (by Swain), a very useful filly, won over 7f at 2yrs and the Group 2 10f Premio Lydia Tesio and listed 10f Lupe Stakes at 3 yrs. She is a half-sister to 6 winners including the Derby winner Erhaab. (Hamdan Al Maktoum).

518. ROSA BURN ★★★

ch.f. Notnowcato – Les Hurlants (Barathea). April 19. Seventh foal. 10,000Y. Tattersalls October Book 2. R Frisby. Half-sister to the useful 7f and 1m 2-y-o winner and Group 3 1m Prix de Chenes third Happy Crusader (by Cape Cross), to the quite useful 1m (including at 2 yrs) and 9f winner of 4 races Roar Of Applause (by Royal Applause) and the quite useful 9f (at 2 yrs) and 12f winner Spear (by Almutawakel). The dam won once over 12f at 3 yrs in France and is a half-sister to 4 minor winners. The second dam, Howlin' (by Alleged), won once in France and is a half-sister to 4 winners. (R C Tooth). *"A very attractive filly and a good mover, she should be running by the end of June".*

519. SEJALAAT (IRE) ★★★

br.c. Kheleyf – Laqataat (Alhaarth). March 30. Third foal. Half-brother to the fairly useful 2011 2-y-o 5f winner and Group 3 6f third Naseem Sea (by Bahri). The dam, placed once over 7f at 2 yrs, is a half-sister to the very useful 2-y-o 6f winner and Group 2 6f Lowther Stakes second Khulan and to the useful 7f (at 2 yrs) and 1m winner Thajja. The second dam, Jawlaat (by Dayjur), a fairly useful dual

6f winner, is closely related to the July Cup winner Elnadim and a half-sister to the Irish 1,000 Guineas winner Mehthaaf. (Hamdan Al Maktoum). *"A good-looking but very big colt, he's a good mover but unlikely to reach the track before mid-summer".*

520. SHABEBEEK (IRE) ★★

b.c. Shirocco – Tanaghum (Darshaan). February 5. Fifth foal. Half-brother to the fairly useful 1m (at 2 yrs) and 10f winner and listed-placed Zahoo (by Nayef), to the smart Group 3 14f winner Tactic (by Sadler's Wells) and the quite useful 1m to 12f and hurdles winner Taaresh (by Sakhee). The dam, a useful listed-placed 10f winner, is a half-sister to 5 winners including the smart Group 2 10f Premio Lydia Tesio winner Najah. The second dam, Mehthaaf (by Nureyev), won the Irish 1,000 Guineas, the Tripleprint Celebration Mile and the Nell Gwyn Stakes and is closely related to the Diadem Stakes winner Elnadim and to the French 2-y-o 7.5f winner Only Seule (herself dam of the Group 1 7f Prix de la Foret and Group 1 6.5f Prix Maurice de Gheest winner Occupandiste). (Hamdan Al Maktoum).

521. SHEBIBI (USA) ★★★

b.c. Mr Greeley – Tashawak (Night Shift). April 3. Half-brother to the fair 2011 2-y-o 7f winner Afnoon (by Street Cry) and to the quite useful 7f and 1m winner Nadawat (by Kingmambo). The dam, a smart 6f (at 2 yrs) and Group 2 1m Falmouth Stakes winner, is a sister to the fair 6f (at 2 yrs) and 1m winner of 8 races Speedfit Free and a half-sister to the Irish 8.5f (at 2 yrs) and 10f winner and Group 1 1m Criterium International third Acropolis and the smart Group 2 12f Ribblesdale Stakes and Group 2 12.5f Prix de la Royallieu winner Fairy Queen. The second dam, Dedicated Lady (by Pennine Walk), a useful Irish 2-y-o 5f and 6f winner, is a half-sister to 5 winners including the German listed winner and Group 3 10.5f Prix de Flore third Silk Petal (herself dam of the listed Sandy Lane Stakes winner Star Tulip). (Hamdan Al Maktoum).

522. WASEELH (IRE) ★★★

br.f. Kheleyf – Winsa (Riverman). February 7. Ninth foal. Half-sister to the very useful 2-y-o 7f and 7.6f winner and listed-placed Mutahayya (by Peintre Celebre), to the fairly useful 10f winner Elmaleeha (by Galileo), the 2-y-o 5f and 6f winner Qusoor (by Fasliyev), the quite useful 10f winner Madhaaq (by Medicean) and the 12f winner Majhub (by Machiavellian) – all quite useful. The dam, a fair 12f winner, is a sister to the Group 1 1m St James's Palace Stakes and Group 1 1m Queen Elizabeth II Stakes winner Bahri and a half-sister to the high-class 2-y-o Group 2 7f Laurent Perrier Champagne Stakes Bahhare. The second dam, Wasnah (by Nijinsky), a fairly useful maiden, was placed at up to 10.5f and is a half-sister to the Group/Graded stakes winners Dance Bid, Northern Plain and Winglet. (Hamdan Al Maktoum).

DAVID ELSWORTH
523. BENTLEYSOYSTERBOY (IRE) ★★★
b.c. Kheleyf – Morality (Elusive Quality). February 17. Third foal. 27,000Y. Tattersalls October Book 2. D Elsworth. Half-brother to the unplaced 2011 2-y-o Downton Abbey (by Dubai Destination). The dam is an unraced half-sister to 3 winners including the dual listed winner and very useful broodmare Swiss Lake. The second dam, Blue Iris (by Petong), a useful winner of 5 races over 5f and 6f including the Weatherbys Super Sprint and the Redcar Two-Year-Old Trophy, is a half-sister to 10 winners. (Corrigan, Dwyer & Partners). "He's a strong colt from a very fast family and he's shown us that he's a precocious type. So he'll be one of our earlier runners, starting off at five furlongs and he'll go six later on. I think he'll be quick, he's strong and mature and should be a challenge for the trainer who doesn't specialise in that sort of horse!"

524. DASHING STAR ★★★
b.c. Teofilo – Dashiba (Dashing Blade). January 28. Half-brother to the dual Group 2 Lancashire Oaks winner of 7 races Barshiba (by Barathea), to the useful 2-y-o listed 1m winner Doctor Dash, the fair 2-y-o 1m winner Dashing Doc (both by Dr Fong) and the modest dual 10f winner Westhaven (by Alhaarth). The dam, a useful 9f and 10f winner, is a half-sister to several winners including the fairly useful 10f and 12f winner Smart Blade. The second dam, Alsiba (by Northfields), a modest winner of one race at 4 yrs, was a staying half-sister to

several winners and to the dam of the Irish St Leger winner Oscar Schindler. (J C Smith). "A big 2-y-o, we've trained a lot of horses from this family. Probably more of a 3-y-o type, but he was an early foal so he may do something later on this year".

525. EMERGING ★★★
b.c. Mount Nelson – Pan Galactic (Lear Fan). March 25. Tenth living foal. 65,000Y. Tattersalls October Book 2. D Elsworth. Half-brother to the fair 2011 dual 1m fourth placed 2-y-o Engrossing (by Tiger Hill), to the fair 7f winner Panoptic (by Dubawi), the fair 2-y-o 6f winner Pan American (by American Post), the 9f and multiple jumps winner Megaton (by Nashwan) and three winners in France by Polish Precedent, Zafonic and Bering. The dam, a French listed-placed 1m winner, is a sister to the French and US winner of 10 races and stakes-placed Jirhan and a half-sister to 5 winners. The second dam, Scierpan (by Sharpen Up), was placed over 5f and 6f at 2 yrs and is a half-sister to 7 winners including the Group/Grade 3 middle-distance winners Tralos and Polemic. (Mr B.C.M Wong). "A good-moving colt, he'll probably be seen out in the first half of the season. I expect him to get a mile later on, but he's forward enough to start off in mid-summer. A good-looking, athletic colt".

526. FAUSTINATHEYOUNGER ★★
b.f. Antonius Pius – Tochar Ban (Assert). March 29. Thirteenth foal. €8,500Y. Goffs Orby. D Elsworth. Half-sister to the French 2-y-o 1m winner and subsequent US Grade 2 San Clemente Handicap and Grade 2 San Gorgonio Handicap winner Uncharted Haven (by Turtle Island), to the fairly useful 12f, 14f and jumps winner Albany (by Alhaarth), the fairly useful 2-y-o 7f winner Torinmoor (by Intikhab), the quite useful 12f winner Tioman (by Dr Devious), the fair 10f winner Ellbeedee (by Dalakhani), the minor US 3-y-o winner Chocolate Reef (by Wild Again) and the placed dam of the Irish Group 3 winner Ferneley. The dam, a quite useful 10f winner, is a half-sister to 6 winners including the listed Italian winner Isticanna (herself dam of the Group 2 Royal Whip Stakes winner Chancellor). The second dam, Guest Night (by Sir Ivor), a very useful 7f and 9f winner, was third in the Group 3 Fred Darling

Stakes and is a half-sister to 4 winners. *"She's going to need some time but she'll be nice later on. She didn't look much when I got her, but she's done really well. Around September time we'll take a look at her and see what we've got".*

527. FRIENDSHIP IS LOVE ★★

b.f. *Byron – Silver Sail (Daylami).* March 31. Second foal. The dam, a poor 1m placed maiden, is a half-sister to 6 winners including Medici Code, a quite useful 1m and 9f winner here and subsequently a Grade 2 winner in the USA. The second dam, Fivefive (by Fairy King), a modest 5f (at 2 yrs) and 1m winner, is a half-sister to 4 winners including the Group 3 6f July Stakes third The Old Firm. (Mrs T. A Foreman). *"Small and neat, but she looks like she'll make a 2-y-o and it's quite a good family".*

528. HALPERION ★★

ch.c. *Halling – Rainbow End (Botanic).* May 13. Fourth foal. Half-brother to the quite useful 2011 2-y-o 6f winner Norse Gold (by Norse Dancer), to the fair 5f winner Morermaloke (by Bahamian Bounty) and to a minor winner abroad by Dr Fong. The dam, a fairly useful 10f winner, is a half-sister to 2 winners. The second dam, High Finish (by High Line), is an unplaced full or half-sister to 11 winners including Munwar (Group 3 Lingfield Derby Trial). (P. A Deal). *"I bred him along with the National Stud and he's a bonny lad that'll be a ten furlong horse next year. The mare has bred 3 winners from 3 runners and this is a particularly attractive, strong colt that I like. He reminds me of Hyperion because he's not over-big, he's got the same blood and the same colour – so I thought we'd tempt providence and give him a similar name!"*

529. LLAREGYB (IRE) ★★★

b.c. *Dylan Thomas – Tango Tonic (Trans Island).* January 25. Second foal. €45,000Y. Goffs Orby. David Elsworth. The dam is a half-sister to the Group 2 Prix Niel winner Housamix and to the French listed 2-y-o 9f winner and US Grade 1 placed Housa Dancer (herself the dam of the Group winners Bushman and Grand Vent) and the unraced dam of the US Grade 1 winner Alexander Tango. The second dam, Housatonic (by Riverman), won over 7f and is a half-sister to 7 winners including the US Grade 2 winner

Globe. (D Elsworth). *"A connoisseur's type of horse, he'll be a back-end 2-y-o and is more of a 3-y-o type. A quality horse, I like him, he's a strong boy and as most good 3-y-o's run with promise as a 2-y-o, I expect he'll do the same".*

530. SENATOR BONG ★★★★

ch.c. *Dutch Art – Sunley Gift (Cadeaux Genereux).* March 6. Second foal. 40,000Y. Tattersalls October Book 2. D Elsworth. Half-brother to the modest 2011 6f and 7f placed 2-y-o Sunley Valentine (by Kyllachy). The dam, a fair 2-y-o 5f winner, is a half-sister to 4 winners. The second dam, Thracian (by Green Desert), a fairly useful 2-y-o 6f and 7f winner, is a half-sister to 12 winners including the Group 2 12f Ribblesdale Stakes winner Third Watch, the Group 3 Prix Foy winner Richard of York, the Group 2 Premio Dormello winner Three Tails (herself the dam three Group winners), the Group 3 Fred Darling Stakes winner Maysoon and the dams of the Group winners Lend A Hand and Talented. (J Dwyer). *"A bonny little colt that shouldn't take long before he's ready. He was an immature yearling but I anticipated he'd improve and thought I'd get him cheap. However, I didn't get him cheap at all! Having said that, no 2-y-o I've got has done better, physically, than he has. Dutch Art is a prolific sire of 2-y-o winners and this is a damn nice horse. He'll start off at five or six furlongs".* Won LS St mdr Notts 15 runners

531. SNOQUALMIE CHIEF ★★★★

b.c. *Montjeu – Seattle Ribbon (Seattle Dancer).* April 5. Brother to the smart listed 10f winner and Group 2 Dante Stakes third Snoqualmie Boy and to the very useful listed 1m (at 2 yrs) and listed 10f winner Snoqualmie Girl, closely related to the fairly useful 2-y-o 7f winner Seattle Drive (by Motivator) and to the quite useful 1m and 10f winner Snoqualmie Star (by Galileo) and half-brother to the quite useful 2-y-o 6f winner Robocop, the modest 9f and 10f winner Seattle Robber, the fair 10f winner Seattle Storm (all by Robellino) and the fair 7f and 10f winner Seattle Express (by Salse). The dam, placed over 9f and 10f at 3 yrs, is a sister to the 2-y-o Group 1 1m winner Seattle Dancer. The second dam, Golden Rhyme (by Dom Racine), was a quite useful 3-y-o 7f winner. (J C Smith). *"One of the more exciting horses we have, his sister and brother were both good winners and this is a strikingly attractive colt".*

532. SORCELLERIE ★★★

ch.f. Sir Percy – Souvenance (Hernando). February 12. Second foal. 15,000Y. Tattersalls October Book 2. Not sold. Half-sister to Nice Rose (by Teofilo), placed fourth over 12f on her debut at 3 yrs in 2012. The dam, a fairly useful 2-y-o 7.2f winner, subsequently won a listed event in Germany, was third in the Group 1 Italian Oaks and is a sister to the 2-y-o Group 3 1m Prix des Reservoirs winner Songerie and a half-sister to 4 winners including the useful listed winners Soft Morning and Sourire. The second dam, Summer Night (by Nashwan), a fairly useful 3-y-o 6f winner, is a half-sister to 7 winners including the Group 3 Prix d'Arenburg winner Starlit Sands. (Miss K Rausing). *"Bred by the owner, this is a 2-y-o type and a nice filly. She looks quite precocious".*

533. UNNAMED ★★★★

b.f. Royal Applause – Dodo (Alzao). January 16. Ninth foal. 50,000Y. Tattersalls October Book 2. D Elsworth. Half-sister to the moderate 2011 6f placed maiden Empressive (by Holy Roman Emperor), to the very smart 6f (at 2 yrs) and 7f winner and Group 3 7f Hungerford Stakes second Tarjman (by Cadeaux Genereux), the smart 2-y-o 6f and 3-y-o listed 6f winner Nota Bene (by Zafonic) and the fairly useful 1m winner of 3 races Porthcawl (by Singspiel). The dam, a fairly useful 3-y-o 6f winner, is a half-sister to 8 winners including the very useful 2-y-o 5f and 6f winner and Cornwallis Stakes second Deadly Nightshade. The second dam, Dead Certain (by Absalom), a very smart winner of the Group 1 6f Cheveley Park Stakes and the Group 2 6.5f Prix Maurice de Gheest, is a half-sister to 7 winners and to the placed dam of the Group 2 Gimcrack Stakes winner Bannister. (Usk Valley Stud 1). *"A filly from a family we're very familiar with, she has a precocious pedigree and should make a 2-y-o, starting off at five furlongs. She's doing well and providing we continue to get encouraging signals from her we'll get on with her, because she could be a Royal Ascot 2-y-o. I thought she was well-bought".*

534. UNNAMED ★★

b.f. New Approach – Gower Song (Singspiel). March 26. First foal. 23,000Y. Tattersalls December. R Frisby. The dam, a very useful listed 10f winner here, subsequently won a Group 3 12f event in Dubai and is a half-sister to 7 winners including the dam of the listed winner and Oaks second Something Exciting. The second dam, Gleaming Water (by Kalaglow), a quite useful 2-y-o 6f winner, is a sister to the Group 3 Solario Stakes winner Shining Water (herself dam of the Group 1 Grand Criterium winner Tenby) and a half-sister to 8 winners. (G.B. Partnership). *"Not very big, she's going to take a bit of time. She was immature when we bought her, she's progressed well but having said that I still feel we won't see her until the back-end of the season".*

535. UNNAMED ★★★

b.c. Bernstein – Hangin Withmy Buds (Roar). April 14. Second foal. 68,000Y. Tattersalls October Book 2. Peter & Ross Doyle. The dam won once at 3 yrs in the USA and is a half-sister to 4 winners including the US listed stakes winner Just You Too. The second dam, Marsh Grass (by Slewpy), is a placed half-sister to the US Grade 1 Acorn Stakes winner of 10 races Cat's Cradle. (Jiang Xi Friends Ltd). *"I like him, he's the first one I've had by the sire and I think he'll make a 2-y-o. I haven't got to grips with him yet but he's progressing well physically".*

536. UNNAMED ★★★★

b.c. Kheleyf – Kissing Time (Lugana Beach). February 2. Sixth foal. £70,000Y. Doncaster Premier. David Elsworth. Half-brother to the quite useful 2011 2-y-o 6f winner Waseem Faris (by Exceed And Excel), to the fair 5f winner of 4 races Baby Queen (by Royal Applause) and the moderate 2-y-o 7f winner Fun Time (by Fraam). The dam, a quite useful 5f winner of 5 races (including at 2 yrs), is a sister to a winner in Germany and a half-sister to 4 winners including the Group 2 6f Diadem Stakes winner and good sire Acclamation and the fairly useful 6f and 7f winner Waypoint (herself dam of the Group 2 Prix Robert Papin winner Never A Doubt). The second dam, Princess Athena (by Ahonoora), a very smart winner of the Group 3 5f Queen Mary Stakes and placed in numerous Group events over sprint distances, is a half-sister to 4 winners. (Lordship Stud 1). *"I have two by the same sire and this is an even better model than the other one. It's a very fast family – one that we know really well and he's a powerfully-built colt that looks the business. You wouldn't find a more attractive 2-y-o anywhere, he has a good attitude and I'd like to think that he'd be running in the first part of the season. We have dreams of getting him to Royal Ascot but we'll have to wait and see".*

537. UNNAMED ★★★★
b.f. Kyllachy – Poldhu (Cape Cross). March 7. First foal. 30,000Y. Tattersalls December. Mark Crossman. The dam is an unraced half-sister to the Group 1 Falmouth Stakes winner Rajeem. The second dam, Magic Sister (by Cadeaux Genereux), a modest 3-y-o 7f placed maiden, is a sister to the very smart 2-y-o Group 1 6f Prix Morny and Group 3 5f Molecomb Stakes winner Hoh Magic and a half-sister to 5 winners. (K A Dasmal). *"From a good family, she has a wonderful temperament, she's kind and only wants to please. I'm looking forward to getting on with her, she's an exciting prospect".*

RICHARD FAHEY
538. AUTUMN SHADOW ★★★
gr.f. Dark Angel – Fall Habit (Hamas). April 24. Fourth foal. €25,000Y. Goffs February. Norman Steel. Half-sister to the French 2-y-o winner Breaking Ice (by Whipper) and to a winner in Japan by Lear Fan. The dam, a listed winner of 3 races at 3 and 4 yrs in Italy, was second the Group 3 10f Prix de Psyche and is a half-sister to 7 winners. The second dam, Hard Bob (by Hard Fought), won 7 races at 3 and 4 yrs in Italy and is a half-sister to 3 winners. (Norman Steel). *"She's a nice, sharp filly and she'll be an early type. One for five/six furlongs and I like her".*

539. AVEC ROSE ★★★
b.f. Tagula – Rose Siog (Bahamian Bounty). March 3. First foal. The dam, a fair 2-y-o dual 5f winner, is a sister to 2 winners including the fairly useful listed-placed sprinter Treasure Cay. The second dam, Madame Sisu (by Emarati), is an unplaced half-sister to 2 winners. (Mike Sweeney). *"The first foal out of mare that won for us, she looks sharp and I can see her being ready when the six furlong races start".*

540. BAYAN KASIRGA ★★★
b.f. Aussie Rules – Gwyllion (Red Ransom). April 14. Second foal. £10,000Y. Doncaster Premier. Robin O'Ryan. The dam, placed fourth once over 7f at 2 yrs, is a half-sister to 3 winners including the Group 3 Nell Gwyn Stakes winner Barefoot Lady. The second dam, Lady Angharad (by Tenby), a winner of 5 races from 6f to 10f including the 2-y-o listed Woodcote Stakes, is a half-sister to 5 minor winners here and in Italy. (Steve Humphreys). *"A six/seven furlong 2-y-o, she's doing everything right".*

541. CASH IS KING ★★★
b.c. Bahamian Bounty – Age Of Chivalry (Invincible Spirit). February 25. First foal. 80,000Y. Tattersalls October Book 2. Robin O'Ryan. The dam won twice over 5f (at 2 yrs) and the Group 3 6f Ballyogan Stakes and is a half-sister to Sebastian Flyte (a winner here and in the USA where he was Grade 1 placed). The second dam, Aravonian (by Night Shift), won once over 1m at 3 yrs. (Penman Bond Partnership). *"A nice, scopey horse, we like him and he'll want six furlongs to begin with and he'll get seven. A grand-moving horse".*

542. CIELO ROJO ★★★
b.c. Red Clubs – Roses From Ridey (Petorius). May 12. Ninth foal. 19,000Y. Tattersalls October Book 2. Robin O'Ryan. Half-brother to the useful 2-y-o Group 2 6f July Stakes second Armigerent, subsequently a winner abroad, (by In The Wings), to the fair 2-y-o 7f winner Sultans Way (by Indian Ridge) and a winner abroad by Invincible Spirit. The dam ran twice unplaced at 2 yrs and is a half-sister to 6 winners including the German and Italian Group 1 winner Kutub and 2 listed winners in Ireland. The second dam, Minnie Habit (by Habitat), an Irish 4-y-o 9f winner, is closely related to the dual Group 3 sprint winner Bermuda Classic (herself dam of the Coronation Stakes winner Shake The Yoke and the Phoenix Sprint Stakes winner Tropical). (Skybet). *"He'll be ready to run by mid-season. A nice, rangy horse and we like him".*

543. DIGGORY DELVET ★★★
b.c. Pastoral Pursuits – Digger Girl (Black Minnaloushe). January 30. Fourth foal. £15,000Y. Doncaster Premier. David Barker. Half-brother to the fair 2011 triple 5f placed

Excavator (by Bahamian Bounty). The dam ran once unplaced and is a half-sister to 5 winners including the listed 14f winner and Group 3 second Art Eyes. The second dam, Careyes (by Sadler's Wells), is an unraced half-sister to 2 minor winners. (David Barker). *"A good, hardy horse, he'll be an early type".*

Won 5f mdn beverley or debut

544. DUSKY QUEEN ★★★   poor card
b.f. *Shamardal – Sanna Bay (Refuse To Bend)*. February 15. First foal. €90,000Y. Goffs Orby. Robin O'Ryan. The dam is an unraced half-sister to 2 winners including Albabilia (Group 3 Sweet Solera Stakes). The second dam, Sonachan (by Darshaan), a minor Irish 14f winner, is a half-sister to the listed 1m Brownstown Stud Stakes and US stakes winner Inchacooley. (Norman Steel). *"A nice filly for when the seven furlong races come along and she's a good mover".*

545. FLIGHTY CLARETS ★★★
ch.f. *Bahamian Bounty – Flying Clarets (Titus Livius)*. January 29. First foal. The dam, a useful 1m (at 2 yrs) to 11f winner, was third in the Group 3 Middleton Stakes, is a half-sister to 4 winners including the fairly useful listed-placed Borders Belle. The second dam, Sheryl Lynn (by Miller's Mate), won 2 races at 3 and 4 yrs in Germany and is a half-sister to 3 winners. (The Matthewman). *"A six furlong type 2-y-o, she seems sharp and she knows her job".*

546. FLYMAN ★★★★ ♠
b.c. *Pastoral Pursuits – Satin Bell (Midyan)*. March 3. Eleventh foal. 40,000Y. Tattersalls October Book 2. Robin O'Ryan. Half-brother to the very useful 6f (at 2 yrs), 9f and subsequent Hong Kong winner Zabaglione (by Zilzal), to the fairly useful 5f to 7f winner Lutine Bell (by Starcraft), the quite useful 5f and 6f winner of 6 races (including at 2 yrs) Sugar Beet (by Beat Hollow), the quite useful 1m and 9f winner Strawberry Leaf (by Unfuwain), the fair 12f winner Snake's Head (by Golden Snake) and a minor winner abroad by Mtoto. The dam, a useful 7f winner, is a half-sister to 4 winners including the useful listed 6f winner Star Tulip and the dam of the dual Group 3 winner Scarlet Runner. The second dam, Silk Petal (by Petorius), a useful German listed 1m winner and third in the Group 3 10.5f Prix de Flore, is a half-sister to 5 winners including the

dam of the Group 2 winners Fairy Queen and Tashawak. (George Murray). *"A grand, scopey horse, he'll be nice in the second half of the season and I'd definitely give him a mention".*

547. GINGER GOOSE ★★★
b.c. *Royal Applause – Eclaircie (Thunder Gulch)*. March 10. Second foal. 37,000Y. Tattersalls December. Robin O'Ryan. The dam, a minor French 3-y-o 10f winner, is a half-sister to 5 winners including the 2-y-o Group 1 Racing Post Trophy third Skanky Biscuit. The second dam, Blushing Gleam (by Caerleon), won the Group 3 Prix du Calvados and the listed Prix de Saint-Cyr and is a half-sister to 8 winners including Gold Away (four Group wins in France) and the Group 3 winner Danzigaway (herself dam of the US Grade 2 winner Silent Name). (City Vaults). *"A six furlong type 2-y-o, he knows his job alright".*

548. GREY STREET ★★★
gr.f. *Royal Applause – Good Enough (Mukaddamah)*. February 25. Seventh foal. 10,000Y. Tattersalls October Book 2. George Robert Hunnam. Half-sister to the useful 7f (at 2 yrs) and listed 6f winner of 6 races Oasis Dancer (by Oasis Dream), to the very useful 1m winner of 4 races and subsequent Scandinavian listed winner Smart Enough (by Cadeaux Genereux), the fair 2-y-o 1m winner Bright Enough (by Fantastic Light) and the Japanese winner of 11 races Night School (by Machiavellian). The dam won once at 3 yrs in the USA and was third in the Group 1 Prix Saint-Alary and is a half-sister to 5 winners including the Group 3 Molecomb Stakes winner Classic Ruler. The second dam, Viceroy Princess (by Godswalk), a modest 2-y-o 7f seller winner, is a half-sister to 7 winners. (George Hunnam). *"She came to us late, but she's catching up and doing well".*

549. INGLEBY ROYALE ★★★
b.f. *Royal Applause – Lay A Whisper (Night Shift)*. March 13. Fourth foal. 800Y. Tattersalls October Book 3. R Fahey. The dam, a modest 3-y-o 1m placed maiden, is a sister to a listed-placed winner and a half-sister to 5 winners including the Group 3 7f winner Express Wish, the useful listed 7f winner Desert Alchemy and the listed 7f winner Madid. The second dam, Waffle On (by Chief Singer), a quite useful

BRILLIANTLY BRED GROUP WINNING SON OF DANZIG

"One of the best yearlings I have ever seen. He should appeal to breeders being a strong sort by Danzig from an illustrious female line."

-Marcus Tregoning

1st January Special Live Foal terms
Limited Books

Asunción
Pineyrúa

HAWATHEEQ   First foals in 2012

Breeders' Delight

CHEVELEY PARK STUD STALLIONS

DUTCH ART

Europe's Leading First Crop Sire in 2011, *(earnings)* with **33** individual 2yo winners *(57% winners to runners)*, including dual **Gr.2** winner **CASPAR NETSCHER** and **Gr.1** placed **MISS WORK OF ART**.

PIVOTAL

One of the world's leading sires. Sire of **20** individual **Gr.1** winners and **100** individual Stakes winners. Sire of two **Gr.1** winners in 2011, *viz* **IMMORTAL VERSE** (x2) and **AMANEE**.

KYLLACHY

Sire of over **114** individual winners in 2011, including **Gr.2** winner **SOLE POWER**. His **24** individual 2yo winners included **Gr.2** winner **DRAGON PULSE**.

VIRTUAL

Gr.1 winning miler by **PIVOTAL**. Three parts brother to **ICEMAN** *(sire of Gr.2 winning 2yo FREDERICK ENGELS in 2011)*. First crop are yearlings in 2012.

MEDICEAN

Sire of seven **Gr.1** winners to date, including **DUTCH ART** and **CAPPONI** (in 2012). Sire of **20** individual Stakes horses in 2011, including **Gr.2** winner **MANIEREE**.

Cheveley Park Stud

Duchess Drive, Newmarket, Suffolk CB8 9DD
Tel: (01638) 730316 Fax: (01638) 730868
enquiries@cheveleypark.co.uk
www.cheveleypark.co.uk

GET THE HOTTEST
INFORMATION THIS
FLAT SEASON

JOIN RACING POST MEMBERS' CLUB
RACING POST.com/membersclub

3-y-o 6f winner here, subsequently won in France and was listed-placed and is a half-sister to 5 winners including the Group 3 Premio Omenoni winner Leap For Joy. *"A scopey filly that's done well. She won't be a star but she was very cheap, she'll definitely win and she was well-bought by me!"* TRAINERS' BARGAIN BUY

550. LEXINGTON PLACE ★★★
ch.c. Compton Place – Elidore (Danetime). March 30. Second foal. £25,000Y. Doncaster Premier. Middleham Park. Half-brother to the fairly useful 2011 2-y-o 6f winner Rex Imperator (by Royal Applause). The dam, a fairly useful 6f and 7f winner at 2 yrs, also won twice over 1m at 4 yrs and is a half-sister to 5 winners including the listed 6f winner Bright Edge. The second dam, Beveled Edge (by Beveled), won once at 4 yrs and is a half-sister to 2 winners. (Middleham Park Racing). *"We've been lucky with the sire and this colt looks a tough sort. One for six furlongs".*

551. LOCH MOY ★★★★
b.c. Kyllachy – Dixielake (Lake Coniston). February 3. Eighth foal. 36,000foal. Tattersalls December. BBA (Ire). Half-brother to the useful Irish 10f winner and Group 2 10f Royal Whip Stakes second Dixie Music (by Montjeu), to the useful 5f and 6f winner Chief Crazy Horse (by Dansili), the quite useful 7f and 1m winner Provost (by Danehill Dancer), the quite useful Irish 12f winner Rossvoss (by Medicean) and the fair 6f winner Dixieanna (by Night Shift). The dam, a quite useful 3-y-o 1m winner, is a half-sister to 6 winners including the listed Masaka Stakes winner Lady Fairfax. The second dam, Rathvindon (by Realm), a fairly useful 5f winner, was third in the Group 3 Mulcahy Stakes and is a half-sister to 4 winners including the dam of the Group 1 Middle Park Stakes winner Balla Cove. (Innercircle). *"A nice, big colt, he'll be a six/seven furlong 2-y-o so he'll take a bit of time but he's quite nice".*

552. MANCHESTAR ★★★
b.c. Elusive City – Grande Terre (Grand Lodge). February 9. Third foal. £31,000Y. Doncaster Festival. Robin O'Ryan. Half-brother to the quite useful 6f (at 2 yrs) and 7f winner The Mellor Fella (by Compton Place) and to the quite useful 2-y-o 6f winner Rock 'N' Royal (by

Royal Applause). The dam, a the modest 7f and 1m winner, is a half-sister to 5 winners including the smart triple 7f winner (at 2 yrs) and Irish 1,000 Guineas third Soul City (by Elusive City) and the French listed 1m winner Sentinelese. The second dam, Savage (by Polish Patriot), won 2 races at 2 and 3 yrs in Germany, was Group 2 placed over 6f at 2 yrs and is a half-sister to 2 other winners abroad. (Jan Calder). *"He's quite a nice horse but he won't be out until late summer at the earliest".*

553. MARY'S DAUGHTER ★★★
b.f. Royal Applause – Aunty Mary (Common Grounds). March 7. Sixth foal. 40,000Y. Tattersalls October Book 2. Robin O'Ryan. Sister to the 5f (at 2 yrs), 7f and hurdles winner King's Bastion and half-sister to the 7f winner Ertikaan (by Oasis Dream) and the 7f and 1m winner Pride Of Kings (by King's Best) – all quite useful. The dam, a quite useful 2-y-o 5f winner, is a half-sister to 4 winners including the 1,000 Guineas, Irish 1,000 Guineas, Coronation Stakes, Matron Stakes and Sun Chariot Stakes winner Attraction. The second dam, Flirtation (by Pursuit Of Love), ran unplaced once over 7f at 3 yrs and is a half-sister to 4 winners including the French listed 12f winner and Group 2 placed Carmita. (John Cotton). *"A sharp filly, she should make a nice 2-y-o".*

Emily won 5f Leicester mdn on 2nd start
554. MIRLO BLANCO ★★★★ ♠
gr.c. Dark Angel – Danzolin (Danzero). February 15. Third foal. 30,000Y. Tattersalls October Book 2. Robin O'Ryan. The dam, a moderate 1m placed maiden, is a half-sister to 5 minor winners. The second dam, Howlin' (by Alleged), won once in France and is a half-sister to 4 winners. (Frank Lenny). *"A lovely horse and a good mover, he'll make a 2-y-o over six and seven furlongs".*

555. MONKEY BAR FLIES ★★★
b.c. Elusive City – Angel Nights (Night Shift). February 8. Second foal. £22,000Y. Doncaster Premier. Robin O'Ryan. The dam is an unraced half-sister to 3 winners including Sacred Nuts, a winner of two stakes events in Hong Kong. The second dam, Sagrada (by Primo Dominie), a minor German 3-y-o winner, is a full or half-sister to 10 winners including two listed winners in Germany. (Penman Bond Partnership). *"A*

grand, hardy horse and a five/six furlong type 2-y-o. We like him".

556. MYSTERY BET ★★★★ ♠

b.f. Kheleyf – Dancing Prize (Sadler's Wells). February 11. Thirteenth foal. €36,000foal. Goffs. Norman Steel. Half-sister to the very useful 6f (at 2 yrs) to 10f winner and Group 3 placed Firebet (by Dubai Destination), to the useful 10f winner Dancing Phantom (by Darshaan), the UAE winner and Group 3 placed Seeking The Prize (by Zafonic), the Italian winner of 16 races and listed-placed Special War (by Warning), the quite useful Irish 1m (at 2 yrs) and 7f winner Sassy Gal (by King's Best), the quite useful dual 7f (at 2 yrs) and hurdles winner Dance In Tune (by Mujtahid), the fair 9f and hurdles winner Marsam (by Daylami) and the French winner at 2 and 3 yrs Dilshaan's Pride (by Dilshaan). The dam, a useful maiden, was third in the listed Lingfield Oaks Trial and is a sister to the Group 1 Fillies Mile second Dance To The Top and a half-sister to 7 winners. The second dam, Aim For The Top (by Irish River), a very useful winner of 4 races including the Group 3 7f Premio Chiusura and two listed events, is a half-sister to 6 winners including the Gimcrack Stakes winner Splendent. (Norman Steel). *"She'll be a nice filly over six and seven furlongs this year. A good mover, we like her and she's done everything asked of her. Worth mentioning in the book".* W.. g.l c.l3 7f m.r Y..r..
s.p.l

557. ORIENTAL ROMANCE ★★★

b.f. Elusive City – My Funny Valentine (Mukaddamah). February 21. Ninth foal. €50,000Y. Goffs Orby. Robin O'Ryan. Sister to the fairly useful 2-y-o dual 6f winner Murbeh and half-sister to the Irish 2-y-o 1m winner Lyle Lady (by Traditionally) and 3 minor winners in Italy by Nashwan, Mark Of Esteem and Singspiel. The dam, a winner of 7 races at 2 to 4 yrs in Italy including two listed events, is a half-sister to 3 minor winners. The second dam, Imperfect Timing (by Coquelin), is an unraced half-sister to 6 winners. (Norman Steel). *"A very sound filly and a good mover, she'll be a six furlong 2-y-o".*

558. ORION'S HERO ★★★

b.c. Oasis Dream – La Reine Mambo (High Yield). April 3. Third foal. €120,000Y. Goffs Orby.

Robin O'Ryan. Half-brother to the quite useful 2-y-o 6f and 7f winner Pearl Arch (by Arch). The dam, a listed-placed winner of 2 races over 1m at 2 and 3 yrs in France, is a half-sister to triple Group/Grade 3 winner and US Grade 1 third Danzon. The second dam, Zappeuse (by Kingmambo), won once over 12f in France. (Norman Steel). *"A 2-y-o for the second half of the season, probably over seven furlongs".*

559. POLSKI MAX ★★★

b.c. Kyllachy – Quadrophenia (College Chapel). March 7. Third foal. £22,000Y. Doncaster Premier. Not sold. Half-brother to the unplaced 2011 2-y-o Gone By Sunrise (by Three Valleys). The dam, a modest 2-y-o 5f winner, is a half-sister to 3 winners. The second dam, Truly Madly Deeply (by Most Welcome), is an unplaced half-sister to 10 winners including the very smart Group 2 5f Flying Childers Stakes and Weatherbys Super Sprint winner Superstar Leo. (Market Avenue Racing). *"A sharp, early 2-y-o, we hope he'll be winning before your book comes out. He's quite a nice horse".*

560. RIGHT TOUCH ★★★

b.c. Royal Applause – Amira (Efisio). March 16. Fourth foal. 46,000Y. Tattersalls October Book 2. Robin O'Ryan. Half-brother to the fair 2011 2-y-o 1m winner Forgive (by Pivotal) and to the quite useful 2-y-o 5f and 6f winner Loki's Revenge (by Kyllachy). The dam, a modest 5f winner, is a half-sister to 5 winners including the Group 2 6f Diadem Stakes winner of 6 races and good sire Acclamation and the fairly useful 6f and 7f winner Waypoint (herself dam of the Group 2 Prix Robert Papin winner Never A Doubt). The second dam, Princess Athena (Ahonoora), a very smart winner of the Group 3 5f Queen Mary Stakes and placed in numerous Group events over sprint distances, is a half-sister to 4 winners. (Wrigley and Hart). *"A really bonny, nice horse that'll be running when the six furlong races start".*

561. SANDSEND ★★★

b.c. Elusive City – Free Lance (Grand Lodge). March 12. Third foal. 26,000Y. Tattersalls October Book 2. Robin O'Ryan. Brother to the 2011 6f placed 2-y-o maiden Poole Harbour and to the Irish 2-y-o 5f winner Machaputo – both very lightly raced. The dam is an unplaced half-sister to 4 winners including the Irish listed winner Flash McGahon. The second dam, Astuti (by Waajib), a quite useful 2-y-o 6f winner, is a half-sister to 6 winners including the Group 2 Kings Stand Stakes and Group 3 5f King George V Stakes winner The Tatling and the fairly useful 5.2f listed and 6f Tattersalls Breeders Stakes winner Amazing Dream. (Rhodes/Timmins). *"He'll be running over five and six furlongs and it won't be long before he's out. A good, hardy, sound horse".*

562. SLIPSTREAM ANGEL ★★★
gr.f. Dark Angel – Ornellaia (Mujadil). April 22. Third foal. 28,000Y. Tattersalls October Book 2. Robin O'Ryan. Sister to the modest 2011 6f and 7f placed 2-y-o Hi There and half-sister to the fair 2-y-o 5f winner Super Tuscan (by Fath). The dam, placed fourth once over 6f at 2 yrs, is a half-sister to 4 winners including the useful 2-y-o 6f and listed 1m winner Henri Lebasque. The second dam, Almost A Lady (by Entitled), was placed over 7f and 1m at 2 yrs in Ireland and is a half-sister to 5 winners including Insatiable (Group 2 Prix Dollar and Group 3 Brigadier Gerard Stakes). (Darras). *"A six furlong type 2-y-o with a great temperament".*

563. TANGHAN ★★★
b.c. Invincible Spirit – Rose De France (Diktat). February 10. First foal. €50,000Y. Goffs Orby. Robin O'Ryan. The dam was placed at 3 yrs in France and is a half-sister to 4 winners including the smart Group 3 1m Prix de Fontainebleau winner Bowman and the dam of the Group 1 winners Kirklees (Gran Criterium) and Mastery (St Leger). The second dam, Cherokee Rose (by Dancing Brave), a high-class winner of 5 races from 6f to 7f including the Group 1 6f Haydock Park Sprint Cup and the Group 1 Prix Maurice de Gheest, is a half-sister to 4 winners. (Norman Steel). *"He'll probably be out before the end of May over six furlongs".*

564. UNSINKABLE ★★★
gr.c. Verglas – Heart's Desire (Royal Applause). March 26. Fifth foal. €75,000Y. Goffs Orby. Robin O'Ryan. Half-brother to the modest 2011 2-y-o 7f winner Hearts And Minds (by Clodovil), to the Irish 2-y-o listed 6f winner Heart Of Fire (by Mujadil) and the fairly useful Irish 1m (at 2 yrs) and 14f winner Knight Eagle (by Night Shift).

The dam, a fair 7f and 1m placed maiden, is a half-sister to 5 winners including the French listed winner and Group 3 placed Bashful. The second dam, Touch And Love (by Green Desert), a 2-y-o winner in France, was second in the Group 2 Prix du Gros-Chene and is a half-sister to 8 winners. (Penman Bond Partnership). *"One for seven furlongs and a mile towards the back-end of the season, but he's shaping alright and he's quite a nice horse".*

565. WOODLAND MILL (IRE) ★★★
br.f. Pastoral Pursuits – Why Now (Dansili). March 25. Fourth foal. £20,000Y. Doncaster Premier. Bobby O'Ryan. Sister to the quite useful triple 5f winner (including at 2 yrs) Here Now And Why and half-sister to the quite useful 2-y-o 6f winner What About You (by Statue Of Liberty). The dam, a fair 5f and 6f winner, is a half-sister to 4 winners including the fairly useful 10.8f and jumps winner In Question. The second dam, Questionable (by Rainbow Quest), is an unraced sister to the Group 3 15f Prix Berteux winner Ecologist and a half-sister to 7 winners including the St James's Palace Stakes second Greensmith, the Group 3 winners Infrasonic and Green Reef and the dam of the St Leger winner Toulon. (Peter Timmins). *"A winner already, she took the race well and we're very pleased with her. She's grand and has quite a quick pedigree so she's probably a five/six furlong 2-y-o".*

566. WYLDFIRE ★★★★ ♠
ch.c. Raven's Pass – Miss Sally (Danetime). March 28. Third foal. €90,000 foal. Goffs. Norman Steel. Half-brother to the useful dual 1m winner Masteroftherolls (by Refuse To Bend). The dam, winner of the Group 3 7f Brownstown Stakes and the Group 3 7.5f Concorde Stakes, is a half-sister to 3 winners. The second dam, Evictress (by Sharp Victor), was placed three times from 6f (at 2 yrs) to 1m in Ireland and is a half-sister to 7 minor winners. (Norman Steel). *"A very nice horse for when the seven furlong races start, we really like him, he's a grand, lovely horse".*

567. UNNAMED ★★★★
b.c. Majestic Missile – Gala Style (Elnadim). April 9. Fifth foal. 55,000Y. Tattersalls October Book 2. Robin O'Ryan. Brother to the very

useful 5f, 6f and listed 7f winner from 2 to 4 yrs Majestic Myles. The dam is an unraced half-sister to 2 minor winners. The second dam, Style N' Elegance (by Alysheba), is a placed half-sister to 11 winners including the Group 2 Premio Legnano winner Easy To Copy (herself the dam of 3 stakes winners) and the Irish 1,000 Guineas winner Trusted Partner (dam of the high-class filly Dress To Thrill). The second dam, Talking Picture (by Speak John), a champion American 2-y-o filly, won at up to 7f. (James Gaffney). *"A full-brother to a very smart 4-y-o of ours called Majestic Myles, he's similar to him and we like him a lot. They're both nice horses and this 2-y-o is a lovely horse to look at".*

568. UNNAMED ★★★

b.f. Duke Of Marmalade – Peaceful Kingdom (King Of Kings). February 4. Second foal. 40,000Y. Tattersalls October Book 1. Middleham Park Racing. Half-sister to the quite useful Irish 2-y-o 1m winner Righteous Man (by Mr Greeley). The dam is an unraced half-sister to 4 winners including the US Grade 1 Man O'War Stakes winner Magistretti. The second dam, Ms Strike Zone (by Deputy Minister), won once in the USA and is a half-sister to 6 other minor winners. (Middleham Park Racing). *"A good mover, she'll be a seven furlong or mile 2-y-o, as the pedigree would suggest. I'd say she's quite nice but she just needs a bit of time".*

JAMES GIVEN

569. AMANDA WOLF (IRE) ★★★

b.f. Amadeus Wolf – Alexander Phantom (Soviet Star). April 14. Fourth foal. 33,000Y. Tattersalls October Book 2. Anthony Stroud. Half-sister to Lone Foot Laddie (by Red Clubs), placed fourth once over 1m from 2 starts at 2 yrs in 2011, to the fairly useful 2-y-o dual 6f winner Alaskan Spirit (by Kodiac) and to the quite useful 7f winner Ghost (by Invincible Spirit). The dam is an unraced half-sister to 4 minor winners. The second dam, Phantom Waters (by Pharly), won twice at 3 yrs and is a full or half-sister to 9 winners including the Group 3 Solario Stakes winner Shining Water (herself dam of the Grand Criterium and Dante Stakes winner Tenby). (Danethorpe Racing Ltd). *"She's done some nice, sharp bits of work but she's going through a bit of a growing phase at the moment. Very much a 2-y-o type although she's*

probably more one for six furlongs rather than a flat out five. We're pleased with her and she's doing everything nicely. We're definitely more forward with all our horses than we were last year when the bad winter held us up".

570. AQUILA CARINA ★★

b.f. Cockney Rebel – Galaxy Of Stars (Observatory). March 20. Second foal. Half-sister to the modest 2011 2-y-o 6f winner Choccywoccydoohdah (by Dr Fong). The dam, a modest 2-y-o 5f winner, is a half-sister to 4 winners including the Group 1 Premio Lydia Tesio winner Aoife Alainn and the Italian listed winner and Group 2 Italian 2,000 Guineas third Adorabile Fong. The second dam, Divine Secret (by Hernando), is an unraced half-sister to 6 minor winners here and abroad. (Danethorpe Racing Ltd). *"We have the 3-y-o half-sister who won for us last year but who didn't run until later on in the year and I suspect this filly will be the same. She's never been quite as strong as the more forward 2-y-o's but I do think she'll be racing this year at some point".*

571. CRYSTAL PEAKS ★★

b.f. Intikhab – Crozon (Peintre Celebre). April 6. Fifth foal. 12,000Y. Tattersalls October Book 2. Anthony Stroud. Sister to the quite useful dual 1m winner Tactful and half-sister to the quite useful 2011 2-y-o 6f and 7f winner Poetic Dancer (by Byron). The dam, a modest 10.2f winner, is a half-sister to 4 winners including the useful Irish 6f (at 2 yrs) and 7f winner Darwin. The second dam, Armorique (by Top Ville), a minor winner and listed placed at 3 yrs in France, is a half-sister to 8 winners including the French Group winners Modhish, Russian Snows and Truly Special. (Danethorpe Racing Ltd). *"She's done some nice, early bits of work and she's just having a growing spell now. She'll make a 2-y-o, if not an early one".*

572. GIRL AT THE SANDS (IRE) ★★★

gr.f. Clodovil – Invincible Woman (Invincible Spirit). March 1. First foal. £8,000 2-y-o. Goffs Kempton Breeze-up. Anthony Stroud. The dam was a fairly useful Irish 2-y-o 5f winner. The second dam, Lady Helen (by Salse), a fair 1m (at 2 yrs) and 9f winner, is a half-sister to 8 winners including the high-class Group 1 6f July Cup, Group 2 6f Moet and Chandon Rennen and dual Group 3 6f winner Owington and the dam of the Group 3 Ballyogan Stakes winner Miss Anabaa. *"She was in the top-ten in the sale in terms of the time she breezed. She'll be out quite early I should think and she certainly looks like a 2-y-o for sprint distances. Not overly-big, but a good, strong, early 2-y-o type"*. TRAINERS' BARGAIN BUY

573. JADANNA (IRE) ★★★★

b.f. Mujadil – Savannah Poppy (Statue Of Liberty). March 13. First foal. 25,000Y. Tattersalls October Book 2. Anthony Stroud. The dam, a fair 3-y-o 7f winner, is a half-sister to 5 winners including the Group 2 6f Mill Reef Stakes winner and Group 1 Golden Jubilee second Galeota (by Mujadil), the 11f and listed 13f winner Loulwa and the fairly useful 2-y-o 5f Weatherbys Supersprint winner Lady Livius. The second dam, Refined (by Statoblest), a fairly useful dual 5f winner, is a half-sister to 6 winners including the very smart Group 3 7f Criterion Stakes winner Pipe Major. (Danethorpe Racing Ltd). *"The most forward of the 2-y-o fillies, she's by Mujadil and her dam is a half-sister to a good horse by that sire in Galeota, so that's encouraging. She's done some sharp bits of work already and she'll be an early 2-y-o. A typical, sprinting 2-y-o type with a big backside and big shoulders and I'm pleased with what she's doing"*.

574. THE POWER OF ONE (IRE) ★★

b.c. Duke Of Marmalade – Mustique Dream (Don't Forget Me). January 17. Sixth foal. 52,000Y. Tattersalls December. Not sold. Half-brother to the quite useful 2-y-o 5f winner Special Day (by Fasliyev), the fair triple 1m winner Marning Star (by Diktat) and the Italian winner of two races at 2 and 3 yrs and listed-placed Looking Back (by Stravinsky and herself dam of the triple Group 1 winner Rip Van Winkle). The dam, a quite useful dual 1m winner, is a half-sister to 6 winners. The second dam, Jamaican Punch (by Shareef Dancer), is an unplaced half-sister to 6 winners including the listed winners Tea House (the dam of four stakes winners including the Australian Grade 1 winner Danish) and Academic (also third in the Grade 1 San Juan Capistrano Handicap) and to the unraced dam of the Group 2 winner

Alderbrook. (Nigel & Suzanne Williams). *"He's not that precocious but he's coming along and he'll certainly run as a 2-y-o although I'm pretty sure he'll be better next year. He may well be out in mid-season, probably over seven furlongs"*.

575. VINO COLLAPSO (IRE) ★★★ ♠

b.c. Jeremy – Compradore (Mujtahid). April 18. Sixth foal. £52,000Y. Doncaster Premier. Anthony Stroud. Half-brother to the listed 6f Cecil Frail Stakes winner Beyond Desire (by Invincible Spirit) and to the fair 6f (at 2 yrs) to 10f winner of 8 races Cherri Fosfate (by Mujahid). The dam, a quite useful 5f to 7f winner of 4 races, is a half-sister to 6 winners including the Group 3 Princess Royal Stakes winner Mazuna. The second dam, the fairly useful 1m (at 2 yrs) and 12f winner Keswa (by Kings Lake), was listed placed and is a half-sister to 5 winners including the listed Zetland Stakes winner Matahif and the dam of the multiple Group 1 winner Mastercraftsman. (Simply Racing Ltd). *"He'd be our most forward 2-y-o and he's done a few nice bits of work. He's just a bit on the small side and we'll have to see how he develops but we'll start him off over five furlongs. Hopefully he'll win his maiden, then we can decide his level and see where we should go with him"*.

576. WOODY BAY ★★★★★ ♠

b.c. New Approach – Dublino (Lear Fan). February 26. Third living foal. 60,000Y. Tattersalls October Book 2. Anthony Stroud. The dam, a French 2-y-o 1m winner, subsequently won the Grade 1 9f Del Mar Oaks and was Grade 1 placed several times and is a half-sister to 6 winners. The second dam, Tuscoga (by Theatrical), was unplaced in 2 starts and is a sister to the Grade 1 Matriarch Stakes winner Duda and a half-sister to 5 winners. (Mr J A Barson). *"An interesting horse because he's by a Derby winner out of a Grade 1 winner in America. You might expect him to need quite a bit of time but that's not the case, because he's quite forward. A very nice, good-sized horse and he's ahead of where he should be in terms of his development. A colt with a good attitude and a nice way of going, he did his first piece of work very well, so he's an exciting horse"*.

577. UNNAMED ★★
ch.c. Redback – Flames (Blushing Flame). May 19. Eighth foal. €30,000Y. Goffs Orby. Anthony Stroud. Brother to the Group 2 6f Rockfel Stakes (at 2 yrs) and Group 1 10f E P Taylor Stakes winner Lahaleeb and a half-sister to the fairly useful dual 6f (at 2 yrs) and listed 1m Masaka Stakes winner Precocious Star (by Bold Fact). The dam is an unraced half-sister to 4 winners including the listed winner Dance Partner. The second dam, Dancing Debut (by Polar Falcon), is a placed half-sister to 4 winners including Virtuous (dam of the Group 1 Lockinge Stakes winner Virtual and the Group 2 Coventry Stakes winner Iceman). (Simply Racing Ltd). *"Not an expensive horse considering his pedigree, he's just taking a little time to come to hand but that's fine because he is a May foal. We haven't had him here that long but he's learning, getting fitter and stronger every week, we just don't know enough about him yet".*

578. UNNAMED ★★
ch.c. Byron – Molly Pitcher (Halling). April 2. First foal. 5,500Y. Tattersalls October Book 3. Not sold. The dam, a dual 3-y-o winner in Holland, is a half-sister to 2 other minor winners. The second dam, American Queen (by Fairy King), placed once at 2 yrs in France, is a three-parts sister to the Italian Group 1 winner Antheus, and a half-sister to 8 winners including the Group 3 10.5f Prix Cleopatre winner Alexandrie (the dam of four Group winners) and the placed dam of the Group 1 winner and sire Indian Danehill. (Ingram Racing). *"A squat, 2-y-o type, he came in a bit late but he's making good progress".*

579. UNNAMED ★★★
br.f. Kheleyf – Pizzicato (Statoblest). May 5. Ninth foal. 70,000Y. Tattersalls October Book 2. Rabbah Bloodstock. Closely related to the quite useful Irish 5f and 1m winner Astonish (by Cape Cross) and half-sister to the 2-y-o Group 2 5f Flying Childers Stakes and Group 3 5f Molecomb Stakes winner Wunders Dream (by Averti), the very useful Irish Group 3 Ridgewood Pearl Stakes winner Grecian Dancer (by Dansili), the fairly useful 6f (at 2 yrs) and 7f winner Go Between (by Daggers Drawn), the quite useful 7f winner Plucky (by Kyllachy) and a winner in Greece by Royal Applause. The dam, a modest 5f and 5.3f winner at 3 yrs, is a half-sister to 5 winners including the high-class Hong Kong horses Mensa and Firebolt. The second dam, Musianica (by Music Boy), was a fairly useful 2-y-o dual 6f winner. (Bolton Grange). *"We know the family well, she's pretty forward and she's a stocky, sprinter-type. She's slightly taller than Wunders Dream was, but a similar colour and with a similar head. She's been showing up well in her few bits of work so far, so I think she's a nice horse in the making".*

580. UNNAMED ★★
ch.c. Dutch Art – Royal Nashkova (Mujahid). February 19. Half-brother to Icewan (by Iceman), unplaced on his debut over 7f at 3 yrs in 2012. The dam is an unraced daughter of the French 11f fourth placed Nashkova (by Nashwan), herself a half-sister to 4 winners. (Ingram Racing). *"A big, tall horse, he didn't get broken until this year so he's a bit behind the others but he's coming along. He's going to need time but being by Dutch Art he'd have a chance".*

GODOLPHIN MAHMOOD AL ZAROONI

581. AUTHORSHIP (IRE) ★★★
b.c. Authorized – Desert Frolic (Persian Bold). February 24. Tenth foal. €150,000foal. Goffs. John Ferguson. Half-brother to the fairly useful 2011 2-y-o 1m and 10f winner Mojave (by Dubawi), to the smart 2-y-o Group 3 7f Killavullan Stakes winner Dubai Prince (by Shamardal), the useful 9f (at 2 yrs), 1m and 12f winner and listed-placed Jakarta Jade, the minor US winner of 4 races Desert Falcon (both by Royal Abjar) and the fairly useful 7f and 1m winner and listed-placed Cadre (by King's Best). The dam, a fairly useful 11f to 13f winner, is a half-sister to 6 winners including the Group 1 Champion Stakes winner Storming Home. The second dam, Try To Catch Me (by Shareef Dancer), won once over 1m at 3 yrs in France and is a half-sister to 8 winners including the Group 2 Criterium de Maisons-Laffitte winner Bitooh and the dam of the Group 2 winners Slip Stream and Porte Bonheur and to the unraced dam of the Group 1 winners Music Note and Musical Chimes. *"A well-balanced, mature type, he's strong and quite forward-going for the moment".*

582. BIRCHAM (IRE) ★★★

ch.c. Dubawi – Royale Danehill (Danehill).
February 6. First foal. 120,000foal. Tattersalls
December. John Ferguson. The dam won 2
minor races at 4 yrs in France and is a half-sister
to 4 winners. The second dam, Royal Ballerina
(by Sadler's Wells), winner of the Group 2 12f
Blandford Stakes and second in the Oaks, is
a half-sister to 7 winners including the dual
Group 2 10f Sun Chariot Stakes winner Free
Guest (herself dam of the Group 1 Fillies Mile
winner and Oaks second Shamshir). *"There's
not much precocity early in this colt's pedigree
but he is well-stamped by Dubawi. A well-made,
lovely, easy-actioned colt".*

583. BORNEAN (IRE) ★★★★

ch.c. Street Cry – Calando (Storm Cat). April
8. Eighth foal. Half-brother to the useful 2-y-o
listed 7f Chesham Stakes winner Champlain (by
Seeking The Gold) and to the modest 5f to 1m
winner of 10 races Sovereignty (by King's Best).
The dam won the Group 3 1m May Hill Stakes,
was second in the Group 1 Fillies Mile and third
in the French 1,00 Guineas and is a half-sister
to 2 winners. The second dam, Diminuendo
(by Diesis), won the Hoover Fillies Mile, Cherry
Hinton Stakes (both at 2 yrs), Epsom Oaks,
Irish Oaks (in a dead-heat), Yorkshire Oaks and
Musidora Stakes. *"This is a strong two-year-old
type who is loving his work at the moment and
should be one of our earlier runners. He has a
very good temperament, which will help him
too".*

584. BOURBON (IRE) ★★★

b.c. Raven's Pass – Traou Mad (Barathea).
February 15. Sixth foal. €80,000 foal. Goffs.
John Ferguson. Half-brother to the French 7.5f
winner and listed-placed Roscoff (by Daylami)
and to the minor French 12f winner Carnac
(by Dalakhani). The dam, a French listed 2-y-o
winner, was Group 3 placed four times and is a
half-sister to 7 winners including the Group 2
6f Gimcrack Stakes and dual Group 3 winner
Josr Algharoud and the dual Group 2 5f Prix du
Gros-Chene winner Saint Marine. The second
dam, Pont-Aven (by Try My Best), a very useful
winner of 3 races including the Group 3 Prix de
Saint-Georges, was second in the French 1,000
Guineas and is a half-sister to 6 winners. *"There*

is a lot of speed and good 2-y-o form in this
colt's family and although it's early days still, he
is well-grown and beginning to shape up nicely".*

585. BUSTOPHER (USA) ★★★

b.br.c. Elusive Quality – Catstar (Storm Cat).
April 19. Third foal. The dam, a very useful 5f (at
2 yrs) and 1m winner and second in the Group
3 Queen Mary Stakes, is out of the US triple
Grade 3 winner and Grade 1 placed Advancing
Star (by Soviet Star), herself a half-sister to the
US Grade 3 winner Darby Fair. *"Catstar was
runner-up in the Queen Mary and this colt will
be quite early too. He is straightforward with a
quick action".*

586. DOLDRUMS (USA) ★★★

b.f. Bernardini – Appealing Storm (Valid
Appeal). February 2. Ninth foal. $300,000Y.
Fasig-Tipton Saratoga August. Mark Johnston.
Sister to the minor US 3-y-o winner Alluring
Storm and half-sister to the US Grade 1 Queen
Elizabeth II Challenge Cup and triple Grade
2 winner Vacare (by Lear Fan) and to the US
Grade 3 winner Single Solution (by Flatter).
The dam, a minor winner in the USA at 2 and
3 yrs, is a half-sister to 2 winners. The second
dam, Storm O'Fire (by Storm Bird), unplaced in
one start, is half-sister to 4 winners including
the dam of the champion filly Serena's Song.
*"Doldrums is a leggy individual who will need
a bit of time, but she is an athletic, attractive
daughter of Bernardini who could be interesting
later in the year".*

587. GROUNDBREAKING ★★★

b.c. New Approach – Ladeena (Dubai
Millennium). February 14. Third foal. 450,000Y.
Tattersalls October Book 1. John Ferguson.
Half-brother to the very useful 6f (at 2 yrs) and
9f winner and dual listed-placed Atlantis Star
(by Cape Cross). The dam, a fair 7f winner at
3 yrs, is a half-sister to 2 winners. The second
dam, Aqaarid (by Nashwan), a smart winner of
the Group 1 Fillies Mile and the Group 3 7.3f
Fred Darling Stakes, was second in the 1,000
Guineas and is a half-sister to 2 winners. *"This
is a good-looking colt, as can be imagined by his
price tag. He is growing at the moment and is
one for later in the year, but is certainly pleasing
at present".*

588. KOSIKA (USA) ★★★

b.f. *Hard Spun – Song Of Africa (Alzao)*. April 18. Eighth foal. $170,000Y. Keeneland September. John Ferguson. Half-sister to the US Grade 3 winner Around The Cape (by Carson City) and to two minor US winners by Hennessy and Songandaprayer. The dam, a US listed winner and Grade 3 placed, is a half-sister to 7 winners including the US Grade 3 winner and Grade 1 placed Intensive Command. The second dam, Intensive (by Sir Wiggle), is an unraced half-sister to a stakes winner. *"She is shaping up to be a tough, athletic filly: she might need some time as she learns her role but has a pleasing attitude and action".*

589. MUSICIANSHIP (IRE) ★★★

b.c. *Cape Cross – Musical Treat (Royal Academy)*. March 31. Seventh living foal. 360,000Y. Tattersalls October Book 1. John Ferguson. Closely related to the Group 2 German 2,000 Guineas winner Frozen Power (by Oasis Dream) and half-brother to the Prix Marcel Boussac, 1,000 Guineas and Irish 1,000 Guineas winner Finsceal Beo (by Mr Greeley), the fairly useful 2-y-o 6f winner and listed-placed Zabeel Park (by Medicean), the quite useful 7f winner and listed placed Musical Bar (by Barathea) and a 3-y-o winner abroad by Red Ransom. The dam, a useful 3-y-o 7f winner and listed-placed twice, subsequently won 4 races at 4 yrs in Canada and the USA and is a half-sister to 6 winners. The second dam, Mountain Ash (by Dominion), won 10 races here and in Italy including the Group 3 Premio Royal Mares and is a half-sister to 7 winners. *"We have had good success with some of this family and, although a similar type to Frozen Power, this colt has more substance. Finsceal Beo has set the bar as a 2-y-o champion so it remains to be seen if this colt can get anywhere close to emulating her!"*

590. PIANOSA (USA) ★★★★

b.f. *Bernardini – Nataliano (Fappiano)*. March 6. Eleventh foal. $600,000Y. Fasig-Tipton Saratoga August. John Ferguson. Closely related to the US Grade 1 Las Virgines Stakes winner A P Adventure (by A P Indy) and half-sister to 4 winners including the US stakes winner Platinum (by Mineshaft) and one in Japan by Red Ransom. The dam is a placed half-sister to 4 winners including the US Grade 2 winner Super Mario. The second dam, Take The Wonder (by Lyphard), is an unraced half-sister to 6 winners. *"This is a very attractive, well-made filly. She has a great temperament, an easy action and hopefully will be one to watch out for in August over seven furlongs".*

591. TEARLESS ★★★★

b.f. *Street Cry – Playful Act (Sadler's Wells)*. March 24. Sister to the fairly useful 2011 2-y-o dual 1m winner Anjaz and half-sister to the US Grade 2 10f winner Giants Play (by Giant's Causeway). The dam, a Group 1 Fillies' Mile, Group 2 Lancashire Oaks and Group 2 May Hill Stakes winner, is a sister to the Group 2 Yorkshire Cup winner Percussionist and a half-sister to the Group 2 Sun Chariot Stakes and Group 2 Park Hill Stakes winner Echoes In Eternity. The second dam, Magnificient Style (by Silver Hawk), won the Group 3 10.5f Musidora Stakes and is a half-sister to the Grade 1 10f Charles H Strub Stakes winner Siberian Summer. *"This filly appears to have plenty of quality, she holds her condition well and has a lovely action. Her unbeaten full-sister Anjaz won on her debut over a mile in August last year and this filly is a similar type".*

592. THALWEG (USA) ★★★

b.br.c. *Hard Spun – Meandering Stream (Gone West)*. February 4. Second foal. $200,000Y. Keeneland September. John Ferguson. Half-brother to a minor 2-y-o winner in Canada by Giant's Causeway. The dam is an unraced sister to 6 winners including the stakes winner and Grade 2 placed Surging River. The second dam, Classic Slew (by Seattle Slew), is an unraced half-sister to numerous stakes winners including the Canadian champion Sky Classic. *"This colt has an American pedigree and a low, daisy-cutting action. He is still lengthy and hasn't quite come together yet, but catches the eye in his canters".*

593. WINTERLUDE (IRE) ★★★

b.c. *Street Cry – New Morning (Sadler's Wells)*. March 17. Brother to Mighty Ambition, a promising 7f winner on his only start at 2 yrs in 2011 and half-brother to the useful 1m and 12f winner Sadeek's Song (by Kingmambo). The dam, a very useful listed 10f winner, is a sister to 6 winners including the high-class Grade 1

Breeders Cup Filly & Mare Turf, Group 1 1m Nassau Stakes and Group 1 Yorkshire Oaks winner Islington, the very smart 10f performer Greek Dance and the smart stayer Election Day and a half-sister to 2 winners. The second dam, Hellenic (by Darshaan), won the Yorkshire Oaks and was second in the St Leger and is a half-sister to numerous winners including the Group 2 Lanson Champagne Vintage Stakes second Golden Wave. *"Winterlude comes from a classy middle-distance family and his full-brother Mighty Ambition won his only start as a 2-y-o last year in September. Physically this colt resembles him more than his Kingmambo half-brother Sadeek's Song, who was unraced as a 2-y-o and is more of a staying type. He is strong, moves well and is pleasing in his exercise".*

594. UNNAMED ★★★★

b.f. Bernardini – Caress (Storm Cat). March 14. Half-sister to the US 2-y-o Grade 1 7f Hopeful Stakes winner Sky Mesa (by Pulpit), to the US dual Grade 3 winner, over 1m and 9f, Golden Velvet (by Seeking The Gold) and the US Grade 2 placed Caressive (by A P Indy). The dam, a triple US Grade 3 winner at up to 9f, is a sister to the US Grade 3 winner Country Cat and to the Group 3 6f Railway Stakes winner and sire Bernstein. The second dam, La Affirmed (by Affirmed), a minor winner at 3 yrs in the USA, is a sister to the US Grade 3 winner Lovelier and is closely related to the champion US two-year-old filly Outstandingly (herself dam of the Group 2 Falmouth Stakes winner Sensation). *"This filly comes from a class family with plenty of 2-y-o form. She is sharp, with a fast ground action and finding her training easy at the moment, so she should be one of our earlier runners, over six furlongs".*

595. UNNAMED ★★★★

ch.c. Exceed and Excel – Dresden Doll (Elusive Quality). January 23. The dam, a fair 2-y-o 5f winner, is a half-sister to 9 winners including the high-class Irish 1,000 Guineas, Coronation Stakes and Nassau Stakes winner Crimplene, the smart Group 3 12.3f Chester Vase winner Dutch Gold and the useful 10f winner Group 2 12f Lancashire Oaks second Loyal Spirit. The second dam, Crimson Conquest (by Diesis), a quite useful 2-y-o 6f winner, is a half-sister

to the US stakes winner at around 1m Sword Blade. *"This is an early foal, from a family with top-class 2-y-o form. He's quite a tall horse who still needs to fill out his frame a bit, so his progress over the next few weeks will determine the kind of season we can expect".*

GODOLPHIN
SAEED BIN SUROOR

596. ABQARI (IRE) ★★★

b.c. Teofilo – Ramona (Desert King). March 29. Eighth foal. 250,000Y. Tattersalls October Book 1. John Ferguson. Closely related to the useful Group 3 7f Athasi Stakes winner Prima Luce, to the fair 12f winner Gakalina (both by Galileo) and half-brother to the fairly useful 3-y-o 1m winner Toraidhe (by High Chaparral), the fair Irish 10f winner Home You Stroll (by Selkirk) and the modest Irish 6f winner Sheer Silk (by Fasliyev). The dam is an unraced half-sister to 9 winners including the Group 2 5f Kings Stand Stakes winner Cassandra Go (herself dam of the triple Group 1 winner Halfway To Heaven) and the smart Group 3 6f Coventry Stakes winner and sire Verglas. The second dam, Rahaam (by Secreto), a fairly useful 3-y-o 7f winner, is a half-sister to 8 winners including the French 2,000 Guineas third Glory Forever. *"A very nice, well-balanced type, he's not that sharp but we would hope to see him late summer".*

597. AMIRR (IRE) ★★★

b.c. New Approach – Dress Uniform (Red Ransom). February 1. First foal. 190,000Y. Tattersalls October Book 1. John Ferguson. The dam, a minor winner at 3 yrs in the USA, is a sister to the Group 1 Oaks winner Casual Look and to the listed 10f winner and Grade 1 Yellow Ribbon Stakes third Shabby Chic (herself the dam of the Group 2 winner Fashion Statement) and a half-sister to 6 winners. The second dam, Style Setter (by Manila), a stakes-placed winner of 3 races in the USA, is a half-sister to 2 winners. *"He is a big scopey horse who will take a little time to fill his frame, but he is light on his feet and certainly pleasing in his canters at the moment. He won't be early and is unlikely to enjoy fast summer ground but will hopefully show ability over seven furlongs a little later in the year".*

598. ARABIAN SKIES (IRE) ★★★★

b.c. Authorized – Chaturanga (Night Shift). February 12. Tenth foal. €75,000Y. Goffs Orby. John Ferguson. Half-brother to the fairly useful Irish 8.5f winner and Group 3 Ridgewood Pearl Stakes second Mooretown Lady (by Montjeu), to the fairly useful 2-y-o 6f winner Ruling (by Footstepsinthesand), the fair 11.7f winner Battledress (by In The Wings), the Irish 7f (at 2 yrs) and 6f winner Cocorica (by Croco Rouge) and the fair 9.4f all-weather winner Folaann (by Pennekamp). The dam is an unraced half-sister to 6 winners including the Irish listed 10f winner and Group 2 9.8f Prix Dollar second Strategic and the Group 2 Prix Eugene Adam winner Sobieski. The second dam, Game Plan (by Darshaan), won the Group 2 10f Pretty Polly Stakes, was second in the Oaks and is a half-sister to 10 winners including the Oaks winner Shahtoush. *"There appears to be plenty of quality about this well-balanced colt, he's good-looking with a lovely action and it's easy to imagine him debuting at Newmarket in July".*

599. ARABIC HISTORY (IRE) ★★★

b.c. Teofilo – Ruby Affair (Night Shift). April 15. Tenth foal. 85,000Y. Tattersalls October Book 1. John Ferguson. Half-brother to the fair 2011 2-y-o 1m winner Madgenta (by Manduro), to the useful 2-y-o 6f and UAE listed 5f winner Hammadi (by Red Ransom), the very useful 6f (including at 2 yrs) and 6.5f winner Khabfair (by Intikhab), the quite useful 7f and 1m winner Roninski, the quite useful 2-y-o 6f winner Frances Cadell (both by Cadeaux Genereux) and the quite useful dual winner (including at 2 yrs) Red Kyte (by Hawk Wing). The dam, a modest 7f placed 3-y-o, is a half-sister to 5 winners including the 2,000 Guineas winner Island Sands. The second dam, Tiavanita (by J O Tobin), is an unplaced half-sister to 8 winners including the Group 2 Great Voltigeur Stakes winner Corrupt. *"A neat, athletic horse, he coughed a bit early on but he should be quite quick coming to hand and have enough speed for six furlong races mid-summer".*

600. BALAD (IRE) ★★★★

b.c. Exceed And Excel – Bright Morning (Dubai Millennium). February 18. Third foal. The dam, a French 2-y-o 6.5f winner, is a half-sister to numerous winners including the top-class National Stakes, Irish 2,000 Guineas and Irish Derby winner Desert King and the useful 2-y-o 6f and 7f winner and Group 2 7f Champagne Stakes third Chianti. The second dam, Sabaah (by Nureyev), a modest 8.2f placed maiden, is a full or half-sister to 8 winners including the Group 1 1m Queen Elizabeth II Stakes winner Maroof and to the placed dam of the Canadian Grade 2 winner Callwood Dancer. *"This colt is one of the more forward types and is showing enough speed at the moment to debut in May, without hold-ups. He's well-grown, athletic and seems to love his job".*

601. DAAREE (IRE) ★★★★

b.c. Teofilo – Mawaakeb (Diesis). January 29. Half-brother to the quite useful 2-y-o 6f winner (from two starts) Tanfeer (by Dansili). The dam is an unraced half-sister to the quite useful 7f and 1m winner Manaal. The second dam, Muwakleh (by Machiavellian), winner of the UAE 1,000 Guineas and second in the Newmarket 1,000 Guineas, is a sister to the high-class Dubai World Cup and Prix Jean Prat winner Almutawakel and to the useful 10f winner Elmustanser and a half-sister to the smart 10f winner Inaaq. *"He is a lovely colt with quality who caught the eye on arrival in the yard. He hasn't come in his coat yet and certainly won't be rushed, but is doing very well physically and should be an interesting prospect in the summer."*

602. EXCELLENT RESULT (IRE) ★★★

b.c. Shamardal – Line Ahead (Sadler's Wells). February 8. Fifth foal. €70,000 foal. Goffs. John Ferguson. Half-brother to the unplaced 2011 2-y-o Blue Ridges (by Dubawi), to the quite useful 2-y-o 7f winner Goldenveil (by Iffraaj) and the Italian 2-y-o winner Linea d'Aria (by Hawk Wing). The dam was unplaced on her only start and is a half-sister to 3 winners. The second dam, Alignment (by Alzao), was placed 3 times including when second in the Group 3 Prestige Stakes and is a half-sister to 5 winners including the Group 2 Great Voltigeur winner Bonny Scot and the dam of the King George and 2,000 Guineas winner Golan. *"He is a big, straightforward colt who is going through a slightly weak patch at the moment. He is light on his feet though for his size and scope and could mature into a pleasing seven furlong type later in the year".*

603. GOLD HUNTER (IRE) ★★★★
b.c. Invincible Spirit – Goldthroat (Zafonic). April 28. Seventh foal. 220,000Y. Tattersalls October Book 1. John Ferguson. Half-sister to the 2-y-o Group 1 Criterium International and dual Group 3 winner Zafisio (by Efisio), to the fairly useful 1m and 9f winner of 4 races Harald Bluetooth (by Danetime) and the quite useful 9.5f (at 2 yrs) and 10f winner New Beginning (by Keltos). The dam, a fair 7f winner at 2 yrs, is a half-sister to 2 winners. The second dam, Winger (by In The Wings), a fair Irish 9f winner, is a half-sister to 6 winners. *"This colt is coming together nicely and is showing pleasing speed. He is strong with a good attitude and all being well should make his debut in May".*

604. GREAT FIGHTER ★★★
b.c. Street Cry – Evil Empire (Acatenango). January 18. Half-brother to the 1m (at 2 yrs) and listed 10f winner Empire Day (by Lomitas) and to the useful 11f and 12f winner Counterpunch (by Halling). The dam, a Group 3 12f winner in Germany, is a sister to the German triple listed winner El Tango and a half-sister to the German listed winner El Tiger. *"A nice, big, rangy type with a lovely action, he catches the eye but is certainly more of a back-end type with a view to middle distances as a three-year-old".*

605. MUSADDAS ★★★
b.c. Exceed And Excel – Zuleika Dobson (Cadeaux Genereux). April 25. Seventh foal. 80,000Y. Tattersalls October Book 1. Angie Loder. Half-brother to the fair dual 10f winner Midnight Dreamer (by Fantastic Light). The dam, a useful 9f winner and third in the Group 3 9f Prix Chloe, is a half-sister to one winner. The second dam, Fresher (by Fabulous Dancer), won twice in France and the USA was second in the Group 2 Prix d'Astarte and is a half-sister to 5 winners including the Group 2 Prix Niel winner Songlines. *"Quite a tall horse with a very good action, he won't be sharp enough for the early six furlong races but if he continues to progress as he is at present, we would hope to see him around July/August time".*

606. MY DIRECTION ★★
ch.c. Singspiel – Ejlaal (Caerleon). May 17. Brother to the French dual 12f winner and Group 3 placed Doe Ray Me and half-brother to the minor French 12f winner Emblazon. The dam won over 1m at 2 yrs in France and is a half-sister to numerous winners including the German dual Group 1 12f winner Mamool and the dam of the Australian Group 2 winner Avienus. The second dam, Genovefa (by Woodman), a useful winner of the Group 3 10.5f Prix de Royaumont, is closely related to the Group 3 10f Prix de la Nonette winner Grafin and a half-sister to the US Grade 3 8.5f winner Miss Turkana. *"This colt is from one of our favourite staying families and he won't be precocious. He is a good-looking, sensible type with scope".*

607. ROYAL FLAG ★★★★
b.c. New Approach – Gonbarda (Lando). April 2. Third foal. Half-brother to the useful 7f (at 2 yrs) and 1m winner Farhh and to the fairly useful 2011 2-y-o 1m winner Welcome Gift (both by Pivotal). The dam, a German dual Group 1 12f winner, is a full or half-sister to numerous winners including Gonfilia, a winner of the Group 3 8.5f Princess Elizabeth Stakes and four listed events. The second dam, Gonfalon (by Slip Anchor), is a half-sister to several winners. *"Gonbarda's two sons to race to date have both been good-looking horses who have shown ability as 2-y-o's and so far this colt is pleasing as well. He is a little weak and immature mentally, as expected at this stage, but he's one to keep an eye on if he continues to go the right way".*

608. TAKAATHUR (USA) ★★★
ch.c. Hard Spun – Vague (Elusive Quality). January 19. First foal. The dam, a very useful 6f (at 2 yrs) and UAE listed 1m winner, was third in the Group 3 6f Albany Stakes and is a half-sister to numerous winners. The second dam, April In Kentucky (by Palace Music), was unplaced in one start and is a half-sister to 7 winners including the US Grade 1 winner Reloy and the Group 2 winner En Calcat. *"This is a tough, good-looking colt with a good temperament and a fast ground action. He's just going through the motions at the moment."*

609. TARIKHI (USA) ★★★

b.c. *Bernardini – Caffe Latte (Seattle Dancer)*. Brother to the very useful 1m to 10f winner and Group 3 10.5f Huxley Stakes third Expresso Star, to the Austrian 10f winner Skarabeus (both by War Chant) and the quite useful 7f (at 2 yrs) and dual 10f winner Raucous Behaviour (by Street Cry). The dam won the Grade 1 9f Ramona Handicap in the USA and is a half-sister to numerous winners including the useful 2-y-o 7f and 1m winner Autonomy. The second dam, Debbie's Next (by Arctic Tern), a quite useful placed maiden, stayed 1m and is a half-sister to 4 minor winners. *"If Tarikhi continues his current rate of progress, he could shape into a nice seven furlong horse with some speed for mid-season".* Won 3d 1m mdn Newmkt cl 4

610. THA'IR (IRE) ★★★

b.c. *New Approach – Flashing Green (Green Desert)*. March 21. Eighth foal. €105,000Y. Goffs Orby. John Ferguson. Half-brother to 5 winners including the German listed winner and Group 3 placed Flashing Colour (by Pivotal) and a minor winner in France by Monsun. The dam, a German 3-y-o winner, is a half-sister to 6 winners including the 2-y-o 5f and 7f Italian listed winner and Group 2 1m Falmouth Stakes second Croeso Cariad, the Irish listed 12f winner and Coronation Stakes and Irish Oaks third Mona Lisa and the Irish 2-y-o listed 7f winner Photogenic. The second dam, Colorsnap (by Shirley Heights), is an unraced half-sister to Colorspin (winner of the Irish Oaks and dam of the Group 1 winners Opera House, Kayf Tara and Zee Zee Top), Bella Colora (winner of the Prix de l'Opera and dam of the very smart colt Stagecraft) and the Irish Champion Stakes winner Cezanne. *"This little colt is pacey and at the moment should be one of Saeed's earlier runners. He can be a little over-enthusiastic however and will have to mature mentally with education".* imp wnr of ck...

JOHN GOSDEN

611. AL FAHIDI ★★★

b.f. *Singspiel – Bastakiya (Dubai Destination)*. February 15. The dam, a fairly useful 2-y-o 6f winner, was listed-placed over 6f at 3 yrs. The second dam, Ting A Folie (by Careafolie), won three Graded stakes events in Argentina and is a sister to Campesino, a winner of 3 Grade 1 events in Argentina. *"She's a nice little filly. Being by Singspiel and out of a sprinter she's probably one to start off in August or September, but she's worth a mention".*

612. ASHLAND ★★★

b.c. *Dansili – Bonash (Rainbow Quest)*. March 25. Brother to the Group 3 7f Prestige Stakes winner Sense Of Joy and half-brother to the multiple Group 3 middle-distance winner and French Derby fourth Day Flight (by Sadler's Wells) and the very useful 2-y-o 7f winner Bionic (by Zafonic). The dam, a very useful filly, won 4 races in France from 1m to 12f including the Prix d'Aumale, the Prix Vanteaux and the Prix de Malleret and is a full or half-sister to 4 winners. The second dam, Sky Love (by Nijinsky), a fairly useful 10f winner, is a half-sister to the high-class Prix de la Cote Normande winner Raft. (Khalid Abdulla). *"He goes fine and he'll be a nice horse by September-time over seven furlongs or a mile. A rangy colt that will appreciate some cut in the ground – like everything else out of the mare does".*

613. BLESSINGTON (IRE) ★★★

b.c. *Kheleyf – Madam Ninette (Mark Of Esteem)*. February 26. Sixth foal. £75,000Y. Doncaster Premier. John Ferguson. Half-brother to the fairly useful 2011 2-y-o dual 5f winner and listed placed Excelette (by Exceed And Excel) and to the modest 9f to 12f winner Waahej (by Haafhd). The dam is an unraced half-sister to 9 winners including the very smart King's Stand Stakes and Temple Stakes winner Bolshoi and the useful sprinters Mariinsky, Great Chaddington and Tod. The second dam, Mainly Dry (by The Brianstan), is an unraced half-sister to 4 winners. *"He goes alright and he's a solid sort of horse. There are no problems with him and I think he'll be out in a six furlong maiden, maybe as early as May".*

614. BREDEN ★★★

b.c. *Shamardal – Perfect Touch (Miswaki)*. April 23. Fifth foal. 140,000foal. Tattersalls December. London Thoroughbred Services. Half-brother to the useful 2-y-o 5f winner and Group 3 Jersey Stakes third Rock Jock (by Rock Of Gibraltar) and to the fairly useful 2-y-o 6f winner Shining Armour (by Green Desert). The dam won 3 races including the Group 3

Brownstown Stakes and is a half-sister to 7 winners including the Italian Group 2 and Irish Group 3 winner King Jock and the dam of the triple US Grade 2 winner Katdogawn. The second dam, Glen Kate (by Glenstal), won three Grade 3 events in the USA and is a half-sister to 3 winners. (Lady Rothschild). *"A nice, strong horse, he'll make a 2-y-o over six furlongs".*

615. CAPE ELIZABETH (IRE) ★★★ ♠
b.f. Invincible Spirit – Maine Lobster (Woodman). February 20. Sixth foal. 180,000Y. Tattersalls October Book 1. Cheveley Park Stud. Half-brother to the very smart Group 2 Sandown Mile and dual Group 3 winner Major Cadeaux (by Cadeaux Genereux), to the useful listed 10f winner of 5 races Beachfire and the fair 7f to 9f winner Lord Of The Dance (both by Indian Haven). The dam, a fair 7f placed 2-y-o, is a half-sister to the US stakes winner Cap Beino. The second dam, Capades (by Overskate), won 11 races including the Grade 1 Selima Stakes and is a half-sister to 3 winners. *"She's fine and a good mover, hopefully a mid-season 2-y-o over six furlongs".*

616. CHAT (USA) ★★★
b.br.f. Dynaformer – Verbal (Kingmambo). February 23. Third foal. $200,000Y. Keeneland September. George Strawbridge. The dam is an unraced half-sister to 5 winners including the Grade 1 Del Mar Oaks winner No Matter What (herself dam of the dual Group 1 winner Rainbow View) and the US dual Grade 2 winner E Dubai. The second dam, Words Of War (by Lord At War), a US stakes winner of 9 races, is a sister to the Grade 3 Miesque Stakes winner Ascutney (the dam of Raven's Pass). *"A neat, active filly from the same family as Rainbow View, she should be in the book".*

Won by cl 5 mdn Mydia

617. CORNROW ★★★
ch.c. New Approach – Needlecraft (Mark Of Esteem). March 6. Fourth foal. Half-brother to the fair 2-y-o 6f winner Manaaber (by Medicean). The dam won 4 races including the Group 3 Prix Chloe and the Group 3 Premio Sergio Cumani and is a half-sister to 3 winners. The second dam, Sharp Point (by Royal Academy), a useful Irish listed 5f winner at 3 yrs, was fourth in the Group 1 5f Nunthorpe Stakes and is a half-sister to the listed winner

High Target. *"A good-looking horse that moves nicely. He's an attractive, scopey horse with a good action and looks like one for a seven furlong maiden on the July course in mid-season".*

618. CROSS PATTEE ★★★
b.f. Oasis Dream – Victoria Cross (Mark Of Esteem). April 21. Seventh foal. Half-sister to the very smart Group 2 12f Hardwicke Stakes and Group 2 12f Jockey Club Stakes winner of 8 races Bronze Cannon, to the quite useful 12f winner Crimson Ribbon (both by Lemon Drop Kid), the useful Irish 2-y-o dual 7f winner Elusive Award (by Elusive Quality) and the fairly useful 2-y-o 7f winner and listed placed Valiance (by Horse Chestnut). The dam, a useful 7f winner here and listed-placed in France, is a half-sister to 6 winners including the Grade 2 San Marcos Handicap winner Prize Giving and to the placed dam of the dual US Grade 1 winner Alpride. The second dam, Glowing With Pride (by Ile de Bourbon), a smart 7f and 10.5f winner, was second in the Park Hill Stakes and is a half-sister to 7 winners. *"A neat filly with a quick action, just like her brother Bronze Cannon who sadly died the other day".*

619. CUSHION ★★★
b.f. Galileo – Attraction (Efisio). April 12. Fourth foal. Closely related to the quite useful 2-y-o 1m winner Devastation (by Montjeu) and half-sister to the fair 2-y-o 7f winner Elation (by Cape Cross). The dam, a high-class 1,000 Guineas, Irish 1,000 Guineas, Coronation Stakes, Matron Stakes and Sun Chariot Stakes winner, is a half-sister to 4 winners. The second dam, Flirtation (by Pursuit Of Love), ran unplaced once over 7f at 3 yrs and is a half-sister to 4 winners including the French listed 12f winner and Group 2 placed Carmita. (Duke of Roxburgh). *"A lovely filly, she's a good mover and I'd expect to see her out on the July course over seven furlongs".*

620. DERWENTWATER (IRE) ★★★
ch.c. Raven's Pass – Waterways (Alhaarth). March 26. Third foal. 72,000Y. Tattersalls October Book 1. John Ferguson. The dam, a 5f winner of 3 races (including a listed event at 2 yrs), was third in the Group 3 Molecomb Stakes and is a half-sister to two minor winners. The

second dam, Buckle (by Common Grounds), a fair dual 1m winner at 3 yrs, subsequently won in France and is a half-sister to 8 winners. "An athletic horse and a good mover, I'd hope to get him out over six furlongs in May".

621. DREAM TO BE MAID ★★★

b.f. Oasis Dream – Maid For The Hills (Indian Ridge). April 16. Twelfth foal. Sister to the fairly useful 2-y-o 6f winner and listed-placed Run For The Hills, closely related to the quite useful 2-y-o 6f winner Green Tambourine (by Green Desert) and half-sister to the useful 7f (at 2 yrs) and 10f winner Maid To Perfection (by Sadler's Wells), to the useful 2-y-o 7f winner Artistic Lad (by Peintre Celebre), the fairly useful 1m to 12f winner of 4 races Maid To Believe (by Galileo), the fairly useful 10f winner Made To Ransom (by Red Ransom) and the quite useful 8.6f winner King's Kama (by King's Best). The dam was a useful 2-y-o and won twice over 6f including the listed Empress Stakes. She is a half-sister to 5 winners including the Group 3 6f Princess Margaret Stakes second Maid For Walking. The second dam, Stinging Nettle (by Sharpen Up), a fairly useful 2-y-o listed 6f winner, is a half-sister to 4 winners including the Group 2 1m Royal Lodge Stakes winner Gairloch. *"Yes, she's a nice, solid type of filly, she's grown a bit and we'd expect her to be happy over six furlongs, like her full-brother".*

622. DRESS DOWN ★★★★

gr.c. Raven's Pass – Bare Necessities (Silver Deputy). May 21. Fourth foal. $200,000Y. Keeneland September. John Ferguson. Half-brother to 2 minor winners in the USA by Seeking The Gold and Tale Of The Cat. The dam, a winner of three Grade 3 stakes in the USA and Grade 1 placed three times, is a half-sister to the US stakes winner Holy Nola (herself dam of the Grade 2 winner Preachinatthebar). The second dam, Shrewd Vixen (by Spectacular Bid), a stakes-placed winner of 6 races, is a half-sister to the winner and Grade 2 placed Tanker Port. *"A late foal but a nice type of horse with a good, even action and I like his attitude".*

623. ENTHUSIASM ★★★

b.f. Dansili – High Praise (Quest For Fame). March 25. Half-sister to Grandiloquent (by Rail Link), placed second over 1m on his only start

at 2 yrs in 2011, to the useful 11f winner and listed-placed Sight Unseen (by Sadler's Wells), the fairly useful 10f winner Eagles Peak (by Galileo) and the quite useful 12f winner Critical Acclaim (by Peintre Celebre). The dam, winner of the Group 2 Prix de Malleret, is a half-sister to 7 winners including the top-class Group 1 1m Queen Elizabeth II Stakes and Group 1 9.3f Prix d'Ispahan winner Observatory. The second dam, Stellaria (by Roberto), won from 5f to 8.5f including the listed 6f Rose Bowl Stakes and is a half-sister to 8 winners. *"She's fine, she's moving nicely and we trained the mother who was a Group 2 winner. I could see this filly being out in August time over seven furlongs or a mile. She'll be a middle-distance filly next year".*

624. ETHEL ★★★

b.f. Exceed And Excel – Agnus (In The Wings). March 19. Half-sister to the listed 1m winner and Group 2 1m Sun Chariot Stakes second Dolores (by Danehill) and herself dam of the Group 2 Doncaster Cup winner Samuel) and to the fairly useful 10f winner Rachel (by Spectrum). The dam, a winner twice in Belgium, is a half-sister to 4 other winners abroad including Wavy Run, a winner of 13 races in Spain, France and the USA including the US Grade 2 San Francisco Mile Handicap. The second dam, Wavy Reef (by Kris), ran once unplaced and is a half-sister to 7 winners including Talented, winner of the Group 2 Sun Chariot Stakes. *"She's a sweet filly and a big girl just like everything out of the mare. The breeding is interesting because it's speed on stamina, but she's got a good attitude and she's a good mover".*

625. EXCESS KNOWLEDGE ★★

br.c. Monsun – Quenched (Dansili). March 16. Third foal. Half-brother to the fairly useful 1m (at 2 yrs) and 10f winner Rain Mac (by Beat Hollow). The dam, a useful listed 12f winner, is a sister to the French dual 13f winner Lifting Cloud and a half-sister to the very useful 7f (at 2 yrs) and 10f winner and Group 2 Dante Stakes second Raincoat (by Barathea). The second dam, Love The Rain (by Rainbow Quest), a winner over 11f in France, is a sister to the very useful Prix d'Aumale, Prix Vanteaux and Prix de Malleret winner Bonash and a half-sister to 3 winners. (Khalid Abdulla). *"Yes, he's fine – he'll be a staying horse, the whole family* stay and he'll fit into that mould. They don't like to be rushed and they want cut in the ground, so he won't see a racecourse until the back-end of the season".

626. FALSAFA ★★★★

b.f. Dansili – Hureya (Woodman). March 14. Seventh foal. Closely related to the useful triple 1m winner Maraheb (by Redoute's Choice) and half-sister to the 2-y-o listed 7f Star Stakes and 3-y-o Group 3 7f Fred Darling Stakes winner Muthabara (by Red Ransom), to the fairly useful 7f (including at 2 yrs) and 1m winner of 4 races Aqmaar (by Green Desert) and the quite useful 9f winner Estiqraar (by Alhaarth). The dam, a quite useful 3-y-o 1m winner, is a half-sister to the very smart listed 7f (at 2 yrs) and listed 10f winner Muqbil. The second dam, Istiqlal (by Diesis), is an unraced half-sister to the Group 1 1m St James's Palace Stakes and Group 1 1m Queen Elizabeth II Stakes winner Bahri and to the high-class 2-y-o Group 2 7f Laurent Perrier Champagne Stakes winner Bahhare. (Hamdan Al Maktoum). "She's an attractive filly, there's a bit of quality about her and all being well we'll start her in a seven furlong maiden in July or August".

627. FLEDGED ★★★

b.c. Dansili – Innocent Air (by Galileo). February 19. The dam won two listed events over 7f and 10f at 2 and 3 yrs and is a half-sister to 6 winners including the French listed and US stakes winner and US Grade 1 placed Skipping and the dual Group 3 placed Minority. The second dam, Minskip (by The Minstrel), won once at 2 yrs and is a sister to the US Grade 2 winner Savinio and a half-sister to the Italian dual Group 1 winner St Hilarion and the dam of the dual Group 1 winner Muhtarram. (Khalid Abdulla). "A nice, rangy type. We had the mare here and she was a dual listed winner. He looks a nice sort of horse for September time".

628. FLIRTINI ★★★

b.f. Nayef – Frappe (Inchinor). March 8. Tenth foal. Half-sister to the 2011 2-y-o Group 1 7f National Stakes and Group 2 6f Coventry Stakes winner Power (by Oasis Dream), to the 7f (at 2 yrs) and Group 2 12f Ribblesdale Stakes winner Thakafaat (by Unfuwain), the fairly useful 10f winner Quantum (by Alhaarth) and

the quite useful 2-y-o 7f winner Applauded (by Royal Applause). The dam, a fairly useful 2-y-o 6f winner, is a half-sister to 2 winners including the 2,000 Guineas winner Footstepsinthesand. The second dam, Glatisant (by Rainbow Quest), winner of the Group 3 7f Prestige Stakes, is a half-sister to 8 winners and to the placed dam of the very smart 2-y-o Superstar Leo. "She's a strong filly, good-looking and a good mover. The dam has done very well and we're happy with her but as she's by Nayef I think we'd want to start her at seven furlongs rather than shorter".

629. FREQUENT ★★★

ch.f. Three Valleys – Arabesque (Zafonic). May 15. Ninth foal. Half-sister to the Group 2 6f Gimcrack Stakes winner Showcasing, to the fairly useful triple 6f winner (including at 2 yrs) and listed-placed Bouvardia (both by Oasis Dream), the very smart listed 6f winner Camacho (by Danehill) and the quite useful 10f winner Almagest (by Diesis). The dam, a useful listed 6f winner, is a sister to 2 winners including the useful 5f and 6f winner Threat and a half-sister to 5 winners including the Group 2 1m Prix de Sandringham winner Modern Look. The second dam, Prophecy (by Warning), was a very useful winner of the Group 1 6f Cheveley Park Stakes and was second in the Group 3 7f Nell Gwyn Stakes. (Khalid Abdulla). "She's no problem at all and she's happy enough. A filly that's bred to be quick, I wouldn't be frightened of trying to get her out in mid-season over six furlongs".

630. GHURAIR ★★★

b.br.c. Elusive Quality – Alta Moda (Sadler's Wells). February 3. Second foal. 180,000Y. Tattersalls October Book 1. Shadwell Estate Co. The dam is an unraced half-sister to 2 winners including the listed Prix Petite Etoile winner Alvarita. The second dam, Alborada (by Alzao), winner of the Champion Stakes (twice), the Group 2 Nassau Stakes and the Group 2 Pretty Polly Stakes, is a sister to the triple German Group 1 winner Albanova and a half-sister to 6 winners including the fairly useful dual middle-distance winner Alakananda (herself dam of the Derby second Dragon Dancer). "He's still at the stud, but when I saw him he was a big, strong, good-looking horse and I think he's worth putting in the book".

Won 2 gd races Newml

631. HARBILIS ★★★

b.f. Harlan's Holiday – Mirabilis (Lear Fan). February 13. The dam, a listed 7f winner in France, was third in the Group 1 7f Prix de la Foret and subsequently won a Grade 3 event in the USA over 1m at 4 yrs. She is a half-sister to the Group 1 1m Prix du Moulin and Group 1 10.5f Prix de Diane winner Nebraska Tornado and the Group 2 10f Prix Eugene Adam winner Burning Sun. The second dam, Media Nox (by Lycius), a useful 2-y-o winner of the Group 3 5f Prix du Bois, is a half-sister to the very useful Bonash, a winner of 4 races in France from 1m to 12f including the Prix d'Aumale, the Prix Vanteaux and the Prix de Malleret. *"I like her, she goes well. We haven't seen a lot of horses by the sire over here but this filly goes very nicely and we're pleased with her. She's got a good attitude and a very good action, so I wouldn't be frightened of six furlongs in mid-season".*

632. HOARDING ★★★

b.c. Elusive Quality – What A Treasure (Cadeaux Genereux). March 30. Second foal. $150,000Y. Keeneland September. John Ferguson. Half-brother to the 2011 7f placed 2-y-o Strada Facendo (by Street Cry). The dam, a fair dual 7f winner, is a half-sister to 4 winners including the German Group 3 6.5f winner Toylsome. The second dam, Treasure Trove (by The Minstrel), is a placed half-sister to the US Graded stakes winners Dance Parade and Ocean Queen. *"A solid horse, he goes OK and I could see him running over six or seven furlongs in mid-season".* Easily won in ~~condi~~ normal ~~undr~~ gd ride

633. KHUDOUA ★★

b.c. Nayef – Danehill Dreamer (Danehill). February 2. Second foal. 70,000Y. Tattersalls October Book 2. Shadwell Estate Co. The dam is an unraced half-sister to 8 winners including the Group 1 10f Coral Eclipse Stakes winner Compton Admiral and the Group 1 1m Queen Elizabeth II Stakes winner Summoner. The second dam, Sumoto (by Mtoto), a useful 6f (at 2 yrs) and 7f winner, is a half-sister to 5 winners including Lalindi (dam of the Group/Graded stakes winners Adagio and Arvada). *"A nice, staying horse, he'll make a 2-y-o but not until the autumn".*

634. MAXI DRESS (IRE) ★★★

b.f. Shamardal – Fashion Trade (Dansili). January 29. First foal. 80,000Y. Tattersalls October Book 1. R O'Gorman. The dam is an unraced half-sister to 3 winners including the Group 1 Cheveley Park Stakes winner Prophecy (herself the dam of 3 stakes winners including the Group 2 Prix de Sandringham winner Modern Look). The second dam, Andaleeb (by Lyphard), was a useful winner of 2 races including the Group 3 12f Lancashire Oaks and was fourth in the Group 1 Yorkshire Oaks and is a half-sister to 5 winners. *"She's fine, a good solid filly with a good attitude to life like a lot of the Shamardal's. There's no reason why she wouldn't be out by the end of May over six furlongs".*

635. MUNHAMER ★★★

ch.c. Iffraaj – Khibraat (Alhaarth). March 30. Second foal. 160,000Y. Tattersalls October Book 2. Shadwell Estate Co. Half-brother to the quite useful 2011 2-y-o dual 1m winner Cavaleiro (by Sir Percy). The dam is an unplaced half-sister to 10 winners including the smart Group 2 14.6f Park Hill Stakes winner Ranin. The second dam, Nafhaat (by Roberto), a fairly useful 12f winner, was listed-placed and stayed 15f. *"He goes alright and he'll be racing over six furlongs. A good, big, strong-looking horse".*

636. NEWFANGLED ★★★

b.f. New Approach – Scarlet Ibis (Machiavellian). Second foal. Half-sister to the fair 2011 Irish 5f placed 2-y-o Red Avis (by Exceed And Excel). The dam, a quite useful French 1m winner, is a half-sister to the US 2-y-o 1m winner and Grade 3 placed Anasheed and to the very useful 1m (in UAE) and 10f winner and listed-placed Marhoob. The second dam, Flagbird (by Nureyev), won the Group 1 Premio Presidente della Repubblica and is a half-sister to the US Grade 1 winners Prospector's Delite and Runup The Colors and the US Grade 2 winner Top Account. *"She goes OK, she's quite neat and should be racing by mid-season. Worth a mention".* Hacked up from well hacked Horses

637. NICKELS AND DIMES (IRE) ★★★

b.f. Teofilo – Neat Shilling (Bob Back). April 15. Seventh foal. 57,000Y. Tattersalls October

horse of mth Murray

Book 1. John Ferguson. Half-sister to the listed winner and UAE Group 2 placed Kalahari Gold (by Trans Island), to the quite useful 7f (at 2 yrs) to 10f and hurdles winner of 8 races Mr Jack Daniells, the fair 6f (at 2 yrs) to 1 winner of 5 races Tidy (both by Mujadil) and the moderate 5f winner Stacey Mac (by Elnadim). The dam is an unraced sister to the Irish 7f (at 2 yrs) and 10f winner and Group 3 placed Fill The Bill and a half-sister to 6 winners including the US Grade 3 winner Riddlesdown. The second dam, Neat Dish (by Stalwart), won once over 6f at 2 yrs in Ireland, was second in the Group 3 Railway Stakes and is a half-sister to 9 winners including the US stakes winner and Grade 1 placed Western Winter. *"She's fine and she goes well, her joints have been a bit immature so I see her as more of a seven furlong type in August or September. A good mover".*

638. PEACE OF LOVE (GER) ★★★

b.f. Galileo – Peace Time (Surumu). May 11. Seventh foal. 600,000Y. Tattersalls October Book 1. Badgers Bloodstock. Sister to the quite useful Irish 11f winner Lastofthemohicans and half-sister to the German dual Group 3 1m winner Peace Royale (by Sholokov), the German Group 3 1m winner Peaceful Love, the fair 1m and 9f winner Prince Evelith and 2 minor winners abroad (all by Dashing Blade). The dam, a German listed-placed winner, is a half-sister to 7 minor winners in Germany and one in Italy. The second dam, Princess Of Spain (by King Of Spain), was a listed-placed winner in Germany and a half-sister to 3 winners. *"A medium-sized, attractive filly and a good mover. She's got a good, laid-back attitude and is a nice type of filly, but her pedigree is all about twelve furlongs as a 3-y-o. She'll start at the back-end over seven furlongs or a mile".*

639. POMEROL ★★★★

ch.c. Kyllachy – Clinet (Docksider). April 18. Second foal. 145,000Y. Tattersalls October Book 2. Blandford Bloodstock. Half-brother to the unplaced 2011 2-y-o La Confession (by Dylan Thomas). The dam won 5 races at 2 to 4 yrs from 7f to 9f, including a listed event in the UAE, was Grade 2 placed in the USA and is a half-sister to 3 winners. The second dam, Oiche Mhaith (by Night Shift), won once at 3 yrs and is a half-sister to 7 winners. *"A nice sort of horse, he's active and athletic. There's no reason why he couldn't make a six furlong 2-y-o by the middle of May. Goes nicely".*

640. POMODORO ★★★

ch.c. Pivotal – Foodbroker Fancy (Halling). March 1. Half-brother to the smart 7f (at 2 yrs), listed 10f and subsequent US Grade 3 12f winner Dalvina (by Grand Lodge) and to the very useful 7f (at 2 yrs) and listed 10f winner Soft Centre (by Zafonic). The dam, a smart 6f (at 2 yrs) and dual listed 10f winner, is a half-sister to the useful listed 2-y-o 6f winner Femme Fatale. The second dam, Red Rita (by Kefaah), a fairly useful 4-y-o 6f winner, was second in the Group 3 6f Cherry Hinton Stakes and the Group 3 6f Princess Margaret Stakes at 2 yrs and is a half-sister to 3 minor winners. (Normandie Stud). *"A big, rangy chestnut colt out of a good mare, being by Pivotal he'll want some juice in the ground. I can see him running over seven furlongs in September".*

641. RANGI ★★★★

ch.c. New Approach – Miss Queen (Miswaki). April 15. Eighth foal. 125,000Y. Tattersalls October Book 2. Blandford Bloodstock. Half-brother to the very useful 2-y-o Group 2 5f Flying Childers Stakes and subsequent Hong Kong winner Chateau Istana (by Grand Lodge), to the very useful 2-y-o Group 3 6f Sirenia Stakes winner Prince Of Light (by Fantastic Light), the very useful 7f (at 2 yrs) and 1m Britannia Handicap winner and listed-placed Mandobi (by Mark Of Esteem), the fair 9f and 10f winner African Cheetah (by Pivotal) and a winner in Japan by High Chaparral. The dam, a minor winner over 6f in the USA, is a half-sister to 8 winners including the useful 2-y-o Group 3 6f Princess Margaret Stakes winner Tajannub. The second dam, Empress Jackie (by Mount Hagen), won 8 races in the USA including two minor stakes and is a half-sister to the Derby and Irish Derby third Star Of Gdansk and the US Grade 3 winner W D Jacks. *"An attractive horse and a good mover, he has some class about him and there's enough speed in the pedigree that I wouldn't be frightened of running him over six furlongs".*

642. REMOTE ★★
b.c. Dansili – Zenda (Zamindar). February 22. Fifth foal. Brother to Panzanella, unplaced over 6f on his only start at 2 yrs in 2011. The dam won the French 1,000 Guineas, was second in the Coronation Stakes and the Grade 1 Queen Elizabeth II Challenge Cup at Keeneland and is a half-sister to the July Cup and Nunthorpe Stakes winner Oasis Dream and the very useful dual listed 1m winner Hopeful Light. The second dam, Hope (by Dancing Brave), is an unraced sister to the very smart filly Wemyss Bight, a winner of five races from 9f (at 2 yrs) to 12f including the Group 1 Irish Oaks and the Group 2 Prix de Malleret. (Khalid Abdulla). *"Obviously we're pleased to have him because of the mare who was so good to us. He's a rather nice sort of horse, we'll take our time with him and he'll appreciate seven furlongs in the autumn".*

643. REQAABA ★★★★ ♠
b.f. Exceed And Excel – Something Blue (Petong). February 21. Ninth foal. 130,000Y. Tattersalls October Book 1. Shadwell Estate Co. Closely related to the fair 6f winner Angel Song (by Dansili) and half-sister to the useful Group 3 5f Prix de Saint-Georges and triple sprint listed winner Mood Music, to the fairly useful 2-y-o 6f winner The Long Game (both by Kyllachy), the fairly useful 5f (including at 2 yrs) to 7f winner of 11 races Steel Blue, the fair 6f and 7f winner of 13 races Yorkshire Blue (both by Atraf) and the quite useful 5f and 6f winner of 13 races (including at 2 yrs) Memphis Man (by Bertolini). The dam is an unplaced sister to one winner and a half-sister to 5 winners including the Group 3 5f Palace House Stakes second Blues Indigo and the 2-y-o winner Indigo (herself dam of the smart sprinters Astonished and Bishops Court). The second dam, Blueit (by Bold Lad, Ire), a useful 2-y-o 5f winner, is a full or half-sister to 3 winners. (Hamdan Al Maktoum). *"A speedy little thing, she's got a bit of 'zip' about her, she's been settled in everything she's been doing and she has a quick, low action. I'd be happy to run her over five furlongs in early May".*

644. SHAMAL ★★★★
b.c. Exceed And Excel – Miss Meltemi (Miswaki Tern). May 8. Eighth foal. 160,000Y. Tattersalls

October Book 1. John Ferguson. Half-brother to the very useful 7f (at 2 yrs) and listed 1m winner and Group 3 Dahlia Stakes third Don't Dili Dali, to the useful 7f and 1m winner and listed-placed Balducci, the fairly useful 1m winner and listed-placed Ada River (all by Dansili), the quite useful 2-y-o 5f winner Haigh Hall (by Kyllachy), the quite useful 12f winner Zafarana (by Tiger Hill) and the fair 7f to 8.7f winner Willie Ever (by Agnes World). The dam, a 7f and 1m 2-y-o winner in Italy, was third in the Group 1 Italian Oaks and is a half-sister to 2 winners. The second dam, Blu Meltemi (by Star Shareef), a winner of 5 races at 2 and 3 yrs in Italy and second in the Italian Oaks, is a half-sister to 3 winners. *"A lovely, big, bay horse. He has a good attitude, he's a good mover and has plenty of scope about him. A lovely sort of horse, his pedigree would suggest six furlongs to start with, but to look at him I'd say seven".*

645. SHE'S LATE ★★★
ch.c. Pivotal – Courting (Pursuit Of Love). April 24. Eighth foal. 120,000Y. Tattersalls October Book 2. John Gosden. Brother to the quite useful 9f to 12f winner Speed Dating and half-brother to the useful 2-y-o dual 7f winner and listed-placed Fury (by Invincible Spirit), to the fairly useful 7f to 10f winner of 6 races Secret Liaison (by Medicean), the fairly useful 7f and 10f winner Tryst (by Highest Honor), the modest 6f winner Vibe (by Danzero) and a minor winner abroad by Zafonic. The dam, a fairly useful winner of four 2-y-o 7f events and two listed races over 1m and 10f at 3 yrs, is a half-sister to 8 winners including the Group 3 Horris Hill Stakes winner Cupid's Glory. The second dam, Doctor's Glory (by Elmaamul), a fairly useful 5.2f (at 2 yrs) and 6f winner, is a half-sister to 6 winners including the listed winner On Call (herself dam of the US Grade 2 winner One Off). *"A nice sort of horse, he's a big, rangy colt and a good mover. Very much the type to start off over seven furlongs in August".*

646. SNOWBRIGHT ★★★
b.f. Pivotal – Snow Gretel (Green Desert). February 13. Second foal. 110,000Y. Tattersalls October Book 2. Cheveley Park Stakes. The dam, a German listed 1m winner, is a half-sister to 3 winners including the 2-y-o Group 2 1m Royal Lodge Stakes winner and 2,000 Guineas

second Snow Ridge. The second dam, Snow Princess (by Ela-Mana-Mou), a smart winner of 6 races at up to 2m including the November Handicap and an Italian listed event, was second in the Group 1 Prix Royal-Oak and is a half-sister to 7 winners. *"A nice type of filly, she goes well. We're pleased with her and she should be able to run in mid-season. I like her".*

647. SNOW KING ★★★

ch.c. *Elusive Quality – Cloudspin (Storm Cat).* March 13. First foal. The dam is an unraced half-sister to the Grade 1 10f Breeders Cup Classic and Group 1 1m Queen Elizabeth II Stakes winner Raven's Pass (by Elusive Quality) and to the US stakes winner and Grade 2 placed Gigawatt. The second dam, Ascutney (by Lord At War), won the US Grade 3 Miesque Stakes and is a sister to the US stakes winner Words Of War (herself dam of the Grade 1 Del Mar Oaks winner No Matter What and the US Grade 2 winner E Dubai) and a half-sister to 8 winners. *"A nice sort of horse, he's a three-parts brother to Raven's Pass and he goes fine. I can see him running over seven furlongs and he's a strong 2-y-o we should see out in mid-season".*

Won 7f 1f Ascor or Sebai

648. SNOW POWDER (IRE) ★★★

ch.f. *Raven's Pass – Multicolour Wave (Rainbow Quest).* March 11. Seventh foal. 170,000Y. Tattersalls October Book 1. John Ferguson. Half-sister to the Group 1 French 1,000 Guineas winner Elusive Wave (by Elusive City), to the Irish 2-y-o 7f winner and listed-placed Million Waves (by Mull Of Kintyre), the quite useful 7f (at 2 yrs) and 1m winner Million Spirits (by Invincible Spirit), the quite useful Irish 2-y-o 7f winner Wealdmore Wave (by Oratorio) and the minor French 9.5f winner Photophore (by Clodovil). The dam is a placed half-sister to 4 winners and to the unraced dam of the Group 2 Queen Mary Stakes winner Langs Lash. The second dam, Echoes (by Niniski), won the Group 3 Prix Corrida, was Group 2 placed and is a half-sister to 5 winners. *"A nice filly, she's very elegant and light on her feet. One for a seven furlong maiden around July time".*

649. SOLACE (USA) ★★★

ch.f. *Langfuhr – Songerie (Hernando).* March 1. The dam won the Group 3 1m Prix des Reservoirs at 2 yrs and was third in the Group

2 Park Hill Stakes and is a sister to the fairly useful 2-y-o 7.2f and German listed winner and Group 1 Italian Oaks third Souvenance and a half-sister to 4 winners including the useful listed winners Soft Morning and Sourire. The second dam, Summer Night (by Nashwan), a fairly useful 3-y-o 6f winner, is a half-sister to 7 winners including the Group 3 Prix d'Arenburg winner Starlit Sands. *"A lovely, big filly, she was quite a character to break in but she enjoys her exercise now. She's a good mover, has a good stride on her and will be a seven furlong filly in mid-season".*

650. SPACE SHIP ★★★

ch.c. *Galileo – Angara (Alzao).* January 17. The dam, winner of Grade 1 10f Beverly D Stakes and Grade 1 9f Diana Stakes in the USA, is a half-sister to numerous winners including the French Group 2 Prix Corrida winner Actrice. The second dam, Ange Bleu (by Alleged), was placed at 3 yrs in France and is a half-sister to 10 winners including the Group 3 Prix de Psyche winner and French 1,000 Guineas and French Oaks placed Agathe (herself dam of the Grade/Group 1 winners Artiste Royale and Aquarelliste), to the Breeders Cup Classic winner Arcangues and the dam of the 1,000 Guineas winner Cape Verdi. (Lady Rothschild). *"An attractive horse, he's well-balanced and a good mover. We'll aim him for the seven furlong maidens".*

651. STREET BATTLE ★★★

b.c. *Street Boss – J J's Kitty (Storm Cat).* March 17. Fourth foal. $165,000Y. Keeneland September. John Ferguson. Half-brother to the US 2-y-o winner and stakes-placed Maria's Kitty (by Maria's Mon). The dam is an unraced half-sister to 2 minor winners. The second dam, J J's Dream (by Glitterman), won two Grade 2 and four Grade 3 events in the USA and is a half-sister to 7 winners and to the unraced dam of the US Grade 1 winner Awesome Gem. *"Certainly worth mentioning, he looks like a little speedy 2-y-o. Sharp, well-rounded and a neat, 2-y-o type for May or June over six furlongs".*

652. TOAST OF THE TOWN (IRE) ★★★★ ♠

b.f. *Duke Of Marmalade – Boast (Most Welcome).* April 14. Sixth foal. 160,000Y.

Tattersalls October Book 1. Blandford Bloodstock. Closely related to the useful 2-y-o listed 5.2f winner and dual Group 3 placed Strut (by Danehill Dancer) and half-sister to the quite useful 2-y-o dual 5f winner and subsequent US Grade 3 placed Vaunt (by Averti) and the quite useful 2-y-o 5f and subsequent US winner Brag (by Mujadil). The dam, a useful 5f and 6f winner, is a half-sister to 6 winners including the fairly useful 2-y-o 5f and 4-y-o 1m winner Great Bear. The second dam, Bay Bay (by Bay Express), a useful 7.6f winner, was listed-placed twice and is a half-sister to 7 winners. *"She's gone through a growing stage, but she's an attractive filly and a good mover that's showing a bit of class".*

653. TRAPEZE ★★★

ch.f. Pivotal – Miss Penton *(Primo Dominie).* April 6. Ninth foal. 240,000Y. Tattersalls October Book 1. Hugo Lascelles. Sister to the Group 2 1m Royal Lodge Stakes winner Leo (by Pivotal), closely related to the Italian 2-y-o 1m listed winner Balkenhol (by Polar Falcon) and half-sister to the quite useful 2011 2-y-o 1m winner Pembrey (by Teofilo), the Italian 2-y-o winner of 4 races Super To Bend (by Refuse To Bend) and the placed dam of the Group 2 Prix Robert Papin winner Irish Field. The dam was placed 3 times at up to 7f and is a half-sister to 8 winners including the very useful listed 6f Sirenia Stakes winner Art of War. The second dam, On The House (by Be My Guest), a high-class winner of 4 races from 5f to 1m including the 1,000 Guineas and the Sussex Stakes, is a half-sister to 3 winners. *"A sister to a good 2-y-o we had called Leo, this is a nice sort of filly and she'll be racing this year but she could do with a bit more scope".*

654. VANITY RULES ★★★

b.f. New Approach – Miss Pinkerton *(Danehill).* February 8. Half-sister to the modest 1m to 12f winner of 12 races General Tufto (by Fantastic Light), the modest 1m and 9f winner Smart Step (by Montjeu) and the moderate 7f winner Hard Ball (by Pivotal). The dam, a useful 6f (at 2 yrs) and 1m listed winner, is a half-sister to 3 winners including the smart 7f (at 2 yrs) and 10f winner Grand Central. The second dam, Rebecca Sharp (by Machiavellian), winner of the Group 1 1m Coronation Stakes, is a half-

sister to 8 winners including the Group 3 11.5f Lingfield Derby Trial winner Mystic Knight. *"She goes nicely, she's a scopey sort of filly with a good, purposeful action and she should be racing by mid-season. Worth watching".*

655. WALLENBERG ★★★

b.c. Rock Of Gibraltar – Waldmark *(Mark Of Esteem).* March 17. Sixth foal. 85,000Y. Tattersalls October Book 1. Blandford Bloodstock. Half-brother to the promising 2011 French 2-y-o 1m winner Walderleche (by Monsun), to the Group 1 St Leger and Group 3 13f Bahrain Trophy winner Masked Marvel (by Montjeu), the fair Irish 10f winner Sadler's Mark (by Sadler's Wells) and the minor French 3-y-o winner Gifted Icon (by Peintre Celebre). The dam, a smart 2-y-o 7f winner, was second in the Group 2 1m Falmouth Stakes and is a half-sister to 6 winners including the Group 1 German Derby winner Waldpark. The second dam, Wurftaube (by Acatenango), a winner of two Group 2 events over 12f and 14f in Germany, was Group 1 placed and is a half-sister to 8 winners. *"A half-brother to our St Leger winner Masked Marvel, he's named after the famous Swedish diplomat who helped a lot of Jewish people escape from the Nazis. This is nice colt, he's obviously going to want seven furlongs or a mile this year but he's a nice sort and we're happy with him".*

656. WANNABE YOUR MAN ★★★

b.c. Halling – Wannabe Posh *(Grand Lodge).* February 8. Second foal. The dam, a winner of four races including the listed 12f Galtres Stakes, was second in the Group 3 14f Lillie Langtry Stakes and is a half-sister to numerous winners including the Group 1 6f Cheveley Park Stakes and Group 2 6f Cherry Hinton Stakes winner Wannabe Grand and the useful Irish listed 1m winner Pirateer. The second dam, Wannabe (Shirley Heights), a quite useful 1m and 10f winner, is a half-sister to 3 winners including the very useful 5f and 6f winner and Group 1 Cheveley Park Stakes second Tanami (herself dam of the Group 2 Rockfel Stakes winner Cairns). (Normandie Stud). *"A nice colt, we like him, he's a good mover with a good attitude. Halling is a good 'owner-breeder' sort of stallion".*

657. WINSILI ★★★

b.f. *Dansili – Winter Sunrise (Pivotal)*. February 1. First foal. The dam, a useful dual 10f winner, is a half-sister to the Group 2 10f Prix Greffulhe winner Ice Blue (by Dansili). The second dam, Winter Solstice (by Unfuwain), a French 2-y-o 1m winner and second in the Group 3 1m Prix d'Aumale, is a half-sister to the Grade 1 Manhattan Handicap winner Meteor Storm, to the Group 2 12.5f Grand Prix de Deauville winner Polish Summer and the French 10f listed winner Morning Eclipse. *"A nice, straightforward filly that just gets on with it. One for seven furlongs in mid-season".*

658. UNNAMED ★★★

ch.c. *Speightstown – Light Jig (Danehill)*. April 13. Fifth foal. Half-brother to the useful 7f (at 2 yrs) and UAE listed 1m and 10f winner Treble Jig (by Gone West). The dam, a US Grade 1 10f Yellow Ribbon Stakes winner, is a half-sister to numerous winners including the very useful French 2-y-o listed 1m winner Battle Dore. The second dam, Nashmeel (by Blushing Groom), was a very smart winner of three races over 1m including the Group 2 Prix d'Astarte and was second in the Prix Jacques le Marois (to Miesque), the Yellow Ribbon Invitational and the Matriarch Stakes. (Khalid Abdulla). *"We like him, he's a good mover with a nice attitude. One for seven furlongs in mid-season – he catches the eye".*

659. UNNAMED ★★★

b.f. *Singspiel – Magic Tree (Timber Country)*. April 21. Third foal. 70,000Y. Tattersalls October Book 1. Badgers Bloodstock. The dam ran once unplaced and is a half-sister to the Group 1 winner Gran Criterium winner Kirklees and the Group 1 St Leger and Group 2 Italian Derby winner Mastery. The second dam, Moyesii (by Diesis), won once and is a half-sister to the Group 3 Prix de Fontainebleau winner Bowman. *"She's done a lot of improving through the winter and has gone the right way. She's a Singspiel and one for September or October, but I'm very happy with her".*

660. UNNAMED ★★

b.c. *Duke Of Marmalade – Overruled (Last Tycoon)*. April 24. Tenth foal. 37,000Y. Tattersalls October Book 2. Blandford Bloodstock. Half-

brother to the 2-y-o 7f and 1m and Irish Oaks winner Vintage Tipple (by Entrepreneur), to the useful 2-y-o 7f and 1m winner and Group 1 1m Gran Criterium third Spettro (by Spectrum), the quite useful 9f to 12f winner and listed-placed Record Breaker (by In The Wings), the fair 9f winners Reclamation (by Red Ransom) and High Cross (by Cape Cross). The dam, a quite useful 1m (at 2 yrs) and 10.2f winner, is a half-sister to 6 winners including the Grade 2 American Derby winner and Italian and German Derby placed Overbury. The second dam, Overcall (by Bustino), a winning Irish middle-distance stayer of 3 races, is a half-sister to 9 winners including the dam of the Melbourne Cup winner Vintage Crop. *"A nice, staying horse for the autumn".*

661. UNNAMED ★★★

b.f. *Manduro – Sugar Mill (Polar Falcon)*. February 25. Half-sister to the Group 2 12f Lancashire Oaks and dual listed winner Gertrude Bell (by Sinndar) and to the fairly useful 10f winner Dick Doughtywylie (by Oasis Dream). The dam won over 10f in France and was listed-placed three times. The second dam, Anastina (by Thatching), a fair 7f and 1m winner, is a half-sister to several winners. *"Owned and bred by my wife, this is a half-sister to Gertrude Bell. She goes nicely but my wife has been far too busy to name her yet! I think she'll be out on the July course in a seven furlong maiden, all being well".*

662. UNNAMED ★★★

b.c. *Galileo – Vallee Des Reves (Kingmambo)*. May 18. Brother to the quite useful 10f, 14f and hurdles winner Corum, closely related to the Irish 7f winner and Group 3 9f placed Uimhir A Haon (by Montjeu) and half-brother to the Group 1 1m Coronation Stakes and Group 2 7f Rockfel Stakes winner Maid's Causeway (by Giant's Causeway) and the fair 7f and 1m winner Manhattan Dream (by Statue Of Liberty). The dam is an unraced half-sister to the Group 2 Prix du Muguet winner Vetheuil, the Group 3 Prix de l'Opera winner Verveine (herself dam of the Grade 1 winners Vallee Enchantee and Volga) and the dam of the Group 1 Grand Prix de Paris winner Vespone. The second dam, Venise (by Nureyev), is an unraced three-parts sister to the Mill Reef Stakes and Richmond Stakes winner Vacarme and a half-sister to the

Prix Jacques le Marois winner Vin de France. *"We had his full-brother Corum many moons ago who was just a staying handicapper. I just hope this horse shows us a bit more zip than that, but he's improved and it looks as if he's got a top of the ground action".*

663. UNNAMED ★★★ ♠

b.c. Authorized – Zam Zoom (Dalakhani). February 11. First foal. 48,000Y. Tattersalls October Book 3. Blandford Bloodstock. The dam is an unraced half-sister to Group 3 10f Winter Derby, listed 7f and listed 10f winner Nideeb. The second dam, Mantesera (by In The Wings), is an unraced sister to the very smart Group 3 Nell Gwyn Stakes winner and Group 1 Yorkshire Oaks and Group 1 Prix Vermeille placed Cloud Castle (herself the dam of 2 stakes winners) and a half-sister to 5 winners including the high-class middle-distance horses and multiple Group 1 winners Warrsan and Luso and the Group 2 winner Needle Gun. *"A nice, staying horse, he's worth a mention in the book and he could be out by August time".*

RAE GUEST

664. FAMOUS TALES ★★

b.f. Zamindar – Fame Game (Fasliyev). April 3. First foal. The dam, a modest dual 5f placed maiden at 2 yrs from 3 starts, is a half-sister to 8 winners including the Group 3 placed Easy Sunshine, Unique Pose and Endless Expense. The second dam, Desert Ease (by Green Desert), an Irish 2-y-o listed 6f winner, is a half-sister to 5 winners including the Group 3 Tetrarch Stakes and Group 3 7f Concorde Stakes winner Two-Twenty-Two. (Mr Mike Beever). *"She had an accident as a foal and she only has one eye, so we've taken our time with her, she's a big filly and very backward. She canters nicely so her handicap hasn't stopped her up to now".*

665. FANTASIOSA ★★★

ch.f. With Approval – Fandangerina (Hernando). February 24. First foal. The dam, a fair 2-y-o 9f winner, is a half-sister to 2 winners. The second dam, Fantastic Belle (by Night Shift), a quite useful 6f winner, is a sister to the Canadian Grade 2 winner Moon Solitaire and a half-sister to 9 winners including the smart Group 3 10f Gordon Richards Stakes winner Germano. (Miss K Rausing). *"She's not very big and we hope to*

get her out quite soon because she's taking all her work without a problem. She's doing well at the moment, she's going forward and all being well she'll be out at the end of May".*

666. GODS GIFT ★★

ch.c. Dalakhani – Guilia (Galileo). February 1. Second foal. Brother to Guiletta, unplaced on her first start at 3 yrs in 2012. The dam, a useful 2-y-o 7f winner, was listed-placed over 10f and 13f and is a half-sister to 2 winners. The second dam, Lesgor (by Irish River), won over 10f in France, was third in the Group 3 10f Prix de Psyche and is a half-sister to 3 winners. (The Hornets). *"We had the dam who was fifth in the Oaks. This is a really nice horse but very much a 3-y-o type. We'll try and give him a run at the back-end if we can, he's a lovely horse that moves well".*

667. MICK DUGGAN ★★

ch.g. Pivotal – Poppy Carew (Danehill). February 22. Ninth foal. 30,000Y. Tattersalls October Book 1. Not sold. Half-brother to the fairly useful 2-y-o 7f winner and Group 2 1m May Hill Stakes fourth Suzy Bliss (by Spinning World), to the fairly useful dual 12f winner Cutting Crew (by Diesis), the fair 1m to 12f winner of 8 races Mad Carew (by Rahy) and 3 winners over hurdles by Affirmed, Medicean and Royal Applause. The dam, a very useful 7f (at 2 yrs) to 12f winner (including a 10f listed event), was third in the Group 2 Sun Chariot Stakes and is a full or half-sister to 9 winners including the very smart dual Group 3 10f winner Leporello and the dam of the US Grade 2 winner Devious Boy. (E P Duggan). *"He's quite a big horse and we'll try and get on with him but he won't be a 2-y-o until July or August. A seven furlong type 2-y-o".*

668. ROSIE FUTURE ★★★

b.f. Azamour – Auspicious (Shirley Heights). April 28. Ninth foal. 25,000Y. Tattersalls October Book 2. Rae Guest. Half-sister to the fair 2011 2-y-o 6f winner Fortrose Academy (by Iceman), to the fairly useful 2-y-o 7f and 1m winner Doctrine (by Barathea), the quite useful 2-y-o 1m winner Australian (by Danzero), the quite useful 1m to 10f winner Prince Picasso (by Lomitas), to the fair 2-y-o 1m winner Perfect Vision (by Starcraft), the fair 7f and 9f winner Brown Butterfly (by Medicean) and the fair dual 7f winner Istiqdaam (by Pivotal). The dam, a fairly useful 10.2f winner, is a sister to the smart Group 2 11.9f Great Voltigeur Stakes winner Sacrament and a half-sister to 5 winners and to the unraced dam of the Group 1 winner Chorist. The second dam, Blessed Event (by Kings Lake), winner of the listed 10f Ballymacoll Stud Stakes and placed in the Yorkshire Oaks and the Champion Stakes, is a half-sister to 4 winners. (Mr E Duggan). *"A very nice filly, she was very small when we bought her and she hasn't grown a lot, so although on pedigree you'd think she'd be much more of a 3-y-o type for twelve furlongs she'll actually be out in mid-summer. She'll either start at six furlongs or we'll wait for seven".* TRAINERS' BARGAIN BUY

669. ROSIE REBEL ★★★

ch.f. *Cockney Rebel – Meandering Rose (Irish River).* March 22. Eighth foal. 9,000Y. Tattersalls October Book 2. Rae Guest. Half-sister to the fair 2m winner of 3 races Rosewood Lad, to the poor 12f winner Primera Rossa (both by Needwood Blade) and the modest 1m (at 2 yrs), 7f and 9f winner Ella Y Rossa (by Bertolini). The dam is an unraced half-sister to 2 minor winners in the USA. The second dam, Sunset Rose (by Shirley Heights), a poor dual 12f winner, is a half-sister to 7 winners. *"She's a big filly but she's doing very well and she'll probably be one of our earlier 2-y-o runners. She'll get better as the season progresses, but she does everything easily and she moves nicely. A 2-y-o type for six furlongs".*

670. UNNAMED ★★★

gr.f. *Dark Angel – Downland (El Prado).* February 21. Fourth foal. 18,000Y. Tattersalls October 2. Rae Guest. Half-sister to a winner in Greece by Camacho. The dam, a moderate 7f placed 3-y-o, is a half-sister to 5 winners including the Group 2 6f Gimcrack Stakes and Group 2 6f Mill Reef Stakes placed Ma Yoram. The second dam, Quelle Affaire (by Riverman), is a French placed sister to the Group 3 7f Concorde Stakes winner and Queen Anne Stakes second Rami and a half-sister to the Group 3 6.5f Prix Eclipse winner Crack Regiment and the listed Prix Yacowlef winner La Grand Epoque. (The Calm Again Partnership). *"She looks like she'll be a 2-y-o although she's not forward now. She's*

not very big, she's the right size and shape to make a 2-y-o but just hasn't come in her coat yet. She'll make a 2-y-o in the summer".*

671. UNNAMED ★★

b.f. *Kyllachy – Fascination Street (Mujadil).* March 29. Fourth foal. 7,500Y. Tattersalls October Book 3. Rae Guest. Closely related to the fair 2011 1m placed 2-y-o Amy Dorrit (by Pivotal). The dam, a modest 7f winner at 3 yrs, is a half-sister to 6 winners including the US triple Grade 1 winner from 9f to 10f Golden Apples and the Group 3 Park Hill Stakes winner Alexander Three D. The second dam, Loon (by Kaldoun), won 4 races in France including the listed 12f Prix de la Porte de Passy and is a half-sister to 3 minor winners. *"A well-bred filly and if everything goes the right way with her she'll make a 2-y-o. A typical sprinting type, she was small with open knees when I bought her, but all that's come good and she's going nicely at the moment. She's still for sale".*

672. UNNAMED ★★★

b.f. *Medicean – Rhumba Rage (Nureyev).* March 27. Tenth foal. 14,000Y. Tattersalls October 2. Rae Guest. Half-sister to the useful 10.3f winner Tough Men, to a minor winner in Spain (both by Woodman), the quite useful 1m winner Rule Maker (by Lemon Drop Kid), the fair 1m winner Atheer (by Lear Fan) and a winner in Japan by Rubiano. The dam is an unplaced sister to the Group 3 1m Prix des Chenes winner and Group 1 placed Fotitieng and a half-sister to 5 winners. The second dam, Dry Fly (by Mill Reef), won 3 times in France and is a half-sister to 6 winners including the Group 1 Grand Prix de Saint-Cloud winner Gay Mecene and the US Grade 3 winner Lassie Dear (herself dam of the Haydock Park Sprint Cup and Prix de la Foret winner Wolfhound). (The Calm Again Partnership). *"She's done very well and although she won't be running until late summer over a seven furlongs or a mile she looks the part, we're just not rushing her yet. She'll be one of the nicer ones".*

673. UNNAMED ★★

b.f. *Jeremy – Sunlit Skies (Selkirk).* March 30. Third foal. 9,000Y. Tattersalls December. Not sold. Half-sister to the fair 2011 2-y-o 1m winner Tingo In The Tale (by Oratorio). The dam is an unplaced sister to the fairly useful 6f and 7f winner Sheltering Sky and a half-sister to 6 winners including the Group 3 Prix d'Arenburg winner Starlit Sands and the listed 6f winner Sea Dane. The second dam, Shimmering Sea (by Slip Anchor), a fairly useful Irish 2-y-o 5f and 7f winner and third in the Group 3 Silken Glider Stakes, is a half-sister to 5 winners including the King George VI and Queen Elizabeth Stakes winner Petoski. *"A nice, big filly, she's backward at the moment, she'll get better as the season goes on but she's one for the back-end of the season".*

674. UNNAMED ★★★

ch.f. Dutch Art – Turban Heights (Golan). April 20. First foal. 19,000Y. Tattersalls October Book 2. Rae Guest. The dam, a fair 1m to 14f winner of 3 races at 3 and 4 yrs, is a half-sister to 7 winners including the listed winner Barboukh (herself dam of the Group 3 winner Barbola). The second dam, Turban (by Glint Of Gold), a fair 10f and 11.7f winner at 3 yrs, is a half-sister to 6 winners including the top-class French and Irish Derby winner Old Vic. (The Calm Again Partnership). *"One for the late-summer over six furlongs, she's a well-made filly that looks like a 2-y-o type. She has a lovely character but we're taking our time with her. The fillies are just starting to bloom now".*

WILLIAM HAGGAS

675. ARAQELLA ★★

b.f. Oasis Dream – Bourbonella (Rainbow Quest). April 23. Seventh foal. Sister to the high-class Group 1 1m Prix du Moulin, Group 2 Summer Mile and Group 3 7f Jersey Stakes winner Aqlaam and half-sister to the fair 12f to 15f winner Curacao (by Sakhee). The dam is an unraced half-sister to 9 winners including the high-class and multiple winning stayer Persian Punch and the Group 3 7f Solario Stakes winner Island Magic. The second dam, Rum Cay (by Our Native), a fair 14.6f winner, is a half-sister to 3 winners including the listed winner of 10 races Gymcrak Premiere. (Mr & Mrs D Hearson). *"Unfortunately she's had an injury, but nothing too dramatic and she's fine now. She'll be back with us soon and she was nice earlier on, so I hope to get her out in September".*

676. ASSEMBLY ★★★★ ♠

ch.c. Kyllachy – Constitute (Gone West). April 11. Seventh foal. 85,000Y. Tattersalls October Book 1. John Warren. Brother to the fairly useful dual 6f winner (including at 2 yrs) and dual listed-placed Enact and to the minor winner abroad Profit Ilias and closely related to another minor winner abroad by Pivotal. The dam, a quite useful 1m winner, is a half-sister to 6 winners including the smart 7f and 1m winner (at 2 yrs) and Group 3 10f Select Stakes second Battle Chant. The second dam, Appointed One (by Danzig), a US stakes winner, was Grade 3 placed and is a sister to the Group 2 1m Lockinge Stakes winner Emperor Jones and the listed 6f Sirenia Stakes winner and Group 1 Middle Park Stakes third Majlood and a half-sister to the Group 1 1m William Hill Futurity Stakes winner Bakharoff. (Highclere Thoroughbred Racing – Coventry). *"This is a nice horse, he's tall, at 16.2 hands already, but he's a nice mover. A classy colt for the second half of the season".*

677. AZIKI (IRE) ★★

ch.c. Duke Of Marmalade – Mubkera (Nashwan). January 21. Sixth foal. 120,000Y. Tattersalls October Book 2. A O Nerses. Half-brother to the very smart Group 3 9f Strensall Stakes and Group 3 11f Dubai Duty Free Arc Trial winner Green Destiny (by Green Desert), to the useful 1m (at 2 yrs) and 10f winner Aqwaal (by Red Ransom), the fair 12f winner First Battalion (by Sadler's Wells) and the minor French 12f winner Manjam (by Almutawakel). The dam, a quite useful 1m winner (at 2 yrs) and listed placed over 10f and 11.5f, is a half-sister to 4 winners. The second dam, Na Ayim (by Shirley Heights), a modest 2-y-o 6f winner, is a half-sister to 5 winners out of a half-sister to the dams of Rainbow Quest, Warning and Commander In Chief. (Saleh Al Homaizi & Imad Al Sagar). *"He's getting more and more like his half-brother Green Destiny by the day. He's not very big, but he's quite strong and I don't suppose he'll be too early. I'd say he'll be a back-end 2-y-o and after all Green Destiny didn't run at two, but he just got better and better, so I hope this colt will be the same. This is a nice horse".*

678. BOTTEEN ★★★

b.c. *Invincible Spirit – Dundel (Machiavellian).* February 28. Eleventh foal. 80,000Y. Tattersalls October Book 1. Shadwell Estate Co. Brother to the fair 2011 1m winner Tina's Spirit and half-brother to the smart 2-y-o 6f and subsequent US stakes winner and Group 2 6f Coventry Stakes third Luck Money (by Indian Ridge), to the 2-y-o Group 3 7f Prix du Calvados winner Charlotte O'Fraise (by Beat Hollow), the modest 2m 1f and hurdles winner Lodgician (by Grand Lodge), the Irish 1m and hurdles winner River Nurey (by Fasliyev), the minor French 3-y-o winner Wing And Wing (by Singspiel) and a dual hurdles winner by Sadler's Wells. The dam, a quite useful 7f winner, is a half-sister to 6 winners including the Group 3 6f Prix de Seine-et-Oise winner Seltitude. The second dam, Dunoof (by Shirley Heights), a fairly useful 2-y-o 7f winner, is a sister to the Premio Roma, Park Hill Stakes and Ribblesdale Stakes winner High Hawk (the dam of In the Wings) and to the winning dams of the Derby winner High-Rise and the Grade 1 Rothmans International winner Infamy. *"He's a sharp horse and he was always going to be our first 2-y-o runner until he had a small problem. Hopefully that won't hold us up too much because he's quite a nice horse. A sharp, six furlong type 2-y-o".*

679. BUTTERFLY DREAM ★★★★ ♠

ch.f. *Kyllachy – Dream Again (Medicean).* March 9. Third foal. The dam is an unplaced half-sister to 2 winners. The second dam, Dance A Dream (by Sadler's Wells), a smart winner of the Cheshire Oaks and second in the Epsom Oaks, is a sister to the 2,000 Guineas winner Entrepreneur and to the very useful middle-distance listed winner Sadler's Image and a half-sister to numerous winners including the Coronation Stakes winner Exclusive. (Cheveley Park Stud). *"She's sharp, a model 2-y-o and I would think she'll run at the end of May. A real five/six furlong 2-y-o type with a very strong second thigh".*

680. CARA GINA ★★★★

b.f. *Bahamian Bounty – Princess Georgina (Royal Applause).* March 4. Second foal. 50,000Y. Tattersalls October Book 1. McKeever Bloodstock. Half-sister to the unplaced 2011 2-y-o Cincinnati Kit (by Cape Cross). The dam,

a fair 2-y-o 5.2f winner, is a sister to the Group 2 6f Richmond Stakes winner and Group 1 Gran Criterium third Mister Cosmi and to the smart 2-y-o listed 6f winner and Group 1 6f Middle Park Stakes third Auditorium and a half-sister to one winner. The second dam, Degree (by Warning), a quite useful 4-y-o 1m winner, is a half-sister to 2 winners including the German listed winner Dark Marble. (Mrs D J James). *"I like her, she's quite long but that wouldn't surprise you considering her pedigree. But she's got some speed, she's definitely a 2-y-o and she'll be in some nice races in the autumn. She'll start off in June/July".*

[handwritten: Won 7f Newbury]

681. COLUMELLA ★★★★ *[handwritten: 4th Warwick.]*

b.f. *Kyllachy – Nausicaa (Diesis).* May 10. Seventh foal. £65,000Y. Doncaster Premier. Not sold. Half-sister to the 2011 2-y-o Group 3 Tyros Stakes winner Remember Alexander (by Teofilo), to the 2-y-o Group 2 Cherry Hinton Stakes and Group 3 Albany Stakes winner Memory, the quite useful 6f (at 2 yrs) and 7f winner Kafuu (both by Danehill Dancer), the quite useful Irish 9f winner Hedaaya (by Indian Ridge) and the quite useful 6f (at 2 yrs) and 1m winner Naughty Frida (by Royal Applause). The dam won 3 races at 2 and 3 yrs in France and the USA over 7f and 1m, was third in the Grade 3 Miesque Stakes and is a half-sister to 3 winners. The second dam, Blushing All Over (by Blushing Groom), won 6 races in France and the USA including a listed event and is a half-sister to 8 winners including the good broodmare Come On Rosi. (Wood Hall Stud Ltd). *"She goes well and she'll be a 2-y-o for sure. Whether she's one for the Albany Stakes or not I don't know yet because she was May foal, but she's not very big, quite strong and she's thrived since we've had her".*

[handwritten: Won very comfortably 5f plused fillies Warwick. Le cannu.]

682. CROSS MY HEART ★★★

b.c. *Sakhee's Secret – Sacre Coeur (Compton Place).* April 29. Second foal. Half-brother to the smart 2011 2-y-o listed 5f winner Stepper Point (by Kyllachy). The dam, a fair 2-y-o 6f winner, is a half-sister to 5 winners including the useful dual 10f winner and listed-placed Lonely Heart (herself dam of the Group 3 Tetrarch Stakes winner Leitrim House) and the useful 6f and 7f winner of 4 races Indian Trail. The second dam, Take Heart (by Electric), a quite useful 7f to 10f winner of 4 races, is a half-sister to 3 winners. (Hot To Trot Partnership). *"She's having a break at the moment but she's definitely a 2-y-o, she's a nice walker, has a good backside on her and I would think she'd be a mid-summer 2-y-o".*

683. CRY PEARL (USA) ★★★
b.f. Street Cry – Onda Nova (Keos). April 11. Fourth foal. $140,000Y. Keeneland September. David Redvers. Half-sister to a minor winner in France by Dubai Destination. The dam, a winner of 3 races in France at 2 and 3 yrs including the listed Prix Imprudence, is a half-sister to 6 winners and to the placed dams of the Group 1 winners Shiva and Light Shift and the Brazilian Grade 1 winners Nonno Luigi and Jeune-Turc. The second dam, Northern Trick (by Northern Dancer), winner of the Prix de Diane and the Prix Vermeille, was second in the Prix de l'Arc de Triomphe and is a half-sister to the US Grade 1 Jockey Club Gold Cup winner On The Sly. (Pearl Bloodstock Ltd). *"A backward filly that needs a bit of time, she's definitely an August/September 2-y-o. A nice mover, she's had a little issue recently but I think she'll be fine".*

684. DARE TO ACHIEVE ★★★
b.c. Galileo – Mussoorie (Linamix). February 8. Second foal. 50,000Y. Tattersalls October Book 1. B Kantor/M Jooste. The dam won over 10f in France, was listed-placed here over 12f and is a half-sister to 4 winners. The second dam, Fascinating Hill (by Danehill), is an unraced half-sister to 7 winners including the French Group 1 winners Fragrant Mix and Alpine Rose. (B Kantor & M Jooste). *"A nice, backward horse, he's a decent mover by a proper sire and it's a good cross so he could be anything. He looks well-bought".*

685. EKHTIZAAL (IRE) ★★★★
ch.c. Haatef – Bezant (Zamindar). February 19. Fourth foal. €100,000Y. Goffs Orby. Shadwell Estate Co. Half-brother to Deposer (by Kheleyf), a 2-y-o 6f and subsequent Hong Kong winner and placed in the Group 3 Jersey Stakes, the Group 3 Diomed Stakes and a US Grade 1 event. The dam, placed once at 3 yrs over 1m, is a half-sister to 3 winners including the Group 2 Beresford Stakes third Sant Jordi. The second dam, Foresta Verde (by Green Forest), is a placed half-sister to 8 winners including the smart broodmare Tanouma. (Hamdan Al Maktoum). *"A nice horse, he was the most expensive Haatef at the sales and he's a strong, well-made 2-y-o. I would think he'd be out by the end of May over five or six furlongs".*

686. EMPRESS ADELAIDE ★★
ch.f. Pivotal – Emperice (Empire Maker). February 21. Second foal. The dam is an unraced half-sister to the Group 3 Princess Royal Stakes and Group 3 Lancashire Oaks winner Sacred Song (herself dam of the Group 2 10f Prix Guillaume d'Ornano winner Multidimensional) and to the Canadian multiple Grade 2 winner Strut The Stage. The second dam, Ruby Ransom (by Red Ransom), won a stakes event over 1m in Canada and is a half-sister to 8 winners including the Grade 1 Breeders Cup Turf winner Chief Bearheart and the Grade 1 Hollywood Derby winner Explosive Red. (Cheveley Park Stakes). *"She'll take some time and looks like a back-end filly. She reminds me very much of the good Pivotal filly we had called Chorist, so I hope she's half as good".*

687. ENFIJAAR (IRE) ★★★★
b.f. Invincible Spirit – Harayir (Gulch). February 3. Half-sister to the smart listed 10f winner Izdiham, to the useful 12f winner Moonjaz (both by Nashwan), the fairly useful 2-y-o 7f and 1m winner Azizi (by Haafhd) and the quite useful 10.5f winner Mulaazem (by King's Best). The dam was a very smart winner of the Lowther Stakes (at 2 yrs), the 1,000 Guineas, the Tripleprint Celebration Mile and the Hungerford Stakes. She is a sister to the useful 10f to 12f winner Ahraar and a half-sister to the useful 7f (at 2 yrs) to 10f winner Min Alhawa. The second dam, Saffaanh (by Shareef Dancer), a quite useful 12.2f winner, is out of the Irish Oaks winner Give Thanks. (Hamdan Al Maktoum). *"She has a lovely pedigree, being out of a Guineas winner, but she's back at the stud after a little setback. Nevertheless she's a definite 2-y-o, she's very strong and well-made, so she'll be one to look out for over six furlongs in mid-summer".*

688. EPIC BATTLE (IRE) ★★★

b.c. Acclamation – Wrong Key (Key Of Luck). February 18. Fourth living foal. 220,000Y. Tattersalls October Book 1. A O Nerses. Half-brother to the useful 2-y-o listed 5f Marble Hill Stakes winner Wrong Answer (by Verglas), to the useful dual 1m winner Albaasil (by Dansili) and the quite useful Irish 2-y-o 1m winner Wrong Number (by King's Best). The dam, an Irish 7f (at 2 yrs) and listed 1m winner, was placed in the Group 2 1m Goffs International Stakes and the Group 2 10f Pretty Polly Stakes and is a sister to the 7f (at 2 yrs) and Group 3 10f and 12f winner Right Key and a half-sister to 3 winners. The second dam, Sarifa (by Kahyasi), is an unraced half-sister to the Group 3 Prix du Palais Royal winner Saratan. (Saleh Al Homaizi & Imad Al Sagar). *"He's a small horse and looks a 2-y-o but he's not as precocious as I expected. So we've backed off him a bit, but he should make a 2-y-o by mid-summer because he's a very strong, very well-made horse".* W.r fair 7f d4 mh Irish

689. ESTIQAAMA ★★★

b.f. Nayef – Ethaara (Green Desert). February 9. First foal. The dam, a useful listed 6f winner, is closely related to the very useful 2-y-o listed 7f Star Stakes winner and Group 3 7f Prestige Stakes second Mudaaraah and a half-sister to the useful 2-y-o listed 7f winner Sudoor. The second dam, Wissal (by Woodman), is an unraced sister to the high-class 2-y-o Group 2 7f Laurent Perrier Champagne Stakes Bahhare and a half-sister to the Group 1 1m St James's Palace Stakes and Group 1 1m Queen Elizabeth II Stakes winner Bahri. (Hamdan Al Maktoum). *"I haven't had her yet because she's at the stud having just arrived from Dubai. I saw her three times over there and every time she'd thrived, so I'm looking forward to her. I trained the mother who did nothing but improve".*

690. FERSAH (USA) ★★

b.f. Dynaformer – Jaleela (Kingmambo). February 16. Second foal. Half-sister to Kahruman (by Mr Greeley), placed fourth over 1m on his only start at 2 yrs in 2011. The dam, a quite useful 1m winner, is closely related to the very useful 7f (at 2 yrs) and subsequent UAE Group 2 1m winner Derbaas. The second dam, Sultana (by Storm Cat), is an unraced sister to the high-class Group 1 7f Prix de la Salamandre and Group 1 1m Sussex Stakes winner Aljabr. (Hamdan Al Maktoum). *"A big, backward filly that hasn't arrived here from Dubai yet".*

691. FEHAYDI ★★★

b.c. Nayef – Red Camellia (Polar Falcon). March 7. Ninth foal. 110,000Y. Tattersalls October Book 1. Shadwell Estate Co. Half-brother to the smart Group 1 Fillies' Mile and dual Group 2 10f Blandford Stakes winner Red Bloom, to the quite useful 2-y-o 1m winner Botanist (both by Selkirk), the smart 10f, 12f and listed 13f winner Red Gala (by Sinndar) and the fair 9f winner Red Blossom by Green Desert). The dam, winner of the Group 3 7f Prestige Stakes and third in the French 1,000 Guineas, is a half-sister to 4 winners including the dam of the listed winners Red Fort and Red Carnation. The second dam, Cerise Bouquet (by Mummy's Pet), a fair 2-y-o 5f winner, is a half-sister to 6 winners including the Irish St Leger winner and Breeders Cup Classic second Ibn Bey and the Yorkshire Oaks winner Roseate Tern. (Sheikh Ahmed Al Maktoum). *"I like him, he's got a bit of speed and a bit of stamina in his pedigree, so I think he'll be alright. A good sort with a good temperament, I'm very happy with him".*

692. GARDEN ROW ★★★

gr.f. Invincible Spirit – Gladstone Street (Waajib). April 1. Tenth foal. 100,000foal. Tattersalls December. Cheveley Park Stud. Sister to the 2-y-o Group 2 6f Flying Childers Stakes and listed St Hugh's Stakes winner Madame Trop Vite and half-sister to the quite useful Irish 5f to 9f winner of 8 races Patrickswell (by Iron Mask), the modest 10f, 12f and hurdles winner Gardasee (by Dashing Blade) and four winners abroad by Nicolette, Dolphin Street, Brief Truce and Perugino. The dam, a winner over 1m at 2 yrs in Germany, is a half-sister to 7 winners. The second dam, Grafton Street (by Pentathlon), a listed-placed winner at 3 yrs in Germany, is a half-sister to 8 winners. (Cheveley Park Stud). *"Quite a leggy, gangly filly but she's got a good backside on her and she's got speed, so I would think we'd be having a closer look at her in May".*

693. GHASABAH ★★★

b.f. Dansili – Muwakleh (Machiavellian). March 6. Half-sister to Tawaasul (by Haafhd), placed second over 7f on her only start at 2 yrs in 2011 and to the quite useful 7f (at 2 yrs) and 1m winner Manaal (by Bahri). The dam, winner of the UAE 1,000 Guineas and second in the Newmarket 1,000 Guineas, is a sister to the high-class Dubai World Cup and Prix Jean Prat winner Almutawakel and to the useful 10f winner Elmustanser and a half-sister to the smart 10f winner Inaaq. The second dam, Elfaslah (by Green Desert), a useful winner of three races from 10f to 10.4f at 3 yrs including a listed event at the Curragh, is a half-sister to the Group 1 12f Italian Derby winner and 'King George' second White Muzzle. (Hamdan Al Maktoum). *"A lovely filly, she's quite small and will need a little time but she's a nice, kind filly. One for the autumn".*

694. I SAY (IRE) ★★★

b.f. Oratorio – Lisieux Orchid (Sadler's Wells). March 3. Fourth foal. 40,000Y. Tattersalls October Book 2. Amanda Skiffington. Half-sister to the fair Irish 10f and 12f winner Notalossonya (by Cadeaux Genereux). The dam, a quite useful Irish 12f winner, is a half-sister to 5 winners including the Group 1 National Stakes third Force Of Will. The second dam, Clear Issue (by Riverman), won once over 7f in Ireland at 3 yrs and is a half-sister to 8 winners including the US Grade 1 winner Twilight Agenda and the dam of the Group 1 winners Media Puzzle, Refuse To Bend and Go And Go. (R C Tooth). *"She's had a problem with a dirty throat but once she's over that we should be able to get on with her. A good, solid type, she's strong and may need a bit of time but she's well-made".* Gd 7x? :- 9? his field 1m f ml. Newbury

695. LADY NOUF ★★★★

b.f. Teofilo – Majestic Sakeena (King's Best). February 3. Fourth foal. Half-sister to the very useful dual listed 10f winner Nouriya (by Danehill Dancer). The dam is an unraced half-sister to the German listed sprint winner Shy Lady (herself dam of the St James's Palace Stakes winner Zafeen) and to the French listed winner Sweet Story. The second dam, Shy Danceuse (by Groom Dancer), a minor French 1m winner, is a half-sister to the very smart colt

Diffident, winner of the Group 3 6f Diadem Stakes, the Group 3 6f Prix de Ris-Orangis and the listed 7f European Free Handicap. (Saleh Al Homaizi & Imad Al Sagar). *"A nice filly, she's a good-mover and one for September-time. A good sort, she's plenty big enough and a very nice mover that'll want fast ground".*

696. MATROOH (USA) ★★★

b.c. Distorted Humor – Rockcide (Personal Flag). January 16. Third foal. $550,000Y. Keeneland September. Shadwell Estate Co. Brother to the minor US 3-y-o winner Afaaf and half-brother to the US dual Grade 3 winner and Grade 1 placed Rule (by Roman Ruler). The dam, placed at 3 and 4 yrs in the USA, is a half-sister to the Kentucky Derby and Preakness Stakes winner and champion 3-y-o colt Funny Cide. The second dam, Belle's Good Cide (by Slewacide), a minor winner of 2 races at 3 yrs, is a half-sister to 3 stakes winners including the Grade 3 winner Belle Of Cozzene. (Hamdan Al Maktoum). *"I haven't got him yet, he looked nice when I saw him in Dubai but with a price tag like that he ought to!"*

697. MUJADORA ★★★★

b.f. Mujadil – Golden Ora (Nordance). January 26. Second foal. 23,000Y. Tattersalls October Book 2. David Redvers. Half-sister to the fair 2011 7f and 1m placed 2-y-o Golden Halo (by Titus Livius). The dam won 6 minor races at 3 to 5 yrs in Italy and is a half-sister to 3 winners including the dual Group 3 winner and Grade 1 placed Golden Titus. The second dam, Oraplata (by Silver Hawk), was placed at 4 yrs in the USA and is a half-sister to 9 winners including the Grade 1 Blue Grass Stakes winner Taylor's Special. (Mr & Mrs Ian Beard). *"She's a nice 2-y-o, she's quite sharp, goes well and will run in May. I hope to go to the Supersprint with her".* TRAINERS' BARGAIN BUY

698. MUNDAHESH (IRE) ★★★★★

ch.c. Tamayuz – Kawn (Cadeaux Genereux). April 27. Fourth foal. Half-brother to the fair 1m winner Jawhar (by Halling). The dam, unplaced on one start, is a half-sister to the Group 2 1m Prix du Rond-Point and Group 3 8.5f Diomed Stakes winner Trans Island, to the Italian Group 3 winner Welsh Diva and the useful 2-y-o 7f winner Nothing Daunted (all by Selkirk). The second dam, Khubza (by Green Desert), a quite useful 3-y-o 7f winner, is a half-sister to 7 winners including the Group 2 winners Barrow Creek and Last Resort and the listed winners Arctic Char and Heard A Whisper. (Hamdan Al Maktoum). "Yes, he's a nice colt. I've trained two out of this mare and they both had ability but some soundness issues. This little Tamayuz colt just wants to please us, he looks sharp and racey".

699. MUTHMIR (IRE) ★★
b.c. Invincible Spirit – Fairy Of The Night (Danehill). March 14. Third foal. 130,000Y. Tattersalls October Book 1. Shadwell Estate Co. Brother to the fairly useful 2-y-o 1m winner and listed-placed Aneedah. The dam, an Irish 7f listed and 9.5f winner, is a sister to one winner and a half-sister to 2 winners including the US Grade 3 12f and Irish listed 11f winner Dress Rehearsal. The second dam, Sassenach (by Night Shift), a winner over 13f at 4 yrs in Ireland, is a half-sister to 5 winners including the Group 3 2m 2f Doncaster Cup winner Far Cry. (Hamdan Al Maktoum). "He's backward, he's grown a lot and gone up behind, so he's going to be an autumn horse now. Hopefully he'll still be alright".

700. NOBLE DEED ★★★
ch.c. Kyllachy – Noble One (Primo Dominie). February 14. Closely related to the Group 1 1m Sun Chariot Stakes and Group 1 1m Lockinge Stakes winner Peeress and to the quite useful 6f and 7f winner Entitled (both by Pivotal) and half-brother to the quite useful 2-y-o 5f winner Carte Royale (by Loup Sauvage). The dam, a useful dual 5f winner (including at 2 yrs), is a half-sister to 5 winners including the fairly useful 10f winner Maiden Castle. The second dam, Noble Destiny (by Dancing Brave), was a fairly useful 2-y-o 7f winner. (Cheveley Park Stud). "He's a very well-made, strong, sprinting type of horse but he got sore shins and we've had to lay off him, so I would think he'll be a June 2-y-o".

701. ODOOJ (IRE) ★★★
b.c. Pivotal – Shabiba (Seeking The Gold). February 17. First foal. The dam, a useful 6f (at 2 yrs) and listed 1m winner, was third in the Group 3 7f Oak Tree Stakes and is a half-sister

to the useful 2-y-o 6f winner and Group 3 placed Darajaat. The second dam, Misterah (by Alhaarth), a very useful listed 6f (at 2 yrs) and Group 3 7f Nell Gwyn Stakes winner, is sister to one winner and a half-sister to the useful 2-y-o 6f winner Muqtarb. (Hamdan Al Maktoum). "He's by Pivotal but he's a real, sharp 2-y-o type. I don't think Pivotal's come that early, but he looks like he wants to be trained so we'll probably get him out by the end of May". *Won 5f Chester on debut despite slow start?*

702. OUR OBSESSION ★★
b.c. Cape Cross – Hidden Hope (Daylami). Half-brother to the modest 11f winner Fine Style (by Pivotal). The dam, a useful listed 11.4f Cheshire Oaks winner, is a half-sister to 9 winners including the Group 1 1m Coronation Stakes winner Rebecca Sharp and the Group 3 11.5f Lingfield Derby Trial winner Mystic Knight. The second dam, Nuryana (by Nureyev), was a useful winner of the listed 1m Grand Metropolitan Stakes and is a half-sister to 5 winners. "A very nice mover, she'll need a bit of time but I think she's worth putting in the book".

Easily won 1m e16 mdn Newmarket

703. PARIS ROSE ★★★★
b.f. Cape Cross – Samira Gold (Gold Away). March 14. First foal. The dam, a very useful dual listed 10f winner, was third in the Group 3 Princess Royal Stakes. The second dam, Capework (by El Gran Senor), is an unplaced full or half-sister to numerous winners. (Jaber Abdullah). "A lovely filly, she's having a break at the moment and will be an autumn 2-y-o, but she's the best of my fillies I'd say. An Oaks type, she's a lovely mover and a cracking first foal".

704. PEMBROKE (IRE) ★★★
b.c. Excellent Art – Mrs Marsh (Marju). February 20. Fourth foal. 210,000Y. Tattersalls October Book 1. John Warren. Half-brother to the top-class miler Canford Cliffs (by Tagula), a winner of five Group 1 events (Irish 2,000 Guineas, Sussex Stakes, St James's Palace Stakes, Lockinge Stakes and Queen Anne Stakes) and to a winner in Sweden by Barathea. The dam is an unraced half-sister to 6 winners including the US Grade 2 and Grade 3 winner Pina Colada. The second dam, Drei (by Lyphard), placed fourth over 1m at 3 yrs on her only outing, is a half-sister to 3 winners. (Highclere Thoroughbred Racing –

Wavertree). *"A nice, backward horse, he won't be early but he has a good physique and he's done well. I won't be getting after him until July but he's got the pedigree to be a good horse".*

705. QUEENSBURY RULES (IRE) ★★★

b.c. Teofilo – Fantastic Spring (Fantastic Light). February 22. Second foal. 72,000Y. Tattersalls October Book 2. Jill Lamb. The dam won 3 minor races in the USA at 4 yrs and is a half-sister to 4 winners including the Hong Kong stakes winner Kid Mambo. The second dam, Spring Pitch (by Storm Cat), is an unplaced half-sister to 8 winners including the Group 1 Queen Elizabeth II Stakes winner and sire Selkirk and the Group/Grade 3 winners Seebe and Rory Creek. (Mr Liam Sheridan). *"A really nice horse but a bit backward at present, he's the type for July onwards. A good mover, he'll be a ten furlong horse next year".*

706. RESILIENT (IRE) ★★★ ♠

b.c. Shamardal – Zither (Zafonic). February 11. Sixth foal. 350,000Y. Tattersalls October Book 1. Blandford Bloodstock. Half-brother to the fair dual 10f winner Lady Gabrielle (by Dansili), to the minor French 2-y-o winner Istimlaak (by Marju) and the fair 8.5f winner Themwerethedays (by Olden Times). The dam, a fairly useful 6f (at 2 yrs) and 7f winner, is a half-sister to 3 winners including the useful 2-y-o listed 6f winner Dowager and the useful 1m (at 2 yrs) and 10f winner Dower House. The second dam, Rose Noble (by Vaguely Noble), a modest 11.5f winner, is a half-sister to 7 winners including the champion two-year-old and Dewhurst Stakes and St James's Palace Stakes winner Grand Lodge. (Silver Arrow Racing). *"He's a big, strong type that cost a lot of money. He had a little injury in the Spring which set him back and he won't be back in training again before June. But I liked what I saw earlier, he's a good sort".*

707. RESPONSE ★★★★ ♠

ch.c. New Approach – Spotlight (Dr Fong). February 15. Fourth foal. 135,000Y. Tattersalls October Book 1. John Warren. Half-brother to the fair 2011 7f placed 2-y-o winner Polydamos (by Nayef). The dam, a listed 1m and subsequent US Grade 2 Lake Placid Handicap winner, is a full or half-sister to 4 winners including the

dam of the Group 1 Phoenix Stakes winner Zoffany. The second dam, Dust Dancer (by Suave Dancer), won 4 races including the Group 3 10f Prix de la Nonette and is a half-sister to 6 winners including the Group 3 7.3f Fred Darling Stakes winner Bulaxie (herself dam of the Group 2 winner Claxon). (Highclere Thoroughbred Racing – Dalmeny). *"This could be my Chesham Stakes horse. He's a nice mover, a good type and keen to please. He'll start over six furlongs but he'll stay much further, I don't think he's too weak to push on with and I like him".*

708. ROCK CHOIR ★★★

b.f. Pivotal – Choir Mistress (Chief Singer). March 27. Sister to the Group 1 10f Curragh Pretty Polly Stakes and dual Group 3 winner Chorist and to the 2-y-o 1m debut winner Hymnsheet and half-sister to the very useful 2-y-o 7f winner and Group 3 7f Prestige Stakes second Choirgirl (by Unfuwain), the fairly useful 1m winner Choir Leader (by Sadler's Wells), the fair 7f (at 2 yrs) and 14.8f all-weather winner Operatic (by Goofalik), the moderate 11f winner Cantor (by Iceman) and a winner in Turkey by Slip Anchor. The dam is an unraced half-sister to 6 winners including the smart Group 2 11.9f Great Voltigeur Stakes winner Sacrament. The second dam, Blessed Event (by Kings Lake), a very useful winner of the listed 10f Ballymacoll Stud Stakes at 3 yrs, was second in the Yorkshire Oaks and fourth in the Champion Stakes. (Cheveley Park Stud). *"A backward full-sister to Chorist, she doesn't look anything like her but she's a nice filly for the Autumn".*

709. ROYAL ASPIRATION ★★★

b.c. Acclamation – Joan Joan Joan (Touch Gold). April 16. Fourth foal. €32,000Y. Goffs Orby. W Haggas. Half-brother to 2 minor winners in the USA by Street Cry and Repent. The dam, a minor US 3-y-o winner, is a half-sister to 9 winners including the Group 3 Acomb Stakes winner Big Timer. The second dam, Moonflute (by The Minstrel), a listed-placed 2-y-o winner, is a half-sister to 4 winners. *"A racey 2-y-o, we're going to aim him for the Supersprint because I think he'll be a five furlong 2-y-o. He'll be out in June".*

710. SONG AND DANCE MAN ★★

b.c. Danehill Dancer – Song (Sadler's Wells). March 15. First foal. The dam is an unraced sister to the Irish 1,000 Guineas winner Yesterday, to the smart 10f winner and Oaks and Irish Oaks third All My Loving and the Group 1 7f Moyglare Stud Stakes winner and triple Group 1 placed Quarter Moon. The second dam, Jude (by Darshaan), a moderate 10f placed maiden, is a sister to the listed 14f winner and Irish Oaks third Arrikala and to the useful Irish 12f listed winner Alouette (herself dam of the Champion Stakes winner Alborada and the German triple Group 1 winner Albanova) and a half-sister to the very smart Group 2 10f Nassau Stakes and Sun Chariot Stakes winner Last Second (dam of the Irish 2,000 Guineas winner Aussie Rules). (Paulyn Ltd). *"He has a wonderful pedigree, but at the moment he's quite an immature horse both physically and mentally. He's a bit of a rebel, but he'll be fine when he grows up. Hopefully he'll thrive throughout the year, but I see him as more of a 3-y-o".*

711. TANAWAR (IRE) ★★★

b.g. Elusive City – Parakopi (Green Desert). March 4. First foal. 125,000Y. Tattersalls October Book 2. W Haggas. The dam, a minor winner at 3 yrs in Germany, is a half-sister to one winner in Japan. The second dam, Siringas (by Barathea), winner of the Grade 2 Nassau Stakes in Canada and the listed 1m Brownstown Stakes in Ireland, was Grade 3 placed twice in the USA and is a half-sister to 4 winners. (Sheikh Ahmed Al Maktoum). *"A strong, well-made 2-y-o type, he was very temperamental so we gelded him and he's much better now, but he's a bit lazy. A strong horse".*

712. TWEED ★★

b.f. Sakhee – Frog (Akarad). May 6. Tenth foal. Half-sister to the promising 2012 3-y-o 10f maiden winner Vow (by Motivator), to the Group 3 12f St Simon Stakes winner Beaten Up (by Beat Hollow), the listed 12f and listed 14f winner Harris Tweed (by Hernando), the fair 2m winner of 3 races Froglet (by Shaamit), the fair 7f (at 2 yrs) to 12f winner Val de Lobo (by Loup Sauvage) and the modest 2-y-o 7f winner Sel (by Selkirk). The dam, a fair 10f and 12f winner of 5 races, is a half-sister to 6 winners. The second dam, Best Girl Friend (by Sharrood), is

an unraced half-sister to 4 winners including the French dual Group 3 winner Comrade In Arms. (Mr B Haggas). *"Very solid, she's like most of the family I suspect in that she won't do much at two but she'll get better as she gets older. A very nice, kind, genuine filly. The sire can still produce winners and after all he does have the winning-most horse in terms of prize money ever trained in England, Luca Cumani's Presvis".*

713. VALTINA ★★★

b.f. Teofilo – Vassiana (Anabaa). April 22. Sixth foal. 160,000Y. Tattersalls October Book 1. Norris/Huntingdon. Half-sister to the fair 2011 2-y-o 6f winner Vassaria (by Rock Of Gibraltar), to the Group 3 Phoenix Sprint Stakes winner Girouette (by Pivotal), the fair Irish 7f winner and listed-placed Paraphernalia (by Dalakhani), the French 1m winner of 5 races at 2 and 3 yrs and listed-placed Prince d'Alienor (by Verglas) and the fair 10f and 12f winner Vallemeldee (by Bering). The dam, a French 3-y-o winner, was listed-placed and is a sister to the Group 3 Prix d'Arenburg winner Villadolide and to the French dual listed winner Victorieux. The second dam, Vassia (Machiavellian), won 3 races at 3 yrs in France and is a half-sister to 7 winners. (MJ & LA Taylor). *"She's had a break and is about to come back into training. She was a backward filly, but a nice mover and I liked her".*

714. VEERAYA ★★

b.c. Rail Link – Follow Flanders (Pursuit Of Love). March 27. Fourth foal. Half-sister to the quite useful 6f winner Bless You (by Bahamian Bounty), to the quite useful dual 10f winner Fever (by Dr Fong) and the fair 1m winner Sir Billy Nick (by Bertolini). The dam, a fairly useful dual 5f winner, is a half-sister to 9 winners including the top-class Group 1 5f Nunthorpe Stakes winner Kyllachy. The second dam, Pretty Poppy (by Song), a modest 2-y-o 5f winner, stayed 7.6f and is a half-sister to 4 winners. (Mr R Farook). *"He's by an Arc winner out of a five furlong sprinter, but he does look quite forward and if you had fifty goes at guessing who his sire is Rail Link wouldn't be one of them! He's a strong, well-made horse that hasn't shown me much yet, but he looks fast".*

715. ZUHD (IRE) ★★

b.c. Cape Cross – Street Star (Street Cry). March 31. First foal. 75,000Y. Tattersalls October Book 2. Shadwell Estate Co. The dam, a quite useful 2-y-o 5f winner, is a half-sister to 7 winners including the listed winners Alva Glen and Lyphard's Honor, the Group 1 placed Shrewd Idea and the dam of the French Group 3 winner Villadolide. The second dam, Domludge (by Lyphard), ran once unplaced and is a full or half-sister to 4 winners including the triple Group 1 winner Mrs Penny and the dam of the Group 1 winners Irish Prize and Hatoof. (Hamdan Al Maktoum). *"A big, solid, typical Cape Cross, he's backward, an autumn type 2-y-o and a 3-y-o in the making"*.

716. UNNAMED ★★★

b.f. Invincible Spirit – Emily Blake (Lend A Hand). April 9. First foal. The dam won the Group 3 7f Athasi Stakes and the Group 3 1m Equestrian Stakes (both at the Curragh). The second dam, Kirri (by Lycius), was unplaced in one start and is a half-sister to 2 minor winners. (Mr & Mrs R Scott). *"She's had a break but she'll be back in soon and when I saw her the other day I thought she'd done really well. She's definitely a summer 2-y-o"*.

717. UNNAMED ★★

b.c. Danehill Dancer – Enticing (Pivotal). February 23. First foal. The dam, a very smart Group 3 5f Molecomb Stakes and Group 3 5f King George Stakes winner, is a sister to one winner and a half-sister to the quite useful dual 5f winner (including at 2 yrs) Speed Song. The second dam, Superstar Leo (by College Chapel), a very smart 2-y-o, won 5 races including the Group 2 5f Flying Childers Stakes and the Weatherbys Super Sprint and is a full or half-sister to numerous winners. (Lael Stable). *"A very backward colt, he's quite plain despite his lovely pedigree and we'll have to see how he goes on"*.

718. UNNAMED ★★★★ ♠

b.f. Oasis Dream – Politesse (Barathea). April 2. Sixth foal. 400,000Y. Tattersalls October Book 1. Amanda Skiffington. Closely related to the fair dual 6f winner Cape Classic (by Cape Cross) and half-sister to the very smart Group 1 6.5f Prix Maurice de Gheest and Group 2 6f

Diadem Stakes winner of 7 races King's Apostle (by King's Best) and the quite useful 7f and 1m winner Kalk Bay (by Hawk Wing). The dam is an unraced half-sister to 4 minor winners out of the Group 1 6f Cheveley Park Stakes and Group 3 6f Princess Margaret Stakes winner Embassy (by Cadeaux Genereux), herself a half-sister to 6 winners including the Group 2 Pretty Polly Stakes winner Tarfshi. (Lael Stable). *"She's lovely and I'm grateful to the owners for buying her. She should be a 2-y-o, I like her very much and I'd love to get to Royal Ascot with her. This is the first time the mare has gone to a sire that can inject proper speed into the foal and I think it's what the mare has been crying out for. A very well-made filly, she's just gone up a bit behind which may halt her being precocious, but she's very well-made and strong"*.

719. UNNAMED ★★★

ch.c. Peintre Celebre – Square The Circle (Second Empire). February 1. Third foal. 135,000Y. Tattersalls October Book 1. William Haggas. The dam, placed once at 3 yrs in Germany, is a half-sister to 5 winners including the US Grade 3 placed Add The Gold. The second dam, Sum (by Spectacular Bid), won the Grade 3 Pucker Up Stakes and is a half-sister to 9 winners including the Group 1 William Hill Futurity winner Bakharoff and the Group 2 Lockinge Stakes winner Emperor Jones. *"A beautiful-looking horse, he's not very big but he's very active and very agile. He could be a Derby horse one day"*.

720. UNNAMED ★★★★ ♠

b.f. Acclamation – Superstar Leo (College Chapel). February 13. Half-sister to the promising 2012 3-y-o 7f winner Sentaril (by Danehill Dancer), to the very smart Group 3 5f Molecomb Stakes and Group 3 5f King George Stakes winner Enticing, the fair 7f winner Map Of Heaven (both by Pivotal) and to the quite useful dual 5f winner (including at 2 yrs) Speed Song (by Fasliyev). The dam, a very smart 2-y-o, won 5 races including the Group 2 5f Flying Childers Stakes and the Weatherbys Super Sprint and is a full or half-sister to numerous winners. The second dam, Council Rock (by General Assembly), a fair 9f and 10f placed 3-y-o, is a half-sister to 6 winners including the Group 3 Prestige Stakes winner Glatisant (dam of the 2,000 Guineas winner and sire Footstepsinthesand) and the listed Virginia Stakes winner Gai Bulga. (Lael Stable). *"She's quite long but has a terrific backside and a very good temperament. She'll be a 2-y-o in June or July, she's well-made with a good head and she's lovely".*

721. UNNAMED ★★★

b.c. Royal Applause – Take The Plunge (Benny The Dip). February 25. First foal. 31,000Y. Tattersalls October Book 2. Norris/Huntingdon. The dam is an unplaced half-sister to 8 winners. The second dam, Pearly River (by Elegant Air), a fair 7f (at 2 yrs) and 12f winner, is a half-sister to 5 winners. (Options O Syndicate). *"A sweet little horse, he's having a break at the moment. He's a 2-y-o alright, quite a well-made, strong, sharp-looking horse that'll be out in June".*

722. UNNAMED ★★★

b.f. Singspiel – Winds Of Time (Danehill). March 21. Third foal. Half-sister to the very useful 2-y-o 6f winner and Group 2 Richmond Stakes second The Paddyman (by Giant's Causeway). The dam, a fairly useful 2-y-o 6f winner, subsequently won in the USA and Canada and is a half-sister to 2 winners. The second dam, Windmill (by Ezzoud), a fair 13.8f winner, is a half-sister to 8 winners including the very smart Group 2 12f Ribblesdale Stakes winner Gull Nook (herself dam of the top-class colt Pentire), the equally smart Group 3 12f Princess Royal Stakes winner Banket and the useful Group 3 Ormonde Stakes winner Mr Pintips. (Mr & Mrs R Scott). *"Quite a small filly, she's done very well and is having a break at present but she'll be back in shortly. She'll be backward but she's lovely and has a great head on her".*

MICHAEL HALFORD

723. ADELA (IRE) ★★★

ch.f. Dr Fong – Adelfia (Sinndar). March 29. Third foal. Half-sister to Afraz (by Red Ransom), placed once over 1m at 2 yrs in 2011 and to the fairly useful 1m (at 2 yrs) and 9f winner Adilapour (by Azamour). The dam, a quite useful 12f winner, is a half-sister to several winners including the smart dual Group 3 winner Adilabad. The second dam, Adaiyka (by Doyoun), was a smart winner of the Group 3 9f Prix Chloe. (H H Aga Khan). *"A nice filly that*

looks like she'll make a 2-y-o. I'm pleased with her so far, she's well put-together and I'd expect her to be racing in the second half of the year. She was picked out as one of the more forward ones of the Aga Khan's, she'll have no problem with seven furlongs and she'll go a mile at the end of the year".

724. ANTRIM (IRE) ★★★★

b.c. Iffraaj – Causeway Song (Giant's Causeway). February 23. Third foal. €42,000foal. Goffs. John Ferguson. Half-brother to the fair 2012 7f and 9f placed 3-y-o Angel Gabrial (by Hurricane Run). The dam is an unraced half-sister to one winner in the USA. The second dam, Colorado Song (by Pine Bluff), a dual winner in the USA, was placed in three Grade 2 events and is a half-sister to 7 winners including the listed winner and dual Grade 2 placed Tomorrows Sunshine. (Sheikh Mohammed). *"He's a nice, well-balanced colt that looks a real 2-y-o. He should be out by the middle of the year, we like him, he has a good attitude and he goes well. A nice, straightforward, very professional horse".*

725. DABADIYAN (IRE) ★★★

b.c. Zamindar – Dabista (Highest Honor). April 20. The dam, placed fourth once over a mile from 3 starts, is a half-sister to 2 winners. The second dam, Dabaya (by In The Wings), a listed-placed 10f winner, is a half-sister to the listed 10f Ballyroan Stakes winner and Group 3 placed Dabtiya from the family of Darshaan. (H H Aga Khan). *"We like him, he has plenty of size and he's a really well-balanced horse with a great temperament. A seven furlong horse that goes well".*

726. MIZZAVA (IRE) ★★★

b.f. Cape Cross – Flamanda (Niniski). March 9. Ninth foal. €38,000foal. Goffs. Not sold. Half-sister to the fair 2-y-o 7f winner Fluvial (by Exceed And Excel), to the 2-y-o Group 2 5f Queen Mary Stakes winner and Group 1 6f Phoenix Stakes third Elletelle (by Elnadim), the German listed 10f winner of 3 races Freedom (by Second Empire) and the German listed-placed 1m winner Fitness (by Monsun). The dam was placed over 9.5f here prior to winning 5 races at 4 yrs in Germany from 1m to 9f and is a half-sister to 8 winners. The second dam, Nemesia (by Mill Reef), a very useful 10.2f and

4-y-o 13.4f listed winner, is a full or half-sister to 8 winners including the smart Tattersalls Rogers Gold Cup winner Elegant Air. (Mr G M O'Leary). *"She's a filly that's grown a lot, we like her and she has a great temperament. She's been going through a growing spurt but she'll make a 2-y-o by the second half of the year, possibly over six furlongs to start with. She's good-looking, does everything well and she gives us a good feel".*

727. ROSE IN WINTER (IRE) ★★★★

b.f. Danehill Dancer – Mount Klinovec (Mujadil). April 4. Third foal. 115,000Y. Tattersalls October Book 2. Margaret O'Toole. The dam, a fair 6f placed maiden (including at 2 yrs), is a half-sister to the Group 3 6f Acomb Stakes winner and Group 1 7f Dewhurst Stakes third Fast Company (by Danehill Dancer). The second dam, Sheezalady (by Zafonic), is an unraced half-sister to 5 winners including Hawajiss, winner of the Group 2 10f Nassau Stakes, the Group 3 1m May Hill Stakes and the Group 3 10.4f Musidora Stakes. (Gigginstown House Stud). *"A nice, well-balanced filly, she has a good way of going and we like her. One for the second half of the season, she looks a real 2-y-o, has a good temperament and goes well".*

728. UNNAMED ★★★

b.c. Shamardal – Dibiya (Caerleon). March 1. Half-brother to the fairly useful Irish 1m (at 2 yrs) to 14f and hurdles winner Dirar (by King's Best), to the quite useful Irish 7f (at 2 yrs) and 1m winner Dilinata (by Spinning World) and the quite useful Irish 12f and hurdles winner Dibella (by Observatory). The dam, a fairly useful 12f and 14f winner, was listed-placed and is a half-sister to one winner. The second dam, Dabtiya (by Shirley Heights), won the listed Ballyroan Stakes. (H H Aga Khan). *"He's a lovely, good-looking horse and I'm pleased with him in his work. He's more precocious than some of the other members of the family we've had, I think he'll make a 2-y-o but he'll want seven furlongs. He's a horse that we like and he works well".*

729. UNNAMED ★★★

b.f. Cape Cross – Nick's Nikita (Pivotal). January 19. First foal. 40,000Y. Tattersalls October Book 1. Emma O'Gorman. The dam, a useful winner

of 4 races in Ireland including the Group 3 12f Noblesse Stakes, was placed in four other Group 3 events and is a half-sister to 5 winners. The second dam, Elaine's Honor (by Chief's Crown), won twice at 2 and 3 yrs in France and is a half-sister to 7 winners including the US Grade 3 winner Savannah's Honor. (Mr N Hartery). *"A filly with a great temperament, she's a bit on the weak side because she's been growing but we like her, she has a good action and I'm pleased with everything she's done so far. One for the second half of the season".*

730. UNNAMED ★★★

b.c. Observatory – Siniyya (Grand Lodge). April 18. Third foal. Half-brother to Sinetta (by Red Ransom), unplaced in one start at 2 yrs in 2011. The dam, placed from 12f to 2m in Ireland, is a sister to the top-class middle-distance colt Sinndar (by Grand Lodge), winner of the Derby, the Irish Derby and the Prix de l'Arc de Triomphe and a half-sister to 7 winners including the fairly useful 1m winner (at 2 yrs) and listed-placed Simawa. The second dam, Sinntara (by Lashkari), won 4 races in Ireland at up to 2m. (H H Aga Khan). *"A nice, well-balanced colt with a great attitude, he'll want seven furlongs and has done everything right so far".*

731. UNNAMED ★★★

b.c. Clodovil – Smoken Rosa (Smoke Glacken). March 10. Second foal. Half-brother to the quite useful 2011 Irish 6f placed 2-y-o Lanett Lady (by Teufelsberg). The dam, placed 3 times in the USA, is a half-sister to 4 winners including Snowdrops (three Graded stakes wins). The second dam, Roses In The Snow (by Be My Guest), a useful 1m winner and listed-placed here, subsequently won in the USA and is a half-sister to 6 winners. (Mr N Hartery). *"A big, tall horse that'll take a bit of time but he's well-balanced and he goes well. We like him and we'll probably start him off at six furlongs but he'll get seven".*

732. UNNAMED ★★★★

b.c. Footstepsinthesand – Your Village (Be My Guest). January 27. Ninth foal. €35,000Y. Goffs Orby. M Halford. Half-brother to the Group 1 5f Heinz 57 Phoenix Stakes second Yara (by Sri Pekan and herself the dam of two listed winners), to the moderate 12f all-weather winner Ink In Gold (by Intikhab) and a winner in Sweden by Verglas. The dam, placed fourth once over 12f in Ireland, is a half-sister to 6 winners including the Middle Park Stakes winner Mister Majestic and the Grand Prix de Paris winner Homme de Loi. The second dam, Our Village (by Ballymore), is an unplaced half-sister to 2 winners. (Dr K Swanick). *"A lovely-looking horse, he's strong and well put-together. He has the right attitude and everything he's done up to now he's done well. He looks a real 2-y-o that'll be out by the middle of the season".*

733. UNNAMED ★★★★
b.c. *Acclamation – Zarkalia (Red Ransom).* February 25. Half-brother to the French 2-y-o 7f winner Zardaba (by Choisir). The dam was placed three times in minor races at around a mile and ten furlongs in France. The second dam, Zarkiya (by Catrail), winner of the Group 3 1m Prix de Sandringham and fourth in the French 1,000 Guineas and the Coronation Stakes, is a half-sister to 5 winners and to the unraced dam of the outstanding filly Zarkava. (H H Aga Khan). *"He's a horse we like, he has a great attitude and he'll make a 2-y-o by the second half of the year. The lads like him and he has a good way of going. A colt from one of the speedier Aga Khan families".*

RICHARD HANNON
734. A LADIES MAN ★★★★★
b.c. *Kyllachy – Ego (Green Desert).* February 17. Fifth foal. 220,000Y. Tattersalls October Book 1. Peter & Ross Doyle. Half-brother to the quite useful 2011 2-y-o 7f winner and listed-placed Self Centred (by Medicean), to the useful 7f (at 2 yrs) and 1m winner and listed-placed Chef, the fair 7f winner I'm Sensational (both by Selkirk) and the fair dual 7f winner (including at 2 yrs) Cut And Thrust (by Haafhd). The dam, a very useful 2-y-o dual 6f winner, was listed-placed twice and is a half-sister to 3 winners including the useful 2-y-o 6f winner and Group 2 7f Champagne Stakes third Ghayth. The second dam, Myself (by Nashwan), a smart winner of the Group 3 7f Nell Gwyn Stakes, is a half-sister to 12 winners including the Group 3 Princess Margaret Stakes winner Bluebook.

(Mrs Julie Wood). *"One of our nicest 2-y-o's, he was an expensive yearling purchase, he's a very good mover and he's doing everything right. He'll make a mid-summer 2-y-o".* The stable jockey Richard Hughes puts this colt in the top five of his picks from the yard".

735. ALHAARTH BEAUTY (IRE) ★★★
b.f. *Alhaarth – Endis (Distant Relative).* February 10. Fourth foal. £15,000Y. Doncaster Premier. Peter & Ross Doyle. The dam, a minor dual winner at 3 yrs in Italy, is a sister to the US Grade 3 and Italian listed winner De Puntillas and a half-sister to 6 winners. The second dam, Enola (by Ela-Mana-Mou), is an unraced half-sister to 8 winners. (Mr A Al Mansoori). *"She wasn't expensive but she's done well recently and she looks quite sharp. A nice filly that's ready to run now".*

Won July Stakes Newmont

736. ALHEBAYEB (IRE) ★★★★ *2nd listed 5f Royal arcot*
gr.c. *Dark Angel – Miss Indigo (Indian Ridge).* March 27. Seventh foal. 170,000Y. Tattersalls October Book 1. Peter & Ross Doyle. Half-brother to the 2011 6f placed 2-y-o Wiltshire Life, to the quite useful 5f and 6f winner of 4 races Humidor (both by Camacho), the modest triple 12f winner Bluebell Ridge, the modest 6f winner Keep Dancing (both by Distant Music) and the moderate 5f winner Mickleberry (by Desert Style). The dam is a placed half-sister to 8 winners including the useful listed 10f Pretty Polly Stakes winner and Oaks fourth Musetta. The second dam, Monaiya (by Shareef Dancer), a French 7.5f and 1m winner, is a full or half-sister to 9 winners including the Canadian Grade 2 winner Vanderlin. (Hamdan Al Maktoum). *"A lovely colt, he's quite sharp, tends to be a bit on his toes but he's calmed down recently. When we get him sweet we'll run him, over five or six furlongs and he should make a nice 2-y-o".*

Ran green Nor small 5 ear rde 5f Now odds or

737. AL ZEIN ★★★★
b.c. *Notnowcato – Luminda (Danehill).* March 22. Sixth foal. 90,000Y. Tattersalls October Book 2. Ed Dunlop. Half-brother to the very useful 6f (at 2 yrs) and listed 1m winner and Group 2 1m second Rhythm Of Light (by Beat Hollow), to the French 1m listed-placed Lazy Afternoon (by Hawk Wing), the quite useful 6f winner Lunar Deity (by Medicean) and the quite useful

triple 7f winner She's In The Money (by High Chaparral). The dam won 2 races in France at 2 and 4 yrs and is a half-sister to 3 winners including the US Grade 2 winner Little Treasure. The second dam, Luminosity (by Sillery), won once at 2 yrs in France and is a half-sister to 4 minor winners. (S H Altayer). *"He's a nice, sound colt and quite a round, sturdy, strong sort. He's very laid-back, so he's the type you'd probably learn more about once he's run but we like him a lot. He ought to make a nice 2-y-o over six or seven furlongs, maybe even a mile".*

738. AMBERLEY HEIGHTS (IRE) ★★★
b.f. Elnadim — Fawaayid (Vaguely Noble). March 30. Sixteenth foal. 37,000Y. Tattersalls October Book 1. Peter & Ross Doyle. Half-sister to the listed 1m Prix de Bagatelle winner Green Lady, to the quite useful 2-y-o 6f winner Shamo (both by Green Desert), the useful 2-y-o 6f winner Desert Realm (by Desert Prince), the fairly useful 12f winner and listed-placed Entisar (by Nashwan), a hurdles winner by Anabaa and to the placed dam of the Group 2 Hungerford Stakes winner Balthazaar's Gift. The dam, a fairly useful winner of 3 races at 2 yrs from 7f to 10f in Ireland including two listed events, is a half-sister to 5 winners. The second dam, Clara Bow (by Coastal), a minor US winner of 3 races, is a half-sister to 4 winners. (Elaine Chivers). *"Not the biggest filly in the world but she's quite sharp, she's done some work and she'll be racing in late April or early May".*

Won by f. Hill Stakes Newbury

739. ANNUNCIATION ★★★★ fair say
br.c. Proclamation – Rockburst (Xaar). February 25. First foal. Doncaster Premier. Peter & Ross Doyle. The dam, a fair 2-y-o dual 6f winner, is a half-sister to 4 winners. The second dam, Topwinder (by Topsider), is an unplaced half-sister to 5 winners. (Middleham Park Racing XXXIX & James Pak). *"A lovely 2-y-o that did one piece of work a week ago and surprised us. We like him and he'll be running by early May, so he's a nice, early sort".* One of Richard Hughes's early favourites, he's pleased him on the gallops.

740. ARCTIC ADMIRAL (IRE) ★★★
gr.c. Verglas – Fag End (Treasure Kay). April 28. Ninth foal. 50,000Y. Tattersalls October Book 2. Peter & Ross Doyle. Half-brother to the fair

2-y-o 7f winner and listed-placed Romany Princess (by Viking Ruler), to the fair 2-y-o 7f winner Bellsbank (by Beckett) and 3 minor winners abroad by Alhaarth, Idris and Bad As I Wanna Be. The dam, a quite useful 2-y-o 6f and 7f winner, was third in the Group 3 Prestige Stakes and is a half-sister to 3 minor winners. The second dam, Gauloise Bleue (by Lyphard's Wish), is a placed half-sister to 5 winners including Gravelines (Group 1 Prix du Moulin) and Grand Pavois (Group 2 Prix d'Harcourt). (Mr P D Merritt). *"We've had quite a few out of this family and he's a nice colt. Good moving and strong, six furlongs will be his trip and he has a sweet temperament. A nice horse".*

741. ASK DAD ★★★
b.c. Intikhab – Don't Tell Mum (Dansili). February 15. Fourth foal. 115,000Y. Tattersalls October Book 2. Dwayne Woods. Brother to the smart 2011 2-y-o Group 3 7f Horris Hill Stakes winner Tell Dad and to the French 2-y-o dual 6f winner and Group 3 6f Prix de Cabourg third Khawatim. The dam, a useful 5f (at 2 yrs) and 6f winner and second in the Super Sprint, is a half-sister to 2 winners including the listed National Stakes winner and Group 3 third Icesolator. The second dam, Zinnia (by Zilzal), ran once unplaced and is a half-sister to 4 winners including the dam of the Group 3 Cornwallis Stakes winner Mubhij. (Mr W A Tinkler). *"He's not showing the same signs and attitude that his brother Tell Dad had, but he's a bit bigger and he seems a nice colt. We've haven't done much with him yet but I'm sure there's an engine there somewhere".*

2nd in gd bf Nwmn mdn debut

742. BALTIC KNIGHT (IRE) ★★★ va- green
b.c. Baltic King – Night Of Joy (King's Best). February 13. Third foal. 50,000Y. Tattersalls October Book 2. Peter 7 Ross Doyle. The dam, a fairly useful 2-y-o dual 1m winner, is a half-sister to 2 winners. The second dam, Gilah (by Saddlers' Hall), is an unraced half-sister to 7 winners including the very useful 10.2f winner Cocotte (the dam of six stakes winners including the top-class colt Pilsudski). (Thurloe Thoroughbreds XXX). *"A nice, big colt, a little bit more forward than he looks, he came in quite late but he seems to go well at the moment. One for seven furlongs I should think".*

743. BLACK MONK (IRE) ★★★

b.c. *Dark Angel – Double Eight (Common Grounds)*. February 26. Tenth foal. £66,000Y. Doncaster Premier. Peter & Ross Doyle. Half-brother to the useful 2-y-o 6f winner and listed-placed Destinate, to the Swedish winner Next Shave (both by Desert Style), the fair 11.6f winner Fiza (by Revoque) and the fair all-weather 13f winner Principal Witness (by Definite Article). The dam, a fair dual 12f winner, is a sister to 4 winners including the useful 2-y-o listed 6f Doncaster Stakes winner Proper Madam and a half-sister to 2 winners. The second dam, Boldabsa (by Persian Bold), won over 9f and 10f in Ireland and is a half-sister to 5 winners. (Mr M Pescod & Mr J Dowley). *"A lovely 2-y-o, he just got tired on his debut so don't be fooled by him getting beat. He's a nice 2-y-o that'll improve for that run and he'll get six furlongs".*

744. BRIGADE (IRE) ★★★

b.c. *Mujadil – Ela Tina (Ela-Mana-Mou)*. May 14. Sixth foal. €20,000Y. Goffs Orby. Peter & Ross Doyle. Half-brother to the quite useful Irish 6f to 1m winner of 6 races Miranda's Girl (by Titus Livius). The dam is an unraced half-sister to 4 minor winners here and abroad. The second dam, Glow Tina (by Glow), ran once unplaced and is a half-sister to 5 winners including the Irish listed winner and Group 3 placed Miss Lilian. (Mr M S Al Shahi). *"He's a done a few nice bits of work and we ought to see him out in May, probably over six furlongs. A nice, professional 2-y-o, he didn't cost too much and he looks good value".* TRAINERS' BARGAIN BUY

745. BROADWAY DUCHESS (IRE) ★★★★ ♠

ch.f. *New Approach – Annee Lumiere (Giant's Causeway)*. March 22. Second foal. 120,000Y. Tattersalls October Book 1. Peter & Ross Doyle. Closely related to the fair 2011 7f and 1m placed 2-y-o Enery (by Teofilo). The dam, a 9f winner in France, was listed-placed over 11f and is a half-sister to several winners including the US Grade 2 and Grade 3 winner Little Treasure and the dam of the listed winner Rhythm Of Light. The second dam, Luminosity (by Sillery), won once at 2 yrs in France and is a half-sister to 4 minor winners. (M Pescod). *"One of our nicest fillies, she's all class. A filly*

with a lovely attitude, we haven't rattled her cage yet and we won't do until mid-summer. A lovely, lovely filly for the back-end and for next year".

746. BROWNSEA BRINK ★★★

b.c. *Cadeaux Genereux – Valiantly (Anabaa)*. February 25. Fourth foal. 50,000Y. Tattersalls December. Peter & Ross Doyle. Brother to the modest 6f to 1m winner Secret Hero. The dam, a 6f winner in France, was second in the listed 6f Cecil Frail Stakes and is a half-sister to 2 winners. The second dam, Valbra (by Dancing Brave), is an unplaced sister to the listed winner and Group 3 placed Cheyenne Dream and a half-sister to 6 winners including the dams of the Group 1 winners Continent and Zambezi Sun. (The Heffer Syndicate). *"He's a nice, strong horse that's had a touch of sore shins but he looks a 2-y-o. We haven't done any work with him yet and I'd say he wants six furlongs".*

747. CAPE APPEAL ★★★★

b.f. *Cape Cross – Sheboygan (Grand Lodge)*. March 21. Third foal. €65,000Y. Goffs Orby. Peter & Ross Doyle. Half-sister to the quite useful 7f and 1m winner of 4 races Master Mylo (by Bertolini). The dam, a fairly useful 7f (at 2 yrs) and 7.5f winner, was listed placed and is a half-sister to one winner. The second dam, White Satin (by Fairy King), a 2-y-o 7f winner and third in the listed 7f Tyros Stakes in Ireland, is a half-sister to 8 winners including the US stakes winner and Grade 2 placed Chenille. (Longview Stud Bloodstock Ltd). *"Quite a round, strong filly, she hasn't done any work yet but we loved her at the sales and she's done nothing wrong yet. She's very nice and she'll want six furlongs".*

748. CARRY ON CLAPPING (IRE) ★★★★ ♠

b.f. *Acclamation – Embassy Belle (Marju)*. March 11. Third foal. €65,000Y. Goffs Orby. Peter & Ross Doyle. Half-sister to the fair 7f winner, from two starts, Embassy Pearl (by Invincible Spirit) and to the modest 1m winner Glass Of Red (by Verglas). The dam, a fair Irish 7f and 1m winner of 3 races at 4 yrs, was Grade 2 placed in the USA and is a half-sister to 6 winners. The second dam, Humble Mission (by Shack), is a placed half-sister to 3 winners including the dual listed winner Fiery Celt. (Mr W A Tinkler).

"A very nice filly, she's working and should be out in May or June over six furlongs".

749. CEELO ★★★
b.c. *Green Desert – Mindsharp (Gone West).* April 25. First foal. 35,000Y. Tattersalls October Book 1. Andrew Tinkler. The dam is an unraced sister to the Grade 1 12f Breeders Cup Turf and Grade 1 Hollywood Derby winner Johar and a half-sister to the Grade 1 Del Mar Oaks winner Dessert. The second dam, Windsharp (by Lear Fan), won 11 races in France, Canada and the USA including the Grade 1 San Luis Rey Stakes and the Grade 1 Beverly Hills Handicap. (Mr W A Tinkler). *"He goes well, we like him, he's done a couple of nice bits of work and he should be out in late May. He has a bit of grey in his tail which we think is very lucky!"*

750. CITIUS (IRE) ★★★
b.c. *Iffraaj – Brave Madam (Invincible Spirit).* January 25. Third foal. £72,000Y. Doncaster Premier. Peter & Ross Doyle. The dam is an unraced half-sister to 4 winners including the US listed stakes winner Insan Mala. The second dam, Madame Claude (by Paris House), a fair 2-y-o 6f winner, is a half-sister to 4 winners including the Irish dual listed winner Nashcash. (Mrs Julie Wood). *"He's working and is doing very well so he'll be out in early May and he's by a stallion that we like a lot".*

751. COLLINGBOURNEDUCIS (IRE) ★★★
b.c. *Bahamian Bounty – Quickstyx (Night Shift).* April 18. Fifth foal. £66,000Y. Doncaster Premier. Peter & Ross Doyle. Half-brother to the fairly useful 6f winner of 4 races (including at 2 yrs) Hairspray (by Bahamian Bounty), to the quite useful 6f (at 2 yrs) and 1m winner Watneya (by Dubawi) and the modest 2-y-o 7.5f and subsequent Swedish winner Blusher (by Fraam). The dam, a fair 1m winner, is a half-sister to 5 winners including the smart 12f listed winner and US dual Grade 1 placed Red Fort and the useful 12f listed winner Red Carnation. The second dam, Red Bouquet (by Reference Point), won 3 minor races from 12f to 13f at 4 yrs in Germany and is a half-sister to 4 winners including the Group 3 7f Prestige Stakes winner Red Camellia (herself dam of the Group 1 Fillies' Mile winner Red Bloom). (Mr W A Tinkler). *"A good-looking, strong 2-y-o type.*

He'll definitely make a 2-y-o, probably over six furlongs".

752. COLMAR KID (IRE) ★★★
b.c. *Choisir – Roselyn (Efisio).* April 28. Seventh foal. £45,000Y. Tattersalls December. Peter & Ross Doyle. Half-brother to the useful 2011 2-y-o 5f and 6f winner West Leake Diman (by Namid), to the fair 2-y-o 6f winner Squires Gate, the fair 1m to 10f winner of 5 races Kimono My House (by Dr Fong) and a minor winner in Italy by Mark Of Esteem. The dam, a modest maiden, was placed fourth 3 times at 2 yrs over 6f and 7f. She is a half-sister to 3 winners including Riberac, a winner of three listed events and third in the Group 2 Sun Chariot Stakes. The second dam, Ciboure (by Norwick), a fair 6f (at 2 yrs) and 1m winner of 3 races, is a half-sister to 4 winners. (The Heffer Syndicate). *"A nice 2-y-o, he hasn't done a lot yet but he's good-looking horse and should make a six furlong 2-y-o".*

Won cl 5 6f mdn Windsor

753. CORREGGIO ★★★
ch.c. *Bertolini – Arian Da (Superlative).* February 26. Ninth foal. 75,000Y. Tattersalls October Book 2. Peter & Ross Doyle. Brother to the smart Group 3 6f Duke Of York Stakes and listed 6f and 7f winner of 8 races Prime Defender. The dam, a fair 2-y-o 5f winner, is a full or half-sister to 7 winners. The second dam, Nell Of The North (by Canadian Gil), won 5 minor races in the USA from 2 to 4 yrs and is a sister to the US Grade 2 and Grade 3 winner Sprink and a half-sister to 5 winners. (J D Manley). *"He was a little bit quirky when we broke him in but he's settled down now. He's a big horse with plenty of speed and he'll be out early".*

754. CURL (IRE) ★★★★
b.f. *Duke Of Marmalade – Fringe (In The Wings).* February 3. Second foal. €40,000Y. Goffs Orby. Peter & Ross Doyle. The dam, a quite useful 10f winner at 4 yrs, is a half-sister to 4 winners including the listed winner Mount Elbrus. The second dam, El Jazirah (by Kris), is an unraced sister to the Group 1 Prix de Diane winner Rafha (herself the dam of 3 stakes winners including the Group 1 Haydock Park Sprint Cup winner Invincible Spirit) and a half-sister to 9 winners. *"We like her a lot, these*

Duke Of Marmalade's seem to be able to run a bit. A nice filly for six/seven furlongs".

755. CYCLONE ★★★★

b.c. Teofilo – Ascot Cyclone (Rahy). April 21. Ninth foal. 62,000Y. Tattersalls October Book 1. A Tinkler. Half-brother to the useful 2-y-o 5f and 7f winner Asia Winds (by Machiavellian), to the useful 2-y-o dual 6f winner Fancy Lady (by Cadeaux Genereux), the fairly useful triple 1m winner Electra Star (by Shamardal)), the quite useful 10f winner Daylami Star (by Daylami), the fair dual 7f winner (including in the UAE) Wadi Wanderer (by Dubai Destination) and the modest 12f winner Kochanski (by King's Best). The dam, a fairly useful 5.7f (at 2 yrs) and 7f winner, is a full or half-sister to 13 winners including the Group 1 7f Prix de la Salamandre second Bin Nashwan and the US Grade 2 winner Magellan. The second dam, Dabaweyaa (by Shareef Dancer), was a smart winner of the 1m Atalanta Stakes and was placed in the 1,000 Guineas and the Kiveton Park Stakes. She is a half-sister to the Group 3 winning sprinter Bruckner, the 12f Galtres Stakes winner Ma Femme and the smart Hoover Fillies Mile and Nassau Stakes winner Acclimatise. (W A Tinkler). *"A nice, big horse that'll take some time. We've done some work with him but he's still a bit weak so there's no rush with him. Seven furlongs should be his trip and we like him a lot".*

756. DAME DE LA NOCHE (IRE) ★★★

b.f. Teofilo – Alessia (Warning). March 12. Seventh foal. €115,000Y. Arqana Deauville August. Peter & Ross Doyle. Half-sister to the smart 1m and 10f winner of 4 races and Group 3 fourth Pinpoint (by Pivotal), to the quite useful 2-y-o 8.5f winner Ahoy (by Danehill Dancer), the quite useful 1m and 10f winner Royal Defence (by Refuse To Bend) and the fair 7f winners Perfect Point (by Cape Cross) and Grand Entrance (by Grand Lodge). The dam won at 2 yrs in Germany and is a half-sister to 5 winners including the German Group winners Arcadio and Assiun. The second dam, Assia (by Royal Academy), a listed-placed winner of 3 races in Germany, is a half-sister to 6 winners including Princess Nana (Group 2 German 1,000 Guineas). (Mr A.T.J Russell). *"A really*

sweet filly, she'll take some time and is one for seven furlongs much later on but she has a lovely action".

757. DANSILI DUAL (IRE) ★★★

b.c. Dansili – Jewel In The Sand (Bluebird). March 29. Third foal. £70,000Y. Doncaster Premier. Dwayne Woods. Half-brother to the fair 2011 5f and 6f placed 2-y-o The Rising (by Pivotal). The dam, a winner of 4 races including the Group 2 6f Cherry Hinton Stakes and the Albany Stakes, is a half-sister to 4 winners including the German 3-y-o listed 6f winner Davignon. The second dam, Dancing Drop (by Green Desert), a useful dual 2-y-o 6f winner, was listed-placed and is a half-sister to 9 winners. (Mr W A Tinkler). *"A nice colt, he's working well and he'll be racing in May. A five/six furlongs type".*

Won 5f scanner mdn c15 windsor

758. DANZ CHOICE (IRE) ★★★

b.c. Kheleyf – Aphorism (Halling). February 8. Second foal. 30,000Y. Tattersalls October Book 2. C McCormack. The dam, a fair 12f to 2m 2f winner, is a half-sister to 10 winners including the Group 2 12f Princess Of Wales's Stakes winner Craigsteel and the Group 1 20f Prix du Cadran winner and Ascot Gold Cup second Invermark. The dam, a smart winner of 3 races from 10f to 13.3f and placed in the Park Hill Stakes and the Princess Royal Stakes, is a half-sister to 6 winners including Coigach (Group 3 Park Hill Stakes). (Dragon Gate Development Ltd). *"A tough little horse, he'll be fairly early and he'll probably win a little race early doors".*

Won ofd 5f 5 runner nursery Sandown

759. DOUGLAS PASHA (IRE) ★★★

b.c. Compton Place – Lake Nayasa (Nayef). February 4. First foal. £40,000Y. Doncaster Premier. Peter & Ross Doyle. The dam is an unplaced half-sister to 4 winners including the useful 1m (at 2 yrs) and 2m winner and listed-placed Coventina. The second dam, Lady Of The Lake (by Caerleon), a useful 2m listed winner of 4 races, is a half-sister to 5 winners including the Italian Group 3 winner Guest Connections and the dam of the Group 1 Irish St Leger winner Sans Frontieres. (Middleham Park Racing). *"A nice, workmanlike colt that looked like being early but actually he'll take a bit of time. A nice, well-made horse for six or seven furlongs".*

760. DROPPING ZONE ★★★★

b.c. Duke Of Marmalade – Blue Azure (American Chance). April 16. Third foal. 80,000Y. Tattersalls October Book 1. Peter & Ross Doyle. Half-brother to Celestrial (by Verglas), unplaced in 2 starts at 2 yrs in 2011 and to the 2-y-o Group 3 6f Firth Of Clyde Stakes winner and Group 3 Ballyogan Stakes third Distinctive (by Tobougg). The dam, a modest 5f placed maiden, is half-sister to 2 minor winners in the USA. The second dam, Kibitzing (by Wild Again), a US stakes-placed winner at 3 yrs, is a half-sister to 6 winners. (P A Byrne). "He did a very nice piece of work yesterday. Pat Dobbs rode him yesterday and was very impressed. A very nice colt".

761. DUST WHIRL ★★★★ ♠

b.c. Bahamian Bounty – Dust (Green Desert). March 6. Eighth foal. £42,000Y. Doncaster Premier. David Barker. Half-brother to the quite useful 2-y-o dual 5f winner Princess Sofie (by Efisio) and to the modest 5f winner Desert Dust (by Vettori). The dam, a modest dual 1m all-weather winner, is a half-sister to 4 winners. The second dam, Storm Warning (by Tumble Wind), a very smart sprinter, won 4 races including the Group 3 Premio Omenoni and the listed Scarbrough Stakes and is a half-sister to 7 winners. (D W Barker). "Right now he's one of our nicest 2-y-o's, he goes well and he'll be out in April. Five furlongs is his trip and he might make the Supersprint if he qualifies".

762. EAST TEXAS RED (IRE) ★★★

ch.c. Danehill Dancer – Evangeline (Sadler's Wells). March 2. 80,000foal. Tattersalls December. Not sold. Closely related to the 2-y-o Group 2 6f Lowther Stakes winner Infamous Angel (by Exceed And Excel) and half-brother to Angelic Note (by Excellent Art), unplaced in 2 starts at 2 yrs in 2012. The dam is an unraced half-sister to 4 winners including the listed winner Sgt Pepper. The second dam, Amandine (by Darshaan), won once at 3 yrs in France and is a half-sister to 3 winners. (G Howard-Spink). "A bright chestnut, he's a nice horse with a good attitude. A workmanlike colt, I'm sure we'll get him out before late May but we haven't tested him yet".

763. ECHION ★★★

b.c. Ishiguru – Glittering Prize (Cadeaux Genereux). January 31. First foal. The dam, a fair 2-y-o 7f winner, half-sister to several winners including the 2-y-o Group 2 7f Rockfel Stakes winner Cairns. The second dam, Tanami (by Green Desert), a very useful 5f and 6f winner and second in the Group 1 Cheveley Park Stakes, is a half-sister to 3 winners including the dam of the Cheveley Park Stakes winner Wannabe Grand. "A tough little horse that doesn't know when to give up. He's ready to run now".

764. EMPOWERMENT (IRE) ★★★

b.c. Elusive City – Maimana (Desert King). April 7. Third living foal. £45,000Y. Doncaster Premier. Peter & Ross Doyle. Half-brother to the 7f (including at 2 yrs) and 1m winner Last Destination (by Dubai Destination). The dam, a useful 12f and 12.6f winner, is a half-sister to 4 winners including the very smart Group 1 10f Premio Presidente della Repubblica and Group 3 8.5f Diomed Stakes winner Polar Prince. The second dam, Staff Approved (by Teenoso), a fairly useful 2-y-o 1m winner, is a half-sister to 11 winners including the US Grade 2 Jockey Club Cup winner Irish Heart. (Mr M S Al Shahi). "A nice horse, he worked on the grass the other day and surprised us a bit. He's one for six or seven furlongs".

765. EQUITANIA ★★★★ ♠

ch.f. Pastoral Pursuits – Clarice Orsini (Common Grounds). March 26. Eighth foal. £65,000Y. Doncaster Premier. Amanda Skiffington. Half-sister to Johnny Jumpup (by Pivotal), a winner of 3 races at 2 yrs from 5f to 7.6f and second in a German Group 2 1m event, the Group 3 Horris Hill Stakes and the Group 3 Greenham Stakes, to the quite useful 5f and 6f winner Lenjawi Pride (by Elusive City), the fair 6f (at 2 yrs) and 7f winner Tiber Tilly (by King Charlemagne), the fair 6f winner Here Comes Danny (by Kyllachy), the modest 6f winner Klarity (by Acclamation) and the modest 6f (at 2 yrs) and 8.3f winner Ally Makbul (by Makbul). The dam was placed over 1m in France and is a half-sister to 6 minor winners. The second dam, Be My Everything (by Be My Guest), won once at 3 yrs and is a half-sister to 9 winners including the Irish 1,000 Guineas winner Nicer.

(Coriolan Links Partnership III). *"A really nice filly, she's classy and has a lot of speed. We like her a lot".*

766. EQUITISSA (IRE) ★★★
b.f. Chevalier – Westcote (Gone West). April 18. First foal. €26,000Y. Tattersalls Ireland. Peter & Ross Doyle. The dam, a fair 9f winner at 4 yrs, subsequently won in Germany and is a half-sister to 7 winners including 4 stakes winners, notably Rainbow Corner (Group 3 1m Prix de Fontainebleau). The second dam, Kingscote (by Kings Lake), won 3 races from 5f to 6f including the Lowther Stakes and is a full or half-sister to 8 winners. (Mrs J I Snow). *"A filly with a really nice pedigree so we'll look after her a bit, she'll probably be a five/six furlongs filly for mid-May onwards".*

767. ERODIUM ★★★★
b.c. Elusive City – Alovera (King's Best). March 23. Second foal. Half-brother to the fair 2011 2-y-o 5f winner Balm (by Oasis Dream). The dam, a fairly useful 2-y-o 6f winner, is a sister to the smart 6f (at 2 yrs) and listed 8.3f winner Army Of Angels and a half-sister to numerous winners including the useful 2-y-o 6f winner and Group 2 Lowther Stakes second Seraphina. The second dam, Angelic Sounds (by The Noble Player), a minor 2-y-o 5f winner, is a half-sister to 7 winners including the Group 1 Prix de la Foret winner Mount Abu. (Rockcliffe Stud). *"A lovely horse, he's grown a lot since he came in, he goes very well and he'll be a six/seven furlong 2-y-o".*

768. EVERLEIGH ★★★
b.f. Bahamian Bounty – Blur (Oasis Dream). January 29. First foal. 35,000Y. Tattersalls October Book 2. Peter & Ross Doyle. The dam, a moderate 10f placed maiden, is a half-sister to 3 winners. The second dam, Easy To Love (by Diesis), a quite useful 4-y-o 11.5f winner, is a sister to the Oaks winner Love Divine (herself dam of the St Leger winner Sixties Icon) and a half-sister to 5 winners including the listed 12f winner Floreeda. (Noodles Racing). *"A nice, very sharp filly bred by Barry Bull, she's not over-big and she goes well. Might win first time out".*

769. FOLLOWEVERYRAINBOW ★★★
b.f. Oasis Dream – Absolute Precision (Irish River). February 9. Fourth foal. 65,000foal. Tattersalls December. Catridge Farm Stud. Half-sister to the fair 10f and hurdles winner Nobunaga (by Beat Hollow). The dam is an unraced half-sister to 5 winners including the Grade 1 9f Kentucky Oaks and the Grade 1 10f Alabama Stakes winner Flute. The second dam, Rougeur (by Blushing Groom), a winner over 10f in France and 12f in the USA, was Grade 2 placed and is a half-sister to 5 winners including the Park Hill Stakes winner and high-class broodmare Eva Luna. (Mrs Julie Wood). *"A very nice filly, we thought she'd be sharp but she's just gone a bit 'empty'. She'll be back for when the six furlong races start and she's a classy-looking filly".*

770. FORT KNOX ★★★
b.c. Dubawi – Savannah Belle (Green Desert). March 30. Eighth foal. 190,000Y. Tattersalls October Book 1. Not sold. Brother to the very smart Group 2 Celebration Mile and dual listed winner and English and Irish 2,000 Guineas second Dubawi Gold and half-brother to 4 winners including the fairly useful 2011 2-y-o 6f winner Campanology (by Royal Applause), the quite useful 7f to 9f winner of 7 races Salient (by Fasliyev), the fair 6f winner Dixieland Boy (by Inchinor) and the Italian winner of 7 races Mac Memory (by Second Empire). The dam, a quite useful 2-y-o 5f winner, is a half-sister to 5 winners including the useful Rainwatch. The second dam, Third Watch (by Slip Anchor), a 7f (at 2 yrs) and Group 2 12f Ribblesdale Stakes winner, is a half-sister to 12 winners including the dual Group 3 winner Richard of York, the Group 2 Premio Dormello winner Three Tails (herself the dam 3 Group winners), the Group 3 Fred Darling Stakes winner Maysoon and the dams of the Group winners Lend A Hand and Talented. (W A Tinkler). *"Not over-big, he's a really good goer. A nice horse that moves well".*

771. FOXY DANCER (IRE) ★★★ ♠
b.f. Jeremy – Date Mate (Thorn Dance). March 19. Eighth foal. 29,000Y. Tattersalls October Book 2. Not sold. Half-sister to the modest 2011 6f and 7f placed 2-y-o Dark Ambition (by Dark Angel), to the 2-y-o Group 3 6f Princess Margaret Stakes winner Soraaya (by

Elnadim), the listed 2-y-o Woodcote Stakes winner and Group 1 Prix Jean-Luc Lagardere second Declaration Of War (by Okawango), the quite useful 6f to 10f winner of 4 races Freak Occurrence (by Stravinsky) and a winner over hurdles by Idris. The dam, placed in the USA, is a half-sister to 4 winners including the dams of the Italian Group 1 winner Le Vie Dei Colori and the Queen Mary Stakes winner Shining Hour. The second dam, Doubling Time (by Timeless Moment), a smart winner at 3 yrs in France and second in the Group 3 10.5f Prix de Flore, is a full or half-sister to 8 winners including the Prix Ganay and Prix d'Ispahan winner Baillamont. (Fox Inn Syndicate 4). *"A very nice filly, she does have a bit of an attitude but that's no bad thing and she's owned by an enthusiastic bunch. One for six or seven furlongs I'd say".*

772. GERRARD'S CROSS ★★★

b.c. Cape Cross – Shin Feign (El Prado). January 30. Second foal. 48,000foal. Tattersalls December. Catridge Farm Stud. The dam won 2 minor races at 3 yrs in the USA and is a half-sister to 4 winners including the Japanese stakes winner Wonderful Days. The second dam, My Cherie (by Woodman), a minor winner at 2 yrs in the USA, is a half-sister to 6 winners including the Group 3 Kiveton Park Stakes and Group 3 Duke of York Stakes winner Green Line Express. (Mrs Julie Wood). *"A really nice, strong, back-end type 2-y-o".*

773. GLOBAL ICON ★★★

b.c. Green Desert – Maganda (Sadler's Wells). March 12. Fifth foal. 50,000Y. Tattersalls October Book 1. Peter & Ross Doyle. Closely related to the useful Irish 2-y-o 6f winner and Group 3 Anglesey Stakes third Rudolf Valentino (by Oasis Dream) and to the quite useful 1m and 10f winner Akhmatova (by Cape Cross). The dam, a quite useful 10f winner, is a sister to the listed winners In The Limelight and On The Nile and a half-sister to 3 winners including the German and Italian Group 1 winner Kutub. The second dam, Minnie Habit (by Habitat), an Irish 4-y-o 9f winner, is closely related to the dual Group 3 sprint winner Bermuda Classic (herself dam of the Coronation Stakes winner Shake The Yoke) and a half-sister to 6 winners. (W A Tinkler). *"Quite nice and he's ready to run now".*

774. GOLD BURST (IRE) ★★★

ch.c. Tamayuz – Mistress Thames (Sharpo). April 16. Ninth foal. 40,000Y. Tattersalls December. Peter & Ross Doyle. Half-brother to the smart 7f (including at 2 yrs) and listed 8.3f winner Father Thames (by Bishop Of Cashel), to the Italian listed winner of 10 races Around Alone (by Rudimentary), the Italian 2-y-o 6f winner and listed-placed Vola Vola (by Danehill Dancer), the quite useful 14f and hurdles winner by Galileo and two winners in Italy by Montjeu and Alhaarth. The dam, placed twice over 6f at 3 yrs, is a half-sister to 5 minor winners. The second dam, Miss Thames (by Tower Walk), won 4 races at 2 and 3 yrs and is a half-sister to 5 winners. (Knockalney Stud Ltd). *"He ought to make a nice, six furlong 2-y-o but he came to us with no tail. Once you get used to it he's alright and he has done some nice bits of work".*

775. GOLD MEDAL (IRE) ★★★

b.c. Dylan Thomas – Sogno Verde (Green Desert). March 16. Third foal. €135,000foal. Goffs. Peter & Ross Doyle. Half-brother to the smart 2011 2-y-o Group 3 6f Railway Stakes winner and Group 1 6f Middle Park Stakes second Lilbourne Lad (by Acclamation) and to the very useful Irish 2-y-o 7f winner and 3-y-o Group 3 10f Gallinule Stakes second Bobbyscot (by Alhaarth). The dam, a fair Irish 9f winner, is closely related to the 7f (at 3 yrs) and 4-y-o listed 12f winner Chartres and a half-sister to 5 winners including the listed 10f and listed 14f winner Pugin. The second dam, Gothic Dream (by Nashwan), a winner over 7f in Ireland at 2 yrs and third in the Irish Oaks, is a half-sister to 3 winners. (Mrs J Wood). *"A lovely, big colt and a half-brother to Lilbourne Lad who we had here. He has a bit of an attitude but once we've sorted that out we'll get on with working him. A mid-season 2-y-o hopefully".*

776. GREAT RUN ★★★★

ch.c. Compton Place – Hasten (Lear Fan). February 13. Seventh foal. 46,000foal. Tattersalls December. Peter & Ross Doyle. Half-brother to the fair UAE 7f winner My Own Way (by Dubawi), to the fair 1m winner Hasty Lady (by Dubai Destination), the modest 2-y-o 7f winner Gassal and a minor winner abroad by Johannesburg. The dam was placed twice in the USA and is a half-sister to 6 winners including the 2-y-o Group 3 Autumn Stakes winner and Group 1 Racing Post Trophy second Fantastic View. The second dam, Promptly (by Lead On Time), a quite useful 6f winner here, subsequently won a minor stakes event over 1m in the USA and is a half-sister to 7 winners. (Mr S Wong). *"A lovely, big horse, one of the nicest 2-y-o's we've got. We've had a lot of luck with the sire and if this colt goes the right way he could be anything. We like him a lot".*

777. HANDS OF TIME ★★★

b.c. Pivotal – Virtuous (Exit To Nowhere). April 27. Eleventh foal. 150,000Y. Tattersalls October Book 1. R Frisby. Brother to the Group 1 1m Lockinge Stakes and dual listed winner Virtual, to the quite useful 10f winner Virtuosity and the fair triple 10f winner Judicial (all by Pivotal), closely related to the very smart 2-y-o Group 2 6f Coventry Stakes winner and Group 1 6f Middle Park Stakes third Iceman (by Polar Falcon) and half-brother to the quite useful 10f winner Peace (by Sadler's Wells) and the fair 2-y-o 6f winner Liberty (by Singspiel). The dam, a fairly useful 2-y-o 1m winner, was third in the listed 11.5f Oaks Trial and is a sister to 3 winners. The second dam, Exclusive Virtue (by Shadeed), a fairly useful 2-y-o 7f winner, stayed 12f and is a half-sister to 9 winners including the 2,000 Guineas winner and Derby fourth Entrepreneur and the Coronation Stakes winner Exclusive. (S H Altayer). *"A very good-looking horse, he'll take his time but he's a half-brother to two Group winners. I haven't done anything with him yet but he's a nice colt".*

778. HAVANA GOLD (IRE) ★★★★

b.c. Teofilo – Jessica's Dream (Desert Style). April 13. Seventh foal. 80,000Y. Tattersalls October Book 1. Mrs A Skiffington. Brother to Skirmish, unplaced in one start at 2 yrs in 2011 and half-brother to the fair 5f winner of 8 races (including at 2 yrs) Rocker (by Rock Of Gibraltar) and a winner in Hong Kong by Royal Applause. The dam, a very smart sprinter, won the Group 3 Ballyogan Stakes and the Group 3 Premio Omenoni and is a half-sister to the listed winner and dual Group 1 placed Majors Cast. The second dam, Ziffany (by Taufan), a 2-y-o 7f seller winner, is a half-sister to one winner abroad. (Coriolan Links Partnership III).

"A lovely big horse, very mature with a good action. A mid-season type 2-y-o, he'll probably want seven furlongs but he's one we like a lot".

779. JANOUB NIBRAS (IRE) ★★★

b.c. Acclamation – Wildsplash (Deputy Minister). February 2. Fourth foal. 105,000Y. Tattersalls October Book 2. R Frisby. Half-brother to the fairly useful 2-y-o 6f winner Princess Severus, to the moderate 9f winner East Of Tara (both by Barathea) and the fair 7f and 1m winner of 7 races Just Five (by Olmodavor). The dam is an unraced half-sister to 4 winners including the French listed winner Royal God. The second dam, Gold Splash (by Blushing Groom), won the Group 1 Prix Marcel Boussac and the Group 1 Coronation Stakes and is a half-sister to the dam of the outstanding filly Goldikova. *"He's a nice horse and he's like all Acclamation's because you can spot them a mile away. They're good-looking, slightly long and they seem to run very well for us. Hopefully he'll be just the same".*

780. JARYAL ★★★★ ♠

b.c. Dubawi – Strings (Unfuwain). March 31. Fifth foal. 190,000Y. Tattersalls October Book 1. Peter & Ross Doyle. Half-brother to the fairly useful 2-y-o 1m winner State Opera (by Shamardal), to the quite useful dual 7f (at 2 yrs) and dual 10f winner Bahamian Flight (by Bahamian Bounty) and a winner abroad by Exceed And Excel. The dam is an unraced half-sister to 6 winners including the French 2,000 Guineas winner Victory Note. The second dam, Three Piece (by Jaazeiro), an Irish placed 2-y-o, is a half-sister to 8 winners including Orchestration (Group 2 Coronation Stakes) and Welsh Term (Group 2 Prix d'Harcourt). (Hamdan Al Maktoum). *"One of our nicest 2-y-o's, he's working really well and he looks great. We won't run him for a while but we're very excited about him".*

781. JUBILEE DIAMOND (IRE) ★★★

b.f. Redback – Nice One Clare (Mukaddamah). April 1. Fourth foal. £32,000Y. Doncaster Premier. Peter & Ross Doyle. Half-sister to a winner in Qatar by Indian Ridge. The dam won 6 races including the Group 3 Diadem Stakes and listed Sceptre Stakes and is a half-sister to 3 minor winners. The second dam, Sarah-Clare (by Reach), a modest 1m and 10f winner of 6 races, is a half-sister to 3 winners. (Mrs Julie Wood). *"We thought she was going to be sharp, but now we're not so sure. She'll probably want six furlongs but she is a nice filly and I'm sure she'll be decent too".*

782. KEEP CALM ★★★

b.c. War Chant – Mayaar (Grand Slam). January 29. First foal. 36,000Y. Tattersalls October Book 3. Will Edmeades. The dam, a fair third over 5f at 2 yrs, is a sister to the winner and US Grade 3 placed Imitation and a half-sister to 5 winners including the US Grade 2 placed El Ballezano. The second dam, Kovna (by Seattle Slew), is an unraced sister to the Group 1 Coronation Stakes winner Magic Of Life (herself dam of the Group 2 Lowther Stakes winner Enthused) and a half-sister to 4 winners. (Richard Hitchcock/Alan King). *"A very strong, tough horse, he'll lovely but he'll probably want six or seven furlongs".*

783. KING OF KUDOS (IRE) ★★★

b.c. Acclamation – Perugina (Highest Honor). March 17. Sixth foal. £54,000Y. Doncaster Premier. Dwayne Woods. Half-brother to four minor winners in France by Anabaa, Cape Cross, Hawk Wing and Zafonic. The dam won the Group 3 Prix Eclipse Stakes in France and is a half-sister to 3 winners. The second dam, Piacenza (by Darshaan), a minor French 3-y-o winner, is a half-sister to 5 winners. (W A Tinkler). *"A nice horse that's done a couple of bits of work. He's sharp and a typical Acclamation".*

784. KING OLIVER ★★★

ch.c. Kyllachy – Confetti (Groom Dancer). March 24. Fourth foal. 35,000Y. Tattersalls October Book 2. Peter & Ross Doyle. Closely related to the quite useful 2-y-o 6f winner Wedding List (by Pivotal) and half-brother to Dust On The Ground (by Dutch Art), unplaced in two starts at 2 yrs in 2011. The dam was unplaced in two starts. The second dam, Fabulous (by Fabulous Dancer), is an unraced sister to 2 winners including the French 2-y-o 7.5f winner and US 1m stakes winner La Piaf and a half-sister to 5 winners including the triple US Grade 1 winner Golden Apples and the Group 3 Park Hill Stakes winner Alexander Three D. (M Pescod). *"It took*

us a long while to get the weight off him but now he's quite sharp, he's a nice colt and one you'll see early on".*

785. LILBOURNE ELIZA (IRE) ★★★

b.f. Elusive City – Midnight Partner (Marju). April 28. Sixth foal. €38,000Y. Goffs Orby. Peter & Ross Doyle. Half-sister to the fair 2-y-o 1m winner Escholido (by Noverre), to the modest 9f and 10f winner of four races Buona Sarah (by Bertolini), the German 3-y-o winner and listed-placed Terre Neuve (by Verglas) and the minor French winner of 4 races at 2 to 4 yrs Desert Nights (by Desert Style). The dam is an unraced half-sister to the winner of 5 races and Group 1 Criterium International second Top Seed. The second dam, Midnight Heights (by Persian Heights), won 5 races including 2 listed events in Italy, was second in the Group 2 10f Premio Lydia Tesio and is a half-sister to Group 3 Sandown Classic Trial winner Galitzin. (Mr A.T.J Russell). *"Yes, she's a nice filly but she's backward and will take a bit of time".*

786. LIONS ARCH (IRE) ★★★

b.c. Rock Of Gibraltar – Swynford Lady (Invincible Spirit). March 19. First foal. €100,000Y. Goffs Orby. Peter & Ross Doyle. The dam is an unraced sister to the Group 1 6f July Cup and dual Group 2 winner Fleeting Spirit and a half-sister to 2 winners. The second dam, Millennium Tale (by Distant Relative), is an unraced half-sister to 5 winners. (Mr A.T.J Russell). *"A lovely horse, he had a bit of a haematoma but he's over that now and he'd one of the nicest moving colts we've got".*

787. LYRIC ACE (IRE) ★★★

b.c. Thousand Words – Aces Dancing (Big Shuffle). February 19. Fourth foal. £23,000Y. Doncaster Premier. Peter & Ross Doyle. Half-brother to the modest 5f and 6f winner of 5 races (including at 2 yrs) Vilnius (by Imperial Dancer). The dam, a quite useful 2-y-o 5f winner, is a sister to the German Group 2 winner Auenklang and to the German listed winner Auenweise and a half-sister to 5 winners. The second dam, Auenglocke (by Surumu), won 2 races in Germany and is a half-sister to 11 winners. (Byerley Racing Ltd). *"A nice colt that we'll start at five furlongs but he'll be better at six".*

788. MAGIC CHANNEL (USA) ★★★
ch.c. English Channel – Arabian Peninsula (Mr Prospector). February 20. Sixth living foal. $12,000Y. BBA (Ire). Fasig-Tipton Kentucky July. £56,000Y. Doncaster Premier. Peter & Ross Doyle. Half-brother to 2 minor winners in the USA by Point Given and Stormy Atlantic. The dam is an unraced half-sister to 5 winners. The second dam, My True Lady (by Seattle Slew), a US stakes winner, is a half-sister to 6 winners. (Mr A Al Mansoori). *"We don't know much about the stallion but this horse has done one piece of work and he did it well. He has a nice temperament, he's going the right way and he looks a nice 2-y-o".*

789. MAGIC LANDO (FR) ★★★
b.c. Lando – Blackberry Pie (Gulch). March 26. Second foal. Tattersalls October Book 2. 60,000Y. Shadwell Estate Co. The dam, a modest 1m placed maiden, is a half-sister to 3 winners including the US stakes winner and Grade 3 third Perilous Pursuit. The second dam, Name Of Love (by Petardia), a very useful 2-y-o Group 3 7f Rockfel Stakes and listed 7f Oh So Sharp Stakes winner, is a half-sister to 5 winners. (Mr A Al Mansoori). *"A backward horse, he'll need time but I like him a lot. One for later on over seven furlongs or a mile, so we'll sit quiet with him until the better type races come along".*

790. MANDEVILLE (IRE) ★★★
b.f. Kodiac – Olympia Theatre (Galileo). March 10. Second foal. 22,000Y. Tattersalls October Book 3. Dwayne Woods. The dam is an unraced half-sister to 3 minor winners. The second dam, Opari (by Night Shift), a French 2-y-o 6f winner, is a half-sister to one winner. (W A Tinkler). *"She's a filly that needs time, so she won't run until the back-end over seven furlongs but I like her".*

791. MASTER OF WAR ★★★
ch.c. Compton Place – Mamma Morton (Elnadim). February 16. Second foal. 28,000foal. Tattersalls December. Peter Doyle. Half-brother to Muaamara (by Bahamian Bounty), a fair 6f winner on her only start at 2 yrs in 2011. The dam, a fair 10f and 11f placed maiden, is a half-sister to 10 winners including the very useful 10f winner Shaya and the dam of the US Grade 1 winner Tamweel. The second dam, Gharam (by Green Dancer), a very useful 2-y-o 6f winner, was third in the French 1,000 Guineas and is a half-sister to 7 winners including the US Grade 1 9f winner Talinum. (Mr M S Al Shahi). *"He's done a couple of bits of work and he ought to make a nice 2-y-o over five or six furlongs".* ̱ₑ̱ₐₜ. ᵈ⸍ ᵂᵐ ᵍ⸍ ᶜˡ ⁵ ᵘᵗⁿ ᴴᵧᵈᶜᵥ. ᵂⁱⁿ ᶜˡ ᴵ ᵗ⸝⸝ˡₒⱼ ᵇⱼ ᴺₑₐₜᵦₘⱼ

792. MERINGUE PIE ★★★★
ch.c. Sakhee's Secret – Queen's Pudding (Royal Applause). April 26. Second foal. €60,000Y. Goffs Orby. Peter & Ross Doyle. Half-brother to the unplaced 2011 2-y-o Arrowroot (by Sleeping Indian). The dam, a quite useful 2-y-o 6f winner, is a half-sister to 5 winners including the Group 2 Yorkshire Cup third Defining. The second dam, Gooseberry Pie (by Green Desert), is a placed half-sister to 8 winners including the dual Group winner Rakaposhi King. *"We're quite excited about him and the Sakhee's Secret's seem to be able to run. We'd like to think he's a Royal Ascot type but it's very early days. He's a nice horse, not the greatest eater in the world but a good mover".*

793. MESHARDAL (GER) ★★★
b.c. Shamardal – Melody Fair (Montjeu). February 10. First foal. 220,000Y. Tattersalls October Book 2. Peter & Ross Doyle. The dam ran once unplaced and is a half-sister to 4 winners including Strawberry Dale (Group 3 Middleton Stakes). The second dam, Manchaca (by Highest Honor), won once at 4 yrs in France and is a half-sister to 3 winners. (Hamdan Al Maktoum). *"We haven't rattled his cage but he's a nice horse that ought to make a 2-y-o – that's what he was bought for".*

794. MIRAAJ (IRE) ★★★
b.c. Iffraaj – My-Lorraine (Mac's Imp). April 24. Eleventh foal. £36,000Y. Doncaster Premier. Peter & Ross Doyle. Half-brother to the useful 7f to 9f and hurdles winner Bolodenka (by Soviet Star), to the fairly useful 5f of 3 races (including at 2 yrs) listed-placed Izmail (by Bluebird), the fair 50 to 7f winner of 5 races Ajara (by Elusive City), the modest 5f and 6f winner of 5 races Cross Of Lorraine (by Pivotal) and a winner in Japan by Captain Rio. The dam, a minor Irish 3-y-o 5f and 6.5f winner, is a half-sister to 6 winners including the Group

3 5f Ballyogan Stakes winner and Group 1 Haydock Park Sprint Cup third Catch The Blues. The second dam, Dear Lorraine (by Nonoalco), won over 10f in France and is a half-sister to 4 winners. (Mr W.A Tinkler). *"A nice horse that goes well, he's very strong and ought to make a nice 2-y-o over five or six furlongs".*

795. MISS DIVA ★★★ ♠

b.f. *Acclamation – Mina (Selkirk).* February 18. Third foal. 23,000Y. Tattersalls October Book 2. Will Edmeades. Half-sister to the fair 5f and 6f winner Peace Seeker (by Oasis Dream). The dam, a modest 6f winner at 4 yrs, is a half-sister to 5 winners including the Group 3 5f Ballyogan Stakes winner Miss Anabaa, the smart 5f and 6f winner of 6 races Out After Dark and the useful 5f and 6f winner of 7 races (here and in Hong Kong) Move It. The second dam, Midnight Shift (by Night Shift), a fair dual 6f winner at 3 yrs, is a half-sister to 8 winners including the Group 1 6f July Cup winner Owington. *"A very, very sharp filly, she'll be racing in April over five furlongs. She's a bit small so she'll be winning her races early".* 2nd Debut

Won 6th race Windsor

796. MISTER MARC (IRE) ★★★★ ♠

b.c. *Acclamation – Fathoming (Gulch).* February 9. First foal. 70,000Y. Doncaster Premier. Peter & Ross Doyle. The dam ran once unplaced and is a half-sister to 2 minor winners. The second dam, Ocean Ridge (by Storm Bird), winner of the Group 2 6f Prix Robert Papin and second in the Group 1 1m Coronation Stakes, is a half-sister to 6 winners including the Group 2 Gimcrack Stakes second Fokine. (Mr A.T.J Russell). *"A lovely colt and one of our nicest. He'll run over five or six furlongs".* Richard Hughes gave me the 'thumbs up' about his colt, he likes him a lot.

Won 6th m h

797. MONTIRIDGE (IRE) ★★★

b.c. *Ramonti – Elegant Ridge (Indian Ridge).* March 14. Seventh foal. $55,000Y. Doncaster Premier. Peter & Ross Doyle. Half-brother to Woodward Park (by High Yield), a minor winner of 3 races in the USA. The dam, a useful German 6.5f winner and second in the German Group 2 1,000 Guineas, subsequently won in the USA and is a half-sister to 8 winners including the smart Irish 5f and listed 6f winner Rolo Tomasi. The second dam, Elegant Bloom

(by Be My Guest), a quite useful Irish 2-y-o 6f winner, stayed 7f and is a full or half-sister to 12 winners including two stakes winners. (M Clarke, J Jeffries, R Ambrose, B Reilly). *"A lovely horse, he's got a bit of a plain head, he ought to get six or seven furlongs so he'll take a little bit of time".* Won 7f c/4 Newbury when not fully f.d

798. MOORTAHAN ★★★ ♠ fully f.d

b.c. *Dutch Art – Rotunda (Pivotal).* February 26. First foal. 75,000Y. Tattersalls October Book 2. Peter & Ross Doyle. The dam is an unraced half-sister to 5 winners including the Group 2 1m May Hill Stakes (at 2 yrs) and Group 2 1m Windsor Forest Stakes winner and 1,000 Guineas second Spacious. The second dam, Palatial (by Green Desert), a useful winner of 4 races over 7f (including at 2 yrs), is a half-sister to 5 winners including the useful listed 10f winners Portal and Ice Palace. (Hamdan Al Maktoum). *"We've done a couple of bits of work with him, he goes well and he's a tall, strong colt".*

2nd to Cooler's Aldon on debut

799. MUTAZAMEN ★★★★

Won by Naprut a.lg

ch.c. *Sakhee's Secret – Disco Lights (Spectrum).* April 24. Third foal. 95,000Y. Tattersalls October Book 2. Peter & Ross Doyle. Half-brother to Mirror Ball (by Notnowcato), placed second over 7f on her only start at 2 yrs in 2011 and to the quite useful 2-y-o 6f winner Tipsy Girl (by Haafhd). The dam, a fair 1m and 9f placed 2-y-o, won at 4 yrs in Germany and is a half-sister to 5 winners including the Ebor Handicap winner Tuning and the useful Group 3 7f Rockfel Stakes second Clog Dance. The second dam, Discomatic (by Roberto), a French 9f winner, is a half-sister to 6 winners including the Phoenix Stakes winner Digamist. (Hamdan Al Maktoum). *"One of our nicest 2-y-o's, we love him and he goes very well. He has loads of bone, he carries a bit of weight and he's very sound".*

800. MYSTERIAL ★★★★★

b.c. *Invincible Spirit – Diamond Dilemma (Sinndar).* February 13. First foal. 150,000Y. Tattersalls October Book 1. John Warren. The dam is an unraced half-sister to 10 winners including the Group 2 11f Blandford Stakes and US dual Grade 2 winner Lisieux Rose. The second dam, Epicure's Garden (by Affirmed), a useful Irish 7f (at 2 yrs) to 9f winner, was Group 3 placed three times and is a sister to the Irish 1,000 Guineas winner Trusted Partner (dam of the high-class filly Dress To Thrill), to the Group 2 winner Easy To Copy (the dam of 3 stakes winners) and the US Grade 3 winner Low Key Affair. (Highclere Thoroughbred Racing – Sloan). *"We're quite excited about him, he goes very well and we might get to Royal Ascot with him. He's not the biggest in the world but he's a nice-looking horse".*

801. MYSTICAL MOMENT ★★★★ ♠

ch.f. Dutch Art – Tinnarinka (Observatory). March 13. First foal. 30,000Y. Tattersalls October Book 2. Peter and Ross Doyle. The dam, a modest 1m winner, is a half-sister to 4 winners. The second dam, Dancing Fire (by Dayjur), is an unraced half-sister to 4 winners including Scintillo (Group 1 Gran Criterium) and the multiple Group 3 winner Jumbajukiba. (Mrs A Turner). *"She's a very nice filly. A big, bright chestnut that hasn't done anything yet but she'll be working soon. She'll want six, maybe seven furlongs and she should make a really nice 2-y-o".*

802. NINJAGO ★★★★

b.c. Mount Nelson – Fidelio's Miracle (Mountain Cat). April 5. Sixth foal. 40,000Y. Tattersalls October Book 2. Peter and Ross Doyle. Half-brother to the quite useful 6f winner Florestans Match (by Medicean). The dam won 3 races from 7f to 10f including a French listed event, was second in the Group 3 Prix de la Grotte and is a half-sister to 3 winners. The second dam, Flurry (by Groom Dancer), a winner in France and the USA and listed-placed twice, is a half-sister to 6 winners and to the dams of the Group/Grade 1 winners Myboycharlie and Snowland. *"He looks a very good horse in the making and he could do his stallion proud. He's tough, I like him a lot and he could be anything".*

803. OLYMPIC GLORY (IRE) ★★★

b.c. Choisir – Acidanthera (Alzao). March 27. Ninth foal. £65,000Y. Doncaster Premier. Peter and Ross Doyle. Half-brother to the fairly useful 1m, 10f and Hong Kong winner Mister Dee Bee (by Orpen), to the fairly useful 5f to 7f winner of 4 races (including at 2 yrs) He's A Humbug and

to the Spanish 1m and 10f winner Pacific Star (both by Tagula). The dam, a quite useful 3-y-o 7.5f winner, is a half-sister to 2 winners. The second dam, Amaranthus (by Shirley Heights), is an unraced half-sister to 6 winners including the dam of the Group winners Wootton Rivers and Magellano. (Mrs Julie Wood). *"A nice, backward horse, he's a strong 2-y-o for the second half of the season".*

Jrreaued up on debut by Edwl

804. OTTAUQUECHEE (IRE) ★★★

b.f. Lawman – Lolita's Gold (Royal Academy). April 18. Sixth foal. 25,000Y. Tattersalls October Book 2. Peter and Ross Doyle. Half-brother to the fair 2010 2-y-o 7f winner Sextons House (by King's Best) and to the modest 2-y-o 7f winner Sienna Lake (by Fasliyev). The dam, placed at 2 and 3 yrs over 9f and 10f, is a half-sister to 3 winners including the Group 3 Jersey Stakes winner Membership. The second dam, Shamisen (by Diesis), a fairly useful 2-y-o 7f winner and second in the Group 2 6f Lowther Stakes, is a sister to the Group 3 8.5f Diomed Stakes winner Enharmonic and a half-sister to 9 winners including the dual listed winner Soprano. (Mr M A Adams). *"This is a nice filly. She's done a couple of bits of work and has done well but still looks a bit backward so we'll give her a bit of time".*

Won 3d 6f — conhr d 3 fyr

805. PEARL ACCLAIM (IRE) ★★★★

b.c. Acclamation – With Colour (Rainbow Quest). March 18. Second foal. 165,000Y. Tattersalls October Book 2. David Redvers. Half-brother to the unplaced 2011 2-y-o Our Phylli Vera (by Motivator). The dam is an unplaced half-sister to 7 winners including the smart 7f (at 2 yrs) and listed 10f winner of 6 races With Interest. The second dam, With Fascination (by Dayjur), won the 2-y-o Group 3 6f Prix de Cabourg and was Group 1 placed twice at 2 yrs and is a half-sister to 5 winners including the US multiple Grade 1 middle-distance winner With Anticipation. (Pearl Bloodstock Ltd). *"One of our nicest 2-y-o's. He's done a few pieces of work and done very well, so we're quite excited about him and he's a typical Acclamation".*

Macked up ord 5f ahn sandown at 2/11

806. PERFECT POSE (IRE) ★★★

b.f. Amadeus Wolf – Interpose (Indian Ridge). April 7. Eighth living foal. €28,000Y. Goffs Orby. A Tinkler. Half-sister to the fairly useful 6f (at

2 yrs) and subsequent US stakes winner and Grade 1 placed Rinterval, to the fair 7f, 10f and hurdles winner Go Figure (both by Desert Prince), the fair 10f winner Interdiamonds (by Montjeu) and a minor winner in France by Sinndar. The dam is an unraced half-sister to 7 winners including the French Group 3 winner Short Pause, the French 1m listed winner Cheyenne Dream and the dams of the Group 1 winners Continent and Zambezi Sun. The second dam, Interval (by Habitat), a high-class sprinting winner of four races from 5f to 1m including the Group 2 Prix Maurice de Gheest, is a half-sister to 5 winners. (Mr W A Tinkler). *"A nice filly, although she has got a few quirks about her. One for six or seven furlongs I'd say".*

807. PIVOTAL MOVEMENT ★★★

ch.c. Pivotal – Selinka (Selkirk). January 16. First foal. 280,000Y. Tattersalls October Book 1. R Frisby. The dam, a useful listed 6f (at 2 yrs) and listed 7f winner, is a half-sister to 2 winners. The second dam, Lady Links (by Bahamian Bounty), a dual listed 6f winner (including at 2 yrs), is a half-sister to 5 winners including the quite useful 2-y-o 6f winner and Group 3 placed Umniya. (Sir A Ferguson, G Mason, R Wood, P Done). *"He surprised us yesterday because we didn't think he was ready but he worked really well. He's not the biggest in the world but he goes very well".* Hely eard when r.o
yoing to win or dont

808. PRINCE'S TRUST ★★★★

b.c. Invincible Spirit – Lost In Wonder (Galileo). February 21. Second foal. Closely related to the fair 2011 7f placed 2-y-o Traveller's Tales (by Cape Cross). The dam, a fairly useful 2-y-o 7.5f winner, is closely related to the 7f (at 2 yrs) and listed 12f winner Juliette and a half-sister to 4 winners including the useful Irish 6f (at 2 yrs) and 1m winner and subsequent US Grade 2 placed Plato. The second dam, Arutua (by Riverman), is an unraced half-sister to the Group 2 Prix Greffulhe Stakes winner Along All. (The Queen). *"We're very excited about this horse. He's one of the nicest we've received from Her Majesty and he's a very good-looking, big colt that ought to make a racehorse. By a stallion that we love".*

809. RAFALE ★★★

b.c. Sleeping Indian – Sweet Coincidence (Mujahid). January 25. Fifth foal. £22,000Y. Doncaster Premier. Peter & Ross Doyle. Half-brother to the quite useful 11f to 14f winner of 6 races Lucky Punt, to the fair 14f and 17f winner May Contain Nuts and the modest 9f winner Llandavery (all by Auction House). The dam, a fair 2-y-o 6f winner, is a half-sister to 3 other minor winners. The second dam, Sibilant (by Selkirk), placed at 3 yrs in France, is a half-sister to 2 winners. (Mr M S Al Shahi). *"A nice colt and as soon as the six furlong races are out he'll be ready to run".*

810. RAGING BEAR (USA) ★★★★

b.c. Leroidesanimaux – Gliding Light (Always A Classic). April 6. Seventh foal. €50,000Y. Goffs Orby. Peter & Ross Doyle. Half-brother to 2 minor winners in the USA by Hold That Tiger and Limehouse. The dam is an unraced half-sister to 8 winners including the dam of the US Graded stakes winners Stanley Park and Mo Cuishle. The second dam, Tricky Squaw (by Clever Trick), won 12 races including two Grade 3 stakes and is a half-sister to 5 winners. *"A very, very nice horse. You won't see him until around Goodwood time and he'll want seven furlongs. He's a very extravagant mover by the sire of the Kentucky Derby winner, Animal Kingdom. We like him a lot".*

811. RAYAHEEN ★★

b.f. Nayef – Natagora (Divine Light). February 9. First foal. The dam, a champion 2-y-o filly and winner of the Group 1 Cheveley Park Stakes and the 1,000 Guineas, is a half-sister to 2 minor winners in France (including one over jumps). The second dam, Reinamixa (by Linamix), a minor French 11f winner, is a half-sister to 6 winners including the French listed winner Reinstate. (Hamdan Al Maktoum). *"A nice filly, she can carry her head a bit high. Obviously with her pedigree we're treating her like a champion until she proves otherwise".*
Fettling debut to win clS bfrl.

812. RED ADAIR (IRE) ★★★ Next nicly

ch.c. Redback – Daanaat (Kheleyf). March 9. First foal. £17,000Y. Doncaster Premier. Peter & Ross Doyle. The dam is an unplaced half-sister to 4 winners including Alzerra (Group 3 Cornwallis Stakes). The second dam, Belle

Argentine (by Fijar Tango), a listed winner in France and third in the French 1,000 Guineas, is a half-sister to one winner. (Mrs S.A.F Brendish). *"This is quite a sharp horse, we'll see him out early, he has a bit of Redback's attitude but he's quite a nice 2-y-o".*

813. RED REFRACTION (IRE) ★★★

b.c. Red Clubs – Dreamalot (Falbrav). February 14. First foal. £55,000Y. Doncaster Premier. Peter & Ross Doyle. The dam is an unraced half-sister to 5 winners including the smart German Group 2 12f winner Baroon, the Group 3 6f Prix de Meautry winner and Group 1 Middle Park Stakes third Vision Of Night, the smart Group 3 5f Prix de Saint-Georges winner Struggler and the useful 10f winner and listed-placed Dream Quest. The second dam, Dreamawhile (by Known Fact), a quite useful 3-y-o 7f winner, is a half-sister to 5 winners including the Group 1 Italian Derby winner My Top and the Hoover Fillies Mile second Mountain Memory. (R Hannon). *"We like him a lot, he'll probably want seven furlongs, he's got white socks and he's quite a big, tall horse so he'll take a bit of time but he goes well".* ~~Bryl 1f n-b~~ ~~Jolibury Jr detbut~~

814. REINVIGORATE (IRE) ★★★ 2nd /last

b.f. Invincible Spirit – Miss Serendipity (Key Of Luck). April 17. Fifth foal. 55,000Y. Tattersalls October Book 2. Peter & Ross Doyle. The dam, an Irish 2-y-o 5f winner, was listed-placed and is a sister to the Group 3 6f Greenlands Stakes winner Miss Emma and a half-sister to 5 winners. The second dam, Disregard That (by Don't Forget Me), is an unraced half-sister to 5 winners including the 2-y-o Group 3 Killavullen Stakes winner Sedulous and the listed Tyros Stakes winner Tapolite (herself the dam of 3 listed winners). *"A nice filly, she had a slight setback but she's on the mend now and she'll be fine. Not very big, but very speedy".*

815. RHAMNUS ★★★

b.c. Sakhee's Secret – Happy Lady (Cadeaux Genereux). March 28. Sixth living foal. 28,000Y. Tattersalls October Book 2. Peter & Ross Doyle. Half-brother to the Group 2 German 1,000 Guineas and listed Bosra Sham Stakes winner and Group 2 6f Lowther Stakes second Penny's Gift (by Tobougg), to the modest 6f (at 2 yrs) and 7f winner Chorus Beauty and the moderate

1m winner Homme Dangereux (both by Royal Applause). The dam, a fair 1m placed maiden, is a half-sister to the smart middle-distance stayer and Group 2 Yorkshire Cup second Rainbow Ways. The second dam, Siwaayib (by Green Desert), a fairly useful winner of 3 races over 6f, is a half-sister to 8 winners here and abroad. (Rockcliffe Stud). *"A nice 2-y-o, slightly upright in front, but he goes well and he's adapted to his new life very well. A nice 2-y-o, we haven't got after him at all yet as he's slightly 'on the leg' and he'll take a bit of time".*

816. RICHARD SENIOR ★★★

b.c. Cape Cross – Sabria (Miswaki). April 7. Twelfth living foal. 160,000Y. Tattersalls October Book 1. Peter & Ross Doyle. Closely related to a minor winner at 3 yrs in Japan by Green Desert and half-brother to the French 2,000 Guineas and Grade 1 Keeneland Turf Mile Stakes winner Landseer (by Danehill), to the very smart listed 10f winner and Group 1 Prince Of Wales's Stakes third Ikhtyar (by Unfuwain), the useful Irish 10f winner Song Of Hiawatha, the fairly useful Irish 9f winner Maurice Utrillo (both by Sadler's Wells), the quite useful 10.2f winner Sabreon (by Caerleon), the moderate triple 11f winner Credential (by Dansili) the French 1m winner Ghita (by Zilzal). The dam is an unraced half-sister to 4 winners including the very useful Grand Criterium third King Sound. The second dam, Flood (by Riverman), won over 6f in the USA and is a half-sister to the US Grade 1 Californian Stakes winner Sabona. (Mr W A Tinkler). *"Not very good-looking, very lazy, he just eats and sleeps. One we've earmarked for Hayley Turner to ride (joke!)".*

817. RISING LEGEND ★★★

ch.c. Rock Of Gibraltar – Miswaki Belle (Miswaki). February 20. 26,000foal. Tattersalls December. Peter & Ross Doyle. Closely related to the very smart sprinter Danehurst (by Danehill), winner of the Cornwallis Stakes (at 2 yrs), the Curragh Flying Five, the Prix de Seine-et-Oise and the Premio Umbria and the modest 6f (at 2 yrs) to 9f winner of 5 races Strike Force (by Dansili) and half-brother to the smart Group 3 10.5f Prix Penelope winner Humouresque, the smart 4-y-o triple 10f winner and Group 2 placed Mighty and the quite useful dual 7f winner Magnitude (all by Pivotal). The dam, second over 7f on her only start, is closely related to the smart Group 3 6f Cherry Hinton Stakes winner and 1,000 Guineas third Dazzle and a half-sister to 7 winners. The second dam, Belle et Deluree (by The Minstrel), won over 1m (at 2 yrs) and 10f in France and is a half-sister to the US Grade 2 winner Doneraile Court and the Cheveley Park Stakes second Dancing Tribute (herself the dam of two Group 2 winners). (Mr M.S Al Shahi). *"We like him a lot, he's a real nice horse and we like him. Probably a seven furlong type 2-y-o".*

818. RONALDINHO (IRE) ★★★★

b.c. *Jeremy – Spring Glory (Dr Fong)*. April 23. Second foal. 52,000Y. Tattersalls October Book 2. Peter & Ross Doyle. The dam, a fair 12f winner, is a half-sister to 6 winners including the useful winner of 7 races at up to 2m On Call (herself dam of the US Grade 2 winner One Off) and the smart broodmare Doctor's Glory (the dam of four stakes winners). The second dam, Doctor Bid (by Spectacular Bid), is an unraced half-sister to 9 winners including the smart Group 3 Prix Thomas Bryon winner Glory Forever and the dam of the Group winners Verglas and Cassandra Go. (Macdonald, Wright, Creed, Smith & Jiggins). *"A nice horse with a good pedigree. He looks a real 2-y-o and when we bought him we thought he looked a possible Royal Ascot type, so let's hope we're proved right".*

Readily won cl 5 nursery Kempton bf

819. ROYAL CHALLIS ★★★

b.c. *Royal Applause – Oh Hebe (Night Shift)*. May 1. Ninth foal. 30,000foal. Tattersalls December. Longview Stud & Bloodstock. Brother to the quite useful 6f and 7f 2-y-o winner of 3 races and subsequent US dual stakes-placed Mr Keppel and half-brother to the smart 2-y-o 5f and 6f and subsequent US Grade 2 Oak Tree Derby winner Devious Boy (by Dr Devious), the fairly useful 6f and 7f winner of 3 races and listed-placed Against The Grain (by Pivotal) and the quite useful 6f and 7f winner of 4 races Special Lad (by Spectrum). The dam, a fair 3-y-o 7f winner, is a half-sister to 8 winners including the Group 3 Select Stakes winner Leporello and the listed winners Calypso Grant and Poppy Carew. The second dam, Why So Silent (by Mill Reef), is an unraced half-sister to 5 winners including the US Grade 3 winner Supreme

Sound. (Longview Stud & Bloodstock Ltd). *"A sharp colt, but he's a big sort and he's had sore shins so we'll sit and wait with him for a bit".*

820. SAM SPADE (IRE) ★★★

gr.c. *Clodovil – Red Empress (Nashwan)*. April 20. Eighth living foal. 26,000Y. Tattersalls October Book 2. Peter & Ross Doyle. Half-brother to the 2011 Scandinavian 6f placed 2-y-o Grey's Electra (by Pivotal). The dam, a quite useful 12.3f winner, is closely related to the smart 7f (at 2 yrs) to 12f winner Happy Valentine, to the very useful Group 3 14f Budweiser Guinness Curragh Cup winner Blushing Flame and the useful dual 12f winner and listed-placed Flaming Quest. The second dam, Nearctic Flame (by Sadler's Wells), a very useful winner of 2 races over 10f and 10.5f and third in the Group 2 12f Ribblesdale Stakes, is a sister to 3 winners including the Irish Derby, Prix Vermeille and 1,000 Guineas winner Salsabil and a half-sister to 8 winners including the St James's Palace Stakes winner Marju. (Mrs V Hubbard). *"He's a very big horse with big feet. Very heavy set, but he goes well, he has a good attitude and we'll get on with him sooner rather than later".*

821. SEA SHANTY (USA) ★★★

b.c. *Elusive Quality – Medley (Danehill Dancer)*. January 23. First foal. The dam, a fairly useful 6f (at 2 yrs) and listed 7f winner, is a half-sister to 8 winners. The second dam, Marl (by Lycius), a fairly useful 2-y-o 5.2f winner, is a half-sister to 4 winners including the very useful 2-y-o listed 5f National Stakes winner Rowaasi. (The Queen). *"He's a very nice colt but he does need a bit of time. One for six/seven furlongs I'd say".*

822. SHAMAHEART (IRE) ★★★

b.c. *Shamardal – Encouragement (Royal Applause)*. April 24. Second foal. 58,000foal. Tattersalls December. Peter Doyle. Half-brother to the fair 6f (at 2 yrs) and 1m winner Joe Eile (by Iffraaj). The dam, a fair dual 6f placed 2-y-o here, was later placed in the USA. She is a sister to the winner and listed-placed Approval and a half-sister to 4 winners including the very useful Group 2 6f Moet and Chandon Rennen winner Sharp Prod and to the unraced dam of the Group 2 German 2,000 Guineas winner Royal Power. The second dam, Gentle Persuasion (by

Bustino), a fairly useful 2-y-o 6f winner, was fourth in both the Princess Margaret Stakes and the Rockfel Stakes and is a half-sister to 11 winners. (Dragon Gate Development Ltd). *"A nice horse, he's grown like mad and done very well. He'll make up into a lovely horse".*

823. SIGN OF THE ZODIAC (IRE) ★★★

gr.c. *Clodovil – Auriga ((Belmez)*. March 28. 24,000foal. Tattersalls December. Catridge Farm Stud. Half-brother to the fairly useful 5f (at 2 yrs) and 7f winner Brae Hill (by Fath), to the fairly useful 6f (including at 2 yrs) and 7f winner of 6 races Morse, the quite useful 2-y-o 6f winner Sylvan (both by Shinko Forest), the fair 2-y-o 6f and 7f winner Good Wee Girl (by Tagula), the 4-y-o 1m seller winner Forest Air (by Charnwood Forest) and a winner in the Czech Republic by Barathea. The dam, a fair 6f and 7f placed 2-y-o, is a half-sister to 8 winners including the listed Blue Riband Trial Stakes winner Beldale Star and the listed winner and smart broodmare Moon Drop. The second dam, Little White Star (by Mill Reef), is an unplaced half-sister to 5 winners. (Mrs Julie Wood). *"A nice horse, he'll be out early and he's been showing up well at home. It came as a bit of a surprise to see him so sharp, but now he looks like he's ready we'll get on and run him".*

824. SIR PRANCEALOT ★★★★

b.c. *Tamayuz – Mona Em (Catrail)*. April 14. Seventh foal. €140,000Y. Goffs Orby. Peter & Ross Doyle. Half-brother to the French listed 10f winner of 9 races Nice Applause, to the quite useful dual 1m winner Dual Attraction (both by Royal Applause), the fair 2-y-o 5f winner Monalini (by Bertolini) and the minor French 2-y-o winner Monatora (by Hector Protector). The dam, a French listed sprint winner, is a half-sister to 5 winners including the Irish 2,000 Guineas fourth Maumee. The second dam, Moy Water (by Tirol), an Irish 1m (at 2 yrs) and 9f winner, is a half-sister to 8 winners including the very useful listed sprint winners Bufalino and Maledetto. (Mr W A Tinkler). *"A lovely horse. Very sharp and he's settled down now because he used to get on his toes and get quite warm. He goes well and you ought to see him a fair bit over five furlongs in the first few months of the season. A very nice colt".* Won Bath 5f on debut imp to win National Stakes

Won gp listed fillies Newl

825. SKY LANTERN (IRE) ★★★★ ♠

gr.f. *Red Clubs – Shawanni (Shareef Dancer)*. January 27. Twelfth foal. €75,000Y. Goffs Orby. Sackville/Donald. Half-sister to the smart 2-y-o Group 3 6f Round Tower Stakes winner Arctic, to the fairly useful 2-y-o 6f winner and Group 3 Greenham Stakes third Shropshire (both by Shamardal), the very useful 10f (including at 2 yrs) and Group 3 2m Queens Vase winner Shanty Star (by Hector Protector), the listed 6f and listed 7f winner Hinton Admiral (by Spectrum), the quite useful 7f to 1m winner of 14 races Mystic Man, the fair dual 7f winner Sharaby (both by Cadeaux Genereux), the quite useful 2-y-o dual 5f winner Twilight Sonnet (by Exit To Nowhere), the fair 9f winner Lucky Token (by Key Of Luck) and a UAE winner by Storming Home. The dam, a useful 2-y-o 7f winner, is a half-sister to 5 winners including the Group 3 winners Blatant and Songlark. The second dam, Negligent (by Ahonoora), a champion 2-y-o filly and winner the 7f Rockfel Stakes at 2 yrs, was third in the 1,000 Guineas and is a full or half-sister to 5 winners including the 1,000 Guineas fourth Ala Mahlik. (Mr B W Keswick). *"She's a nice, well-made filly with a very pretty head and long ears. A sweet filly, we're getting excited about her and she may be a Royal Ascot 2-y-o. We think a lot of her".*

Won nicely small on Gwd. ain it always

826. SPANISH ART ★★★

b.c. *Byron – Spanish Gold (Vettori)*. March 6. Fourth foal. £26,000Y. Doncaster Premier. Dwayne Woods. Half-brother to the fairly useful 6f winner of 4 races (including at 2 yrs) and listed-placed Spanish Bounty (by Bahamian Bounty), to the quite useful dual 6f winner King Ferdinand (by Tobougg) and the fair dual 6f winner Spanish Acclaim (by Acclamation). The dam, a fair 8.5f winner, is a half-sister to 4 winners including the useful 1m Victoria Cup winner Bold King and the Group 2 Railway Stakes second Spanish Ace. The second dam, Spanish Heart (by King Of Spain), a quite useful winner of 4 races over 7f and 1m, is a half-sister to 7 winners including the Group 3 Phoenix Sprint Stakes winner and smart broodmare Northern Goddess. (Mr W A Tinkler). *"A very nice colt, but he's big and will want seven furlongs at least".*

827. STIFF UPPER LIP (IRE) ★★★

b.c. Sakhee's Secret – Just In Love (Highest Honor). April 28. Fourth foal. 38,000Y. Tattersalls October Book 2. Sackville/Donald. Half-brother to the quite useful 2-y-o 1m winner and listed-placed Dauberval (by Noverre), to the fair 1m winner Nassmaan (by Alhaarth) and the modest dual 7f and hurdles winner Ginger Grey (by Bertolini). The dam is an unraced sister to the French listed winner of 10 races Justful and a half-sister to 2 winners. The second dam, Just Class (by Dominion), a useful winner over 7f and 1m here, subsequently won three Grade 3 events in the USA at around 8.5f and is a half-sister to 5 winners including the Group 3 12f St Simon Stakes winner and smart broodmare Up Anchor. (Richard Hitchcock/Alan King). *"A tall horse, he'll hopefully be running over six or seven furlongs around June or July. A horse with a lot of scope".*

828. TAMAYUZ STAR (IRE) ★★★ ♠

ch.c. Tamayuz – Magical Peace (Magical Wonder). February 20. Ninth foal. 58,000Y. Tattersalls October Book 1. Peter & Ross Doyle. Half-brother to the smart Group 3 winning sprinter and 2-y-o Group 2 placed Hoh Mike, to the fairly useful Irish 6f (at 2 yrs) and 7f winner and listed-placed Intapeace (both by Intikhab), the useful 5f and 6f winner and listed-placed Hogmaneigh (by Namid), the useful 2-y-o 5f and 6f winner and listed-placed Dario Gee Gee, the fair 5f and 6f winner of 6 races Magical Speedfit (both by Bold Fact) and the quite useful 7f (at 2 yrs) and 1m winner Mt Topaz (by Celtic Swing). The dam, a quite useful Irish 6f winner, is a half-sister to one winner. The second dam, Peace In The Woods (by Tap On Wood), is an unraced half-sister to 2 winners and to the unraced dam of the multiple staying Group 1 winner Vinnie Roe. (Mr A Al Mansoori). *"He's had a bit of a throat infection but he's back to his best now, he's thriving and he'll run over five and six furlongs in mid-season".*

2nd *pair* 7f 1: *April* (*hill*)

829. TASSEL ★★★★ ♠

b.f. Kyllachy – Xtrasensory (Royal Applause). February 4. Fifth foal. £42,000Y. Doncaster Premier. John Warren. Sister to the quite useful 2-y-o 5f and 6f winner Tishtar and half-sister to the quite useful 2011 2-y-o 6f winner

Responsive (by Dutch Art), the fair 7f (at 2 yrs) and 1m winner Redsensor (by Redback) and the fair 6f winner Fenella Rose (by Compton Place). The dam, a fairly useful 2-y-o 6f winner, is a half-sister to 7 winners. The second dam, Song Of Hope (by Chief Singer), a useful 2-y-o 5f winner and second in the listed Firth of Clyde Stakes, is a half-sister to 10 minor winners. (Highclere Thoroughbred Racing – Herbert Jones). *"She'll be our first 2-y-o filly to run and we're hoping she's going to be useful. Hughesy has ridden her a couple of times and he likes her a lot. We're very excited about her, she's small and racy.*

830. TAWTHEEQ (IRE) ★★★

b.c. Acclamation – Grand Slam Maria (Anabaa). February 22. Third foal. 165,000Y. Tattersalls October Book 2. Peter & Ross Doyle. Brother to the useful 7f winner King Of Jazz. The dam, a moderate 9f placed Irish maiden, is a half-sister to 7 winners. The second dam, Kate Marie (by Bering), a listed-placed winner of 3 races in France, is a half-sister to 6 winners. (Hamdan Al Maktoum). *"He's got quite open knees so we've laid-off him for a bit. So he's quite immature but he's a nice horse that'll want seven furlongs I should think".*

831. THE GATLING BOY (IRE) ★★★

ch.c. Tamayuz – Miniver (Mujtahid). April 4. Tenth foal. 32,000Y. Tattersalls October Book 1. Peter & Ross Doyle. Half-brother to the fairly useful 2-y-o 1m winner Minos, to the fair 4-y-o 7f winner Chateau (both by Grand Lodge), the Irish 10f and 12f winner and Group 3 placed Mon Michel (by Montjeu), the modest 1m to 12f winner of 5 races Night Warrior (by Alhaarth), the minor French 3-y-o winner Unveiled (by Galileo) and a winner in Japan by Footstepsinthesand. The dam ran once unplaced at 2 yrs and is a half-sister to 6 winners including the Champion Stakes winner Legal Case and the useful 10f winner and Group 3 12f Lancashire Oaks second La Sky (herself dam of the Oaks winner Love Divine). The second dam, Maryinsky (by Northern Dancer), won twice at up to 9f in the USA and is a half-sister to 10 winners. (Kennet Valley Thoroughbreds I). *"This colt goes well, he's quite long and slack of his pasterns, but he's a very well-made 2-y-o type who is showing up well on the gallops so far. He could win first time out over six furlongs".*

832. THE MASCOT ★★★
b.c. Assertive – All Business (Entrepreneur). March 17. Sixth foal. £25,000Y. Doncaster Premier. Peter & Ross Doyle. Half-brother to the quite useful 6f (at 2 yrs) and 7f winner The Kyllachy Kid (by Kyllachy) and a winner in Hungary by Zafeen. The dam, a fair 12f winner, is a half-sister to 3 winners including the French Group 3 winner Espirita. The second dam, Belle Esprit (by Warning), is an unraced sister to the German Group 2 winner Torch Rouge and a half-sister to the dam of the dual Group 2 winner Simonas. (Mason Brown Partnership). *"A nice horse. When we bought him he had splints but he's over that now and he moves well. A real 'trainer's type' of horse, he has a good attitude and hopefully he'll make up into a nice horse. A sharp, five furlongs type".*

833. TILSTARR (IRE) ★★★★
b.f. Shamardal – Vampire Queen (General Monash). February 1. Fifth foal. 70,000Y. Tattersalls October Book 2. Peter & Ross Doyle. Half-brother to the minor Italian winner of 5 races at 3 to 5 yrs Passi De Sanza (by Bertolini) and to the modest Irish 10f winner Vampire Blues (by Azamour). The dam, a modest 3-y-o 6f winner, is a sister to the winner and dual Group 2 placed Bram Stoker and a half-sister to 4 winners. The second dam, Taniokey (by Grundy), won at 3 yrs and is a half-sister to 5 winners including Kittyhawk (Group 3 Lowther Stakes). (H Hunt). *"She's a very nice filly, sharp and racey – just what you're looking for in a 2-y-o filly. Hopefully she won't let us down".*

834. TOBACCO ROAD (IRE) ★★★★ ♠
b.c. Westerner – Virginias Best (King's Best). March 3. First foal. 38,000Y. Tattersalls October Book 2. Peter & Ross Doyle. The dam is an unplaced half-sister to 5 winners including Lavirco (Group 1 German Derby), Laveron (Group 2 German St Leger) and Lyonels Glory (German Group 3 winner). The second dam, La Virginia (by Surumu), won twice at 3 yrs in Germany and is a sister to 2 winners including the German Group 3 winner La Colorada (herself dam of the dual Group 1 winner and

sire Lomitas) and a half-sister to 4 winners. (Noodles Racing). *"We weren't expecting him to show up quite as early as he has done. He's a nice horse that will improve as the weeks go on and he'll probably want six furlongs to start with, but he's surprisingly sharp".*

835. TORONADO (IRE) ★★★★ ♠
b.c. High Chaparral – Wana Doo (Grand Slam). February 20. Fourth foal. €55,000Y. Arqana Deauville August. Amanda Skiffington. Half-brother to a winner over jumps in France by Tagula. The dam, a French 2-y-o 1m winner, is a half-sister to 4 winners including the 2-y-o Group 1 1m Racing Post Trophy and Group 2 1m Beresford Stakes winner Casamento and the very useful 6f (at 2 yrs) and 7f winner Inler. The second dam, Wedding Gift (by Always Fair), a French 2-y-o listed 1m winner, was Group 3 placed twice and is a half-sister to 7 winners. (Coriolan Links Partnership III). *"One of our nicest, but you won't see him for a bit. It wouldn't surprise me to see him in some very nice races later on and he could be anything".*

Won easily bolted up 1¾f cl 4 Newbury

836. VICTIX LUDORUM (IRE) ★★★★
b.f. Invincible Spirit – Matikanehamatidori (Sunday Silence). March 21. Sixth foal. 75,000Y. Tattersalls October Book 1. Peter & Ross Doyle. Half-sister to the fair Irish 9f winner Flying Plover (by Danehill Dancer), to the 2-y-o 7f and hurdles winner Space Telescope (by Galileo) and two winners in Japan by Danehill. The dam, placed once at 3 yrs in Japan, is a full or half-sister to 7 winners including two listed winners in Japan. The second dam, Matikaneebenizakura (by Royal Academy), won 3 races in Japan and is a half-sister to 8 winners including Generous (Derby, Irish Derby, King George VI etc) and Imagine (Oaks and Irish 1,000 Guineas). (Mrs Julie Wood). *"A very racey filly with a good pedigree, she'll be a six furlong type. The way she moves she looks really classy. Her owner Julie is mad about her and so are we, so let's hope we're all right!"*

837. WENTWORTH (IRE) ★★★★ ♠
b.c. Acclamation – Miss Corinne (Mark Of Esteem). February 8. Fourth foal. 200,000Y. Tattersalls October Book 2. Peter & Ross Doyle. Half-brother to the modest 2-y-o 6f and 7f

One of Hannon's best runners 2f +win

winner Captain Loui (by Verglas), to the Spanish 2-y-o winner Irish Cliff (by Marju) and a winner in the Czech Republic by Denon. The dam won 6 races in Italy from 3 to 5 yrs and is a half-sister to 4 minor winners here and abroad. The second dam, Percy's Girl (by Blakeney), a useful 10f and 10.3f winner, is a sister to the Group 3 September Stakes winner Percy's Lass (herself dam of the Derby winner Sir Percy) and a half-sister to 5 winners including the very smart Grade 1 E P Taylor Stakes and Group 2 Sun Chariot Stakes winner Braiswick. (Coolmore). *"A very big, gorgeous-looking colt. He'll take a good bit of time but we're very excited about him. We don't need to get on with him until July or August but I'm sure that when we do he'll come alive". Richard Hughes tells me he's very taken by this colt.* *Won Maiden Hannon Newbury*

838. WHATEVER YOU DO (IRE) ★★★★
ch.f. Barathea – Petite Spectre (Spectrum). March 4. Fourth foal. €90,000Y. Goffs Orby. Peter & Ross Doyle. Half-sister to the fair 2011 2-y-o 6f winner Ballyea (by Acclamation) and to the useful 5.7f (at 2 yrs) to 7f winner and Group 2 6f Coventry Stakes third Rakaan (by Bahamian Bounty). The dam, a fair 2-y-o 6f winner, is a half-sister to 8 winners including the useful 2-y-o Group 3 7f C L Weld Park Stakes winner Rag Top. The second dam, Petite Epaulette (by Night Shift), a fair 5f winner at 2 yrs, is a full or half-sister to 3 winners. (Mrs Julie Wood). *"A beautiful filly, she's the image of a filly we had called Rag Top. She has the same look, the same strong shoulder and she looks like a colt. Very strong and sharp, she has her head in the right place all the time. We're mad about her".*

839. ZURIGHA (IRE) ★★★
b.f. Cape Cross – Noyelles (Docksider). March 31. Second foal. 72,000Y. Tattersalls October Book 2. Ed Dunlop. Half-sister to the useful 2011 2-y-o 5f and listed 6f winner and Group 3 7f Sweet Solera Stakes second Lily's Angel (by Dark Angel). The dam is an unraced half-sister to 8 winners including the Group 3 Prix de Flore winner In Clover and the French listed winners Bayourida and Bellona. The second dam, Bellarida (by Bellypha), won the Group 3 Prix de Royaumont and is a half-sister to 2 winners.

(S H Altayer). *"A really nice filly, she hasn't done anything other than routine canters as yet, but she's a nice mid-season type".*

Curry or Sydney

840. UNNAMED ★★★
ch.c. Notnowcato – River Fantasy (Irish River). April 19. Eighth foal. 20,000Y. Tattersalls December. Peter & Ross Doyle. Brother to the modest 2011 2-y-o 1m winner Plym and half-brother to the smart Group 2 7f Prix du Palais-Royal winner and 2,000 Guineas third Frenchman's Bay (by Polar Falcon) and to the modest 9f winner Zerzura (by Oasis Dream). The dam is an unplaced half-sister to 5 winners including the Group 3 Norfolk Stakes winner Romeo Romani, the US stakes winner Herb Wine and the dam of the Cherry Hinton Stakes winner Chicarica. The second dam, Harbor Wine (by Herbager), won 3 races at up to 1m in the USA and is a half-sister to 6 winners including the dam of the top-class US filly Life's Magic. *"This is a nice horse, he qualifies for the Chesham Stakes, we've worked him a couple of time and he goes very well. He probably wants seven furlongs but he's a really likeable horse, always looks great and looks after himself".*

Won g1 bf wtr Newbury

841. UNNAMED ★★★
b.f. Duke Of Marmalade – Square Pants (King Of Kings). March 27. Second foal. 100,000Y. Tattersalls October Book 1. Peter & Ross Doyle. Half-sister to the fair 3-y-o 6f winner Passing Stranger (by Dixie Union). The dam, a minor US 4-y-o winner, is a half-sister to the Group 2 Cherry Hinton Stakes and Group 3 Albany Stakes winner Sander Camillo. The second dam, Staraway (by Star de Naskra), a US winner of 20 races including 3 stakes events, is a half-sister to 5 winners. (Coolmore). *"A lovely filly, we're excited about her but we'll leave her until the middle of the season".*

I'm indebted to Richard Hannon's Head Lad Steve Knight for helping me out with comments on a few more of the Everleigh trained two-year-olds I've added below.

842. CHORAL RHYTHM ★★★
b.f. Oratorio – Sierra (Dr Fong). February 15. Half-sister to the fairly useful 9f winner and listed-placed Mister Music (by Singspiel). The

dam, a moderate 7f and 1m winner at 5 yrs, is a half-sister to several winners out of Warning Belle (by Warning). *"I like this filly a lot – she's a tough sort".*

843. CIO CIO SAN ★★★

ch.c. *Dalakhani – Unreachable Star (Halling).* February 12. Second foal. 11,000Y. Tattersalls October Book 2. Peter & Ross Doyle. The dam, a fair dual 7f placed maiden at 3 yrs, is a half-sister to the 2-y-o Group 1 7f Moyglare Stud Stakes and US Grade 1 placed Necklace. The second dam, Spinning The Yarn (by Barathea), ran once unplaced and is a half-sister to the Group 1 winners Opera House, Kayf Tara and Zee Zee Top. (Ms V O'Sullivan). *"She'll probably want a bit of a trip so although we could run her now she'll be better for seven furlongs".*

844. JIMMY ELDER ★★★

b.c. *Invincible Spirit – Hijab (Green Desert).* April 30. First foal. 14,000Y. Tattersalls October Book 2. Not sold. The dam is an unraced half-sister to 2 winners out of the listed Pretty Polly Stakes winner Hi Dubai (by Rahy), herself a sister to Fantastic Light. *"Not very big, he came in late but he's sharp and ready to run. I would imagine he'd be fairly early and he's nice as well".*

845. LAW ENFORCEMENT ★★★

b.c. *Lawman – Broken Spectre (Rainbow Quest).* April 27. Eight foal. £18,000Y. Doncaster Premier. Not sold. Half-brother to one winner in Germany by Dansili. The dam, unplaced in two starts, is a half-sister to several winners including the Group 1 1m Racing Post Trophy winner and St Leger second Armiger. The second dam, Armeria (by Northern Dancer), a fair 3-y-o 10f winner, is a half-sister to the Park Hill Stakes winner I Want To Be. *"He's ready to run now. Sharp and early, he'll probably win first time out but he's got a bit of scope as well".*

846. LISA'S LEGACY ★★★

b.c. *Kyllachy – Lisathedaddy (Darnay).* March 26. First foal. The dam was a quite useful 10f winner of 4 races over 10f at 4 and 5 yrs. The second dam, Erith's Chill Wind (by Be My Chief), was a poor 10f winner at 3 yrs. (Mrs P. S Wilson). *"A little Kyllachy that I like a lot – he's done so well since he came in. He's no world-beater, but he could win a few races early on".*

847. PAELLA ★★★

b.f. *Oasis Dream – Chibola (Roy).* February 8. The dam won 5 races in Argentina including a Group 3 over 7f. *"I like this filly. She's got plenty of speed and she looks sharp".*

848. PETHER'S MOON (IRE) ★★

b.c. *Dylan Thomas – Softly Tread (Tirol).* April 15. Third foal. €52,000Y. Tattersalls Ireland. Peter & Ross Doyle. The dam won 3 races in Ireland including the Group 3 Gladness Stakes and the listed Tyros Stakes. The second dam, Second Guess (by Ela-Mana-Mou), a listed-placed winner of one race at 3 yrs in Ireland, is a half-sister to 5 winners including the Group 1 Moyglare Stud Stakes second Heed My Warning. (J D Manley). *"Big and backward, he has plenty of light under him and is a bit on the leg, so he'll take time but he's a nice horse".*

849. PRIMO D'ORO (USA) ★★

b.c. *Medaglia D'Oro – First Glimmer (Glitterman).* May 15. Eighth foal. 85,000Y. Tattersalls October Book 1. Peter & Ross Doyle. Half-brother to the US 3-y-o listed stakes winner Exclusive Quality (by Elusive Quality) and to the minor US winner of 3 races Magic Jade (by Jade Hunter). The dam is an unraced half-sister to the US winner and Grade 1 second Brave Deed. The second dam, First Stand (by Big Spruce), a US stakes-placed winner, is a half-sister to 6 winners. (Macdonald, Wright, Smith, Creed and Jiggins). *"A backward horse now, but a very imposing sort for the back-end of the season".*

850. REBEL MAGIC ★★★

b.f. *Cockney Rebel – Aastral Magic (Magic Ring).* February 17. £1,000Y. Ascot November. Not sold. The dam, a quite useful dual 6f (at 2 yrs) and 7f winner, is a half-sister to 2 winners out of Robanna (by Robellino). *"We trained the dam and she was a quirky mare. This filly is a bit similar but she's shown plenty of speed. One for six furlongs I would say".*

JESSICA HARRINGTON

851. CALISSA (IRE) ★★★★

b.f. *Danehill Dancer – Mauralakana (Muhtathir).* February 27. The dam, US Grade 1 Beverly D Stakes, dual US Grade 2 and Group 3 Prix de

Cabourg winner, is a half-sister to the French listed winner over 6f (at 2 yrs) and 1m Petit Calva. The second dam, Jimkana (by Double Bed), a minor winner, is a sister to the Grade 1 Hong Kong International Cup winner Jim And Tonic. (Mr Robert Scarborough). *"A very nice filly, she's very well-bred and so far she's going really well. She's a good size for a 2-y-o, fairly compact and I expect her to be out around mid-May over six furlongs. She looks the part and she has the pedigree to go with it".*

852. LIBERATING ★★★★

b.f. Iffraaj – Ros The Boss (Danehill). March 27. Sixth foal. €50,000foal. Goffs. BBA (Ire). Half-brother to the quite useful Irish dual 1m winner Alsalwa, to the modest 1m winner Makyaal (both by Nayef) and the quite useful 2-y-o 5f winner Kate The Great (by Xaar). The dam, a quite useful 7f and 1m winner, is a half-sister to 6 winners including the Irish 2-y-o listed 9f winner and Group 1 second Yehudi. The second dam, Bella Vitessa (by Thatching), is an unplaced half-sister to 6 winners including the German Group 1 12f Aral-Pokal winner and Epsom Oaks second Wind In Her Hair (herself dam of the Japan Cup winner Deep Impact). (Mr P Barnett, Mrs Y Nicoll & Mr J Throsby). *"A nice filly that will have started her career well before your book comes out. She's been very forward all along and although she'll be better over six furlongs we'll start her at five. I like her a lot – she's a very straightforward, professional filly".*

853. NO PROBLEM (IRE) ★★★

b.c. Holy Roman Emperor – Two Marks (Woodman). April 5. Fifth foal. €42,000Y. Goffs Orby. John Wholey. Half-brother to the quite useful 9f winner Stock Market (by Rahy) and to a minor winner in the USA by Forestry. The dam, a fair 8.5f and 12f winner, is a half-sister to 8 winners including the French listed winner and Group 3 placed Mystic Melody. The second dam, Munnaya (by Nijinsky), winner of the Group 3 11.5f Lingfield Oaks Trial and third in the 10f Pretty Polly Stakes, is a half-sister to 8 winners. (Mr John Wholey). *"A nice colt, he's done some growing but he needed to because he was small when we bought him. He should be racing in mid-May over six furlongs and he's goes nicely".*

854. PASS EXPRESS (IRE) ★★★★

ch.c. Raven's Pass – Red Top (Fasliyev). January 31. Second foal. 125,000foal. Tattersalls December. BBA (Ire). Half-brother to the fair Irish 4-y-o 1m winner Aragorn Rouge (by Aragorn). The dam, a fairly useful 7.6f and subsequent US 1m winner, was listed-placed and is a half-sister to 7 winners including the useful 2-y-o Group 3 7f C L Weld Park Stakes winner Rag Top and the dam of the 2-y-o listed winner Elhamri. The second dam, Petite Epaulette (by Night Shift), a fair 5f winner at 2 yrs, is a sister to the listed Sweet Solera Stakes second The Jotter and a half-sister to 2 winners. *"A fine, big, strong colt. I like him a lot and I think he'll be out in May over six furlongs. We don't know about the sire yet because this is his first season, but this is a smashing horse".*

855. RUPA ★★★

b.f. Acclamation – Claustra (Green Desert). March 2. Seventh foal. €85,000Y. Goffs Orby. Course Investment Corp. Half-sister to 6 winners including the US Grade 3 winner No Explaining, the quite useful 7f and 1m winner Azameera (both by Azamour), the fair 2-y-o 7f winner Weld II Balad (by Alhaarth), to the fair 2-y-o 7f winner Inspector Clouseau (by Daylami) and a minor 4-y-o winner abroad by Zafonic. The dam, an Irish 4-y-o 9f winner, is a half-sister to 6 winners including the US Grade 2 winner Bayamo and the German Group 3 7f winner Wessam Prince. The second dam, Clare Bridge (by Little Current), won the Group 3 1m Gilltown Stud Stakes, was second in the Group 2 Prix de Malleret and is a half-sister to 6 winners including the dam of the Group 1 winners Silver Patriarch and Papineau. (Niarchos Family). *"A very nice filly that seems reasonably forward, so I hope to have her racing in May and I see her as a six/seven furlong 2-y-o".*

856. SINMIEBO (IRE) ★★★

br.c. Intikhab – Xaviera (Xaar). February 2. First foal. €9,000Y. Goffs Orby. J Harrington. He dam is an unraced half-sister to 4 winners including the US Grade 2 San Luis Rey Handicap winner Champion Lodge. The second dam, Legit (by Runnett), is a placed half-sister to 5 winners. (Favourite Racing Ltd). *"He's a very nice horse and he's surprised me because he's a big, strong colt. If he doesn't start growing again he'll be running before the end of April. He was cheap and cheerful at the sales but he's a very nice 2-y-o".*

RON HARRIS
857. GOWERTONIAN (IRE) ★★★
b.c. Auction House – Fabuleux Cherie (Noverre). April 8. First foal. £400Y. Ascot December. Ron Harris. The dam, a fair 2-y-o 5f and 6f winner of 3 races, is a half-sister to 3 minor winners here and abroad. The second dam, Ashover Amber (by Green Desert), a fair 5f and 6f winner of 3 races at 3 yrs, is a half-sister to 2 winners. (David & Gwyn Joseph). *"There's a race in him alright, he's very sharp and not over-big but all in proportion. He knows his job and he'll be a five furlong type, starting around late April".* TRAINERS' BARGAIN BUY

858. HALUL ★★★
b.c. Dutch Art – Bella Bertolini (Bertolini). March 26. Third foal. £28,000Y. Doncaster Premier. Mubarak Said Al Naemi. The dam is a placed half-sister to one winner. The second dam, Fly Like The Wind (by Cyrano de Bergerac), a fair 3-y-o 5f winner, is a half-sister to 6 other minor winners. (Mr A N Mubarak).

859. MRS BROWN'S BOY ★★★
gr.c. Verglas – Brazilian Style (Exit To Nowhere). April 22. Second foal. £5,000Y. Doncaster Premier. Ron Harris. Half-brother to the modest 7f winner Loving Thought (by Oasis Dream). The dam was placed in all three of her starts over 5f at 2 yrs and is a half-sister to 2 minor winners. The second dam, Cosmic Star (by Siberian Express), was a modest 7f (at 2 yrs) and 10f winner. (Ridge House Stables Ltd). *"I'm really pleased with him, he's growing into a nice horse and although he had a little setback with a sore shin he'll be having a run in late April".*

BEN HASLAM
860. DIAKTOROS (IRE) ★★★★
b.c. Red Clubs – Rinneen (Bien Bien). March 12. Fourth foal. 42,000Y. Tattersalls October Book 2. Charlie Gordon-Watson. Brother to the fair 2011 2-y-o 6f winner The Blue Banana. The dam, a modest 6f (at 2 yrs) and 12f placed

maiden, is a half-sister to 5 winners including the dual listed 6f winner (including at 2 yrs) Lady Links (herself dam of the dual listed winner Selinka). The second dam, Sparky's Song (by Electric), a moderate 10.2f and 12f winner, is a half-sister to the very smart Group 1 6.5f winner Bold Edge and to the listed winner and Group 3 5f Temple Stakes second Brave Edge. (Sir Alex Ferguson & Mr S Hassiakos). *"A big, rangy horse that will need a minimum of six furlongs, starting off in June. He's a nice type with scope and although I haven't pressed any buttons he's showing plenty already considering his size. He stands out physically and I see him being a nice 2-y-o over seven furlongs by the end of the summer".*

861. DUNLAOGHAIRE (IRE) ★★★
b.f. Bachelor Duke – Dunbrody (Jeune Homme). April 13. Fourth foal. Brother to Chic Fabric, placed third over 10f at 3yrs at Deauville in 2012 and half-brother to the French dual 10f winner and subsequent US Grade 3 9f second Kilmore Quay (by Traditionally) and the quite useful 5f and 6f winner of 4 races (including at 2 yrs) Azzurra Du Caprio (by Captain Rio). The dam won 2 minor races at 3 yrs in France at around 11f and is a half-sister to 8 winners including the US Grade 2 winner Shir Dar. The second dam, Irish Sea (by Irish River), was placed at 2 yrs here and won at 4 yrs in France and is a half-sister to 8 winners. (Blue Lion Racing). *"She done a few bits upsides and I can see her being a nice horse later on. She looks weak but she's showing up well, so when she strengthens up she'll probably be a nice filly over seven furlongs, probably in June or July I would have thought".*

862. UNNAMED ★★
b.c. Byron – City Maiden (Carson City). March 22. Sixth living foal. 8,000Y. Tattersalls October Book 2. Ben Haslam. Half-brother to the very useful 6f (at 2 yrs) and UAE Group 2 1m winner First City (by Diktat) and to the quite useful dual 1m winner Metropolitan Miss (by Bertolini). The dam is an unraced half-sister to the French listed winner and Group 3 placed Vernoy. The second dam, Marble Maiden (by Lead On Time), won the Grade 2 All Along Stakes and the Group 3 Prix de Sandringham

and is a half-sister to 5 winners. (Mr B Haslam). *"A very big, very solid horse that won't be particularly early. Probably one for six furlongs at the end of the summer because he's done plenty of growing so I haven't pressed him too hard. I'm still looking for an owner for him".*

863. UNNAMED ★★★★

b.f. Diamond Green – Dancing Steps (Zafonic). February 21. Sixth foal. £10,000Y. Doncaster Premier. Ben Haslam. Half-sister to the fair 6f (at 2 yrs), 10f and hurdles winner Dance For Julie (by Redback) and to the moderate dual 12f and hurdles winner Dance For Livvy (by Kodiac). The dam is an unraced sister to the winner and UAE Group 3 placed Seeking The Prize and a half-sister to 7 winners including the Group 3 placed Firebet. The second dam, Dancing Prize (by Sadler's Wells), a useful maiden and third in the listed Lingfield Oaks Trial, is a sister to 3 winners including the Group 1 Fillies Mile second and good broodmare Dance To The Top and a half-sister to 5 winners. (Go Alfresco Racing Club). *"She looks like being quite early. I trained both her half-sisters and they both won races but this filly looks the most precocious of the three. She's showing plenty at the moment and I could see her starting off in May in a fillies' maiden. She looks sharp enough to start off at five furlongs and run well, but I think she'll do better when she steps up in trip to six/ seven".*

864. UNNAMED ★★★

b.c. Indesatchel – Day By Day (Kyllachy). January 21. First foal. £14,000Y. Doncaster Festival. Ben Haslam. The dam, a fairly useful 5f and 6f winner, was listed-placed twice and is a half-sister to 4 winners including the dam of the 2-y-o Group 1 Gran Criterium winner Hearts Of Fire. The second dam, Dayville (by Dayjur), a quite useful triple 6f winner, is a half-sister to 4 winners including the Grade 1 Yellow Ribbon Handicap winner Spanish Fern and to the unraced dams of the Grade 1 winners Lord Shanakill and Heatseeker. (Go Alfresco Racing Club). *"A very big, solid horse, he's done bits 'upsides' and shown enough but he's one for the back-end of the summer. A good-looking horse that's done well but I'm not pressing on with him just yet".*

865. UNNAMED ★★★

b.f. Clodovil – Green Life (Green Desert). April 2. Thirteenth foal. £6,000Y. Doncaster Festival. Ben Haslam. Half-sister to the fairly useful 2-y-o dual 6f winner Zuzu (by Acclamation), to the fairly useful 2-y-o 7f and 1m winner Agilis (by Titus Livius), the fair 5f (at 2 yrs) and 6f winner Bohobe (by Noverre), the Italian winner of 4 races at 2 and 3 yrs including over 5f Green Band (by College Chapel) and the fair triple 6f winner (including at 2 yrs) Tappit (by Mujadil). The dam, placed fourth once over 7f at 2 yrs, is a half-sister to 6 winners including the Group 3 Molecomb Stakes winner Classic Ruler. The second dam, Viceroy Princess (by Godswalk), a modest 2-y-o 7f seller winner, is a half-sister to 7 winners. (Go Alfresco Racing Club). *"She's grown a lot, looks speedy and she's a half-sister to plenty of winners. A stocky, strong little filly, she has a good attitude but her knees are slightly immature still, so we have to wait a bit with her. She hasn't done a lot of work, but looking at her I don't think she'll need to before starting her career at the end of May".*

866. UNNAMED ★★

ch.f. Sakhee's Secret – May Day Queen (Danetime). February 2. First foal. £16,000Y. Doncaster Premier. Ben Haslam. The dam, a quite useful 2-y-o 6f winner and Group 3 6f third in Ireland, is a half-sister to 2 winners. The dam is an unraced half-sister to 3 winners including the Group 1 Moyglare Stud Stakes third Supposition. (Miss Karen Theobald). *"A lovely mover up the gallops and she seems to be going well, but she does look a bit weak. We're in no rush so we've backed off her and I can see her running in sprint maidens at the end of the summer".*

867. UNNAMED ★★

b.c. Byron – Balwarah (Soviet Star). April 1. Fourth foal. £5,000Y. Doncaster Premier. B Haslam. The dam is an unraced half-sister to 7 winners including the useful 3-y-o 7f and 1m winner Tahirah. The second dam, Kismah (by Machiavellian), a very useful dual 1m winner, is a half-sister to 10 winners. (Go Alfresco Racing Club). *"He was a cheap purchase but he's showing me plenty and providing he doesn't get sore shins I can see him running in early*

May in auction maidens and running well. He has a bit of a knee action, so he wouldn't run on fast ground". TRAINERS' BARGAIN BUY

CHARLES HILLS

868. ANNA LAW (IRE) ★★★
b.f. Lawman – Portelet (Night Shift). May 13. Twelfth foal. 42,000Y. Tattersalls October Book 2. BBA (Ire)/C Hills. Half-sister to the very smart 2-y-o Group 2 7f Champagne Stakes winner and Group 1 6f July Cup third Etlaala, to the useful 7f and 1m winner and listed-placed Selective, the modest 5f winner Come What May, the fairly useful dual 1m winner Splendorinthegrass (all by Selkirk), the useful 6f and 7f winner Overspect (by Spectrum), the quite useful 6f winner and listed-placed Button Moon (by Compton Place) and the modest 7f to 10f winner of 11 races Marmooq (by Cadeaux Genereux). The dam, a fairly useful 5f winner of 4 races, is a half-sister to 4 winners. The second dam, Noirmont (by Dominion), is an unraced half-sister to the Group winners Braashee, Adam Smith and Ghariba. *"She was a late foal but she's a nice, neat filly with a good temperament. She'll not be running until June but she ought to have a bit of speed, she's nice and she goes well".*

869. AVANZARE ★★★
b.f. Kyllachy – Never Away (Royal Applause). March 9. Third foal. £42,000Y. Doncaster Premier. BBA (Ire)/C Hills. The dam, a moderate 1m and 10f placed maiden, is a half-sister to 4 winners including the 2-y-o Group 2 5.5f Prix Robert Papin winner Never A Doubt (herself dam of the listed winner Royal Confidence). The second dam, Waypoint (by Cadeaux Genereux), a fairly useful 6f and 7f winner, is a half-sister to 5 winners including the Group 2 6f Diadem Stakes winner and good sire Acclamation. *"She's done a bit of work, she's very laid back and I think she'll need a couple of runs before the penny drops really. Other than that she's a nice, scopey filly".*

870. BARBS PRINCESS ★★★★
ch.f. Bahamian Bounty – Halland Park Girl (Primo Dominie). April 21. Eighth foal. 34,000Y. Doncaster Premier. BBA (Ire). Half-sister to the quite useful 2011 2-y-o dual 6f winner Imelda

Mayhem (by Byron), to the quite useful 5.2f and 6f winner Lindbergh, the modest 7f 2-y-o winner Hallandale (both by Bold Edge), the quite useful 2-y-o 5f winner Top Town Girl (by Efisio) and the modest dual 7f winner Party In The Park (by Royal Applause). The dam won 5 races at 2 yrs including the listed Doncaster Stakes and is a half-sister to 2 minor winners. The second dam, Katsina (by Cox's Ridge), a useful 2-y-o 7f winner, was placed in two listed events and is a half-sister to 9 winners including the listed 10f Virginia Stakes winner Rambushka. *"A nice filly, she looks very tough and genuine and she goes well. We'll probably start her off at six furlongs".*

871. BESPOKE JOE ★★
b.g. Royal Applause – Spinning Lucy (Spinning World). February 24. First foal. 5,000Y. Tattersalls October Book 2. Not sold. The dam, a 2-y-o listed 6f winner, is a half-sister to the 2-y-o listed 6f Bosra Sham Stakes winner Midris (by Namid). The second dam, Dolara (by Dolphin Street), is an unraced half-sister to 4 winners including Idris, a winner of four Group 3 races in Ireland. *"He's just 'on the leg' and plain at the moment but he's certainly growing into his frame. He has a nice temperament and he's probably one for the second half of the season although we've done a bit of work with him just to get him going".*

872. BOSSA NOVA BABY (IRE) ★★★
b.f. High Chaparral – Attilia (Tiger Hill). February 12. Third foal. 35,000Y. Tattersalls October Book 1. BBA Ire/C Hills. Half-sister to the German listed winner Ambria and to the German 2-y-o winner and Group 3 third Anjella (both by Monsun). The dam, a 7f (at 2 yrs) and listed 9f winner in Germany, is a half-sister to 9 winners including the Group 2 German 2,000 Guineas winner Aviso and the dam of the Group 2 German Oaks winner Amarette. The second dam, Akasma (by Windwurf), won 3 minor races in Germany and is a half-sister to 5 winners including the German Group 2 winner Ajano. *"A nice filly for the second half of the season over seven furlongs to start with, we like the sire very much and this is a good-looking filly who was quite good value".*

873. CALLMEAKHAB (IRE) ★★★

b.f. Intikhab – Viola Royale (Royal Academy). March 25. Ninth foal. €65,000Y. Goffs Orby. BBA (Ire)/C Hills. Half-sister to the listed 1m winner of 6 races (including at 2 yrs) and Group 3 Darley Stakes third St Andrews, to the fairly useful 1m to 10f and hurdles winner Celticello, the quite useful 1m winner Shady Lady, the 10f to 14f winner Hurricane Thomas (all by Celtic Swing) and the fair 1m winner Colour Trooper (by Traditionally). The dam, an Irish 2-y-o 6f and 7f winner, was listed-placed and is a half-sister to 3 minor winners. The second dam, Wood Violet (by Riverman), is an unraced half-sister to 4 minor winners. *"The sire does well with his fillies and this one should off in July over seven furlongs. We'll see how she goes but she's got a nice temperament and she's an attractive filly".*

874. CAMISOLE (IRE) ★★★

br.f. Teofilo – Sleeveless (Fusaichi Pegasus). February 12. First foal. 78,000Y. Tattersalls October Book 1. BBA (Ire). The dam, a fair Irish 7f placed maiden, is a half-sister to 5 winners including the Group 3 Beresford Stakes winner and dual Group 1 second Castle Gandolfo. The second dam, Golden Oriole (by Northern Dancer), won at 3 yrs and is a sister to the champion 2-y-o's El Gran Senor and Try My Best. *"She's a little bit backward but she's a nice big filly that should strengthen up throughout the summer. We like her but she just wants a bit of time".*

875. COUNTRY WESTERN ★★★

b.c. Oasis Dream – Musical Horizon (Distant View). May 22. Third foal. Half-brother to the fair 2011 2-y-o 5f winner Musical Valley (by Three Valleys). The dam is an unplaced sister to the champion 2-y-o Distant Music (winner of the Group 1 7f Dewhurst Stakes, the Group 2 7f Champagne Stakes and the Group 2 9f Goffs International Stakes) and a half-sister to 3 winners including the useful 10f winner and Group 3 Lancashire Oaks third New Orchid (herself dam of the Group 1 6f Haydock Sprint Cup winner African Rose). The second dam, Musicanti (by Nijinsky), a French 14.5f winner, is a half-sister to the top-class American middle-distance colt Vanlandingham, winner of the Washington D.C. International, the Jockey Club

Gold Cup and the Suburban Handicap. *"A nice horse and we all seem to like him, but he was a late foal and he's one for the second half of the year. A nice, big, scopey horse that should so well".*

876. DALI'S LOVE (IRE) ★★★

b.f. Excellent Art – Hendrina (Daylami). March 7. Third foal. 18,000Y. Tattersalls October Book 2. BBA (Ire)/C Hills. Half-sister to Sweet Liberta (by Cape Cross), unplaced in one start at 2 yrs in 2011. The dam, unplaced in 2 starts, is a half-sister to 5 winners including the Irish Group 3 7.5f Concorde Stakes winner Hamairi and the Irish 5f (at 2 yrs) and 3-y-o listed 6f winner Hanabad. The second dam, Handaza (by Be My Guest), a 1m winner at 3 yrs in Ireland, is a half-sister to 6 winners including the Group 3 winners Hazariya and Hazarista. *"She was excellent value for what she cost and is a nice, big scopey filly that looks like she's got a bit of speed as well. It'll be June before we think of running her but she's a good-looking filly with a nice action".* TRAINERS' BARGAIN BUY

877. DESERT IMAGE ★★★

b.f. Beat Hollow – Western Appeal (Gone West). February 10. Half-sister to the quite useful French 1m winners Full Steam (by Oasis Dream) and Calm (by Montjeu). The dam, a 7f winner at 3 yrs in France, was third in the listed 7f Prix de Saint-Cyr and is a sister to the champion 2-y-o and 3-y-o Zafonic, winner of the 2,000 Guineas, the Dewhurst Stakes, the Prix de la Salamandre and the Prix Morny and to the smart Zamindar – winner of the Group 3 6f Prix de Cabourg and second in the Prix Morny. The second dam, Zaizafon (by The Minstrel), a dual 2-y-o 7f winner, was placed in the Group 1 1m Queen Elizabeth II Stakes and the Group 3 1m Child Stakes and is a half-sister to the dam of the Eclipse Stakes and Phoenix Champion Stakes winner Elmaamul. (Khalid Abdulla). *"A nice-looking filly that hasn't been here long, she's done nothing wrong, she's been cantering and we'll just give her a bit of time. She has a nice action and a good temperament".* I'd stay turned up will any an in tral running

878. ENGLISHMAN ★★★★ 7f 6|5 mle

b.c. Royal Applause – Tesary (Danehill). February 7. Fourth foal. £36,000Y. Doncaster Premier. Hillwood Bloodstock. Half-brother to the quite useful 2011 2-y-o 5f winner Verbeeck (by Dutch Art) and to the modest 1m winner Merton Lady (by Beat Hollow). The dam, a useful 5f (at 2 yrs) to 7f winner, is a half-sister to 4 winners including the fairly useful 7f and 1m winner Baldour. The second dam, Baldemara (by Sanglamore), is an unraced half-sister to 5 winners including the Group 1 5.5f Prix Robert Papin winner Balbonella (herself dam of the top-class sprinter Anabaa, the French 1,000 Guineas winner Always Loyal and the useful sire Key Of Luck). *"He goes well and he'll be running soon. Very straightforward and professional in everything he does, he should run well first time out but he'll certainly improve for it. He's showing plenty of pace and has a nice flowing action and a good cruising speed".*

879. ESTIBDAAD (IRE) ★★★
b.c. Haatef – Star Of Siligo (Saratoga Six). April 9. Sixth foal. 70,000foal. Tattersalls December. Shadwell Estate Co. Half-brother to the Italian Group 3 6f (at 2 yrs) and dual listed winner Magritte (by Modigliani) and to 2 minor winners in Italy by Almutawakel and Tout Seul. The dam was placed once at 4 yrs in Italy and is a half-sister to 5 winners. The second dam, Molly Seven (by Dewan), won 2 minor races in the USA and is a half-sister to 2 winners. *"He's grown an awful lot, so he's now a nice, scopey horse with a good temperament that should make a 2-y-o. We'll probably start him off at six furlongs".*

880. ESTIFZAAZ (IRE) ★★★★ ♠
b.c. Invincible Spirit – Lulua (Bahri). April 11. Third foal. 280,000Y. Tattersalls October Book 1. Shadwell Estate Co. Half-brother to the fair 2011 5f and 7f placed 2-y-o Marcus Augustus (by Holy Roman Emperor) and to the fair Irish 7f and subsequent US winner Samba School (by Sahm). The dam, a minor winner of 2 races at 3 yrs in the USA, is a half-sister to 7 winners. The second dam, Sajjaya (by Blushing Groom), a useful 2-y-o 7f and 3-y-o 1m winner, was second in the Group 3 Matron Stakes and is a half-sister to 8 winners including the top-class Group 1 1m Queen Elizabeth II Stakes winner Lahib. *"They paid quite a bit for him at the sales and I'm not surprised because he's an attractive looking colt. We'll start him at six furlongs in May and it would be nice to think*

he could be one for Royal Ascot. A nice colt that both Richard Hills and Paul Hanagan have ridden and reported they like".

881. FUNK SOUL BROTHER ★★★★
b.c. Cockney Rebel – Sweet Afton (Mujadil). March 8. Second foal. £65,000Y. Doncaster Premier. BBA (Ire). The dam, a fairly useful 5f (at 2 yrs) and 6f winner, was listed placed twice and is a half-sister to 4 winners. The second dam, Victory Peak (by Shirley Heights), is an unplaced half-sister to 6 winners out of the French Oaks winner Lypharita. *"We like him. He's a nice horse that we'll start off in May, probably over six furlongs at Haydock Park. He's an attractive colt and we've always liked him. He's never been difficult to handle, the more work he's done the better he's become and he's taken it all well".*

882. GLENARD ★★★
b.c. Arch – Olaya (Theatrical). February 23. Third foal. 65,000Y. Tattersalls October Book 1. BBA Ireland/C Hills. The dam won 4 races in France and the USA including the Grade 2 Long Island Handicap and is a half-sister to 3 winners. The second dam, Solaia (by Miswaki), won the listed Cheshire Oaks, was second in the Group 3 Lancashire Oaks and is a half-sister to 3 winners. *"An attractive-looking colt with size and scope, we'll wait for the second half of the season with him, but everyone seems to like him, he's got a good action and he's light on his feet".* Now to win gd c (3 ah. in Dunc

883. GLEN GINNIE (IRE) ★★★
br.f. Red Clubs – Belsay (Belmez). April 12. Eleventh foal. €65,000Y. Goffs Orby. BBA (Ire)/C Hills. Sister to the fair 2011 6f placed 2-y-o Red Senor and half-sister to the 6f, 7f (at 2 yrs) and Group 3 Craven Stakes winner and Group 2 second Killybegs (by Orpen), to the fairly useful Irish 1m (at 2 yrs) and 7.5f winner Pyrenees, a minor winner in Switzerland (both by Rock Of Gibraltar), the fairly useful Irish 2-y-o 6f winner Lady's Mantle (by Sri Pekan), the quite useful Irish 7f winner Dreamalittledream (by Danehill Dancer), the fair 6f (at 2 yrs) and 1m winner Tsaroxy (by Xaar) and minor winners abroad by Rock Of Gibraltar, Xaar and Cape Cross. The dam ran unplaced twice and is a half-sister to 4 winners including the Group 3 7f Nell Gwyn

Stakes winner and 1,000 Guineas third Crystal Gazing. The second dam, Crystal Bright (by Bold Lad, Ire), won once in the USA and is a half-sister to 4 minor winners. *"She's pretty forward and we'll probably see her out in late April or early May. She looks quite fast".*

884. GOLDEN CAUSEWAY ★★★★★

ch.f. *Giant's Causeway – Cast In Gold (Elusive Quality).* January 29. First foal. 60,000Y. Tattersalls October Book 1. BBA (Ire). The dam, a quite useful 2-y-o 7f winner, is a half-sister to 3 winners including Rule Of Law (Group 1 St Leger and Group 2 Great Voltigeur Stakes). The second dam, Crystal Crossing (by Royal Academy), winner of the listed 6f Doncaster Bloodstock Rose Bowl Stakes, is a sister to the very useful 2-y-o Group 3 7f Prestige Stakes winner and subsequent US Grade 2 placed Circle Of Gold and a half-sister to 5 winners. *"She's a very nice filly that's done really well recently and she goes very much like Maids Causeway did in her style of running. She has a nice temperament and I think she's a very nice filly".*

Wor g4 listed 7f newbury

885. JUST THE JUDGE (IRE) ★★★

br.f. *Lawman – Faraday Light (Rainbow Quest).* April 19. Third foal. €50,000Y. Goffs Orby. BBA (Ire)/C Hills. Sister to the fair 2011 7f placed 2-y-o Amber Silk. The dam ran twice unplaced and is a half-sister to the Group 3 St Simon Stakes winner and dual Group 1 placed High Heeled. The second dam, Uncharted Haven (by Turtle Island), won two Grade 2 events in the USA and is a half-sister to 5 winners. *"A nice filly that's just hanging onto her coat at the minute, she's probably a little bit better model than her sister who we have here. There's a bit of substance about her and she probably won't run until around August time, but she'll make a 2-y-o".* *Won g1 7f mdr in g0 style Newbury*

imply won Accepted Wormul

886. KERBAAJ (USA) ★★

b.c. *Dixie Union – Mabaahej (Belong To Me).* January 22. Second foal. The dam, a 1m placed maiden, is a half-sister to the smart 2-y-o 6f winner and Group 1 6f Middle Park Stakes third Tajdeef and to the listed 7f winner Alyarf (by Dixie Union). The second dam, Tabheej (by Mujtahid), a useful 2-y-o 5f and 6f winner, was

Wor g1 7f mdr or debut Jordan

third in the Lowther Stakes and is a sister to the Group 3 5f Cornwallis Stakes winner Mubhij. (Hamdan Al Maktoum). *"A nice, big scopey sort of horse. He's only just arrived from Dubai".*

887. LUCKY BEGGAR (IRE) ★★★

gr.c. *Verglas – Lucky Clio (Key Of Luck).* March 27. Second foal. €25,000Y. Goffs Orby. BBA (Ire)/C Hills. The dam was placed 3 times at 3 yrs in France and is a half-sister to Special Kaldoun (by Alzao), a winner of 9 races including the Group 2 Prix Daniel Wildenstein Casino Barriere (twice) and to the French listed-placed and subsequent Canadian winner Privalova (by Alhaarth). The second dam, Special Lady (by Kaldoun), was placed at 2 yrs in France and is a half-sister to 5 minor winners. *"He worked nicely yesterday under Michael Hills and we made an entry for him at Newmarket in a Conditions race. He'll improve a lot for the race but he's got a bit of speed and a good temperament".*

Wor 5f pln Windsor day5 snD

888. MAWJTAMMY (USA) ★★

b.c. *Invasor – Plenty Of Sugar (Ascot Knight).* March 21. Half-brother to the US 2-y-o 6f to 9f winner Sugar Mom (by Monarchos) and to a US Grade 1 jumps winner by Pulpit. The dam, second in the Grade 1 CCA Oaks, is out of Lemons To Lemonade (by Conquistador Cielo). (Hamdan Al Maktoum). *"He's just come in from Dubai, he's a big horse but we know nothing about him as yet".*

889. MAYAASEM ★★★★ ♠

b.c. *Royal Applause – Rolexa (Pursuit Of Love).* March 3. Second foal. 90,000Y. Tattersalls October Book 2. Shadwell Estate Co. The dam, a fair dual 1m placed 3-y-o, is a half-sister to 9 winners including the smart Green Card, a winner from 1m to 10.3f and Group 3 placed three times. The second dam, Dunkellin (by Irish River), a minor 3-y-o winner in the USA, is a half-sister to the Group 1 Criterium des Pouliches winner Oak Hill. (Hamdan Al Maktoum). *"He's just starting to work now but I'll wait for the six furlong races to start him off. He should improve, they all like him and he has a good action – an action like his Dad actually. A nice horse".*

890. MOJO MISS (IRE) ★★★

br.f. Shirocco – Starring (Ashkalani). April 10. Sixth foal. Tattersalls October Book 2. BBA (Ire)/C Hills. Half-sister to the 2011 2-y-o listed 1m winner Letsgoroundagain (by Redback), to the quite useful 7f to 9f winner of 11 races Spinning (by Pivotal), the quite useful 7f to 12f and hurdles winner Goodwood Starlight (by Mtoto), the fair 1m winner L'Astre De Choisir (by Choisir) and the fair 2-y-o 5f winner Daisy Moses (by Mull Of Kintyre). The dam, placed once at 3 yrs in France, is a half-sister to 5 winners the very smart dual listed 5f winner Watching. The second dam, Sweeping (by Indian King), a useful 2-y-o 6f winner, is a half-sister to 10 winners. *"She's very straightforward, she wants to please and won't take a lot of teaching because she knows her job and has a nice cruising speed. We'll just take our time with her because she is by Shirocco after all".*

891. MOSES OACS (IRE) ★★

b.c. Aussie Rules – Reinstated (Galileo). March 20. First foal. €17,000Y. Goffs Orby. BBA (Ire)/C Hills. The dam, a fair 10f to 17f placed maiden, is a half-sister to 3 winners including the smart Irish 10f and 13f winner Changingoftheguard. The second dam, Miletrian (by Marju), won the Group 2 Ribblesdale Stakes and Group 3 Park Hill Stakes and is a half-sister to the Group 2 Geoffrey Freer Stakes winner and Group 1 St Leger third Mr Combustible. *"I think he's done really well since he came in – he looks a different horse to be honest with you. He's really grown and strengthened up, but all the same he'll still need time and is one for autumn over seven furlongs.*

892. MOVEMENTNEVERLIES ★★★

ch.f. Medicean – Frabjous (Pivotal). March 12. Second foal. 30,000Y. Tattersalls October Book 2. Not sold. The dam is an unraced half-sister to 6 winners including the Group 1 Prix Maurice de Gheest winner May Ball. The second dam, Minute Waltz (by Sadler's Wells), is an unraced full or half-sister to 7 winners including the Lincoln Handicap winner King's Glory. *"She's just gone a bit weak and backward at the moment because she's growing. When you see her in the string she stands out because she's got size and scope, so she should do well in the second half of the season".*

893. MRS WARREN ★★★★

b.f. Kyllachy – Bold Bunny (Piccolo). January 23. Second living foal. £45,000Y. Doncaster Premier. Chris Powell. Half-sister to a winner in Sweden by Needwood Blade. The dam, a moderate 6f placed 3-y-o, is a half-sister to 6 winners including the listed winners Warbler and Silly Bold. The second dam, Bold And Beautiful (by Bold Lad, Ire), a useful 1m winner, was Group 3 placed twice in Germany is a half-sister to 4 winners. *"A nice filly, she'll be out at Newmarket in April and she's an attractive, very well-balanced filly that seems to go nicely. She should do quite well and I can't say anything against her really".*

894. MY HEART'S RACING (IRE) ★★

b.f. Montjeu – Nuriva (Woodman). March 25. Sister to the fairly useful 10f winner Awe Inspiring and half-sister to the fairly useful 7f (including at 2 yrs) and 6f winner of 3 races State Dilemma (by Green Desert), the quite useful 8.3f winner Dahman (by Darshaan) and the modest 9f, 10f and hurdles winner Brave Dane (by Danehill). The dam, a fairly useful 2-y-o 6f winner, is a sister to the champion 2-y-o colt Mujtahid, winner of the Group 2 6f Gimcrack Stakes and the Group 3 6f Anglia TV July Stakes and a half-sister to the smart Group 2 10f Guillaume d'Ornano and 1m Thirsk Classic Trial winner Just Happy and the very useful 10f winner and Lingfield Derby Trial second Tanaasa. The second dam, Mesmerize (by Mill Reef), is an unraced half-sister to the champion Italian 2-y-o filly Marina Duff. *"She's an attractive-looking filly that just needs a bit of time. She has a very good temperament for a Montjeu but she's just cantering away for now and is one for the autumn".*

895. NOBLE BULL (IRE) ★★

b.c. Papal Bull – Fernlawn Hope (Danehill Dancer). February 2. First foal. 23,000Y. Tattersalls October Book 2. BBA (Ire)/C Hills. The dam, a modest 2-y-o 1m winner, is a half-sister to 3 winners including the Group 3 Winter Derby winner Sri Diamond. The second dam, Hana Marie (by Formidable), a useful 2-y-o sprint winner, is a half-sister to 9 winners including the smart Group 3 and multiple listed winner Compton Bolter. (Magnier/Tabor/Smith & Mrs F Hay). *"He probably wants a bit of time but he's done a couple of bits of work and seems to go well. We'll give him some time off now and let him come to himself, because he's one for a bit later on in the season".*

896. NO TRUTH (IRE) ★★

b.f. Galileo – State Crystal (High Estate). May 12. Fourteenth foal. Closely related to the 10f winner True Crystal, to the 12f winner Time Crystal (both fairly useful), the 17f and hurdles winner Malakiya (all by Sadler's Wells) and the modest 12f winner Mount Crystal (by Montjeu) and half-sister to the quite useful 10f and hurdles winner Crystal Rock (by Rock Of Gibraltar), the fairly useful 2-y-o 7f winner Crystal Curling (by Peintre Celebre) and the fair 8.5f and multiple hurdles winner Jack The Giant (by Giant's Causeway). The dam was a very useful winner of the Group 3 12f Lancashire Oaks and was placed in the Yorkshire Oaks and the Prix Vermeille. She is a half-sister to 6 winners including the Group 1 Fillies' Mile winner Crystal Music, the Group 3 winners Dubai Success and Solar Crystal and the Irish Derby third Tchaikovsky. The second dam, Crystal Spray (by Beldale Flutter), a minor Irish 4-y-o 14f winner, is a half-sister to 8 winners. *"A very hardy filly from a good family, she's not the biggest but she's got a good temperament. She was a late foal so she's just cantering for now, but she looks very tough and genuine".*

897. ONE WORD MORE (IRE) ★★★

b.c. Thousand Words – Somoushe (Black Minnaloushe). March 18. Fourth foal. £36,000Y. Doncaster Premier. G Howson. Half-brother to the useful 5f winner of 4 races and Group 3 Molecomb Stakes third Archers Road (by Titus Livius) and to a minor 3-y-o winner in Italy by Clodovil. The dam is an unraced half-sister to 8 winners including the 1m 2-y-o and subsequent German Group 1 10f winner Ransom O'War. The second dam, Sombreffe (by Polish Precedent), a fair 7f winner, is closely related to the Group 2 Mill Reef Stakes winner Russian Bond and the Group 2 Temple Stakes winner Snaadee and a half-sister to 9 winners including the Group 3 Prix de Conde winner Cristofori. *"He's a nice horse that's done a bit of work, he's got a very good temperament and looks like he wants to please. We'll just give him a short break but it won't be long before he's racing".*

898. OVERRIDER ★★★

b.c. Cockney Rebel – Fustaan (Royal Applause). April 22. Second foal. Half-brother to the unplaced 2011 2-y-o Make A Fuss (by Proclamation). The dam, a fair 7f winner, is a sister to the Group 2 7f Lennox Stakes and 2-y-o Group 3 5f Molecomb Stakes winner Finjaan. The second dam, Alhufoof (by Dayjur), a fairly useful 2-y-o 6f winner, was fourth in the Group 3 7f Nell Gwyn Stakes and is a half-sister to 5 winners including the dam of the 1,000 Guineas winner Lahan. *"He can get a little hot, but with work he's settling down nicely. We're taking our time with him because he's probably a seven furlong type and we don't want to buzz him up too much. He has a nice, athletic action on him and he could be anything really".*

899. PENANG POWER ★★

b.f. Manduro – Penang Pearl (Bering). April 10. Ninth foal. Half-sister to the Group 1 12f King George VI Queen Elizabeth Stakes and Group 2 12f Hardwicke Stakes winner Harbinger (by Dansili), to the fair 7f to 12f winner of 12 races Penang Cinta (by Halling), the fair 12f winner Penangdouble O One (by Starcraft) and the modest 2-y-o 5f winner Penang Sapphire (by Spectrum). The dam was a very useful 3-y-o 1m listed winner of 3 races. The second dam, Guapa (by Shareef Dancer), won twice over 1m and is a half-sister to 7 winners including the Group 2 winners Dusty Dollar and Kind Of Hush. *"She was a bit small but she's grown and done well. We'll give her a bit of time, she's got a nice temperament and with patience she'll hopefully come good".*

900. PREMIUM ★★★★

b.f. Dansili – Arum Lily (Woodman). February 21. Fourth foal. Half-sister to the very useful 2011 2-y-o 1m winner and Group 3 1m Autumn Stakes second Perennial (by Motivator) and to the very smart Canadian Grade 1 12f and Group 3 12f Glorious Stakes winner Redwood (by High Chaparral). The dam, a minor French 1m and 9f winner, is a half-sister to several winners. The second dam, Jolypha (by Lyphard), won the Group 1 Prix Vermeille and the Group 1 Prix de Diane. *"A very nice filly with a bit of size and scope and she's from a good family. I think we'll wait until mid-season before we do anything with her but she's a filly we like a lot".*

2nd g4 Newbury b7f d 4 mln

901. PULIGNY (IRE) ★★★

b.f. Holy Roman Emperor – Le Montrachet (Nashwan). April 30. Sixth foal. 20,000Y. Tattersalls October Book 2. Will Edmeades. Closely related to the quite useful 2-y-o 6f winner Barzan (by Danehill Dancer) and half-sister to the fair 2-y-o 1m winner Fly By White (by Hawk Wing), the quite useful 12f winner Baba Ganouge (by Desert Prince) and a minor winner in New Zealand by Green Desert. The dam is an unraced sister to one minor winner and a half-sister to the Group 1 Coronation Stakes and Group 1 Prix Marcel Boussac winner Gold Splash and the good broodmare Born Gold (dam of the outstanding Goldikova). The second dam, Riviere d'Or (by Lyphard), winner of the Group 1 10f Prix Saint-Alary, is closely related to the Group 3 winner Chercheur d'Or and the French 2,000 Guineas second Goldneyev. *"She's a fairly late foal and she's coughed a bit so we're giving her a bit of time. She's grown an awful lot but I'd say that when she comes she'll come fairly quick. Probably one for June or July"*.

902. RED DRAGON (IRE) ★★★

b.c. Acclamation – Delphie Queen (Desert Sun). April 2. Fourth foal. 60,000Y. Tattersalls October Book 2. BBA (Ire)/C Hills. Half-brother to the fair 2011 5f and 6f placed 2-y-o Fast Finian (by Clodovil). The dam, a fairly useful 6f (at 2 yrs) and 7f winner of 3 races, is a half-sister to 4 winners. The second dam, Serious Delight (by Lomond), is an unraced half-sister to 8 winners. *"He's done well recently and I'd like to think we could get him out in May. He was a very attractive yearling and he should be a nice 2-y-o, probably over six furlongs"*.

903. RED INVADER (IRE) ★★★

b.c. Red Clubs – Tifariti (Elusive Quality). April 18. First foal. 92,000Y. Tattersalls October Book 1. BBA (Ire)/C Hills. The dam is an unraced half-sister to 6 winners including the Group 2 Flying Childers Stakes winner Land Of Dreams (herself dam of the multiple Group 1 winner Dream Ahead). The second dam, Sahara Star (by Green Desert), won the Group 3 Molecomb Stakes and is a half-sister to 6 winners including the Group 3 Greenham Stakes winner Yalaietanee. *"He's a very attractive horse with a lovely temperament. We'll hopefully get on with him quite soon"*.

904. REGAL DAN (IRE) ★★★

b.c. Dark Angel – Charlene Lacy (Pips Pride). April 7. Tenth foal. 36,000Y. Tattersalls October Book 2. BBA (Ire)/C Hills. Half-brother to the very useful 2-y-o listed 5f winner of 6 races Star Rover, to the fairly useful 2-y-o dual 5f winner and listed-placed Jamesway (both by Camacho), the minor Italian 2-y-o winner Bod Common Pride (by Bad As I Wanna Be) and the modest 4-y-o 8.6f winner Tetcott (Definite Article). The dam won once over 5f at 2 yrs and is a half-sister to 4 winners. The second dam, Friendly Song (by Song), is a placed sister to the winner of 7 races and sire Fayruz. *"He starts his career in April, he's very precocious and he's a nice, neat colt that looks a proper 2-y-o"*.

Won competitive c/ 2 Hdcp 7f Donc

905. REYAADAH ★★★★

b.f. Tamayuz – Tafaani (Green Desert). January 28. Second foal. Half-sister to the fair 2011 7f placed 2-y-o Kaafel (by Nayef). The dam is an unraced half-sister to numerous winners including the high-class 7.3f Hungerford Stakes and Tripleprint Celebration Mile winner and French 2,000 Guineas second Muhtathir. The second dam, Majmu (by Al Nasr), a useful winner of the Group 3 1m May Hill Stakes at 2 yrs, was third in a listed event over 10f at 3 yrs and is a half-sister to 5 minor winners. (Hamdan Al Maktoum). *"A nice, big filly, she's correct, quite forward and a good mover. One for the second half of the season"*.

906. SAND BOY (IRE) ★★★★

b.c. Footstepsinthesand – Farbenspiel (Desert Prince). April 22. Third foal. 70,000Y. Doncaster Premier. BBA (Ire)/C Hills. The dam won once at 3 yrs in Germany and is a half-sister to 6 winners including the US Grade 3 Miesque Stakes winner Louvain. The second dam, Flanders (by Common Grounds), a very useful sprint winner of 6 races including the listed Scarbrough Stakes, was second in the Group 2 Kings Stand Stakes and is a half-sister to 8 winners. *"He's done really well recently and although he's not an early foal he'll certainly make a 2-y-o. We'll try and get him out before Royal Ascot to give him a run and see if he's good enough to go there"*.

907. SHAISHEE (USA) ★★★

b.br.c. *Indian Charlie – Hatpin (Smart Strike)*. April 18. Third foal. $325,000Y. Keeneland September. Shadwell Estate Co. The dam, a winner and Grade 3 placed in Canada, is a half-sister to 14 winners including the dual Grade 3 placed Eden Lodge. The second dam, Lafayette's Lady (by Young Commander), won 3 races at 3 yrs in the USA and is a sister to a stakes winner. *"He's just come in from Dubai, he has a good temperament and he 's a good-looking horse but we're just learning about him really"*.

908. SINGLE MAST ★★★★

ch.f. *Mizzen Mast – Single Market (Dynaformer)*. February 20. Sister to Multilateral, unplaced in two starts at 2 yrs in 2011. The dam over 1m in the USA and is a half-sister to the Group 1 Grand Prix de Saint-Cloud second Perfect Sunday (by Quest For Fame) and the smart US 10f winner Barter Town. The second dam, Sunday Bazaar (by Nureyev), won over 12f in France and is a half-sister to numerous winners including the US Grade 1 winners Bates Motel and Hatim and the Horris Hill Stakes winner Super Asset. (Khalid Abdulla). *"Everyone seems to like her a lot. She's got a lovely action and we're just giving her a bit of time. She looks like she'll have a bit of pace about her and she's very straightforward. A nice filly"*.

909. SOCIETY PEARL (IRE) ★★★

b.f. *Kheleyf – Mamonta (Fantastic Light)*. March 12. Third foal. €37,000Y. Goffs Orby. David Redvers. Half-sister to the fair 2-y-o 10f winner Marhaba Malyoon (by Tiger Hill). The dam, placed once over 2m, is a half-sister to 6 winners including the Group 2 12.5f Prix de Royallieu winner Mouramara. The second dam, Mamoura (by Lomond), won over 10f and 12f in Ireland and is a half-sister to 5 winners. *"She goes well and early on she looked as if she was quite precocious, but as it turns out she needs a bit more time. She is out of a Fantastic Light mare after all. We're taking our time with her, but she's got a good cruising speed and she wants to please"*.

910. THE WELSH WIZARD (IRE) ★★★

b.c. *Dylan Thomas – Golden Dew (Montjeu)*. February 25. Third living foal. 110,000Y. Tattersalls October Book 1. BBA (Ire). Half-brother to the fair 2011 2-y-o 6f winner Purple 'n Gold (by Strategic Prince). The dam, placed fourth twice over 12f in Ireland, is a half-sister to 5 winners including the Breeders Cup Juvenile Turf winner Pounced. The second dam, Golden Cat (by Storm Cat), won over 1m at 3 yrs in Ireland and was listed-placed and is a half-sister to 9 winners including the Irish listed winners and subsequent US winner Eurostorm and Bowmore. *"He's a lovely, attractive horse. One for the back-end of the year but he's got a lovely temperament, he's light on his feet and I've always liked him"*.

911. UNMOOTHAJ ★★★

b.c. *Green Desert – Sundus (Sadler's Wells)*. April 7. Half-brother to the fair 1m winner Atraas (by King's Best). The dam, a quite useful 10f winner on her only start, is a half-sister to 5 winners including the 1,000 Guineas and Coronation Stakes winner Ghanaati and the Group 3 12f Cumberland Lodge Stakes winner Mawatheeq out of the listed 1m winner Sarayir (by Mr Prospector), herself a half-sister to Nashwan, Nayef and Unfuwain. *"He's just come in from Dubai. He's a good-sized horse with a good temperament but that's all we know about him for now"*.

912. WINTER SONG ★★★

b.f. *Pivotal – Speed Song (Fasliyev)*. March 31. First foal. 110,000Y. Tattersalls October Book 2. BBA (Ire)/C Hills. The dam, a quite useful dual 5f winner (including at 2 yrs), is a half-sister to the very smart Group 3 5f Molecomb Stakes and Group 3 5f King George Stakes winner Enticing. The second dam, Superstar Leo (by College Chapel), a very smart 2-y-o, won 5 races including the Group 2 5f Flying Childers Stakes and the Weatherbys Super Sprint and is a full or half-sister to 10 winners. *"Not the biggest but she's all there, very stocky and she should have plenty of speed. She has a nice temperament and there's nothing wrong with her at all. I'll start to get more serious with her soon"*.

913. ZIPP (IRE) ★★★

b.f. *Excellent Art – Subito (Darshaan)*. March 10. Eighth foal. €65,000Y. Goffs Orby. BBA (Ire). Half-sister to the quite useful Irish 9f winner

Silk Mascara (by Barathea), to the modest 11f and 12f winner Onemoreandstay (by Dr Fong) and the minor US winner of 8 races Chasm (by Gulch). The dam, a fairly useful 2-y-o 7f winner, is a half-sister to 3 winners. The second dam, Rapid Repeat (by Exactly Sharp), a 2-y-o 7f winner, is a half-sister to 5 winners including the Group 3 Derrinstown Stud Derby Trial and US stakes winner Artema. *"A very nice filly, she looks like she has plenty of speed and we'll probably wait until mid-season with her. A filly that we like".*

914. UNNAMED ★★★
b.f. *Excellent Art – Bali Breeze (Common Grounds).* March 30. Fourth foal. €105,000Y. Goffs Orby. BBA (Ire)/C Hills. Half-sister to the 2011 placed 2-y-o Soulside (by Whipper) and to the useful dual 10f winner and Group 3 10f second Alkimos (by High Chaparral). The dam, a quite useful 10f, 12f and hurdles winner, is a sister to the fairly useful listed-placed winner Amicable and a half-sister to 3 minor winners. The second dam, Bahia Laura (by Bellypha), a minor winner over 10.5f at 4 yrs in France, is a sister to the Group 3 10.5f Prix de Flore winner Benicia and a half-sister to 6 winners. *"She's had a problem that set her back for a while but she's coming right now and she's a very attractive filly with a good temperament. She should be quite nice".*

915. UNNAMED ★★★
FIRE FAIRY

b.br.f. *Henrythenavigator – Fabulous Fairy (Alydar).* March 13. Half-sister to the US Grade 2 winner Chinese Dragon, to the quite useful 2-y-o 6f winner Mythical Echo (both by Stravinsky), the quite useful 2-y-o 6f winner Truly Bewitched (by Affirmed), the minor US 4-y-o winner Calming (by Wild Again) and the fair 7f winner Marfooq (by Diesis). The dam, a fair 3-y-o 10f winner, is a half-sister to 5 winners including the Group 3 10.5f Prix Penelope third Fleet Fairy and to the dam of the top-class miler Desert Prince. The second dam, Fairy Footsteps (by Mill Reef), won the 1981 1,000 Guineas and is a half-sister to the St Leger winner Light Cavalry. *"She's done well this filly and she shouldn't be too backward either. A good-looker, she has a bit of spirit*

about her which I suppose is what you want and we'll probably start her off at six furlongs".*

916. UNNAMED ★★★
b.c. *Mizzen Mast – Geographic (Empire Maker).* February 6. First foal. The dam is an unraced half-sister to the Grade 1 9f Hollywood Oaks winner Sleep Easy and to the dual US Grade 1 winner Aptitude. The second dam, Dokki (by Northern Dancer), is an unraced half-sister to the champion US colt Slew O'Gold and the Belmont Stakes winner Coastal. (Khalid Abdulla). *"A nice, big, scopey horse that everyone likes. He has a good action and he should make a 2-y-o".* Ogbourne Dwn

917. UNNAMED ★★★
b.c. *Royal Applause – Helen Sharp (Pivotal).* February 17. Fourth foal. £42,000Y. Doncaster Premier. BBA (Ire). Half-brother to the fair 5f winner Sharp Eclipse (by Exceed And Excel) and to the fair 5f winner of 5 races Angelo Poliziano (by Medicean). The dam ran once unplaced and is a half-sister to 7 winners including the useful 6f (at 2 yrs) to 1m (in Sweden) winner Warming Trends. The second dam, Sunny Davis (by Alydar), was a fair 2-y-o 7f winner. *"A nice horse, he's done some bits of work and he's improved every time. One for the second half of the season, he has a good temperament, good conformation and there's nothing wrong with him".* Won fair 3yo 1m Mkt Windsor 33/1

918. UNNAMED ★★★
ch.f. *Rock Of Gibraltar – Penny Cross (Efisio).* April 22. Fifth foal. Half-sister to the very useful 2-y-o 7f winner and Group 3 1m Autumn Stakes second Prompter (by Motivator) and to the fair 10f to 14f winner of 6 races Quinsman (by Singspiel). The dam, a useful 7f to 8.5f winner of 3 races, was listed placed twice and is a half-sister to 6 winners including the Group 2 Celebration Mile winner Priors Lodge. The second dam, Addaya (by Persian Bold), ran once unplaced and is a half-sister to 8 winners abroad. *"She's done well, she's still hanging onto her coat a bit and just needs a bit of time really. One for the second half of the year, we'll be patient with her and she ought to stay quite well I would have thought".*

JOHN HILLS

919. A GOOD YEAR ★★
b.f. Montjeu – Noble Pearl (Dashing Pearl). March 31. Tenth foal. Sister to the French listed 15f and subsequent jumps winner Noble Prince and half-sister to the US Grade 2 and triple Grade 3 winner Noble Stella (by Monsun) and 2 winners in Germany by Acatenango and Kornado. The dam won the 2-y-o Group 1 Gran Criterium and is a half-sister to 3 winners. The second dam, Noble Girl (by Esclavo), won 4 races at 3 and 5 yrs in Germany and is a half-sister to 6 winners. (Corinthian). *"A lovely filly that'll take time, as her pedigree would suggest, even though her dam was pretty useful as a 2-y-o. A scopey filly with a rather peculiar 'wall eye' which I've seen on Montjeu's before. She's probably the best mover in the yard but she'll be one for the autumn and next year".*

920. ARMS ★★★★
b.c. Excellent Art – Enchanting Way (Linamix). March 29. Second foal. €40,000foal. Goffs. Camas Park. The dam is an unraced half-sister to 2 winners including the US Grade 1 Citation Handicap and dual Grade 2 winner Ashkal Way. The second dam, Golden Way (by Cadeaux Genereux), a fairly useful 10f and 10.5f winner, is a half-sister to 8 winners including the French listed 11f winner Go Boldly and the US listed stakes winner Polish Spring. *"This is my favourite, as things stand at the moment. He's a big, raw, lengthy colt. He has presence and he's scopey so we need to be patient with him and we may have to wait until September with him. He just has a classy look about him and he reminds me of a very nice Excellent Art 3-y-o I have called Johnno".*

921. DUCHESS OF HYGROVE ★★
b.f. Duke Of Marmalade – Elegant Pride (Beat Hollow). March 2. Second foal. 17,000Y. Tattersalls October Book 1. J W Hills. The dam is an unraced half-sister to 3 winners including the Australian Group 2 winner Trick Of Light. The second dam, Stardom (by Known Fact), is an unraced half-sister to 14 winners including the dual Group 1 winner Xaar and the dam of the dual Grade 1 winner Senure. (Huw Francis). *"She's all legs at the movement, she has a lovely action and has grown a lot just lately.*

A very attractive filly but one for much later in the year and next year".

922. ELUSIVE GOLD ★★★
b.f. Elusive City – Lady Angola (Lord At War). April 6. Sixth foal. £12,000Y. Doncaster Premier. Amanda Skiffington. Half-sister to Duntle (by Danehill Dancer), unplaced in one start at 2 yrs in 2011, to the fair 2-y-o dual 6f and subsequent US winner of 3 races Raiding Party (by Orpen) and the fair 6f and 7f winner of 4 races Tislaam (by With Approval). The dam, a quite useful 12f winner, is a half-sister to 6 winners including the dam of the US Grade 1 winner Honor In War. The second dam, Benguela (by Little Current), won twice at 4 yrs in the USA and is a half-sister to 12 winners including the US Grade 1 winners Al Mamoon and La Gueriere (herself dam of the US Grade 1 winner Icon Project). *"She's quite fast, I trained her half-sister Raiding Party who won here and then in the USA. She's a strong, sturdy filly and would have been almost ready to run if she hadn't coughed in February. She's clear now and it's just a case of getting her fit, so she'll start off in May and she'll race over five and six furlongs this year".*

923. KEENE'S POINT ★★★
br.c. Avonbridge – Belle's Edge (Danehill Dancer). March 14. Fourth foal. £28,000Y. Doncaster Premier. John Hills (private sale). The dam is an unraced half-sister to 6 winners including the listed 6f winner of 4 races Bright Edge. The second dam, Beveled Edge (by Beveled), won once at 4 yrs and is a half-sister to 2 winners. (Mrs D Abberley). *"A lovely horse, very attractive with a good action and he'll definitely make a 2-y-o. He'll also have speed and he could be running in May".*

924. KONZERT (ITY) ★★★
b.c. Hurricane Cat – Known Alibi (Known Fact). March 27. €17,000Y. Italy. Gordon Trollier. Half-brother to 5 winners including the dam of the Group 3 Prix des Chenes winner Vizir Bere (by Hurricane Cat). The dam is an unraced half-sister to 4 winners including Dockage (the grandam of Rail Link). *"The sire has been doing quite well in France and although this colt won't be early he floats along and we really like him".*

925. MICK DUNDEE (IRE) ★★★

b.c. Aussie Rules – Lucky Oakwood (Elmaamul). February 28. Eighth foal. £17,000Y. Doncaster Premier. Amanda Skiffington/John Hills. Half-brother to a winner in Japan by Grand Lodge and another winner abroad by Spectrum. The dam, a fair 2-y-o 7f winner, is a half-sister to 11 winners including the listed 1m Cecil Frail Handicap winner Incisive and the listed 10f Lupe Stakes winner Gisarne and to the unraced dam of the Australian Grade 1 winner Bezeal Bay. The second dam, Fair Sousanne (by Busted), a fair 6f and 10f placed maiden, is a half-sister to 5 minor winners. (R J Tufft). *"He's done a couple of bits of work and he's improving all the time. He probably wouldn't be as quick as the last Aussie Rules colt I had, Boomerang Bob, in other words he looks more of a six furlong type rather than five, but he should be ready to run around Guineas time onwards. He's a very good-looking horse, but he doesn't do anything more than you ask him to, so we'll have to let the racecourse do the talking".*

926. MOONLIT DANCER (IRE) ★★★

gr.f. Dark Angel – Wohaida (Kheleyf). January 17. First foal. €19,000Y. Goffs Orby. A Skiffington/J Hills. The dam, a fair 2-y-o 6f winner, is a half-sister to 5 winners including the useful Group 3 7f Horris Hill Stakes second Samhari. The second dam, Cambara (by Dancing Brave), a useful winner of three 1m events at 3 yrs, is a half-sister to 7 winners including the dual French Group 3 Pluralisme, the German Group 3 and listed Virginia Stakes winner Singletta, the useful winners Classic Tale, Only and Cambrian and the dam of the high-class miler Markofdistinction. *"She looks pretty quick and strong, but she did some coughing a couple of months so we gave her a break which meant she got a bit fat and happy. She's got natural speed and looks all over a 2-y-o. She could start at five furlongs but I think she'll be better at six – now all we have to do is get her fit".*

927. RIOJA DAY (IRE) ★★★★

b.c. Red Clubs – Dai E Dai (Seattle Dancer). April 17. Ninth foal. 17,500Y. Tattersalls October Book 3. John Hills/Amanda Skiffington. Half-brother to the modest 2011 Irish 6f placed 2-y-o Fibril (by Kheleyf), to the fairly useful Irish 2-y-o 7f and subsequent Hong Kong winner Monashee Star (by Monashee Mountain) and two winners in Italy (including at 2 yrs) by Brief Truce and Second Empire. The dam won 8 minor races in Italy and was listed-placed and is a half-sister to 9 winners including the Group 2 Premio Ribot winner Pater Noster and the Italian Group 3 winner and Group 1 placed Miscrown. The second dam, Sainera (by Stop The Music), a minor 2-y-o winner, is a half-sister to 11 winners. *"He's been working and he'll be on the racecourse in April. He's well-balanced and has a great temperament –so much so that you could do anything you want with him. A horse with natural speed, he looks all over a winner".* TRAINERS' BARGAIN BUY

928. SNOW ANGEL (IRE) ★★★

b.f. Danehill Dancer – Snowy Day In LA (Sadler's Wells). March 24. Second foal. Closely related to the fairly useful 2011 2-y-o 5f winner and dual listed placed Snowflake Dancer (by Dylan Thomas). The dam is an unplaced Kistena (Group 1 Prix de l'Abbaye). The second dam, Mabrova (by Prince Mab), a French 2-y-o 7f winner, is a half-sister to 6 winners. *"She's quick and she's started working now so I expect her to be out in May over five furlongs. She's quite small and all pretty face and big bottom!"*

929. TESTA ROSSA (IRE) ★★★

b.c. Oratorio – Red Rita (Kefaah). April 30. Eleventh foal. £52,000Y. Doncaster Premier. Amanda Skiffington/John Hills. Half-brother to the 6f (at 2 yrs) and smart dual listed 10f winner Foodbroker Fancy (by Halling and herself the dam of 2 stakes winners), the useful dual 6f winner (including a listed event at 2 yrs) Femme Fatale (by Fairy King) and the modest 1m winner Bob Stock (by Dubai Destination) and a winner in France by Halling. The dam, a fairly useful 4-y-o 6f winner, was second in the Group 3 6f Cherry Hinton Stakes and the Group 3 6f Princess Margaret Stakes at 2 yrs and is a half-sister to 3 minor winners. The second dam, Katie Roche (by Sallust), won over 1m in Ireland and is a half-sister to 6 winners. (Gary & Linnet Woodward). *"A good-looking horse, I bought him to replace a nice horse we had last year by Oratorio who we sold to Hong Kong. This fellow has grown, he's a good mover and he's probably one for June or July. He has a lot of substance and quality but we have to wait for him to pull himself together because he's gone up behind".*

930. TOFFEE SHOT ★★★

ch.f. Dutch Art – Toffee Vodka (Danehill Dancer). February 24. Second living foal. £2,100Y. Ascot November. Not sold. Sister to the fair 2011 2-y-o 6f winner Toffee Tart. The dam, a fair 6f (at 2 yrs), to 1m winner, is a half-sister to 6 winners. The second dam, Vieux Carre (by Pas de Seul), is an unplaced half-sister to 6 winners. (Gary & Linnet Woodward). *"A full sister to Toffee Tart who did quite well for us last year and was only beaten a nose in the Sales race at Ascot. She has a little bit more substance than her sister, she goes very well and she's a natural 2-y-o".*

931. WATCHEROFTHESKIES ★★★

b.c. Dutch Art – Red Heaven (Benny The Dip). February 2. Fourth foal. 38,000Y. Tattersalls October Book 2. J W Hills/Amanda Skiffington. Half-brother to the minor US dual winner at 4 yrs Heaven Forbid (by Pivotal). The dam, unplaced in one start, is a half-sister to 4 winners including the US triple Grade 1 winner Megahertz and to the dual Group 3 9f winner Heaven Sent. The second dam, Heavenly Ray (by Rahy), a fairly useful 7f and 1m winner, is a half-sister to 3 winners. (R J Tufft). *"A beautiful horse, he's been on a growing spree so we'll have to wait until he levels out, but he goes well and really takes the eye every time you see him in the string. I'm looking forward to him and he'll make a 2-y-o later on".*

932. ZIGGIE STARDUST ★★★

b.c. Sixties Icon – Aileen's Gift (Rainbow Quest). March 24. Seventh foal. 58,000Y. Tattersalls October Book 1. J W Hills/Amanda Skiffington. Half-brother to Nijoom Dubai (by Noverre) and Samitar (by Rock Of Gibraltar), both winners of the 2-y-o Group 3 6f Albany Stakes, to the fair 7f winner of 6 races La Gifted (by Fraam) and a winner in Greece by Xaar. The dam is an unraced half-sister to 5 winners including the fairly useful listed-placed Roker Park and the dam of the Group 2 Gimcrack Stakes winner Shameel. The second dam, Joyful (by Green Desert), a fair 7f winner at 3 yrs, is a half-

sister to 7 winners including the Group 1 1m Coronation Stakes winner Golden Opinion. (Gary & Linnet Woodward). *"An interesting horse because he's a half-brother to two Albany Stakes winners. He's a gorgeous horse that had a cyst in his sinus which we had to deal with in January. So that put us back a bit, but he's the best looking horse in the yard, he goes nicely but he's just a bit short on experience for the moment because he had to spend time at the vets recovering from the surgery. He looks to me like he'll definitely make a 2-y-o but it'll be from July onwards. If he'd been by Galileo he'd have made half a million because of the conformation and the pedigree".*

933. UNNAMED ★★★

b.f. Danehill Dancer – Amethyst (Sadler's Wells). April 2. Half-sister to the fairly useful 2-y-o 6f winner Sydney Harbour and half-sister to the quite useful 11f, 12f and hurdles winner Audit (by Fusaichi Pegasus), to the fair 6f winner Fifty (by Fasliyev) and a minor winner abroad by Kingmambo. The dam, winner of the Leopardstown 1,000 Guineas Trial, was second in the Irish 1,000 Guineas. She is a sister to the 2,000 Guineas and Group 1 National Stakes winner King Of Kings and the Group 3 Athasi Stakes winner Lucky and a half-sister to the Group 2 5.5f Prix Robert Papin winner General Monash. The second dam, Zummerudd (by Habitat), is an unplaced sister to the Irish Group 3 and US Grade 3 winner Ancestral. (Corinthian). *"She was a bit late coming in but she's racy, looks quite classy and is going to be a 2-y-o from June onwards. Everyone who rides her likes her and she looks like a six furlong 2-y-o".*

934. UNNAMED ★★★

ch.c. Danehill Dancer – Arosa (Sadler's Wells). January 22. Second foal. 50,000Y. Tattersalls December. J W Hills. The dam, a fairly useful Irish 9f and subsequent US stakes winner, is a sister to the smart German Group 2 8.5f and Italian Group 2 1m winner Crimson Tide and to the Group 3 12f Give Thanks Stakes winner Tamarind and a half-sister to the US Grade 2 and Group 3 Prix de Sandringham winner Pharatta and the US stakes listed stakes winner and Grade 2 placed La Vida Loca. The second dam, Sharata (by Darshaan), is an unraced half-sister to the Derby and Irish Derby winner Shahrastani. *"The dam is a full sister to a good horse I trained called Crimson Tide who is now a very successful stallion in Brazil. This is a very nice horse, but he's big and although he can do anything with any of them I need to ensure his bones and joints are bedded in. So he looks like he'll make a 2-y-o later on, over seven furlongs to start with".*

935. UNNAMED ★★★

ch.f. Singspiel – Carson Dancer (Carson City). March 5. Seventh foal. €20,000Y. Goffs Orby. Not sold. Half-sister to the quite useful Irish 2-y-o dual 7f winner Mistress Bailey (by Mister Baileys), to the fair 2-y-o 7f and 1m winner Digger Derek (by Key Of Luck) and the French 2-y-o 6.5f winner Irish Heart (by Efisio). The dam is an unplaced half-sister to 8 winners including the Japan Cup winner Tap Dance City. The second dam, All Dance (by Northern Dancer), a minor French 3-y-o winner, is a half-sister to 8 winners including the Kentucky Derby winner Winning Colors. *"She's a lovely filly, Singspiel's nearly always get better with age and yet this filly looks like she'll be slightly earlier than some. The dam is a half-sister to a Japan Cup winner and Singspiel himself won that race. She's a thoroughly likeable filly and I would have thought we'd be starting with her in June or July over six/seven furlongs".*

936. UNNAMED ★★★

b.c. Galileo – Flamingo Guitar (Storm Cat). March 21. Second foal. 50,000Y. Tattersalls December. Jamie Osborne. Brother to Jungle Beat, a promising 7f winner on his only start at 2 yrs in 2011. The dam, a quite useful Irish 7f winner, is a sister to 2 winners including the US Grade 2 9f Super Derby winner Fantasticat and a half-sister to 3 winners. The second dam, Lotta Dancing (by Alydar), a winner of 7 races in the USA including the Grade 3 8.5f Affectionately Handicap, was third in the Grade 1 Top Flight Handicap and is a half-sister to 8 winners. (Prolinx Ltd). *"A beautiful horse, he won't be ready until later in the year but he's a lovely, scopey type and he's one of my favourites in terms of the future. He does everything easily, even now".*

937. UNNAMED ★★★

b.f. Hurricane Run – Foreign Relation (Distant Relative). March 4. Sixth foal. €40,000Y. Goffs Orby. Not sold. Half-sister to Red Rioja (by King's Theatre), a winner of 4 races here and in the USA including the Group 3 C L Weld Park Stakes and the Grade 3 Brown Bess Handicap and third in the Group 2 Ribblesdale Stakes. The dam is a placed half-sister to 4 minor winners. The second dam, Nicola Wynn (by Nicholas Bill), a quite useful 12f winner, is a half-sister to 6 winners including the good broodmare Canton Silk. *"She's a very nice filly, she'll make a 2-y-o by mid-summer and she might start at six furlongs but she'll love seven. She has natural speed and a beautiful action".*

938. UNNAMED ★★★

b.f. Galileo – Tea Break (Daylami). January 28. Second foal. 50,000Y. Tattersalls October Book 1. Not sold. Closely related to the unplaced 2011 2-y-o Panettone (by Montjeu). The dam is an unraced half-sister to 7 winners including the French Group 3 winner Short Pause, the French 1m listed winner Cheyenne Dream and the dams of the Group 1 winners Continent and Zambezi Sun. The second dam, Interval (by Habitat), a high-class sprinting winner of four races from 5f to 1m including the Group 2 Prix Maurice de Gheest, is a half-sister to 5 winners including the Group 2 winner Interim (dam of the US Grade 1 winner Midships) and the dams of the Group 2 winners Invited Guest and Much Faster. *"A beautifully-bred filly. She has an Oaks winner's type shoulder and depth but very unattractive hocks. So she wasn't a sales type animal but she's by the best stallion there is, she has a great frame and we just have to be patient. She probably wouldn't run until September anyway".*

WILLIAM JARVIS
939. ARGENT KNIGHT ★★

gr.c. Sir Percy – Tussah (Daylami). May 8. Fifth foal. 55,000Y. Tattersalls October Book 2. W Jarvis. Brother to Noble Silk, unplaced in one start at 2 yrs in 2011, and to the fair 10f to 12f winner Watered Silk (by Encosta De Lago). The dam is an unraced half-sister to 7 winners including the Group 2 13f Prix de Pomone winner Armure and the listed winners Gravitas, Affirmative Action and Seta. The second dam, Bombazine (by Generous), a useful listed-placed 10f winner, is a half-sister to 7 winners including the Breeders Cup Mile, Irish 2,000 Guineas and Queen Anne Stakes winner Barathea, the Fillies Mile and Irish 1,000 Guineas winner Gossamer and the multiple Group 3 winner Zabar. (Dr J Walker). *"I loved him as a yearling and was pleased to buy him. He's a May foal so he's still a bit on the weak side and is one for the second half of the season. A middle-distance horse in the making, I quite like him and he has a good action".*

940. ARTORIUS CASTUS ★★★

ch.c. Dutch Art – Miss Madame (Cape Cross). March 12. Third foal. 17,000Y. Tattersalls October Book 2. Blandford Bloodstock. Half-brother to the unplaced 2011 2-y-o La Passionata (by Proclamation). The dam, a modest 7f and 1m winner, is a half-sister to 2 winners. The second dam, Cosmic Countess (by Lahib), a fair 2-y-o 6f winner, is a half-sister to 7 winners. (The Round Table Partnership). *"A very big, strong colt, but he's going through a growing stage so he's gone a bit weak on us at the moment through immaturity. When he grows into himself I think he'll be quite a nice sprinter".*

941. JODIES JEM ★★

br.g. Kheleyf – First Approval (Royal Applause). March 15. Third foal. 9,000Y. Tattersalls October Book 3. Bobby O'Ryan. Half-brother to the fair 2011 9f placed 2-y-o I'm Harry (by Haafhd). The dam, a fair 6f winner, is a half-sister to 6 winners including the high-class 7f to 11f winner Hawksley Hill (by Rahy), winner of the Arcadia Handicap, El Rincon Handicap and San Francisco Mile (all US Grade 2 events) and the dam of the Group 1 Prix de l'Abbaye winner Benbaun. The second dam, Gaijin (by Caerleon), a useful 2-y-o 6f winner, is a full or half-sister to 5 winners including Thousla Rock (Group 3 Premio Umbria). *"He was a cheap yearling and we've gelded him, but he's by a stallion that gets plenty of winners. There's no reason why he won't be a fun horse for his owner".*

942. LAUDATION ★★★

b.c. Royal Applause – Calamanco (Clantime).

April 4. Twelfth foal. 30,000Y. Tattersalls October Book 2. Ric Wylie. Half-brother to the smart listed 5f winner and Group 3 second Corrybrough, to the fair dual 5f winner (including at 2 yrs) Crimson Cloud, the fair 5f winner Fairy Shoes (all by Kyllachy), the fairly useful 5f to 6f winners Kingscross (by King's Signet) and Artie (by Whittingham) and the dam of the dual Group 3 winning sprinter Amour Propre. The dam, a fair 5f winner at 3 and 4 yrs, is a sister to the sprint winner Cape Merino (herself dam of the Group 1 Golden Jubilee Stakes winner Cape Of Good Hope) and a half-sister to 3 winners. The second dam, Laena (by Roman Warrior), is a placed half-sister to one minor winner. (The Laudation Partnership). *"I like him, there's a lot of speed in the pedigree and he's got it as well. I'd expect him to be running in June".*

943. RASKOVA (USA) ★★★★

b.f. Henrythenavigator – Diamond Necklace (Unbridled's Song). April 16. Second foal. 130,000Y. Tattersalls October Book 1. Ric Wylie. The dam, a useful 9f listed-placed maiden in Ireland, is a half-sister to 5 winners notably Shamardal (Dewhurst Stakes, French 2,000 Guineas, French Derby and St James's Palace Stakes). The second dam, Helsinki (by Machiavellian), a winner and listed placed over 10f at 3 yrs in France, is a sister to the Dubai World Cup and US Grade 1 winner Street Cry and a half-sister to 8 winners out of the Irish Oaks winner Helen Street. (Mr K J Hickman). *"If we've only got one good 2-y-o this will be the one. She was our most expensive yearling and she comes from a good family. The sire stands in America, so there weren't an awful lot of his yearlings to choose from at the Sales over here. This filly has done everything right so far, she's a good-sized 2-y-o with good conformation. A good, solid filly, her natural ability might see her running in late June or early July over six furlongs".*

944. UNNAMED ★★★

b.c. Oratorio – Always Attractive (King's Best). January 29. First foal. £45,000Y. Doncaster Premier. Blandford Bloodstock. The dam is an unplaced half-sister to 6 winners including the fairly useful 2-y-o 6f and 7f winner and smart broodmare Witch Of Fife. The second dam, Fife (by Lomond), a fairly useful 1m winner, is a half-sister to 5 winners including Piffle (dam of the Group 1 winners Frenchpark and Pearly Shells). (Tony Foster & Partners). *"He's a nice horse, I like him and I think the stallion is still capable of getting a good horse. He had a tiny setback but I can still see him being a late-July type 2-y-o over seven furlongs".*

945. UNNAMED ★★★
b.f. Sakhee's Secret – Bolsena (Red Ransom). March 2. Sixth foal. 16,000Y. Tattersalls October 3. Blandford Bloodstock. Half-sister to the quite useful dual 1m winner Cactus Rose (by Zamindar) and to the fair 2-y-o 6f seller winner Wolf Slayer (by Diktat). The dam is an unraced half-sister to 8 winners including the US Grade 3 winner De Niro and the Italian Group 3 winner Vidalia. The second dam, Waya (by Faraway Son), won four Grade 1 events in the USA and the Group 2 Prix de l'Opera and is a half-sister to the US Grade 1 winner Warfever. (A Partnership). *"She's sweet – I really like this filly. I expect she'll be our first 2-y-o runner, she has a lovely attitude and covers plenty of ground for her size. She may need six furlongs a bit later on, rather than five, but she's certainly showing us a bit of speed at the moment". TRAINERS' BARGAIN BUY*

EVE JOHNSON HOUGHTON
946. CARDMASTER ★★
gr.c. Red Clubs – El Morocco (El Prado). March 23. First foal. 14,000Y. Tattersalls October Book 2. Eve Johnson Houghton. The dam is an unraced half-sister to 2 winners including the Group 3 placed Smart Coco. The second dam, Djebel Amour (by Mt. Livermore), won 2 minor races at 3 yrs in the USA and is a half-sister to 4 winners including Almushahar (Group 2 Champagne Stakes). *"When I bought him I thought he's be sharp and early but since I've had him he's done nothing but grow. I still think he's nice but we won't see him until late May/June time now, over six furlongs. A deep-chested colt, he was a bit immature but he seems to have grown into himself now and I can get stuck into him a bit".*

947. CLEMENT (IRE) ★★
b.c. Clodovil – Winnifred (Green Desert). March 31. Second foal. 15,000Y. Tattersalls October

Book 2. Eve Johnson Houghton. Brother to the quite useful 2011 2-y-o dual 6f winner Kimbali. The dam is an unraced sister to 2 winners including the listed 1m winner and Group 1 1m Coronation Stakes third Dolores (herself dam of the listed winners Duncan and Samuel). The second dam, Agnus (by In The Wings), a winner twice in Belgium, is a half-sister to 5 winners including Wavy Run (Grade 2 San Francisco Mile Handicap). (P Deal & C Brown). *"A big, backward baby – something of a spotty teenager at the moment! But he'll be very nice later in the year, probably over seven furlongs".*

948. KNIGHT CHARM ★★★
b.c. Haafhd – Enchanted Princess (Royal Applause). April 17. Sixth foal. 18,000Y. Tattersalls October Book 2. Eve Johnson Houghton. Half-brother to the fairly useful 6f winner of 4 races (including at 2 yrs) and listed-placed Morache Music (by Sleeping Indian), to the fairly useful 6f and 7f winner and listed-placed Never Lose (by Diktat) and a winner in the Czech Republic by Dr Fong. The dam, a fair 3-y-o 8.3f winner, is a half-sister to 5 winners including the useful 7f and 1m winner Bishr and the dam of the Group 3 winner High Standing. The second dam, Hawayah (by Shareef Dancer), a modest 2-y-o 7f winner, is a half-sister to 7 winners including the quite useful 6f and subsequent US stakes winner Promptly. (Fairweather Friends). *"He's a lovely horse, he shows bags of pace and once we get some better weather and he looks better in his coat he'll be ready to run. He'll be sharp and early and a five/six furlong type. I bought him because I love the sire and as he's unfashionable I can buy a nice horse at a reasonable price".*

Won cl5 5f mdn Warwick

949. MUST BE ME ★★★
b.f. Trade Fair – Roodeye (Inchinor). March 22. Third foal. Half-sister to the unraced 2011 2-y-o Hoonose (by Cadeaux Genereux) and to the quite useful 5f (at 2 yrs) and 7f winner Roodle (by Xaar). The dam, a useful 5f (at 2 yrs) and 7f winner, was listed-placed and is a half-brother to 5 winners including the Group 1 Prix Morny second Gallagher and the useful 7f and 1m winner Quick Wit. The second dam, Roo (by Rudimentary), a quite useful 2-y-o 5f and 6f winner, is a half-sister to 5 winners including the Group 2 6f Gimcrack Stakes winner

Bannister. (Eden Racing IV). *"She was bred by my mother, she's sharp and she'll be ready to start over five furlongs by late May. We should have some fun with her and she's similar to the rest of the family in that they're all little minxes and she's definitely got that naughtiness in her!"*

950. PEACE TREATY ★★
b.c. *Lucky Story – Peace Lily (Dansili).* May 6. Third foal. The dam, a modest 7f winner at 4 yrs, is a half-sister to 5 winners including the Group 2 6f Gimcrack Stakes winner Bannister and the quite useful 2-y-o 5f and 6f winner Roo. The second dam, Shall We Run (by Hotfoot), placed once over 5f at 2 yrs, is a full or half-sister to 8 winners including the Group 1 6f Cheveley Park Stakes winner Dead Certain. (Eden Racing IV). *"He's a nice horse that'll take time. One for September-time over seven furlongs to a mile".*

951. ROCK GOD ★★★★
br.c. *Shirocco – Melatonina (King Charlemagne).* February 3. Second foal. 16,000Y. Tattersalls October Book 2. Eve Johnson Houghton. Half-brother to the 2012 French placed 3-y-o Faraway Run (by Hurricane Run). The dam won twice at 2 yrs in Italy and is a half-sister to 5 winners including the Group 2 Prix Eugene Adam winner Look Honey and two listed winners in the USA and Italy. The second dam, Middle Prospect (by Mr Prospector), is an unraced half-sister to 5 winners. *"He's a very nice colt that's done nothing but please me. He's the most beautiful mover and will most likely be out in July or August over seven furlongs".*

952. STARLIGHT SYMPHONY ★★★★
b.f. *Oratorio – Phillippa (Galileo).* April 11. Second foal. €10,000Y. Tattersalls Ireland. Bobby O'Ryan. Half-sister to the fair 2011 6f to 1m placed 2-y-o Naseem Alyasmeen. The dam is an unraced half-sister to 4 winners including the listed winner Ayam Zaman. The second dam, Kardashina (by Darshaan), won 3 races at 3 yrs in France and is a half-sister to two listed winners. *"She could be very nice. She looks all class, she's a lovely mover and very willing. We'll start her off at six furlongs".*

953. TAGALAKA ★★
b.c. *Tagula – Queeny's Princess (Daggers Drawn).* April 6. Third foal. €10,000Y. Tattersalls

Ireland. Eve Johnson Houghton. The dam is an unraced half-sister to 12 winners including the US stakes winner Fawlty Towers and the dam of the Group 1 Prix du Cadran winner Give Notice. The second dam Queen Of The Brush (by Averof), won at 3 yrs and is a half-sister to 6 winners including the triple Group 1 winner Old Country. (Eden Racing IV). *"A sharp, early 2-y-o, he should give the Eden Racing syndicate members some fun".*

954. VESTIBULE ★★★
ch.f. *Kheleyf – Lobby Card (Saint Ballado).* February 28. Fifth living foal. £5,000Y. Doncaster Premier. Not sold. Half-sister to a minor winner in the USA by Flying Chevron. The dam, placed at 3 yrs in the USA, is a half-sister to 6 winners including the Japanese stakes winner Biko Pegasus. The second dam, Condessa (by Condorcet), won the Group 1 Yorkshire Oaks and is a half-sister to 3 winners. *"A nice filly, she'll start off in mid-April. She's so laid-back that you can do whatever you want with her and she doesn't bat an eyelid. She does whatever you want, not flamboyantly but better than any horse she works with".* TRAINERS' BARGAIN BUY

MARK JOHNSTON
955. AMBLESIDE
b.c. *Cape Cross – Zarara (Manila).* April 2. Eighth foal. 50,000Y. Tattersalls October Book 1. Mark Johnston. Half-brother to the very useful 10f (at 2 yrs) to 14f and subsequent Australian Group 1 12f Caulfield Cup winner All The Good (by Diesis), to the fair 2-y-o 7f winner Hudoo (by Halling) and the minor Italian winner of 5 races Grey Latino (by Daylami). The dam is an unraced half-sister to 10 winners including the Oaks, Irish Oaks and Yorkshire Oaks winner Ramruma and the Lingfield Oaks Trial winner Ausherra (herself dam of the Group 2 winner Strategic Prince). The second dam, Princess Of Man (by Green God), won three races including the Group 3 Musidora Stakes and is a half-sister to 6 winners. (Sheikh Hamdan Bin Mohammed Al Maktoum).

956. BAILEY'S JUBILEE
b.f. *Bahamian Bounty – Missisipi Star (Mujahid).* April 19. Second foal. Doncaster Premier. £19,000Y. Bobby O'Ryan. The dam, a fairly

useful 1m winner, was listed placed and is a half-sister to one winner. The second dam, Kicka (by Shirley Heights), is a placed half-sister to 8 winners. (G R Bailey Ltd). *Won 1/v 2*

Kempron, Newmv

957. DISCERNABLE

ch.f. *Elusive Quality – Louve Mysterieuse (Seeking The Gold)*. April 29. Sixth foal. 160,000Y. Tattersalls October Book 1. John Ferguson. Sister to the US Grade 2 winner True Quality and half-sister to the minor US winner Indy Express (by A P Indy). The dam, a French listed 10f winner, is a half-sister to 5 winners. The second dam, Louve Bleue (by Irish River), a very useful 10f winner and second in the Group 1 Prix Saint-Alary, is a sister to the French Group 2 winner Lascaux and a half-sister to the Group 1 Prix de Diane and Group 1 Prix Saint-Alary placed Louve Romaine and to the very smart 1m winners Legend of France and Louveterie (herself dam of the Group 1 winners Loup Sauvage and Loup Solitaire). (Sheikh Hamdan Bin Mohammed Al Maktoum). *Won clSwd,*

Kempton Aug

958. DOUBLE YOUR MONEY (IRE)

b.c. *Shamardal – Zeiting (Zieten)*. May 5. Ninth foal. €60,000Y. Arqana Deauville August. Not sold. Half-brother to 5 winners including the useful 2-y-o 7f winner and triple Group 3 placed Bikini Babe (by Montjeu), to the French 2-y-o 6f winner and Group 3 7f Prix Miesque third Zut Alors (by Pivotal), the useful 2-y-o 6f winner Mutawajid (by Zafonic) and the quite useful 1m winner Mohathab (by Cadeaux Genereux). The dam won 6 races from 6f to 1m including the listed Prix Zeddaan and 3 minor US stakes events and is a half-sister to 5 winners including the Group 3 Prix du Bois winner Dolled Up out of the Irish 13f winner Belle de Cadix (by Law Society), herself a half-sister to 5 winners. (A D Spence).

959. DREAMILY (IRE)

b.br.f. *New Approach – Idilic Calm (Indian Ridge)*. March 15. Seventh foal. 100,000Y. Tattersalls October Book 1. Mark Johnston. Half-sister to the UAE Group 2 Godolphin Mile and listed King Charles II Stakes winner Calming Influence (by King's Best), to the Irish listed and subsequent Canadian Grade 2 Nearctic Handicap winner Steel Light (by Stravinsky), the fairly useful 2-y-o 7f winner Dark Humour

(by Bahri) and the fair 6f winner Marajel (by Marju). The dam, a fair Irish 7f winner, is a half-sister to 2 winners. The second dam, Miracle Drug (by Seattle Slew), ran unplaced twice and is a half-sister to 9 winners including the US Grade 1 winner Twilight Agenda and the dams of the Group 1 winners Go And Go, Refuse To Bend and Media Puzzle. (Sheikh Hamdan Bin Mohammed Al Maktoum).

960. EXCELLENT MARINER (IRE)

b.f. *Henrythenavigator – Castara Beach (Danehill)*. February 1. Seventh foal. €39,000Y. Arqana Deauville August. Not sold. Half-brother to the very smart 6f (at 2 yrs) and Group 3 1m Solonaway Stakes winner, Group 1 Dewhurst Stakes fourth and subsequent Hong Kong Group 3 9f winner Steinbeck (by Danehill Dancer), to the fairly useful 2-y-o 7.5f winner and Italian listed-placed Varenka (by Fasliyev) and the fair 2-y-o 7f winner Corsicanrun (by Fasliyev). The dam, placed fourth once over 7f at 2 yrs, is a sister to the useful Group 3 7f Criterion Stakes winner Hill Hopper and a half-sister to 5 winners including the Australian Grade 1 winner Water Boatman. The second dam, Sea Harrier (by Grundy), ran twice unplaced and is a half-sister to 5 winners including the Group 2 12f King Edward VII Stakes winner Sea Anchor. (Ian Harland, Excellence Racing).

961. FLASHLIGHT (IRE)

b.c. *Shamardal – Jazzy Jan (Royal Academy)*. April 14. Second foal. €135,000foal. Goffs. John Ferguson. Half-brother to the modest 2011 2-y-o 10f winner Enjoying (by Marju). The dam is an unplaced daughter of the 2-y-o listed 1m winner and Group 3 Prix Saint-Roman second La Vita E Bella (by Definite Article), herself a half-sister to 3 winners including the 2-y-o dual listed 5f winner and Group 2 Criterium de Maisons-Laffitte third Bella Tusa. (Sheikh Hamdan Bin Mohammed Al Maktoum).

962. HOUSE OF ORANGE

b.c. *Kheleyf – Cox Orange (Trempolino)*. May 13. Half-brother to the very useful listed 1m winner and 1,000 Guineas third Vista Bella, to the fair 1m and 9f winner Ochre (both by Diktat), the fair 10f winner The Hague (by Xaar) and the minor French 2-y-o winner Orlena (by Gone West). The dam won the Group 3 7f Prix du Calvados at 2 yrs and four US Grade 3 events and is a half-sister to 6 winners including the Group 1 Prix Marcel Boussac winner Amonita. The second dam, Spectacular Joke (by Spectacular Bid). (Sheikh Hamdan Bin Mohammed Al Maktoum).

963. LIGHT ROSE (IRE)
b.f. Cape Cross – Laureldean Lady (Statue Of Liberty). February 14. First foal. €45,000Y. Goffs Orby. Mark Johnston. The dam, a minor French 3-y-o winner, is a half-sister to 5 winners including the smart Group 3 Sandown Classic Trial and Group 3 Mooresbridge Stakes winner Regime (by Golan) and to the very useful 2-y-o 5f listed winner and Group 2 Cherry Hinton second Salut d'Amour (by Danehill Dancer). The second dam, Juno Madonna (by Sadler's Wells), is an unraced half-sister to 5 winners including the Group 3 5f King George Stakes winner Title Roll and the Irish listed sprint winner Northern Express. (J Abdullah).

964. LIMIT UP
b.c. Shamardal – Love Me Tender (Green Desert). February 23. Third foal. 78,000Y. Tattersalls October Book 1. Mark Johnston. The dam, a fair 3-y-o dual 7f placed maiden, is a half-sister to 3 winners. The second dam, Easy To Love (by Diesis), a quite useful 4-y-o 11.5f winner, is a half-sister to 6 winners including the high-class Group 1 12f Oaks and listed Lupe Stakes winner Love Divine (dam of the St Leger winner Sixties Icon), the listed 12f winner Floreeda and the dam of the dual Group 3 winner Dunboyne Express. (Sheikh Hamdan Bin Mohammed Al Maktoum).

965. MAPUTO
b.c. Cape Cross – Insijaam (Secretariat). May 10. Half-brother to the smart 7f (at 2 yrs) and Group 3 10f winner and Group 1 7f Moyglare Stud Stakes second Pictavia (by Sinndar), to the US 2-y-o 6.5f and UAE 1m winner of 7 races Janadel (by Machiavellian), the fairly useful 7f and 10f winner of 7 races Master Marvel (by Selkirk), the quite useful 2-y-o 7.5f winner River Lena and the fair 7f (at 2 yrs) to 12f winner of 5 races Safebreaker (by Key Of Luck). The dam, a dual listed 10f winner at 3 yrs in France, is

a half-sister to the 1,000 Guineas and Prix de l'Opera winner Hatoof and the 1m (at 2 yrs) and 12f listed winner Fasateen. The second dam, Cadeaux d'Amie (by Lyphard), a 1m (at 2 yrs) and 10f winner in France, was third in the Group 3 1m Prix d'Aumale and is a half-sister to the Prix Vermeille and Prix de Diane winner Mrs Penny. (Sheikh Hamdan Bin Mohammed Al Maktoum).

966. NELLIE BLY
b.f. Exceed And Excel – La Presse (Gone West). April 12. Second foal. Half-sister to the modest 2012 3-y-o 10f winner News Desk (by Cape Cross). The dam, a useful 2-y-o 6f winner, was third in the Group 3 6f Firth Of Clyde Stakes and is a half-sister to the useful 7f and 1m winner Paper Talk. The second dam, Journalist (by Night Shift), a useful 2-y-o 6f winner, was second in the Group 3 6f Princess Margaret Stakes and is a half-sister to the useful sprinter Sheer Viking. (Sheikh Hamdan Bin Mohammed Al Maktoum).

967. OPEN LETTER (IRE)
b.f. New Approach – Deveron (Cozzene). April 18. Third foal. 100,000Y. Tattersalls October Book 1. Mark Johnston. Half-brother to the quite useful 2-y-o 7f winner Dffar (by Shamardal). The dam, a very useful 2-y-o 7f winner, was third in the Group 1 1m Prix Marcel Boussac and is a sister to the Canadian dual Grade 2 winner Windward Islands and a half-sister to 5 winners including the minor US stakes winner Hunter Cruise. The second dam, Cruisie (by Assert), won 3 minor races at 3 yrs in the USA and is a half-sister to 4 stakes winners including the dam of the US Grade 1 winner Capote Belle. (Sheikh Hamdan Bin Mohammed Al Maktoum).

968. OPT OUT
ch.c. Pivotal – Easy Option (Prince Sabo). May 16. Half-brother to the Group 1 1m Sussex Stakes and Group 1 7f Prix de la Foret winner Court Masterpiece (by Polish Precedent), to the useful 6f (at 2 yrs) and 7f winner Easy Air, the French 5f winner (including at 2 yrs) Maybe Forever (both by Zafonic), the quite useful 2-y-o 7f winner Layali Al Arab (by Cape Cross), the quite useful 6f (at 2 yrs) and 7f winner

Generous Option (by Cadeaux Genereux) and the fair 6f winner Pride In Me (by Indian Ridge). The dam, a smart winner of the listed 5f St Hugh's Stakes and second in the Group 2 5f Prix du Gros-Chene, is a half-sister to 8 winners including the useful 2-y-o 5f winner and Group 2 Flying Childers Stakes third Wanton (herself dam of the Irish 1,000 Guineas winner Classic Park). The second dam, Brazen Faced (by Bold And Free), a quite useful 2-y-o 5f winner, is a half-sister to 8 winners including the Musidora Stakes winner Lovers Lane. (Sheikh Hamdan Bin Mohammed Al Maktoum).

969. OUTSET (USA)

h-und of by cl 5 nursery Gdwl.

ch.c. Street Boss – Now It Begins (Two Punch). April 4. First foal. $100,000Y. Fasig-Tipton Saratoga August. Blandford Bloodstock. The dam, a US stakes winner of 4 races, is a half-sister to 2 winners. The second dam, Carna (by Dehere), a minor winner in the USA at 3 and 4 yrs, is a half-sister to 6 winners including the US Grade 3 winner Algar. (Sheikh Hamdan Bin Mohammed Al Maktoum).

970. PARTY ROYAL

b.c. Royal Applause – Voliere (Zafonic). February 2. First foal. 30,000Y. Tattersalls October Book 2. Mark Johnston. The dam, a fairly useful listed-placed 9f and 10f winner, is a half-sister to 4 minor winners here and abroad. The second dam, Warbler (by Warning), a listed 11.5f winner in France, is a half-sister to 5 winners. (Mark Johnston Racing Ltd). *Won gd by cl 4 mln ago early y*

971. PENNY ROSE

b.f. Danehill Dancer – Love Everlasting (Pursuit Of Love). March 16. Sixth foal. 55,000Y. Tattersalls October Book 1. Mark Johnston. Closely related to Yours Ever (by Dansili), placed third over 7f and 1m on her two starts at 2 yrs in 2011 and half-sister to the fairly useful 12f winner and listed Cheshire Oaks second Acquainted (by Shamardal). The dam, a very useful 2-y-o 7.5f and 3-y-o listed 12f winner, is a half-sister to 6 winners including the smart Group 3 10f Scottish Classic winner Baron Ferdinand. The second dam, In Perpetuity (by Great Nephew), a fairly useful 10f winner, is a half-sister to 6 winners including the Derby winner Shirley Heights and to Bempton

(dam of the Group 2 winner Gull Nook and the Group 3 winners Mr Pintips and Banket). (Greenland Park Stud). *Won fair 7f fillies cnls Newbury*

972. PRIVATE CAPTAIN (IRE)

ch.c. Astronomer Royal – Private Whisper (Roar). March 14. First foal. 26,000Y. Tattersalls October Book 2. Mark Johnston. The dam won 3 minor races in the USA at 3 to 5 yrs and is a half-sister to 7 winners including the dam of the listed winners Lickety Lemon and Cry Of Freedom. The second dam, Salon Prive (by Private Account), is a placed half-sister to 5 winners including the Group 1 Prix Morny winners Seven Springs (dam of the Sussex Stakes winner Distant View) and Regal State (dam of the Dubai World Cup and Breeders Cup Classic winner Pleasantly Perfect). (J Abdullah).

973. SALUTATION (IRE)

b.c. Iffraaj – Totally Yours (Desert Sun). March 1. 78,000foal. Tattersalls December. John Ferguson. Half-brother to the fair 2011 5f placed 2-y-o Tahnee Mara (by Sleeping Indian) and to the fairly useful 7f (at 2 yrs) and 1m winner and listed-placed Totally Ours (by Singspiel). The dam, a quite useful 2-y-o 6f winner, is a half-sister to 3 winners including the 2-y-o Group 1 7f Dewhurst Stakes winner Tout Seul (by Ali-Royal). The second dam, Total Aloof (Groom Dancer), a fair dual 5f winner at 3 yrs, is a half-sister to 3 winners in Japan. (Sheikh Hamdan Bin Mohammed Al Maktoum).

974. SANDYS ROW (USA)

b.f. Street Cry – Carry On Katie (Fasliyev). February 22. Fifth foal. Half-sister to the useful 2011 2-y-o dual 5f winner and Group 3 6f Sirenia Stakes second Vocational (by Exceed And Excel). The dam won 3 races at 2 yrs including the Group 1 6f Cheveley Park Stakes and the Group 2 6f Lowther Stakes and is a half-sister to 2 winners. The second dam, Dinka Raja (by Woodman), a minor French 3-y-o 1m winner, is a half-sister to 3 winners. (Sheikh Hamdan Bin Mohammed Al Maktoum).

975. SKYTRAIN

ch.c. Exceed And Excel – Viola Da Braccio (Vettori). January 23. Fourth foal. €70,000Y.

Arqana Deauville August. Mark Johnston. Half-brother to the quite useful 6f (at 2 yrs) and 7f winner Bowmaker (by Dubawi) and to the fair 7f to 9f winner Sham Sheer (by Cape Cross). The dam, placed once at 3 yrs in France, is a half-sister to 5 winners including the dam of Rock Of Gibraltar. The second dam, Push A Button (by Bold Lad, Ire), won once at 2 yrs and is a half-sister to 6 winners including the French 2,000 Guineas winner and top-class sire Riverman. (A D Spence).

976. STORM MOON (USA)

b.c. Invincible Spirit – Storm Lily (Storm Cat). February 19. Second foal. Half-brother to the useful 2011 2-y-o dual 7f winner and listed second Gold City (by Pivotal). The dam is an unplaced half-sister to the useful 2-y-o dual 6f winner and Group 3 placed Crimson Sun. The second dam, Crimplene (by Lion Cavern), won the Irish 1,000 Guineas, the Coronation Stakes and the Nassau Stakes and is a half-sister to numerous winners including the smart Group 3 12.3f Chester Vase winner Dutch Gold. (Sheikh Hamdan Bin Mohammed Al Maktoum).

977. SUPEROO (IRE)

ch.c. Bahamian Bounty – Roo (Rudimentary). April 7. Seventh living foal. 40,000Y. Tattersalls October Book 2. Mark Johnston. Brother to the very smart 6f (at 2 yrs) and 7f winner and Group 2 Prix Morny second Gallagher and half-brother to the quite useful 2011 2-y-o 6f winner Cockney Dancer (by Cockney Rebel), the useful 7f (including at 2 yrs) and 1m winner Quick Wit (by Oasis Dream), the useful 5f (at 2 yrs) and 7f winner and listed-placed Roodeye (by Inchinor), the quite useful 7f (at 2 yrs), 10f and hurdles winner Roodolph (by Primo Valentino) and the fair 6f and 7f winner of 6 races and subsequent US stakes-placed Averoo (by Averti). The dam, a quite useful 2-y-o 5f and 6f winner, was listed-placed and is a half-sister to 5 winners including the Group 2 6f Gimcrack Stakes winner Bannister. The second dam, Shall We Run (by Hotfoot), placed once over 5f at 2 yrs, is a full or half-sister to 8 winners including the Group 1 6f Cheveley Park Stakes winner Dead Certain. (M J Pilkington).

978. TUSSIE MUSSIE

b.f. Royal Applause – Loveleaves (Polar Falcon). February 22. Sixth foal. 60,000Y. Tattersalls October Book 2. Mark Johnston. Sister to the very smart Group 2 1m Oettingen Rennen and Group 3 7f Supreme Stakes winner of 9 races Lovelace and half-sister to the quite useful 12f winner Greyfriars Drummer (by Where Or When), the fair 6f (at 2 yrs) to 1m winner of 4 races Avonrose (by Avonbridge) and a bumpers winner by Observatory. The dam, a fairly useful 8.3f winner, is closely related to the South African Group 3 winner Headstrong and a half-sister to 5 winners. The second dam, Rash (by Pursuit Of Love), is an unraced half-sister to 6 winners including the useful 2-y-o dual 6f winner Maid For The Hills and the useful 2-y-o 5f and 6f winner Maid For Walking (herself dam of the US Grade 1 winner Stroll) and to the placed High Savannah (the dam of three Group winners). (Mark Johnston Racing Ltd).

979. WINDHOEK

b.c. Cape Cross – Kahlua Kiss (Mister Baileys). February 3. First foal. 110,000Y. Tattersalls October Book 1. Mark Johnston. The dam, a fairly useful 7f (at 2 yrs) and 10f winner of 4 races, was listed-placed twice and is a half-sister to the 2-y-o winner and dual Group 3 placed Mister Genepi. The second dam, Ring Queen (by Fairy King), is an unraced half-sister to 8 winners including the US dual Grade 1 winner Special Ring. (Sheikh Hamdan Bin Mohammed Al Maktoum). *Ver gl bf m de or dobw Nott*

SYLVESTER KIRK

980. ADMIRALS WALK (IRE) ★★

b.c. Tagula – Very Racy (Sri Pekan). June 6. Seventh foal. 20,000Y. Tattersalls December. S Kirk. Half-brother to two minor winners in the USA by Clure and Anziyan. The dam, a minor winner in the USA, is a half-sister to 3 winners including the US stakes winner and multiple Graded stakes placed Dianehill. The second dam, Very Subtle (by Hoist The Silver), won four races including the 6f Breeders Cup Sprint, the 1m Hollywood Starlet Stakes and the 8.5f Fantasy Stakes (all Grade 1 events) and is a half-sister to 5 winners including the stakes winner Schematic. (N Pickett). *"A late foal, but he's very precocious mentally. Quite strong and mature, I might get him going in May over six furlongs".*

981. BANOVALLUM ★★★★

b.c. Invincible Spirit – Sinduda (Anabaa). March 23. Second foal. 95,000Y. Tattersalls October Book 1. Peter & Ross Doyle. The dam, a French 3-y-o 1m winner, is a half-sister to 8 winners including the very useful 2-y-o 5f and 6f winner and Cornwallis Stakes second Deadly Nightshade, the useful Irish 7f and 10f winner Hamad and the quite useful 6f winner Dodo (herself the dam of 2 stakes winners). The second dam, Dead Certain (by Absalom), a very smart winner of the Group 1 6f Cheveley Park Stakes, the Queen Mary Stakes, the Lowther Stakes (all at 2 yrs) and the Group 2 6.5f Prix Maurice de Gheest, is a half-sister to 7 winners. (Mr C Wright & the Hon Mrs J.B Corbett). *"He's just starting to grow a little bit, he's a really nice horse with a good attitude and he's getting stronger. I really like him and I might be able to get him started at six furlongs".*

982. EXOTIC LADY (IRE) ★★

b.br.f. Excellent Art – Princess Sabaah (Desert King). February 28. Fourth foal. 13,000Y. Tattersalls October Book 3. Not sold. Half-sister to the quite useful 9f winner Prince Sabaah (by Spectrum). The dam, a fairly useful 2-y-o 6f winner, is a half-sister to 2 winners including the fairly useful 6f (at 2 yrs) and dual 7f winner Oasis Star. The second dam, Sound Tap (by Warning), won 7 races in France from 6f to 1m and is a half-sister to 4 minor winners in Europe. (Mr D Brocock). *"A tall, leggy filly, she's straightforward and a beautiful mover but because of her size I'll have to hang on with her. One for the second half of the season".*

983. HURRICANE EMMA (USA) ★★★

b.br.f. Mr Greeley – Victorica (Exbourne). March 31. Eighth foal. €40,000Y. Goffs Orby. Rathmore Stud. Half-sister to the Irish 2-y-o listed 6f Rochestown Stakes winner and Group 3 Superlative Stakes third King Hesperus (by Kingmambo). The dam, a stakes winner of 5 races in the USA, was third in the Grade 3 Dogwood Stakes and is a half-sister to 5 winners including the French 2,000 Guineas second and Hollywood Derby third Noble Minstrel. The second dam, Noble Natisha (by Noble Commander), a stakes winner of 7 races in the USA, is a half-sister to 4 winners. (Ms C Cleary). *"A lovely filly, she's grown and*

lengthened and is the best-moving filly I've had for a long time. One for a bit later on, we'll take our time with her and she'll be a seven furlong type".*

984. LITTLE MISS ZURI (IRE) ★★★

ch.f. Choisir – Miss Kinabalu (Shirley Heights). March 4. Ninth foal. €16,000Y. Goffs Orby. S Kirk. Closely related to the Irish 2-y-o 5f winner and 6f listed-placed Joyce and to a winner in Hong Kong (both by Danehill Dancer) and half-sister to the fair 10f winner Miss Uluwatu (by Night Shift), the fair triple 1m winner Apres Ski (by Orpen), the modest sprint winner of 4 races Spinetail Rufus (by Prince Of Birds) and the Irish 9f to 12f winner of 3 races Miskilette (by Nicolotte). The dam was placed twice at up to 1m and is a half-sister to 4 minor winners here and abroad including Miss Ranjani (dam of the Group winners Asian Heights and St Expedit) and to the unraced dam of the very smart Group 3 6f Prix de Meautry winner Andreyev. The second dam, Miss Kuta Beach (by Bold Lad, Ire), a fairly useful 6f to 10f winner, is a half-sister to 8 winners. (I.A.N Wight). *"There are confusing messages because she's by Choisir, she's very sharp-looking and there's plenty of speed in the pedigree, but she's also out of a Shirley Heights mare which should slow things down a bit. I've only just started to do anything with her, so we'll just see how she goes on".*

985. ROYAL BAR ★★★★ ♠

b.c. Royal Applause – Our Faye (College Chapel). January 29. First foal. £38,000Y. Doncaster Premier. Peter & Ross Doyle. The dam, a fairly useful winner of 7 races from 6f to 1m including the Group 3 Summer Stakes, is a half-sister to one winner. The second dam, Tamara (by Marju), a fairly useful 2-y-o 5f winner, is a half-sister to 2 winners. (Mr H Balasuriya). *"A nice horse out of a filly I trained to win seven races. This colt is sharp and early and I'll try to get a run into him in May, just to see if he's good enough to get to Royal Ascot.*

986. SECRET REBEL ★★★

ch.c. Sakhee's Secret – Indiana Blues (Indian Ridge). February 21. Half-brother to the quite useful dual 7f winner (including at 2 yrs) Norse Blues (by Norse Dancer). The dam, a fair 6f winner, is a half-sister to several winners including the useful 2-y-o listed 5.2f winner and Group 2 Flying Childers Stakes third Speed Cop and the fairly useful triple 5f winner (including at 2 yrs) and listed-placed Siren's Gift. The second dam, Blue Siren (by Bluebird), a very useful winner of three races from 5f to 7f, was disqualified from first place in two more, notably the Group 1 5f Nunthorpe Stakes (the winner on merit) and is a half-sister to several winners including the quite useful 9f winner Northern Habit. (Mr J C Smith). *"A huge horse, but he's very precocious and if he wasn't so big I'd be cracking on with him. He can lead the string already, he's forward-going and I like him but I need to hang on to him for a bit. Everything he's done so far has been straightforward".*

987. SEE AND BE SEEN ★★★

b.c. Sakhee's Secret – Anthea (Tobougg). March 22. Second foal. 13,000Y. Tattersalls October Book 3. S Kirk. Half-brother to the unplaced 2011 2-y-o Aloysia (by Amadeus Wolf). The dam, a modest 7f (at 2 yrs) to 10f placed maiden, is a half-sister to 2 winners including the useful 1m (at 2 yrs) and subsequent US Grade 3 winner Genre. The second dam, Blue Indigo by Pistolet Bleu), was placed 5 times in France and is a half-sister to 6 winners. (Mr T Pearson). *"He keeps growing all the time. I had his half-sister last year who was small but he's a stronger model and I'm just doing a bit of work with him now. Probably one for six or seven furlongs a bit later on".*

988. SHOW MORE FAITH ★★★

b.c. Pastoral Pursuits – Lalina (Trempolino). March 28. Third foal. 21,000Y. Tattersalls October Book 3. Peter & Ross Doyle. Half-brother to the modest 2-y-o 7f winner Wotsthehurry (by Proclamation). The dam, a minor winner at 3 yrs in Germany, is a half-sister to the German winner and Group 3 second Lancetto. The second dam, Lanciana (by Acatenango), a minor winner of 2 races in France and Germany, was listed-placed and is a half-sister to 3 winners including the German Group 2 winner Lanciano. (R Hannon & I.A.N Wight). *"He's the most improved 2-y-o I've got because he was very weak at first and now he's just blossomed and come to himself, so I couldn't be happier with him. He's turned into a*

good-looking horse and I might even start him at six furlongs because he's showing up well".

989. SOMETHING MAGIC ★★★★

b.f. Proud Citizen – Comeback Queen (Nayef). March 23. First foal. The dam, a fairly useful 2-y-o 1m winner, was listed-placed and is a half-sister to numerous winners including the high-class 2-y-o Grade 1 1m Breeders Cup Juvenile winner Donativum, the useful 2-y-o 7f winner Tasdeed and the 2-y-o 8.6f and subsequent dual US Grade 3 winner Worldly. The second dam, Miss Universe (by Warning), a useful 2-y-o 6f winner and third in the Group 3 Solario Stakes, is a half-sister to 5 winners including the useful German 7f (at 2 yrs) to 11f winner Silver Sign. (Chris Wright). *"She's quite precocious mentally and she's forward-going, but physically she needs to improve. A filly with a lovely pedigree, I could run her anytime but I'll let her come to herself and she'll be nice a bit later on".*

990. STAR BREAKER ★★★

b.c. Teofilo – Bunditten (Soviet Star). January 23. Fourth foal. 50,000foal. Tattersalls December. Littleton Stud. Half-brother to the quite useful 2011 2-y-o 5f winner Airborne Again (by Acclamation). The dam, a fairly useful 2-y-o 5f winner, was listed-placed and fourth in the Group 3 5f Queen Mary Stakes and a half-sister to 3 winners. The second dam, Felicita (by Catrail), won 3 races in France at 2 yrs including two 5f listed events, was Group 3 placed and is a half-sister to 5 winners. (J C Smith). *"He's precocious and I might give him a try in May just to see if he's good enough for Royal Ascot. He might just be a nice horse".*

991. UNNAMED ★★★

b.c. Medaglia d'Oro – Becky In Pink (Formal Gold). March 4. Third foal. 85,000Y. Tattersalls October Book 1. Peter & Ross Doyle. Half-brother to a winner in Russia by Saint Liam. The dam, a listed stakes winner of 7 races from 2 to 4 yrs in the USA, is a sister to the US Grade 3 winner and Grade 2 placed Miss Matched and a half-sister to 6 winners. The second dam, Ivory Princess (by Cure The Blues), a listed stakes winner of 8 races in the USA, is a half-sister to 13 winners. (Mr H Balasuriya). *"A smashing horse, he's backward and has sore* shins at the moment. *He's heavy topped and I'll have to try and keep the weight off him, but he's a beautiful mover and has a great attitude. One for the second half of the season".*

992. UNNAMED ★★★
b.f. Indesatchel – Four Legs Good (Be My Guest). January 24. Seventh foal. 5,500Y. Tattersalls October 3. S Kirk. Sister to the fair 2011 2-y-o 6f winner The Noble Ord and half-sister to the fairly useful 6f and 7f winner of 9 races Bennlech (by Lujain) and to the fair 5f (at 2 yrs) and 7f winner of 4 races Perfect Friend (by Reel Buddy). The dam is an unplaced half-sister to 4 minor winners here and abroad. The second dam, Karine (by Habitat), ran twice unplaced and is a half-sister to the Group 3 Oaks Trial winner Heaven Knows and to the Irish listed winner Kizzy. *"I've had all the family and this is a nice filly too. She's a bit leggier and leaner than the others, but she was cheap, she has ability and I'm happy to keep her myself, win a race with her and then sell her. She's done one piece of work and she went well, so I could run her whenever I want to".* TRAINERS' BARGAIN BUY

993. UNNAMED ★★★
ch.c. Sakhee's Secret – Intermission (Royal Applause). January 29. First foal. 25,000Y. Tattersalls October Book 3. Peter & Ross Doyle. The dam is an unraced half-sister to the US Grade 1 Citation Handicap and dual Grade 2 winner Ashkal Way. The second dam, Golden Way (by Cadeaux Genereux), a fairly useful 10.5f winner, is a half-sister to 8 winners including the useful Polish Spring (a winner here and a dual US stakes winner) and the French listed 11f winner and Group 3 placed Go Boldly. (Verano Quartet). *"He's a smashing horse that's just coming to himself. He's strong and we're just about to start working him to see how he copes. I like him, he's a good-looking horse and a real 'Richard Hannon' type".*

994. UNNAMED ★★
ch.c. Ad Valorem – Lapis Lazuli (Rainbow Quest). April 12. Fifth living foal. €10,000Y. Tattersalls Ireland. S Kirk. Half-brother to the quite useful 2011 Irish 2-y-o 6f winner Sophies Echo (by Footstepsinthesand). The dam is an unraced half-sister to 3 winners. The second dam, Nimphidia (by Nijinsky), a useful triple 6f winner (including at 2 yrs), was third in the Group 3 Phoenix Sprint Stakes and is a half-sister to 7 winners including Dancing Dissident (Group 3 Temple Stakes). *"He'll probably be the first 2-y-o I run. He's big and strong with a big backside and he's behaving like an early 2-y-o".*

995. UNNAMED ★★
b.f. Rock Of Gibraltar – Yaky Romani (Victory Note). April 13. Third foal. €15,000Y. Tattersalls Ireland. Peter & Ross Doyle. Half-sister to the placed 2011 Italian 2-y-o Yaky Mahori (by Oratorio). The dam won 10 races from 2 to 6 yrs in Italy and is a half-sister to 5 winners including the Group 3 winning sprinter Al Qasi. The second dam, Delisha (by Salse), won once at 3 yrs in Germany and is a half-sister to 6 winners including the Group 1 Hong Kong Mile winner Ecclesiastical. *"A smashing filly, if I'd have sold her earlier she'd have been ready now. But she'll start over six furlongs no bother because she's sharp enough. A nice filly".*

WILLIAM KNIGHT
996. AEOLIAN BLUE ★★
ch.f. Bahamian Bounty – Blue Mistral (Spinning World). February 12. Second foal. 10,000Y. Tattersalls October Book 3. Blandford Bloodstock. Half-sister to the unplaced 2011 2-y-o Raffinn (by Sakhee). The dam, a modest 1m and 10f winner, is a half-sister to winners including the useful 6f winner of 6 races (including at 2 yrs) and listed-placed Johannes. The second dam, Blue Sirocco (by Bluebird), ran once unplaced and is a half-sister to 8 winners including the listed 7f winner and Group 1 7f Moyglare Stud Stakes second Tamnia, the Group 2 13.3f Geoffrey Freer Stakes winner Azzilfi and the Group 3 15f Coppa d'Oro di Milano winner Khamaseen. (Mrs S M Mitchell). *"I trained the dam and she's quite similar to her. I don't think she's going to be too early because she's just growing a bit. I can see her being a fast ground 2-y-o around July or August time over seven furlongs and a mile. I don't think she'll be a world beater, but I think she'll win her races".*

997. AUSSIE REIGNS (IRE) ★★★

b.c. Aussie Rules – Rohain (Singspiel). April 15. Second foal. €36,000Y. Goffs Orby. Portanova Bloodstock. The dam is an unraced half-sister to the useful listed 1m winner of 3 races Zayn Zen and to the fairly useful winner and listed-placed Zaafran. The second dam, Roshani (by Kris), a fair 1m and 10f winner at 3 yrs, is a half-sister to 8 minor winners here and in the USA. (The Old Brokers). *"He should be my earliest 2-y-o and he's a well put-together, mature, medium-sized colt. He has a very good temperament, has done everything asked of him at the moment and I would hope he'll be starting off in May over six furlongs".*

Wor 7f NAWWY G. GLWA

998. EXCLUSIVE WATERS (IRE) ★★★

b.c. Elusive City – Pelican Waters (Key Of Luck). May 11. Second foal. €50,000Y. Goffs Orby. Portanova Bloodstock. The dam, a fairly useful 9.5f winner, is a half-sister to 2 winners. The second dam, Orlena (by Gone West), a minor 2-y-o 7f winner in France, is a half-sister to 6 winners including the listed winner and 1,000 Guineas third Vista Bella. (The Old Brokers). *"He's a big lad and a May foal so I haven't rushed him, but he'll probably be a mid-season 2-y-o over seven furlongs and want a mile next year. I quite like him, he's got a big back-end, a good temperament and has done everything right so far".*

999. KEEP THE SECRET ★★★★

ch.f. Sakhee's Secret – Starfleet (Inchinor). February 14. Fifth living foal. 19,000Y. Tattersalls October Book 2. Portanova Bloodstock. Half-sister to the useful 2-y-o 7f and subsequent US Grade 2 San Francisco Mile winner Mr Napper Tandy (by Bahamian Bounty) and to the quite useful 1m to 10f winner of 5 races Wind Star (by Piccolo). The dam, a modest maiden, was placed over 7f and 10f and is a half-sister to 6 winners including the listed National Stakes winner Pool Music. The second dam, Sunfleet (by Red Sunset), is a placed half-sister to 7 winners including the Group 3 Curragh Stakes winner Peace Girl. (Mrs N J Welby). *"She's a really nice mover but she's grown a lot and has a lot of scope. I still think she'll make a 2-y-o around mid-season, over seven furlongs to begin with. I like her and think she has a bit of class".* TRAINERS' BARGAIN BUY

1000. MOTION LASS ★★★

b.f. Motivator – Tarneem (Zilzal). March 6. Eleventh foal. 16,000Y. Tattersalls October Book 2. Not sold. Half-sister to the smart 7f (at 2 yrs) and Group 3 9f Darley Stakes winner and Group 1 Coronation Cup third Enforcer, to the quite useful 2-y-o dual 5f winner Lord Of The Inn, the modest 1m winner Uncle Brit (all by Efisio), the fair dual 10f winner Canaveral (by Cape Cross), the fair 5.7f winner Innstyle (by Daggers Drawn) and the Italian winner of 9 races at up to 13.5f Kris's Bank (by Inchinor). The dam, a quite useful 3-y-o 1m winner, is a half-sister to 4 minor winners abroad. The second dam, Willowy Mood (by Will Win), won 14 races including two Grade 3 events in the USA and is a half-sister to 9 winners. (R C Tooth). *"I don't expect we'll see her out before August time. She just needs to relax a bit on the gallops – I'm not worried about it but she just tries to do a bit too much at present. She's going to want a trip next year, but I reckon we bought her well and although she has a pedigree to suggest she'll make a nice 3-y-o I can certainly see her winning this year over seven furlongs or a mile".*

1001. WHIPPER SNAPPER ★★★

b.c. Whipper – Topiary (Selkirk). April 14. Fifth foal. 32,000Y. Tattersalls December. Portanova Bloodstock. Brother to the fairly useful triple 6f winner (including at 2 yrs) Gramercy and half-brother to the fair 2011 dual 7f placed 2-y-o Berwin (by Lawman) and the quite useful 7f (at 2 yrs) and 6f winner Bassett Road (by Byron). The dam, a minor winner in France at 3 yrs, is a half-sister to 4 winners including the French dual Group 3 winner Top Toss. The second dam, Tossup (by Gone West), won the listed Irish 1,000 Guineas Trial and is a full or half-sister to 6 winners. (The Oil Merchants). *"A likeable colt, he's not over-big and he was a late foal that we bought at the December Sales so I haven't rushed him. I can see him being out in July/ August time, he has a nice action and his full brother turned into a nice horse. I think he has a bit of class".*

DANIEL KUBLER

Dan and his partner Claire Middlebrook have recently set up their first training yard at Whitsbury Manor in Hampshire – a beautiful place to train racehorses. They've learned their trade from a long list of top-class trainers and bloodstock experts over the past few years. People like the Queen's bloodstock advisor John Warren, Roger Charlton, Jeremy Noseda, Francis Doumen, California-based trainers Ben Cecil and Paddy Gallagher and the champion Australian trainer Gai Waterhouse – an impressive list if ever there was one. Despite all that, setting up a training yard on their own must be a scary, if exciting venture, but they've started well because from a small string they've had a winner already. I do hope they have plenty of success this season and who knows – in ten years time they may find themselves in a similar position that their mentors occupy right now.

1002. GHETTO DIVA ★★★

b.f. *Compton Place – Like A Virgin (Iron Mask)*. January 23. Second foal. 8,000Y. Tattersalls October Book 2. Kubler Racing. Half-sister to the unplaced 2011 2-y-o King Fong (by Dr Fong). The dam, placed once at 2 yrs in Italy, is a half-sister to 4 winners. The second dam, Future Treasure (by Habitat), won over 7f at 3 yrs on her only start and is a half-sister to 8 winners. *"She just went a bit weak on us so we backed off her a bit, otherwise she would have been early. We're about to start her off again, she's well put-together and it's a nice family further back so we were pleased to get her for only 8,000gns. A January foal, she ought to make a 2-y-o by mid-season over five/six furlongs but she isn't just an early 2-y-o type, so she ought to go on as a 3-y-o as well".*

1003. MONT SIGNAL ★★★

ch.c. *Pivotal – Anse Victorin (Mt Livermore)*. March 24. Second foal. 55,000Y. Tattersalls October Book 1. BBA (Ire). Half-brother to the unplaced 2011 2-y-o Surrey Spirit (by Invincible Spirit). The dam is an unraced half-sister to 10 winners including the French Oaks, French 1,000 Guineas, Prix Marcel Boussac, Prix d'Astarte and Prix Morny winner (all Group 1's) Divine Proportions and the Prix Jacques Le Marois, Prix Maurice de Gheest and Prix Morny winner (all Group1's) Whipper. The second dam, Myth To Reality (by Sadler's Wells), a triple listed winner of 4 races at 3 yrs in France, was second in the Group 3 Prix de Minerve and is a full or half-sister to 6 winners. *"A well put-together little*

colt, I see him being out in mid-season and he's from a fantastic family. Although he's by Pivotal who doesn't get that many forward types, you would think he'd make a reasonably nice 2-y-o. I think we'll start him over six furlongs and then step him up to seven".*

1004. MULTI FOURS ★★

ch.f. *Medicean – Spiralling (Pivotal)*. February 20. Second foal. 8,000Y. Tattersalls October Book 2. Kubler Racing. Sister to Master Chipper, unplaced on his only start at 2 yrs in 2011. The dam is an unraced half-sister to 4 winners. The second dam, River Saint (by Irish River), is a placed half-sister to 5 winners including the multiple US Grade 1 winner Serena's Song (herself the dam of 4 Group winners including Group 1 Coronation Stakes winner Sophisticat). (Michael Grayson & Ian O'Brien). *"She's well put-together but through having had a setback she's had some time off and she's grown a lot in the meantime. There's quite a bit of the damsire Pivotal about her I think, she's just started cantering again now and she's quite green, so we haven't done enough with her to comment on how good she is. You're probably looking at July or August before she's out, but I think she was well-bought considering her half-brother brought 34,000 as a foal last year".*

1005. ROSACEOUS ★★

ch.f. *Duke Of Marmalade – Briery (Salse)*. April 3. Sixth foal. Half-sister to the quite useful 6f and 7f winner of 6 races Great Charm (by Orpen), to the quite useful 7f to 15f winner of 5 races Fregate Island, the fair 10f, 11f and hurdles winner Pearl (both by Daylami) and the Swiss 2-y-o winner Story Of Dubai (by Dubai Destination). The dam, a modest 3-y-o 7f winner, is out of the unraced Wedgewood (by Woodman), herself a half-sister to 10 minor winners. *"Quite a big filly, but she's well-balanced and straightforward. She's lovely and although some of the family can be a bit hot-headed she's not that way at all. She takes everything in her stride and although she'll definitely train on to be a lovely 3-y-o I wouldn't be surprised if we got her out at the end of May or the beginning of June. She seems to find it all easy, we're not going to rush her but when she's ready we'll start her off at six furlongs".*

DAVID LANIGAN

1006. BRAVESTAR (IRE) ★★★★

b.c. Lawman – High Fidelity (Peintre Celebre). March 26. Second foal. 80,000Y. Tattersalls October Book 1. Charlie Gordon-Watson. The dam, a minor French 12f winner, is a half-sister to 5 winners including the multiple Group 1 winner Hurricane Run and the German Group 3 winner and Group 1 Europa Preis second Hibiscus. The second dam, Hold On (by Surumu), a listed winner in Germany at 3 yrs, is a half-sister to 7 winners including the German Group winners Hondo Mondo and Hondero. *"A nice horse that goes well, he's a horse that I like and he's doing everything alright. He's bred for middle-distances but he looks much sharper than that, so hopefully he'll be out by mid-summer".*

1007. BRIGHT GLOW ★★★

ch.f. Exceed And Excel – Lighthouse (Warning). February 13. Eighth foal. 170,000Y. Tattersalls October Book 1. J Brummitt. Half-sister to the very useful 7f and 1m winner Kehaar, to the fairly useful 2-y-o 5f winner and listed placed All For Laura (herself dam of the Group 2 Cherry Hinton Stakes winner Misheer), the fair 6f (at 2 yrs) and 1m winner Present Danger (all by Cadeaux Genereux), the fair 10f to 12f and hurdles winner Point Of Light (by Pivotal) and a minor US winner at 4 yrs by Barathea. The dam, a fairly useful 3-y-o 8.3f winner, is a half-sister to 4 winners including the Group 1 Middle Park Stakes, Group 3 July Stakes and Group 3 Richmond Stakes winner First Trump. The second dam, Valika (by Valiyar), was placed three times from 1m to 12f at 3 yrs and is a half-sister to 6 winners including the high-class sprinter Mr Brooks. *"I was hoping she'd be early but she's a bit light and I've backed off her a bit. One for six furlongs in mid-season and she's doing alright".*

1008. INTERCEPTION ★★★

ch.f. Raven's Pass – Badee'a (Marju). March 29. Fifth foal. 160,000Y. Tattersalls October Book 1. J Brummitt. Half-sister to the smart multiple listed 7f and 1m winner Dunelight (by Desert Sun), to the very useful dual 7f and subsequent UAE winner Leahurst (by Verglas) and the fair 2-y-o 6f winner Writingonthewall (by Danetime). The dam is an unraced sister

to the Group 3 Prix Quincey winner Mahboob and a half-sister to 4 winners. The second dam, Miss Gris (by Hail The Pirates), won the Group 1 Italian 1,000 Guineas and the Group 1 Italian Oaks and is a half-sister to two US stakes winners. *"She had a little setback but it won't affect her for the season and she looks a 2-y-o type. A compact and racey filly, I'll be getting on with her now".*

1009. MASQUERADING ★★★

b.c. Singspiel – Moonlight Dance (Alysheba). May 15. Half-brother to the listed winner and Group 1 French Oaks second Millionaia (by Peintre Celebre), to the 2-y-o 7f winner and Group 1 7f Dewhurst Stakes second Fencing Master (by Oratorio), the French 2-y-o 1m winner and Group 3 second Memory Maker (by Lure), the minor French winner Maitre du Jeu (by Rock Of Gibraltar) and the 10f winner Memoire (by Sadler's Wells). The dam, winner of the Group 1 10f Prix Saint-Alary, is a half-sister to the Dante Stakes winner Claude Monet and the smart winners Magdalena and Marignan. The second dam, Madelia (by Caro), won the French 1,000 Guineas, the Prix Saint-Alary and the Prix de Diane and is a half-sister to the Prix du Moulin winner Mount Hagen and two other good French horses in Monsanto and Malecite. (B E Nielsen). *"He had a setback but it wasn't too serious and the time off has done him good. He's about to start cantering again now, being by Singspiel you'd expect him to be a later type and he's a scopey colt that should be alright".*

1010. NO JET LAG (IRE) ★★★★

b.c. Johar – Desert Sky (Green Desert). January 24. Fourth foal. Half-brother to the French 2-y-o dual 6f winner and Group 3 6f Prix de Cabourg third Optari (by Diesis). The dam, a 2-y-o listed 6f Silver Flash Stakes winner, is a sister to the 6f winner and listed placed Moonis and a half-sister to 2 winners. The second dam, Badrah (by Private Account), is a placed half-sister to 5 winners including the Group 3 Brigadier Gerard Stakes winner Husyan. *"A nice horse, he goes well and although he's not the best walker he moves very well in his faster paces. He's done very well and I think he's a horse we can have some fun with from June onwards. He does everything nicely and even*

*Won fair. If same mdn Lingfield
2nd race well backed fav*

DAVID LANIGAN **213**

though he's a big horse he carries himself well, so he's a nice type".

1011. NUR JAHAN ★★

b.f. *Selkirk – Have Faith (Machiavellian)*. January 27. Fourth foal. 180,000Y. Tattersalls October Book 1. Charlie Gordon-Watson. Half-sister to the quite useful 7f and 1m winner and listed-placed Faithful One (by Dubawi) and to a winner in Qatar by Cape Cross. The dam, a quite useful 2-y-o 7f winner, is a sister to the useful UAE winner of 7 races and Group 3 third Opportunist and a half-sister to the Group 1 Nassau Stakes and Group 2 1m Matron Stakes winner Favourable Terms and the French listed winner Modern History. The second dam, Fatefully (by Private Account), a smart winner of 4 races at 3 yrs including two listed events over 1m, is a half-sister to 6 winners including the Canadian Grade 2 winner Points Of Grace. *"A big, backward filly that goes very well, but she just wants minding this season because she'll be a better 3-y-o. She does everything well, but she's very tall and needs to strengthen so if I can get her out in September this year I'd be delighted".*

1012. PINK ANEMONE ★★

b.f. *Dansili – Crystal Reef (King's Best)*. March 24. First foal. 45,000Y. Tattersalls October Book 1. Not sold. The dam was placed at 3 yrs in France and is a half-sister to 5 winners including Reefscape (Group 1 Prix du Cadran) and the Group 2 winners Coastal Path and Mortaline. The second dam, Coraline (by Sadler's Wells), won over 12f in France and is a full or half-sister to 6 winners including the Group 1 Irish Oaks winner Wemyss Bight (herself dam of the multiple Group 1 winner Beat Hollow) and to the unplaced dam of the Group 1 winners Oasis Dream and Zenda. *"A nice sort but backward and immature. Hopefully she'll be a nice type later in the season over seven furlongs plus".*

1013. TYPHON ★★★

b.c. *Proud Citizen – Seven Moons (Sunday Silence)*. April 29. Fifth foal. Half-brother to the quite useful 12f winner Protaras (by Lemon Drop Kid) and to the fair triple 7f winner Alpha Tauri (by Aldebaran). The dam is a half-sister to a 10f winner in France. The second dam, Moon Is Up (by Woodman), a listed 1m winner and

Group 3 placed in France, is closely related to the French 2,000 Guineas, the St James's Palace Stakes and Prix du Moulin winner Kingmambo and the smart Group 3 6f Prix de Ris-Oranges winner Miesque's Son and a half-sister to the high-class French 1,000 Guineas, Prix de Diane and Prix Jacques le Marois winner East of the Moon. (Niarchos Family). *"He's done really well since I saw him at the farm in America where he as very tall and leggy. He's strengthening up and improving all the time now, but you won't see him out until September. He's pleasing me the longer I have him".*

1014. UNNAMED ★★★

b.c. *Mujadil – Bradamante (Sadler's Wells)*. February 24. Fourth foal. 50,000Y. Tattersalls October Book 2. J Brummitt. The dam, a French 2-y-o 1m winner, is a half-sister to 3 winners including the listed Godolphin Stakes winner and Group 2 placed Galactic Star. The second dam, Balisada (by Kris), won the Group 1 1m Coronation Stakes and is a half-sister to 2 winners. *"A nice sort of horse, he's cantering now, I haven't done a lot with him but he should be out around June time. A 2-y-o type".*

1015. UNNAMED ★★

b.c. *Galileo – Egyptian Queen (Storm Cat)*. January 29. Third foal. $525,000Y. Fasig-Tipton Saratoga August. R V La Penta. Closely related to the minor US 3-y-o winner Turns My Head (by Montjeu). The dam is an unraced half-sister to the US dual Grade 2 winner A P Warrior. The second dam, Warrior Queen (by Quiet American), winner of the listed 6f Round Tower Stakes in Ireland and third in the Group 3 5f Queen Mary Stakes, is a half-sister to 4 winners. *"A very good-looking and attractive horse, but he's very big and backward. He has a nice action but he'll take time because he's as big as any of the 2-y-o's I have and if I get him out in September I'll be happy".*

1016. UNNAMED ★★★

br.c. *Monsun – Geminiani (King Of Kings)*. May 8. Sixth foal. 80,000Y. Tattersalls October Book 1. Charlie Gordon-Watson. Half-brother to the fairly useful 11f and 14f winner and Group 3 2m Queen's Vase second Amerigo (by Daylami). The dam, winner of the Group 3 7f Prestige Stakes and second in the Group 3 Musidora

Stakes, is a half-sister to 4 winners including the 2-y-o Group 1 6f Phoenix Stakes and Group 2 5f Queen Mary Stakes winner Damson (herself dam of the Group 3 Molecomb Stakes winner Requinto). The second dam, Tadkiyra (by Darshaan), won over 10f at 3 yrs in France and is a half-sister to 8 winners including the Group 3 winners Tashtiya, Tassmoun and Tashkourgan. *"A nice horse and I like him, he goes very well but he'll be a back-end 2-y-o and is more of a 3-y-o type. He does everything nicely and he's an attractive colt, but being by Monsun he'll probably want two or three runs this year before we put him away".*

1017. UNNAMED ★★★
b.c. Compton Place – Guermantes (Distant Relative). February 14. Sixth foal. 58,000foal. Tattersalls December. Yeomanstown Stud. Half-brother to the very useful French 5f to 10f winner of 6 races and Group 1 Prix de l'Abbaye third Mar Adentro (by Marju), to the quite useful 2-y-o 5f winner Kinlochrannoch (by Kyllachy) and the minor French 3-y-o winner Encanto (by Singspiel). The dam, a listed-placed French winner at 2 and 3 yrs, is a half-sister to 4 winners including the smart 7.2f (at 2 yrs) and Group 3 1m Leopardstown 2,000 Guineas Trial winner Yasoodd and to the French listed 1m Prix Montenica winner Gript. The second dam, Needwood Epic (Midyan), a modest 14f winner, is a half-sister to 7 winners. *"Not as forward as I'd hoped he'd be, but he's going along doing two canters at the moment and he's fine. A nice little horse that will hopefully make a 2-y-o in July or August".*

1018. UNNAMED ★★★
b.br.f. Street Cry – Meribel (Peaks And Valleys). March 2. First foal. $110,000Y. Keeneland September. David Lanigan. The dam, a US Grade 3 winner and placed in three Grade 2 events, is a half-sister to the US stakes winner Knox. The second dam, Count To Six (by Saratoga Six), a minor US winner of 7 races from 2 to 5yrs, is a half-sister to 6 winners. *"She's a nice filly that was very backward at the sales. She's going along nicely and she should make a 2-y-o around six or seven furlongs".*

1019. UNNAMED ★★★
b.f. Cape Cross – Nantyglo (Mark Of Esteem). March 28. Third foal. 95,000Y. Tattersalls October Book 1. Tally-Ho Stud. Half-sister to the moderate 9f winner Valley Tiger (by Tiger Hill). The dam, a useful 6f (at 2 yrs) and listed 1m winner, was third in the Group 2 6f Mill Reef Stakes and is a half-sister to 3 minor winners. The second dam, Bright Halo (by Bigstone), a minor French 3-y-o 9f winner, is a half-sister to 8 winners including the Group 1 Irish Oaks winner Moonstone, the Breeders Cup second L'Ancresse and the Group 1 10f Prix Saint-Alary winner Cerulean Sky (herself dam of the Group 2 Doncaster Cup winner Honolulu). *"A nice filly that's going through a bit of a growth spurt now. She's a filly I like and she's going the right way so I should think she'll start off at seven furlongs this year".*

1020. UNNAMED ★★★
ch.c. Danehill Dancer – One So Wonderful (Nashwan). February 26. Seventh foal. 210,000Y. Tattersalls October Book 1. Charlie Gordon-Watson. Half-brother to the US Grade 2 8.5f winner Sun Boat, to the modest French 10f winner Alqaayid (both by Machiavellian) and the fair 9f winner Sensationally (by Montjeu). The dam won the Group 1 Juddmonte International Stakes and the Group 2 Sun Chariot Stakes and is a half-sister to 8 winners including the Rockfel Stakes winner Relatively Special and the Dante Stakes and Craven Stakes winner Alnasr Alwasheek. The second dam, Someone Special (by Habitat), won over 7f, was third in the Coronation Stakes and is a half-sister to the Queen Elizabeth II Stakes winner Milligram. *"A big horse, he had a lot of daylight under him when he came from the sales but he's done nothing but improve and furnish. He's one for September onwards, he goes very well and he'll strengthen up into a nice 3-y-o. The more we get into the summer the more we'll know about him, but he has done well".*

1021. UNNAMED ★★
b.c. Dansili – Palmeraie (Lear Fan). February 15. Half-brother to the multiple French Group 2 middle-distance winner Policy Maker (by Sadler's Wells), to the very useful listed 11f winner Place Rouge (by Desert King), the useful 1m (at 2 yrs) and listed 2m winner

Pushkin (by Caerleon), the quite useful 11f and 12f winner Planetoid (by Galileo), the French middle-distance winners Pinacotheque (by In The Wings) and Petrograd (by Peintre Celebre), the French 2-y-o 1m winner Palme Royale (by Red Ransom). The dam is a half-sister to the Grade 2 12f Long Island Handicap winner Peinture Bleue (herself dam of the Prix de l'Arc de Triomphe winner Peintre Celebre), to the US Grade 3 1m William P Kyne Handicap winner Provins, the Irish 2-y-o winner and Group 3 Gladness Stakes second Chateau Royal and the Group 3 11f Andre Baboin winner Parme. The second dam, Petroleuse (by Habitat), won the Group 3 8.5f Princess Elizabeth Stakes and the 6f Blue Seal Stakes and is a half-sister to Pawneese (winner of the King George VI and Queen Elizabeth Stakes, the Oaks and the Prix de Diane). (Mr B Nielsen). *"A nice horse, he's much bigger and stronger than anything else we've had out of the family. He's going to be a 3-y-o but I'd like to think he'll have enough ability to be out this year from September onwards".*

1022. UNNAMED ★★★★★
b.c. *Shamardal – Prima Luce (Galileo).* March 22. First foal. 330,000Y. Tattersalls October Book 1. Blandford Bloodstock. The dam, a useful Group 3 7f Athasi Stakes winner, was second in the Group 3 Solonaway Stakes and is a half-sister to 4 minor winners. The second dam, Ramona (by Desert King), is an unraced half-sister to 9 winners including the Group 2 5f Kings Stand Stakes winner Cassandra Go (herself dam of the triple Group 1 winner Halfway To Heaven) and the smart Group 3 6f Coventry Stakes winner and Irish 2,000 Guineas second Verglas. *"A horse I like a lot and hopefully he'll make a nice 2-y-o. He looks very strong and scopey, but I think the further we get into the summer the better he'll be because there's a lot of stamina in the female side of the pedigree. A nice type, he's the spitting image of his father, he could start off at six furlongs but if we do wait a bit we won't miss the boat because he's very likeable".*

1023. UNNAMED ★★★
b.c. *Dansili – Private Life (Bering).* April 6. Half-brother to the 7f (at 2 yrs) and dual German Group 3 10f winner Persian Storm (by Monsun).

The dam won over 1m (at 2 yrs) and 12f and was listed-placed twice in France and is a half-sister to the French listed winners Pretty Tough and Parisienne. The second dam, Poughkeepsie (by Sadler's Wells), won once at 3 yrs in France and is a daughter of the King George and Oaks winner Pawneese. (B E Nielsen). *"A nice type of horse that's done well since he came in. I'd like to see him out in July or August and he's done well".*

GER LYONS
1024. ABBEY VALE (IRE) ★★★ ♠
b.c. *Moss Vale – Cloonkeary (In The Wings).* April 20. Second foal. £15,000Y. Doncaster Premier. BBA (Ire). The dam is an unraced half-sister to 6 winners including the listed winner Esyoueffcee. The second dam, Familiar (by Diesis), a fairly useful 3-y-o 1m winner, is a half-sister to 8 winners including the high-class Prix du Moulin winner and Epsom Oaks second All At Sea and the smart French dual Group 3 winner Over The Ocean. (Mr V Gaul). *"A lovely, big, scopey 2-y-o. I like him, he does his job well and I'd like to run him over six/seven furlongs from the end of May".*

1025. BEATBOXING (USA) ★★
b.c. *Street Sense – Make My Heart Sing (King Of Kings).* March 14. Brother to Layali Dubai, unplaced in 2 starts at 2 yrs in 2011. The dam, a stakes winner of 3 races at 3 and 4 yrs in the USA, is a half-sister to 3 winners. The second dam, Songlines (by Diesis), a stakes winner of 7 races and Grade 2 placed, is a half-sister to 2 winners. (Sheikh Mohammed). *"A huge horse, hopefully he's done all his growing and although he has ability he won't be out until the end of the season. I'm very pleased with my 2-y-o's but I haven't pressed any buttons with them yet and a lot of them won't appear until mid-season. I'll be disappointed if we don't have a few black-type horses amongst them though".*

1026. BUMBLE BEE SLIM ★★★
ch.c. *Bertolini – Questama (Rainbow Quest).* April 2. Third foal. €11,500Y. Tattersalls Ireland. Ger Lyons. The dam, a minor 3-y-o winner in France, is a half-sister to two more minor winners there. The second dam, Xinca (by Green Dancer), a listed-placed French

3-y-o winner, is a half-sister to 3 winners. (Mr S Jones). *"A good, solid, Bertolini horse with a great temperament, he's very straightforward and you'll see him out anytime from May onwards, probably starting at six furlongs. Music fans might notice that a lot of the names of my two-year-olds this year are named after Jazz artists!"*

1027. CAMPESTRAL SCENE ★★

ch.c. Pastoral Pursuits – Raindrop (Primo Dominie). May 7. Seventh living foal. 30,000Y. Tattersalls October Book 2. BBA (Ire). Half-brother to the useful 1m listed winner of 6 races Kasumi (by Inchinor), to the fair 5f winner of 5 races (including at 2 yrs) Enodoc (by Efisio) and the modest 6f and 7f winner of 3 races Glencal (by Compton Place). The dam, placed fourth once over 7f, is a half-sister to 5 winners. The second dam, Thundercloud (by Electric), is a placed half-sister to 9 winners including the St Leger winner Julio Mariner, the Oaks winner Scintillate and the Irish Oaks winner Juliette Marny. (Mr V Gaul). *"A straightforward colt with a lovely temperament, he's very much a seven furlong type of 2-y-o from July onwards. He does all his work grand but we'll take our time with him".*

1028. DR FUNKENSTEIN (IRE) ★★★ ♠

ch.c. Excellent Art – Romancing (Dr Devious). April 25. Sixth foal. €23,000Y. Goffs Orby. Ger Lyons. Half-brother to the quite useful 5f and 6f winner Another Wise Kid (by Whipper), to the fair 6f winner Romanticize and the modest dual 7f (including at 2 yrs) and 6f winner Romantic Verse (both by Kyllachy). The dam, a fair 10f placed maiden, is a sister to the listed 6f winner Irresistible (herself dam of the Group 3 Nell Gwyn Stakes winner Infallible). The second dam, Polish Romance (by Danzig), a minor 7f winner in the USA, is a sister to the US stakes winner Polish Love and a half-sister to 4 minor winners. (Mr S Jones). *"A lovely, big horse, he's still a bit weak and he's one for the mid-to-back-end of the season. A big, scopey horse, he's gorgeous looking and has a great temperament. One for seven furlongs plus".*

1029. HARD WALNUT (IRE) ★★★

b.f. Cape Cross – Yaria (Danehill). March 30. Second foal. £42,000Y. Doncaster Premier.

Not sold. Half-sister to the fair dual 1m winner Hurricane Lady (by Hurricane Run). The dam, an Irish 6f (at 2 yrs) and 7f winner, was fourth in two Group 3 events in Ireland and is a half-sister to 5 winners including the UAE listed 1m winner Emirates Gold and the French listed 10f winner Yarastar. The second dam, Yara (by Sri Pekan), was placed second ten times including in the Group 1 5f Heinz 57 Phoenix Stakes. (Pearl Bloodstock). *"She's ready to run, so we'll probably start her off at five furlongs but she'll be more of a six/seven furlong 2-y-o. An early type and a very nice filly, She hasn't grown a lot but she's big enough if she's good enough".*

1030. HOUND DOG TAYLOR ★★★

b.c. Sir Percy – Mrs Brown (Royal Applause). March 22. Fifth foal. 22,000Y. Half-brother to the moderate 2011 5f placed 2-y-o Kaylee (by Selkirk), to the quite useful 2-y-o 5f winner Kings Of Leo and the modest 2-y-o 6f winner Fleet Captain (both by Compton Place). The dam, a moderate 7f placed 3-y-o, is a half-sister to 5 winners including the Italian Group 3 winner Shifting Place. The second dam, Shifting Mist (by Night Shift), a modest 10f to 14f winner of 5 races, is a half-sister to 7 winners including the dam of the Group/Grade 3 winner Needwood Blade. (Mr S Jones). *"One for the middle of the season, he's a horse with a good temperament and I see him running over six furlongs from the end of May. He's always been a sort of 'good feeling' horse".*

1031. KEEPING (IRE) ★★★★

b.f. Teofilo – My (King's Best). March 22. Second living foal. 50,000Y. Tattersalls October Book 1. Rabbah Bloodstock. The dam is an unplaced half-sister to 4 winners including the very smart dual Group 3 12f winner Laaheb. The second dam, Maskunah (by Sadler's Wells), is an unraced half-sister to 6 winners including the high-class middle-distance horses and multiple Group 1 winners Warrsan and Luso, the Nell Gwyn Stakes winner Cloud Castle and the Group 2 Gallinule Stakes winner Needle Gun. (Sheikh Mohammed). *"I think I have some nice fillies again this year and she'd be one of them. Very straightforward, she'll be running over six furlongs in May or June. She has an engine and a good temperament".*

1032. LIGHTNIN HOPKINS (IRE) ★★★

b.c. Kodiac – Bundle Of Joy (Golan).
April 4. Second foal. 20,000Y. Tattersalls October Book 2. BBA (Ire). The dam is an unraced half-sister to one minor winner. The second dam, Alenteja (by Danehill), a modest 5f placed maiden, is a half-sister to 10 winners including the Group 1 Prix de Diane winner Rafha (dam of the Group 1 Haydock Park Sprint Cup winner and high-class sire Invincible Spirit). (Mr S Jones). *"Another nice horse, he's very straightforward and like a lot of mine he'll start out over six furlongs. I like the sire and this colt will be running in May".* TRAINERS' BARGAIN BUY

1033. MARVELOUS JAMES ★★

b.g. Captain Marvelous – Answer Do (Groom Dancer). April 4. Third foal. 19,000Y. Doncaster Premier. Not sold. Half-brother to the minor Italian winner, at 2 and 3 yrs, Para Muslera (by Kheleyf). The dam ran once unplaced and is a sister to one winner and a half-sister to 4 winners including the dam of the multiple Group 3 winner and Group 1 second Mac Love. The second dam, Be My Lass (by Be My Rose), won once at 4 yrs in France and is a half-sister to the US Grade 1 winner Bonne Ile and the Group 3 winners Ile de Nisky and Hi Lass. (Mr C Dineen). *"He's just been gelded but he'll be ready to run as soon as he gets over the operation. He's straightforward enough and he'll run over five/six furlongs. A horse that looks as if he'll win a maiden and then be a nursery type 2-y-o".*

1034. MEMPHIS RED (IRE) ★★

ch.c. Danehill Dancer – Rain Flower (Indian Ridge). May 8. Ninth foal. €37,000Y. Goffs Orby. Ger Lyons. Brother to the Group 1 Oaks and Group 1 German Oaks winner Dancing Rain and to the fair 7f (at 2 yrs) and 1m winner Captain Dancer, closely related to the 2-y-o listed 5f St Hugh's Stakes winner Sumora (herself dam of the Group 1 Moyglare Stud Stakes winner Maybe) and the useful Irish 2-y-o 7f winner Fleeting Shadow (both by Danehill) and half-brother to the fairly useful 12f winner Mikhail Fokine (by Sadler's Wells). The dam is an unraced three-parts sister to the top-class Epsom Derby, Irish Champion Stakes and Dewhurst Stakes winner Dr Devious

and a half-sister to 5 winners including the Japanese listed winner Shinko King and the Group 3 winners Royal Court and Archway. The second dam, Rose Of Jericho (by Alleged), is an unraced half-sister to 5 winners. (Mr S Jones). *"If he runs at all this year it'll be right at the back-end because he's a real backward type. He's growing up all the time though and physically he's done great. He's obviously got a cracking pedigree, but he'll be trained with the back-end of the season in mind and we won't be disappointed if he doesn't run until next year".*

1035. MINISTER OF MAYHEM ★★

ch.c. Sakhee's Secret – First Fantasy (Be My Chief). February 15. Eighth foal. €40,000Y. Goffs Orby. Ger Lyons. Half-brother to the quite useful 1m winner Infatuate (by Inchinor), to the modest dual 12f winner Sitwell (by Dr Fong), the Italian 2-y-o winner Aces Romanorum (by Beat Hollow), the fair 12f and hurdles winner First Fandango and the hurdles winner Nicene Creed (both by Hernando). The dam, a fairly useful listed winner of 6 races from 9.7f to 10.5f, is a half-sister to 3 winners. The second dam, Dreams (by Rainbow Quest), a quite useful 10.3f winner, is a half-sister to 4 winners including Jeune (winner of the Melbourne Cup and the Group 2 12f Hardwicke Stakes) and the Group 2 12f King Edward VII Stakes winner Beneficial. *"A real smart colt, his temperament was questionable but he's turned a corner in the last month. A lovely horse to look at and hopefully he's more of a Sakhee's Secret than Sakhee. I like him and he gallops well, but I won't be pushing any buttons with him until June".*

1036. MISSISSIPPI JOHN (IRE) ★★

b.c. Lawman – Requested Pleasure (Rainbow Quest). March 17. Third foal. Half-brother to the modest 1m winner Govenor General (by Araafa). The dam, a fairly useful 1m and 10f winner in Ireland, is a half-sister to 9 winners including the very useful Group 3 1m Desmond Stakes winner Swift Gulliver and the useful 2-y-o 6f and subsequent dual US stakes winner Abderian. The second dam, Aminata (by Glenstal), a useful winner of the Group 3 5f Curragh Stakes, is a half-sister to 3 winners. (Mr S Jones). *"A small, butty horse that's carrying plenty of condition at the moment. He's definitely one for the middle of the season because I'm not going to rush to get the weight of him. Whilst he's smaller than my 2-y-o Beatboxing he's in the same league and I won't run him before July over seven furlongs".*

1037. PEARL CAUSEWAY (USA) ★★★★

ch.c. Giant's Causeway – Northern Mischief (Yankee Victor). May 7. Third foal. 80,000Y. Tattersalls October Book 1. David Redvers. The dam, a dual winner in the USA at 2 and 3 yrs, was third in the Grade 1 Hollywood Starlet Stakes and is a half-sister to 5 winners including the US champion older mare and triple Grade 1 winner Gourmet Girl. The second dam, Rhondaling (by Welsh Pageant), won twice at 2 yrs and was third in the Group 3 C L Weld Park Stakes and is a half-sister to 3 minor winners. (Pearl Bloodstock). *"A lovely, big, beautiful horse and one for the middle of the season, starting over seven furlongs. He's a gorgeous, imposing horse to look at and he can gallop".*

1038. PEARL MUSIC (IRE) ★★★★

b.c. Oratorio – Balamiyda (Ashkalani). March 16. Fifth foal. €42,000Y. Goffs Orby. David Redvers. Half-brother to the Italian winner and dual listed-placed Escalada (by American Post) and to the minor French dual winner (including at 2 yrs) Hidden Magic (by Bering). The dam is an unraced half-sister to 6 winners including the very smart Group 2 10f King Edward VII Stakes winner Balakheri and the Group 3 Irish 1,000 Guineas Trial winner Baliyana. The second dam, Balanka (by Alzao), a French listed winner and third in the Group 2 9.2f Prix de l'Opera, is a half-sister to 7 winners. (Pearl Bloodstock). *"He'd be one of my favourites in terms of 'types' of horses. He's going through a growth spurt at the minute and you won't see him out before June over six furlongs, but he's a gorgeous horse that's doing really well. He's growing into a nice physical specimen and he can gallop as well".*

1039. PEARL TURN (USA) ★★★★ ♠

b.f. Bernardini – Turn Me Loose (Kris S). March 19. Fourth foal. $225,000Y. Keeneland September. David Redvers. Half-sister to a minor 3-y-o winner in the USA by Medaglia d'Oro. The dam

is a placed half-sister to 5 winners including the US Grade 2 winner Saint Anddan. The second dam, Adoradancer (by Danzig Connection), a US stakes-placed winner, is a half-sister to 3 stakes winners. (Pearl Bloodstock). *"A lovely filly with a lot of quality, she's not an early type but she'll be racing by the middle of the season over six/seven furlongs and we like her a lot".*

1040. ROCKABILLY RIOT (IRE) ★★★★

b.c. Footstepsinthesand – Zawariq (Marju). March 16. Second foal. €46,000Y. Goffs Orby. Ger Lyons. Half-brother to the unplaced 2011 2-y-o Red Hot Penny (by Kheleyf). The dam is an unplaced half-sister to 4 winners including the fairly useful triple 7f winner (including at 2 yrs) Silk Fan. The second dam, Alikhlas (by Lahib), a fair 3-y-o 1m winner, is a half-sister to 4 winners including the listed winner and Group 2 Lancashire Oaks second Sahool and to the dam of the dual Group 2 winner Maraahel. (Mr S Jones). *"A very straightforward colt, I love him to death. He's typical of the sire and we've been very lucky with him. He's ready to run whenever we want, so you'll see him out in May and we like him a lot".*

1041. SCRAPPER BLACKWELL ★★★★

b.c. Zamindar – Kythia (Kahyasi). May 19. Fifth foal. 15,000Y. Tattersalls October Book 2. BBA (Ire). Half-brother to the fair 1m and 10f winner Phoenix Enforcer (by Bahamian Bounty). The dam, a fair 2-y-o 8.5f winner, is a half-sister to 2 minor winners. The second dam, Another Rainbow (by Rainbows For Life), is a placed half-sister to 8 winners including Reunion (Group 3 Nell Gwyn Stakes). *"He's mentally very forward despite his late foaling date, so he'll be earlier than you'd think. A lovely, big, scopey horse for the end of May onwards and I like him a lot".*

1042. TENNESSEE WILDCAT ★★★

b.c. Kheleyf – Windbeneathmywings (In The Wings). February 3. First foal. €19,000Y. Tattersalls Ireland. Ger Lyons. The dam, a fair dual 12f winner, is a half-sister to 2 winners including the Group 2 1m Prix du Muguet and dual listed 1m winner Dandoun. The second dam, Moneefa (by Darshaan), a fair 10f winner, is a half-sister to 6 winners including the Group 3 5f Duke Of York Stakes second Garah (herself dam of the Group 1 winner Olden Times). (Mr S Jones). *"He's ready to run and so he's very much like my other earlyish types, such as Bumble Bee Slim. We can just get on with them, start them at six furlongs, win their maiden and see where we go from there. I like them – they're a nice bunch of colts".*

1043. UNCLE MUF (USA) ★★★
b.br.c. Curlin – Peak Maria's Way (Pyramid Peak). January 29. First foal. $55,000Y. Keeneland September. David Redvers. The dam, a stakes winner of 8 races in the USA, was Grade 3 placed and is a half-sister to 3 winners. The second dam, Illusoria (by Maria's Mon), a US 2-y-o winner and third in the Grade 1 Matron Stakes, is a half-sister to the dam of the Matron Stakes winner Meadow Breeze. (Pearl Bloodstock). *"A lovely horse that's having a short break at the minute. He's a gorgeous, quality horse to look at, but you won't see him out until the middle of the season at the earliest. A big, scopey horse that will take a bit of time".*

1044. WYOYO (IRE) ★★
b.c. Moss Vale – Jersey Lillie (Hector Protector). March 9. Fifth foal. £15,000Y. Doncaster Premier. BBA (Ire). Half-brother to the fair 12f winner Island Myth (by Inchinor) and to the modest 5f and 6f winner Juarla (by Tagula). The dam is an unraced half-sister to 3 winners including the useful Italian 2-y-o listed 6f winner and Group 3 6f Prix de Seine-et-Oise third Jezebel. The second dam, Just Ice (by Polar Falcon), a fairly useful winner of 3 races over 5f and 6f here and in France including a listed event at Bordeaux, is a half-sister to 11 winners including the listed winners Always On A Sunday and Palmetto Express. (Mr D Nolan). *"He's a small, grand horse that'll be running at the end of May. He's doing his work straightforward, no 'bells and whistles', but hopefully he's good enough to win a little auction maiden".*

1045. UNNAMED ★★
b.c. Excellent Art – Chameleon (Green Desert). May 2. Seventh living foal. €16,000Y. Tattersalls Ireland. Ger Lyons. Half-brother to the fairly useful 6f (at 2 yrs) to 14.7f winner of 7 races and listed-placed Merchant Of Dubai (by Dubai Destination) and to the fair 6f winner Youhavecontrol (by Hawk Wing). The dam, a

fair 4-y-o 7f winner, is a sister to the Group 1 6f July Cup winner Owington and a half-sister to 7 winners. The second dam, Old Domesday Book (by High Top), a fairly useful 10.4f winner, was listed-placed over 10f. (Mr C Dineen). *"He's a small, handy 2-y-o but his knees were very open so we put him out in the paddock to grow. He'll come back in after the May grass and we'll make a plan with him then, once we see how he's developed".*

1046. UNNAMED ★★
b.f. Cape Cross – Recite (Forty Niner). February 28. Third foal. Closely related to the fairly useful Irish 1m winner and listed placed One Spirit (by Invincible Spirit). The dam, a fair Irish 2-y-o 1m winner, is a half-sister to 4 winners including the Group 1 Haydock Park Sprint Cup and Group 1 Prix Maurice de Gheest winner and sire Diktat. The second dam, Arvola (by Sadler's Wells), a fair 3-y-o 8.2f winner, is a sister to the 12.5f listed placed Lord of Appeal and a full or half-sister to 8 winners including the Group 1 Lockinge Stakes winner and high-class sire Cape Cross. (Miss A H Marshall). *"A strapping filly but she won't be racing before September".*

GEORGE MARGARSON
1047. AMIRAH (IRE) ★★★
b.f. Holy Roman Emperor – Nadwah (Shadeed). January 31. Eighth foal. £20,000Y. Doncaster Premier. Jarvis, Louch, Hodgson. Closely related to the fair 6f winner Golden Taurus (by Danehill Dancer) and half-sister to the fairly useful French and UAE 6f to 1m winner Estihdaaf (by Distant View), to the 6f and 7f winner Dash Back (by Sahm) and the modest 1m winner Macanta (by Giant's Causeway). The dam, winner of the Group 3 5f Queen Mary Stakes and third in the Group 2 Lowther Stakes and is a half-sister to 7 winners. The second dam, Tadwin (by Never So Bold), was a very useful sprint winner of 3 races including the listed Hopeful Stakes and is a half-sister to 4 winners including the very smart sprinter Reesh and the dam of the smart sprinter Averti. (Hodgson, Jarvis, Louch). *"She's done a lot of work and has done really well. She was a very difficult filly to deal with for a while, but we've persevered and hopefully if we wait a bit now she'll be alright from May onwards. If her temperament goes the right way she could win her maiden first time out because she*

knows her job – in fact she probably knows it a bit too well! She has the speed for five furlongs but she'll be better at six".

1048. EXOTIC GUEST ★★★

ch.c. Bahamian Bounty – Mamoura (Lomond). March 2. Fourteenth foal. 67,000Y. Tattersalls October Book 2. George Margarson. Half-brother to the Group 2 12.5f Prix de Royallieu winner Mouramara (by Kahyasi and herself the dam of two listed winners), to the French listed-placed winner of 10 races Pares (by Catrail), the minor French winner Mouriyana (by Akarad and herself dam of the Group 3 Prix Edmond Blanc winner Skins Game), the French 3-y-o winner and listed-placed Mourasana (by Shirocco) and 2 minor winners in France and Germany by Barathea. The dam won over 10f and 12f in Ireland and is a half-sister to 5 winners including the Group 3 12f Meld Stakes third Mirana (herself dam of the Group 3 Prix de Flore winner Miliana). The second dam, Mamouna (by Vaguely Noble), won once at 3 yrs and was third in the Group 2 10f Nassau Stakes. (John Guest Racing Ltd). "He's quite a nice type and one I'm hoping to get out by mid-summer. He's a bit immature mentally so I've stepped back with him a touch, but he's growing up quite a lot now. A well-grown horse, there are mixed messages in his pedigree as to what sort of trip he'll want, but he looks a six/seven furlong 2-y-o in the making".

1049. JAMMY GUEST ★★★★

b.c. Duke Of Marmalade – Ardbrae Lady (Overbury). April 3. Third foal. 68,000Y. Tattersalls October Book 1. George Margarson. Half-brother to the useful Irish 7f (at 2 yrs) and 11f winner and listed-placed Jackaroo (by Galileo). The dam, a useful winner of the Group 3 1m Park Express Stakes and second in the Irish 1,000 Guineas, is a half-sister to 5 winners including the useful listed 5f (at 2 yrs) to 7f winner of 15 races Obe Gold (by Namaqualand). The second dam, Gagajulu (by Al Hareb), won 5 races over 5f at 2 yrs and is a half-sister to 4 winners. (John Guest Racing Ltd). "He's the apple of my eye at the moment. A serious horse and his aim will be the Chesham Stakes at Royal Ascot. He should be able to win a small maiden (without anything special in it) first time out, although I haven't done a great

deal with him yet because he's a big, powerful colt. He does everything effortlessly, he's very straightforward and mentally he's grown up already".

1050. MADAME MORETON ★★★

ch.f. Zafeen – Limegreen Bow (Efisio). April 2. Second foal. The dam, unraced due to an injury, is a half-sister to 3 minor winners. The second dam, Sioux Chef (by Be My Chief), a fair 2-y-o 6f winner, is a sister to the German 2-y-o Group 2 winner Flying Squaw and a half-sister to 6 winners. (M.V.S & Mrs Aram). "A very small, sharp filly and a nice type, she should make her mark from late April onwards. Quite a well-made 2-y-o".

1051. RED CATKIN ★★

b.f. Notnowcato – Red Salvia (Selkirk). February 5. First foal. 22,000Y. Tattersalls December. George Margarson. The dam is an unraced sister to the Group 1 Fillies' Mile and Group 2 10f Blandford Stakes winner Red Bloom and a half-sister to 3 winners including the listed winner Red Gala. The second dam, Red Camellia (by Polar Falcon), won of the Group 3 7f Prestige Stakes, was third in the French 1,000 Guineas and is a half-sister to 4 winners. (Mrs E L Hook). "We picked her up quite reasonably at the Sales because she's a nice type of filly for later in the year. She's shown me already that she has a good attitude and a fair level of ability, but I haven't done much with her yet. She'll be trained with an eye towards seven furlongs or a mile later this season and she's probably more of a 3-y-o type".

1052. SPEEDFIT BOY ★★★

b.c. Red Clubs – Princess Speedfit (Desert Prince). March 9. Sixth foal. €30,000Y. Goffs Orby. G Margarson. Half-brother to the useful 6f winner of 5 races (including a 2-y-o listed event) Imperial Guest (by Imperial Dancer), to the fairly useful 6f (at 2 yrs) and 7f winner Excellent Guest (by Exceed And Excel) and a winner abroad by Barathea Guest. The dam, a fair 8.3f winner at 3 yrs, is a half-sister to 5 winners including the French listed 12f winner and dual Group 2 placed Sibling Rival. The second dam, Perfect Sister (by Perrault), a minor French winner, is a sister to the US Grade 1 winner Frankly Perfect and a half-sister to the

French listed winner and US Grade 1 placed Franc Argument. (John Guest Racing Ltd). *"He has all the traits of his half-brother Excellent Guest, although he may be a little bit lighter. I've given him a bit of time but he's done work and I expect to get him out around July time. He's shown me that he's got the pace and the right attitude".*

1053. UNNAMED ★★

b.f. Zafeen – Nihal (Singspiel). April 21. Third foal. Half-sister to the modest 2-y-o 7f winner Al Jabreiah (by Bertolini). The dam, a quite useful dual 7f (at 2 yrs) and 12f winner, is a half-sister to 7 winners including the Irish 9f to 14f winner and listed-placed Catherina and the fairly useful 7f (at 2 yrs) to 10f winner Secretary General. The second dam, Katie McLain (by Java Gold), an Irish 3-y-o 7f and 10f winner, is a half-sister to 6 winners including the Group 3 Desmond Stakes and Group 3 7f C L Weld Park Stakes winner Asema. (Stableside Racing Partnership). *"She's done particularly well in a short space of time and she's quite strong and powerful. Her knees are still a bit open but she should be out in May and she's shown me that she's quite a nice filly".*

ALAN McCABE

1054. BOUGALOO ★★

b.c. Tobougg – Benjarong (Sharpo). April 11. Seventh living foal. £6,000Y. Doncaster Festival. T Malone/A McCabe. Half-brother to the fair dual 6f winner Ben Lomand (by Inchinor) and to the moderate 5f and 6f winner Senate Majority (by Avonbridge). The dam, a modest 5f (at 2 yrs) and 1m winner, is a half-sister to 8 other minor winners. The second dam, Rose And The Ring (by Welsh Pageant), ran twice unplaced and is a half-sister to 5 winners. *"A nice, big, strong horse. We'll probably wait for the six and seven races for him and I think he has a future".*

1055. PROVENTI ★★★

b.c. Auction House – Miss Poppy. March 3. First foal. £15,000 2-y-o. Goffs Kempton breeze-up. A McCabe. The dam, a modest 6f placed maiden (including at 2 yrs), is a half-sister to 10 winners including the top-class Group 1 5f Nunthorpe Stakes winner Kyllachy and the fairly useful 2-y-o 5f winner Follow Flanders.

The second dam, Pretty Poppy (by Song), a modest 2-y-o 5f winner, stayed 7.6f and is a half-sister to 4 winners. *"We've done well with the sire, this colt goes well and we're hoping to run him towards the end of April in an auction maiden. We only bought him at the breeze-ups but he's ready to go and he's a sharp 2-y-o, well put-together and a typical Auction House".*

1056. ZAITSEV ★★★

ch.c. Refuse To Bend – Zuniga's Date (Diesis). March 7. Fourth living foal. 19,000Y. Doncaster Festival. T Malone/A McCabe. Half-brother to the fair 2-y-o 6f winner Dr Noverre (by Noverre) and the fair dual 6f winner (including at 2 yrs) Mark Anthony (by Antonius Pius). The dam, a minor winner at 3 yrs in France, is a half-sister to 2 other minor winners. The second dam, Zalamalec (by Septieme Ciel), a listed-placed winner of 2 races at 2 yrs in France, is a half-sister to 6 winners including the Group 1 placed River Drummer. (Mrs Z Wentworth). *"He's named after the Soviet sniper Vassili Zaitsev. A lovely, well-made horse, he's above average and he'll be a six/seven furlong 2-y-o".*

1057. UNNAMED ★★

b.f. Dubai Destination – Blinding Mission (Marju). April 3. Eighth foal. 800Y. Tattersalls October Book 3. Alan McCabe. Half-sister to the fair 7f and subsequent Spanish winner Langston Boy, to the moderate 4-y-o 1m winner Todwick Owl (both by Namid), the modest 9f and 10f winner Kyle Of Bute (by Kyllachy) and a minor winner abroad by Danehill Dancer. The dam, a fair 9f placed maiden, is a full or half-sister to 4 winners including the dual listed-placed High Priority. The second dam, Blinding (by High Top), ran unplaced twice and is a half-sister to 3 winners including the triple Group 3 winner Hadeer. *"She goes very well and she'll probably start off over a stiff six furlongs or maybe seven. We're looking for an owner for her, she was cheap but I like her. A nice, tall filly that going to need a bit of time because she needs to fill her frame".* TRAINERS' BARGAIN BUY

1058. UNNAMED ★★★

b.c. Antonius Pius – Consultant Stylist (Desert Style). April 30. Fifth foal. £20,000Y. Doncaster Festival. T Malone/A McCabe. Brother to the fair 1m winner Veni Vedi Vici and half-brother to the modest 6f placed maiden (including at 2 yrs in 2011) Miss Purity Pinker (by One Cool Cat) and the fair 7f (at 2 yrs) to 9f winner of 4 races Whodathought (by Choisir). The dam is an unraced half-sister to 5 minor winners. The second dam, Grannys Reluctance (by Anita's Prince), is a placed half-sister to 9 winners including the US Grade 3 winner Down Again. (Mrs Z Wentworth). *"We hope to be racing him by the end of April or early May. I'd say he's more of a six furlong type but he looks a 2-y-o".*

ED McMAHON
1059. ARLECCHINO (IRE) ★★★
b.c. Hernando – Trullitti (Bahri). March 19. Third foal. 62,000Y. Tattersalls October Book 2. Oliver St Lawrence. Half-brother to the 12f Swiss Derby winner Fabrino (by Elnadim). The dam, a quite useful German listed-placed 11f winner, is a half-sister to 3 other minor winners. The second dam, Penza (by Soviet Star), is a placed half-sister to 5 winners including the Group 1 12f Italian Derby winner and 'King George' second White Muzzle, the Group 2 German St Leger winner Fair Question and the listed winner Elfaslah (herself dam of the Dubai World Cup winner Almutawakel). (The LAM Partnership). *"A nice sort of colt, he's a bit immature mentally although he's cantering and doing everything alright. He's got a Derby entry, he's starting to fill out a bit now and he looks a nice type with a very good action. He's very athletic and he won't be out until July or August, possibly over seven furlongs, but we'll just have to wait and see".*

1060. COLOUR MY WORLD ★★
gr.c. With Approval – Nadeszhda (Nashwan). March 14. Fourth foal. 30,000Y. Tattersalls October Book 2. Ed McMahon. Half-brother to the fair 2011 2-y-o 6f winner Nimiety (by Stormy Atlantic) and to the minor Italian 3-y-o winner Aroundthestar (by Pulpit). The dam, a quite useful triple 12f winner, subsequently won once in the USA and was second in the Grade 2 Santa Barbara Handicap and is a half-sister to 2 winners including the useful 2-y-o 6f winner and 7f Group 3 placed Nataliya. The second dam, Ninotchka (by Nijinsky), a listed winner in Italy and third in the Group 3 12f Lancashire Oaks and the Group 3 12f Princess Royal Stakes, is a half-sister to 7 winners. (Philip

Wilkins). *"He's a nice, big horse that we won't be racing until the latter part of the year. He has a Derby entry, he's a very nice horse that moves well and we can only hope that he performs well when he does run. He'll definitely need at least seven furlongs this year and he's more of a 3-y-o type".*

1061. DUSTY STORM (IRE) ★★★
ch.f. Kyllachy – Halliwell House (Selkirk). April 8. First foal. 30,000Y. Tattersalls October Book 2. Ed McMahon. The dam ran once unplaced and is a half-sister to 3 winners including the Group 2 Italian Oaks second Counterclaim. The second dam, Dusty Answer (by Zafonic), a quite useful 2-y-o 7f winner, was listed placed over 1m and is a half-sister to 4 winners including the listed 1m and subsequent US Grade 2 winner Spotlight and the dam of the Group 1 Phoenix Stakes winner Zoffany. (R L Bedding). *"Quite a feminine looking filly, she's a bit weak at the moment but she's got a nice action. She's a typical Kyllachy in that she's just a bit fiery, but the sire can produce winners alright. A sharp, sprinting-type filly, hopefully she'll be OK. We'll see her out in late May or early June".*

1062. FLIRTINASKIRT ★★★
b.f. Avonbridge – Talampaya (Elusive Quality). January 11. First foal. £11,000Y. Doncaster Festival. Ed McMahon. The dam is an unraced half-sister to 3 winners. The second dam, Argentina (by Storm Cat), a minor US 2-y-o winner, is a sister to a US stakes-placed winner and a half-sister to 4 winners. (Mr P A Wilkins). *"She was bought fairly cheaply, so anything's a bonus with her. She's progressed well throughout the winter and I should think she'll be racing from late April onwards, then we'll see where we go with her. She's nearly up to full tilt now and she's showing me that she should win a little race somewhere".*

1063. FORRAY ★★★
ch.c. Choisir – Selique (Selkirk). March 21. Second foal. 31,000Y. Tattersalls October Book 2. J C Fretwell. The dam ran once unplaced and is a half-sister to 3 minor winners here and abroad. The second dam, Elle Questro (by Rainbow Quest), a modest 12f winner, is a half-sister to 5 winners including the Group 1 Racing Post Trophy winner Be My Chief. *"A very flashy horse*

with four white socks – he wouldn't look out of place in a Cowboy film! But he's a nice sort and he's coming to hand now so I think we'll have him out in April. He's fairly professional and I don't think he'd want it too fast underfoot because his action is a little bit rounded".

Won 1f Leic mdn soft

1064. LOOK ON BY ★★

gr.g. Byron – Where's Carol (Anfield). February 28. Half-brother to the smart listed 6f winner Now Look Here (by Reprimand), to the fairly useful 6f and 7f winner of 3 races and listed-placed Look Here's Carol (by Safawan), the fair 6f winner of 6 races Look Here Now (by Ardkinglass), the fair 2-y-o 5f winner Now Look Out (by Bahamian Bounty) and the fair 5f winner Look Who's Kool (by Compton Place). The dam, a fair 2-y-o 6f winner of 4 races, is a half-sister to several winners including the useful 7.5f to 1m winner Weet-A-Minute. The second dam, Ludovica (by Bustino), is an unraced half-sister to 6 winners. (S L Edwards). *"A big-topped horse, we'll just have to see how he goes because he doesn't have the best conformation. As long as he stays sound we'll get him on the track and then we'll see how he goes".*

1065. MISS METICULOUS ★★★★

ch.f. Bahamian Bounty – Umniya (Bluebird). February 26. Fourth foal. £29,000Y. Doncaster Premier. Ed McMahon. The dam, a quite useful 2-y-o 6f winner, was fourth in the Group 1 Moyglare Stud Stakes and third in the Group 3 Premio Dormello and is a half-sister to 5 winners including the dual listed 6f winner Lady Links (herself dam of the dual listed winner Selinka). The second dam, Sparky's Song (by Electric), a moderate 10.2f and 12f winner, is a half-sister to 3 winners including the very smart Group 1 6.5f winner Bold Edge and the listed winner and Group 2 5f Temple Stakes second Brave Edge. (The LAM Partnership). *"A nice-enough filly, she's just had a couple of niggling problems but she's been going fairly well. She's fairly sharp and has a nice action, so I can see her being out sometime in May over five furlongs. I find that Bahamian Bounty's are generally good value for money".*

1066. PUCKER UP ★★★

b.f. Royal Applause – Smooch (Inchinor).

February 12. Third foal. £30,000Y. Doncaster Premier. J C Fretwell. The dam, a quite useful 2-y-o dual 5f winner, was listed-placed twice and is a half-sister to 6 winners. The second dam, Two Step (by Mujtahid), a modest 5f and 7f winner at 4 and 5 yrs, is a half-sister to 3 winners. *"She's OK, she's not over-big and she's coming to hand quicker than most of the 2-y-o fillies. She's got quite a good action so she wouldn't want it too soft, I can see her being out in late April and she's going the right way".*

1067. SECRET LOOK ★★★

ch.c. Sakhee's Secret – Look Here's Carol (Safawan). March 23. Fourth foal. Half-brother to the modest 2011 2-y-o dual 5f winner Look Here's Lady (by Kyllachy), to the fair 2-y-o 5f winner Look Whos Next (by Compton Place) and the modest 2-y-o 1m winner Imperial Look (by Royal Applause). The dam, a fairly useful 6f and 7f winner of 3 races, was listed-placed and is a half-sister to several winners including the smart listed 6f winner Now Look Here. The second dam, Where's Carol (by Anfield), was a fair 2-y-o 6f winner of 4 races. (S L Edwards). *"I've got two Sakhee's Secret and they're both similar in that they need to stop growing and fill out a bit. I don't think this colt will be early and he might want six or seven furlongs, maybe even a mile. We'll start him in mid-season and although you might think on pedigree that he'd end up a sprinter he doesn't really look that way".*

1068. TRUTH HURTS ★★★

br.c. Cockney Rebel – Vino Veritas (Chief's Crown). March 29. Ninth foal. £35,000Y. Doncaster Premier. J C Fretwell. Half-brother to the quite useful 2011 2-y-o 7f winner Na Zdorovie (by Cockney Rebel), to the useful 2-y-o 7f winner and listed placed Slim Shadey (by Val Royal), the fair Irish 12f and 13f winner Nora Chrissie (by Bahhare) and two minor winners abroad by Choisir and Fath. The dam, placed fourth once over 7f at 2 yrs from two starts, is a half-sister to several winners including the multiple Hong Kong and Japanese Group 1 winner Bullish Luck. The second dam, Wild Vintage (by Alysheba), a minor French 10f winner, is a half-sister to 7 winners including the Group 1 Prix Marcel Boussac winner Juvenia and the Group 3 Prix de Guiche winner In Extremis. *"I think all*

Cockney Rebel's have a bit of something about them and he does live on his nerves to some extent. I think he'll get seven furlongs or a mile, he looks fairly athletic, he's started to do some work now and I'll bring him along gradually. As long as he settles he'll be OK".

1069. UNNAMED ★★★

b.f. Compton Place – Ashover Amber *(Green Desert).* March 31. Seventh foal. 7,500Y. Doncaster Festival. J C Fretwell. Half-sister to the fair 2-y-o 5f and 6f winner of 3 races Fabuleux Cherie (by Noverre), to the modest dual 7f (including at 2 yrs) and subsequent Spanish winner Sir Jasper (by Sri Pekan) and 2 winners in Greece by Celtic Swing and Muhtarram. The dam, a fair 5f and 6f winner of 3 races at 3 yrs, is a half-sister to 2 winners. The second dam, Zafaaf (by Kris), a useful 7f and 1m winner, is a half-sister to 8 winners including the useful 6f winner Siwaayib (dam of the smart middle-distance stayer Rainbow Ways). *"She's got quite a nice action, although her attitude leaves a bit to be desired. But she's doing everything asked of her and I'm expecting her out in late April or early May. She wouldn't want it too soft and although she isn't a world-beater I think she has every chance of picking up a little contest somewhere".*

1070. UNNAMED ★★★★

b.f. Kodiac – Berenica *(College Chapel).* March 20. Third foal. £26,000Y. Doncaster Premier. J C Fretwell. Half-sister to the quite useful 6f (at 2 yrs) to 1m winner of 7 races Kingswinford (by Noverre). The dam, a dual Irish 6f winner (including at 2 yrs) was listed-placed and is half-sister to 3 winners including the fairly useful 5f winner of 4 races and listed-placed Gaelic Princess. The second dam, Berenice (by Marouble), was unraced. *"I wouldn't say she's over-big, she's quite short coupled and her action is a bit rounded so she probably wants a bit of cut in the ground. She's a bit on the weak side at this moment in time, so although she's doing strong canters up the hill it'll be sometime in May before she's ready to run".*

1071. UNNAMED ★★★

b.c. Oratorio – Blue 'Reema *(Bluebird).* March 20. Fourth foal. £28,000Y. Doncaster Premier. J C Fretwell. Half-brother to the modest 12f

winner Marju King (by Marju). The dam, a fairly useful 7f winner, was listed-placed over 1m and is a half-sister to 14 winners including the Japanese Grade 1 winner Meisho Doto and the Italian St Leger winner Pay Me Back. The second dam, Princess Reema (by Affirmed), is an unraced half-sister to the dam of a Grade 1 winner in Peru. *"He's not over-big and he reminds me of another horse I had by Oratorio called Indian Ballad. He's got a nice action on him but he's a bit of a teenager at the moment in that he's likely to whip round and drop his rider. I think he'll be better waiting for the six furlong races to start in May, he hasn't grown a lot but as long as he's got a bit of an engine that's all we want".*

1072. UNNAMED ★★★

b.c. Royal Applause – Cherokee Stream *(Indian Ridge).* April 29. Third foal. 50,000Y. Tattersalls October Book 2. J C Fretwell. Half-brother to the quite useful 2-y-o 5f and 6f winner of 4 races Indian Ballad (by Oratorio). The dam, a fair Irish 7f to 9f placed maiden, is a sister to the winner and Group 3 placed Maimee and a half-sister to 4 winners including the listed winner Mona Em. The second dam, Moy Water (by Tirol), an Irish 1m (at 2 yrs) and 9f winner, is a half-sister to 8 winners including the very useful listed sprint winners Bufalino and Maledetto. *"He's a big, leggy type of colt and he's not doing anything too serious yet because of his fairly late foaling date. He's a lot taller than his half-brother Indian Ballad but we've got to find out if he's got the will to do it like he had".*

1073. UNNAMED ★★★

ch.c. Iffraaj – Dance On *(Caerleon).* April 30. Eighth living foal. 32,000Y. Tattersalls October Book 2. J C Fretwell. Half-brother to the fairly useful 2-y-o 5f winner Dance Away (by Pivotal), to the quite useful 6f winner Strictly (by Falbrav) and the fair 7f winner Dance Card (by Cape Cross). The dam, a fairly useful 2-y-o dual 5f winner, was listed-placed and is a half-sister to 5 winners. The second dam, Dance Sequence (by Mr Prospector), a very useful winner of the Group 2 6f Lowther Stakes, is a sister to 3 winners including the US dual Grade 2 winner Souvenir Copy and the Japanese Grade 2 1m winner Shake Hand. *"He has quite a late foaling date and he needs to grow a bit yet, so he's just going through the motions without us having pushed any buttons for now. He's likely to be out around May or June time".*

1074. UNNAMED ★★★
b.c. Haatef – Fantastic Account (Fantastic Light). April 8. Fourth foal. 25,000Y. Tattersalls October Book 2. J C Fretwell. Half-brother to the useful 2011 2-y-o 7f and listed 1m winner Coupe de Ville (by Clodovil), to the US stakes winner and Grade 3 placed Fantastico Roberto (by Refuse To Bend) and the fairly useful Irish 2-y-o 7f winner and listed-placed Tell The Wind (by Mujadil). The dam is an unraced half-sister to 3 minor winners. The second dam, Fabulous Account (by Private Account), is a placed half-sister to 9 winners including the US Grade 1 winner Joyeux Danseur and the Group 3 placed Danseur Fabuleux (dam of the outstanding 2-y-o Arazi and the Sussex Stakes winner Noverre). *"He's a big, leggy sort and out of a Fantastic Light mare so I don't see him coming out before mid-summer because he'll probably want at least seven furlongs. He's still growing and he's very green, so he's just cantering for now".*

1075. UNNAMED ★★★
ch.c. Sakhee's Secret – Lark In The Park (Grand Lodge). March 25. Fourth foal. Half-brother to the fair 2011 2-y-o 5f winner Passionada (by Avonbridge) and to the quite useful 1m and 10f winner Dolphin Rock (by Mark Of Esteem). The dam, a moderate 1m winner at 3 yrs, is a half-sister to several winners including the quite useful 1m to 12f winner of 8 races Invasian. The second dam, Jarrayan (by Machiavellian), is an unplaced half-sister to several winners including the 2-y-o listed 6f Silver Flash Stakes winner, is a sister to the 6f winner and listed placed Moonis. *"He's similar to my other Sakhee's Secret in that he's a very big horse. He'll probably need at least six and more likely seven furlongs to start with and he's one for the middle of the season".*

BRIAN MEEHAN
1076. BAIRAM ★★★★
gr.g. Haatef – Intishaar (Dubai Millennium). February 8. Third foal. The dam is an unraced half-sister to 2 winners. The second dam, Bint

Shadayid (by Nashwan), a very useful winner of the Group 3 7f Prestige Stakes, was placed in the 1,000 Guineas and the Fillies Mile. (Hamdan Al Maktoum). *"A very sharp colt, he's got a lot of speed and hopefully he'll be running in May. He's very nice and although he'll get six furlongs I think he's quick enough to win over five".* win of nursery 6 runners [handwritten] Chester

1077. BATASH ★★★
b.c. Royal Applause – Regal Asset (Regal Classic). May 6. Third foal. 30,000Y. Tattersalls October Book 2. Rabbah Bloodstock. Half-brother to the modest 2011 2-y-o 7f and 1m winner Regal Gold (by Exceed And Excel). The dam is an unplaced half-sister to 7 winners including the Grade 1 Hong Kong Mile winner Ecclesiastical and the dam of the Group 3 sprint winner Al Qasi. The second dam, Rachael Tennessee (by Matsadoon), was placed once in the USA and is a half-sister to 7 winners including the top-class miler Lear Fan and the triple Group 2 winner Pirate Army. (Mr Sultan Ali). *"A sharp sort and a typical 2-y-o, he should be running in May, possibly over five furlongs to start with, but six will be his trip".*

1078. BIX (IRE) ★★★
b.c. Holy Roman Emperor – Belle Rebelle (In The Wings). March 22. Third foal. 20,000Y. Tattersalls October Book 2. Angie Loder. The dam is an unraced half-sister to 3 winners including Utrecht (Group 3 Prix Chloe). The second dam, Maria Isabella (by Kris), a fairly useful 8.2f winner, was listed placed over 8.5f and 10f and is a half-sister to the classic winners Bosra Sham, Hector Protector and Shanghai. (I Parvizi). *"He'll probably be better when he gets to seven furlongs but he works well. We'll wait until May or June and start him over six, he's a typical of the sire, good-looking with a good temperament".*

1079. CARD HIGH (IRE) ★★★
b.c. Red Clubs – Think (Marchand de Sable). March 13. Second foal. £26,000Y. Doncaster Premier. McKeever Bloodstock. Half-brother to the unplaced 2011 2-y-o Calusa Bay (by Bertolini). The dam, a French 2-y-o 6f winner, was third in the Group 3 Prix du Bois and is a half-sister to 7 minor winners. The second dam, Montagne Bleue (by Legend Of France), is a

placed half-sister to 5 winners. *"Similar to the Holy Roman Emperor colt Bix in that he'll want seven furlongs, he has a good temperament and he's a good-looking horse we'll start off in late May"*.

1080. CORRESPONDENT ★★★

ch.c. Exceed And Excel – Indian Love Bird (Efisio). February 28. Fifth foal. Half-brother to the Group 2 6f Duke Of York Stakes and Group 3 1m Craven Stakes winner and Group 1 placed Delegator (by Dansili). The dam is an unraced sister to the smart Group 1 7f Prix de la Foret winner Tomba and the French Derby winner Holding Court. The second dam, Indian Love Song (by Be My Guest), a modest middle-distance placed maiden, is a full or half-sister to 4 winners. *"A nice, strong colt and very similar to his half-brother Delegator. He still needs a bit of time and he'll be one for seven furlongs in July or August"*.

1081. DISCO INFERNO ★★★★

b.c. Lawman – Pink Sovietstaia (Soviet Star). April 30. Ninth foal. 65,000Y. Tattersalls October Book 2. Angie Loder. Half-brother to the fairly useful 2-y-o 6f winner and multiple listed-placed Russian Rosie (by Traditionally), to the quite useful 6f (at 2 yrs) and 1m winner King's Icon (by King's Best), the quite useful 2-y-o 6f and 7f winner Russian Ruby (by Vettori) and the fair dual 6f winner (including at 2 yrs) Observatory Star (by Observatory). The dam, awarded a 9f event at 4 yrs in France, is a half-sister to 9 winners including the listed winner Pinaflore (herself dam of the Group/Graded stakes winners Pinakaral, Pinfloron and Pinmix). The second dam, Pink Satin (by Right Royal V), won once at 2 yrs and is a half-sister to the French Group 1 winners Amber Rama and Blue Tom and to the placed dam of the French 2,000 Guineas winner Fast Topaze. *"A very nice horse with a lot of class I'd say. He has a great attitude and he'll be one for the mid-season onwards over seven furlongs and a mile"*.

1082. DOWNHILL DANCER (IRE) ★★★

b.f. Montjeu – Wiener Wald (Woodman). May 5. Thirteenth foal. Half-sister to the high-class 2-y-o Group 1 1m Racing Post Trophy winner Crowded House, to the French listed 11f winner and Group 3 placed On Reflection (both by Rainbow Quest), the useful 12f winner Heron Bay (by Hernando), the fairly useful 6f (at 2 yrs) and 1m winner and listed-placed Forest Crown, the fairly useful dual 6f winner (including at 2 yrs) and listed-placed Riotous Applause (both by Royal Applause), the quite useful 7.5f winner Woodland River (by Irish River), the New Zealand winner Bering Island (by Bering), the moderate 10f winner Harry Lime (by Cape Cross) and the placed dam of the US dual Grade 1 winner Ticker Tape. The dam is an unplaced half-sister to 6 minor winners abroad. The second dam, Chapel Of Dreams (by Northern Dancer), a dual Grade 2 winner in the USA, is a three-parts sister to the champion sire Storm Cat. (Car Colston Hall Stud). *"A filly that's very easy to deal with, she enjoys her work and she probably won't take as long as you'd expect from her pedigree. One for the middle of the season onwards"*.

1083. ETIJAAH (USA) ★★

b.c. Daaher – Hasheema (Darshaan). March 12. Half-brother to the fairly 1m (at 2 yrs) and 10f winner Badeel, to the quite useful Irish 7f winner Ma Ani (both by El Prado) and the fair 7f winner Ghafeer (by War Chant). The dam, a quite useful 3-y-o Irish 7f winner, is a half-sister to numerous winners including the Irish 2-y-o 6f winner and Group 3 7f Killavullen Stakes third Dance Clear (subsequently a winner of 4 races and Grade 3 placed in the USA). The second dam, Dance Ahead (by Shareef Dancer), a quite useful 2-y-o 7f winner, is a half-sister to 6 winners including the useful 12f winner Shoot Ahead. (Hamdan Al Maktoum). *"He's only just arrived from Dubai so I don't know much about him but he's a nice-looking colt, he's in good shape and has an excellent temperament"*.

Won over 7f mdn Sandown

1084. FANTACISE ★★★

ch.f. Pivotal – My First Romance (Danehill). March 27. Thirteenth foal. 70,000Y. Tattersalls October Book 1. Not sold. Half-sister to the Group 3 5f Queen Mary Stakes winners Romantic Myth (by Mind Games) and Romantic Liason (by Primo Dominie), the useful 2-y-o 5f winner Power Packed (by Puissance), the fairly useful 2-y-o 6f winner Alkhafif (by Royal Applause), the fairly useful dual 5f winner Zargus (by Zamindar), the quite useful 2-y-o 7f winner Wedaad (by Fantastic Light), the fair 7f winner Romantic Destiny (by Dubai Destination), the fair 2-y-o 5.5f winner Chance For Romance (by Entrepreneur) and the UAE 7f winner Maath Gool (by Dubawi). The dam ran twice unplaced and is a half-sister to 6 minor winners here and abroad. The second dam, Front Line Romance (by Caerleon), won once and was Group 3 placed over 1m at 2 yrs in Ireland and is a full or half-sister to 10 winners including the multiple Italian Group 3 winner Knight Line Dancer. (Mr T.G & Mrs M.E Holdcroft). *"A very nice, very sharp filly, she should be ready to run in late May and she's looks a decent filly".*

1085. FORBIDDEN FRUIT ★★★

b.c. Acclamation – Perils Of Joy (Rainbow Quest). April 8. Twelfth foal. €50,000Y. Goffs Orby. Angie Loder. Half-brother to the Irish listed 1m winner Hymn Of Love, to the modest Irish 1m winner Joyful Tears (both by Barathea), the fair 2-y-o 5f winner Jennifers Joy (by Green Desert) the Irish 6f and subsequent US winner Still As Sweet (by Fairy King), the modest 12f and 14f winner Aura Of Calm (by Grand Lodge) and the minor US winner Epic Pursuit (by Salse). The dam, a 3-y-o 1m winner in Ireland, is a half-sister to 5 winners including the Italian Group 3 winner Sweetened Offer. The second dam, Sweet Mint (by Meadow Mint), won the Group 3 Cork And Orrery Stakes. *"He was due to run soon but he's had a little setback and he needs a few days off. He has a lot of speed and hopefully we can get him out in early May".*

1086. FREEPORT ★★★

b.c. Bahamian Bounty – Perdicula (Persian Heights). January 25. Tenth foal. 50,000Y. Tattersalls October Book 2. Angie Loder. Half-brother to the useful 10f winner and listed-placed Markovitch (by Mark Of Esteem), to the quite useful 6f (at 2 yrs) and 1m winner of 16 races here and in Italy Zandicular (by Forzando), the fair 10f winner Azizam (by Singspiel) and the poor 12f winner Laura Land (by Lujain). The dam won twice at 4 yrs in Germany and is a half-sister to 7 winners including the Derby winner High-Rise and the dual listed winner Supremacy and to the placed dam of the Italian Oaks and E P Taylor Stakes winner Zomaradah.

The second dam, High Tern (by High Line), a fairly useful winning stayer, is a half-sister to 9 winners including the Group 1 Premio Roma and Group 2 Ribblesdale Stakes winner High Hawk (herself dam of the Breeders Cup Turf winner In The Wings and the Group 2 winners Hunting Hawk and Hawker's News) and the dam of the Group winners Infamy, Amfortas and Legend Maker. *"Typical of the sire, he's very tough and resilient. He'll probably get seven furlongs but he'll be good enough over six and he'll be ready from the middle of May onwards".*

1087. GIVE WAY NELSON (IRE) ★★★★

b.f. Mount Nelson – Give A Whistle (Mujadil). February 9. Seventh foal. €42,000Y. Goffs Orby. Newsells Park Stud. Half-sister to the Irish 2-y-o listed 5f and subsequent US Grade 3 6f winner Pasar Silbano (by Elnadim), to the useful listed 6f winner Gerfalcon (by Hawk Wing), the quite useful UAE 3-y-o 6f winner Call For Liberty and the fair Irish 2-y-o 6f winner Laldie (both by Statue Of Liberty). The dam, a dual 5f winner at 3 and 4 yrs, is a half-sister to one winner. The second dam, Repique (by Sharpen Up), a fair 6f and 7f winner, is a half-sister to the Group winners Indian Lodge, Sarhoob and Sifting Gold. *"A tall filly and a little bit leggy, she has a lot of speed and looks very decent. I'd say she might be racing from late May onwards".*

1088. GREAT HALL ★★★

b.c. Halling – L'Affaire Monique (Machiavellian). April 23. Seventh foal. 65,000Y. Tattersalls October Book 1. Angie Loder Bloodstock. Half-brother to the Italian 7.5f (at 2 yrs) and 10f winner and Group 3 1m Premio Dormello second Short Affair, to the Italian 9f to 11f winner and listed-placed Bon Spiel (both by Singspiel), the quite useful triple 10f winner Bourne (by Linamix) and the modest 1m winner Majestic Bright (by Pivotal). The dam, a useful 10f winner, is a full or half-sister to 11 winners including Little Rock (Group 2 Princess Of Wales's Stakes), Whitewater Affair (Group 2 Prix de Pomone and the dam of two Japanese Group 1 winners) and Short Skirt (Group 3 Musidora Stakes). The second dam, Much Too Risky (by Bustino), won twice at 2 yrs and is a half-sister to the Group 1 winners Arctic Owl and Marooned. *"Typical of the sire, he's got a lot of class but he wants plenty of time. I'm sure he'll get a mile and he'll be ready in August or September".*

1089. HARRY BOSCH ★★★
b.c. Kyllachy – Fen Guest (Woodborough). April 10. Second foal. £78,000Y. Doncaster Premier. McKeever Bloodstock. Half-brother to the fair 2011 2-y-o 7f winner Vinnie Jones (by Piccolo). The dam, a moderate 6f winner, is a half-sister to 5 winners including the listed winner of 4 races Ronaldsay. The second dam, Crackling (by Electric), a modest 9f and 12f winner, is a half-sister to 4 winners including the Group 1 7f Moyglare Stud Stakes winner Bianca Nera and the dam of the Group 1 Fillies' Mile winner Simply Perfect. *"He'll want six furlongs to start with in late May and I think he has a bit of class about him".*

1090. IGHRAA ★★★★
b.f. Tamayuz – Frond (Alzao). March 15. Tenth foal. 110,000foal. Tattersalls December. Shadwell Estate Co. Half-sister to the smart multiple listed winner (from 7f to 10f) Nashmiah (by Elusive City), to the useful 2-y-o 7f and listed 1m winner Streets Ahead (by Beat Hollow), the fairly useful 2-y-o 6f winner and listed-placed Ridder (by Dr Fong), the fair dual 10f winner Addikt (by Diktat), the German 10f winner Portcullis (by Pivotal) and the Scandinavian 1m and 10f winner Azolla (by Cadeaux Genereux). The dam, a quite useful 2-y-o 7f winner, is a half-sister to 8 winners. The second dam, Fern (by Shirley Heights), a useful 12f winner and third in the listed 10f Lupe Stakes, is a half-sister to 6 winners including the Group 1 Fillies Mile winner and Oaks second Shamshir. *"A very sharp filly with a superb attitude, she goes really well and will be a five/six furlong 2-y-o".*

1091. INDEX WAITER ★★★★
ch.c. Exceed And Excel – Snowy Indian (Indian Ridge). March 27. First foal. 70,000Y. Tattersalls October Book 2. McKeever Bloodstock. The dam, a modest 7f (at 2 yrs) to 10f placed maiden, is a sister to the 2-y-o Group 1 1m Royal Lodge Stakes winner and 2,000 Guineas second Snow Ridge and a half-sister to 3 winners including the German listed 1m winner Snowy Gretel. The second dam, Snow Princess

(by Ela-Mana-Mou), a smart winner of 6 races at up to 2m including the November Handicap and an Italian listed event, was second in the Group 1 Prix Royal-Oak and is a half-sister to 7 winners. *"A lovely horse, he goes really well and I like him. I see him being ready from mid-May onwards and he'll get seven furlongs this year".*

1092. INVINCIBLE WARRIOR (IRE) ★★★
b.c. Invincible Spirit – Riotous Applause (Royal Applause). January 30. Second foal. Half-brother to Riot Of Colour (by Excellent Art), placed second over 6f on both her starts at 2 yrs in 2011. The dam, a fairly useful dual 6f winner (including at 2 yrs), is a sister to one winner and a half-sister to the high-class 2-y-o Group 1 1m Racing Post Trophy winner Crowded House, the French listed 11f winner and Group 3 placed On Reflection and the useful 12f winner Heron Bay and to the placed dam of the US dual Grade 1 winner Ticker Tape. The second dam, Wiener Wald (Woodman), is an unplaced half-sister to 6 minor winners abroad. *"A strong, forward, very sharp colt. He's been sick so he'll probably need a bit more time but I still see him as a five/six furlong 2-y-o from late May onwards".*

[handwritten: will Coventry wnr g1 6f rds]

1093. KING DRAGON ★★★ **[handwritten: wnr list]**
b.g. Iffraaj – Reign Of Fire (Perugino). April 22. Fourth foal. €80,000Y. Goffs Orby. McKeever Bloodstock. Half-brother to the fair 2011 2-y-o 7f winner Not Bad For A Boy (by Elusive City) and to the multiple Italian winner Very Glamour (by Pyrus). The dam was placed at 2 yrs and is a half-sister to 4 winners including the US Grade 3 winner Media Mogul. The second dam, White Heat (by Last Tycoon), was placed at 2 yrs and is a half-sister to 5 winners including the dual listed winner Watching. *"He's sharp so it shouldn't take too long before we get him out and six furlongs should do for him from mid-May onwards although he'll probably get further".*

[handwritten: Ran late in jd 6f mdn Nwm]

1094. MASTER MING (IRE) ★★★
b.c. Excellent Art – China Pink (Oasis Dream). March 16. First foal. 26,000Y. Tattersalls October Book 2. McKeever Bloodstock. The dam, a moderate 11f winner, is a half-sister to 5 winners including the smart listed 12f winner and US Grade 1 second Red Fort and the useful

listed 12f winner Red Carnation. The second dam, Red Bouquet (by Reference Point), won 3 minor races from 12f to 13f at 4 yrs in Germany and is a half-sister to 4 winners including the Group 3 7f Prestige Stakes winner Red Camellia (herself dam of the Group 1 Fillies' Mile winner Red Bloom). *"He still needs a bit of time because he's got a lot of size and scope to him, but we like him a lot and he'll be a seven furlong 2-y-o in mid-season".* *Easily won 1m seq m/m 7k:1py*

1095. MEETING IN PARIS (IRE) ★★★ *1st*

b.f. Dutch Art – Sharplaw Star (Xaar). March 23. The dam, a fairly useful 2-y-o dual 5f winner, was third in the Group 3 5f Queen Mary Stakes and is a half-sister to 2 winners. The second dam, Hamsah (by Green Desert), a quite useful 2-y-o dual 5f winner, was listed-placed and is a half-sister to the Irish 2,000 Guineas winner Wassl and to the dam of the Queen Mary Stakes winner On Tiptoes. (Sir Robert Ogden). *"She had a little setback recently so she's having a couple of months off, but she has a lot of speed and she's a good-looking filly I'll be glad to see back in training".*

1096. MUTASHABEK (USA) ★★★

b.c. Arch – Siyadah (Mr Prospector). February 16. Half-brother to the useful 9f winner and listed-placed Musanid, to the minor French 12f winner Sahabah (both by Swain), the French listed-placed Mahara (by Diesis), the fair 1m winner Tasjeel (by Aljabr), the minor French 2-y-o 7f winner Tawaaleef (by Haafhd) and a hurdles winner by Bahri. The dam, a useful listed 10f winner, is a half-sister to numerous winners including the dual listed 10f winner Esloob. The second dam, Roseate Tern (by Blakeney) won the Group 1 12f Yorkshire Oaks, the Group 2 12f Jockey Club Stakes and the Group 3 12f Lancashire Oaks, was second in the Epsom Oaks and third in the St Leger. She is a half-sister to several winners including the high-class middle distance colt Ibn Bey, winner of the Irish St Leger, the Gran Premio d'Italia, two Group 1 events in Germany and second in the Breeders Cup Classic. (Hamdan Al Maktoum). *"A lovely, big horse that wants a bit of time. He's just come in from Dubai, so we're still getting to know him".*

1097. PEARL BELL (IRE) ★★★★

b.f. Camacho – Magnificent Bell (Octagonal). February 12. Fourth foal. £25,000Y. Doncaster Premier. David Redvers. Half-sister to the fairly useful 10f to 2m and hurdles winner Inventor (by Alzao), to the quite useful 5f (at 2 yrs) to 1m winner Las Verglas Star (by Verglas) and a winner in Russia (by Celtic Swing). The dam is an unraced half-sister to 6 winners including the very useful 7.5f (at 2 yrs) and listed 10f winner Esyoueffcee (by Alzao). The second dam, Familiar (by Diesis), a fairly useful 3-y-o 1m winner, is a half-sister to 8 winners including the high-class Prix du Moulin winner and Epsom Oaks second All At Sea and the smart French dual Group 3 winner Over The Ocean. (Pearl Bloodstock). *"A very sharp, big, strong filly with a lot of speed. She should be running soon and I like her a lot".*

1098. RUN IT TWICE (IRE) ★★★

b.c. Dark Angel – Alinda (Revoque). February 18. Fourth foal. 75,000Y. Tattersalls October Book 1. Angie Loder. Half-brother to the fair 2011 2-y-o 7f winner Alabanda and to the fair 6f (at 2 yrs) and 7f winner Camache Queen (both by Camacho). The dam, a fair 6f (at 2 yrs) and dual 7f winner, is a half-sister to 5 winners including the Group 3 July Stakes winner Rich Ground and the fairly useful 5f and 6f winner of 6 races (including at 2 yrs) and Group 2 Princess Margaret Stakes third Bandanna. The second dam, Gratclo (by Belfort), a modest winner of 5 races from 2 to 4 yrs, is a half-sister to 3 winners. (I Parvizi). *"A typical Dark Angel, he's strong, good-looking, a little bit lazy but a good sort that goes well. He'll probably get seven furlongs this year".*

1099. SAVED BY THE BELL (IRE) ★★★★

b.c. Teofilo – Eyrecourt (Efisio). February 24. Fourth foal. €100,000foal. Goffs. Camas Park. Half-brother to Wreaths Of Empire (by Dalakhani), unplaced in two starts at 2 yrs in 2011. The dam ran twice unplaced and is a sister to the Group 1 Prix Vermeille and Group 2 Prix de Malleret winner Pearly Shells and a half-sister to 3 winners including the US Grade 1 Hollywood Turf Handicap and Group 3 Beresford Stakes winner Frenchpark. The second dam, Piffle (by Shirley Heights), a quite useful 12f winner, is a sister to the useful stayer

El Conquistador and a half-sister to 4 winners. *"A lovely colt, he shows plenty of speed and he seems to have a lot of ability. I thought originally he'd be one for August-time, but now I'd say he'll be running by early June".*

1100. SECRET SIGN ★★★★

ch.c. Sakhee's Secret – Barboukh (Night Shift). March 15. Eleventh foal. 23,000Y. Tattersalls October Book 2. McKeever Bloodstock. Half-brother to the Group 3 10f Prix Exbury winner and Group 1 Premio Presidente della Repubblica third Barbola (by Diesis), to the fairly useful 1m to 10f and jumps winner Tarboush (by Polish Precedent) and a hurdles winner by Fantastic Light. The dam, a fairly useful winner of the 1m listed Fern Hill Stakes, is a half-sister to 7 winners. The second dam, Turban (by Glint Of Gold), a fair 10f and 11.7f winner at 3 yrs, is a half-sister to 6 winners including the top-class French and Irish Derby winner Old Vic. *"A very sharp colt, he'll be running in May, he'll get six furlongs but he's got a lot of speed".*

1101. SMOOTHTALKINRASCAL (IRE) ★★★★

b.c. Kodiac – Cool Tarifa (One Cool Cat). April 14. First foal. £21,000Y. Doncaster Premier. Ned Sangster. The dam, a quite useful Irish 2-y-o 5f winner, is a half-sister to 4 minor winners. The second dam, Tarafiya (by Trempolino), won once in France over 12.5f and is a half-sister to 6 winners. (Invictus). *"We were very pleased with his debut run when he was second and just got tired towards the end. He was very professional, showed a lot of speed and he'd been working well previously. We'll keep him at five furlongs for the moment but I'm sure he'd have no trouble getting six".* TRAINERS' BARGAIN BUY *won in a canter Sptr Leicester*

1102. THANKSGIVING DAY (USA) ★★★★

b.c. Harlan's Holiday – Frappay (Deputy Minister). March 20. Fifth foal. 42,000Y. Tattersalls October Book 2. McKeever Bloodstock. Half-brother to 2 minor winners in the USA by Cherokee Run and Smart Strike. The dam is an unplaced daughter of the US Grade 2 Railbird Stakes and multiple listed stakes winner Supercilious (by Skywalker). *"A lovely horse, one for the back-end of the season because he's still a bit weak and wants a bit of time, but he's a lovely, lovely*

colt and I think the world of him. Seven furlongs or a mile will suit him".

1103. WHIPPER'S BOY (IRE) ★★★

b.g. Whipper – Glympse (Spectrum). May 19. Fifth foal. €52,000Y. Goffs Orby. McKeever Bloodstock. Half-brother to the fair 5f winner Supercharged (by Iffraaj) and to the fair Irish 2-y-o 7f winner Westering Home (by Mull Of Kintyre). The dam, placed fourth once over 9f in Ireland, is a half-sister to 4 winners including the Group/Graded stakes winners Rekindled Interest, Simple Exchange, Sights On Gold and Where We Left Off. The second dam, Seasonal Pickup (by The Minstrel), won four listed races in Ireland and is a half-sister to the dam of Grey Swallow. *"He's showing a lot of flair and he has a good attitude. I can see him starting at six furlongs and then moving on to seven".*

1104. UNNAMED ★★★

b.c. Amadeus Wolf – Cantaloupe (Priolo). March 23. Seventh foal. £24,000Y. Doncaster Premier. McKeever Bloodstock. Half-brother to the winner Cantabilly (by Distant Music) and a winner in Poland by Singspiel. The dam is an unraced half-sister to 8 winners including the French Group 3 12f Prix de Royaumont winner Cantilever. The second dam, Cantanta (by Top Ville), won over 2m at 3 yrs and is a sister to the Irish Oaks winner Princess Pati and a half-sister to 8 winners including the Group 2 Great Voltigeur Stakes winner Seymour Hicks. *"He's got plenty of speed, but I can see him getting seven furlongs later on. A nice colt with a good attitude".*

1105. UNNAMED ★★★★

b.c. Kheleyf – Catching Stars (Halling). February 6. Third foal. £55,000Y. Doncaster Premier. McKeever Bloodstock. Half-brother to the fairly useful 2011 Irish 2-y-o 1m winner Cloudracer (by Rail Link). The dam is an unraced half-sister to the Group 1 Pretty Polly Stakes winner Chinese White. The second dam, Chiang Mai (by Sadler's Wells), won the Group 3 12f Blandford Stakes and is a half-sister to 9 winners including the Group 1 10.5f Prix de Diane winner and top-class broodmare Rafha and the quite useful 1m 6f Ebor Handicap winner Sarawat. *"He looks really good on the* gallops at the moment. He seems to have a lot of ability and just needs a bit of time, but he'll be out in mid-season".

1106. UNNAMED ★★★

b.c. Royal Applause – Fantastic Santanyi (Fantastic Light). April 30. Third foal. 38,000Y. Tattersalls October Book 2. McKeever Bloodstock. The dam, a winner in Italy at 3 yrs and listed-placed in France, is a half-sister to the winner and Group 3 third Zuleika Dobson. The second dam, Fresher (by Fabulous Dancer), won twice in France and was second in the Group 2 Prix d'Astarte and is a half-sister to 5 winners including the Group 2 Prix Niel winner Songlines. "A nice horse, he's strong, wants a bit of time but he's a good-looking colt. We haven't done a lot with him yet, but I like him and we'll probably start him at six furlongs".

1107. UNNAMED ★★★

ch.c. Redback – Feet Of Flame (Theatrical). February 10. Seventh foal. £32,000Y. Doncaster Premier. McKeever Bloodstock. Brother to the fairly useful 2-y-o 8.7f winner Fullback and half-brother to the fairly useful 7f to 10f winner and Group 3 third Kinky Afro (by Modigliani) and the fair 2-y-o 7f winner Orpen Fire (by Orpen). The dam is a placed half-sister to one winner in the USA. The second dam, Red Hot Dancer (by Seattle Dancer), is a US placed half-sister to 5 winners including the minor US stakes winner at around 1m Madame Secretary (herself dam of the French 1,000 Guineas winner Ta Rib) and the Stewards Cup winner Green Ruby. "A very genuine colt, he has a good temperament, he wants six furlongs and as soon as those races appear he'll run. A typical Redback".

1108. UNNAMED ★★★

ch.c. Excellent Art – Granny Kelly (Irish River). March 27. Ninth foal. €55,000Y. Goffs Orby. McKeever Bloodstock. Half-brother to the fairly useful 2011 2-y-o 6f winner Right To Dream, to the minor French 3-y-o winner Aisy (both by Oasis Dream), the quite useful 2-y-o 6f and Italian 7.5f listed winner Six Hitter (by Boundary), the quite useful dual 7f winner (including at 2 yrs) of 4 races Hustle (by Choisir) and the minor French 10f and 11f winner of 3 races Heavenly Light (by Montjeu). The dam, placed once over 7f at 2 yrs in Ireland, is a half-

sister to 4 minor winners. The second dam, Deviltante (by Devil's Bag), a minor US 3-y-o winner, is a half-sister to 5 winners including the US stakes winner and Grade 2 placed Arrowtown. "He wants time because he's still a bit weak, but he's very straightforward and genuine. One for seven furlongs around July time". 2nd ????? ?? ?? Newbury ????? ?? debut

1109. UNNAMED ★★★

b.c. Royal Applause – Just Julie (Gulch). April 6. Second foal. €55,000Y. Goffs Orby. BBA. Half-brother to Julie Moss (by Moss Vale) placed third over 5f on her only start at 2 yrs in 2011. The dam, modest dual 12f placed maiden, is a half-sister to 2 minor winners. The second dam, Julie Jalouse (by Kris S), won 4 races in the USA including the Grade 2 Orchid Handicap and is a half-sister to 4 winners including the US Grade 2 winner Mariensky. "A typical Royal Applause, he's very straightforward, does it all well and he should be racing in May over six furlongs".

1110. UNNAMED ★★★

ch.f. Shamardal – La Vita E Bella (Definite Article). April 14. Fifth foal. 80,000Y. Tattersalls October Book 2. McKeever Bloodstock. Sister to the fair 9f winner Lifetime. The dam, a 2-y-o listed 1m winner and second in the Group 3 Prix Saint-Roman, is a half-sister to 3 winners including the useful 2-y-o dual listed 5f winner and Group 2 third Bella Tusa. The second dam, Coolrain Lady (by Common Grounds), was placed 12 times in Ireland from 1m to 10f and is a half-sister to 4 winners. "A lovely filly, she'll want six furlongs and she'll probably be ready in late May".

1111. UNNAMED ★★★★

b.f. Danehill Dancer – Myth And Magic (Namid). February 6. First foal. 150,000Y. Tattersalls October Book 1. Hugo Merry. The dam is an unraced half-sister to 11 winners including the Grade 1 9f Matriarch Stakes, Group 2 1m Sun Chariot Stakes and triple Group 3 winner Dress To Thrill. The second dam, Trusted Partner (by Affirmed), winner of the Group 3 7f C L Weld Park Stakes (at 2 yrs) and the Irish 1,000 Guineas, is a sister to the 3 stakes winners including Easy to Copy (herself the dam of 3 stakes winners) and Epicure's Garden (dam of the Group 2 Blandford Stakes winner Lisieux

Rose). *"She wants plenty of time, she's a big, strong filly and I can see her being out around July time. She'll get seven furlongs and she never misses a day. A very nice filly".*

1112. UNNAMED ★★★

ch.g. Exceed And Excel – Our Sheila (Bahamian Bounty). February 9. Third foal. 31,000Y. Tattersalls October Book 2. McKeever Bloodstock. Brother to Selective Spirit, unplaced in one start at 2 yrs in 2011. The dam, a fair 6f winner of 4 races at 3 yrs, is a half-sister to 4 winners including the Italian Group 3 winner and Group 2 Prix Robert Papin second Shifting Place. The second dam, Shifting Mist (by Night Shift), a modest 10f to 14f winner of 5 races, is a half-sister to 7 winners including the dam of the dual Group 3 winner Needwood Blade. *"A nice, sharp gelding with a good attitude. One for six furlongs".*

1113. UNNAMED ★★★★ ♠

ch.c. Exceed And Excel – Psychic (Alhaarth). March 21. Sixth foal. 80,000Y. Tattersalls October Book 1. McKeever Bloodstock. Half-brother to the fair triple 7f winner Mr Tinktastic (by Noverre), to the fair 6f winner Psychic Dream (by Oasis Dream) and the minor French and Qatar winner Barapsy (by Barathea). The dam, a fair 3-y-o 5f winner, is a half-sister to 7 winners including the Group 3 Gallinule Stakes winner Grand Ducal and the dam of the dual Group 3 winner Azmeel. The second dam, Mood Swings (by Shirley Heights), a fair 2-y-o 6f winner, is a sister to the listed 2-y-o Sweet Solera Stakes winner Catwalk and a half-sister to 6 winners. *"A very sharp colt, he could be racing in early May. A six furlong type, he could be one for Royal Ascot".*

1114. UNNAMED ★★★

ch.f. Stormy Atlantic – Rebuke (Carson City). January 23. First foal. The dam, a minor winner of 4 races in the USA at 3 and 4 yrs, is a half-sister to 6 winners including the 2-y-o Group 1 Middle Park Stakes second Rebuttal and the US stakes winner Summer Cruise. The second dam, Launch Light Tek (by Relaunch), a stakes winner of 6 races in the USA and Grade 3 placed, is a half-sister to 4 winners. (Mr A Rosen). *"She'll want six furlongs from late May onwards and she's going well".*

1115. UNNAMED ★★★

br.c. Shamardal – Red Bandanna (Montjeu). March 18. Third foal. €50,000Y. Goffs Orby. Oliver St Lawrence. Half-brother to the quite useful 1m winner Finest Reserve (by Royal Applause). The dam, placed once over 9f at 3 yrs in Ireland, is a half-sister to 4 winners including the smart dual listed 10f winner and good broodmare Foodbroker Fancy and the listed winner Femme Fatale. The second dam, Red Rita (by Kefaah), a fairly useful 4-y-o 6f winner, was second in the Group 3 6f Cherry Hinton Stakes and the Group 3 6f Princess Margaret Stakes at 2 yrs and is a half-sister to 3 minor winners. *"A lovely, big colt, he'll want a bit of time but he'll be out in mid-season over seven furlongs".*

1116. UNNAMED ★★★

ch.c. Duke Of Marmalade – Santa Sophia (Linamix). March 29. Sixth foal. 62,000Y. Tattersalls October Book 2. McKeever Bloodstock. Half-brother to the quite useful 2-y-o 1m and subsequent US winner Dover Street Art (by Alhaarth) and to the fair 1m to 10f winner of 3 races Snow Magic (by Marju). The dam won the listed Oaks Trial and is a half-sister to 2 winners. The second dam, Samara (by Polish Patriot), a winner of two listed events over 1m and 8.5f, was third in the Group 3 Park Stakes and is a half-sister to 8 winners including the German Group 2 winner Soto-Grande. *"He wants a bit of time but he works well and shows plenty. He'll get a mile this year and we'll probably start him in July or August".*

1117. UNNAMED ★★★

ch.f. Teofilo – Scarlett Rose (Royal Applause). March 24. Fourth foal. €180,000Y. Goffs Orby. Hugo Merry. Half-sister to the smart 2-y-o Group 2 6f Railway Stakes winner and Group 2 6f Mill Reef Stakes second Formosina (by Footstepsinthesand). The dam, a modest 6f and 7f placed maiden, is a half-sister to 7 winners including the multiple Group 3 winner Tumbleweed Ridge and the dam of the Group 2 Queen Mary Stakes winner Gilded. The second dam, Billie Blue (by Ballad Rock), is a placed half-sister to 4 winners. *"She's got a lot of speed but needs a bit more time before she's ready. I might start her over six furlongs but she'll stay seven".*

Lazarus 604

1118. UNNAMED ★★★★

ch.c. Bahamian Bounty – Snake's Head (Golden Snake). January 26. Second foal. £38,000Y. Doncaster Premier. The dam, the fair 12f winner, is a half-sister to the 5 winners including the very useful 6f (at 2 yrs) and 9f winner Zabaglione. The second dam, Satin Bell (by Midyan), a useful 7f winner, is a half-sister to 4 winners including the useful listed 6f winner Star Tulip. *"A nice horse, he had a minor injury in early April but he's still cantering and he should be ready to start sometime in May over six furlongs. I like him, he's very genuine and shows ability".* *Easily Won 4 corale 7f Newmar*

1119. UNNAMED ★★★

b.c. Moss Vale – Street Style (Rock Of Gibraltar). March 1. First foal. £30,000Y. Doncaster Premier. Agent Allison. The dam, a fair 9f winner, is a half-sister to 4 winners including the US Grade 1 winner and Irish 1,000 Guineas third Luas Line. The second dam, Streetcar (by In The Wings), is a placed half-sister to 9 winners including Intimate Guest (Group 3 May Hill Stakes). *"A sharp, early sort, he probably wants six furlongs though, but we'll run him soon enough".*

1120. UNNAMED ★★★

b.c. Invincible Spirit – Three Wrens (Second Empire). February 10. Third foal. 80,000Y. Tattersalls October Book 1. McKeever Bloodstock. Half-brother to the modest 2011 7f and 1m placed 2-y-o Courtesy Call (by Manduro). The dam, a listed 1m winner of 4 races from 2 to 4 yrs, is a half-sister to 7 winners including the listed winner and Group 2 placed Thames. The second dam, Three Terns (by Arctic Tern), won over 9f in France and is a half-sister to 3 winners including the Group 3 1m Prix des Reservoirs winner Three Angels. *"A colt with a lot of size about him, he's one for the second half of the season. We haven't done an awful lot with him yet but he seems to go well".*

1121. UNNAMED ★★★★

b.f. Speightstown – Unrestrained (Unbridled). February 27. Sixth foal. 65,000Y. Tattersalls October Book 1. McKeever Bloodstock. Half-sister to the US winner and stakes-placed Stormy The Cat (by Storm Cat) and a minor

US stakes winner by Tale Of The Cat. The dam, a dual stakes winner in the USA, was Grade 3 placed and is a half-sister to 10 winners including the US Grade 3 winners Colonial Minstrel and Minidar. The second dam, Minstrella (by The Minstrel), won the Cheveley Park Stakes, the Moyglare Stud Stakes and the Phoenix Stakes (all Group 1 events). *"A lovely filly with plenty of size and scope. She has a great attitude and shows plenty of ability. One for the middle of the season over six/seven furlongs".*

1122. UNNAMED ★★★

br.c. Kheleyf – Upskittled (Diktat). May 5. Third foal. £28,000Y. Doncaster Premier. McKeever Bloodstock. Half-brother to a winner abroad by Medicean. The dam, placed twice at 3 yrs in France, is a half-sister to 9 winners including the listed winner and dual Group 1 third Musicanna and to the dam of the champion sprinter Overdose. The second dam, Upend (by Main Reef), won 3 races from 10f to 12f including the Group 3 St Simon Stakes and the listed Galtres Stakes, was second in the Group 3 Princess Royal Stakes and is a half-sister to 6 winners including the dam of the high-class stayer and champion hurdler Royal Gait. *"A very nice colt that shows he has ability, I'll start him off over six furlongs from mid-May onwards and he'll get seven later on".*

1123. UNNAMED ★★★

b.c. Holy Roman Emperor – Web Of Intrigue (Machiavellian). March 13. Eighth living foal. Tattersalls October Book 2. McKeever Bloodstock. Half-brother to the fair 6f winner Francis Walsingham (by Invincible Spirit), to the modest 1m and 10f winner Chapter (by Sinndar), the moderate 4-y-o 1m seller and hurdles winner Dubonai (by Peintre Celebre) and a bumper winner by In The Wings. The dam is a placed half-sister to 9 winners including the high-class Group 1 12f Yorkshire Oaks and Group 3 12f Lancashire Oaks winner Catchascatchcan (herself dam of the Group 2 winner and triple Group 1 placed Antonius Pius). The second dam, Catawba (by Mill Reef), a useful 3-y-o listed-placed 10.5f winner, is a half-sister to 7 winners including Strigida (Group 2 Ribblesdale Stakes). *"A colt with a* good temperament, he's a straightforward, typical Holy Roman Emperor and a six/seven furlong type".

ROD MILLMAN

1124. ASTRUM ★★

ch.c. Haafhd – Vax Star (Petong). March 16. Tenth foal. 30,000Y. Tattersalls October Book 2. Rod Millman. Half-brother to the fairly useful 2-y-o dual 6f winner Negligee (by Night Shift), to the quite useful 6f (at 2 yrs) and 5f winner of 5 races Yurituni (by Bahamian Bounty), the quite useful 3-y-o 7f winner Vandal (by Entrepreneur), the fair 2-y-o 5f winner River Crossing (by Zafonic), the 2-y-o 5f seller winner Trick Or Two (by Desert Style) and the French 2-y-o 6f winner Silver Shadow (by Fasliyev). The dam, a fairly useful 2-y-o 5f listed winner, is a half-sister to 4 winners. The second dam, the fairly useful listed sprint winner Vax Lady (by Millfontaine), is a half-sister to 2 winners. (The Links Partnership). "A very correct, good-looking horse that had a virus in the winter which put him back a few weeks. He looked the type we could have got on with but now it's looking like the end of May before he'll be out. A nice horse otherwise, but we haven't been able to press any buttons with him. I think he'd have been much more expensive if the sire wasn't out of fashion. I see him being a sprinter but he'll probably get seven furlongs later on".

1125. BLACKDOWN SPIRIT ★★

b.g. Ishiguru – Shielaligh (Aragon). March 26. Third foal. 15,000Y. Ascot Autumn. Rod Millman. Half-brother to the quite useful 2011 2-y-o 6f winner Blackdown Fair (by Trade Fair) and to the modest 6f winner Blackdown Boy (by Sampower Star). The dam, a fair 2-y-o winner, is a sister to 2 winners including the quite useful 5f (at 2 yrs) and 6f winner of 4 races Seamus Shindig and a half-sister to one winner. The second dam, Sheesha (by Shadeed), was unplaced in one start and is a half-sister to 8 winners including the smart 12f King George V Handicap winner and St Leger fourth Samraan and the useful 6f (at 2 yrs) and 7f winner Star Talent. "We know the family well and I think he takes after his half-sister Blackdown Fair. A sharp type that should be racing by the end of May and he's still for sale if anyone would like to take a look at him". TRAINERS' BARGAIN BUY

1126. ISIS BLUE ★★

b.c. Cockney Rebel – Bramaputra (Choisir). February 7. First foal. The dam, a quite useful 1m winner, is a half-sister to 2 winners including the Group 2 7f Champagne Stakes winner and 2,000 Guineas second Vital Equine. The second dam, Bayalika (by Selkirk), is an unraced half-sister to 5 winners including an Italian listed winner. (Cantay Partnership). "A lovely horse that was working very well in the spring but unfortunately he's had a setback and he won't run now until late summer over seven furlongs. He's well-bred and I trained the dam who was very good. She was massive – about 530kgs, whereas this is a 'tidy' type of horse".

1127. PHOEBE'S PERFECT ★★★

b.f. Tobougg – Water Flower (Environment Friend). March 28. Fifth foal. Half-sister to the moderate 10f and hurdles winner Lucy's Perfect (by Systematic) and to a hurdles winner by Double Trigger. The dam, a fair 12f winner of 5 races, also won over jumps and is a half-sister to the very useful Group 3 1m Prix Saint-Roman winner and Group 2 9.8f Prix Dollar third Eco Friendly. The second dam, Flower Girl (by Pharly), a very useful winner of 5 races including the Group 3 6f Goldene Peitsche and the listed 6f Sandy Lane Stakes, is a sister to the useful listed 9.4f winner Farmost and a half-sister to 3 winners. "Her mother was a staying mare, but this filly takes after her sire a bit because she's got quite a bit of speed about her. A racey type, she was broken-in late but I think she'll be racing over six furlongs by the end of May and she's showing a fair bit of form at the moment".

1128. SHAHDAROBA (IRE) ★★★

b.c. Haatef – Gold Script (Script Ohio). March 18. Twelfth foal. £25,000Y. Doncaster Premier. G Howson. Half-brother to the Group 3 6f Railway Stakes winner and Group 1 7f Prix de la Salamandre second Honours List (by Danehill), to the fairly useful dual 6f winner (including at 2 yrs) Cnocan Gold (by Danehill Dancer), the Italian 1m winner of 3 races and listed placed Zina La Belle (by Mark Of Esteem), the minor French 1m winner Ballpoint (by Oasis Dream) and the minor French winner of 5 races Supreme Talent (by Desert King). The dam, a French 5.5f (at 2 yrs) and listed 12f

Prix de Thiberville winner, is a half-sister to 5 winners. The second dam, Quiet Thoughts (by Thatching), won the Group 3 7f Athasi Stakes. (The Links Partnership). *"A really nice, masculine horse and a very correct individual that shows ability. He'll probably be running by the end of April, he looks sharp enough for five furlongs but he'll stay a bit further".*

1129. SWEET ALABAMA ★★★

gr.f. *Johannesburg – Alybgood (Alydeed).* March 3. Seventh foal. 22,000Y. Tattersalls October Book 2. Rod Millman. Half-sister to 3 minor winners in the USA by Consolidator, Grand Slam and Gone West and to a winner in Japan by Mr Greeley. The dam, a US listed stakes winner of 5 races at 2 and 4 yrs, is a half-sister to 10 winners including the German Oaks winner Que Belle (herself the dam of two Group 3 winners) and the dams of the Group 2 winners Quelle Amore and Johann Zoffany. The second dam, Qui Bid (by Spectacular Bid), is an unraced sister to the US Grade 3 winner Sum and a half-sister to 9 winners including the Group 1 winner Bakharoff and the Group 2 winner Emperor Jones. (The Links Partnership). *"A nice, quality filly and well-bred, she's had a small setback but she'll still be running at the end of May. I see her staying a mile later on".*

1130. WINNIE PERRY ★★

ch.g. *Assertive – Hayley's Flower (Night Shift).* March 4. First foal. The dam, a modest 7f winner at 3 yrs, is a half-sister to a winner. The second dam, Plastiqueuse (by Quest For Fame), won over 10.7f and 12f in France. *"Quite a nice horse, he was broken-in a bit late but he's a real sprinting-type 2-y-o".*

1131. YES TOO ★★★

b.c. *Indesatchel – Charlie Girl (Puissance).* March 3. Ninth foal. £11,000Y. Doncaster Premier. Rod Millman. Half-brother to the useful 2-y-o dual 6f winner and listed-placed Josh (by Josr Algharoud), to the quite useful 2-y-o 6f winner Russian Reel (by Reel Buddy), the quite useful 5f (including at 2 yrs) and 6f winner of 9 races and listed-placed Feelin Foxy and the 2-y-o 5f seller winner Gone To Ground (both by Foxhound). The dam, a 2-y-o 5f winner, is a half-sister to 4 winners. The second dam, Charolles (by Ajdal), is a placed half-sister

to 5 winners including the French dual Group 1 winner Creator. (Mustajed Partnership). *"A bit leggy but a great walker, he'll probably start off at five furlongs but I think he'll be better over six. He's well-forward, he catches the eye and he's a good-tempered horse".*

1132. UNNAMED ★★

b.c. *Auction House – Lady Of Limerick (Thatching).* April 21. Ninth foal. 5,000Y. Tattersalls October Book 3. G Howson. Half-brother to the fairly useful 5f to 7f winner of 5 races High Reach (by Royal Applause), to the fair dual 5f winner (including at 2 yrs) Our Acquaintance (by Bahamian Bounty), the fair 2-y-o 5f winner Marechal George (by Deerhound) and the modest 5f and 6f winner of 5 races Lady Algarhoud (by Josr Algarhoud). The dam ran unplaced in the USA and is a half-sister to 5 winners including the Group 2 Kings Stand Stakes third Funny Valentine and the dam of the Group 3 winner Resplendent Glory. The second dam, Aunt Hester (by Caerleon), a modest 2-y-o 5f winner, is a half-sister to 7 winners including the Group 3 9f Prix Daphnis winner L'Irresponsable. *"He put quite a bit of weight on over the winter so we're working on reducing that now. He probably won't be running until May but he looks a 2-y-o type and he's still for sale".*

ROBERT MILLS
1133. CLUB HOUSE ★★★★

b.c. *Marju – Idesia (Green Desert).* March 4. First foal. 36,000Y. Tattersalls October Book 2. R A Mills. The dam, a modest 1m and 10f placed maiden, is a half-sister to 2 minor winners. The second dam, Indaba (by Indian Ridge), a fairly useful 6f and 7f winner, was listed-placed twice and is a half-sister to 8 winners including the dam of the multiple Group 1 winner and sire Shirocco. (Mr Trevor Jacobs & Mrs B B Mills). *"A nice horse, I like him a lot. We'll be looking at starting him off as soon as the six furlong maiden races appear and although he'll probably be seen to best advantage over seven he does have the speed for six. He goes well, he's forward and shows ability".*

1134. DREAM ABOUT YOU ★★★★

br.f. *Amadeus Wolf – Peshawar (Persian Bold).* March 4. €10,000Y. Goffs Orby. TG & BB Mills.

Half-sister to the quite useful 6f (at 2 yrs), 7f and hurdles winner American Art (by Statue Of Liberty) and to 6 winners in Germany and Italy by Platini, Second Set and Monsun. The dam is an unraced half-sister to 7 winners including the German 1,000 Guineas winner Princess Nana. The second dam, Alys (by Blakeney), won two listed events in France, was third in the Group 2 Prix d'Astarte and is a half-sister to 7 winners. *"She had a setback during the winter but she's catching up fast and we like her a lot. Very forward, very tough and a filly with a great attitude. I'd say five or six furlongs will suit her, her dam has bred plenty of winners and I've no doubt this will win too".*

1135. MOSSTANG ★★★★

b.c. *Moss Vale – Lovely Dream (Elnadim).* January 30. First foal. €6,000Y. Goffs Orby. TG & BB Mills. The dam, a fair Irish dual 7f placed 3-y-o, is a half-sister to 8 winners including the US dual Grade 1 winner Janet. The second dam, Bid Dancer (by Spectacular Bid), won at 3 yrs in France and is a half-sister to 7 winners. (Pinehurst Racing). *"He was very cheap but he goes well, he's matured and he's very forward. Not your usual sharp, early type but he has plenty of speed and he'll pay his way. A five/six furlong 2-y-o that should start off in April".* TRAINERS' BARGAIN BUY

1136. RAVENS NEST ★★

b.c. *Piccolo – Emouna (Cadeaux Genereux).* January 31. Third foal. £18,000Y. Doncaster Premier. T.G. & B.B. Mills. The dam, a minor winner at 3 yrs in France, is a half-sister to 6 other minor winners. The second dam, Red Rabbit (by Suave Dancer), was placed three times over 7f including at 2 yrs and is a half-sister to 8 winners including the listed 1m winner Barboukh (herself dam of the Group 3 10f Prix Exbury winner Barbola). *"A big, long-striding horse that may well want seven furlongs. I thought he'd be earlier but he's tall and lean and is going to need a bit of time".*

1137. UNNAMED ★★★

b.c. *Zamindar – Shahmina (Danehill).* January 29. Third foal. 21,000Y. Tattersalls October Book 2. R A Mills. Half-brother to the modest 2011 5f and 6f placed maiden Lady Jameela (by Acclamation). The dam, a fair 12f and 13f

placed maiden, is a sister to the useful 2-y-o 6f and 1m winner and Group 3 Cherry Hinton Stakes third Sundari and a half-sister to 6 winners including the US Grade 3 placed Twin Spires. The second dam, My Ballerina (by Sir Ivor), a fairly useful 10f and 12f winner, is a half-sister to 3 winners including the very useful dual 6f winner and Group 1 1m Coronation Stakes third Zarani Sidi Anna and to the dam of the US Grade 2 winner Striking Dancer. (Mrs B B Mills). *"He's matured a lot over the winter and he's a big, tall colt with a lot of class. He'll be a seven furlong/mile 2-y-o at the back-end but he has a long term future".*

1138. UNNAMED ★★★ *SWING EASY*

ch.c. *Hurricane Run – Vale View (Anabaa).* April 24. Third foal. €47,000Y. Goffs Orby. TG & BB Mills. The dam, placed fourth twice in France over 7f and 1m, is a half-sister to 11 winners including the Irish 2,000 Guineas winner Saffron Walden, the Grade 1 E P Taylor Stakes winner Insight and the Group 1 Prix de la Foret winner Dolphin Street. The second dam, Or Vision (by Irish River), won over 5.5f and 7f at 2 yrs and the listed 7f Prix de l'Obelisque at 3 yrs and is a full or half-sister to 7 winners including the dams of Listen (Fillies Mile), Sequoyah (Moyglare Stud Stakes) and the US Grade 2 winner Dance Master. (Mr B Kerr). *"He had a heavy cold during the winter which knocked him back, but he's a great mover and he'll catch up quick. I've no doubt he'll be a mid-summer horse and he goes well. We only have a small bunch of 2-y-o's but there's something to like about all of them, they're a nice bunch".*

GARY MOORE

2nd run v- well ¶¶ 1m m 1o ✗ ea p'sn

1139. BUY ART ★★★

b.c. *Acclamation – Kondakova (Soviet Star).* February 9. Second foal. 100,000Y. Tattersalls October Book 2. G L Moore Racing. Half-brother to Tooley Woods (by Cape Cross), unplaced on her only start at 2 yrs in 2011. The dam, a fair dual 6f winner (including at 2 yrs), was listed-placed and is a half-sister to 5 winners including the US stakes winner and Grade 3 1m placed Solar Bound. The second dam, Solar Star (by Lear Fan), a useful 2-y-o dual 6f winner, is a half-sister to 7 winners including the US triple Grade 3 winner Gold Land. (Mr R Green). *"A big, strong colt with a great attitude. He's still at the backward stage at the moment but he's a really nice type and I like him a lot. He'll be racing in June over six furlongs".* ꙮꙮ ꙮꙮ ꙮꙮ

1140. DELPHICA ★★★

b.f. *Acclamation – Expectation (Night Shift).* March 8. Tenth foal. 55,000Y. Tattersalls October Book 1. G L Moore Racing. Half-sister to the 2-y-o Group 2 6f Richmond Stakes winner and Group 1 6f Prix Morny third Always Hopeful, to the fairly useful 6f and 1m winner Extraterrestrial, the quite useful 2-y-o 6f winner All About You (all by Mind Games), the useful 2-y-o 6f winner and listed-placed Nacho Libre (by Kyllachy), the quite useful 2-y-o dual 6f winner Enford Princess (by Pivotal) and the quite useful 3-y-o dual 1m winner Polly Plunkett (by Puissance). The dam, a modest 6f placed 2-y-o, is a half-sister to 5 minor winners here and abroad. The second dam, Phantom Row (by Adonijah), was a poor half-sister to 10 winners including the Horris Hill Stakes winner Long Row and the Norfolk Stakes winner Colmore Row. (Mr C Bird). *"A lovely, big filly that's doing everything right at the moment. A June/July type for six furlongs, she's a very willing 2-y-o with plenty of scope".*

1141. LYBICA ★★★

b.f. *Galileo – Tingling (Storm Cat).* January 11. First foal. 75,000Y. Tattersalls October Book 1. Not sold. The dam, a quite useful 7f and 1m placed 2-y-o in Ireland, is a half-sister to 3 winners including the Canadian Grade 3 winner Rosberg. The second dam, Bosra Sham (by Woodman), an outstanding filly and winner of three Group 1 events, is a sister to the multiple Group 1 winner Hector Protector and a half-sister to the French 2,000 Guineas winner Shanghai and the dam of the Group/Grade 1 winners Ciro and Internallyflawless. (Mr C Bird). *"She's gorgeous, not the most correct filly in the world but she has a great way about her and makes it all look very easy. We won't be rushing her at all but she's really strong – more like a colt than a filly".*

1142. OUR THREE GRACES ★★★

b.f. *Red Clubs – Villa Nova (Petardia).* January 23. Ninth foal. 19,000Y. Tattersalls October Book 2. G L Moore. Half-sister to the fairly

useful 5f (at 2 yrs) to 9f winner and listed-placed Prince Of Denmark, to the modest 7f winner Alexander Family (both by Danetime), the fairly useful triple 10f and subsequent Hong Kong winner Six Of Diamonds (by Redback), the US 2-y-o winner and stakes-placed Forbidden Paradise (by Chineur) and the fair dual 11f and hurdles winner Star Of Canterbury (by Beckett). The dam is an unplaced half-sister to 6 winners including the Group 3 winner and Group 1 Dewhurst Stakes third Impressionist. The second dam, Yashville (by Top Ville), is an unraced half-sister to 8 winners. (Patrick Moorehead). *"A lovely filly that's grown quite a lot since we've had her, she goes really well and I couldn't be more pleased with her. She should be racing from mid-season onwards".* TRAINERS' BARGAIN BUY

1143. UNNAMED ★★

b.c. *Exceed And Excel – Stormy Weather (Nashwan).* March 26. Fifth foal. 14,000Y. Tattersalls October Book 2. G L Moore Racing. Half-brother to a hurdles winner by Hernando. The dam is an unraced half-sister to 8 winners including the Group 3 Prix d'Arenberg winner Starlit Sands. The second dam, Shimmering Sea (by Slip Anchor), a fairly useful Irish 2-y-o 5f and 7f winner and third in the Group 3 Silken Glider Stakes, is a half-sister to 5 winners including the King George VI and Queen Elizabeth Stakes winner Petoski. *"A bit backward at the moment, he has a great attitude and he's laid-back which is unusual for the sire, but he won't be out until September. I'm still looking for an owner for him if anyone's interested".*

GEORGE MOORE

1144. BELLA CINDERELLA ★★

b.f. *Tiger Hill – Design Perfection (Diesis).* April 15. Fifth foal. Half-sister to the fairly useful dual 12f winner Awsaal (by Nayef) and to the quite useful 7f and 1m winner Capucci (by King's Best). The dam, a useful 10f winner, was listed-placed and is a half-sister to one winner. The second dam, Bella Ballerina (by Sadler's Wells), a quite useful 3-y-o 9f winner, is a sister to the high-class Group 2 10f Prince of Wales's Stakes and Group 3 10f Brigadier Gerard Stakes winner Stagecraft and to the useful listed 9f winner Balalaika and a half-sister to 4 winners. (A Crute & Partners). *"A filly that wants time.*

She was broken-in and seemed to learn very quickly, but we sent her home for a break so she's not going to be ready until the back-end. A lovely, big filly, we're very hopeful of her but she's more of a 3-y-o type".

1145. DON'T TELL ★★★

ch.f. *Sakhee's Secret – Starry Sky (Oasis Dream)*. January 21. First foal. 5,500Y. Tattersalls October Book 3. Portanova Bloodstock. The dam, a fair 2-y-o 7f winner, is a half-sister to one winner. The second dam, Succinct (by Hector Protector), a useful listed 10f winner, is a half-sister to 3 winners including the German listed winner Succession. (Duchess Of Sutherland). *"She's been cantering upsides but she came into the yard late so we don't know much about her yet. I'm very happy with her and she's done everything we've asked, but it'll be mid-summer before she's out. She looks like being a sprinter because she has a good back-end on her and she uses herself well".*

1146. LADY POPPY ★★★

b.f. *Kyllachy – Poppets Sweetlove (Foxhound)*. February 12. First foal. £26,000Y. Doncaster Premier. George Moore. The dam, a the modest 7f and 1m winner, is a half-sister to 5 winners including the champion sprinter and German 6f Group 2 and Group 3 winner Overdose and the fairly useful French 2-y-o 7f winner and listed-placed Poppet's Treasure. The second dam, Our Poppet (by Warning), unplaced in one outing at 2 yrs, is a half-sister to the Group 1 Falmouth Stakes third Musicanna, the 10f and 10.5f winner Shortfall and the 1m (at 2 yrs) and 12f winner Al Azhar – all useful. (Ingham Racing Syndicate). *"She ran in the Brocklesbury and I was very pleased with her. She'll be winning fairly shortly because she'll come on a ton for the run, like all my 2-y-o's do. She'll get six furlongs later on but no more than that".*

1147. RED KOKO (IRE) ★★

ch.f. *Sleeping Indian – Aunt Sadie (Pursuit Of Love)*. March 20. Half-sister to the fair 7f and 1m winner of 4 races Montboli (by Bahamian Bounty), to the modest 1m (at 2 yrs), 11f and hurdles winner Shaydreambeliever (by Daggers Drawn) and a winner over hurdles by Bob Back. The dam, a fair 6f placed 2-y-o, is a half-sister to several winners including the Irish

fairly useful 1m 10f and bumper winner and listed-placed Crossing. The second dam, Piney River (by Pharly), was placed over 6f and 7f and is a half-sister to 8 winners including the smart Group 3 Prix De Ris-Orangis winner Monaasib. (A Crute & Partners). *"A bigger filly than Lady Poppy, she'll be running fairly quickly in lower grade races. I think she'll stay further and she's a big, strong filly so she's one that could go on".*

STAN MOORE

1148. ALEXANDRAKOLLONTAI ★★

b.f. *Amadeus Wolf – Story (Observatory)*. March 6. Second foal. €11,000Y. Goffs Orby. Stan Moore. The dam is an unraced half-sister to the Group 3 Somerville Tattersall Stakes winner Thousand Words. The second dam, Verbose (by Storm Bird), a fairly useful listed-placed 1m winner, is a half-sister to 3 winners including the useful 9f and 10f winner and subsequent US dual Grade 2 placed Exterior. (Norton Common Farm Racing & Mr S Moore). *"Named after a Russian Communist revolutionary. This filly will be sharp, she'll win her auction race and she's a nursery type. One we'll have a lot of fun with this year, she's speedy and mature enough to run plenty of times".*

1149. EVERREADYNEDDY ★★

ch.g. *Ad Valorem – Maugwenna (Danehill)*. April 24. Fifth foal. €8,200Y. Tattersalls Ireland. Stan Moore. Half-brother to the useful 2-y-o dual 5f winner and Group 2 5f Flying Childers second Bould Mover (by Kyllachy) and to the modest 5f and 6f winner of 5 races including sellers at 2 yrs Mac Dalia (by Namid). The dam, a fair 2-y-o 5f winner, is a half-sister to 3 winners. The second dam, River Abouali (by Bluebird), is an unraced half-sister to 3 winners including the Irish Group 3 winner Psalm. (Ever Equine & J S Moore). *"This is a nice little 2-y-o, his half-sister Bould Mover was apparently on the small side as well. He's taking a while to come in his coat but I think he'll be a six furlong 2-y-o and he seems to be pacey enough to win his races".*

1150. KUBERA (IRE) ★★★

b.c. *Cape Cross – Paris Glory (Honour And Glory)*. April 6. Fourth foal. Half-brother to the unplaced 2011 2-y-o Electric Daydream (by Elusive Quality) and to the moderate 5f placed

2-y-o Ezzles (by Speightstown). The dam is an unraced half-sister to 3 winners including the Group 1 Prix Morny winner and sire Elusive City. The second dam, Star Of Paris (by Dayjur), is an unraced half-sister to 8 winners including Millions, winner of the Grade 3 Laurel Futurity. *"A horse with a really nice pedigree, he has plenty of size and scope and he'll make a 2-y-o by mid-season. Definitely one to follow over seven furlongs or a mile".*

1151. PADDY SLANTES ★★★
b.c. *Redback – Shall We Tell (Intikhab).* April 2. Fourth foal. €6,000Y. Tattersalls Ireland. Stan Moore. The dam is an unraced half-sister to 5 winners including Group 1 Prix de Diane winner and 1,000 Guineas second Confidential Lady. The second dam, Confidante (by Dayjur), a fairly useful 3-y-o dual 7f winner, is a half-sister to 7 winners including the Group/Grade 3 winners White Crown and Drilling For Oil. (The Wall to Wall Partnership). *"A good, strong colt, his main aim will be the Sales race in Ireland over seven furlongs. He's a typical Redback in that he's a good-bodied colt and all the ones I've had by that sire before have been really tough. He won't run until the six furlong races and as he wasn't expensive he should be good enough to win his maiden auction and then go to the sales race".*

1152. RAKTICATE (IRE) ★★★
b.f. *Rakti – Authenticate (Dansili).* April 16. Second foal. €7,500Y. Goffs Open. Stan Moore. The dam, a modest 7f winner, is a half-sister to 2 winners. The second dam, Exact Replica (by Darshaan), is an unraced sister to the Group 2 winner and Group 1 placed Darnay. (Mr G V March & J S Moore). *"She wasn't expensive but I think she'll be one of my better 2-y-o's. She seems to have gears but I think she'll be better over seven furlongs or a mile.*

1153. SALUTE TO SEVILLE (IRE) ★★★
b.f. *Duke Of Marmalade – Vingt Et Une (Sadler's Well).* March 29. Tenth foal. £30,000Y. Doncaster Premier. Stan Moore. Half-sister to 4 winners including the very useful 12f winners Sayadaw and Year Two Thousand (both by Darshaan), the fair 9f and 2m winner Gaselee (by Toccet) and 3 minor French winners by Numerous, Inchinor and Linamix. The dam, a

minor French 3-y-o winner, is a sister to the very useful Group 1 10.5f Prix Lupin and US Grade 2 1m winner Johann Quatz and to the smart French 10.5f to 13.5f listed winner Walter Willy and a half-sister to the top-class middle-distance colt Hernando, winner of the Group 1 Prix du Jockey Club and Group 1 Prix Lupin. The second dam, Whakilyric (by Miswaki), won the Group 3 7f Prix du Calvados and was third in the Prix de la Salamandre and in the Prix de la Foret. *"She's very well bred, we'll kick start her over six furlongs and we definitely think she's one to follow. She's got a bit about her and hopefully she'll be one of my better ones. She didn't have a lot of size about her at the sales and hence she didn't cost much considering her pedigree. She's grown since then and the ugly duckling has turned into a swan".*

1154. THE BLACK JACOBIN ★★★★
b.c. *Piccolo – Greenfly (Green Desert).* February 3. Fifth foal. £1,000Y. Ascot December. Not sold. Half-brother to the fair 7f winner Desert Bump (by Medicean) and a winner in Greece by Vettori. The dam, a winner in France, is a half-sister to 2 winners. The second dam, Exact Replica (by Darshaan), is an unraced sister to the Group 2 Sea World International Stakes winner and Group 1 placed Darnay. *"A very big, very mature horse that seems to be quite pacey. He's a horse that I think might run in the Supersprint because although he's big he's quick with it. If he does on the track what he does at home he'll be a very nice horse and definitely one to follow this year".* TRAINERS' BARGAIN BUY

1155. UNNAMED ★★
b.f. *Amadeus Wolf – Fortress (Generous).* March 19. First foal. £10,000Y. Doncaster Premier. Stan Moore. The dam, a modest 6f winner, is a half-sister to 6 winners including the high-class sprinter Reverence, winner of the Haydock Park Sprint Cup and the Nunthorpe Stakes and the very useful 2-y-o listed 6f Chesham Stakes winner Helm Bank. The second dam, Imperial Bailiwick (by Imperial Frontier), was a useful winner of 3 races at around 5f including the Group 2 Flying Childers Stakes, was Group 3 placed twice and is a half-sister to 3 winners in France. (Mrs E O'Leary & Mr S Moore). *"She was sharp, but she's just had a bit of an injury*

which will keep her out until mid-season at the earliest. She's bred to be speedy, she'll win her races alright and she's an out-and-out 2-y-o".

1156. UNNAMED ★★★
ch.f. Shamardal – Shakti (Indian Ridge). January 25. First foal. £10,000Y. Doncaster Premier. Stan Moore. The dam is an unraced daughter of the useful 2-y-o 6f and 1m winner and Group 3 Cherry Hinton Stakes third Sundari, herself a full or half-sister to 6 winners. (Norton Common Farm Racing & Mr S Moore). *"She's big and scopey, we didn't break her until after Christmas but she's got a bit of class and she'll be well worth following. Hopefully she'll have two or three runs and then we'll take her to Dubai for the carnival early next year. Shamardal's are usually tough and this one seems the same. I think she'll have ability as well".*

HUGHIE MORRISON
1157. ANOTHER COCKTAIL ★★★
b.c. Dalakhani – Yummy Mummy (Montjeu). February 20. First foal. 85,000Y. Tattersalls October Book 1. Anthony Stroud. The dam, a fair Irish 10f winner, is a sister to the multiple Group 1 winner Fame And Glory (Ascot Gold Cup, Irish Derby, Coronation Cup etc) and a half-sister to 6 winners including the listed-placed Grampian and Guaranda (herself dam of the Group 3 winner Gravitation). The second dam, Gryada (by Shirley Heights), a fairly useful 2-y-o 7f and 8.3f winner and third in the Group 3 1m Premio Dormello, is a full or half-sister to 4 middle-distance winners. (Mr M Kerr-Dineen). *"A very nice horse, you wouldn't think he was bred for a mile and half plus because he's quite a close-coupled colt that finds it all very easy and he's enjoying himself. Nevertheless he's too nice too push on with too early and hopefully he'll be a really nice autumn 2-y-o. A quality colt, he's quite naughty but he's attractive".*

1158. BANOFFEE (IRE) ★★
b.f. Hurricane Run – Nanabanana (Anabaa). April 12. Second foal. €60,000Y. Arqana Deauville October. Anthony Stroud. The dam won at 2 yrs in France, was second in the Group 3 Prestige Stakes and is a half-sister to 3 winners. The second dam, Tanabata (by Shining Steel), is a placed sister to the US Grade

2 winner Gold And Steel and a half-sister to 7 winners. (M Kerr-Dineen, The Hon. W. Smith & Partners). *"A strong-looking filly that finds it all easy. It's not a 2-y-o family so she'll be one for the autumn because she's a nice filly that's bred to get a trip".*

1159. BURGOYNE (USA) ★★
b.c. Officer – Married For Money (Not For Love). March 20. Sixth foal. 35,000Y. Tattersalls October Book 2. Hugh Morrison. Half-brother to the minor US 3-y-o winners Yore (by Yes It's True) and Moe Money (by More Than Money) and to a minor 2-y-o winner abroad by More Than Money. The dam is an unraced half-sister to 4 winners including the US Grade 3 winner Lovely Afternoon and the US multiple stakes winner and Grade 3 placed With Patience. The second dam, Lovely Later (by Green Dancer), is an unraced half-sister to 3 winners including the dam of the US Grade 2 winner Points Of Grace. (Lord Margadale, Mr M Kerr-Dineen, Mr H Scott-Barrett & The Hon. W. Henry Smith). *"A big colt, he's a bit of a lad and we probably won't see him until towards the end of the season".*

1160. CHURCH OF ENGLAND ★★★
bl.c. Pastoral Pursuits – Lawyers Choice (Namid). March 13. First foal. The dam, a fair 7f and 1m winner, is a half-sister to several winners including the Italian listed winner Far Hope. The second dam, Finger Of Light (by Green Desert), a fairly useful 2-y-o 6f winner, stayed 7f and is a half-sister to 6 winners including the listed winners Lady Shipley and Ellie Ardensky and to the dams of the Australian Grade 1 winner Serenade Rose and the Group 3 Solario Stakes and US Grade 3 winner Brave Act. (Mr R C Tooth). *"A nice, neat, typical Pastoral Pursuits. He has a bit of growing to do but he's done well since he came in and he'll be racing by late summer".*

1161. CODEBREAKER ★★★★
ch.c. Sakhee's Secret – Folly Lodge (Grand Lodge). February 28. First foal. 47,000Y. Tattersalls October Book 2. Will Edmeades. The dam, a quite useful 7f (including at 2 yrs) and 1m winner, is a half-sister to 2 winners. The second dam, Marika (by Marju), a useful 6f listed and 1m winner, is a half-sister to 8

winners including the Group 3 7.3f Fred Darling Stakes winner and Group 2 10f Nassau Stakes third Sueboog (herself dam of the Group 1 Prix d'Ispahan winner Best Of The Bests). (Thurloe Thoroughbreds XXX). *"A really nice horse, he looks very much like the sire and reflects all the nice things about him. I could start training him now but I'm waiting with him because he's a nice, scopey horse. Hopefully he'll be out in July and I'm looking forward to him"*.

1162. COUNTRYMAN ★★★★

b.br.c. Pastoral Pursuits – Baileys Silver (Marlin). February 15. Sixth foal. 22,000Y. Tattersalls October Book 2. G Howson. Half-brother to the quite useful 2-y-o 5f winner Bahama Baileys (by Bahamian Bounty). The dam is an unraced half-sister to 4 winners including the Group 3 Nell Gwyn Stakes second Zaheemah. The second dam, Port Of Silver (by Silver Hawk), a US 2-y-o stakes winner, is a half-sister to 5 winners. (H Scott-Barrett, S de Zoete & A Pickford). *"He looks like he'll make a nice 2-y-o from the midsummer onwards. Initially I was going to get on with him early but he's continued to grow. A horse with a nice character, he's willing and I'll be disappointed if he doesn't win this year"*. TRAINERS' BARGAIN BUY

1163. FELIX FABULLA ★★★

b.c. Lucky Story – Laser Crystal (King's Theatre). April 15. Fifth foal. 10,000Y. Tattersalls December. Hugh Morrison. Half-brother to the modest 1m and 10f winner of 4 races D'Urberville (by Auction House) and to a minor winner abroad by Desert Prince. The dam was placed once over 10f and is a half-sister to 4 winners including the Group 1 Racing Post Trophy third Feared In Flight. The second dam, Solar Crystal (by Alzao), a smart 2-y-o winner of the Group 3 1m May Hill Stakes and third in the Group 1 1m Prix Marcel Boussac, is a half-sister to 6 winners including Crystal Music (Group 1 Fillies' Mile), State Crystal (Group 3 12f Lancashire Oaks), Dubai Success (Group 3 John Porter Stakes) and the Irish Derby third Tchaikovsky. (Mrs I Eavis). *"He finds everything really easy, he's never been a problem and he moves well. I think he was a good buy – for ten grand he was a snip, he goes well and he'll make a 2-y-o around July or August over seven furlongs to a mile".*

1164. JUBILANTE ★★

b.f. Royal Applause – Lavinia's Grace (Green Desert). March 6. Third foal. 14,000Y. Tattersalls October 2. Hughie Morrison. Halfsister to the fairly useful 7f and 1m winner Justonefortheroad (by Domedriver). The dam, a minor 2-y-o winner in France, is a half-sister to 2 winners including the dual listed-placed Guilia. The second dam, Lesgor (by Irish River), won over 10f in France, was third in the Group 3 10f Prix de Psyche and is a half-sister to 2 winners. (Mr S de Zoete, Mr A Pickford & Mr R.A.C Hammond). *"She's still got a bit of growing to do but I'm getting to like her. She found the winter quite hard but she's done well lately and she'll be one for later in the summer, over six furlongs I would think".*

cou v late url bf Ada Epsom

1165. MINT CRISP ★★

gr.f. Dalakhani – Peppermint Green (Green Desert). March 30. First foal. 20,000Y. Tattersalls December. Not sold. The dam is an unplaced half-sister to 3 winners including the US Grade 2 winner Sun Boat. The second dam, One So Wonderful (by Nashwan), won the Group 1 Juddmonte International and the Group 2 Sun Chariot Stakes and is a half-sister to 8 winners including the Group 2 Dante Stakes winner Alnasr Alwasheek. (Helena Springfield Ltd). *"She's only been here a week but she looks like making a nice autumn filly. She's a nice size, quite compact and although she's only trotting at the moment she looks nice".*

1166. REVEILLE ★★★ ♠

ch.f. Sakhee's Secret – Up At Dawn (Inchinor). March 5. Third foal. 28,000Y. Tattersalls October Book 2. Hugh Morrison. Half-sister to the fair 2011 2-y-o 1m placed Don't Take Me Alive (by Araafa) and to the useful 7f (at 2 yrs) and subsequent US 1m Grade 2 and Grade 3 stakes winner Up In Time (by Noverre). The dam is an unplaced half-sister to 5 winners including the dam of the Group 3 winner Summer Fete. The second dam, Up And About (by Barathea), a fair 14.8f winner, is a half-sister to 8 winners including the listed Atalanta Stakes winner and Group 1 placed Musicanna and to the unplaced dam of the champion European 3-y-o sprinter Overdose. (Mr C Harper & Mr N Poole). *"Compared with our other 2-y-o by Sakhee's Secret she's quite small, so she hasn't* grown a lot but quite a few of the sire's family are on the small side. She's just beginning to get it together now, but mentally she's got quite a lot of growing up to do. If that comes we'll be able to train her quite quickly because it'll only take six weeks to get her ready. She'll be a five/six furlong 2-y-o".

1167. SPICY DAL ★★★

ch.f. Dalakhani – Salsa Steps (Giant's Causeway). January 30. First foal. The dam, a fairly useful dual 6f winner, was fourth in a Group 3 event over 7f and is a half-sister to several winners. The second dam, Dance Design (by Sadler's Wells), won the Irish Oaks. (Mr B Arbib & Sir M Arbib). "The dam was huge and only her talent got her onto the racecourse really. This filly is strong and she looks as if she'll make a 2-y-o at some point, but not until later in the year over seven furlongs".

1168. SUSPENSION ★★

b.f. Avonbridge – Summertime Parkes (Silver Patriarch). February 27. Third foal. £5,000Y. Doncaster St Leger Festival. Hughie Morrison. Half-sister to the modest 2011 5f placed 2-y-o Summathisnthat (by Auction House). The dam, placed once over 7f from 2 starts at 2 yrs, is a half-sister to 8 winners including the listed Cecil Frail Stakes winner Summerhill Parkes and the useful dual 5f winner and Moyglare, Lowther and Queen Mary Stakes placed My Melody Parkes. The second dam, Summerhill Spruce (by Windjammer), a fair winner of a 6f seller at 3 yrs, is a half-sister to 6 winners. (Mr Simon Malcolm). "She's growing a lot, she's quite backward and the penny needs to drop at the moment, but she's likely to make a late summer 2-y-o over six furlongs".

1169. TOWN MOUSE ★★

ch.c. Sakhee – Megdale (Waajib). April 22. Eleventh living foal. 15,000Y. Tattersalls October Book 2. G Howson. Half-brother to the smart 7f (at 2 yrs) and triple listed middle-distance winner Frank Sonata (by Opening Verse), to the useful 2-y-o listed 7f Sweet Solera Stakes winner Peaceful Paradise (by Turtle Island), the fairly useful dual 7f winner Coup d'Etat (by Diktat), the quite useful 7f and 1m (at 2 yrs) and 10f winner Kinetic Quest (by Haafhd), the fair 2-y-o 6f winner Castellano (by Mujahid), the modest 12f and 13f winner Gems (by Haafhd), the French 3-y-o winner Lunch Time (by Zamindar) and the German 10f and 11f winner Meg (by Be My Chief). The dam, a fair middle-distance placed maiden, is a sister to the useful 7f to 9f winner Wijara and a half-sister to 10 winners including Alhijaz, a winner of four Group 1 events in Italy. The second dam, Nawara (by Welsh Pageant), was a fair 10.2f winner. (Justin Dowley & Mouse Hamilton-Fairley). "He's done well lately, he'll need time but he's forward-going and he moves well. He's not over-big but he's still a big baby and I don't think we'll see him out until September time".

1170. UNNAMED ★★★

ch.f. Raven's Pass – Rosinka (Soviet Star). February 22. First foal. The dam, a useful 2-y-o 6f winner, subsequently won a US Grade 3 event over 11f and was Grade 1 placed twice. She's a half-sister to numerous winners including the US Grade 1 12f and triple Grade 2 winner King's Drama and the US Grade 1 placed Self Feeder. The second dam, Last Drama (by Last Tycoon), won and was listed placed twice over 10f in France. (Capt J Macdonald-Buchanan). "Quite a neat filly, I'm sure she'll make a 2-y-o when we start to push on".

WILLIE MUIR
1171. FOIE GRAS ★★★

b.c. Kyllachy – Bint Zamayem (Rainbow Quest). March 8. Thirteenth foal. 28,000Y. Tattersalls October Book 2. Not sold. Closely related to the useful 7f (at 2 yrs) to 9f winner of 9 races (including a 1m listed event) Mia's Boy (by Pivotal) and half-brother to the useful Irish 6f (at 2 yrs) and 7f winner and Group 3 Debutante Stakes third Sweet Deimos (by Green Desert), the quite useful 7.6f winner Queenie (by Indian Ridge) and the fair 2-y-o 1m winner Rumbalara (by Intikhab). The dam, a fairly useful 10f winner, was listed-placed over 10f and is a half-sister to the Group 3 Prix Chloe winner Rouquette and the US stakes winner Moody's Cat. The second dam, Zamayem (by Sadler's Wells), is an unraced half-sister to 4 winners. (Mrs G .E Rowland-Clark). "He's one of the few 2-y-o's I've done a bit with, he's shown he's got something about him and I like the sire. He's in the same mould as my nice Kyllachy 2-y-o of last year, Stepper Point. He will win this year, I *like him and he's done very well. I would guess he'd be a six furlong type".*

1172. GRAYSWOOD ★★

gr.c. *Dalakhani – Argent Du Bois (Silver Hawk).*
May 4. Sixth foal. 75,000Y. Tattersalls October
Book 1. Willie Muir. Half-brother to the
2-y-o 6.5f and 7f and subsequent US Grade 1
9f and 10f winner Ticker Tape, to the modest
7f all-weather winner Silver Bark, the modest
10f winner Centime (all by Royal Applause),
the quite useful dual 6f winner (including at
2 yrs) and subsequent Canadian listed-placed
Sant Elena (by Efisio) and the fair French
2-y-o 1m winner Woodland Faery (by Act
One). The dam was placed five times at 2 and
3 yrs in France, stayed 1m and is a half-sister to
7 winners including the 2-y-o Group 1 Racing
Post Trophy winner Crowded House and the
French listed winner and Group 3 placed On
Reflection. The second dam, Wiener Wald
(by Woodman), is an unplaced half-sister to
6 minor winners abroad. (C.L.A Edginton). *"A
really nice individual, he moves well and looks
the part. You won't see him out until the back-
end of the season and although I couldn't say
anything negative about him I don't know
about his ability yet".*

1173. UNNAMED ★★★

b.c. *Sakhee's Secret – Malelane (Prince Sabo).*
March 9. Third foal. £45,000Y. Doncaster
Premier. Willie Muir. The dam, a poor 5f placed
maiden, is a half-sister to 6 winners including
the Group 3 Prix du Petit Couvert winner
Bishops Court and the listed winning sprinter
Astonished. The second dam, Indigo (by Primo
Dominie), a quite useful 2-y-o 5f winner, is a
half-sister to 5 winners. *"I really like him and he
looks like being a sharpish 2-y-o but I've taken
my time with him. He's a big, strong colt and I'll
start winding him up now because he might be
pretty special. A colt from a very good sprinting
family".*

1174. UNNAMED ★★

b.f. *Singspiel – Portmeirion (Polish Precedent).*
January 28. Third foal. The dam, a quite useful
triple 6f winner, was listed-placed and is a
half-sister to 8 winners including the smart US
Grade 2 1m Colonel F W Koester Handicap and
German Group 3 1m winner Ventiquattrofogli

and to the German 6f to 11f listed winner
Irish Fighter. The second dam, India Atlanta
(by Ahonoora), is an unraced half-sister to 6
winners including the German Group 3 1m
winner Sinyar. *"A lovely, big filly that moves
well, she's one for the end of the season but
she's got a real strong body and being by
Singspiel she could be anything".*

1175. UNNAMED ★★★

b.f. *Mount Nelson – Purring (Mountain Cat).*
April 5. Sixth foal. 11,500Y. Tattersalls Book 3.
Willie Muir. Half-sister to the fairly useful 9f and
subsequent US winner and dual listed-placed
Lady Francesca (by Montjeu), to the quite useful
10f and 12f winner of 7 races Jeer (by Selkirk)
and the fair 12f and 14f winner of 4 races Cat
O' Nine Tails (by Motivator). The dam, a quite
useful 7f winner, is a half-sister to the Group 2
1m Falmouth Stakes and Group 3 1m Prix de
Sandringham winner Ronda (herself dam of a
Group 3 winner) and to the smart 1m (at 2 yrs)
and listed 2m winner Silver Gilt. The second
dam, Memory's Gold (by Java Gold), a modest
3-y-o 7.6f winner, is a half-sister to 5 winners
including the useful middle-distance filly and
German Group 3 winner Fields Of Spring. *"I
love her, I've trained two out of the dam and
they're both quite nice but in looks this filly is
the best of the three. She looks the strongest
and that may be due to Mount Nelson because
they are very good-looking horses. She'll tell
me when she's ready, but I guess that will be
around August or September time".*

1176. UNNAMED ★★★

b.f. *Jeremy – Staceymac (Elnadim).* April 19.
Third foal. 10,000Y. Doncaster Premier. Not
sold. The dam, a modest 5f winner at 3 yrs,
is a half-sister to several winners including the
listed 7f winner Kalahari Gold. The second
dam, Neat Shilling (by Bob Back), is an unraced
full or half-sister to 7 winners including the US
Grade 3 winner Riddlesdown. *"I like her, she's
very sharp and I've done some bits of work
with her. I'm going to step up her work now
and she looks a sharp, early type".* TRAINERS'
BARGAIN BUY

1177. UNNAMED ★★

b.f. *Haafhd – Welsh Valley (Irish River).* April
13. Sixth foal. Half-sister to the moderate 2011

6f fourth placed 2-y-o Armiger (by Araafa), to the fairly useful 2-y-o 7f winner Brecon (by Unfuwain) and the fair 4-y-o 9.5f and 10f winner Man Of Gwent (by In The Wings). The dam, a modest 6f placed maiden, is a half-sister to 9 winners including the Group 2 6f Gimcrack Stakes winner Chilly Billy, the US Grade 3 placed Mister Approval and the dam of the Italian Group 2 winner Fisich. The second dam, Sweet Snow (by Lyphard), won over an extended 10f in France and is a half-sister to 9 winners including the US stakes winners Windansea and Sing And Swing. *"A big, strong, nice-looking filly, she looks like being stronger than the Singspiel 2-y-o we have but I'll still take my time with her. She does things nicely, she has a nice pedigree and I like the way she does things".*

JEREMY NOSEDA

1178. AGERZAM ★★★★
br.c. Holy Roman Emperor – Epiphany (Zafonic). February 27. Fourth foal. Half-brother to the fair 1m winner Zakiy (by Selkirk). The dam, a fair 2-y-o 6f winner, is a half-sister to one winner abroad. The second dam, Galette (Caerleon), a fairly useful 12f winner, is a half-sister to 6 winners including the Irish 2,000 Guineas winner Indian Haven, the smart Group 1 Gran Criterium winner Count Dubois and the dam of the Group winners Imperial Stride and High Pitched. *"He's in fast work and he's a strong, quite precocious colt. Definitely a sharp, early type, he goes along OK and I could see him being out before the end of May. He's got a bit of speed and I'm sure he'll win races this year".*

1179. BEAMING STAR (USA) ★★
b.f. Giant's Causeway – Wandering Star (Red Ransom). April 26. Eleventh foal. $130,000Y. Keeneland September. John Black. Closely related to the Group 3 Prix de Conde winner Naval Officer and the minor winner Wonder Woman (dam of two stakes winners in France) and half-sister to 5 winners including the French 1m winner War Czar (by Pulpit). The dam won the Grade 2 E P Taylor Stakes and is a half-sister to numerous winners including the US stakes winner and Grade 3 placed Major Hero. The second dam, Beautiful Bedouin (by His Majesty), is an unraced half-sister to 6 winners including the Group 3 Craven Stakes

winner and Irish Derby second Silver Hawk. *"A nice, scopey filly, she'll take a bit of time and is one for September time but she's a filly I like and physically she's done really well in the last few weeks. A good mover, she's more of a 3-y-o type but I think she'll be out and running at the back-end of the season".*

1180. BLUE NOVA ★★★
b.f. Nayef – Blue Rhapsody (Cape Cross). February 9. First foal. €50,000Y. Arqana Deauville August. Not sold. The dam, a fair 2-y-o 7f winner, is a half-sister to the very smart Group 3 7f Prestige Stakes (at 2 yrs) and Group 3 Nell Gwyn Stakes winner and dual Group 1 placed Fantasia and the Group 3 winner Pink Symphony. The second dam, Blue Symphony (by Darshaan), a fair 10f winner, is a half-sister to one winner out of the Group 1 6f Cheveley Park Stakes winner Blue Duster. *"This filly's working, she's a good mover and I'm happy with what she's showing us at the moment. She'll be running in May so clearly she's takes more after the dam's side of the pedigree than Nayef. A neat, handy filly that'll win this year".*

~~~ Hayras a Hou or

1181. CHIEF HAVOC (USA) ★★★
ch.c. Giant's Causeway – La Reina (A P Indy). March 2. Fourth foal. $325,000Y. Keeneland September. Jeremy Noseda. Brother to the minor US winner at 2 and 3 yrs Tia. The dam, winner of the Grade 3 Tempted Stakes and Grade 2 placed twice, is a half-sister to 4 winners including the US Grade 1 winner Brahms. The second dam, Queena (by Mr Prospector), won three Grade 1 events in the USA and is a sister to the US Grade 1 winner Chic Shirine. *"He arrives from America this weekend. I've seen him a few times over there and he's a lovely, rangy horse with a lot of scope. More of a back-end of the season type 2-y-o that'll go on at 3, but I've been thrilled with him. I know that they're delighted with him at Vinery Stud and they love the way he goes. A good prospect for the future".* ran green but finished well 1m Kempton nde

1182. CONSIGN ★★★
b.c. Dutch Art – Maid To Dance (Pyramus). February 19. Seventh foal. 68,000Y. Tattersalls October Book 1. Brian Grassick Bloodstock. Half-brother to the quite useful 2-y-o 7f winner Right Step (by Xaar), to the quite useful 6f (at

2 yrs) and 10f winner Bussa (by Iceman), the moderate dual 10f winner Everyman (by Act One) and a winner over hurdles by King's Best. The dam is an unplaced half-sister to the triple German Group 2 winner and Group 1 second Filia Ardross (herself dam of the Group 1 Fillies' Mile winner Sunspangled). The second dam, Sari Habit (by Saritamer), won twice at 3 and 4 yrs in Italy and is a half-sister to the Italian Group 3 winner How To Go. *"Very much a 2-y-o type, he's been held up the spring with a dirty nose and a cough but he's back on the go now. A good-moving horse, he'll soon be ready to start work and I'd hope to see him over five/ six furlongs from the middle of May onwards. I quite like him, he's a good, strong individual and just the type to do a job early on".*

1183. DUTIFUL SON (IRE) ★★★
b.c. *Invincible Spirit – Grecian Dancer (Dansili).* March 14. Second foal. €150,000Y. Goffs Orby. Sackville/Donald. The dam, a very useful Irish Group 3 Ridgewood Pearl Stakes winner, is a half-sister to 5 winners including the 2-y-o Group 2 5f Flying Childers Stakes and Group 3 5f Molecomb Stakes winner Wunders Dream. The second dam, Pizzicato (by Statoblest), a modest 5f and 5.3f winner at 3 yrs, is a half-sister to 5 winners including the high-class Hong Kong horses Mensa and Firebolt. *"An athletic, good-moving horse, I haven't made up mind whether to crack on with him or wait until mid-summer. A good mover, I'm sure he'll do well at 2, although the mare did get better as she got older".*

1184. ELAS LAW ★★
gr.f. *Lawman – Ela Athena (Ezzoud).* March 11. Seventh foal. Half-sister to the fairly useful 2-y-o 1m winner and listed placed Elas Diamond (by Danehill Dancer). The dam, a winner of 3 races including the Group 3 Lancashire Oaks, was placed in 7 Group/Grade 1 events and is a half-sister to 5 winners. The second dam, Crodelle (by Formidable), a French 3-y-o 9.5f winner, is a half-sister to 7 winners. *"Quite a backward filly and one for the back-end of the season, so I don't know too much about her yet".*

1185. ENVIABLE (IRE) ★★★
b.c. *Kyllachy – Eternal Beauty (Zafonic).* March

10. Fifth foal. 75,000Y. Tattersalls October Book 2. Brian Grassick Bloodstock. Half-brother to the German 2-y-o winner and Group 3 7f third Eternal Power (by Tiger Hill), to the quite useful 6f winner Ziraun (by Cadeaux Genereux), the fair French (over 6f at 2 yrs) and German winner Eternal Flash (by One Cool Cat) and the fair 2-y-o triple 5f winner Artdeal (by Fasliyev). The dam was unplaced in France and is a half-sister to 3 winners and to the unraced dam of the Group 2 winner Cape Dollar. The second dam, Strawberry Roan (by Sadler's Wells), an Irish 7f and 1m listed winner, was second in the Irish 1,000 Guineas and is a sister to the Oaks and Irish 1,000 Guineas winner Imagine and a half-sister to the top-class colt Generous. *"He's cantering away, he's a little bit coarse and immature at present but he's pulling himself together and I can see him making a 2-y-o from the middle of the season onwards, possibly over seven furlongs".*

1186. EVIDENT (IRE) ★★★
b.c. *Excellent Art – Vestavia (Alhaarth).* April 7. Second foal. €95,000Y. Goffs Orby. Sackville/Donald. The dam is an unraced half-sister to 6 winners including the Group 3 placed 2-y-o Rosabee. The second dam, Tilbrook (by Don't forget Me), won over 1m at 3 yrs in Ireland and is a half-sister to 8 winners including the listed winner and Group 1 Phoenix Stakes second Maledetto. *"A lovely, scopey horse that moves well. A July-onwards type 2-y-o, he's a good mover and has a good way of going. I do like him but he's just going to take a bit of time".*

1187. EVOKE (IRE) ★★★
b.f. *Dark Angel – Happy Talk (Hamas).* April 6. Sixth foal. €30,000Y. Tattersalls Ireland. Brian Grassick Bloodstock. Half-sister to the fairly useful 2011 2-y-o 5f winner Nagham (by Camacho), to the fair 2-y-o dual 5f winner Frisky Talk (by Fasliyev), the modest 5f and 6f winner of 5 races Foreign Rhythm (by Distant Music) and the fair 7f winner of 3 races Mica Mika (by Needwood Blade). The dam, a minor Irish 10f and hurdles winner, is a half-sister to 7 winners including the US Grade 3 winner Storm Dream. The second dam, Mamara Reef (by Salse) won once at 3 yrs and once over hurdles and is a half-sister to 9 winners including the listed Galtres Stakes winner and smart broodmare

Nibbs Point. *"She's taking a bit longer to come to hand than the pedigree suggests, but the penny is starting to drop now. A neat filly, she'll make a 2-y-o from mid-summer. I haven't done an awful lot with her as yet".*

Won by nursery c15 Yarmouth

1188. EXEMPT ★★★
ch.f. *Exceed And Excel – Miss University (Beau Genius).* February 8. Ninth foal. 55,000Y. Tattersalls October Book 1. Sackville/Donald. Half-sister to the US Grade 2 winner and triple Grade 1 placed Three Degrees, to the minor US winner Megaspiel (both by Singspiel) and a winner over hurdles by Erhaab. The dam ran unplaced twice and is a half-sister to 9 winners. The second dam, Gorgeously Divine (by Al Hattab), is an unplaced half-sister to 3 winners. *"A good-sized filly that moves well, she has a good attitude and I quite like her. She's done well, I'd be hopeful of running her in June and she's got some strength and size to her".*

1189. FANTASTIC MOON ★★★★ ♠
ch.c. *Dalakhani – Rhadegunda (Pivotal).* March 8. First foal. 210,000Y. Tattersalls October Book 1. Rabbah Bloodstock. The dam, a fairly useful dual 1m winner here, won a listed 9f event in France and is a half-sister to 5 winners. The second dam, St Radegund (by Green Desert), a fairly useful 7f winner, is a half-sister to 7 winners including the very useful listed 6f Sirenia Stakes winner Art of War. *"A good-moving horse and very forward-going, considering his pedigree it's surprising that he appears quite precocious but I'm taking that as a positive sign. He goes well and we'll see how he develops over the next month but he could be out in a maiden at the back-end of May. I don't want to push him too soon, but he could just be a Chesham Stakes type".*

1190. GIDDY HEIGHTS ★★
b.c. *Pivotal – Light Hearted (Green Desert).* February 12. First foal. 48,000Y. Tattersalls October Book 1. Not sold. The dam, a quite useful 6f winner, is a sister to 2 winners including the smart 2-y-o Group 2 6f Mill Reef Stakes winner Byron, closely related to the fairly useful 7f and 1m winner Resort and half-sister to 4 winners including the useful 1m and 10.3f winner Gallant Hero, the fairly useful 9f winner and US Grade 3 placed Gallant and

the useful 10.4f listed-placed maiden Gay Heroine. The second dam, Gay Gallanta (by Woodman), a very smart winner of the Group 1 6f Cheveley Park Stakes and the Group 3 5f Queen Mary Stakes, was second in the Group 2 1m Falmouth Stakes and is a half-sister to 11 winners including the smart Group 2 10f Gallinule Stakes winner Sportsworld. *"He's more of a 3-y-o type, but he's a good-moving, straightforward type of horse".*

1191. HAVELOVEWILLTRAVEL (IRE) ★★
b.f. *Holy Roman Emperor – Strategy (Machiavellian).* February 26. Fourth foal. 38,000Y. Tattersalls October Book 1. Global Equine Group. Closely related to the US Grade 3 winner and Grade 1 placed Justaroundmidnight (by Danehill Dancer) and half-sister to the useful Irish 2-y-o 5f winner and Group 3 6f Anglesey Stakes third (by Excellent Air). The dam, a quite useful 10f and 11f winner, is a half-sister to 2 winners. The second dam, Island Story (by Shirley Heights), a quite useful 10f winner, is a half-sister to 6 winners. *"Quite a backward type with a bit of size and scope, so she's not typical of the sire, but she moves well. She hasn't been in that long so I need to see a bit more of her but I'm happy with what she's done so far. A back-end type 2-y-o I'd say".*

1192. HENRIETTA ROSE (USA) ★★★★
b.f. *Henrythenavigator – Shermeen (Desert Style).* March 7. The dam, a useful 2-y-o 5f and 5.7f winner, was third in the Group 3 Cornwallis Stakes and a Grade 3 stakes in the USA and is a sister to the very useful dual listed 6f winner Mister Manannan. The second dam, Cover Girl (by Common Grounds), a fair 2-y-o 6f and 7f and subsequent Scandinavian listed winner, is a half-sister to 2 winners. *"In fast work now, she's a neat filly and definitely a 2-y-o. She goes about her job and will definitely be winning this year. Very much a sprinter type".*

1193. HI FILWAH (USA) ★★★
b.c. *Medaglia d'Oro – Star Landing (Caller I D).* January 29. Sixth foal. €160,000Y. Arqana Deauville August. Sackville/Donald. Half-brother to 4 winners including the US stakes winner Loch Dubh (by Friends Lake) and 2 minor winners in the USA by Limehouse and

Malibu Moon. The dam is a placed half-sister to 6 winners including the US Grade 3 winner Epic Honor. The second dam, Poage's Landing (by Heart), is a placed half-sister to 5 winners including the US Grade 3 winner Wild Gale. *"He's just started working, he's a definite 2-y-o type and a good-moving horse that's most probably a six furlong 2-y-o. I'm hopeful that he'll be up and running by the middle of May and for what he's done at this moment I'm pleased with what he's shown me".*

1194. HOMAGE (IRE) ★★★
b.c. Acclamation – Night Sphere (Night Shift).
April 23. Third foal. €80,000Y. Goffs Orby. John Warren. Half-brother to the fair 2011 2-y-o 7f and 1m placed Parisian Princess (by Teofilo) and to the minor German 3-y-o winner Bitter Green (by Choisir). The dam, a quite useful Irish 2-y-o 7f winner, is a half-sister to the very useful 2-y-o 6f and subsequent US Grade 2 Providencia Stakes winner and Group 2 7f Rockfel Stakes second Missit (by Orpen). The second dam, High Spot (by Shirley Heights), was placed over middle-distances and is a half-sister to 3 winners. *"A great-framed horse, he just needs to fill out and mature but he moves well and he's a colt I like. He'll be a nice type from July onwards and he's an athletic individual".*

1195. HORNBOY ★★★
b.c. Medicean – Soar (Danzero). March 26. Fourth foal. 115,000Y. Tattersalls October Book 1. Sackville/Donald. Brother to the quite useful 2-y-o 6f winner Racy and half-brother to the fair 2011 6f placed 2-y-o Uprise and the quite useful 6f winner Levitate (both by Pivotal). The dam, winner of the Group 2 6f Lowther Stakes and the Group 3 Princess Margaret Stakes at 2 yrs, is a half-sister to 5 winners including the very smart 6f and 7f winner of 7 races Feet So Fast. The second dam, Splice (by Sharpo), a smart winner of the listed 6f Abernant Stakes, is a full or half-sister to 7 winners. *"He's just coming together now after going through a backward stage. He's a good-moving horse, strong and definitely on an upward curve. He looks well, the dam was a good 2-y-o and I like the way he's going forward now, so he's a decent type for the back-end of June onwards. When I saw him at the sale, Cheveley Park's John Marsh mentioned that he was the first*

foal out of the mare that was like herself. He's a bonny horse and he'll definitely make a 2-y-o type by mid-summer".

1196. IAN'S DREAM ★★★★ ♠
ch.c. Speightstown – She's Loaded (Deputy Minister). February 25. Second foal. $220,000Y. Keeneland September. Not sold. The dam, unplaced in one start, is a half-sister to the US 2-y-o stakes winner Rights Reserved and to the Grade 2 placed Miner's Reserve. The second dam, Royal Reserves (by Forty Niner), is a placed half-sister to 8 winners. *"He's in America and arrives this weekend. He's working out there, he's a strong type and he goes well. I'd hope to be running him in mid-May because he looks a real 2-y-o type and they like the way he goes out there".*

1197. INFINITE MAGIC (USA) ★★★
b.c. More Than Ready – Truly Enchanting (Danehill Dancer). February 23. First foal. $7,000 2-y-o. Keeneland January. The dam, a useful 7f and 1m winner, is a half-sister to the 1m winner and Group 3 Prix Miesque third Arabian Spell. The second dam, Truly Bewitched (by Affirmed), a quite useful 2-y-o 6f winner, is a half-sister to 6 winners including the US Grade 2 winner Chinese Dragon. *"A 2-y-o that's coming in from America this week. I saw him working out there in March, he's a precocious type that'll be running in May. He looks a good, solid individual that should be doing his job as a 2-y-o".* TRAINERS' BARGAIN BUY

1198. INTIMIDATE ★★★
b.c. Royal Applause – Crystal Power (Pleasant Colony). March 7. Fifth foal. 88,000Y. Tattersalls October Book 1. Brian Grassick Bloodstock. Brother to the fair 2011 6f and 7f placed 2-y-o Ashbina and half-brother to the useful 2-y-o 7f winner and Group 3 Sweet Solera second Misdaqeya (by Red Ransom) and to a winner in Belgium by Averti. The dam won once at 3 yrs in the USA and is a half-sister to 5 winners including the US Grade 1 Flower Bowl Invitational Handicap winner Chelsey Flower (herself dam of the French Group 3 winner Kentucky Dynamite). The second dam, Chelsey Dancer (by Affirmed), is an unplaced half-sister to 10 winners. *"A good-moving horse that's*

2-1 on debut 7f + mdn (nippel)

Run wd have won 3 more still

just coming together now. He's improving and should be doing some work soon with the intention of getting him out in June. He's definitely got the make and shape of a 2-y-o and I like what I've seen so far".

Hacn't up 7f mdn Yarmouth cl 5

1199. INTREPID (IRE) ★★★★ *1 runner*

b.c. Invincible Spirit – Imiloa (Kingmambo). March 5. First foal. €110,000Y. Goffs Orby. Sackville/Donald. The dam is an unraced half-sister to 3 winners including the 2-y-o Group 1 6f Middle Park Stakes and Group 2 6f Gimcrack Stakes winner Balmont and the US Grade 1 Wood Memorial Stakes winner Eskendereya (by Giant's Causeway). The second dam, Aldebaran Light (by Seattle Slew), a winner of 3 races at around 1m in the USA, is a half-sister to 3 winners including the 2-y-o 5.2f and subsequent US Grade 2 Blazonry. *"He's working and he's a precocious, forward-going kind of horse. I'm not quite sure yet whether I should start him at five furlongs or wait for six, but he looks solid and he'll win races for sure".*

1200. INVESTMENT EXPERT (IRE) ★★★

b.c. Tamayuz – Kindling (Dr Fong). March 21. Third foal. 125,000Y. Tattersalls October Book 2. Sackville/Donald. Half-brother to Bayan (by Danehill Dancer), unplaced in one start at 2 yrs in 2011. The dam, a useful 9f, 12f and listed 2m winner, is a half-sister to 9 winners including the French listed 9f winner Thattinger. The second dam, Isle Of Flame (by Shirley Heights), was unraced. *"He went very backward through the winter but he's coming along now and he moves well. I'm pleased with him and he's a good, straightforward individual for July time onwards".*

1201. IRIDESCENCE ★★★★

b.f. Dutch Art – Radiate (Sadler's Wells). February 23. Third foal. Sister to the quite useful 2011 2-y-o 6f winner Princess Of Orange and half-sister to the fair 7f and 10f winner Icebuster (by Iceman). The dam is an unraced half-sister to 4 winners including the Group 1 Phoenix Stakes third Polar Force. The second dam, Irish Light (by Irish River), a fairly useful dual 1m winner at 3 yrs, is a half-sister to 5 winners including the US stakes winner and Grade 3 placed Solar Bound. *"She was a bit late coming in but she's strengthened up really well*

and she moves well cantering. Hopefully we can think about getting her out in June or July, she's on an upward curve now and I'm pleased with her. Definitely a 2-y-o type".

1202. JOE PALOOKA (IRE) ★★★★

b.c. Galileo – Glinting Desert (Desert Prince). February 20. Fourth foal. 155,000Y. Tattersalls October Book 1. Badgers Bloodstock. Half-brother to the Group 1 Phoenix Stakes and Group 2 Railway Stakes winner Alfred Nobel (by Danehill Dancer) and to the fair 1m winner Starbound (by Captain Rio). The dam, a fair 2-y-o 7f winner, is a half-sister to 3 minor winners. The second dam, Dazzling Park (by Warning), a very smart winner of the Group 3 1m Matron Stakes and a listed 9f event, was placed in the Group 1 Irish Champion Stakes and the Irish 1,000 Guineas and is a half-sister to 7 winners including the Derby, Champion Stakes, Dewhurst Stakes and National Stakes winner New Approach. *"He was late coming in but we've got him going now and he's a lovely-moving horse. Quite backward at the moment, I think he's one for August onwards but he's got a bit of quality and he's a horse I like a lot. A really nice type, I'm keeping my fingers crossed for him. He's named after the most famous cartoon boxing character in America".*

1203. KAJOKSEE (IRE) ★★

ch.c. Verglas – Dazzling Dancer (Nashwan). April 3. Fifth foal. €35,000Y. Goffs Orby. Jane Allison. Brother to the Irish listed-placed 2-y-o 7f winner and subsequent US 1m winner and Grade 3 placed Driving Snow and half-brother to the fairly useful Irish 2-y-o 7f winner Dazzling Day (by Hernando). The dam, a quite useful Irish 12f winner, is a half-sister to 2 winners. The second dam, Danse Classique (by Night Shift), a listed-placed winner in Ireland, is a half-sister to 5 winners including the triple Group 1 winner Petrushka. (Mrs Susan Roy). *"A back-end type 2-y-o and much more of a 3-y-o type, he's a good, strong individual but an immature horse we need to be patient with this year".*

1204. MAGIQUE (IRE) ★★★★

b.f. Jeremy – Misskinta (Desert Sun). April 21. Third foal. €38,000Y. Goffs Orby. Brian Grassick Bloodstock. Half-sister to the quite useful 2011

2-y-o 7f winner Grandeur (by Verglas) and to the winner modest Irish 12f winner Sixty Eight Guns (by Noverre). The dam, a minor Irish 12f winner at 4 yrs, is a half-sister to 5 winners including the Group 3 2m 2f Doncaster Cup winner Far Cry and the dam of the US Grade 3 winner Dress Rehearsal. The second dam, Darabaka (by Doyoun), is an unraced half-sister to 6 winners including the Group 3 Prix Minerve winner Daralinsha (herself the dam of numerous winners) and the listed winner Darata (dam of the French Oaks winner Daryaba). *"This filly's done well, she'll be a mid-season type 2-y-o and she moves well, has some size and scope and is quite an athletic filly. I'm pleased with her at this stage, she's a nice type and we like her".*

1205. MARCIANO (IRE) ★★
b.c. Pivotal – Kitty Matcham (Rock Of Gibraltar). January 15. First foal. 360,000Y. Tattersalls October Book 1. Badgers Bloodstock. The dam, winner of the 2-y-o Group 2 7f Rockfel Stakes, is a sister to the Irish 10f winner and dual Group 1 placed Red Rock Canyon, closely related to the 2-y-o Group 1 7f Prix Jean Luc Lagardere winner Horatio Nelson and a half-sister to the listed 7f winner and Group 1 Eclipse Stakes third Viscount Nelson. The second dam, Imagine (by Sadler's Wells), winner of the Irish 1,000 Guineas and Epsom Oaks, is a sister to the dual listed winner Strawberry Roan and a half-sister to 7 winners notably Generous, winner of the Derby, the Irish Derby, the King George VI and Queen Elizabeth Diamond Stakes and the Dewhurst Stakes. *"A big 2-y-o, but he needs a bit of time to get his strength and although I hope he'll win this year he's one for September onwards and his game is going to be as a 3-y-o. That's not knocking him at all because he's nice, but we need to be a little patient with him".*

1206. MARIA LOMBARDI ★★
b.f. Medicean – Fabulously Fast (Deputy Minister). May 7. Seventh living foal. 32,000Y. Tattersalls October Book 2. Cheveley Park Stud. Half-sister to the fairly useful 2011 listed 1m placed Humungosaur (by Red Ransom), to the fair 1m winner Fabulouslyspirited (by Selkirk) and two winners in Japan by A P Indy and Kingmambo. The dam won 4 races including

the Grade 1 Spinaway Stakes, was placed in two more Grade 1 stakes and is a half-sister to 6 winners. The second dam, Fabulous Notion (by Somethingfabulous), won the Grade 1 Santa Susana Stakes in the USA and is a half-sister to 5 winners including Cacoethes (Grade 1 Turf Classic) and the dam of the US dual Grade 1 winner Subordination. *"I like this filly, she moves well and has size and scope, but she's going to take time and I'll have to be patient with her".*

1207. MORE THAN AMAZING (USA) ★★★★
b.f. More Than Ready – Baffled (Distorted Humor). February 7. First foal. $125,000Y. Keeneland September. Sackville/Donald. The dam, a fairly useful 2-y-o 6f winner and third in the Group 3 Albany Stakes, subsequently won a minor event in the USA and is a half-sister to the US stakes winner Spring Party. The second dam, Surf Club (by Ocean Crest), won 6 minor races in the USA and is a half-sister to the US Grade 1 winner Awesome Humor. *"She arrives from America in the next few days, she's working out there and they like the way she goes. I trained the dam and this filly has been working well on the grass, so I'm hoping she'll be out over six furlongs in the second half of May. Hopefully she'll be even better than her dam".*

1208. PROPHETS PRIDE ★★★
b.c. Sakhee – Winner's Call (Indian Ridge). February 18. First foal. The dam is an unraced daughter of Damsel (by Danzero), herself a quite useful 2-y-o 1m winner and a half-sister to 13 winners including the US Grade 1 Oaklawn Handicap winner Jovial, the US Grade 3 winner Brave Note and the minor US stakes winner Never Force. *"I like this horse, he'll take a bit of time but he's a good mover and a lovely balanced horse. One for August onwards but he's a nice individual and I'm really pleased with the way he's done things".*

1209. RED BATON ★★★★ ♠♠
b.f. Exceed And Excel – Ruby Rocket (Indian Rocket). March 9. Fourth foal. 200,000Y. Tattersalls October Book 1. Cheveley Park Stud. Half-sister to the fairly useful Irish 4-y-o 5f and 6f winner Maarek (by Pivotal). The dam, a listed

5f and listed 6f winner, was Group 3 placed twice and is a half-sister to 8 winners including the Irish 2-y-o 6f listed winner Alexander Alliance and the German listed winner and Group 3 6.5f Prix Eclipse second Inzar's Best. The second dam, Geht Schnell (by Fairy King), is a placed half-sister to one winner abroad. *"A good type and a good mover, she's a little 'up behind' at present, so she's a bit less precocious than the pedigree would suggest. Definitely one for the second half of the season, she goes well and I like her".*

1210. RED TURBAN ★★★

b.f. *Kyllachy – Red Tiara (Mr Prospector).* March 20. Eighth foal. Sister to the useful 2-y-o 6f winner and Group 1 6f Cheveley Park Stakes fourth Adorn, closely related to the US 5f (minor stakes) to 8.5f winner Red Diadem (by Pivotal) and half-sister to the modest 8.3f winner Argent (by Barathea). The dam, a moderate 7.6f fourth-placed maiden, is closely related to the Japanese sprint stakes winner Meiner Love and a half-sister to 2 winners. The second dam, Heart Of Joy (by Lypheor), won 10 races including the Grade 2 Palomar Handicap and the Group 3 Nell Gwyn Stakes, is a half-sister to 8 winners. *"This filly moves well, she a bit light-framed but she goes about her job well and is forward-going. She'll definitely make a 2-y-o, she's on an upward curve and I think she'll definitely do a job this year".*

Win vf cl 5 mln f Hydock despite green

1211. REGAL SILK ★★★

b.f. *Pivotal – Regal Velvet (Halling).* February 16. Third foal. Half-sister to the quite useful 1m winner Robemaker (by Oasis Dream). The dam, a quite useful 10f winner, is a half-sister to 8 winners including the Group 1 6f Cheveley Park Stakes winner Regal Rose and the Japanese dual listed winner Generalist. The second dam, Ruthless Rose (by Conquistador Cielo), ran twice unplaced and is a half-sister to 9 winners including the high-class miler Shaadi. *"She's a good mover, a bit immature at present but strengthening up all the time. I've moved her up a bracket now and she'll definitely run as a 2-y-o".*

1212. THE BEST DOCTOR (IRE) ★★★

ch.c. *Pivotal – Strawberry Fledge (Kingmambo).* March 3. First foal. 110,000Y. Tattersalls

October Book 1. Sackville/Donald. The dam, placed once at 2 yrs in France, is a sister to 2 winners including the Group 1 12f Oaks winner Light Shift and a half-sister to 6 winners including the Group 2 10.5f Tattersalls Gold Cup and Group 3 10f Brigadier Gerard Stakes winner Shiva, the Group 2 12f Prix Jean de Chaudenay and Group 3 12f Prix Foy winner Limnos and the useful 7f and listed 1m winner Burning Sunset. The second dam, Lingerie (by Shirley Heights), placed 6 times in France, is a half-sister to 7 winners and to the placed dam of two Grade 1 winners in Brazil. *"He's grown a lot and has some size and scope, so he's a bigger horse than I expected him to be. He'll make a July type 2-y-o, he moves nicely and I like the way he's come on, so I think he's a horse with a future".*

1213. WARRIGAL (IRE) ★★

ch.c. *Mount Nelson – Waldblume (Halling).* April 24. Third living foal. €42,000Y. Goffs Orby. Sackville/Donald. Half-brother to a minor 3-y-o winner abroad by Tiger Hill. The dam, a quite useful Irish 2-y-o 9f winner, is a half-sister to 6 winners including the Group 1 German Derby winner Waldpark, the German listed winner and Group 3 placed Waldvogel and the Group 2 1m Falmouth Stakes second Waldmark (herself dam of the St Leger winner Masked Marvel). The second dam, Wurftaube (by Acatenango), won two Group 2 events over 12f and 14f in Germany and is a half-sister to 8 winners. *"A tall, rangy horse and a nice mover, he's athletic but backward and if everything went smoothly he'll be running over a mile in September. For what he cost he's a really nice individual".* decer horse wor lfr mdn Lingfield

1214. WHITFIELD (USA) ★★★

b.br.c. *Private Vow – Seda Fina (Known Fact).* March 15. Ninth foal. $190,000 2-y-o. Ocala Breeze-up. Hugo Merry. Half-brother to 4 winners including the US stakes winner of 4 races from 5f to 7f winner Su Casa G Casa (by During) and the stakes-placed Smooth Rocket (by Golden Missile). The dam, unplaced in one start, is a half-sister to 9 winners including the US stakes winners Downtown Clown and Tucky's Girl. The second dam, Tucked Inside (by Great Above), was a US stakes winner of 3 races. *"He breezed well at the sale and I think* he's very much a seven furlong/mile horse. One we should be running in July".

rahly 3rd when 1/2 fw Newcastle mile

1215. WHY AREEB (IRE) ★★

b.c. Galileo – Piquetnol (Private Account). January 29. Eleventh foal. €200,000Y. Arqana Deauville August. FBA. Half-brother to the Group 3 5f King George Stakes and Group 3 5f Ballyogan Stakes winner Dietrich (by Storm Bird and herself dam of the Group 3 winner Beauty Bright) and the German listed 1m winner Mambo Light (by Kingmambo). The dam, a minor French 3-y-o winner and second in the Group 1 Prix Marcel Boussac, is a sister to the very smart Moyglare Stud Stakes, Coronation Stakes, Child Stakes and Cherry Hinton Stakes winner Chimes of Freedom and a half-sister to the useful 2-y-o 6f listed Firth of Clyde Stakes and 3-y-o 7f winner Imperfect Circle (by Riverman) – herself dam of the Breeders Cup Mile, Irish 2,000 Guineas and Prix Jacques le Marois winner Spinning World. The second dam, Aviance (by Northfields), won the Group 1 6f Heinz 57 Phoenix Stakes at 2 yrs and is out a winning half-sister to the US Grade 1 winner Blush With Pride and the unraced Sex Appeal (dam of El Gran Senor and Try My Best). *"Quite a backward horse, we haven't done an awful lot with him but he moves well. Very much a back-end of the season type and for next year".*

1216. WILD OCEAN ★★★

b.f. Pivotal – Mystery Ocean (Dr Fong). March 18. Second foal. 140,000foal. Tattersalls December. Cheveley Park Stud. Half-sister to the fair 2011 2-y-o 5f winner Ocean Myth (by Acclamation). The dam, a quite useful 2-y-o 5f winner, was third in the listed Masaka Stakes and is a half-sister to 4 winners including the useful Group 3 7f Dubai Duty Free (Fred Darling Stakes) and 2-y-o 7f listed winner and Irish 1,000 Guineas second Penkenna Princess. The second dam, Tiriana (by Common Grounds), is a placed half-sister to 6 winners including the 2-y-o listed 5.2f winner Head Over Heels. *"She's just been taking a bit of time to furnish but she's getting herself together now and she moves well. She handles her cantering easily and in May we'll have a closer look at her. She'll definitely run as a 2-y-o and I'm pleased with the way she's coming forward".*

1217. ZAMOYSKI ★★★ ♠

ch.c. Dutch Art – Speech (Red Ransom). April 17. First foal. 55,000Y. Tattersalls October Book 2. Jane Allison. The dam is an unraced half-sister to 4 winners. The second dam, Spout (by Salse), a very smart winner of the Group 3 12f John Porter Stakes and the Group 3 Lancashire Oaks and second in the Group 2 Sun Chariot Stakes, is a half-sister to 5 winners including the French listed winner Mon Domino. *"I did a bit of work with him but I've eased off now because he's a little tall and unfurnished. He's shown us enough at this stage for me to say he'll make a 2-y-o by July time and it's pleasing that he showed us such precocity quite early on".*

1218. UNNAMED ★★★

b.f. Kheleyf – Blinking (Marju). February 9. First foal. 50,000Y. Tattersalls October Book 2. Michael Youngs. The dam is an unraced sister to Viva Pataca, a winner of 18 races and nearly £6 million in prize money here and in Hong Kong from 6f (at 2 yrs) to 12f and a half-sister to 3 winners including the Irish listed 11f winner Laughing. The second dam, Comic (Be My Chief), a quite useful 10f and 11.5f winner, is a half-sister to 4 winners including the very useful 2-y-o Group 3 Solario Stakes winner Brave Act and the dual listed winner Jellaby Ashkir. *"A strong, good type that moves well, she had a minor issue which kept her back for a few weeks so I'm not sure how soon she'll be out, but I'm pleased with what she's done so far".*

1219. UNNAMED ★★★

b.br.f. Medaglia d'Oro – Chandelle No. Five (Yes It's True). February 1. Second foal. $70,000Y. Keeneland September. Sackville/Donald. The dam, a stakes winner of 4 races at 3 yrs in the USA, is a sister to the US Grade 3 winner Chandtrue. The second dam, Chandelle (by Crafty Prospector), a winner US winner of 3 races at 2 and 3 yrs, is a half-sister to 10 winners. *"She's been at Vinery Stud in America where she's been working. She looks like a filly for July or August and she's done well physically over there".*

1220. UNNAMED ★★★

b.br.f. Johannesburg – Elle Nicole (El Corredor). April 26. Fourth foal. 27,000Y. Tattersalls October Book 2. Sackville/Donald. Half-sister to Make A Grand (by Grand Reward), a minor winner at 2 and 3 yrs in the USA. The dam, placed once at 2 yrs in the USA, is a half-sister to 5 winners including two US stakes winners. The second dam, Gold Premieress (by Premiership), was placed once in the USA and is a full or half-sister to 9 winners including three US stakes winners. *"She's in work and I'm just about to get a bit more serious with her. She looks like she's got a bit of speed and she should be running in May over five, maybe six furlongs. A solid type of 2-y-o that should win a race or two".*

1221. UNNAMED ★★★★

b.f. Red Clubs – Fuerta Ventura (Desert Sun). January 25. First foal. 70,000Y. Tattersalls October Book 1. Badgers Bloodstock. The dam, a useful Irish 1m to 9.5f winner, is a half-sister to 3 winners including the useful 2-y-o listed 6f winner and Group 2 6f Mill Reef Stakes second Sir Xaar. The dam is an unraced half-sister to the Group 3 6f Greenlands Stakes winner Tiger Royal. *"A good, strong type that moves well. I'm pleased with what I've seen and she should start work soon with an eye on getting her out by the end of May or early June. I think she could be a decent 2-y-o and she reminds me of the nice Red Clubs filly I had last year, Illaunglass".*

1222. UNNAMED ★★★

ch.c. Pivotal – Jamboretta (Danehill). March 2. First foal. 215,000Y. Tattersalls October Book 1. Michael Youngs. The dam, a quite useful 9f winner, is a half-sister to 2 winners including the very useful listed winner and Group 3 second Excusez Moi. The second dam, Jiving (by Generous), a fair 6f placed 2-y-o, is a half-sister to 7 winners including the outstanding broodmare Hasili (dam of the Group 1 winners Banks Hill, Cacique, Champs Elysees, Heat Haze and Intercontinental and the Group 2 winner and leading sire Dansili) and the listed winner Arrive (dam of the Group 1 Pretty Polly Stakes winner Promising Lead) and to the unraced dam of the US Grade 1 winner Leroidesanimaux. *"A horse for August onwards, he moves well and is quite immature at present*

but he'll improve throughout the summer and I'm happy with him at this stage. A colt with a good temperament and he's done everything right for the type of individual he is".*

1223. UNNAMED ★★★

b.br.c. Lion Heart – Sadler's Charm (Honour And Glory). March 22. Third foal. $70,000Y. Keeneland September. Sackville/Donald. The dam is a US unplaced half-sister to 5 winners. The second dam, Wild Rumour (by Sadler's Wells), a fairly useful 2-y-o 6f winner, is a sister to the quite useful 11f winner and listed-placed Grapevine and a half-sister to 5 winners including the very useful 6f Cherry Hinton Stakes, 7f Rockfel Stakes and 7.3f Fred Darling Stakes winner Musicale and the Group 2 King Edward VII Stakes third Theatre Script. *"A strong, forward-going horse, we took him straight from the breeze-up sale to Vinery Stud and he remained in training there. He'll be here shortly and he should be running by mid-May. A sprinting type 2-y-o that should do his job".*

1224. UNNAMED ★★★

b.br.c. Mr Greeley – Sand Pirate (Desert Wine). February 9. Ninth foal. $150,000Y. Keeneland September. Sackville/Donald. Half-brother to the US Grade 2 winner Sweet Vendetta (by Stephen Got Even) and to the US stakes winners Half Heaven (by Regal Classic), Love Cove (by Not For Love) and Doll Baby (by Citidancer). The dam won 7 minor races in the USA. The second dam, Wayward Pirate (by Pirate's Bounty), won the Grade 3 Anoakia Stakes and was third in the Grade 1 Oak Leaf Stakes. *"He's coming in from America this week and he's a good type with size and scope. He needs a bit of time because he's more of a 3-y-o type, but I like the way he goes and he's a really nice individual with a future".*

1225. UNNAMED ★★★

ch.f. Street Boss – Special Grayce (Smart Strike). March 7. Third foal. $75,000Y. Keeneland September. Sackville/Donald. $220,000 2-y-o. Ocala Breeze-Up. Not sold. The dam, a winner at 3 and 4 yrs in the USA, was Grade 3 placed and is a half-sister to 3 winners. The second dam, Trust Your Heart (by Relaunch), a stakes-placed winner in the USA, is a half-sister to several winners including the US Grade 3 winner Aunt Henny and the dam of the US Grade 1 winner Ever A Friend. *"We bought her at Keeneland, put her in the Ocala breeze-up and bought her back. A good-moving filly for the second half of the season, probably over seven furlongs. A good-moving filly, she looks like she's got a bit of quality and she's done nothing but progress throughout the winter. I'm looking forward to her arriving here, she's quite a nice filly with a future".*

AIDAN O'BRIEN

1226. CODRINGTON COLLEGE (IRE)

ch.c. Duke Of Marmalade – A P Easy (A P Indy). April 2. Second foal. 100,000Y. Tattersalls October Book 1. Demi O'Byrne. The dam, a minor winner at 3 yrs in the USA, is a half-sister to the French 2,000 Guineas winner Astronomer Royal and to the US Grade 2 Pan American Handicap winner Navesink River. The second dam, Sheepscot (by Easy Goes), a minor stakes winner of 5 races in the USA, is a half-sister to the dual US Grade 1 winner Vicar.

1227. COUNT OF LIMONADE (IRE)

b.c. Duke Of Marmalade – Hoity Toity (Darshaan). April 24. Fifth foal. €140,000Y. Goffs Orby. Demi O'Byrne. Closely related to the Group 1 1m Coronation Stakes and Group 1 1m Matron Stakes winner Lillie Langtry (by Danehill Dancer). The dam is an unraced half-sister to 5 winners. The second dam, Hiwaayati (by Shadeed), is an unraced half-sister to 6 winners including the dual Group 3 winner Great Commotion and the dual Group 2 winner Lead on Time.

1228. DELIGHT (IRE)

ch.f. Danehill Dancer – Northern Gulch (Gulch). May 2. Eighth foal. 220,000Y. Tattersalls October Book 1. Charlie Gordon-Watson. Closely related to the moderate 2011 5f and 6f placed 2-y-o Mount McLeod (by Holy Roman Emperor) and half-sister to the 2-y-o Group 2 6f Richmond Stakes winner Hamoody (by Johannesburg) and the US winner and Grade 3 placed Arcodoro (by Medaille d'Or). The dam, placed three times in the USA, is a half-sister to 9 winners including the US dual Grade 3 winner Stylish Star. The second dam, Northern Style (by Ack Ack), a US stakes winner, was Grade 3 placed.

1229. FORESTER (IRE)

gr.c. Danehill Dancer – Amenixa (Linamix). February 6. Tenth foal. €260,000Y. Arqana Deauville August. Demi O'Byrne. Half-brother to the 2-y-o Group 2 6f Criterium de Maisons-Laffitte and Group 3 Prix Eclipse winner Zinziberene (by Zieten and herself the dam of two stakes winners), to the quite useful 7f, 1m (both at 2 yrs) and subsequent UAE winner Palm Court (by Green Desert) and the fairly useful French 9f winner Iron Age (by Pivotal). The dam, a 4-y-o 10f winner, is a sister to Amilynx (dual Group 1 Prix Royal-Oak winner) and a half-sister to Amiwain (Group 2 Criterium de Maisons-Laffitte). The second dam, Amen (by Alydar), was a Grade 3 placed winner in the USA.

1230. FRANCIS OF ASSISI (IRE)

b.c. Danehill Dancer – Queen Cleopatra (Kingmambo). January 27. Second foal. Brother to the Irish 7f (at 2 yrs) and listed 1m winner and Group 2 10f Blandford Stakes second Look At Me and half-brother to the quite useful 2011 Irish 2-y-o 5f winner Wave (by Dansili). The dam, won the Group 3 Irish 1,000 Guineas Trial, was third in the Irish 1,000 Guineas and the Prix de Diane and is a sister to Henrythenavigator. The second dam, Sequoyah (by Sadler's Wells), winner of the Group 1 7f Moyglare Stud Stakes, is a sister to the Fillies' Mile winner Listen and a half-sister to the listed 5.6f winner Oyster Catcher.

1231. FREEDOM FIGHTER (IRE)

b.c. Danehill Dancer – Rose Of Petra (Golan). February 16. Second foal. 170,000Y. Tattersalls October Book 1. Demi O'Byrne. The dam, a quite useful 7f (at 2 yrs) and 10f winner, is a half-sister to 4 winners. The second dam, Desert Beauty (by Green Desert), a fairly useful 7f and 1m winner, is a half-sister to the Group 1 winners Islington, Mountain High and Greek Dance.

1232. GALE FORCE TEN *2nd Norfolk*

b.c. Oasis Dream – Ronaldsay (Kirkwall). February 20. First foal. £280,000Y. Doncaster Premier. Eddie Fitzpatrick. The dam, a listed 11f winner of 4 races, is a half-sister to 5 winners including the dam of the US dual Grade 3 winner Pickle. The second dam, Crackling (by Electric), a modest 9f and 12f winner, is a half-sister to the Moyglare Stud Stakes winner Bianca Nera and to the dam of the Fillies' Mile winner Simply Perfect.

1233. ILLUSTRATE (IRE)

b.c. *Oasis Dream – Kassiopeia (Galileo).* March 22. Third foal. 700,000Y. Tattersalls October Book 1. Demi O'Byrne. Closely related to the quite useful 7f (at 2 yrs) to 10f winner of 4 races Arabian Star (by Green Desert). The dam, a quite useful 12f winner, is a half-sister to 5 winners. The second dam, Brush Strokes (by Cadeaux Genereux), is a half-sister to the Racing Post Trophy second Mudeer.

1234. INFANTA BRANCA (USA)

b.f. *Henrythenavigator – Totemic (Vanlandingham).* February 16. Half-sister to the Group 3 Round Tower Stakes winner Cherokee, to the Irish 2-y-o listed 6f winner Art Museum (both by Storm Cat) and the US Grade 2 winner and Grade 1 placed Lil's Lad (by Pine Bluff). The dam won the Grade 3 Honeybee Stakes in the USA.

1235. INKERMAN (IRE)

b.c. *Duke Of Marmalade – Lady Taufan (Taufan).* April 14. Eleventh foal. €140,000Y. Goffs Orby. Demi O'Byrne. Half-brother to numerous winners including the 2-y-o Group 3 7f Prestige Stakes winner Gracefully, to the listed 6f winner and dual Group 3 placed Lady Grace, the 2-y-o 6f winner and Group 3 Sirenia Stakes third Visionist (all by Orpen), the 2-y-o 6f winner Speedball (by Waajib) – all useful. The dam was placed 5 times and is a sister to the listed National Stakes winner Princess Taufan. The second dam, Guindilla (by Artaius), is an unraced half-sister to the US Flower Bowl Handicap winner Gaily Gaily and the Premio Parioli winners Gay Burslem and Crisos II Monaco.

1236. KING GEORGE RIVER

b.c. *Danehill Dancer – Butterfly Blue (Sadler's Wells).* March 12. Sixth foal. Brother to the fairly useful 9f winner and Group 3 Irish 1,000 Guineas Trial third Sapphire Pendant and half-brother to the Canadian winner and listed-placed Lacadena (by Fasliyev). The dam, a quite useful Irish 9f winner, is a sister to the winner and Fillies' Mile second Maryinski

(herself dam of the Criterium International winner Thewayyouare and the multiple Group 1 winner Peeping Fawn) and a half-sister to Better Than Honour (Demoiselle Stakes), Turnberry Isle (Beresford Stakes) and Smolensk (Prix d'Astarte). The second dam, Blush With Pride (by Blushing Groom), won the Kentucky Oaks and the Santa Susana Stakes and is a half-sister to the dams of Xaar, El Gran Senor and Try My Best.

1237. MOHAWK LANE (USA)

b.c. *Henrythenavigator – Crystal Crossing (Royal Academy).* May 12. Eleventh foal. $625,000Y. Keeneland September. Demi O'Byrne. Closely related to the St Leger and Great Voltigeur Stakes winner Rule Of Law (by Kingmambo) and half-brother to the 1m winner and listed-placed Totally Devoted (by Seeking The Gold). The dam, winner of a listed 6f event, is a sister to the Group 3 7f Prestige Stakes winner Circle Of Gold, subsequently Grade 2 placed in the USA. The second dam, Never So Fair (by Never So Bold), is an unplaced three-parts sister to the Amaranda (Queen Mary Stakes) and a half-sister to Favoridge (Nell Gwyn Stakes).

1238. MONTCLAIR

b.c. *Montjeu – Minaccia (Platini).* April 7. Tenth living foal. €340,000Y. Arqana Deauville August. Demi O'Byrne. Half-brother to 5 winners including Macleya (Group 2 Prix de Pomone). The dam, a dual listed winner in France, is a half-sister to 4 winners out of the modest 12f winner Maji (by Shareef Dancer), a half-sister to the German Group 2 winner Malinas.

1239. PARLIAMENT SQUARE (IRE)

b.c. *Acclamation – Bold Desire (Cadeaux Genereux).* February 23. Third foal. 370,000Y. Tattersalls October Book 1. Demi O'Byrne. Half-brother to the quite useful 2-y-o 6f and 7f winner Bunce (by Good Reward). The dam, placed once over 6f, is a sister to the listed 6f winner Irresistible (herself dam of the Group 3 Nell Gwyn Stakes winner Infallible). The second dam, Polish Romance (by Danzig), a minor 7f winner in the USA, is a full or half-sister to 6 winners.

1240. PEDRO THE GREAT

b.c. *Henrythenavigator – Glatisant (Rainbow*

Quest). March 27. Eleventh foal. 150,000Y. Tattersalls October Book 1. John Magnier. Half-brother to the 2,000 Guineas winner Footstepsinthesand (by Giant's Causeway) and to the fairly useful 2-y-o 6f winner Frappe (by Inchinor and herself dam of the Group 1 National Stakes winner Power and the Ribblesdale Stakes winner Thakafaat). The dam won the Group 3 7f Prestige Stakes at 2 yrs and is a half-sister to 8 winners including the Group 1 placed Rockerlong and the very useful triple 10f winner Gai Bulga and to the placed dam of Superstar Leo. The second dam, Dancing Rocks (by Green Dancer), won over 5f and 6f at 2 yrs and the Group 2 10f Nassau Stakes at 3 yrs and is a half-sister to 4 winners.

Maced up bf mln leopder

1241. PERFORMANCE (IRE)

b.c. Danehill Dancer – Ahdaab (Rahy). March 1. Seventh foal. Brother to the Canadian Grade 2 Nassau Stakes winner Callwood Dancer, to the Group 2 Italian Oaks winner Contredanse and the fairly useful Irish 2-y-o 7f winner and Group 1 Juddmonte International third Set Sail and closely related to the fair 2-y-o 5f and subsequent US winner and Grade 3 placed Walklikeanegyptian (by Danehill). The dam, placed once over 10f, is a half-sister to 8 winners including Maroof (Group 1 1m Queen Elizabeth II Stakes) and to the placed dam of the Irish Derby winner Desert King. The second dam, Dish Dash (by Bustino), won the Group 2 12f Ribblesdale Stakes.

1242. PIET MONDRIAN

b.c. Danehill Dancer – Last Second (Alzao). April 5. Eleventh living foal. Brother to the quite useful 2011 2-y-o 7f winner Gooseberry Fool, closely related to the French 2,000 Guineas and US Grade 1 winner Aussie Rules (by Danehill) and half-brother to 6 winners including the listed 10f winner and US Grade 2 second Approach and the very useful 2-y-o 8.5f winner Intrigued (both by Darshaan). The dam, winner of the Nassau Stakes and the Sun Chariot Stakes, is a half-sister to 7 winners including the Moyglare Stud Stakes third Alouette (herself dam of the Group 1 winners Albanova and Alborada) and the Group 2 Doncaster Cup winner Alleluia (dam of the Group 1 winner Allegretto) and to the placed dam of the Group 1 winners Yesterday and Quarter Moon. The

second dam, Alruccaba (by Crystal Palace), was a quite useful 2-y-o 6f winner.

1243. POINT PIPER (USA)

b.c. Giant's Causeway – Imagine (Sadler's Wells). Brother to the Irish listed 7f winner and Group 2 Champagne Stakes second Viscount Nelson and half-brother to the 2-y-o Group 1 7f Prix Jean Luc Lagardere winner Horatio Nelson (by Danehill), the 2-y-o Group 2 7f Rockfel Stakes winner Kitty Matcham and the Irish 10f winner and Group 1 placed Red Rock Canyon (both by Rock Of Gibraltar). The dam, winner of the Irish 1,000 Guineas and Epsom Oaks, is a half-sister to Generous. The second dam, Doff The Derby (by Master Derby), is an unraced half-sister to the Prix Ganay winner Trillion (herself the dam of Triptych).

1244. RENEW (IRE)

b.c. Dansili – Hold Me Love Me (Sadler's Wells). March 16. First foal. The dam, a fairly useful 13f winner and third in the Group 2 Park Hill Stakes, is a sister to the Irish 1,000 Guineas winner Yesterday, the Group 1 7f Moyglare Stud Stakes winner Quarter Moon and the 10f winner and Epsom Oaks third All My Loving. The second dam, Jude (by Darshaan), a moderate 10f placed maiden, is a sister to the Irish listed 14f winner and Irish Oaks third Arrikala and to the Irish 12f listed winner Alouette (herself dam of the Group 1 winners Albanova and Alborada) and a half-sister to the Group 2 10f Nassau Stakes and Sun Chariot Stakes winner Last Second (dam of the dual Group 1 winner Aussie Rules) and the Group 2 Doncaster Cup winner Alleluia (dam of the Group 1 winner Allegretto).

1245. SURREALIST (IRE)

b.c. Montjeu – Spritza (Spectrum). March 26. Second foal. €200,000Y. Goffs Orby. Demi O'Byrne. Brother to the quite useful 7f and 10f (at 2 yrs in 2011) and 3-y-o 10f winner Rougemont. The dam, a modest 11f and 12f winner, is a half-sister to 3 winners including the fairly useful 12f winner of 3 races and listed-placed Portrait Of A Lady. The second dam, Starlight Smile (by Green Dancer), is an unraced half-sister to 4 winners including the dam of the Irish Derby winner Grey Swallow.

1246. TWILIGHT ZONE (IRE)

b.c. Danehill Dancer – All My Loving (Sadler's Wells). February 28. Second foal. Closely related to the 2011 2-y-o 1m winner Thomas Chippendale (by Dansili). The dam, a 10f winner and third in the Oaks and Irish Oaks, is a sister to the Irish 1,000 Guineas winner Yesterday and to the Moyglare Stud Stakes winner Quarter Moon. The second dam, Jude (by Darshaan), a moderate 10f placed maiden, is a sister to the listed 14f winner and Irish Oaks third Arrikala and to the 12f listed winner Alouette (herself dam of the Group 1 winners Alborada and Albanova) and a half-sister to the Group 2 10f Nassau Stakes and Sun Chariot Stakes winner Last Second (dam of the Irish 2,000 Guineas winner Aussie Rules).

1247. VESTIGE

b.c. Montjeu – Llia (Shirley Heights). February 28. Tenth foal. 150,000Y. Tattersalls October Book 1. Demi O'Byrne. Closely related to the 7f (at 2 yrs), Group 1 Irish St Leger and Group 2 12f Princess Of Wales's Stakes winner Sans Frontieres (by Galileo) and half-brother to 5 winners including the very useful triple listed 1m winner (including at 2 yrs) and Group 2 Falmouth Stakes third Kootenay (by Selkirk). The dam, a fairly useful 2-y-o 7f winner, was third in the listed 10f Pretty Polly Stakes and is a half-sister to 5 winners including the Italian Group 3 winner Guest Connections and the 2m listed winner Lady Of The Lake. The second dam, Llyn Gwynant (by Persian Bold), won the Group 3 1m Desmond Stakes and the Group 3 1m Matron Stakes.

1248. VICTORY SONG (IRE)

b.c. Dansili – All Too Beautiful (Sadler's Wells). April 9. Fourth foal. Half-brother to the listed 11f winner, Group 1 Oaks second and Group 1 Irish Oaks third Wonder Of Wonders (by Kingmambo). The dam, a Group 3 10.5f Middleton Stakes winner, is a sister to Galileo and to Black Sam Bellamy and a half-sister to Sea The Stars. The second dam, Urban Sea (by Miswaki), won 8 races from 1m (at 2 yrs) to 12f including the Group 1 Prix de l'Arc de Triomphe and is closely related to the 2,000 Guineas winner King's Best.

1249. WHERE (IRE)

b.f. Danehill Dancer – Virginia Waters (Kingmambo). March 28. Fourth foal. Half-sister to the very useful 6f (at 2 yrs), 7f and listed 1m winner Emperor Claudius (by Giant's Causeway). The dam won the 1,000 Guineas and is a half-sister to the Group 3 Gallinule Stakes winner and Irish Derby second Alexander Of Hales and to the Group 1 1m Criterium International second Chevalier. The second dam, Legend Maker (by Sadler's Wells), won the Group 3 10.5f Prix de Royaumont, was third in the Group 2 13.5 Prix de Pomone and is a half-sister to the Group 2 12f King Edward VII Stakes winner Amfortas.

1250. UNNAMED *The United States*

ch.c. Galileo – Beauty Is Truth (Pivotal). February 19. Second foal. Half-sister to the 2011 Group 3 6.3f Anglesey Stakes winner and dual Group 1 placed Fire Lily (by Dansili). The dam won the Group 2 5f Prix de Gros-Chene and is a half-sister to the French listed 9f winner Glorious Sight. The second dam, Zelda (by Caerleon), a 6.5f in France at 3 yrs, is closely related to the dam of the French 1,000 Guineas winner Valentine Waltz and a half-sister to Last Tycoon (Breeders Cup Mile and William Hill Sprint Championship) and the Group winners Astronef and The Perfect Life.

1251. UNNAMED *Won on debut 7f Curragh nice horse*

b.c. Danehill Dancer – Chenchikova (Sadler's Wells). March 20. Second foal. Closely related to the useful 2011 2-y-o 7f winner Unex Michelangelo (by Dansili). The dam, a fairly useful Irish 2-y-o 7f winner, is a sister to High Chaparral (Derby, Irish Derby and Breeders Cup Turf) and to Black Bear Island (Group 2 Dante Stakes). The second dam, Kasora (by Darshaan), is an unraced full or half-sister to 8 winners including two listed winners.

1252. UNNAMED

b.c. Montjeu – Cherry Hinton (Green Desert). January 14. Second foal. Brother to the 2011 2-y-o Group 2 7f Rockfel Stakes winner Wading. The dam was second in the Group 3 10f Blue Wind Stakes and third in a listed event over 9f and is closely related to the outstanding colt Sea The Stars and a half-sister to the top-class Galileo, the dual Group 1 winner Black Sam

THE LIVING LEGEND RACING PARTNERSHIP

For an inexpensive way to enjoy the benefits of being a racehorse owner, join us in 2012.

Call Steve Taplin on 07754 094204
or e-mail stevetaplin@blueyonder.co.uk

"Betting must-have".

★★★★★
APP STORE REVIEW - MARCH 15, 2012

The Racing Post App. The five-star betting app.

★★★★★* 1,840 RATINGS

RACING POST MOBILE APP

Bellamy and the Group 2 winner Urban Ocean. The second dam, Urban Sea (by Miswaki), won 8 races from 1m (at 2 yrs) to 12f including the Arc and is closely related to the 2,000 Guineas winner King's Best.

1253. UNNAMED

b.c. Montjeu – Dance Parade (Gone West). March 6. Sixth foal. 520,000Y. Tattersalls October Book 1. Demi O'Byrne. Brother to Warwick Avenue, unplaced in one start at 2 yrs in 2011, and half-brother to 4 winners including the useful 6f and 7f winner of 5 races Castles In The Air (by Oasis Dream). The dam won the Grade 2 Buena Vista Handicap, the Group 3 Queen Mary Stakes and the Group 3 Fred Darling Stakes and is a half-sister to the Grade 3 9f Bay Meadows Derby winner Ocean Queen. The second dam, River Jig (by Irish River), a useful 2-y-o 9f winner here, won over 12f in Italy.

1254. UNNAMED

b.c. Dansili – Flawly (Old Vic). March 2. Fifth foal. 480,000Y. Tattersalls October Book 1. Demi O'Byrne. Half-brother to the Group 3 10f Prix du Prince d'Orange winner and French Derby second Best Name (by King's Best) and to the German Group 3 11f winner February Sun (by Monsun). The dam, a French 12f winner, was second in a US Grade 1 9f event and is a half-sister to 6 winners including Ombre Legere (Group 3 10.5f Prix Penelope). The second dam, Flawlessly (by Rainbow Quest), is a placed half-sister to the French listed winners and Group-placed Video Rock and Lady Day.

1255. UNNAMED

ch.c. Galileo – Halfway To Heaven (Pivotal). February 21. First foal. The dam, winner of the Irish 1,000 Guineas, Nassau Stakes and Sun Chariot Stakes, is a half-sister to the Group 3 6f Summer Stakes winner Theann. The second dam, Cassandra Go (by Indian Ridge), winner of the Group 2 5f Kings Stand Stakes, is a full or half-sister to 7 winners including the smart Group 3 6f Coventry Stakes winner and Irish 2,000 Guineas second Verglas.

1256. UNNAMED

b.c. Galileo – La Chunga (More Than Ready). February 13. Second foal. The dam won the

2-y-o Group 3 6f Albany Stakes and the Group 3 6f Summer Stakes. The second dam, Gypsy Monarch (by Wavering Monarch), a minor US winner, is a half-sister to the US Grade 3 6f winner Mint.

1257. UNNAMED

b.c. Giant's Causeway – Liscanna (Sadler's Wells). March 4. Second foal. $550,000Y. Fasig-Tipton Saratoga August. Blandford Bloodstock. The dam, winner of the Group 3 6f Ballyogan Stakes, is a half-sister to the Group 3 10f Kilternan Stakes winner and dual Group 2 placed The Bogberry. The second dam, Lahinch (by Danehill Dancer), a listed 5f (at 2 yrs) and listed 6f winner, was second in the Group 2 Rockfel Stakes and is a half-sister to 7 winners including the smart 2-y-o 5f and subsequent US stakes winner Perugino Bay.

1258. UNNAMED

ch.c. Galileo – Love Me True (Kingmambo). March 17. Closely related to the quite useful 2-y-o 7f winner So In Love With You (by Sadler's Wells) and half-brother to the multiple Group 1 winner Duke Of Marmalade (by Danehill), the US Grade 3 placed Countess Lemonade and the quite useful 2-y-o 6f winner Looking Lovely (both by Storm Cat). The dam, a 1m winner, was third in the Group 3 Killavullan Stakes and is a half-sister to the Grade 2 Sanford Stakes winner Bite The Bullet and the listed 10f winner Shuailaan. The second dam, Lassie's Lady (by Alydar), a US stakes-placed winner, is a half-sister to the dual US Grade 3 winner Weekend Surprise and the high-class sprinter Wolfhound.

1259. UNNAMED

ch.c. Galileo – Luas Line (Danehill). January 28. Third foal. The dam won the US Grade 1 Garden City Breeders Cup Stakes, was third in the Irish 1,000 Guineas and is a half-sister to 2 winners. The second dam, Streetcar (by In The Wings), was placed fourth once over 8.5f at 2 yrs and is a half-sister to 9 winners including Intimate Guest (Group 3 May Hill Stakes) and the dam of the US Grade 1 winner Prince Arch.

1260. UNNAMED

ch.c. Galileo – Massara (Danehill). February 24. Fifth foal. Half-brother to the smart 2011 2-y-o

Group 1 1m Gran Criterium winner Nayarra (by Cape Cross), to the fair Irish 1m winner Middle Persia (by Dalakhani) and the fair 10f winner Tebee (by Selkirk). The dam, a useful listed 6f winner and second in the Group 2 Prix Robert Papin at 2 yrs, is closely related to the Group 1 6f Haydock Park Sprint Cup winner Invincible Spirit and a half-sister to the Group 3 winners Acts Of Grace and Sadian. The second dam, Rafha (by Kris), winner of the Group 1 10.5f Prix de Diane, is a half-sister to 9 winners.

1261. UNNAMED

b.c. Dansili – Moonstone (Dalakhani). February 21. First foal. The dam, winner of the Irish Oaks, is closely related to the Breeders Cup second L'Ancresse and to the Prix Saint-Alary winner Cerulean Sky (dam of the Group 2 Doncaster Cup winner Honolulu). The second dam, Solo de Lune (by Law Society), a French 11f winner, is a half-sister to the Grade 2 E P Taylor Stakes winner Truly A Dream and the French Group 2 winner Wareed.

1262. UNNAMED

b.c. Galileo – Mora Bai (Indian Ridge). April 30. Brother to the 2011 2-y-o Group 2 1m Beresford Stakes winner and Group 1 7f National Stakes second David Livingston and closely related to the fair 10f winner Tupelo Honey (by Sadler's Wells). The dam is an unraced full or half-sister to 8 winners including High Chaparral. The second dam, Kasora (by Darshaan), is an unraced full or half-sister to 8 winners.

1263. UNNAMED

b.c. Duke Of Marmalade – Night Frolic (Night Shift). March 28. Fifth foal. 340,000Y. Tattersalls October Book 1. Demi O'Byrne. Closely related to the fair 2-y-o 5f winner Chicita Banana (by Danehill Dancer) and half-brother to the very smart 2011 2-y-o 1m winner and Group 1 Criterium International third Bonfire (by Manduro), the Musidora Stakes winner Joviality (by Cape Cross) and the fair 7f and 1m winner Burns Night (by Selkirk). The dam, a modest 1m winner, is a half-sister to 5 winners including the US Grade 3 Cardinal Handicap winner Miss Caerleona (dam of the Group winners Karen's Caper and Miss Coronado). The second dam, Miss d'Ouilly (by Bikala), a listed 9f winner in France, is a half-sister to 6 winners including

Miss Satamixa (Prix Jacques le Marois).

1264. UNNAMED

b.c. Galileo – Rumplestiltskin (Danehill). January 17. Brother to the fairly useful 2-y-o 7f winner Why. The dam won the Prix Marcel Boussac and the Moyglare Stud Stakes and is a full or half-sister to 4 winners. The second dam, Monevassia (by Mr Prospector), is a placed sister to Kingmambo and to Miesque's Son (Group 3 6f Prix de Ris-Oranges) and a half-sister to East of the Moon (French 1,000 Guineas, Prix de Diane and Prix Jacques le Marois).

1265. UNNAMED

b.c. Montjeu – Shadow Song (Pennekamp). April 28. Fourth foal. Brother to the 2-y-o Group 1 1m Criterium International winner and Irish Derby third Jan Vermeer and closely related to the 2-y-o Group 3 7f Silver Flash Stakes and subsequent US Grade 1 9f winner Together (by Galileo). The dam, a minor French 3-y-o winner, is a half-sister to the Group 3 May Hill Stakes winner Midnight Air (dam of the Group 3 and US Grade 2 winner Midnight Line) and to the placed dam of Imperial Beauty (Prix de l'Abbaye). The second dam, Evening Air (by J O Tobin), is an unraced half-sister to 5 winners.

1266. UNNAMED

b.c. Galileo – Sharp Lisa (Dixieland Band). April 3. The dam won the Grade 1 1m Las Virgines Stakes and two Grade 2 stakes in the USA and is a half-sister to the US Grade 1 9f winner Spring At Last and the US Grade 2 9f winner Sharp Susan. The second dam, Winter's Gone (by Dynaformer), is an unplaced half-sister to the multiple US Grade 1 winner Bien Bien.

1267. UNNAMED

b.c. Galileo – Shouk (Shirley Heights). March 12. Closely related to the 1m (at 2 yrs), Oaks, Irish Oaks and Yorkshire Oaks winner Alexandrova, to the listed 2-y-o 1m winner and Epsom Derby third Masterofthehorse, the useful dual 12f winner Clearwater Bay (all by Sadler's Wells), the Cheveley Park Stakes winner Magical Romance, the fairly useful 2-y-o 7f winner and Canadian Grade 3 placed Saree (both by Barathea) and the 10f winner and Group 2 placed Washington Irving (by Montjeu). The dam, a quite useful 10.5f winner, is closely related to the listed winner and Park Hill Stakes third Puce. The second dam, Souk (by Ahonoora), was a fairly useful 7f winner.

1268. UNNAMED

b.c. *Galileo – Theann (by Rock Of Gibraltar)*. February 6. Second foal. The dam, winner of the Group 3 6f Summer Stakes, is a half-sister to several winners including Halfway To Heaven (Irish 1,000 Guineas, Nassau Stakes and Sun Chariot Stakes). The second dam, Cassandra Go (by Indian Ridge), won the Group 2 5f Kings Stand Stakes and is a half-sister to Verglas (Coventry Stakes winner and Irish 2,000 Guineas second).

1269. UNNAMED

b.c. *Montjeu – Time Over (Mark Of Esteem)*. February 25. Second foal. 270,000Y. Tattersalls October Book 1. Demi O'Byrne. Brother to the quite useful 2011 2-y-o 7f and 1m winner Repeater. The dam, a fair 1m winner, is closely related to the Musidora Stakes winner and Prix de Diane third Time Away (herself dam of the Group 2 winner Time On) and a half-sister to the French Oaks second Time Ahead. The second dam, Not Before Time (by Polish Precedent), is an unraced half-sister to the dual Group 3 winner Time Allowed.

JEDD O'KEEFFE

1270. BRONTE BELLE ★★★

b.f. *Pastoral Pursuits – Katy O'Hara (Komaite)*. March 22. Fourth foal. 20,000Y. Doncaster November. Paul Chapman. Half-sister to the quite useful 2011 2-y-o 5f and 6f winner Kune Kune (by Sir Percy) and to the fair 6f winner of 4 races Katy's Secret (by Mind Games). The dam, a modest 2-y-o dual 5f winner, is a half-sister to one winner. The second dam, Amy Leigh (by Imperial Frontier), was a moderate 5f (including at 2 yrs) and 6f winner. (Caron & Paul Chapman). "I've known the dam for quite some time, be*cause she was trained by and is still owned by my landowner and next door neighbour Sally Hall. She was very quick and this daughter of hers is a lovely, sprinting type. Quite stocky and powerful, she has a great temperament and she's going really well. I'd expect her to start off in early May and I'm*

looking forward to some happy days with her. She's entered in the Weatherbys Supersprint". TRAINERS' BARGAIN BUY

1271. CAPTAIN'S DREAM (IRE) ★★★

b.c. *Kheleyf – Somaggia (Desert King)*. February 18. Third foal. 28,000Y. Tattersalls October Book 2. Jedd O'Keeffe. Half-brother to the fair 2011 2-y-o 6f winner Mention (by Acclamation). The dam is an unplaced half-sister to 8 winners including the listed winner and Group 1 Prix de la Salamandre third Speedfit Too. The second dam, Safka (by Irish River), a useful 2-y-o 5f winner, was third in the Group 3 5f Cornwallis Stakes and is a half-sister to 9 winners including the Group 2 7f Lockinge Stakes winner Safawan. (Mr & Mrs Bruce McAllister). *"A lovely, big horse, we're taking our time with him because of his size but he's already showing lots of promise. I expect he'll debut over six furlongs around June-time and I think he's the sort of horse that should train on nicely to be a 3-y-o as well. I really like him".*

1272. CREDITAS ★★

b.f. *Avonbridge – Jade Pet (Petong)*. April 29. £8,000Y. Doncaster Premier. Jedd O'Keeffe. Half-sister to the useful winner of 17 races from 7f to 10f including a US Grade 2 handicap Hail The Chief (by Be My Chief), to the quite useful 7f and 1m winner Chilli Green (by Desert Sun), the fair 7f to 10f and hurdles winner Just Wiz (by Efisio), the fair 2-y-o 5f winner Smirfys Diamond (by Mujahid), the fair 6f winner Champagne Future (by Compton Place) and the hurdles winner Jade Warrior (by Sabrehill). The dam, a fairly useful sprint winner of 3 races at 2 and 4 yrs, is a half-sister to 4 minor winners and to the dam of the very smart Group 2 6f Diadem Stakes winner Sampower Star. The second dam, Pea Green (by Try My Best), was a useful winner of the listed 5f St Hugh's Stakes at 2 yrs. (Ken & Delia Shaw Racing). *"A filly from quite a speedy family, she was a fairly late foal so we haven't been rushing her but she should be worth putting in the book".*

1273. DARK OCEAN (IRE) ★★★

b.c. *Dylan Thomas – Neutral (Beat Hollow)*. February 11. First foal. 13,500Y. Tattersalls October Book 2. Oliver St Lawrence. The dam is an unraced half-sister to 5 winners including the 2-y-o Group 2 7f Debutante Stakes winner Silk And Scarlet (herself dam of a dual Group 2 winner in Japan) and the Group 3 6f Prix de Seine-et-Oise winner Danger Over. The second dam, Danilova (by Lyphard), is an unraced half-sister to the high-class middle-distance colt Sanglamore – winner of the French Derby and the 9.3f Prix d'Ispahan – and the very useful listed 10f winner Opera Score. (Miss S Long). *"We really like him, he's not bred to be early but I can see him making his debut in early summer over seven furlongs and he's not backward at all. He's been coping so easily with the work we've been giving him".*

1274. DREAM ALLY (IRE) ★★★★

b.c. Oasis Dream – Alexander Alliance (Danetime). February 15. First foal. £65,000Y. Doncaster Premier. Jedd O'Keeffe. The dam, an Irish 2-y-o 6f listed winner, is a half-sister to 8 winners including the listed 5f and 6f winner and dual Group 3 placed Ruby Rocket and the German listed winner and Group 3 6.5f Prix Eclipse second Inzar's Best. The second dam, Geht Schnell (by Fairy King), is a placed half-sister to one winner abroad. (Caron & Paul Chapman). *"A lovely colt, he's not particularly tall but he's very strong, I'm very taken with him and he's coping very easily with all the work we're giving him. He could possibly debut in early May, he'll be going for the Bonus races and we like him a lot. At this moment in time I'm quite excited about him".*

1275. ROYAL JENRAY ★★★

gr.c. Royal Applause – In The Highlands (Petong). March 26. Tenth foal. £16,000Y. Doncaster Premier. J O'Keeffe. Half-brother to the fair Irish 9f winner Trust In Me (by Spartacus), to the quite useful 2-y-o 5f and 6f winner Glenmorangie (by Danzig Connection), the modest dual 6f winner Strathmore (by Fath) and a winner in Jersey by Missed Flight. The dam is an unplaced full or half-sister to 5 winners. The second dam, Thevetia (by Mummy's Pet), is a placed half-sister to 7 winners. (Jenny & Ray Butler). *"An early, sprinting type and he's coping very well with the work I'm giving him on the gallops. There's a fair chance he could run in April, we like him and we should have some fun with him. The pedigree is all speed, he's showing plenty and he's eligible*

for the Racing Post Yearling Bonus, so we'll be trying to win one of those".*

1276. UNNAMED ★★

b.c. Byron – Fresher (Fabulous Dancer). April 23. Eighth foal. £3,000Y. Doncaster Festival. Jedd O'Keeffe. Half-sister to the useful 9f winner and Group 3 9f Prix Chloe third Zuleika Dobson and to the Italian 3-y-o winner and French listed 10f placed Fantastic Santanyi (by Fantastic Light). The second dam, Fresher (by Fabulous Dancer), won twice in France and the USA was second in the Group 2 Prix d'Astarte and is a half-sister to 5 winners including the Group 2 Prix Niel winner Songlines. The second dam, Aborigine (by Riverman), a listed winner in France and Group 2 placed twice, is a half-sister to 5 winners. (Highbeck Racing). *"He was a bit weak-looking at the sales and he was a late foal anyway, but he's done really well, he's strengthened up and now he's a nice athlete. We like him and I think he could have been a good buy for what we paid for him. One that should debut in mid-summer".*

DAVID O'MEARA

1277. ARCH EBONY (USA) ★★★★

b.c. Arch – Dot C C (Cozzene). February 27. Sixth foal. 38,000Y. Tattersalls October Book 2. Guy Stephenson. Half-brother to 3 minor winners in the USA by Chief Seattle, Hold That Tiger and Yonagusta. The dam is an unplaced half-sister to 7 winners including the US Grade 3 winners High Tech Friend and Sergeant Stroh. The second dam, Tasha Lanae (by Air Forbes Won), is an unraced full or half-sister to 10 winners. *"A good, strong colt, he's showed us quite a bit and he's very well-made. We do quite like him and he'll make a 2-y-o around May time over six furlongs".*

1278. GRANDORIO (IRE) ★★★

b.g. Oratorio – Grand Splendour (Shirley Heights). January 27. Eighth foal. £15,000Y. Doncaster Premier. Guy Stephenson. Half-brother to the useful 2-y-o 1m winner and listed-placed Fantasy Ride (by Bahhare), the fair 6f to 1m winner Smith N Allan Oils, the moderate 1m seller winner Seejay (both by Bahamian Bounty) and a hurdles winner by Xaar. The dam, a quite useful 4-y-o 10f winner, is a half-sister to 6 winners abroad out of the

2-y-o 5f winner Mayaasa (by Green Desert), herself a half-sister to 3 winners. *"A good, big 2-y-o, he'll be racing by late May or early June I expect, he's showing plenty at home and there's a lot to like about him. I think he'll be a six/seven furlong 2-y-o".*

1279. SLEEPING APACHE (IRE) ★★★

ch.c. Sleeping Indian – Remedy (Pivotal). April 18. Fifth foal. €16,500Y. Tattersalls Ireland. Emma O'Gorman. Half-brother to the French 1m and 11f winner Remedial (by Verglas), to the French 2-y-o 6f winner Race Driver (by Domedriver) and a minor winner abroad by Bachelor Duke. The dam, a modest dual 1m winner, including at 2 yrs, is a half-sister to 6 winners including the useful On Call, a winner of 7 races at up to 2m and herself dam of the US Grade 2 winner One Off. The second dam, Doctor Bid (by Spectacular Bid), is an unraced half-sister to 9 winners including the smart Group 3 Prix Thomas Bryon winner Glory Forever and the dam of the Group winners Verglas and Cassandra Go. *"He was very small when we bought him, but he's grown quite a bit. Very laid-back, he's a nice colt and a typical 2-y-o that looks a five/six furlong type".*

1280. VITAL EDITION (IRE) ★★★

b.c. Pivotal – Triple Edition (Lear Fan). May 4. Third foal. 14,000Y. Tattersalls October Book 2. Guy Stephenson. Half-brother to the fair dual 7f and UAE 9f winner Ana Emarati (by Forestry). The dam, placed at 2 yrs in France, is a sister to the winner and listed-placed Starfan and a half-sister to the Group 1 Prix de la Foret winner Etoile Montante. The second dam, Willstar (by Nureyev), a minor French 3-y-o winner, is a sister to the listed winner Viviana (herself dam of the Grade 1 winners Sightseek and Tates Creek) and a half-sister to US Grade 2 winner Revasser. *"A bit small when he came in, he's grown tremendously in the last couple of months but he needed to. He was a May foal as well, so he's one for the middle of the summer onwards. A nice colt and very good-looking, he's probably a seven furlong type 2-y-o".*

1281. DIL LANEY (IRE) ★★★

b.c. Mujadil – Maddie's Pearl (Clodovil). April 28. Second foal. €11,000Y. Tattersalls Ireland. Helmsley Bloodstock. Half-brother to the moderate 2011 6f placed 2-y-o Masivo Man (by Titus Livius). The dam is an unplaced half-sister to 6 winners including the French 11f and 12f listed winner Paraiyor and the dual Group 3 placed Excelerate. The second dam, Perle d'Irlande (by Top Ville), a listed-placed winner of 3 races in France, is a half-sister to 4 winners including the Prix Marcel Boussac winner Sierra Madre (herself dam of the Sussex Stakes winner Aljabr). *"He's showing quite a bit and he might be one of the first ones to come out, starting off over five furlongs. He's not over-big, but well put-together".*

1282. MOSS QUITO (IRE) ★★★

b.g. Moss Vale – Gold Majesty (Josr Algarhoud). March 7. Fourth foal. £7,000Y. Doncaster Premier. Guy Stephenson. Half-brother to the fair Irish 7f (at 2 yrs) and 1m winner Miss Minnies (by Fraam). The dam is an unplaced half-sister to the smart Group 3 Fred Darling Stakes and Group 3 Oak Tree Stakes winner and multiple Group 1 second (including the Cheveley Park Stakes) Majestic Desert. The second dam, Calcutta Queen (by Night Shift), was placed twice over 1m. *"He looks a 2-y-o type and he's showing us quite a bit, so it shouldn't be long before he's out. He's a good sized gelding and well put-together".*

JAMIE OSBORNE

1283. CASH RICH ★★★

ch.c. Assertive – Dahshah (Mujtahid). March 7. Seventh foal. £30,000Y. Doncaster Premier. Jamie Osborne. Half-brother to the fair 7f (at 2 yrs) and 1m winner of 5 races and listed-placed Eastern Gift (by Cadeaux Genereux), to the modest dual 5f winner (including at 2 yrs) Mini Bon Bon (by Kyllachy) and a winner in Spain by Cherokee Run. The dam, a fair 3-y-o 1m winner, is a half-sister to 6 winners including the Group 3 Horris Hill Stakes winner La-Faah. The second dam, Rawaabe (by Nureyev), a quite useful dual 5f winner, is a half-sister to 4 winners including the Gimcrack Stakes winner Doulab and the dam of the champion US 2-y-o filly Chilukki. *"Quite sharp, he'll be out in May and he goes OK. He's got a bit of speed and he's a real 2-y-o type. He's a smaller version of his father in that he's very strong and he's a five/six furlong 2-y-o".*

1284. DARKEST NIGHT (IRE) ★★★

b.g. *Dark Angel – Vadarousse (Numerous)*. April 28. First foal. €40,000Y. Goffs Orby. Jamie Osborne. The dam, a fair Irish 9f placed maiden, is a half-sister to the French listed winner Valima. The second dam, Vadlawysa (by Always Fair), a minor winner at 3 yrs in France, is a sister to the Group 2 Prix Hocquart winner Vadlawys and a half-sister to 9 winners including Val Royal (Grade 1 Breeders Cup Mile). (Miss E Asprey & Mr C Wright). *"He's been gelded, he won't be as early I expected he'd be because he's grown quite a lot and he does have a bit of stamina on the dam's side. A horse with a good action, he's a 2-y-o for the mid-summer onwards, but a nice one".*

1285. DEEPEST BLUE ★★★

b.c. *Sakhee's Secret – Midnight Sky (Desert Prince)*. February 21. Second foal. 40,000Y. Tattersalls October Book 2. Amanda Skiffington. The dam, a moderate 5f winner, is a half-sister to 5 winners including the Group 3 5f Ballyogan Stakes winner Miss Anabaa, the smart 5f and 6f winner of 6 races Out After Dark and the useful 5f and 6f winner of 7 races (here and in Hong Kong) Move It. The second dam, Midnight Shift (by Night Shift), a fair dual 6f winner at 3 yrs, is a half-sister to 8 winners including the Group 1 6f July Cup winner Owington. (Mr & Mrs I H Bendelow). *"I ran him in the Brocklesby and he finished last, but he'd gone very well at home beforehand, he just fluffed his lines and the signs where all there in the paddock beforehand. I've given him a little bit of time since and I think he'll come back and prove that run to be all wrong. He's sharp, he's all 2-y-o, he's from a fast family and he's got plenty of speed".*

1286. DEVOUT (IRE) ★★★

b.f. *Holy Roman Emperor – Raphimix (Linamix)*. March 3. Third foal. £12,000Y. Doncaster Premier. Not sold/Jamie Osborne private sale. Half-sister to the quite useful 12f winner Reflect (by Hurricane Run). The dam is an unraced half-sister to 2 minor winners in France. The second dam, Restifia (by Night Shift), a listed winner in France, is a half-sister to 3 winners. (Hearn, Margolis, Pennick). *"She's quite forward, she'll run in May and she goes well. Being out of a Linamix mare she's not just going to be about* speed, I like her and I think she'll be quite a nice filly. We've done a few bits of work with her and she goes nicely".* TRAINERS' BARGAIN BUY

1287. HARDY BLUE (IRE) ★★

b.f. *Red Clubs – Alexander Wonder (Redback)*. March 11. First foal. €35,000Y. Tattersalls Ireland. David Redvers. The dam is an unraced half-sister to 5 winners including the dual Group 3 sprint winner Triple Aspect and the French 2-y-o listed winner Wonderfilly. The second dam, Wicken Wonder (by Distant Relative), a fair 2-y-o 6f winner, is a half-sister to 7 winners including the dams of 4 stakes winners. (Patrick Gage & Tony Taylor). *"She'll be out in May, she's not very big but she goes OK and might be one for the nurseries later on".*

1288. HARDY RED (IRE) ★★★

b.c. *Mujadil – Salonga (Shinko Forest)*. April 5. First foal. 27,000Y. Tattersalls October Book 2. David Redvers. The dam, a modest 9f winner, is a half-sister to 4 winners. The second dam, Alongside (by Slip Anchor), an Irish 4-y-o 9f winner, is a half-sister to 4 winners including the Group 2 Prix Eugene Adam and US Grade 2 winner Kirkwall. (Tony Taylor & Patrick Gage). *"He goes very well, has slightly sore shins at the moment but he could be running in May. We've had good luck with the sire and although this horse might lack a bit of pedigree on his dam's side, he has got speed. Very strong, very forward, he knows how to gallop and he ought to win a maiden at least".*

1289. LORAINE ★★★

b.f. *Sir Percy – Emirates First (In The Wings)*. February 13. Third foal. 27,000Y. Tattersalls October Book 2. Simon Christian. Half-sister to the modest 2011 dual 6f placed Arabian Flight (by Exceed And Excel) and to the minor Italian 3-y-o winner Tiger Of Emirates (by Tiger Hill). The dam, a modest 9f winner, is a half-sister to 4 winners including the smart 1m (at 2 yrs) and German dual Group 1 12f winner Mamool and the dam of the Australian Group 2 winner Avienus. The second dam, Genovefa (by Woodman), a useful winner of the Group 3 10.5f Prix de Royaumont, is closely related to the Group 3 10f Prix de la Nonette winner Grafin and a half-sister to the US Grade 3 8.5f winner Miss Turkana. (Mrs F Walwyn, Mr & Mrs

A Pakenham, A Taylor). *"A real 2-y-o type, she was bred by Sir Percy's owners and when they came to see her they commented that she looks more like her sire than any other horse they've seen. I like her, she's a bit feisty but in a nice way. She's a good mover and I'm hoping she'll be a May 2-y-o even though the Sir Percy's haven't been that early as yet".*

1290. ORATORIO'S JOY (IRE) ★★
b.f. Oratorio – Seeking The Fun (Alhaarth). March 21. First foal. £22,000Y. Doncaster Premier. Simon Christian. The dam, a minor winner at 3 yrs in France, is a half-sister to the Group 3 Prix Exbury winner Polynechnicien. The second dam, Golden Party (by Seeking The Gold), is a placed half-sister to 10 winners including the US Grade 1 winners Dare And Go and Go Deputy. (Mr D Christian). *"She's grown and gone very backward, so she'll be an autumn filly over seven furlongs plus".*

1291. SYCOPHANTIC (IRE) ★★
b.c. Cape Cross – Amarice (Suave Dancer). April 18. Seventh living foal. €70,000 foal. Goffs. Redpender Stud. Half-brother to the US triple Grade 2 12f and 14f winner The Acorn (by Inchinor) and a winner in Greece by Key Of Luck. The dam won over 7f at 2 yrs and is a half-sister to 5 winners including the Italian Group 2 winner Dancer Mitral. The second dam, Almitra (by Targowice), won once at 3 yrs and is a half-sister to 4 winners. (Lady Blyth). *"He's not bred to be particularly early but he will be a 2-y-o at some point. He's a lovely mover and although I haven't taken his hand brake off yet he's a nice horse and more of a seven furlong plus type from mid-season onwards".*

1292. UNNAMED ★★
br.f. Byron – Bella Beguine (Komaite). April 19. Half-sister to the fairly useful 5f and 6f winner of 8 races Beat The Bell (by Beat All) and to the modest 6f and 7f winner of 5 races Boy The Bell (by Choisir). The dam, a modest dual 6f winner, is a half-sister to several winners including the listed winning sprinter Lago di Varano. The second dam, On The Record (by Record Token), a fair dual sprint winner at 2 and 4 yrs, is a half-sister to 3 winners. (Michael Turner). *"The mare has bred some quite fast horses and this filly*

is fairly strong, she's been a bit wayward but she's fine and she goes OK".

1293. UNNAMED ★★★ CONTINENTAL DIVIDE
ch.c. Kheleyf – Leenane (Grand Lodge). April 3. Fourth foal. €26,000Y. Goffs Orby. Jamie Osborne. The dam is an unraced half-sister to 5 winners including the very smart dual listed 5f winner and Group 2 second Watching. The second dam, Sweeping (by Indian King), a useful 2-y-o 6f winner, was listed-placed twice and is a half-sister to 10 winners. *"A very nice horse and a lovely mover. He's not that early because he's grown a fair bit but he's beautifully balanced and although I haven't had his hand brake off yet he does everything really nicely. At the moment he belongs to me – but a new owner would be welcome".*

1294. UNNAMED ★★★
b.f. Bertolini – Lighted Way (Kris). March 7. Third foal. £9,000Y. Doncaster Premier. Not sold. Half-sister to 2 minor winners abroad by Compton Place. The dam was placed twice at 2 yrs and is a half-sister to 2 minor winners. The second dam, Natchez Trace (by Commanche Run), is a placed half-sister to 10 winners including the Group 3 winner and good broodmare Lighted Glory. (Brightwalton Stud & Partners). *"She goes nicely and she could be racing in May. She didn't make a lot of money through the ring but she's changed and done very well. She's OK".*

1295. UNNAMED ★★
b.f. Dalakhani – Shesasmartlady (Dolphin Street). February 2. Seventh foal. 75,000Y. Tattersalls October Book 1. Not sold. Half-sister to the smart Group 2 6f Criterium de Maisons-Laffitte winner and Group 1 Middle Park Stakes third Captain Marvelous (by Invincible Spirit), to the fairly useful 10f and 12f winner Hero Worship (by Kalanisi), the fair Irish 6f winner Smartest (by Exceed And Excel) and the minor US 4-y-o winner French Fern (by Royal Applause). The dam is an unplaced half-sister to 8 winners including the listed winners Dashing Colours and Dash Of Red. The second dam, Near The End (by Shirley Heights), is an unraced half-sister to 2 minor winners. (Hearn, Margolis, Pennick). *"She has a lovely pedigree*

and she's a good type of filly, but we'll just have to be patient with her. She's a good mover and she has a bit of quality but she just needs a bit of time to develop".

1296. UNNAMED ★★★

b.c. *Amadeus Wolf – Yasmin Satine (Key Of Luck).* April 21. Second foal. 42,000Y. Tattersalls December. Dr Brendan McDonald. Half-brother to the 2011 French 7f placed 2-y-o Dancinginmydreams (by Aussie Rules). The dam is an unraced half-sister to 3 winners including the smart Group 2 5f King's Stand Stakes winner Mitcham. The second dam, Arab Scimetar (by Sure Blade), is an unraced half-sister to 2 minor winners and to the placed dam of the dual Group 3 winner Mr Martini. (Dr B McDonald). *"A nice horse and he could be a May runner. A fluent mover, he's strong and although he hasn't got five furlong pace he'll probably be quite nice".*

JOHN OXX

1297. ABU NEYEF (IRE) ★★★

ch.c. *Nayef – Queen's Logic (Grand Lodge).* March 27. Half-brother to the Group 2 6f Lowther Stakes, Group 3 6f Princess Margaret Stakes (both at 2 yrs) and Group 2 6f Diadem Stakes winner Lady Of The Desert (by Rahy), to the quite useful 2-y-o 1m and subsequent UAE 6f winner Go On Be A Tiger (by Machiavellian), the fair UAE 1m winner Enjoy Today (by Kingmambo) and the fair 9f winner Dunes Queen (by Elusive Quality). The dam, a champion 2-y-o filly and winner of the Group 1 6f Cheveley Park Stakes and the Group 2 6f Lowther Stakes, is a half-sister to the top-class multiple Group 1 winner Dylan Thomas. The second dam, Lagrion (by Diesis), was placed 5 times in Ireland and stayed 12f and is a full or half-sister to 3 winners. (Jaber Abdullah). *"A good-looking horse and quite sharp-looking. The pedigree is a bit of mixture, as he's by Nayef who wouldn't normally get precocious horses and Queen's Logic who was one. He looks like his mother and he's behaving that way, so it'll be interesting to see how he takes his early work but he looks like a horse that could run in the summer. I'm hopeful that he'll make a nice 2-y-o".*

1298. AKIRA (IRE) ★★★

b.f. *Acclamation – Saik (Riverman).* April 25. Ninth foal. €24,000Y. Goffs Orby. Not sold. Half-sister to the quite useful 3-y-o 7f winner Wistman (by Woodman), to the fair 7f (including at 2 yrs) to 10f winner Hallingdal (by Halling), the fair 9f and hurdles winner Halling Gal (both by Halling), the modest dual 1m winner Ryedale Dancer (by Refuse To Bend) and two winners in Japan by Jade Robbery. The dam is an unraced half-sister to 5 winners including the smart Group 3 10f Brigadier Gerard Stakes and Group 3 10f Scottish Classic winner Husyan and the dam of the triple Group 2 winner Mubtaker. The second dam, Close Comfort (by Far North), is an unraced half-sister to the champion French 2-y-o filly Ancient Regime (herself dam of 3 good winners in Crack Regiment, Rami and La Grande Epoque) and to the Group 2 Prix Maurice de Gheest winner Cricket Ball. (Mr M Morris). *"A nice filly, but she's well-grown and will take a bit of time. She's not very precocious but she's a good-looking filly with a very good temperament. We like her".*

1299. ALAZAYA (IRE) ★★★★

b.f. *Shirocco – Alasha (Barathea).* April 8. Sixth foal. Half-sister to the 6f (at 2 yrs), Group 3 7f Sceptre Stakes and dual listed winner Alanza (by Dubai Destination) and to the quite useful dual 12f winner Alajan (by Alhaarth). The dam, a useful 7f (at 2 yrs) and listed 1m winner, is a half-sister to 7 winners including the Irish listed winner Alaiyma. The second dam, Alasana (by Darshaan), won twice in France over 1m and 9f and is a half-sister to the Prix Maurice de Nieuil winner Altayan and the Grand Prix de Vichy winner Altashar. (HH Aga Khan). *"She's a good-looker and a very nice filly that's had a good winter. She's quite forward but you don't expect to do too much at two with a Shirocco. Nevertheless I like her a lot – she's a good sort".*

1300. BRECCBENNACH ★★★★

b.c. *Oasis Dream – Next (In The Wings).* February 19. Second foal. 190,000Y. Tattersalls October Book 1. BBA (Ire). The dam, a French 10f winner, is a half-sister to the smart listed 1m and listed 10f winner and dual Group 3 third Perfect Stride and to the French 2-y-o listed 6f winner Law Lord. The second dam, First (by Highest Honor), a listed 1m winner at 3 yrs in

France, is a half-sister to 12 winners including the smart Group 3 winners Bluebook and Myself. (Mr T Barr). *"A nice, sharp-looking colt, he's had a good winter and he goes well, so time will tell but he certainly looks like making a 2-y-o and he'll go beyond a mile next year".*

1301. DALUKA (IRE) ★★★

b.f. Dylan Thomas – Daliya (Unfuwain). April 3. Fourth foal. Half-sister to the fairly useful 12f and 2m winner Dimona (by Alhaarth) and to the fair Irish 2-y-o 1m winner Dalkan (by Sinndar). The dam, a fair 6f (at 2 yrs) and 9f placed maiden, is a half-sister to the high-class Group 1 12f Coronation Cup winner and Derby second Daliapour, to the useful 12f and 14f winner Dalaram and the smart 2m Queens Vase winner Dalampour. The second dam, Dalara (by Doyoun), a smart winner of the Group 2 12.5f Prix de Royallieu, was third in the Group 1 Prix Royal-Oak and is a half-sister to the French Derby winner and high-class sire Darshaan and to the Prix Vermeille winner Darara. (H H Aga Khan). *"She's OK, quite a nice filly and a very good mover. The sire's stock haven't been precocious yet so it's difficult to know, but she's well-made and not backward-looking so she might be one for the middle of the season onwards".*

1302. FLASHY APPROACH ★★★★

ch.c. New Approach – Flashy Wings (Zafonic). February 20. Second foal. The dam, a winner of 4 races including the Group 2 6f Lowther Stakes and Group 2 5f Queen Mary Stakes, was Group 1 placed three times and is a half-sister to 5 winners. The second dam, Lovealoch (by by Lomond), a very useful 7f (at 2 yrs) and 9f winner here and placed in the Group 2 Falmouth Stakes and the Group 2 Premio Lydia Tesio, subsequently won once in the USA and is a half-sister to 7 winners. (Jaber Abdullah). *"A nice horse, he's very agile and has a very fluent action. He looks a little bit backward now, but he'll certainly be out in the second half of the year. A nice colt".*

1303. HARASIYA (IRE) ★★★★

br.f. Pivotal – Hazariya (Xaar). February 20. Third foal. Half-sister to the useful dual 10f winner and Group 3 second Haziyna (by Halling) and to the useful listed 12f winner Hazarafa (by Daylami). The dam, winner of the Group 3 7f Athasi Stakes and a listed event over 7f, is a half-sister to the Group 3 Blue Wind Stakes winner Hazarista and a half-sister to numerous minor winners. The second dam, Hazaradjat (by Darshaan), won twice at 2 and 3 yrs and is a half-sister to 10 winners including the Group 1 Flying Childers Stakes winner Hittite Glory. (H H Aga Khan). *"A very well-made, strong and mature filly. A good sort, it looks like she'll make a 2-y-o and although Pivotal's aren't generally early she should show ability at two. She's a good looker and you'd be very happy with her".*

1304. JUMAIRA TOWER (IRE) ★★

b.c. Dubawi – Jumaireyah (Fairy King). May 3. Brother to the smart listed 10f winner Afsare and half-brother to the useful 8.6f to 10.4f winner and listed placed Reem Three (by Mark Of Esteem), the quite useful 12f winner Qahriman (by Tiger Hill) and the quite useful 12f to 14f and hurdles winner of 13 races Trip The Light (by Fantastic Light). The dam, a fairly useful 8.3f (at 2 yrs) and 10.3f winner, is a half-sister to numerous winners including the useful 10f to 14f winner Lost Soldier Three and the useful 10.5f and 12f winner Altaweelah. The second dam, Donya (by Mill Reef), was placed once over 10f from two outings and is a half-sister to the Rothmans International winner French Glory. (Sheikh Mohammed Obaid Al Maktoum). *"He's a nice sort of horse but he's small, a bit backward and he was a May foal. An autumn horse for sure".*

1305. KARLIDI (USA) ★★

ch.c. Smart Strike – Kastoria (Selkirk). March 18. Third foal. Half-brother to the fair 12f winner Kastania (by Gone West). The dam, winner of the Group 1 14f Irish St Leger, is a half-sister to several winners. The second dam, Kassana (by Shernazar), winner of the Group 3 12.5f Prix Minerve, is a half-sister to the Group 2 15f Prix Kergorlay winner Kassani. (H H Aga Khan). *"He's a good, strong colt and a good mover but he needs a bit of time and I see him as an autumn horse. We're very fond of the mare, she had a lot of ability and hopefully she'll breed a good one. There's nothing much wrong with him but he isn't precocious".*

1306. MAJESTIC JASMINE (IRE) ★★

ch.f. *New Approach – Majestic Roi (Street Cry)*. March 4. First foal. The dam won the Group 1 1m Sun Chariot Stakes and the Group 3 7f Fred Darling Stakes and is a half-sister to the very useful 7f (at 2 yrs) and 1m winner and Grade 2 Prix Guillaume d'Ornano third Black Spirit, the US Grade 3 placed Heza Gone West and the useful 2-y-o 7f winner and listed placed Hiddnah. The second dam, L'Extra Honor (by Hero's Honor), won a listed race in France over 10f and is a half-sister to 11 winners including the Group 2 Gallinule Stakes winner Montelimar. (Jaber Abdullah). *"She had a little setback after breaking but she's back in harness now and cantering. She just needs a little bit of time because she needs to furnish a bit. A nice filly but we don't know too much about her yet".*

1307. NOOR AL WATAN ★★★★★

b.c. *Raven's Pass – Shy Lady (Kaldoun)*. May 8. Ninth foal. Half-brother to the high-class Group 1 1m St James's Palace Stakes and Group 2 6f Mill Reef Stakes winner Zafeen (by Zafonic), to the very useful listed 7f winner Atlantic Sport (by Machiavellian), the useful 2-y-o Group 3 7f Prix du Calvados winner Ya Hajar (by Lycius), the useful 2-y-o 1m winner and listed-placed Happy Today (by Gone West), the fairly useful 7f and 1m winner Youm Mutamiez (by Seeking The Gold) and the fair dual 7f winner Fantastic Dubai (by Fantastic Light). The dam, winner of a listed event over 6f in Germany, was fourth in the Group 2 6f Moet and Chandon Rennen and is a half-sister to 4 winners. The second dam, the minor French 3-y-o winner Shy Danceuse (by Groom Dancer), is a half-sister to the dual Group 3 winner Diffident. (Jaber Abdullah). *"A nice horse and a good mover, he'll probably grow a bit but he's a real good-looking colt and he goes very well. We'll have to wait until the autumn before we see him on the track, but he looks promising and he's a very nice horse".*

1308. PALACE OF WINGS (IRE) ★★★★

b.f. *Monsun – Exciting Times (Jeune Homme)*. March 25. Sixth foal. 125,000foal. Tattersalls December. Kern/Lillingston. Half-sister to the 2011 2-y-o 1m winner Jupiter Storm (by Galileo), to the US Grade 1 Beverly D Stakes, Group 2 Prix de Sandringham and dual US

Grade 2 winner Gorella (by Grape Tree Road), the US stakes and French listed winner and dual US Grade 2 second Porto Santo (by Kingsalsa), the fair 1m winner Squall (by Dubawi) and the French listed-placed winner Thanks Again (by Anabaa Blue). The dam is a placed half-sister to 7 winners. The second dam, Eloura (by Top Ville), won twice in France and is a half-sister to 4 other minor winners. (Mrs B Keller). *"A nice filly, she's not over-big but she has a good length to her and a very good, long stride. She's very athletic looking and although Monsun's are not noted for being 2-y-o's she isn't particularly backward and we'll see her in the summer. She's had a good winter and will come to hand quickly enough, even though she's not bred for it. I like her".*

1309. PAPAYA (IRE) ★★★

ch.f. *Teofilo – Janaat (Kris)*. April 8. Half-sister to the very smart Group 1 1m Gran Criterium winner and 2,000 Guineas second Lend A Hand (by Great Commotion), to the fairly useful 1m to 11f winner Emirates Champion (by Haafhd), the quite useful 2-y-o 5f winner Grand Fleet (by Green Desert), the quite useful 10f and 12f winner Soldiers Quest (by Rainbow Quest) and the quite useful 10f to 14f winner Double Deputy (by Sadler's Wells). The dam, a fair 12f winner, is a sister to the French 3-y-o listed 10.5f winner Trefoil and a half-sister to numerous winners including the smart middle-distance winners Maysoon, Richard of York, Three Tails (dam of the high-class middle-distance colt Tamure) and Third Watch. The second dam, Triple First (by High Top), won seven races including the Group 2 10f Nassau Stakes and the Group 2 10f Sun Chariot Stakes. (Sheikh Mohammed). *"A nice filly, she looks as if she'll benefit by a gradual build-up of work but she's a very fluent mover, covers a lot of ground and she's very athletic. I quite like her and she looks a forward-going filly but physically you'd say she would benefit by not rushing her".*

1310. STEPWISE (IRE) ★★★★

b.c. *Azamour – Cadence (Cadeaux Genereux)*. March 11. Brother to the very useful Irish 2-y-o 7f winner and Group 3 1,000 Guineas Trial third History Note and to the quite useful Irish 1m winner Aznavour and half-brother to the 12f winners Blues In Cee and Rhythm 'N' Blues (both by Sinndar). The dam, a quite useful Irish 9f winner, is out of the quite useful 1m winner Cambrel (by Soviet Star). (CDA Bloodstock). *"A particularly good-looking colt, he's very fluent and he's quite well-grown so he's not an early season horse, but I hope he's one for the second half of the season onwards".*

1311. TARANA (IRE) ★★★★

b.f. Cape Cross – Tarakala (Dr Fong). January 29. Half-sister to the useful Irish 7f and 1m winner Tarankali (by Selkirk). The dam, a useful listed 11.9f Galtres Stakes winner, is a half-sister to numerous winners. The second dam, Tarakana (by Shahrastani), won 9f in Ireland at 3 yrs, was placed in four listed events from 7f to 12f and is a half-sister to 6 winners. (H H Aga Khan). *"The dam was very smart and this is a nice filly and a very good-looker. She's very straightforward and a nice mover with a good temperament. She hasn't put a foot wrong all year and hopefully she'll be out from mid-season onwards".*

1312. WAAHY (IRE) ★★★

b.c. Manduro – Wonder Why (Tiger Hill). March 14. Second foal. Half-brother to the smart 2011 Irish 2-y-o 7f winner and Group 2 1m Beresford Stakes second Akeed Mofeed (by Dubawi). The dam is an unraced half-sister to 5 winners including the German listed winners Whispered Secret and Wells Present. The second dam, Wells Whisper (by Sadler's Wells), was placed over 1m and 10f and is a sister to the very useful Group 1 10.5f Prix Lupin and US Grade 2 1m winner Johann Quatz and to the smart French 10.5f to 13.5f listed winner Walter Willy and a half-sister to the top-class middle-distance colt Hernando. (Jaber Abdullah). *"He's a nice, lengthy horse and a good sort. A very fluent mover with a nice temperament, I like him".*

1313. WHAT STYLE (IRE) ★★★

ch.f. Teofilo – Out Of Time (Anabaa). April 5. Second foal. €68,000Y. Goffs Orby. Kevin Ross Bloodstock. The dam is an unraced half-sister to 3 winners including the dual Group 2 placed Drill Sergeant. The second dam, Dolydille (by Dolphin Street), won 7 races (including two listed events) from 9f to 12f and is a half-sister to 9 winners including the Irish listed 1m

winner and high-class broodmare La Meilleure. (Mr C Jones). *"She's a nice filly, a good mover, athletic and a willing sort of worker. I think she'll be out in July, she seems to want to do her work she's very straightforward".*

1314. ZAINDA (IRE) ★★★

b.f. Dr Fong – Zafayra (Nayef). March 2. First foal. The dam, a fairly useful 3-y-o 1m winner, was listed-placed over 9f and is a half-sister to 2 winners. The second dam, Zafayana (by Mark Of Esteem), is an unplaced half-sister to 4 winners. (H H Aga Khan). *"A very good mover, very fluent and a good sort of filly. She should be out over the summer and might be capable of doing a bit at two".*

1315. UNNAMED ★★

b.f. Montjeu – Fashion Statement (Rainbow Quest). April 16. Second foal. 35,000Y. Tattersalls December. Not sold. The dam, a 1m (at 2 yrs) and Group 2 Italian Oaks winner, is a half-sister to 2 winners. The second dam, Shabby Chic (by Red Ransom), winner of the listed 10f Prix de Liancourt and third in both the Grade 1 Yellow Ribbon Stakes and the Group 3 Prix Chloe, is a sister to the Oaks winner Casual Look and a half-sister to 7 winners. (Mrs C McStay). *"A nice filly and very athletic, she's a fluent mover but she'll take time".*

1316. UNNAMED ★★★★

b.c. Giant's Causeway – Hasanka (Kalanisi). February 23. The dam, a very useful 1m (at 2 yrs) and listed 12f and listed 14f winner, was second in the Group 3 12f Give Thanks Stakes and is a half-sister to 5 winners. The second dam, Hasainiya (by Top Ville), a useful listed 10f winner, is a half-sister to numerous winners. (H H Aga Khan). *"A very nice, medium-sized, good-moving, athletic horse with a good temperament. I like him and he's a horse for the second half of the year".*

1317. UNNAMED ★★★★

b.f. Rock Hard Ten – High Maintenance (Danehill). April 18. Sixth foal. $70,000Y. Keeneland September. Margaret O'Toole. Half-sister to the French 3-y-o winner and Group 3 Prix Djebel third Silver Black (by Hennessy) and to 2 minor winners in the USA by Aragorn and Lemon Drop Kid. The dam, a minor US stakes winner, was Grade 3 placed and is a half-sister to 3 winners. The second dam, Speak Softly To Me (by Ogygian), is an unraced half-sister to 8 winners including Soundings (dam of the French Group 1 winners Green Tune and Pas de Reponse). (Mr P Garvey). *"She's a lovely filly. A beautiful mover with a very good temperament and quite forward. The sire line (Rock Hard Ten, by Kris S) have done well in Europe and although the dam line isn't noted for sharp 2-y-o's this filly is nice and precocious-looking, so I think she could be out in July".*

1318. UNNAMED ★★★ ~~Karamaju~~

b.f. *Invincible Spirit – Karawana (King's Best).* February 6. Third foal. The dam, a fairly useful Irish 1m and 10f winner, is a half-sister to 2 winners. The second dam, Karaliyfa (by Kahyasi), a quite useful 9f winner, is a half-sister to 6 winners including the 2-y-o Group 3 1m May Hill Stakes winner Karasta and to the Group 2 2m 2f Doncaster Cup dead-heat winner Kasthari. (H H Aga Khan). *"A nice filly, well-made and strong. I hope she'll be out in mid-summer, particularly as Invincible Spirit's win as 2-y-o's – they come to hand early and they're quick learners. So although the dam line might take a bit of time, he might add some precocity to it".* ~~Carr. 9/12f~~

~~Won on debut Moving up a lift of ground~~

1319. UNNAMED ★★★★ ~~of ground~~

b.f. *Azamour – Kerania (Daylami).* March 2. Half-sister to the useful Irish 2-y-o 7f winner and Group 3 9f Kilboy Estates Stakes second Kirinda (by Tiger Hill) and to the fairly useful 7f (at 2 yrs) and listed 12f winner Karasiyra (by Alhaarth). The dam, unplaced in one start, is a half-sister to the useful Irish 12f winner and Group 2 placed and dual Australian Group 2 placed Kerdem. The second dam, Kermiyana (by Green Desert), won the listed 1m Brownstown Stakes at 3 yrs in Ireland. (H H Aga Khan). *"A very nice filly, very strong and well-made. It looks like she'll perform at two, she's had a good winter and I think she'll come to hand by June or July – which is early for me!"*

1320. UNNAMED ★★★

b.c. *Lawman – Sharesha (Ashkalani).* May 3. Sixth foal. Half-brother to the useful Irish Group 3 8.5f winner Shareen (by Bahri), to the

useful 6f (at 2 yrs) and 7f winner and listed-placed Sharleez (by Marju) and the fairly useful 1m winner Sharestan (by Shamardal). The dam, a fairly useful Irish 10f winner, is a half-sister to 4 winners out of the 1m placed Sharemata (by Doyoun). (H H Aga Khan). *"A nice colt that was quite small when he arrived here, but he's been developing well over the past couple of months. Because of that I think he'll benefit with a bit of time. A good sort, a good-looker and a good mover".*

1321. UNNAMED ★★★★

b.f. *Zamindar – Sharleez (Marju).* February 4. First foal. The dam, a useful 6f (at 2 yrs) and 7f winner, was listed-placed twice and is a half-sister to 3 winners including the useful Irish Group 3 8.5f winner Shareen. The second dam, Sharesha (by Ashkalani), a fairly useful Irish 10f winner, is a half-sister to 4 winners. (H H Aga Khan). *"She's very nice, very strong and a precocious-looking filly. Very correct, well put-together and a good mover, she'll be one for the mid-season onwards".*

1322. UNNAMED ★★★

b.br.f. *More Than Ready – Sindirana (Kalanisi).* May 5. Second foal. Half-sister to the quite useful 2011 2-y-o 1m winner Sindjara (by Include). The dam won over 7f (at 2 yrs) and the listed 11f Lingfield Oaks Trial and is a half-sister to 2 winners. The second dam, Sinndiya (by Pharly), won over 13f and is a half-sister to Sinndar. *"She's a bit of a mixture because the sire is noted for getting 2-y-o winners but the family takes a bit of time. It'll be interesting to see how it goes, but she's quite a precocious-looking filly that looks as if she wants to go and the dam did win at two. We'll be aiming for July time with her".*

HUGO PALMER

It was very nice to meet Hugo for the first time on my visit to Newmarket in the spring. He's one of several young trainers this year who are setting out to try and turn their dreams into reality. It won't be easy for any of them, but Hugo seems a talented, personable and enthusiastic young man and he won't fail for lack of effort. Like everyone else in this game if he gets a slice of luck (maybe a stakes winner this year) and new owners are attracted, then further success might well follow. I wish him the best of luck.

1323. B BARDOT (IRE) ★★

b.f. Sixties Icon – Indiannie Moon (Fraam).
April 17. Second foal. £28,000Y. Doncaster Premier. Amanda Skiffington. The dam ran once unplaced and is a sister to the winner and listed-placed Indiannie Star and a half-sister to the German 2-y-o Group 2 6f winner Ajigolo and the listed-placed winner Silver Guest. The second dam, Ajig Dancer (by Niniski), a quite useful 7f winner of 4 races, is a half-sister to 2 winners. (Coriolan Links Partnership III). *"She hasn't come in yet, she's being broken-in by Malcolm Bastard who is delighted with her and says she moves beautifully. She was a gorgeous yearling but despite the fact that the sire has already had winners I think this filly will be a back-end 2-y-o".*

1324. BORN TO RUN ★★

b.f. Ishiguru – Maid For Running (Namaqualand).
March 28. Fifth foal. £20,000Y. Doncaster Premier. Hugo Palmer. Sister to the fair 2-y-o 5f winner Sheka and half-sister to a winner in Hong Kong by Fraam. The dam, a quite useful 2-y-o 5f winner, is a half-sister to the useful winners Polar Kingdom and Goodwood Prince. The second dam, Scarlet Lake (by Reprimand), is an unplaced half-sister to 6 winners and to the dams of the US Grade 1 winner Stroll and the Group 2 Sun Chariot Stakes winner Lady In Waiting. (Born To Run Racing). *"I thought she'd be early but she's grown a huge amount and has probably changed the most of all my 2-y-o's. She'll make a July/August 2-y-o".*

1325. CERNANOVA ★★

b.f. Strategic Prince – Ellanova (Kyllachy). March 3. Second foal. €28,000Y. Tattersalls Ireland. Amanda Skiffington. Half-sister to the fair 2011 2-y-o 7f winner Choice Of Remark (by Choisir). The dam is an unraced half-sister to 2 winners including the Group 2 Lancashire Oaks and Group 2 Prix de Royallieu winner Anna Pavlova. The second dam, Wheeler's Wonder (by Sure Blade), a moderate 12f, 2m and jumps winner, is a half-sister to 9 winners including the US Grade 3 winner Kirov Premiere (herself dam of the US Grade 1 winner and champion Japanese

filly Cesario) and the dam of the dual Group 2 winner Gothenburg. (Chisholm, Vestey, Kerr-Dineen & Gibbs). *"She's sharp and hopefully she'll be out at the Craven meeting".*

1326. CONDIZIONANTE ★★★

b.f. Excellent Art – Desert Classic (Green Desert).
March 18. Fourth foal. Half-sister to the 2011 2-y-o Grade 1 1m Breeders Cup Juvenile Turf winner Wrote (by High Chaparral) and to a winner in Germany by Hawk Wing. The dam, placed fourth over 9f and 12f, is a sister to 2 winners and a half-sister to 5 winners including the very useful 12f winner and listed-placed Al Moulatham. The second dam, High Standard (by Kris), a fairly useful 2-y-o 8.2f winner, is a half-sister to the 6 winners. (Mr N E Sangster). *"A stunning filly, she's quite big now but she moves effortlessly, finds life very easy and she's an exciting filly to have in the yard".* Wjn 6f mlo fillies Kempton

1327. EARLY ONE MORNING ★★★

b.f. Medicean – Still Small Voice (Polish Precedent). February 24. First foal. 28,000Y. Tattersalls October Book 1. The dam is an unraced sister to 3 winners including Pure Grain (Group 1 12f Irish Oaks and Group 1 12f Yorkshire Oaks) and the dam of the Japanese Group 1 winner Fine Grain and a half-sister to 6 winners. The second dam, Mill Line (by Mill Reef), a fair 14.6f winner at 3 yrs, is a half-sister to 6 winners. (Mrs M Bryce). *"She's the only filly from Book One here and it shows, because she oozes class. She isn't big, so she's a typical first foal, but she is beautiful and moves very well. One for August or September time".*

1328. RED RED WINE ★★★

b.c. Dutch Art – Atnab (Riverman). March 14. Eleventh foal. 62,000Y. Tattersalls October Book 2. Armando Duarte. Half-brother to Sequoia (by Shamardal), placed fourth over 6f on both his starts at 2 yrs in 2011, to the useful French 9.5f (at 2 yrs) to 15f winner and listed-placed Grey Mystique (by Linamix), the quite useful 2-y-o 8.3f and subsequent US winner Millestan (by Invincible Spirit), the fair 7f (at 2 yrs) and 6f winner Seeking Magic (by Haafhd) and two winners in Greece by Fasliyev and Refuse To Bend. The dam, a modest 12f winner, is a half-sister to 6 winners including the useful 2-y-o 6f and 7f winner Muhab. The second dam, Magic

Slipper (by Habitat), a useful 10f and 11.5f winner, is a half-sister to the 1,000 Guineas winner Fairy Footsteps and to the St Leger winner Light Cavalry. (Mr K. J. P Gundlach). *"A big, strong colt, he's just had a tiny setback but hopefully he'll be back on the road in mid-May and he's one of the best moving horses I've ever seen. He'll be racing in August, I haven't worked him yet but I'd say he'd be a seven furlong type to begin with".*

1329. TIPPING OVER (IRE) ★★★

b.f. Aussie Rules – Precipice (Observatory). February 27. First foal. €8,500Y. Tattersalls Ireland. Amanda Skiffington. The dam, a quite useful Irish 5f to 7f placed 2-y-o, is a half-sister to 3 winners. The second dam, On The Brink (by Mind Games), a quite useful 2-y-o listed 5f winner, is a full or half-sister to 5 winners including the very useful listed 5f winner Eastern Romance. (Anglia Bloodstock Syndicate). *"One of our earlier types, she should be racing in late May and she's shown enough to suggest she'll pick up a maiden at some point this year, then we'll search for one of the £10k bonus races".* TRAINERS' BARGAIN BUY

Won gd bf mdn Nwmkr

1330. TWO IN THE PINK (IRE) ★★★★

b.f. Clodovil – Secret Circle (Magic Ring). April 21. Ninth foal. £32,000Y. Doncaster Premier. Armando Duarte. Sister to the quite useful 2-y-o 5f and 6f winner Alben Star and half-sister to the fairly useful 5f and 7f winner of 7 races Secret Place (by Compton Place), the quite useful 7f winner of 4 races Ektimaal (by Bahamian Bounty), the fair 6f (at 2 yrs) and 7f winner So Surreal (by Avonbridge), the fair dual 1m winner Ambrosiano (by Averti) to the fair 2-y-o 6f winner Full Of Nature (by Monsieur Bond) and the fair 6.5f winner Secret Affair (by Piccolo). The dam is an unraced half-sister to 8 winners including the Group 1 1m St James's Palace Stakes winner Bijou d'Inde. The second dam, Pushkar (by Northfields), is an unraced half-sister to the Group 3 1m Brownstown Stakes winner Red Chip. (Mr K. J. P Gundlach). *"She's been working really well and we're quite excited about her. More of a six furlong type than five, I'm hoping she can win her maiden in May before we dream about something a little smarter!"*

AMANDA PERRETT

1331. CAST A VISION (USA) ★★★

b.c. E Dubai – Shoogle (A P Indy). April 12. Half-brother to the fairly useful 2-y-o 1m winner Close Alliance (by Gone West), to the quite useful French 1m winner Cross Purposes (by Distant View) and the fair 2-y-o 6f winner Moral Duty (by Silver Deputy). The dam, a quite useful 2-y-o 7f winner, is closely related to the US Grade 1 winner Sleep Easy and a half-sister to the US Grade 1 winner Aptitude and the smart 6f (at 2 yrs) to 8.5f (in the USA) winner Electrify. The second dam, Dokki (by Northern Dancer), is an unraced half-sister to the US Grade 1 winners Coastal and Slew O'Gold. (Khalid Abdulla). *"I like him. A colt with a good attitude, he's still growing quite a bit at the moment but he's done enough nice early work to suggest that he'll be running by the middle of the season, probably over seven furlongs".*

1332. CZECH IT OUT ★★★

b.c. Oratorio – Naval Affair (Last Tycoon). March 8. Seventh foal. 58,000Y. Tattersalls October Book 2. Peter & Ross Doyle. Half-brother to the 7f (at 2 yrs) and listed 1m Valiant Stakes winner and Group 3 1m Prix de Lieurey second Field Day (by Cape Cross), to the quite useful 1m and 12f winner War At Sea (by Bering) and the Japanese 3-y-o winner Meiner Corvette (by Green Desert). The dam, a useful 2-y-o 7f winner, is a half-sister to 3 listed winners and to the dam of the dual French Group 2 winner Cut Quartz. The second dam, Sailor's Mate (by Shirley Heights), won the Group 2 Meld Stakes and is a half-sister to 8 winners including the good broodmare Grecian Sea. (G. D. P Materna). *"Quite a forward sort of horse, he's mature in his knees and shows a good attitude in his work. He'll start over six furlongs and should go on from there. A nice individual, he's a strong sort and ready to go".*

1333. EBONY ROC (IRE) ★★★

b.br.c. Shirocco – Chia Laguna (Ela-Mana-Mou). March 2. Seventh foal. 38,000Y. Tattersalls October Book 2. Peter & Ross Doyle. Half-brother to the quite useful 2011 2-y-o dual 6f winner Wise Venture (by Kheleyf) and to 2 minor winners in Italy by Kris Kin and Celtic Swing. The dam, a minor 3-y-o winner in Italy, is a half-sister to 2 winners including the Italian

Group 3 and triple listed winner Miss Carolina. The second dam, Lalla's Rock (by Ballad Rock), won two listed events at 2 yrs in Italy and is a half-sister to 3 winners. (The To-Agori-Mou Partnership). *"He's more than likely going to debut later in the year, although his half-brother was quite a good 2-y-o last year. He has a nice bit of size and scope and is one for seven furlongs from the middle of the season onwards. Having said that, he's not slow".*

1334. EMPIRICIST (IRE) ★★★

b.c. Holy Roman Emperor – Charaig (Rainbow Quest). March 10. Second foal. 67,000Y. Tattersalls October Book 2. The dam ran once unplaced and is a half-sister to 2 minor winners. The second dam, Chesnut Bird (by Storm Bird), a dual listed 10f winner, is a half-sister to 4 winners including the French Group 3 winner and Group 2 placed Caesarion. (John Connolly & Odile Griffith). *"He's grown quite a bit since we bought him and he stands at sixteen hands now so he'll want a little bit of time. The Danehill/Rainbow Quest cross is a good one and the second dam was rated 106, so I think this colt is a nice middle-distance prospect for next year".*

1335. ENSURE ★★★

ch.f. Three Valleys – Tentative (Distant View). February 6. Third foal. Half-sister to the French 3-y-o 9f winner Provisional (by With Approval). The dam, a fairly useful 2-y-o triple 5f winner, was listed-placed and is a half-sister to numerous winners including the Grade 1 Eddie Read handicap winner Monzante and the useful French 2-y-o 7f winner Alpha Plus. The second dam, Danzante (by Danzig), a sprint winner in France and in the USA, is a half-sister to the Breeders Cup Classic winner Skywalker and to the French Group 3 7f winner Nidd. (Khalid Abdulla). *"She's a compact, racey filly and she should have enough speed to win over six furlongs. A February foal, there's no reason why she shouldn't be out by mid-season".*

1336. EXTRASOLAR ★★★

b.c. Exceed And Excel – Amicable Terms (Royal Applause). March 5. First foal. €90,000Y. Arqana Deauville August. Peter & Ross Doyle. The dam, a quite useful 10f and 11f winner of 4 races, is a half-sister to 6 winners including the Japanese

stakes winner Kei Woman. The second dam, Friendly Finance (by Auction Ring), is an unraced half-sister to 7 winners including Riverman. (Odile Griffith & John Connolly). *"He looked quite sharp but he's going through a growth spurt now. I would think that from June time onwards we'll be getting him going".*

1337. FIRST WARNING ★★

b.c. Rail Link – Tricked (Beat Hollow). January 28. Second foal. The dam is an unraced half-sister to the dual Champion Stakes, Juddmonte International and Eclipse Stakes winner Twice Over. The second dam, Double Crossed (by Caerleon), a useful listed 10.5f winner, is a half-sister to 6 winners including Clepsydra (herself dam of the Group 1 winners Timepiece and Passage Of Time and the Group 2 winner Father Time). (Khalid Abdulla). *"A nice individual for around September time and next year. He has a Derby entry and it's a lovely family".*

1338. FORMERLY HOT ★★★

b.c. Sakhee – Photogenic (Midyan). April 20. Half-brother to the fairly useful 7f winners Johnny Castle (by Shamardal) and Baby Houseman (by Oasis Dream) and to the quite useful 12f winner Gifted Musician (by Sadler's Wells). The dam, a fairly useful 6f and listed 7f winner at 2 yrs, is a half-sister to numerous winners including the listed winner and Group 1 placed Mona Lisa and the very useful 2-y-o 5f and 7f Italian listed winner and Group 2 1m Falmouth Stakes second Croeso Cariad. The second dam, Colorsnap (by Shirley Heights), is an unraced half-sister to 8 winners including the Irish Oaks winner Colorspin (dam of the Group 1 winners Opera House, Zee Zee Top and Kayf Tara), the Prix de l'Opera winner Bella Colora (dam of the very smart colt Stagecraft) and the Irish Champion Stakes winner Cezanne. (Normandie Stud). *"He's a nice, neat colt with a good, straight action. We've got three from the mare at the moment and this is a nice sort that won't take too long coming to hand. I like him – he's very athletic".*

1339. HERO'S STORY ★★★★

b.c. Mount Nelson – Red Roses Story (Pink). April 30. Seventh foal. 62,000Y. Tattersalls October Book 2. Amanda Perrett. Half-brother to the fair 2012 11f debut winner Red Orator (by Osario), to the quite useful 2-y-o 6f winner In Full Cry (by Grand Lodge) and a hurdles winner by Dr Fong. The dam won the Group 1 Prix Royal-Oak and the Group 3 Prix Exbury and is a half-sister to 2 winners. The second dam, Roses For The Star (by Stage Door Johnny), a listed winner and second in the Oaks, is a half-sister to 7 winners including the Irish Derby winners Ribocco and Ribero. (The Recitation Partnership). *"A lovely horse, he does want some time but I really like him. You'd think that on pedigree he'd make up into a nice middle-distance type 3-y-o, he's a lovely individual and he'd be the pick of my 2-y-o's at the moment. We won't see him out until September time over seven furlongs".*

1340. KNIGHT'S PARADE (IRE) ★★★

b.c. Dark Angel – Toy Show (Danehill). April 25. Sixth foal. 36,000Y. Tattersalls October Book 2. Peter & Ross Doyle. Half-brother to the quite useful 1m to 10f winner of 5 races from 2 to 4 yrs Wing Play (by Hawk Wing) and to the Italian flat and hurdles winner of 5 races Capo Malfatano (by Hurricane Run). The dam, a quite useful triple 10f winner (including at 2 yrs), is a half-sister to 3 winners. The second dam, March Hare (by Groom Dancer), a modest middle-distance placed maiden, is a half-sister to 7 winners including the smart 1m and 10f listed winner Inglenook. (The Recitation Partnership). *"A sharp, nice, compact, ready-to-go 2-y-o type".*

1341. OVATORY ★★★★ ♣

b.c. Acclamation – Millsini (Rossini). February 13. Second foal. 220,000Y. Tattersalls October Book 1. Peter & Ross Doyle. Brother to the unplaced 2011 2-y-o Periwinkle Way. The dam is an unplaced half-sister to 4 winners including the useful 6f winner and listed 6f placed Millybaa. The second dam, Millyant (by Primo Dominie), winner of the Group 2 5f Prix du Gros-Chene, is a half-sister to 5 winners including the Group 2 5f Flying Childers winner and very useful sire Prince Sabo and to the Irish listed winner Bold Jessie (herself dam of the Gimcrack Stakes winner Abou Zouz). (John Connolly & Odile Griffith). *"He'd be one of the most forward that we've got and he'd have enough speed to run over five furlongs before moving up to six. He's a nice individual and*

although he cost a pretty penny he'll hopefully prove well worth it. Possibly a Royal Ascot 2-y-o if all goes well".

1342. PIVOTAL SILENCE ★★

ch.f. Vita Rosa – Tara Moon (Pivotal). April 28. Fourth foal. Half-sister to the Group 3 8.5f Princess Elizabeth Stakes and Group 3 10f Select Stakes winner Lady Gloria (by Diktat). The dam is an unraced daughter of the fairly useful 2-y-o 5f winner Tarf (by Diesis), herself a half-sister to 7 winners including Nadwah (Group 2 Queen Mary Stakes). (M. H & Mrs G Tourle). *"A nice, big, scopey individual, we're not likely to see her before the second half of the season, but she's done nothing wrong and just hasn't been cantering for that long".*

1343. SAUCY MINX (IRE) ★★★★

b.f. Dylan Thomas – Market Day (Tobougg). April 9. Second foal. 42,000Y. Tattersalls October Book 2. Peter & Ross Doyle. Half-sister to the moderate 2011 2-y-o 1m seller winner Coach Montana (by Proud Citizen). The dam, a fairly useful dual 6f winner here at 2 yrs, subsequently won a stakes event in the USA and is a half-sister to 3 winners. The second dam, Makhsusah (by Darshaan), is an unraced half-sister to 6 winners. (Mr & Mrs F Cotton, Mr & Mrs P Conway). *"I like her, she's bred to want middle-distances but she's a strong filly that's done everything right so far. One for seven furlongs a bit later on in the year I should think, but nevertheless I think she's my favourite of all the fillies".*

1344. SUBLIMATE (USA) ★★

gr.f. Mizzen Mast – Complex (Unbridled's Song). January 30. Third foal. The dam is an unraced half-sister to 3 winners including the dam of the dual Group 3 winner Announce. The second dam, Choice Spirit (by Danzig), was a listed winner in France and is a half-sister to Zafonic and Zamindar. (Khalid Abdulla). *"She's a big filly and although she was a January foal she'll be given time to mature. A Salisbury seven furlong maiden in September is likely to be her first target if all goes well".*

1345. UNNAMED ★★★

b.c. Beat Hollow – Second Of May (Lion Cavern). April 20. Third foal. 7,000Y. Tattersalls

October Book 2. Not sold. Half-brother to the quite useful 2-y-o 7f winner Baariq (by Royal Applause). The dam, a modest 3-y-o 1m winner, is a half-sister to 3 winners including the Group 3 Brigadier Gerard Stakes winner Take A Bow. The second dam, Giant Nipper (by Nashwan), ran once unplaced and is a half-sister to 3 winners. (Mr A. J Chandris). *"A nice, big, strapping horse for later in the year. He's got size and scope and is probably the nicest individual out of the mare so far".*

1346. UNNAMED ★★★

b.c. Danehill Dancer – Showbiz (Sadler's Wells). May 3. Fourth foal. 85,000Y. Tattersalls October Book 2. James Delahooke. Brother to the quite useful 2011 Irish 5f and 6f placed Hongkong Dancer and to the fairly useful 2-y-o 6f winner Conniption. The dam, a quite useful Irish 2-y-o 7f winner, is a half-sister to two listed-placed winners. The second dam, Movie Legend (by Affirmed), was placed over 1m in Ireland and is a sister to the Irish 1,000 Guineas winner Trusted Partner (dam of the high-class filly Dress To Thrill), to the Italian Group 2 winner Easy To Copy (dam of the Irish triple Group 3 winner Two-Twenty-Two), the US Grade 3 winner Low Key Affair and the Irish listed winner Epicure's Garden (dam of the Irish Group 2 Blandford Stakes winner Lisieux Rose). (Guy Harwood). *"A nice, compact individual and he should make up into a 2-y-o from mid-season onwards. He's growing a lot at the moment but he has plenty of time and he's owned by Mr Harwood so he won't be rushed!"*

1347. UNNAMED ★★★

b.br.c. Arch – Valentine Band (Dixieland Band). May 22. Half-brother to the Irish 1m (at 2 yrs), Group 2 12f Hardwicke Stakes and Group 3 10f winner Await The Dawn (by Giant's Causeway), the French 1m, 10f (both at 2 yrs) and listed 9f winner Putney Bridge (by Mizzen Mast) and the fairly useful 11f to 13f winner of 4 races Spruce (by Maria's Mon). The dam, the very useful 10f winner, is a half-sister to the French 7f (at 2 yrs) and listed 1m winner Multiplex, to the very useful 10f and Irish Group 3 14f winner Memorise, the useful 7.5f winner and listed 1m placed Sparkling Water and the useful 2-y-o 7f winner Fully Invested. The second

dam, Shirley Valentine (by Shirley Heights), a useful 12f winner, was fourth in the Park Hill Stakes and the Lancashire Oaks and is a sister to the high class Irish Derby second Deploy and a half-sister to the Derby and Irish Derby winner Commander in Chief, the champion 2-y-o and miler Warning and the Grade 1 10f Flower Bowl Invitational Handicap winner Yashmak. (Khalid Abdulla). *"A late foal but a lovely horse that's very well-related. Seven furlongs or a mile later in the year should suit him, he stands about 15.2 now and he'll grow into a big horse by the end of the season. A lovely colt".*

TIM PITT

1348. KATIE GALE ★★

b.f. Shirocco – Karla June (Unfuwain). February 6. Sixth foal. 26,000Y. Tattersalls October Book 2. McKeever Bloodstock. Half-sister to the quite useful 1m and 10f winner of 4 races Uncle Fred (by Royal Applause), to the fair 2-y-o 7f winner Little Eskimo (by Johannesburg) and a winner in Greece by Danehill Dancer. The dam, a US stakes-placed winner, is a sister to the listed 15f winner of 10 races Sweetness Herself and the US listed winner Unrivalled and a half-sister to 8 winners. The second dam, No Sugar Baby (by Crystal Glitters), was placed 8 times at 2 and 3 yrs in France and is a half-sister to 11 winners including three French listed winners. (Ferrybank Properties Ltd). *"More of a 3-y-o type, but she's from a very solid, honest family and she's a big girl that's just cantering away at the minute. We won't ask her any questions at all until she's ready, but she's all there and seven furlongs this year would see her in a proper light. A lovely, straightforward filly with a very good temperament and quite correct".*

1349. LAVENDER BAY ★★★

b.f. Needwood Blade – In Good Faith (Dynaformer). April 14. Third foal. Sister to the quite useful 2011 2-y-o 7f winner Nelson's Bay. The dam, a French 3-y-o 1m winner, is a half-sister to 2 minor winners in the USA. The second dam, Healing Hands (by Zafonic), won once at 3 yrs in France and is a half-sister to 10 winners. (Invictus). *"A very nice filly and very forward, she could well start off over five furlongs in May, so she has a bit of quality to go with her precocity".*

1350. UNNAMED ★★★

ch.f. Iffraaj – Radiancy (Mujtahid). February 16. Eighth foal. 32,000Y. Tattersalls October Book 2. McKeever Bloodstock. Half-sister to the fair 7f and 1m winner and listed-placed Chicken Soup (by Dansili), to the poor 7f to 2m winner Radiant Bride (by Groom Dancer) and a winner in Italy by Emperor Jones. The dam, placed once over 7f from two starts, is a half-sister to 6 winners including the listed 10f Zetland Stakes (at 2 yrs) and listed 2m George Stubbs Stakes winner Upper Strata (herself dam of the Group 1 winner Lord Of Men and the Group 2 winner Her Ladyship). The second dam, Bright Landing (by Sun Prince), won 3 races at 3 yrs in France and is a half-sister to 6 winners. (Ferrybank Properties Ltd). *"I know her half-sister Chicken Soup very well. This filly wouldn't have the sharpest of 2-y-o pedigrees but she was a very striking individual at the sales and did look like making a 2-y-o. She hasn't told me otherwise yet and she's going nicely but we probably won't see her until May or June time, starting off at six furlongs. Mentally she's very forward but we have to let her mature physically as well".*

JON PORTMAN

1351. DOUBLE STAR ★★

b.f. Elusive City – Tease (Green Desert). April 18. Fifth foal. £16,000Y. Doncaster Premier. G154 Bloodstock. Half-sister to the fairly useful 2-y-o 7f winner and listed-placed Jazz Police (by Beat Hollow) and to the fair dual 10f winner Sit Tight (by Act One). The dam, a fair 3-y-o 7f winner, is a half-sister to the Irish listed winner Galistic. The second dam, Mockery (by Nashwan), won 2 minor races in France over 10.5f and 15f and is a half-sister to 3 other minor winners. (Mrs D.O Joly). *"She was broken-in and ridden away but the owner wanted her turned out for a bit so I can't comment on her really, other than to say she looks the part and she looks a bit stronger and more scopey than the half-sister I have here by Shamardal".*

1352. MONSIEUR RIEUSSEC ★★★

bl.c. Halling – Muscovado (Mr Greeley). March 20. First foal. 45,000Y. Tattersalls October Book 2. J Portman. The dam ran twice unplaced and is a half-sister to 4 minor winners here and abroad. The second dam, Only Royale (by Caerleon), won 9 races including the Group 1 Yorkshire Oaks (twice) and the Group 2 Jockey Club Stakes and is a half-sister to 5 winners. (Mr J.T Habershon-Butcher). *"He's a nice, big, strong horse – hopefully not too big. He's been straightforward from day one and he does everything easily. We wouldn't be rushing him until June or July at the earliest because he'll benefit if we're patient with him. We like him and hope he'll be a nice ten furlong horse next year".*

1353. PASAKA BOY ★★★

ch.c. Haafhd – Shesha Bear (Tobougg). April 2. First foal. £1,000Y. Ascot. Not sold. The dam, a fair 10f to 12f winner of 5 races, is a half-sister to numerous winners including the useful 6f (at 2 yrs) to 1m (in Sweden) winner Warming Trends. The second dam, Sunny Davis (by Alydar), was a fair 2-y-o 7f winner. (RWH Partnership). *"A smashing little horse and we won a Derby with the dam last year. She won the Epsom Jump Jockey's Derby! He was a bit small and weedy-looking when he first came in but he's done really well lately. You wouldn't think he'd be a five furlong type, so we'll wait for six in May/June I should think. He's been very straightforward and he's ready to go whenever he want him to. A super little horse".*

TRAINERS' BARGAIN BUY

Won at Salisbury on debut fair 6f mdn Salisbury

1354. UNNAMED ★★

b.f. Footstepsinthesand – Ringmoor Down (Pivotal). May 8. Fourth foal. Sister to the moderate 6f placed maiden Adaeze and half-sister to the unplaced 2011 2-y-o Ladram Bay (by Oratorio) and the modest 9f winner Cuckoo Rock (by Refuse To Bend). The dam won 6 races from 2 to 5 yrs including the Group 3 5f King George Stakes and the Group 3 Flying Five and is a half-sister to 6 winners. The second dam, Floppie (by Law Society), a minor 3-y-o winner in France, is a sister to a listed-placed winner there and a half-sister to 4 winners including the French listed winner Love Shack. (Prof C. D Green). *"All the family tend to need a bit of time, both mentally and physically. She does show a lot of speed but she hasn't been with me long and she'll need a bit of time".*

1355. UNNAMED ★★

b.f. Lucky Story – May Fox (Zilzal). March 14.

£1,000Y. Ascot December. Not sold. Half-sister to the quite useful 2-y-o 6f winner Meglio Ancora (by Best Of The Bests), to the moderate 10f and hurdles winner Britannia Mills (by Nordico) and another hurdles winner by Absalom. The dam was unraced. *"We acquired her privately after the sales from her breeder, she's quite nice and we'll aim her for the six furlong races from May or June. It would be nice to find an owner for her".*

KEVIN PRENDERGAST

1356. ANTARCTIC PRINCE ★★★

gr.g. Verglas – Queenie (Indian Ridge). March 28. Seventh foal. €25,000Y. Tattersalls Ireland. Frank Berry. Brother to a winner in Greece and half-brother to two other minor winners abroad, both by Efisio. The dam, a quite useful 3-y-o 7f winner, is a half-sister to 3 winners including the listed winner Mia's Boy and the useful Irish 6f (at 2 yrs) and 7f winner and Group 3 Debutante Stakes third Sweet Deimos. The second dam, Bint Zamayem (by Rainbow Quest), a fairly useful 3-y-o 10f winner, was listed-placed over 10f and is a half-sister to the Group 3 Prix Chloe winner Rouquette. (J McGrath). *"He'll be racing by the end of May, we like him and he seems to go nicely. One for six/seven furlongs this year".*

1357. CAGED LIGHTNING ★★★

b.c. Haatef – Rainbow Melody (Rainbows For Life). April 28. Sixth living foal. €20,000Y. Goffs Orby. Frank Barry. Half-brother to the quite useful dual 7f winner (including at 2 yrs) and US Grade 3 placed Musical Rain (by Val Royal) and to the fair 1m winner Sapphire Spray (by Viking Ruler). The dam, a quite useful dual 7f winner (including at 2 yrs), is a half-sister to 6 winners including the smart 3-y-o listed 5f winner Indian Prince. The second dam, Lingering Melody (by Nordico), was placed at up to 1m in Ireland and is a half-sister to 3 winners including the Group 2 Queen Anne Stakes and the Group 2 Sea World International Stakes winner Alflora. *"He'll be a six/seven furlong horse from July onwards. He moves nicely and we like him a lot".*

1358. COTTRELL ★★★

b.c. Acclamation – Asheyana (Soviet Star). February 24. Third foal. €47,000Y. Goffs Orby.

Kevin Prendergast. Half-brother to the quite useful 2-y-o dual 7f winner Dubarshi (by Dubawi) and to the modest 1m and 10f winner Ashkalara (by Footstepsinthesand). The dam is an unraced sister to the high-class miler Ashkalani, winner of the Group 1 Prix du Moulin and the Group 1 French 2,000 Guineas. The second dam, Ashtarka (by Dalsaan), won over 1m in France and is a half-sister to 4 winners including Shafaraz (Group 1 Prix du Cadran) and Ajarann (Group 1 Premio Roma second). *"A nice horse but backward-looking and we'll have to wait with him. We might start him at six furlongs before moving him up to seven".*

1359. COQUETTE NOIRE ★★★

b.f. Holy Roman Emperor – Coquette Rouge (Croco Rouge). February 6. Third foal. 55,000Y. Tattersalls October Book 1. Not sold. Closely related to the 2-y-o winner, Group 1 1,000 Guineas second and Group 1 Coronation Stakes third Jacqueline Quest (by Rock Of Gibraltar). The dam, a quite useful Irish 12f and 17f winner, is a half-sister to 5 winners including the Group 3 Classic Trial winner Regime and the 2-y-o 5f listed winner and Group 2 Cherry Hinton second Salut d'Amour. The second dam, Juno Madonna (by Sadler's Wells), is an unraced half-sister to 5 winners including the Group 3 5f King George Stakes winner Title Roll and the Irish listed sprint winner Northern Express. (Lady O'Reilly). *"A nice filly that we'll see out in May, she goes nicely and I'd expect her to be a six furlong type. Not a big filly, but she's muscular".*

1360. DAYMOOMA ★★★★

ch.f. Pivotal – Adaala (Sahm). April 22. Fourth foal. Half-sister to the useful 2011 2-y-o 6f winner and Group 3 7f Killavullan Stakes third Aaraas (by Haafhd), to the useful Irish 2-y-o 6f winner and Group 3 7f Silver Flash Stakes third Alshahbaa (by Alhaarth) and the fairly useful Irish 7f winner and listed placed Asheerah (by Shamardal). The dam, an Irish 7f (at 2 yrs) and listed 9f winner, is a half-sister to 2 winners. The second dam, Alshoowg (by Riverman), is an unraced half-sister to 4 winners. (Hamdan Al Maktoum). *"I like her an awful lot and we'll start her over six or seven furlongs in June. I trained the dam and all three of her foals and they've all won. I think this could be the best of* them so far and I see her getting a mile later on".

1361. EMPEROR'S HERO ★★

b.c. Holy Roman Emperor – Serengeti Day (Alleged). April 30. Tenth foal. €44,000Y. Goffs Orby. Frank Barry. Half-sister to the moderate 2011 1m placed 2-y-o Daring Damsel and to three winners including two in the USA by Belong To Me and Danzig. The dam, a minor 3-y-o winner in the USA, is a half-sister to 11 winners including the dual US Grade 3 winner Weekend Surprise (dam of the top-class colts A P Indy and Summer Squall) and the high-class sprinter Wolfhound. The second dam, Lassie Dear (by Buckpasser), won 5 races including the Grade 3 Villager Stakes and is a half-sister to the high-class middle-distance colt Gay Mecene. (Mr J Foley). "He wants seven furlongs, I like him but we won't see him until later in the season".

1362. ESTINAAD (USA) ★★

b.f. Street Sense – Dawla (Alhaarth). The dam, a fairly useful 1m and 11f winner, is a half-sister to several winners including Moiken (Group 3 10f Ballysax Stakes) and the Group 2 1m Beresford Stakes second Rekaab. The second dam, Za Aamah (by Mr Prospector), is an unraced half-sister to the listed Pretty Polly Stakes winners Esloob and Siyadah. (Hamdan Al Maktoum). "She only arrived last night and I just saw her this morning. She's a nice filly, the dam was quite useful and this filly has a good way about her. A lovely big filly that looks like she'll want at least seven furlongs".

1363. FROZEN NORTH ★★★

gr.c. Verglas – Lazaretta (Dalakhani). April 7. Second foal. €22,000Y. Goffs Orby. Skymarc Farm. Half-brother to the quite useful 2011 2-y-o 6f and 7f winner Greek Canyon (by Moss Vale). The dam is an unraced half-sister to 2 winners abroad. The second dam, Siringas (by Barathea), won the Grade 2 Nassau Stakes in Canada and is a half-sister to 4 winners. (Lady O'Reilly). "A nice horse, he'll want six furlongs around June time".

1364. GOLDEN SILENCE ★★★

b.c. Shirocco – Guarantia (Selkirk). February 21. Second foal. 30,000Y. Tattersalls October

Book 2. K Prendergast. Half-brother to the fair 2011 2-y-o 6f winner Daraa (by Cape Cross). The dam, a fairly useful listed-placed 7f winner, is a half-sister to the very smart dual Group 3 12f winner Laaheb (by Cape Cross). The second dam, Maskunah (by Sadler's Wells), is an unraced half-sister to 6 winners including the high-class middle-distance horses and multiple Group 1 winners Warrsan and Luso, the Nell Gwyn Stakes winner Cloud Castle and the Group 2 Gallinule Stakes winner Needle Gun. (Mrs Prendergast). "He's bred to want a trip but he goes nicely and we like him a lot. He shows plenty and he might be out when the first seven furlong races start, possibly at Gowran Park. We're looking for an owner for him".

1365. HAWAIIAN HEAT ★★★

b.f. Galileo – Miss Hawai (Peintre Celebre). February 26. Fifth foal. 85,000foal. Tattersalls December. Not sold. Closely related to the Irish listed 9f winner and Group 1 Pretty Polly Stakes second Beach Bunny (by High Chaparral) and half-sister to the quite useful 6f winner Robinson Cruso (by Footstepsinthesand). The dam is an unraced half-sister to 4 winners including the French dual listed winner Mer de Corail. The second dam, Miss Tahiti (by Tirol), won the Group 1 Prix Marcel Boussac and is a half-sister to 3 winners. (Lady O'Reilly). "I like her an awful lot, but although we've had her cantering we've turned her out and she's one for the back-end".

1366. JACKAMO ★★

ch.c. Tamayuz – Cradle Brief (Brief Truce). March 24. Eighth foal. €50,000Y. Goffs Orby. Frank Barry. Half-brother to the useful 2-y-o listed 6f winner and Group 2 6f Mill Reef Stakes second Sir Xaar (by Xaar), to the useful Irish 1m to 9.5f winner Fuerta Ventura (by Desert Sun), the quite useful triple 6f winner Redvers (by Ishiguru) and the quite useful 13f and hurdles winner Mamlook (by Key Of Luck). The dam is an unraced half-sister to the Group 3 6f Greenlands Stakes winner Tiger Royal. The second dam, Lady Redford (by Bold Lad), ran once unplaced and is a half-sister to 5 winners. (Mrs Prendergast/David Brennan). "He's had a slight setback so we won't see him out until towards the back-end of the season".

1367. KALAWMA ★★★

b.f. Lawman – Kazinoki (Timber Country).
February 27. Second foal. €40,000Y. Goffs Orby.
K Prendergast. The dam is an unraced half-
sister to 4 winners including the 10f winner
and 12f listed placed Flow Chart. The second
dam, Kartajana (by Shernazar), won the Group
1 10.5f Prix Ganay, the Group 1 10f Grosser
Preis Bayerisches Zuchtrennen, the Group 2
10f Nassau Stakes and the Group 2 10f Sun
Chariot Stakes and is a sister to a French listed
winner and a half-sister to 3 winners including
the dual Australian Group 1 placed Karasi. (Mr
Vasicheck). *"We like her a lot, she goes very well
and she'll be racing in May"*.

1368. LADY MEDICI ★★★

ch.f. Medicean – Jesting (Muhtarrram).
February 5. Seventh foal. €22,000Y. Tattersalls
Ireland. Frank Barry. Half-sister to the useful
2-y-o 5f winner and listed-placed Raggle
Taggle (by Tagula) and to three winners abroad
by Definite Article (2) and Revoque. The dam
is an unraced half-sister to 6 winners out of
the Galtres Stakes winner Sans Blague (by The
Minstrel). (J McGrath). *"She's going very nicely,
we like her a lot and she's definitely one for six/
seven furlongs this year"*.

1369. LUMUQAABIL ★★★

gr.c. Verglas – Anne Tudor (Anabaa). February
15. Third foal. €140,000Y. Goffs Orby. Shadwell
Estate Co. Brother to the useful Irish 2-y-o 5f
winner and Group 2 Railway Stakes second
Alhaban. The dam, a quite useful 3-y-o 7f
winner, is a half-sister to 3 winners including
the fairly useful triple 7f winner (including at
2 yrs) Silk Fan. The second dam, Alikhlas (by
Lahib), a fair 3-y-o 1m winner, is a half-sister
to 4 winners including the listed winner and
Group 2 Lancashire Oaks second Sahool and to
the dam of the dual Group 2 winner Maraahel.
(Hamdan Al Maktoum). *"I like him a lot but he'll
definitely need some ease in the ground and six
furlongs plus"*.

1370. MADEIRA TIME ★★

*b.f. High Chaparral – Danse Classique (Night
Shift).* April 6. Eighth foal. €20,000Y. Tattersalls
Ireland. Frank Barry. Half-sister to the Irish
dual 7f (at 2 yrs) and dual 1m winner Defi
(by Rainbow Quest), to the Irish 12f winner

Dazzling Dancer (by Nashwan and herself dam
of the US listed winner and Grade 3 placed
Driving Snow) and the fair 7f winner Hierarch
(by Dansili). The dam, an Irish listed-placed 7f
winner, is a half-sister to 5 winners including
the high-class Irish Oaks, Yorkshire Oaks and
Prix de l'Opera winner Petrushka. The second
dam, Ballet Shoes (by Ela-Mana-Mou), a
fair 3-y-o dual 5f winner, is a half-sister to 5
winners including the Irish 2,000 Guineas and
Dubai Champion Stakes winner Spectrum
and the US Grade 2 winner Stream Of Gold.
(Comerford Brothers). *"A nice, quality filly, but
High Chaparral's take time and she'll want
seven furlongs"*.

1371. MAKTOOB ★★★★

b.c. Tamayuz – Walayef (Danzig). February 18.
Fifth foal. Half-brother to the fairly useful Irish
2-y-o 6f and 7f winner and 3-y-o listed-placed
Jamaayel (by Shamardal), the quite useful Irish
1m winner Estithmaar (by Pivotal) and the
quite useful Irish 2-y-o 7f winner Reyaada (by
Daylami). The dam, a listed 6f (at 2 yrs) and
Group 3 7f Athasi Stakes winner, is a sister to
the smart 2-y-o 6f winner Haatef and to the
Irish dual listed 6f winner Ulfah. The second
dam, Sayedat Alhadh (by Mr Prospector), a
US 7f winner, is a sister to the US Grade 2 7f
winner Kayrawan and a half-sister to the useful
winners Amaniy, Elsaamri and Mathkurh.
(Hamdan Al Maktoum). *"A very nice horse, he
hasn't been in long but we like him a lot and I
trained the dam and most of the family. He'll
make a 2-y-o alright"*.

1372. MONACO MIST ★★

b.f. Montjeu – Madeira Mist (Grand Lodge).
March 29. Fifth foal. 120,000Y. Tattersalls
October Book 1. Not sold. Sister to the Group
2 1m Royal Lodge Stakes (at 2 yrs) and Grade
1 Canadian International winner Joshua Tree
(by Montjeu) and half-sister to Stencive (by
Dansili), placed third over 1m from one start
at 2 yrs in 2011. The dam won 8 races in the
USA and Canada including the Grade 3 Dance
Smartly Handicap and is a half-sister to 7
winners including the Irish listed winner Misty
Heights. The second dam, Mountains Of Mist
(by Shirley Heights), a quite useful 10f winner,
is a half-sister to 8 winners including the Group
2 Lowther Stakes winner Enthused. (Lady

O'Reilly). *"She goes well, but you can see by her pedigree that she'll take some time. She's having a break at the moment and is one for seven furlongs at the back-end".*

1373. MOOQTAR (USA) ★★★
b.c. Invasor – Sayedat Alhadh (Mr Prospector). Half-brother to the Group 2 6f Diadem Stakes winner Haatef, to the listed 6f (at 2 yrs) and Group 3 7f Athasi Stakes winner Walayef, the Irish dual listed 6f winner Ulfah (all by Danzig) and the smart 2-y-o listed 6f winner and Group 1 7f Moyglare Stud Stakes second Shimah (by Storm Cat). The dam, a US 7f winner, is a sister to the US Grade 2 7f winner Kayrawan and a half-sister to the useful winners Amaniy, Elsaamri and Mathkurh. The second dam, Muhbubh (by Blushing Groom), a winner of the Group 3 6f Princess Margaret Stakes at 2 yrs, is a half-sister to the quite useful 6f and 10f winner Mathaayl. (Hamdan Al Maktoum). *"He's only just arrived from Dubai so I can't say much about him, but he looks the part and the family have been very lucky for me. He looks to me like he'll want seven furlongs this year".*

1374. MURJANAH ★★★
ch.f. Tamayuz – Millay (Polish Precedent). March 14. Fifth foal. €140,000Y. Goffs Orby. Shadwell Estate Co. Half-sister to the fairly useful 2011 2-y-o 6f winner and Group 1 Fillies' Mile fourth Salford Art (by Sir Percy), to the moderate 2m winner M'Lady Rousseur (by Selkirk) and a winner in Switzerland by Red Ransom. The dam, a minor winner at 3 yrs in France, is a half-sister to 6 winners including the listed winner Millstreet. The second dam, Mill Path (by Mill Reef), ran once unplaced and is a half-sister to 4 winners including the Irish Oaks winner Give Thanks. (Hamdan Al Maktoum). *"She seems to be precocious and dry ground over five/six furlongs would be her thing. Not too big, she's very sharp and an early type".*

1375. NURPUR ★★★
b.f. Dark Angel – The Good Life (Rainbow Quest). May 4. Eighth foal. €22,000Y. Goffs Orby. Skymarc Farm. Half-sister to the French listed 1m winner Double Vie (by Tagula), to two minor winners abroad by Whipper and Indian Lodge and a winner over hurdles King's Theatre. The dam won once at 3 yrs in France

and is a half-sister to 3 minor winners. The second dam, Once In My Life (by Lomond), won the Group 3 Prix de Sandringham and is a half-sister to 8 winners including No Pass No Sale (French 2,000 Guineas). (Lady O'Reilly). *"A nice filly, we like her a lot and she goes well. A big, strong filly for six or seven furlongs".*

1376. REBEL FORCE ★★★
b.f. Dalakhani – Rebelline (Robellino). April 1. Sixth foal. Half-sister to the smart Group 3 Irish 2,000 Guineas Trial and listed 1m winner and Group 1 10.5f Tattersalls Rogers Cup second Recharge (by Cape Cross) and to the fair Irish 1m winner Regalline (by Green Desert). The dam won 6 races from 7f to 10.5f including the Group 1 10.5f Tattersalls Gold Cup and the Group 2 10f Pretty Polly Stakes and is a half-sister to 4 winners including the Group 2 Blandford Stakes winner Quws. The second dam, Fleeting Rainbow (by Rainbow Quest), a modest 10f placed 3-y-o, is a half-sister to 3 winners. (Lady O'Reilly). *"She goes nicely and she'll come into her own over seven furlongs and a mile. We like her and she goes well".*

1377. ROSSERAIE ★★★
b.f. Lawman – Red Feather (Marju). February 4. Half-sister to the very useful listed 6f and listed 7f winner Rose Bonheur (by Danehill Dancer). The dam, a Group 3 1m winner in Ireland, is a half-sister to the smart dual 10f winner and dual Group 3 12f placed Frankies Dream. The second dam, Galyph (by Lyphard), a modest Irish 10f winner at 4 yrs, is a half-sister to 2 minor winners. (Lady O'Reilly). *"We'll see her racing in May, probably over six furlongs. She's a nice filly and I like her a lot".*

1378. SAKHIB ★★
b.c. Haatef – Jeed (Mujahid). March 6. Half-brother to the very useful 2-y-o listed 6f winner and Group 3 6f Princess Margaret Stakes second Nidhaal (by Observatory), to the fairly useful 12f winner of 11 races on the Flat and dual hurdles winner Maslak (by In The Wings) and the fair 9f winner Riqaab (by Peintre Celebre). The dam, a quite useful 2-y-o 6f winner, is a half-sister to 2 winners. The second dam, Secretary Bird (by Kris), is an unraced half-sister to the classic winners Assert (French and Irish Derby), Bikala (French Derby) and Eurobird

(Irish St Leger). (Hamdan Al Maktoum). *"A nice horse, he's just a bit backward at the moment and we'll take our time with him".*

1379. SPINACRE ★★★
gr.f. Verglas – Spinamix (Spinning World). March 22. Half-sister to the French listed 10f winner and subsequent Hong Kong Group 1 Hong Kong Derby second Some World (by Hawk Wing), to the smart dual listed 5f winner Spin Cycle (by Exceed And Excel), the useful Group 3 7f winner of 3 races San Sicharia (by Daggers Drawn) and the fairly useful 2-y-o 6f winner and subsequent US Grade 3 placed Codeword (by Dansili). The dam was placed at 2 yrs in France and is a half-sister to 2 winners. The second dam, Vadsagreya (by Linamix), a French 7f (at 2 yrs) and 1m winner, was listed-placed and is a half-sister to 12 winners including the dams of the French 1,000 Guineas winner Vahorimix and the Breeders' Cup Mile winner Val Royal. (Lisa Kelly). *"She would have run at the opening meeting at the Curragh but she got a touch of sore shins. She's back now and we like her a lot. Six furlongs will be great for her".*

1380. STARBRIGHT ★★★★
b.f. Duke Of Marmalade – Starry Messenger (Galileo). April 15. Second foal. €48,000Y. Goffs Orby. BBA (Ire). Closely related to the fair 2-y-o 1m winner The Giving Tree (by Rock Of Gibraltar). The dam, a fair 12f winner, is a half-sister to 2 winners including the US Grade 1 Gamely Handicap and multiple Grade 2 1m winner Tuscan Evening. The second dam, The Faraway Tree (by Suave Dancer), a very useful 6f (at 2 yrs) and 14f winner, was second in the Group 2 Park Hill Stakes and is a half-sister to 12 winners including the high-class 9.3f Prix d'Ispahan winner Sasuru, the high-class Challenge Stakes and Jersey Stakes winner Sally Rous and the dam of the French 1,000 Guineas winner Rose Gypsy. (Lady O'Reilly). *"A nice filly, her pedigree suggests she'll want six furlongs plus and she's more of a 3-y-o type perhaps but I'd be surprised if she didn't win at two and I'd watch out for her. She goes well".*

1381. TAFKEER ★★★★
b.c. Marju – Lidanski (Soviet Star). April 10. Third foal. €140,000Y. Goffs Orby. Shadwell Estate Co. Half-brother to the Group 2 5f Prix du Gros-Chene winner Wizz Kid (by Whipper). The dam, a fairly useful Irish 7f winner, was listed-placed and is a half-sister to 5 winners including the listed winner Yaa Wayl and the Irish 2-y-o 5f and subsequent Hong Kong listed winner Prince Monalulu. The second dam, Lidanna (by Nicholas), a dual Group 3 winner in Ireland over 5f and 6f, is a half-sister to 5 winners. (Hamdan Al Maktoum). *"Quite a nice horse, he goes well and seven furlongs will suit him. He should be worth following".*

1382. UNTIL MIDNIGHT ★★★
b.g. Moss Vale – Emma's Star (Darshaan). February 1. Eighth foal. €50,000Y. Goffs Orby. Frank Barry. Closely related to the Group 3 6f Chipchase Stakes winner and Group 1 placed Genki (by Shinko Forest) and half-brother to the useful 2-y-o 6f winner and listed 7f second Za Za Zoom, the fair 6f winner Hazelrigg (by Namid) and the modest 7f and 1m winner of 4 races The Happy Hammer (by Acclamation). The dam, a winner over 8.5f in Italy at 3 yrs, is a half-sister to 4 other winners in Italy. The second dam, Notte Chiara (by Artaius), won the listed Premio Minerva and is a half-sister to 8 winners. (Mrs Prendergast & Lady O'Reilly). *"He grew a lot and became quite heavy so we gelded him to keep the weight off him. He's a nice horse and he'll definitely be winning as a 2-y-o over six or seven furlongs".*

1383. UNNAMED ★★★
b.f. Holy Roman Emperor – Seamstress (Barathea). Seventh foal. €20,000Y. Goffs Orby. Frank Barry. Half-sister to the very useful 2-y-o listed 5f Windsor Castle Stakes and 5.2f Weatherbys Super Sprint winner Elhamri (by Noverre). The dam, a fair 2-y-o 7f winner, subsequently won over 1m in the USA and is a sister to 2 winners including the useful 2-y-o Group 3 7f C L Weld Park Stakes winner Rag Top and a half-sister to 5 winners including the fairly useful 7.6f and subsequent US 1m winner Red Top and the fairly useful 2-y-o dual 5f winner Lady Sarka. The second dam, Petite Epaulette (by Night Shift), a fair 5f winner at 2 yrs, is a full or half-sister to 3 winners. (Norman Ormiston). *"She looks a winner and she'll be racing by the end of April or early May. A tidy filly, five or six furlongs wouldn't be a problem to her".*

SIR MARK PRESCOTT

During our conversation Sir Mark pointed out that, in general, no matter how many 2-y-o's he has in his yard around 50% of them win as juveniles. He was equally quick to point out that only a few of his trainer colleagues could boast a similar record. He has thirty 2-y-o's in training this year, so I'm guessing that he was also trying to point out that my job is to choose the fifteen 2-y-o's that will win as opposed to those that won't – so here goes. Except that I've cheated a bit to give myself a better chance and chosen twenty instead of fifteen!

1384. ALCAEUS ★★ ♠

b.c. Hernando – Alvarita (Selkirk). February 23. Fourth foal. 43,000Y. Tattersalls October Book 2. Sir Mark Prescott. Brother to the fair 12f winner Albert Bridge and half-brother to the useful 2011 Irish 2-y-o 1m winner and listed 9f placed Alla Speranza (by Sir Percy). The dam, a French listed 10.5f winner, is a half-sister to one winner. The second dam, Alborada (by Alzao), was a high-class winner of the Champion Stakes (twice), Nassau Stakes and Pretty Polly Stakes and is a sister to the German triple Group 1 winner Albanova and a half-sister to 6 winners. (Ne'er Do Wells IV). *"A nice, big colt, he'll make a back-end 2-y-o over seven furlongs plus".*

1385. ALWILDA ★★★

gr.f. Hernando – Albanova (Alzao). February 12. Fourth foal. Half-sister to the quite useful 2011 2-y-o 9f winner Albamara (by Galileo) and to the fair 10f winner Albertus Pictor (by Selkirk). The dam, a triple Group 1 12f winner in Germany, is a sister to the dual Group 1 10f Champion Stakes winner Alborada and a half-sister to numerous winners. The second dam, Alouette (by Darshaan), a 1m (at 2 yrs) and listed 12f winner, is a half-sister to the Nassau Stakes and Sun Chariot Stakes winner Last Second (dam of the Group 1 winner Aussie Rules) and the dams of the Group 1 winners Yesterday, Quarter Moon and Allegretto. (Miss K Rausing). *"She's not over-big so she'll be a 2-y-o of sorts, her pedigree is marvellous and he should be racing around September-time".*

1386. HELICONIA ★★★

b.f. Hernando – Flor Y Nata (Fusaichi Pegasus).

February 28. Second foal. Half-sister to the fair 2011 2-y-o 7f winner Fresa (by Selkirk). The dam, a fairly useful 2-y-o dual 7f winner, was listed placed twice in Germany and is a half-sister to 2 winners. The second dam, Rose Of Zollern (Seattle Dancer), won 9 races including the German 1,000 Guineas and a stakes event in the USA and is a half-sister to 3 winners. (Miss K Rausing). *"A July/August 2-y-o over a mile. She's a big, strong filly".*

1387. HYPNOTISM ★★

ch.c. Pivotal – Hypnotize (Machiavellian). March 21. Eighth foal. Brother to the quite useful 2-y-o 6f winner Hip and half-brother to the 2-y-o Group 1 6f Cheveley Park Stakes and Group 2 6f Lowther Stakes winner Hooray (by Invincible Spirit), the useful 2-y-o listed 8.3f winner of 7 races Hypnotic (by Lomitas), the fairly useful 2-y-o 1m winner Notorize (by Hernando) and the quite useful dual 7f winner Macedon (by Dansili). The dam, a useful 2-y-o dual 7f winner, is closely related to 2 winners including the Group 3 6f Cherry Hinton Stakes winner Dazzle and a half-sister to 5 winners including the useful 7f (at 2 yrs) and 1m listed winner Fantasize and to the placed dam of the Group 2 winning sprinter Danehurst. The second dam, Belle et Deluree (by The Minstrel), won over 1m (at 2 yrs) and 10f in France and is a half-sister to the very useful 6f and 1m winner and Cheveley Park Stakes second Dancing Tribute (herself dam of the Group/Grade 2 winners Souvenir Copy and Dance Sequence). *"He looks a much taller, leggier type than his half-sister Hooray and he won't run until September".*

1388. JULY WAITS (USA) ★★★

b.f. Mr Greeley – Unique Pose (Sadler's Wells). April 2. Fourth foal. Sister to the modest triple 7f winner Drive Home. The dam, an Irish 6f (at 2 yrs) and 10f winner, was listed-placed and is a sister to the Irish 3-y-o 7f winner and 2-y-o Group 3 7f C L Weld Park Stakes third Easy Sunshine and a half-sister to 5 winners. The second dam, Desert Ease (by Green Desert), an Irish 2-y-o listed 6f winner, is a half-sister to several winners including the Group 3 Tetrarch Stakes and Group 3 7f Concorde Stakes winner Two-Twenty-Two. (Moyglare Stud Farms Ltd). *"She needed more time than one would have thought with her pedigree and she's grown a lot, so we gave her a break. She'll run in September, probably over seven furlongs or a mile".*

1389. LIBER ★★★★
b.c. Ishiguru – Startori (Vettori). February 12. Second foal. £28,000Y. Doncaster Premier. Kern/Lillingston. Brother to the fair 2011 2-y-o dual 5f winner Guru Girl. The dam, a quite useful 2-y-o dual 7f winner, was listed-placed and is a half-sister to 3 winners. The second dam, Celestial Welcome (by Most Welcome), a useful 7f to 12f winner of 8 races, is a full or half-sister to 5 winners including the smart Group 2 12f King Edward VII Stakes second Snowstorm. (William Charnley & Richard Begum). *"An early sort, he's not over-big but he's strong and he canters well. He'll be racing in late May and he'll be one of our first 2-y-o runners. I've got four relatively early types (early for me anyway). Fortunately I don't have to lie to you because I haven't worked them fast enough to be able to say if they're any good or not. But if you work four slow ones together they look alright!"* 2nd debut, won wn 5f mdn Carlisle easily

1390. LYRIC PIECE ★★★
ch.f. Dutch Art – Humouresque (Pivotal). February 16. Fifth foal. Half-sister to the fairly useful 10f and 11f winner Piano (by Azamour) and to the fair Irish 7f and 1m winner Solid Air (by Linamix). The dam, a smart Group 3 10.5f Prix Penelope winner, is a sister to 2 winners including the Group 2 placed Mighty and a half-sister to the very smart sprinter Danehurst, winner of the Cornwallis Stakes (at 2 yrs), the Curragh Flying Five, the Prix de Seine-et-Oise and the Premio Umbria (all Group 3 events). The second dam, Miswaki Belle (by Miswaki), second over 7f on her only start, is a half-sister to 8 winners including the smart Group 3 6f Cherry Hinton Stakes winner and 1,000 Guineas third Dazzle. (Cheveley Park Stud). *"A July/August type filly for six/seven furlongs, she's good-looking and correct. The mare did very well for us on the racecourse and we had a wonderful time with her – but she showed nothing at this time of her life! But this is a Dutch Art and she should be a bit more quick to hand then her Mum was".*

1391. MEDICOE ★★★★
ch.g. Medicean – Blue Dream (Cadeaux Genereux). January 28. Third foal. The dam, a useful 6f winner, was listed-placed and is a half-sister to 5 winners including the 1m (at 2 yrs) and 9.2f winner and listed-placed Equity Princess. The second dam, Hawait Al Barr (by Green Desert), a useful 12f to 2m winner, is a half-sister to 3 winners. (J B Haggas). *"He'll run early, he's a home-bred but I don't know much about the family. He's done a bit of work, he's not very big but he's well put-together and a thoroughly good-looking horse that might need six furlongs".*

1392. MISS VISTAERO ★★
b.f. Montjeu – Miss Corniche (Hernando). February 25. Sixth foal. Half-sister to the very useful 1m winner and listed-placed Moyenne Corniche (by Selkirk), to the quite useful 6f (at 2 yrs) and dual 7f winner Miss Eze and the modest dual 9f winner Miss Villefranche (both by Danehill Dancer). The dam, a 7f (at 2 yrs) and listed 10f winner, is a sister to 2 winners and a half-sister to numerous winners including the listed 1m winner Miss Riviera Golf. The second dam, Miss Beaulieu (by Northfields), was a useful 6f and 10f winner. (J. L. C Pearce). *"She's very much a 3-y-o type by Montjeu but she's very good-looking and the pedigree says that one day she'll be alright".*

1393. NORTH POLE ★★★★
b.c. Compton Place – Cool Question (Polar Falcon). March 17. Sixth foal. Half-brother to the useful 2-y-o 5f and 6f winner and subsequent Group 3 UAE 2,000 Guineas third Krypton Factor (by Kyllachy), to the quite useful dual 5f winner (including at 2 yrs) Fairfield Princess (by Inchinor), the quite useful 2-y-o dual 6f winner Haven't A Clue (by Red Ransom) and a winner in Sweden by Diktat. The dam, a useful 2-y-o 5f and listed 6f winner, is a half-sister to 4 winners. The second dam, Quiz Time (Efisio), a fairly useful 2-y-o 5f winner, was second in the listed St Hugh's Stakes and is a half-sister to 6 winners including the Group 3 Premio Dormello winner Brockette. (Lady Fairhaven & The Hon C & H Broughton). *"A half-brother to Krypton Factor who was the winning-most 2-y-o of his generation in England when I had him. He won five races, we sold him and he*

then drew a blank at three but this year he's returned and has won the Group 1 Golden Shaheen in Meydan. Unfortunately for us the mare has just produced a dead foal that was his full brother. The family all come to hand early and this colt has done a bit of work already, so he'll be ready to run by the end of May."

1394. OASIS CANNES ★★★
b.c. Oasis Dream – Miss Provence (Hernando). February 27. Third foal. Half-brother to the unplaced 2011 2-y-o Le Cagnard (by Danehill Dancer) and to the quite useful 10f winner Miss Aix (by Selkirk). The dam, a quite useful 9f winner, is a sister to 2 winners including the 7f (at 2 yrs) and listed 10f winner Miss Corniche and a half-sister to 5 winners. The second dam, Miss Beaulieu (by Northfields), was a useful 6f and 10f winner. (J L C Pierce). "He'll make a 2-y-o because he's not over-big. The sire is seemingly capable of doing anything – some can sprint and some can stay. He seems mature enough to work, so surprisingly he's earlier than expected".

1395. PEARL ANGEL (IRE) ★★★★
b.f. Dark Angel – Serious Delight (Lomond). February 12. Ninth foal. €85,000Y. Goffs Orby. David Redvers. Half-sister to 5 winners including the fairly useful dual 7f winner and listed-placed Maid In Heaven (by Clodovil), to the fairly useful 6f (at 2 yrs) and 7f winner of 3 races Delphie Queen, the fair 5f and 6f winner Everygrainofsand (both by Desert Sun), the fairly useful 2-y-o 6f and 8.5f winner Wathiq (by Titus Livius) and the Irish 5f to 7f winner of 4 races Foxhollow Lady (by Goldmark). The dam is an unraced half-sister to 8 winners including the dam of the Group 1 Haydock Park Sprint Cup winner Pipalong. The second dam, Grey Goddess (by Godswalk), won 5 races from 7f to 8.5f including two Group 3 events in Ireland and is a half-sister to 2 winners. (Pearl Bloodstock Ltd). "A jolly nice filly, she had a minor setback at Christmas but she's back cantering now. Because of that time off she won't be able to run before July".

1396. PEARL SPICE (IRE) ★★★★
ch.c. Dalakhani – Cinnamon Rose (Trempolino). February 22. Ninth living foal. €165,000Y. Arqana Deauville August. David Redvers.

Half-brother to the Group 1 7f Moyglare Stud Stakes winner of 5 races Chelsea Rose (by Desert King), to the Irish 6f (at 2 yrs) and listed 1m and subsequent US winner and Grade 2 placed European (by Great Commotion), the quite useful 7f (at 2 yrs) and 12f winner Woodcutter (by Daylami), the Japanese 3-y-o winner Admire Golgo (by Fasliyev), the 2-y-o 7f winner Next Move (by Tiger Hill) and the minor French and Spanish winner of 4 races Ruente (by Persian Bold). The dam, an Irish 10f winner, is a half-sister to 6 winners including the Group 2 Prix Eugene Adam winner River Warden and the US Grade 3 winner Sweettuc. The second dam, Sweet Simone (by Green Dancer), is a placed half-sister to 7 winners. (Pearl Bloodstock). "He looks like a seven furlong to a mile 2-y-o and he has a firm ground action. Much more mature than you might think on pedigree".

1397. PIGEON POWER ★★
b.f. Byron – Making Waves (Danehill). March 5. Fourth foal. £14,000Y. Doncaster November. Jeremy Gask. Half-sister to the Irish 2-y-o 6f winner and subsequent US Grade 2 fourth Wave Of Applause (by Royal Applause) and to the moderate 6f (at 2 yrs) and 7f winner Top Flight Splash (by Bertolini). The dam is an unplaced half-sister to the French winner and Group 2 Prix de Malleret second Buoyant. The second dam, Wavey (by Kris), a quite useful 2-y-o 7f winner here, subsequently won a listed event in France and is a half-sister to 5 winners including two French listed winners. (P Bamford). "She comes back to us in mid-May after a break because her limbs needed time. She's big and very robust but might make a 2-y-o if she has ability. I haven't seen her since January so I couldn't tell you any more".

1398. PORTRAIT ★★★
ch.f. Peintre Celebre – Annalina (Cozzene). February 15. Fourth foal. Half-sister to Hepworth (by Singspiel), placed second over 1m on her only start at 2 yrs in 2011, to the quite useful 12f winner Sagamore (by Azamour) and the Japanese Group 3 placed Kyoei Basara (by Aussie Rules). The dam is an unraced half-sister to 4 winners including the US Grade 2 Long Island Handicap winner Olaya. The second dam, Solaia (by Miswaki),

won the listed Cheshire Oaks and was second in the Group 3 Lancashire Oaks and is a half-sister to 3 winners. (Denford Stud). *"It's quite a stamina laden pedigree but she's not very big and she might be running in July or August. We should capitalise on her limited size by racing her as a 2-y-o".*

1399. SAGESSE ★★★★

ch.f. Smart Strike – Summer Night (Nashwan). January 23. Ninth foal. Half-sister to the 2-y-o Group 3 1m Prix des Reservoirs winner Songerie, to the fairly useful 2-y-o 7.2f winner and Group 3 1m Prix des Reservoirs third Souvenance (both by Hernando), the useful listed 9.5f winner of 3 races Soft Morning (by Pivotal), the fairly useful 7f (at 2 yrs) and Scandinavian listed 8.5f winner Sourire (by Domedriver), the fair triple 10f winner Aestival (by Falbrav) and a minor winner of 6 races in Italy by Selkirk. The dam, a fairly useful 3-y-o 6f winner, is a half-sister to 7 winners including the Group 3 Prix d'Arenburg winner Starlit Sands and the listed 6f winner Sea Dane. The second dam, Shimmering Sea (by Slip Anchor), a fairly useful Irish 2-y-o 5f and 7f winner and third in the Group 3 Silken Glider Stakes, is a half-sister to 5 winners including the King George VI and Queen Elizabeth Stakes winner Petoski. (Miss K Rausing). *"She came in late, was broken in January, canters well but wouldn't be running until August. She's not over-big, I've had nearly all the foals out of the mare – they're good and the sire is good as well".*

1400. SAVANNAH LA MAR (USA) ★★★

ch.f. Curlin – Soft Morning (Pivotal). March 12. First foal. The dam, a useful listed 9.5f winner of 3 races, is a half-sister to numerous winners including the 2-y-o Group 3 1m Prix des Reservoirs winner Songerie, the fairly useful 2-y-o 7.2f winner and Group 3 1m Prix des Reservoirs third Souvenance and the fairly useful 7f (at 2 yrs) and Scandinavian listed 8.5f winner Sourire. The second dam, Summer Night (by Nashwan), a fairly useful 3-y-o winner, is a half-sister to 7 winners including the Group 3 Prix d'Arenburg winner Starlit Sands and the listed 6f winner Sea Dane. (Miss K Rausing). *"She'll be a seven furlong type in July and she's out of a mare that was a good, tough performer. This filly has plenty of scope*

and the sire was a tough racehorse although we don't know if he'll be a good sire or not yet".*

1401. SLIP OF THE TONGUE ★★★

ch.c. Zamindar – Kiswahili (Selkirk). March 10. Third foal. €42,000Y. Goffs Orby. Sir M Prescott. Half-brother to the 2011 2-y-o listed 7f winner and dual Group 3 third Kinetica (by Stormy Atlantic) and to the fair 10f winner Four Nations (by Langfuhr). The dam won 4 races including a listed 14f event in Germany and is a half-sister to 3 winners. The second dam, Kiliniski (by Niniski), a very smart winner of the Group 3 12f Lingfield Oaks Trial, was second in the Yorkshire Oaks and fourth in the Epsom Oaks and is a half-sister to 5 winners including the dam of the US triple Grade 1 winner Bienamado. (J E Fishpool – Osborne House). *"A half-brother to a decent 2-y-o we had last year in Kinetica. This fellow will need more time and I don't see him running before September. He's a big, fine, smashing horse".*

1402. SZABO'S ART ★★

br.f. Excellent Art – Violette (Observatory). April 11. Third foal. 10,000Y. Tattersalls December. Not sold. Half-sister to the quite useful 2011 2-y-o 7f winner Beaufort Twelve (by Hurricane Run). The dam, a Group 3 6f Firth Of Clyde Stakes winner, was second in the Group 2 Rockfel Stakes and is a half-sister to 4 winners including the useful 2-y-o 5f and 6f winner and Group 3 placed Virginia Hall and the listed 6f (at 2 yrs) and Group 3 7f Nell Gwyn Stakes winner Silca's Gift. The second dam, Odette (by Pursuit Of Love), a fair 3-y-o 5f and 5.7f winner, is a half-sister to 4 winners including the useful 6f (at 2 yrs) and 7f winner and Group 2 5f Flying Childers Stakes fourth Caballero. (C. G Rowles-Nicholson). *"We've had all the family and they're quick. She went to the Sales but didn't sell, so she came to us. She's having a break now, she might make a 2-y-o but not until later in the season".*

1403. WILD DIAMOND (IRE) ★★

b.f. Hernando – Step With Style (Gulch). April 16. Half-sister to the useful 6f (at 2 yrs) and 9f winner and Group 3 1m Irish 1,000 Guineas Trial third Firey Red (by Pivotal), to the quite useful Irish 12f winner Comedic Art (by Dansili), the minor Irish 2-y-o 1m winner Sansibar (by

Linamix) and the modest Irish 1m winner Shy Smile (by Peintre Celebre). The dam, a quite useful Irish 1m winner at 3 yrs, is a half-sister to several winners including the Group 3 placed Absolute Glee. The second dam, Looking Brill (by Sadler's Wells), won over 12f in Ireland and is a half-sister to numerous winners. (Moyglare Stud Farms Ltd). *"She has a grand pedigree, as you'd expect from a Moyglare family. Like a lot of Hernando's she'll need time, she came in late after having a hold-up at stud".*

NOEL QUINLAN

1404. LOUCAL ★★★

b.c. *Lucky Story – Penny Ha'Penny (Bishop Of Cashel)*. March 12. Fifth foal. £10,000Y. Doncaster Premier. Noel Quinlan. Half-brother to the fair dual 6f winner (including at 2 yrs) Celtic Sixpence, to the fair 7f winner Celtic Sovereign (both by Celtic Swing) and the moderate 5f and 6f winner Half A Crown (by Compton Place). The dam, a quite useful 3-y-o 5f winner of 3 races, is a half-sister to 4 winners including the Group 2 Temple Stakes winner Celtic Mill. The second dam, Madam Millie (by Milford), a useful winner of 3 races over 5f at 2 yrs, is a full or half-sister to 6 winners. *"I like all the two-year-olds I have this year because I got rid of anything that wasn't worth keeping. This colt is a half-brother to a Goodwood winner for us called Celtic Sixpence. He's a workmanlike, tough horse that'll win races".*

1405. REBERTY LEE ★★

b.g. *Three Valleys – Query (Distant View)*. April 24. Second foal. £2,800Y. Doncaster November. Not sold. Half-brother to the fairly useful 2-y-o 7f winner and listed-placed Sensei (by Dr Fong). The dam is an unraced half-sister to 7 minor winners here and abroad. The second dam, Questonia (by Rainbow Quest), a useful winner at around 1m, is a half-sister to 2 winners including the listed 10f winner Zante. (Burns Farm Racing). *"He'll have had a run before your book comes out and my only reservation is that he may have got a bit too clever for his own good. A real 2-y-o type".*

1406. VITRUVIAN LADY ★★

b.f. *Manduro – Vas Y Carla (Gone West)*. February 8. Fifth foal. 28,000Y. Tattersalls

October Book 1. Not sold. Half-sister to the fair 2011 9f placed 2-y-o Confirmed (by Authorized) and to the quite useful 7f (at 2 yrs) and 6f winner Alice Alleyne (by Oasis Dream). The dam, a quite useful 7f placed 2-y-o, is a half-sister to 4 winners including the Group 2 Great Voltigeur Stakes third Avalon. The second dam, Lady Carla (by Caerleon), won over 1m (at 2 yrs) and the Group 1 12f Oaks, is a half-sister to a minor winner. *"You won't see her until later in the season, although she is strong considering her pedigree".*

1407. UNNAMED ★★★★

b.f. *Bahamian Bounty – Gee Kel (Danehill Dancer)*. February 9. Second foal. Half-sister to the fair 2011 dual 7f placed 2-y-o Arley Hall (by Excellent Art). The dam, a useful 6f winner at 2 yrs in Ireland and second in the Group 3 6f Swordlestown Sprint Stakes, is a half-sister to 4 winners. The second dam, Shir Dar (by Lead On Time), won the US Grade 2 Palomar Handicap and is a half-sister to 9 winners. (David O'Rourke). *"A nice colt bred by Plantation Stud and I think he's a right horse. He didn't go to the sales but if he had done he'd have easily made 80,000. He'll be a six furlong 2-y-o to start off with. I like him an awful lot and I think of all our 2-y-o's he's the one with the most potential".*

1408. UNNAMED ★★★

b.c. *Celtic Swing – Cape Finisterre (Cape Cross)*. Third foal. Brother to the fair 7f (including at 2 yrs) and 1m winner Abriachan. The dam is an unraced half-sister to one winner. The second dam, Trim Star (by Terimon), is a placed half-sister to 6 winners including the listed Galtres Stakes winner Startino. *"He'll be a nice colt and worth putting in the book. We train his full-brother Abriachan".*

1409. UNNAMED ★★

b.c. *Oasis Dream – Pinacotheque (In The Wings)*. April 1. Second foal. The dam, a French 12f winner, was listed-placed over 10f and is closely related to the multiple French Group 2 middle-distance winner Policy Maker and a half-sister to numerous winners including the very useful listed 11f winner Place Rouge and the useful 1m (at 2 yrs) and listed 2m winner

Pushkin. The second dam, Palmeraie (by Lear Fan), is a half-sister to the Grade 2 12f Long Island Handicap winner Peinture Bleue (herself dam of the Prix de l'Arc de Triomphe winner Peintre Celebre), to the US Grade 3 1m William P Kyne Handicap winner Provins, the Irish 2-y-o winner and Group 3 Gladness Stakes second Chateau Royal and the Group 3 11f Andre Baboin winner Parme. (R.G & T. E Levin). *"A colt with a lovely pedigree, he's a big 2-y-o that'll need time".*

1410. UNNAMED ★★★
b.c. Red Clubs – Solo Symphony (Fayruz). April 30. Tenth foal. £60,000 2-y-o. Goffs Kempton Breeze-Up. Noel Quinlan. Half-brother to the fair 2-y-o 5f winner Abzolutely (by Chineur), to the fair 2-y-o 5f winner Streaky, the modest 3-y-o 5f winner Correct Time (both by Danetime) and two winners abroad by Brave Act and Inzar. The dam was placed 4 times over 5f at 2 and 3 yrs and is a half-sister to 3 winners. The second dam, Keen Note (by Sharpo), won 2 races at 4 yrs in Belgium and is a half-sister to 4 winners including the triple listed winner Whittingham. *"He cost plenty of money considering his pedigree, but he's a lovely horse and he did a real good breeze at the sales".*

KEVIN RYAN
1411. ANA EMARATIYA
b.f. Sleeping Indian – Vale Of Belvoir (Mull Of Kintyre). January 12. First foal. £35,000Y. Doncaster Festival. Stephen Hillen. The dam, a useful 2-y-o 5f winner of 3 races, was listed-placed and is a half-sister to one winner. The dam, Sunrise (by Sri Pekan), a modest 5f placed 2-y-o, is a half-sister to 5 winners including the Group 3 Phoenix Sprint Stakes winner March Star. (A Al Shaikh).

1412. ANGILINA
b.f. Teofilo – Finnmark (Halling). February 22. Third foal. Half-sister to the modest 2012 3-y-o 1m winner Cape Safari (by Cape Cross). The dam is an unraced half-sister to 8 winners including the very smart Group 2 15f Prix Hubert de Chaudenay winner Affadavit, the French listed 12f winner Nalani, the 10f and 12f listed winner Altamura and the Italian listed

winner Tea Garden. The second dam, Narwala (by Darshaan), won the Group 3 12f Princess Royal Stakes and was second in the Grade 2 12f Long Island Handicap. (S Ali).

1413. A STAR IN MY EYE (IRE)
b.f. Authorized – Vyatka (Lion Cavern). March 31. Third foal. 20,000Y. Tattersalls October Book 1. Rabbah Bloodstock. Half-sister to the Group 3 10f Ballysax Stakes and multiple jumps winner Bobs Pride (by Marju). The dam is an unraced half-sister to 6 winners including the French listed 1m winner Queen Catherine (herself dam of the Group 3 Premio Dormello winner Lady Catherine) and the useful 2-y-o 7f winner and Group 3 1m May Hill Stakes third Gretel. The second dam, Russian Royal (by Nureyev), a useful winner over 6f at 2 yrs and 7f at 3 yrs and placed in the Jersey Stakes, the Fred Darling Stakes, the Supreme Stakes and the Beeswing Stakes, is a half-sister to 8 winners here and in the USA. (S Ali).

1414. AYR MISSILE
b.f. Cadeaux Genereux – Venoge (Green Desert). February 14. Second foal. £12,000Y. Doncaster Premier. Middleham Park Racing. The dam is an unraced half-sister to 2 winners. The second dam, Horatia (by Machiavellian), won the Grade 3 Matchmaker Stakes in the USA and was third in the Grade 2 Long Island Handicap and is a half-sister to 6 winners including Opinion Poll (Group 2 Lonsdale Cup). (Middleham Park Racing XLV).

1415. BAIN'S PASS (IRE)
ch.c. Johannesburg – Rose Bourbon (Woodman). April 18. Twelfth foal. €37,000Y. Tattersalls Ireland. Stephen Hillen. Brother to the French 2-y-o 5f and 6f winner and dual listed placed Princess Roseburg and half-brother to the useful 2-y-o listed 7f winner and Group 3 7f Vintage Stakes second Bourbonnais (by Singspiel), the fair Irish dual 1m winner Georgina (by Polish Precedent) and the minor US 3-y-o winner Artefacto (by Officer). The dam was listed-placed twice in France at up to 1m and is a half-sister to 5 stakes winners including the French 1,000 Guineas winner Baiser Vole, the smart French sprinter Tenue de Soiree and the very smart 1m to 10f colt Squill.

The second dam, River Rose (by Riverman), was a listed winner of 5 races over 5f at 2 yrs. (Mrs M Forsyth).

1416. BAPAK BESAR
ch.c. Speightstown – Valid Move (Valid Expectations). April 25. Third foal. $185,000Y. Keeneland September. Stephen Hillen. The dam, a minor stakes winner in the USA, is a sister to the US listed stakes winner Stage Stop. The second dam, Winning Move (by Strike The Gold), a US stakes winner of 3 races at 2 and 3 yrs, is a half-sister to another stakes winner. (Mr Shah).

1417. DELORES ROCKET
b.f. Firebreak – Artistic (Noverre). March 22. Third foal. £19,000Y. Doncaster Premier. Stephen Hillen. Half-sister to the fair 2011 2-y-o 5f winner Ortea (by Vital Equine). The dam is an unraced half-sister to 3 winners including the dam of the 2-y-o listed winner Geesala. The second dam, Shmoose (by Caerleon), a useful 6f winner at 2 yrs and third in the Group 3 6f Prix de Seine-et-Oise, is a half-sister to 6 winners and to the good broodmare June Moon. (J Nixon).

1418. DILADY
b.f. Bertolini – Flying Highest (Spectrum). February 2. Fourth foal. £16,500Y. Doncaster Premier. Stephen Hillen. The dam ran once unplaced and is a half-sister to 6 sprint winners. The second dam, Mainly Sunset (by Red Sunset), ran once due to an injury and is a half-sister to 9 winners including the high-class sprinter Bolshoi. (Mr P Beirne).

1419. EASTERN DRAGON (IRE)
b.c. Elnadim – Shulammite Woman (Desert Sun). March 6. Third foal. €30,000Y. Goffs Orby. Stephen Hillen. Half-brother to a minor 2-y-o winner abroad by Statue Of Liberty. The dam is an unraced half-sister to 7 winners including the dual listed-placed Judicial Field. The second dam, Bold Meadows (by Persian Bold), won twice in Ireland at 2 and 3 yrs, was second in the Group 2 Blandford Stakes and is a half-sister to 8 winners including the dam of the triple Group 1 winner Kilijaro. (C. G. J Chua).

1420. GREAT PHILOSOPHER (IRE)
ch.c. Choisir – Sandbox Two (Foxhound). February 20. Third foal. £33,000Y. Doncaster Premier. Stephen Hillen. Half-brother to a minor winner of 3 races at 2 yrs in Italy by Spartacus. The dam is an unplaced half-sister to 4 minor winners. The second dam, Moorfield Daisy (by Waajib), is an unplaced half-sister to 7 winners. (A & A).

1421. HOTOTO *Won 5f listed by/ Ascot*
ch.c. Sleeping Indian – Harlem Dancer (Dr Devious). March 9. Fourth foal. £22,000Y. Doncaster Festival. Stephen Hillen. The dam, a French 10f and 11f winner and listed-placed, is a half-sister to 2 winners. The second dam, Hymenee (by Chief's Crown), a minor French 3-y-o winner, is a half-sister to 7 winners including the US Grade 2 winner Globe and the dam of the Group 2 Prix Niel winner Housamix. (Kenneth MacPherson). *Won 5f cl 4 2 x to Cny Verde mdn ayr*

1422. LADY OF THE HOUSE (IRE)
b.c. Holy Roman Emperor – Miss Delila (Malibu Moon). February 8. Second foal. 18,000Y. Tattersalls October Book 2. Stephen Hillen. Half-brother to the fair 2011 6f and 7f placed 2-y-o Marching On (by Rock Of Gibraltar). The dam is an unplaced half-sister to 3 winners including Sander Camillo (Group 2 Cherry Hinton Stakes and Group 3 Albany Stakes). The second dam, Staraway (by Star de Naskra), won 20 races in the USA including three listed stakes and is a half-sister to 5 winners.

Won d-vel 6f Alr Thirsk
1423. LEXI THE PRINCESS (IRE)
b.f. Holy Roman Emperor – Star Profile (Sadler's Wells). March 13. Eleventh foal. 28,000Y. Tattersalls October Book 2. Stephen Hillen. Half-sister to the useful 2011 2-y-o dual 5f winner Dozy (by Exceed And Excel), to the 11f and 12f winner and French Group 2 15f third Without A Trace, the fair 1m winner Just A Fluke (both by Darshaan), the quite useful dual 1m winner Kindest (by Cadeaux Genereux), the moderate 12f winner Lady Asheena and a winner in Greece (both by Daylami). The dam, an Irish 2-y-o 6f winner, is closely related to the very useful Group 3 6.3f Anglesey Stakes and Group 3 5f Molecomb Stakes winner Lady Alexander (herself dam of the Group 3 winner Dandy Man). The second dam, Sandhurst

Goddess (by Sandhurst Prince), a useful winner of 4 races from 5f to 7f in Ireland including the listed Topaz Sprint Stakes, is a half-sister to 5 winners. (Dr M Koukash).

1424. MARHABA MALAYEEN
b.c. Dutch Art – Poyle Caitlin (Bachir). March 14. Third living foal. 62,000Y. Tattersalls October Book 2. Stephen Hillen. Half-brother to the quite useful 2-y-o 5f and 6f winner of 3 races Puddle Duck (by Pastoral Pursuits). The dam, a modest 1m fourth placed maiden, is a half-sister to 4 winners including the Group 2 Lowther Stakes winner Jemima. The second dam, Poyle Fizz (by Damister), is an unraced full or half-sister to 4 winners. (A Al Shaikh).

1425. PEARL RANSOM (IRE)
b.c. Intikhab – Massada (Most Welcome). February 15. Ninth foal. 62,000Y. Tattersalls October Book 2. David Redvers. Half-brother to the multiple listed winner Les Fazzani, to the minor French and German 3-y-o winner Marangu (both by Intikhab), the German listed winner and Group 3 6f placed Miss Lips, the minor German winner Moody Blues (both by Big Shuffle) and a minor 2-y-o winner in Spain by King Charlemagne. The dam, a listed-placed 7f and 1m winner at 2 yrs in Germany, is a half-sister to 3 minor winners. The second dam, Maracuja (by Riverman), won over 1m at 2 yrs in France and is a half-sister to 3 minor winners. (Pearl Bloodstock Ltd).

1426. PROJECTISLE (IRE)
b.f. Tagula – Erne Project (Project Manager). March 15. Eighth living foal. £15,000Y. Doncaster Premier. Stephen Hillen. Brother to the useful 5f to 7f winner of 9 races (including at 2 yrs) and Group 2 Hungerford Stakes third Beaver Patrol, to the Italian winner of 16 races at up to 1m Golden Tagula and the quite useful 2-y-o 6f winner Eternal Luck. The dam won over 13f at 3 yrs in Ireland and is a half-sister to 2 winners. The second dam, Erneside (by Lomond), is a placed half-sister to 10 winners including the Group 2 Sandown Mile winner and sire Almushtarak. (Mrs Bailey).

1427. RED PALADIN (IRE)
b.c. Red Clubs – Alexander Goldmine (Dansili). March 16. Second foal. £20,000Y. Doncaster

Premier. Stephen Hillen. Half-brother to the fair 2011 2-y-o winner Redair (by Redback). The dam, a winner, is a half-sister to a winner in Italy. The second dam, Key Virtue (by Atticus), is a placed half-sister to 3 winners including Among Men (Group 1 Sussex Stakes). (Hambleton Racing Ltd XXII).

1428. SETFIRETOTHERAIN
ch.c. Compton Place – Tembladora (Docksider). January 24. Third foal. £21,000Y. Doncaster Premier. Stephen Hillen. Half-brother to the quite useful 2011 2-y-o 6f winner Desert Philosopher (by Pastoral Pursuits). The dam, placed once at 3 yrs, is a sister to the UAE listed winner and US Grade 2 placed Clinet and a half-sister to 3 winners. The second dam, Oiche Mhaith (by Night Shift), won once at 3 yrs and is a half-sister to 7 winners. (Mrs A Bailey).

1429. UNASSAILABLE
ch.c. Bahamian Bounty – Reeling N' Rocking (Mr Greeley). April 30. Second foal. 22,000Y. Tattersalls October Book 2. Stephen Hillen. The dam, a fair 7f winner of 4 races at 3 and 4 yrs, is a half-sister to 4 winners including the useful listed-placed 6f winner of 3 races Entrap. The second dam, Mystic Lure (by Green Desert), a fair 5f and 6f placed 2-y-o, is a half-sister to 5 winners including the Grade 1 Hollywood Derby and Group 3 Prix Daphnis winner Thrill Show and the Grade 3 Pilgrim Stakes winner David's Bird. (J Nixon).

DEREK SHAW
1430. APHRODITE'S DREAM ★★★
b.f. Manduro – Trick Of Ace (Clever Trick). May 4. Tenth foal. 25,000Y. Tattersalls October Book 2. Derek Shaw. Half-sister to the Group 3 12f Princess Royal Stakes winner of 7 races and Group 1 Yorkshire Oaks third Trick Or Treat, to the bumper winner Kick For Touch (both by Lomitas), the modest 10f and hurdles winner Trickstep (by Imperial Ballet) and a winner in Sweden by Fraam. The dam, a stakes-placed winner of 4 races in the USA over 1m or more, is a half-sister to 5 winners including the US Grade 2 La Prevoyante Handicap winner Prospectress and the Group 3 winner Across The Rhine. The second dam, Seductive Smile (by Silver Hawk), is an unraced half-sister to 6 winners including the Group 1 Premio Roma

winner Nizon, the US Grade 3 winner Don Roberto and the South African Grade 3 winner Lord Balmerino. (Mr Brian Johnson). *"A nice filly and physically she's done really well over the winter. She was bought with the intention of racing her from July and August onwards. Looking at the pedigree you'd expect her to need seven furlongs and she's a lovely-moving filly with a great attitude".*

1431. LADY ELALMADOL (IRE) ★★★
gr.f. Shamardal – Elitista (Linamix). February 14. Fifth foal. 45,000Y. Tattersalls October Book 2. Derek Shaw. Half-sister to the fair 2011 dual 6f placed 2-y-o Poseidon Grey (by Kheleyf) and to the fair 2-y-o 5f winner and listed-placed Riotista (by Captain Rio). The dam is an unplaced half-sister to 5 winners. The second dam, Elacarta (by Acatenango), won the Group 3 Prix Corrida and is a half-sister to 7 winners including the Group 2 German St Leger winner Elsurimo. (Mr Brian Johnson). *"She's not going to be early because she had a little setback, but she's a nice-moving filly with a lovely attitude and she did well over the winter. We're just cracking on with her now and she'll make a 2-y-o in May or June over five furlongs".*

1432. TOP BOY ★★★
b.c. Exceed And Excel – Injaaz (Sheikh Albadou). February 2. Third foal. 42,000Y. Tattersalls October Book 2. Derek Shaw. Half-brother to the fair 2-y-o 6f winners Fardyieh (by King's Best) and Classic Fortune (by Royal Applause). The dam, a quite useful 6f winner, was listed-placed and is a sister to the fairly useful 6f winner of 3 races Corndavon (herself dam of the smart 2-y-o Nevisian Lad) and a half-sister to the placed dam of the listed winners Pyman's Theory and Forthefirstime. The second dam, Ferber's Follies (by Saratoga Six), a winning 2-y-o sprinter, was third in the Grade 2 6f Adirondack Stakes and is a half-sister to 11 winners including the US 2-y-o Grade 2 6f winner Blue Jean Baby. (Mr Brian Johnson). *"A colt with a good attitude, he goes about his job really nicely and he should be racing by the end of April. It's a good family and he could be anything from five to seven furlongs".*

1433. UNNAMED ★★
b.c. Manduro – Rakata (Quiet American). April

11. Second foal. £800Y. Doncaster November. Derek Shaw Racing. The dam, a fair winner of 4 races over 7f and 1m, was listed-placed and is a half-sister to 4 winners. The second dam, Haleakala (by Kris), a useful 3-y-o 13.3f winner, is a half-sister to the 5 winners including the dual US Grade 1 placed Blue Burner. *"We've just got him broken-in and cantering and we're taking our time with him. He's a lovely, big horse that won't be racing until August over seven furlongs or more and I thought he was very good value for what he cost".* TRAINERS' BARGAIN BUY

DAVID SIMCOCK
1434. AL BANDAR ★★★★
ch.c. Pivotal – Kotsi (Nayef). April 8. First foal. 26,000Y. Tattersalls October Book 1. David Simcock. The dam, a smart 2-y-o 7f winner, was second in the Group 2 1m May Hill Stakes and is a half-sister to 8 winners including the Canadian Grade 2 winner Miss Keller, the very useful listed placed Tissifer and the useful dual Group 3 placed Sir George Turner and the dams of the Group 2 winners Fantastic Pick and Hatta Fort. The second dam, Ingozi (by Warning), a fairly useful winner over 7f and 1m at 3 yrs including a listed event at Sandown Park, is a half-sister to 7 winners including the very smart and tough triple Group 3 7f winner Inchinor. *"He's probably our sharpest 2-y-o, he's quick, very natural and shows plenty of speed. I'm very happy with him".*

1435. AL EMIRATI (IRE) ★★★
b.c. Tamayuz – Corrine (Spectrum). March 12. Fourth foal. £19,000Y. Doncaster Premier. Blandford Bloodstock. Half-brother to the fairly useful Irish 1m (at 2 yrs) and 14f winner Liszt (by Galileo). The dam won 4 races, including a listed event, in Norway and is a half-sister to 6 winners. The second dam, La Luna (by Lyphard), a winner over 9f at 3 yrs in France, is a sister to the Group 3 Prix Daphnis and Group 3 Prix Thomas Bryon winner Bellypha and a half-sister to 6 winners including the Prix Eugene Adam winner Bellman and the Peruvian Grade 1 winner Run And Deliver. *"He's very forward, very natural and shows plenty of speed. He'll be racing in May and for what he cost I'm delighted with him".* TRAINERS' BARGAIN BUY

1436. ARE YOU SURE ★★★

ch.f. Mount Nelson – Dancing Mirage (Machiavellian). February 6. Sixth foal. 55,000Y. Tattersalls October Book 2. Blandford Bloodstock. Half-sister to the Group 3 Jersey Stakes winner and Group 1 Lockinge Stakes second Ouqba (by Red Ransom), to the very useful 7f (at 2 yrs) and 12f winner and listed-placed Foxhaven (by Unfuwain), the quite useful 1m winner Robby Bobby (by Selkirk), the quite useful 8.3f (at 2 yrs) and 12.5f winner Swiss Act (by Act One) and a winner in South Africa by Danehill. The dam, a quite useful 2-y-o 7f winner, is a half-sister to 4 winners including the dam of the good Hong Kong horse Housemaster. The second dam, Kraemer (by Lyphard), winner of the listed 8.5f Bay Meadows Oaks, was second in the Grade 2 Del Mar Oaks and is a half-sister to 5 winners including the Prix du Rond-Point and Prix d'Astarte winner Shaanxi. *"The mare is a good producer and this is a very attractive filly that probably won't start before the seven furlong/ mile races. Very likeable".*

1437. BEAUTIFUL LIFE ★★★

b.f. Footstepsinthesand – My Heart's Deelite (Afternoon Deelites). April 14. Half-sister to the fair 7f winner Lighthearted (by Fantastic Light) and to a minor winner in Italy at 3 and 4 yrs by Johannesburg. The dam won races in the USA and 3 and 4 yrs and was stakes-placed and is a half-sister to 8 winners. The second dam, Frozen Rope (by Clever Trick), a stakes-placed winner of 4 races in the USA, is a half-sister to 9 winners. *"Not the prettiest filly to look at, but she's got a great action and is showing up very nicely in the first group of 2-y-o's. I'd like to think she'd be starting off at six furlongs in May. Everything's she's done so far she's done very well".*

1438. BRAZEN ★★★

b.c. Kyllachy – Molly Brown (Rudimentary). March 25. Eighth foal. £80,000Y. Doncaster Premier. Blandford Bloodstock. Half-brother to the smart 2-y-o dual 6f winner and Group 2 Mill Reef Stakes second Doctor Brown (by Dr Fong), to the fairly useful 6f (at 2 yrs) and 1m winner Insaaf (by Averti), the quite useful 2-y-o 5f and 6f winner Bright Moll, the quite useful 2-y-o 6f winner Ballyalla (both by Mind

Games) and the modest 7f winner La Fanciulla (by Robellino). The dam, a fairly useful 5f (at 2 yrs) and 6f winner, is a half-sister to 4 winners including the listed 1m Premio Nearco winner Stato King. The second dam, Sinking (by Midyan), is an unraced half-sister to 3 winners. *"He's a very likeable, good-looking horse that hasn't done a great deal at the moment, but what he has done is pleasing on the eye. A six furlong type, he probably wouldn't want the ground too quick but I like him and he's a real attractive horse".*

1439. BRETON ROCK (IRE) ★★★

b.c. Bahamian Bounty – Anna's Rock (Rock Of Gibraltar). February 12. First foal. £20,000Y. Blandford Bloodstock (private sale). The dam, a useful Irish 7f (at 2 yrs) and listed 7.5f winner, is a half-sister to the useful 1m winner and listed-placed Sugar Mint. The second dam, Anna Karenina (by Atticus), is an unraced half-sister to the Group 3 Prix de Psyche winner and French 1,000 Guineas and French Oaks placed Agathe (herself dam of the Grade/Group 1 winners Artiste Royal and Aquarelliste), to the Breeders Cup Classic winner Arcangues and the dams of the Group/Grade 1 winners Cape Verdi and Angara. *"A horse that hits the ground hard, he's just thrown a splint and we look on him as a six/seven furlong horse with cut in the ground. He's showing up well and doing everything right at home".*

1440. DREAM CAST (IRE) ★★★

b.c. Refuse To Bend – Star Studded (Cadeaux Genereux). March 9. Fifth foal. €90,000Y. Arqana Deauville August. Mark Crossman. Brother to the useful 1m winner and triple listed-placed Say No Now and half-brother to the useful 2011 2-y-o 6f winner and Group 3 7f Acomb Stakes third Zumbi (by Dubawi). The dam is an unraced sister to the Group 2 5f Flying Childers Stakes and Group 3 5f King George V Stakes winner Land Of Dreams (herself the dam of the multiple Group 1 winner Dream Ahead) and a half-sister to 5 winners. The second dam, Sahara Star (by Green Desert), won the Group 3 5f Molecomb Stakes, was third in the Lowther Stakes and is a half-sister to 6 winners. *"Closely related to Dream Ahead, unfortunately he's by a stallion that hasn't done a lot with his colts, but he has a likeable attitude, he shows up well and I'd expect him out over six or seven furlongs around June time".*

1441. EXCELLENT HIT ★★★★
b.c. *Exceed And Excel – Broadway Hit (Sadler's Wells).* April 23. Fourth foal. 145,000Y. Tattersalls October Book 1. Hugo Merry. Half-brother to the French 10f winner Coutances (by Shamardal). The dam is an unraced half-sister to 5 winners including the smart 2-y-o Group 1 1m Prix Marcel Boussac winner and Group 1 10f Nassau Stakes second Sulk, the Group1 Hong Kong Cup winner and Epsom Derby second Eagle Mountain and the smart 1m listed winner Wallace. The second dam, Masskana (by Darshaan), a minor 9f and 10f winner in France, is a half-sister to 3 winners including Madjaristan (US Grade 3 Arcadia Handicap) and Massyar (Group 2 Gallinule Stakes). (Mrs F H Hay). *"He's a lovely horse. A scopey, seven furlong type 2-y-o with a lovely action, a great brain and a smashing attitude. One of those types of horses that never seems to get tired. Very likeable".*

1442. FATIMA'S GIFT ★★
b.f. *Dalakhani – Heavenly Whisper (Halling).* April 12. Seventh foal. 38,000foal. Tattersalls December. Not sold. Half-sister to the useful triple 1m winner River Tiber (by Danehill), to the 2-y-o 1m and 9f winner Premier Banker (by Cape Cross), the triple 1m winner Twilight Star (by Green Desert) and the dual 1m winner Sweet Clementine (by Shamardal) – all 3 quite useful. The dam, a useful listed 1m winner and second in the Group 2 Falmouth Stakes, is a half-sister to 4 winners including the German listed winner Gipsy Moth (herself dam of the Group 2 Goodwood Cup winner Illustrious Blue). The second dam, Rock The Boat (by Slip Anchor), a modest 6f (at 2 yrs) and 1m placed maiden, is a half-sister to 9 winners including the smart Cherry Hinton Stakes winner Kerrera and the high-class colt Rock City. *"We're getting mixed messages from her because she's very forward and very natural and yet being by Dalakhani you'd expect her to be one for later in the season. So I would think she takes more after the dam. I would imagine she'd start at seven furlongs, but as she's not very big I might push on with her a bit sooner".*

1443. GLASS OFFICE ★★★
br.c. *Verglas – Oval Office (Pursuit Of Love).* March 16. Third foal. €60,000Y. Goffs Orby. Stephen Hillen. The dam, a fairly useful 3-y-o dual 1m winner, is a half-sister to 12 winners including the smart 6f (at 2 yrs) and Nell Gwyn Stakes winner Myself and the smart 2-y-o 6f Princess Margaret Stakes and 3-y-o 6f Prix de Seine et Oise winner Bluebook. The second dam, Pushy (by Sharpen Up), a very useful 2-y-o winner of 4 races including the Queen Mary Stakes, is a half-sister to 10 winners including the good winners Precocious and Jupiter Island. *"Although he's by Verglas he's a very good-actioned horse that wouldn't want it too soft. I'd be looking to start him over six furlongs in May, I'm very happy with him and he's done one piece of work where he showed up very well. He has a great attitude and I'm very pleased with him".* ~my wkf J.Crow Kempton bf~

1444. KELDIVA ★★★
b.f. *Dixie Union – Keladora (Crafty Prospector).* February 7. First foal. 30,000Y. Tattersalls October Book 2. David Simcock. The dam, a French listed-placed winner of 3 races, is a half-sister to 2 winners including the French winner and Group 1 Prix Marcel Boussac second On Verra. The second dam, Karmifira (by Always Fair), winner of the listed Prix Finlande and second in the French 1,000 Guineas, is a half-sister to 5 winners including the listed 1m Prix Coronation winner Kart Star. *"She's really started to come to hand and I see her as a seven furlong prospect. She's changed quite dramatically for the better in the last month and she's likeable".*

1445. MAJEED ★★★★
b.c. *Mount Nelson – Clever Millie (Cape Canaveral).* February 19. First foal. €120,000Y. Arqana Deauville August. Mark Crossman. The dam, a fair Irish 7f winner at 4 yrs, is a half-sister to 6 winners including the US Grade 2 winner Dance Smartly and the smart listed 1m winner Fatefully (herself dam of the Group 1 Nassau Stakes winner Favourable Terms). The second dam, Fateful (by Topsider), a fairly useful 6f (at 2 yrs) and 7f winner, is a half-sister to 2 winners. *"He's probably the most attractive 2-y-o in the yard – an absolute belter to look at. He has a very fluent, very natural action and I see him*

as a seven furlong/mile horse later in the year. I'm very pleased with him, he's a lovely horse".

1446. POSTE RESTANTE ★★★
b.f. Halling – Postage Stampe (Singspiel). January 27. Second foal. Half-sister to Fulney (by Dr Fong), placed over 7f on both her starts at 2 yrs in 2011. The dam, a quite useful 7f (at 2 yrs) and 10f winner, is a half-sister to numerous winners. The second dam, Jaljuli (by Jalmood), a very useful 2-y-o 5f and 6f winner, was placed in the Cheveley Park, Rockfel, Lowther and Princess Margaret Stakes and is a half-sister to the top-class Coronation Stakes, Coral-Eclipse Stakes and Irish 1,000 Guineas winner Kooyonga. *"I trained the mother who won her first two starts. Even though this filly is by Halling she's very forward and very natural. She does everything easily and is a very likeable filly. She'll be a mile 2-y-o but I like what I see – she's nice".*

1447. RAY WARD (IRE) ★★★
b.c. Galileo – Kentucky Warbler (Spinning World). March 27. Second foal. €205,000Y. Goffs Orby. Stephen Hillen. The dam, a modest 12f winner, is a half-sister to 2 winners including the listed-placed Higher Love. The second dam, Dollar Bird (by Kris), a useful 2-y-o 8.2f winner and second in the listed 11.5f Oaks Trial, is a half-sister to 7 winners including the Group 2 12f King Edward VII Stakes winner Amfortas and the Group 3 10.5f Prix de Royaumont winner Legend Maker (herself dam of the 1,000 Guineas winner Virginia Waters). *"A horse that came in late, he hasn't done a lot yet but he has a likeable pedigree and he's a very attractive horse. We don't know much about him yet but whatever he's done has been pleasing".*

1448. ZEVA ★★★
b.f. Zamindar – Mennetou (Entrepreneur). March 21. Fifth foal. 180,000Y. Tattersalls October Book 1. Not sold. Half-sister to the Irish 3-y-o Group 3 9f winner Obama Rule (by Danehill Dancer). The dam is an unraced half-sister to 5 winners including the Prix de l'Arc de Triomphe winner Carnegie, the Group 2 10f Prix Guillaume d'Ornano winner Antisaar and the Group 3 St Simon Stakes winner Lake Erie. The second dam, Detroit (by Riverman), won the Prix de l'Arc de Triomphe and is a half-

sister to 7 winners including the Cheveley Park Stakes winner Durtal. *"She was very expensive but she's a very attractive filly. She hasn't done a massive amount because I see her as more of a seven furlong/mile filly later in the season. A belter to look at".*

1449. UNNAMED ★★★
ch.f. Kheleyf – Areyaam (Elusive Quality). February 6. Second foal. Half-sister to the quite useful 2011 2-y-o dual 6f winner My Lucky Liz (by Exceed And Excel). The dam, a fair maiden, was placed three times over 1m and is a half-sister to 2 winners. The second dam, Yanaseeni (by Trempolino), is an unplaced sister to the German-trained middle-distance dual Group 1 winner Germany (by Trempolino) and to 4 minor winners in the USA. *"I trained the half-sister My Lucky Liz last year who was as tough as old boots, a real hard-knocking filly. This filly looks very similar. She's probably a bigger, scopier type but she shows plenty of speed and I'm delighted with what I've seen so far. I should imagine she'll be starting out over six furlongs in May".*

1450. UNNAMED ★★
b.f. Oasis Dream – Ever Rigg (Dubai Destination). January 23. First foal. The dam, a fair 12f winner, is a half-sister several winners including the Irish 2-y-o 7f winner and listed placed Pietra Dura (herself dam of the US Grade 3 winner and Grade 1 second Turning Top). The second dam, Bianca Nera (by Salse), a smart 2-y-o winner of the Group 1 7f Moyglare Stud Stakes and the Group 2 6f Lowther Stakes, is half-sister to 4 winners including the very useful Group 1 Moyglare Stud Stakes second Hotelgenie Dot Com (herself dam of the dual Group 1 winner Simply Perfect). *"The mare wasn't particularly quick but she was beautifully bred and she cost a lot of money. This is a very attractive filly that won't be particularly early, I should imagine we'll see her later in the year but I like what I see so far".*

1451. UNNAMED ★★★ ̶B̶l̶a̶ ̶a̶ ̶a̶
b.c. Danehill Dancer – Gilded Vanity (Indian Ridge). May 3. Sixth foal. 68,000Y. Tattersalls October Book 2. Blandford Bloodstock. Brother to the Irish 2-y-o Group 3 6f placed maiden A Mind Of Her Own, closely related

to the fair 2011 2-y-o 5f winner Roman Seal (by Holy Roman Emperor) and half-brother to the fair 6f winner of 4 races (including at 2 yrs) Desert Icon (by Desert Style). The dam, a minor Irish 5f winner, is a sister to 2 winners including the smart 1m winner and Irish 2,000 Guineas second Fa-Eq and a half-sister to 4 winners including the smart listed 7.3f and 1m winner Corinium and the useful dual 5f winner (including at 2 yrs) Ellway Star. The second dam, Searching Star (by Rainbow Quest), a modest 6f (at 2 yrs) to 11.3f placed maiden, is a half-sister to 8 winners including the smart listed Blue Riband Trial winner Beldale Star. *"I had his half-brother Desert Icon for a short while and he won me two races. This is a very natural 2-y-o, slightly hot, but he shows up very well. He probably wouldn't want the ground too quick but I'll look forward to seeing him out in May".* ʳᵘⁿ ᵇʸ ʷⁱⁿ Bʳⁱᵍʰᵗᵒⁿ ᵇ ᶠ ᵐᵈⁿ

1452. UNNAMED ★★★
b.f. *Soviet Star – Gravieres (Saint Estephe).* April 4. Fifteenth foal. €36,000Y. Goffs Orby. Blandford Bloodstock. Half-sister to the Irish 9f winner and Group 1 National Stakes second Coliseum, to the quite useful 2-y-o 8.2f winner Ballerina Suprema, the Irish 2-y-o 1m and subsequent hurdles winner Homer, the fair 10f winner Bolero Again, the modest 4-y-o 10f all-weather winner Stroller, the minor Irish 11f winner Savieres (all by Sadler's Wells) and the fairly useful 1m to 11f winner Adare Manor (by Galileo). The dam won the Grade 1 Santa Ana Handicap and the Grade 3 California Jockey Club Handicap and is a half-sister to 9 winners. The second dam, Gay Spring (by Free Round), won at 2 yrs in France and is a half-sister to 4 winners. *"She shows plenty of speed and I would imagine she'd start at six furlongs. Very attractive, she's a little hot, but the first piece of work she did was very pleasing".* Wᵒⁿ ᵍˡ cˡˢ ᵐᵈⁿ ᵒⁿ ᵈᵉᵇᵘᵗ ᵇᶠ ⁿᵒʳᵐᵃˡ

1453. UNNAMED ★★
b.g. *Kheleyf – Pelican Key (Mujadil).* April 6. Second foal. 15,000Y. Doncaster Festival. Mark Crossman. Half-brother to the unplaced 2011 2-y-o Plum Bay (by Nayef). The dam, a quite useful 2-y-o 5f winner, is a half-sister to one winner. The second dam, Guana Bay (by Cadeaux Genereux), is an unraced sister to one winner and a half-sister to 5 winners including

the Group 2 winners Prince Sabo and Millyant, and the listed winner Bold Jessie (dam of the Group 2 Gimcrack Stakes winner Abou Zouz). *"I trained the dam and she was quite quick – she won first time out at Windsor. He's been gelded already which is probably no bad thing and he's a horse for the early part of the season. I don't know how good he is, but he's certainly no mug".*

1454. UNNAMED ★★
b.f. *Authorized – Princess Danah (Danehill).* April 7. Second foal. The dam, a modest 9f winner, is a half-sister to numerous winners including the very useful dual 1m winner Kismah. The second dam, Thaidah (Vice Regent), was a useful winner from 5f (at 2yrs) to 7f and is a half-sister to the champion US 2-y-o Devil's Bag and to the top-class filly Glorious Song (the dam of Singspiel and Rahy). *"A neat filly, not overly big, her pedigree suggests a staying type but she shows up remarkably well at this time of the year. I would imagine she'd be starting at seven furlongs and she's far more forward than I'd expected".*

TOMMY STACK

1455. ADDICTEDTOPROGRESS (IRE) ★★★
b.f. *Holy Roman Emperor – Farthingale (Nashwan).* March 27. Fifth foal. €80,000Y. Goffs Orby. Cormac McCormack. Closely related to the dual listed winner over 7f and 1m and Group 3 second Lisvale (by Danehill Dancer). The dam, placed once over 12f in Ireland, is a half-sister to the winner and Group 2 Richmond Stakes third Cedarberg. The second dam, Crinolette (by Sadler's Wells), ran once unplaced and is a half-sister to the triple Group 3 winner Desert Style. *"A good-moving filly, she should make up into a 2-y-o but it'll more in the middle of the summer over six/ seven furlongs. She seems quite nice".*

1456. ALMANAC ★★★
b.c. *Haatef – Openness (Grand Lodge).* February 26. Third foal. £40,000Y. Doncaster Premier. C McCormack. The dam is an unraced half-sister to 3 winners including the Group 1 1m Coronation Stakes winner Balisada (herself the dam of a listed winner). The second dam, Balisada (by Lomond), a modest 3-y-o 1m winner, is a sister to Inchmurrin (winner of the

Child Stakes and herself dam of the very smart and tough colt Inchinor), closely related to the very useful 1m winner Guest Artiste and a half-sister to 6 winners including the Mill Reef Stakes winner Welney. *"He'll be racing in May, he'll want good ground and he's a strong colt that seems to go OK".*

1457. ASTER CASS (IRE) ★★

b.f. Duke Of Marmalade – Mayfair Lane (Sadler's Wells). March 25. First foal. The dam is an unplaced sister to 4 winners including the Irish 1m (at 2 yrs), 12f and German listed 14f winner and French dual Group 2 placed Poseidon Adventure and the Irish 2-y-o 1m winner and listed-placed Kisses For Me. The second dam, Fanny Cerrito (by Gulch), is an unraced half-sister to 7 winners including the US stakes winners Al Sabin and Sabina. *"She's not over-big so despite her middle-distance pedigree she'll definitely make a 2-y-o. More of a seven furlong/mile filly".*

1458. CLANCY AVENUE ★★★★

b.c. Henrythenavigator – Saintly Speech (Southern Halo). February 20. Eighth foal. 100,000Y. Tattersalls October Book 1. Cormac McCormack. Half-brother to the fairly useful 7f (at 2 yrs) and 1m winner Pure Illusion (by Danehill) and to the minor French 3-y-o winner Well Spoken (by Sadler's Wells and herself the dam of the Irish Group 3 winner Chrysanthemum). The dam won 2 races including the Group 3 6f Princess Margaret Stakes and is a half-sister to 5 winners including the Group 3 7f Prix du Calvados winner Woodland Melody and the good Japanese 10f winner Maruka Diesis. The second dam, Eloquent Minister (by Deputy Minister), a very useful sprint winner of 2 listed events at Doncaster and in Ireland, also won in the USA and is a half-sister to 8 winners including the dam of the US Grade 2 winner The Tender Track. *"A fine, big, strong horse. He looks like a horse that won't be short of speed and he goes well, so look out for him".*

1459. DYLANBARU (IRE) ★★★

b.c. Footstepsinthesand – Nubar Lady (Danetime). March 20. First foal. The dam, a fairly useful Irish 2-y-o dual 5f winner, was listed-placed over 5f and is a half-sister to one

winner. The second dam, Sarah Stokes (by Brief Truce), a fair 3-y-o 6f winner, is a half-sister to 5 winners including the very useful Group 3 5f Curragh Stakes and Group 3 5f Molecomb Stakes winner Almaty. *"He finished fourth at the Curragh on his debut and he'll have another run before your book comes out. He's like his mother as far as the trip is concerned – I don't think he'll get further than five, maybe six furlongs. Hopefully he'll grow up from his first run and he'll win".*

1460. GMAC (IRE) ★★

b.br.c. Excellent Art – Kafayef (Secreto). April 27. 19,000Y. Tattersalls October Book 2. C McCormack. Half-brother to the fairly useful 12f to 2m winner of 4 races Blimey O'Riley (by Kalanisi), to the Italian winner at 2 and 3 yrs and listed-placed Persian Filly (by Persian Bold), the French 2-y-o winner and listed-placed Ascot Dream (by Pennekamp), the fairly useful 2-y-o 7f winner Almaviva (by Grand Lodge), the fair 12f and hurdles winner Non Dom (by Hawk Wing), the modest 6f winner Gardrum (by Lycius) and a winner over hurdles by Spinning World. The dam is an unplaced half-sister to 10 winners including 3 stakes winners. The second dam, Sham Street (by Sham), a minor winner of 4 races in the USA, is a sister to the Italian Group 3 winner Stramusc and a half-sister to the dam of the Group 1 July Cup winner and champion sprinter Sakhee's Secret. *"A late April foal, he's a good mover that's done well of late, but again he's probably one we'll introduce later on".*

1461. GREAT MINDS (IRE) ★★★

ch.c. Bahamian Bounty – Raja (Pivotal). February 2. First foal. 54,000Y. Tattersalls October Book 2. C McCormack. The dam, a fairly useful Irish and French 6f winner of 4 races (including at 2 yrs), is a half-sister to 11 winners including the Group 1 6f Haydock Park Sprint Cup and Group 3 5f Palace House Stakes winner Pipalong (by Pips Pride and herself dam of the Group 3 winner Walk On Bye), the Group 2 5f Flying Childers Stakes second China Eyes, the Group 3 6f placed 2-y-o Silver Shoon and the 2-y-o 6f listed winner Out Of Africa. The second dam, Limpopo (by Green Desert), a poor 5f placed 2-y-o, is a half-sister to 8 winners here and abroad. *"He's just starting* to grow a little bit but he's a good mover that'll probably take a bit more time than his pedigree would suggest. He'll be racing by the summer and he'll be a sprinter like the rest of the family".

1462. MISCHIEF N MAYHEM ★★★

b.f. Nayef – Mail The Desert (Desert Prince). April 6. Sixth foal. £70,000Y. Doncaster Premier. C McCormack. Half-sister to the 2011 2-y-o winner abroad Mail Princess, to the fair 1m winner Al Muthanaa (both by Pivotal) and the modest 1m winner of 5 races Postman (by Dr Fong). The dam, winner of the Group 1 7f Moyglare Stud Stakes and third in the Coronation Stakes, is a half-sister to 2 winners. The second dam, Mail Boat (by Formidable), is an unraced half-sister to 4 winners including the Group 3 Chester Vase winner and St Leger third Dry Dock. "A good-moving filly, she's quite forward and will probably want fastish ground. I see her starting off over six furlongs in mid-May".

1463. MISTER AVIATION (IRE) ★★★★

b.c. Montjeu – Gamra (Green Desert). February 3. Fourth foal. 90,000Y. Tattersalls October Book 1. Bobby O'Ryan. Brother to the quite useful Irish 12f winner Boulay and half-brother to the 2-y-o listed 5f winner and Group 3 Firth Of Clyde Stakes second Roxan (by Rock Of Gibraltar). The dam, a fair 3-y-o 1m winner, is a full or half-sister to 6 winners including the very smart Group 2 9.7f Prix Dollar winner Wiorno and the very smart Trusthouse Forte Mile, Gimcrack Stakes and Earl of Sefton Stakes winner Reprimand. The second dam, Just You Wait (by Nonoalco), is an unraced half-sister to 7 winners including the dam of the Group winners Ozone Friendly, Ardkinglass and Soft Currency. "A pretty mature horse for a Montjeu, he's a good mover and quite strong. He'll definitely make a 2-y-o and I think he's going to want seven furlongs. We won't have to wait too long for him and he's one to look out for".

1464. OVERLAND EXPRESS (IRE) ★★★★

b.f. Dylan Thomas – No Way (Rainbows For Life). April 17. Seventh foal. €80,000Y. Goffs Orby. Cormac McCormack. Half-sister to the smart Irish 2-y-o listed 7f and 5-y-o US Grade 2 1m winner Ryehill Dreamer (by Catcher In

The Rye) and to the French 3-y-o and hurdles winner Fair Attitude (by King's Theatre). The dam, a French 3-y-o 9f winner, is a sister to the French listed winner No Lies and a half-sister to 7 winners including the French 2,000 Guineas winner No Pass No Sale and the Group 3 winner Once In My Life. The second dam, No Disgrace (by Djakao), won at 2 yrs in France and was Group 3 placed and is a half-sister to 3 winners. "She's a fine, big, good-looking filly. She moves quite well and seems very straightforward. She'll probably want a bit of a trip, but hopefully she should be quite nice and I'd watch out for her".

1465. PUSSYCAT LIPS (IRE) ★★★

b.f. Holy Roman Emperor – On The Nile (Sadler's Wells). March 8. Seventh foal. £6,000Y. Doncaster Premier. John O'Byrne. Sister to the modest 2011 7f placed Emperors Pearl and closely related to the fairly useful 1m and 10f winner Tommy Toogood (by Danehill). The dam, an Irish 2-y-o listed 9f winner, is a sister to the Irish listed 1m winner In The Limelight, closely related to the Singapore Gold Cup and Gran Premio del Jockey Club winner Kutub and a half-sister to 3 winners. The second dam, Minnie Habit (by Habitat), an Irish 4-y-o 9f winner, is closely related to the dual sprint Group 3 winner Bermuda Classic (herself dam of the Coronation Stakes winner Shake The Yoke) and a half-sister to 6 winners. "She'll be racing in late May over six furlongs and she seems to go quite nicely at the minute. She was very cheap, all things considered". TRAINERS' BARGAIN BUY

1466. SPEAK SLOWLY ★★

ch.f. Dubawi – Blond Moment (Affirmed). March 8. Eight living foal. 10,000Y. Tattersalls October Book 2. C McCormack. Half-sister to the fair 7f (at 2 yrs) and 1m winner Dancer's Legacy (by Nayef) and to 3 minor winners in the USA by Dynaformer, El Prado and Mt. Livermore. The dam, a US stakes winner at 2 yrs, is a half-sister to 11 winners including 2 stakes-placed horses in the USA. The second dam, Nijinsky's Beauty (by Nijinsky), is an unraced sister to the US Grade 1 winner Nijinsky's Secret. "A hardy little filly, I can see her being out in May and I'm quite happy with her so far. She'll start off over six furlongs but she'll probably want seven".

1467. YOUR PAL TAL ★★★

b.c. Dark Angel – Good Health (Magic Ring).
February 24. Fourth foal. 45,000Y. Tattersalls
October Book 2. C McCormack. Half-brother
to the quite useful 2-y-o 5f and 6f winner of 4
races The Magic Of Rio (by Captain Rio) and to
the poor 6f winner Amoureuse (by Needwood
Blade). The dam was a fair 2-y-o 5f winner.
The second dam, Fiddling (by Music Boy), won
once at 3 yrs and is a half-sister to 4 winners
including the Group 2 and Group 3 placed
sprinter Clantime. *"A big, strong horse and
whatever we've done with him so far he's done
it quite nicely. He'll start off at five furlongs and
probably wouldn't get beyond six".*

1468. UNNAMED ★★

*br.c. Rock Of Gibraltar – Almaaseh (Dancing
Brave).* May 9. Thirteenth living foal. €65,000Y.
Tattersalls Ireland. John O'Byrne. Half-brother to
8 winners including the promising 2011 2-y-o
1m winner Plutorius (by Holy Roman Emperor),
the very useful Group 3 5f Curragh Stakes and
Group 3 5f Molecomb Stakes winner Almaty
(by Dancing Dissident), the very useful triple
1m winner Race (by Oratorio), the useful 10f
winner and listed-placed Salee (by Caerleon)
and the fairly useful 7f (at 2 yrs) to 10f winner
of 9 races Impeller (by Polish Precedent). The
dam, placed once over 6f at 3 yrs, is a half-sister
to 8 winners including Haafhd (2,000 Guineas
and Champion Stakes) and Munir (Group 2
Challenge Stakes) and to the unraced dam of
Gladiatorus (Group 1 Dubai Duty Free Stakes).
The second dam, Al Bahathri (by Blushing
Groom), won the Irish 1,000 Guineas and is a
half-sister to the US Grade 2 winner Geraldine's
Store and to the dam of the US Grade 1 winner
Spanish Fern. *"A late foal, he's obviously going
to take a bit of time but he's a fine, big colt and
a good mover. He'll run as a 2-y-o but it won't
be until later on".*

1469. UNNAMED ★★

b.f. Galileo – Banquise (Last Tycoon). April 2.
Tenth foal. Sister to Shada, placed third over 7f
on her only start at 2 yrs in 2011 and to the
2-y-o 7f winner and Group 2 Blandford Stakes
third Robin Hood, closely related to the minor
Irish 10f winner Snow Lord (by Sadler's Wells)
and half-sister to 3 winners including the fairly
useful Irish dual 9f and subsequent US stakes

winner Cold Cold Woman (by Machiavellian).
The dam won over 2m in France and is a half-
sister to 8 winners including the dual Group 2
winner Modhish, the Group 2 winner and Irish
Oaks second Russian Snows and the Group 3
winner Truly Special. The second dam, Arctique
Royale (by Royal And Regal), won the Irish
1,000 Guineas and the Moyglare Stud Stakes
and is a half-sister to the dam of the top-class
middle-distance stayer Ardross. *"Quite a tall
filly, she'll probably take a bit of time but she
seems to be a good mover for what she's done
so far and we're quite happy with her at the
minute. One for the second half of the year".*

1470. UNNAMED ★★

b.c. Jeremy – Birdsong (Dolphin Street). April
12. Seventh foal. €35,000Y. Goffs Orby. John
O'Byrne. Half-brother to the fairly useful
2-y-o dual 5f winner Mubaashir, to the fair 10f
winner Mecox Bay (both by Noverre) and the
minor French 1m winner of 4 races Filimeala
(by Pennekamp). The dam, a fair dual 6f winner
at 3 yrs, is a half-sister to 7 winners including
the 2-y-o listed 6f Sweet Solera Stakes winner
Lucayan Princess (herself the dam of four
Group winners including the Group 1 winners
Luso and Warrsan). The second dam, Gay
France (by Sir Gaylord), a fairly useful 2-y-o 6f
winner, is a half-sister to 10 winners including
the dam of the Group 1 winner and sire
Common Grounds. *"He's quite a nice, biggish
horse. He seems to go OK for what he's done
at the minute and he'll probably be one for the
second half of the year".*

1471. UNNAMED ★★★★

*b.f. Duke Of Marmalade – Higher Love
(Sadler's Wells).* April 19. Fourth foal. 125,000Y.
Tattersalls October Book 1. John O'Byrne. Half-
sister to the fair 1m winner Frances Stuart (by
King's Best). The dam, a fairly useful 9.7f winner,
was second in the listed Cheshire Oaks and is a
half-sister to 2 winners. The second dam, Dollar
Bird (by Kris), a useful 2-y-o 8.2f winner and
second in the listed 11.5f Oaks Trial, is a half-
sister to 7 winners including the Group 2 12f
King Edward VII Stakes winner Amfortas and
the Group 3 10.5f Prix de Royaumont winner
Legend Maker (dam of the 1,000 Guineas
winner Virginia Waters). *"A fine, big, good-
looking filly and a very good mover. Probably*

one for the second half of the year over seven furlongs, she's a very nice filly".

1472. UNNAMED ★★★

b.f. Oratorio – Holly Blue (Bluebird). April 17. Eighth foal. €30,000Y. Goffs Orby. Not sold. Closely related to the Irish 2-y-o and subsequent South African triple Group 2 winner Gibraltar Blue (by Rock Of Gibraltar) and half-sister to 3 minor winners including one over jumps by Dr Fong. The dam, a useful listed 1m winner, is a half-sister to 6 minor winners. The second dam, Nettle (by Kris), a useful listed 7f winner, is a half-sister to 5 winners. *"A good moving filly that looks to be quite sharpish and I imagine she won't take too long to come to hand".*

1473. UNNAMED ★★★

b.f. Shamardal – Nassma (Sadler's Wells). April 16. Fourteenth foal. €48,000Y. Goffs Orby. Not sold. Half-sister to the useful 2011 Irish 2-y-o 7f and listed 1m placed Lady Wingshot (by Lawman), to the 2-y-o listed 5f Dragon Stakes and dual German listed winner and Group 2 5f Flying Childers Stakes second Bahama Mama (by Invincible Spirit), the useful 2-y-o 6f and 7f and subsequent UAE winner Calchas (by Warning), the quite useful 9f and 10f winner Traprain (by Mark Of Esteem), the quite useful 9f winner Dansker (by Darshaan), the moderate 12f winner Harlequinn Danseur (by Noverre) and two winners abroad by Indian Ridge and Marju. The dam, a listed middle-distance winner of 2 races, is a half-sister to 5 minor winners. The second dam, Pretoria (by Habitat), a useful 7f (at 2 yrs) and listed 10f winner (in Italy), was Group 3 placed in Italy and is a half-sister to 4 winners including Ivanka (Group 1 Fillies' Mile). *"A strong filly, she's probably one for mid-summer and I see her a sprinting type 2-y-o. She seems to move well and I'm quite happy with her at the minute".*

SIR MICHAEL STOUTE

1474. AVIETTA (IRE)

gr.f. Dalakhani – Alabastrine (Green Desert). April 21. Sixth foal. 340,000Y. Tattersalls October Book 1. Cheveley Park Stud. Half-sister to Albaspina (by Selkirk), a winner over 7f on her only start at 2 yrs in 2011 and to the

useful Irish 7.5f (at 2 yrs) and 9f winner Hail Caesar (by Montjeu). The dam, placed over 7f at 2 yrs, is a half-sister to 8 winners including the Nassau Stakes and Sun Chariot Stakes winner Last Second (dam of the French 2,000 Guineas winner Aussie Rules), the Doncaster Cup winner Alleluia (dam of the Prix Royal-Oak winner Allegretto), the Moyglare Stud Stakes third Alouette (dam of the dual Champion Stakes winner Alborada and the triple German Group 1 winner Albanova) and to the placed dam of the Group 1 winners Yesterday and Quarter Moon. The second dam, Alruccaba (by Crystal Palace), a quite useful 2-y-o 6f winner, is out of a half-sister to the dams of Aliysa and Nishapour.

1475. BEDOUIN INVADER (IRE) ♠

b.c. Oasis Dream – Hovering (In The Wings). March 16. Second foal. €200,000Y. Goffs Orby. Charlie Gordon-Watson. The dam, a fairly useful Irish 1m and hurdles winner, was listed placed and is a half-sister to 2 winners. The second dam, Orlena (by Gone West), a minor 2-y-o 7f winner in France, is a half-sister to 6 winners including the listed winner and 1,000 Guineas third Vista Bella.

1476. DUKE COSIMO

ch.c. Pivotal – Nannina (Medicean). March 31. Second foal. 130,000Y. Tattersalls October Book 1. Not sold. Brother to the quite useful 2011 2-y-o 6f winner Duke Of Firenze. The dam, winner of the Group 1 Fillies' Mile and the Group 1 1m Coronation Stakes, is a half-sister to 5 winners. The second dam, Hill Hopper (by Danehill), a useful winner of 4 races including the Group 3 7f Criterion Stakes, is a half-sister to 5 winners including the Australian Grade 1 winner Water Boatman.

1477. ENOBLED

b.c. Dansili – Peeress (Pivotal). May 2. Third foal. Half-brother to Ladyship (by Pivotal), placed second over 6f on both her starts at 2 yrs in 2011. The dam, a very smart winner of 7 races including the Group 1 1m Lockinge Stakes and the Group 1 1m Sun Chariot Stakes, is a half-sister to 2 winners. The second dam, Noble One (by Primo Dominie), a useful dual 5f winner, is a full or half-sister to 5 winners.

1478. FANTASY IN BLUE ♠

b.f. Galileo – Blue Symphony (Darshaan). April 17. Sixth foal. 410,000Y. Tattersalls October Book 1. Cheveley Park Stud. Closely related to the very smart Group 3 7f Prestige Stakes (at 2 yrs), Group 3 Nell Gwyn Stakes and US Grade 3 winner and Group/Grade 1 placed Fantasia (by Sadler's Wells) and to the useful Group 3 12f Give Thanks Stakes winner Pink Symphony (by Montjeu) and half-sister to the fair 2-y-o 7f winner Blue Rhapsody (by Cape Cross). The dam, a fair 10f winner, is a half-sister to one winner. The second dam, Blue Duster (by Danzig), winner of the Group 1 6f Cheveley Park Stakes, the Group 3 6f Princess Margaret Stakes and the Group 3 5f Queen Mary Stakes, is a sister to the smart Group 1 6f Middle Park Stakes and Group 2 7f Challenge Stakes winner Zieten and a half-sister to 9 winners.

1479. HILLSTAR

b.c. Danehill Dancer – Crystal Star (Mark Of Esteem). February 22. Fifth foal. Half-brother to the very smart dual Group 2 12f Pride Stakes, Group 2 12f Princess Of Wales's Stakes and Group 3 10.3f Middleton Stakes winner Crystal Capella (by Cape Cross) and to the fairly useful 1m and 10f winner Sandor (by Fantastic Light). The dam, winner of the listed Radley Stakes and second in the Group 3 Fred Darling Stakes, is a half-sister to 6 winners. The second dam, Crystal Cavern (by Be My Guest), a fairly useful 2-y-o 7f winner here and subsequently a dual winner in Canada, is a half-sister to 5 winners including the French 1,000 Guineas winner Rose Gypsy.

1480. INTEGRAL

b.f. Dalakhani – Echelon (Danehill). March 13. Second foal. The dam won the Group 1 1m Matron Stakes, the Group 2 Celebration Mile and four Group 3 events and is a half-sister to the dual Group 2 1m Celebration Mile winner Chic. The second dam, Exclusive (Polar Falcon) winner of the Group 1 1m Coronation Stakes, is a half-sister to the 2,000 Guineas winner and Derby fourth Entrepreneur, the smart Cheshire Oaks winner and Epsom Oaks second Dance a Dream, the very useful middle-distance listed winner Sadler's Image and the useful French 2-y-o listed 7f winner Irish Order.

1481. INTRINSIC

b.c. Oasis Dream – Infallible (Pivotal). April 2. First foal. The dam, a very smart 7f (at 2 yrs) and Group 3 7f Nell Gwyn Stakes winner, was second in the Coronation Stakes and the Falmouth Stakes and is a full or half-sister to 3 winners. The second dam, Irresistible (by Cadeaux Genereux), was a fairly useful 5f (at 2 yrs) and listed 6f winner and is a half-sister to one winner.

1482. JUST DARCY

b.f. Danehill Dancer – Jane Austen (Galileo). January 20. First foal. 175,000Y. Tattersalls October Book 1. Not sold. The dam, a useful Irish listed 12f winner, is a sister to the listed-placed winner Acapulco and a half-sister to 3 winners. The second dam, Harasava (by Darshaan), is an unraced half-sister to 5 winners.

1483. KING'S REQUEST (IRE)

ch.c. New Approach – Palace Weekend (Seattle Dancer). February 5. Ninth foal. €90,000Y. Goffs Orby. Charlie Gordon-Watson. Half-brother to 6 winners including the 2-y-o Group 1 Racing Post Trophy winner Palace Episode (by Machiavellian) and to the dam of the US Grade 2 winner Laughing Lashes. The dam is an unraced half-sister to the Grade 2 Futurity winner Tejano Run and the Grade 2 Jersey Derby winner and Group 2 Royal Lodge Stakes second More Royal. The second dam, Royal Run (by Wavering Monarch), is an unraced half-sister to three US Graded stakes winners.

1484. LOVE MAGIC

b.f. Dansili – Magical Romance (Barathea). February 24. Third foal. Sister to the quite useful 10f winner Dean Swift. The dam, a 2-y-o Group 1 6f Cheveley Park Stakes winner, is a sister to the fairly useful 2-y-o 7f winner and subsequent Canadian Grade 3 placed Saree and closely related to the Oaks, Irish Oaks and Yorkshire Oaks winner Alexandrova and the smart listed 2-y-o 1m winner and Group 2 1m Beresford Stakes third Masterofthehorse. The second dam, Shouk (by Shirley Heights), a quite useful 10.5f winner, is closely related to the listed winner and Group 3 Park Hill Stakes third Puce and a half-sister to 6 winners.

1485. MADAME VESTRIS (IRE)

ch.f. Galileo – Mrs Lindsay (Theatrical). February 26. First foal. 350,000Y. Tattersalls October Book 1. Cheveley Park Stud. The dam won 4 races at 3 yrs in France and Canada including the Group 1 Prix Vermeille and the Grade 1 E P Taylor Stakes and is a half-sister to one winner. The second dam, Vole Vole Monamour (by Woodman), won once at 3 yrs in France.

1486. MUTAJALLY

b.c. Teofilo – Dhelaal (Green Desert). March 31. Fourth foal. Half-brother to the 2,000 Guineas and Prix Jacques le Marois winner Makfi (by Dubawi). The dam is an unraced half-sister to 7 winners including the champion 2-y-o Alhaarth, winner of the Dewhurst Stakes, the Laurent Perrier Champagne Stakes, the Prix Dollar, the Budweiser American Bowl International Stakes and the Prix du Rond-Point and the very useful 2-y-o Group 3 7f Prix du Calvados winner Green Pola. The second dam, Irish Valley (by Irish River), is an unplaced half-sister to 10 winners, notably the Observer Gold Cup, French 2,000 Guineas and 10.5f Prix Lupin winner and good sire Green Dancer, the US Grade 3 winner Ercolano and the US Graded stakes winner Val Danseur.

1487. NAZYM (IRE)

ch.f. Galileo – Brigid (Irish River). February 1. Eleventh foal. 1,700,000Y. Tattersalls October Book 1. Charlie Gordon-Watson. Closely related to the Group 1 7f Moyglare Stud Stakes winner Sequoyah (herself dam of the multiple Group 1 winner Henrythenavigator), to the 2-y-o Group 1 Fillies' Mile winner Listen, the fairly useful 2-y-o 1m winner Purple Heart and the fair 7f winner Clara Bow (all by Sadler's Wells) and half-sister to the Irish listed 5.6f winner and Group 3 7f placed Oyster Catcher (by Bluebird). The dam, a minor French 3-y-o 1m winner, is a sister to 2 winners including the French listed 7f winner Or Vision (herself dam of the Group/Grade 1 winners Dolphin Street, Insight and Saffron Walden) and a half-sister to 5 winners. The second dam, Luv Luvin' (by Raise a Native), won 2 races in the USA and was stakes-placed.

1488. PERSEPOLIS (IRE) ♠

b.c. Dansili – La Persiana (Daylami). April 23. Fourth foal. 55,000Y. Tattersalls October Book 1. John Warren. Half-brother to the quite useful 7f (at 2 yrs) and 12f winner Qushchi (by Encosta De Lago). The dam, a very useful dual listed 10f winner, is a half-sister to 7 winners including the champion 2-y-o Grand Lodge (Group 1 7f Dewhurst Stakes and Group 1 1m St James's Palace Stakes winner) and the useful 1m listed winner Papabile. The second dam, La Papagena (by Habitat), is an unraced half-sister to 7 winners including the listed winners Lost Chord and Eagling.

1489. PIRA PALACE (IRE) ♠

b.f. Acclamation – Takrice (Cadeaux Genereux). March 7. Third foal. €110,000Y. Goffs Orby. Charlie Gordon-Watson. Half-sister to the fair 2-y-o 6f winner Dynamo Dane (by Danehill Dancer) and the minor Italian 4-y-o winner Mascagni (by Galileo). The dam, a 2-y-o 7f winner, was third in the Group 3 Killavullen Stakes. The second dam, Hasanat (by Night Shift), won over 7f (at 2 yrs) and 9f and was third in the Group 3 Concorde Stakes.

gentle debut 4th 6f cl 5 rh

1490. QAREENAH (USA)   *Kempton*

b.f. Arch – Princess Kris (Kris). February 5. Tenth foal. €340,000Y. Goffs Orby. Shadwell Estate Co. Sister to the US Grade 1 11f winner Prince Arch and to the minor US winner of 4 races Art Crafty and half-sister to the 2-y-o Group 1 National Stakes winner Kingsfort (by War Chant). The dam, a quite useful 3-y-o 1m winner, is half-sister to 8 winners including the Group 3 May Hill Stakes winner Intimate Guest and the dam of the US Grade 1 winner Luas Line. The second dam, As You Desire Me (by Kalamoun), won 2 listed events in France over 7.5f and 1m and is a half-sister to 7 winners including the Group 2 King Edward VII Stakes winner Classic Example. (Hamdan Al Maktoum).

1491. RAUSHAN (IRE)

gr.f. Dalakhani – Chiang Mai (Sadler's Wells). February 20. Fifth foal. 400,000Y. Tattersalls October Book 1. Charlie Gordon-Watson. Sister to the Group 1 Pretty Polly Stakes and Group 2 Blandford Stakes winner Chinese White. The dam won the Group 3 12f Blandford Stakes and is a half-sister to 9 winners including the very smart Group 1 10.5f Prix de Diane winner Rafha (the dam 4 stakes winners including Invincible Spirit). The second dam, Eljazzi (by Artaius), a fairly useful 2-y-o 7f winner, is a half-sister to the high-class miler Pitcairn and the Blandford Stakes winner Valley Forge.

1492. RUN WITH PRIDE (IRE)

b.c. Invincible Spirit – Zibilene (Rainbow Quest). May 14. Eighth foal. 200,000Y. Tattersalls October Book 1. Charlie Gordon-Watson. Brother to Zimira, a winner over 1m on his only start at 2 yrs in 2011 and half-brother to the smart 2-y-o 7f winner and Irish 2,000 Guineas third Oracle (by Danehill Dancer), the French 6f (at 2 yrs) and 7.5f winner and Group 2 1m third Mathematician (by Machiavellian) and the quite useful 10f winner Aryaamm (by Galileo and herself dam of the 2-y-o Group 2 winner Saamidd). The dam, a useful 12f winner and listed-placed over 10f, is a half-sister to 7 winners including the Breeders Cup Mile, Irish 2,000 Guineas and Queen Anne Stakes winner Barathea, the Fillies Mile and Irish 1,000 Guineas winner Gossamer and the dams of the Group 2 winners Armure and Coretta. The second dam, Brocade (by Habitat), won 5 races including the Group 1 7f Prix de la Foret and is a half-sister to 7 winners.

1493. RUSSIAN REALM

b.c. Dansili – Russian Rhythm (Kingmambo). February 9. Fourth foal. Half-brother to the fairly useful 7f winner and listed 1m placed Safina (by Pivotal). The dam won the 1,000 Guineas, Coronation Stakes, Nassau Stakes and Lockinge Stakes and is a half-sister to several winners including the 2-y-o Group 2 1m Royal Lodge Stakes winner Perfectperformance. The second dam, Balistroika (Nijinsky), is an unraced half-sister to numerous winners including Park Appeal (winner of the Cheveley Park Stakes and the Moyglare Stud Stakes and the dam of Cape Cross), Alydaress (Irish Oaks) and Desirable (winner of the Cheveley Park Stakes and the dam of Shadayid). (Cheveley Park Stud).

1494. SHADES OF SILVER ♠

b.c. Dansili – Silver Pivotal (Pivotal). February 18. First foal. 260,000Y. Tattersalls October Book 1. Charlie Gordon-Watson. The dam, a listed 1m winner of 3 races, was second in the Group 3 Winter Derby. The second dam, Silver Colours (by Silver Hawk), a useful 2-y-o

listed 1m winner, is a half-sister to 4 winners including the Japanese Grade 2 winner God Of Chance and to the unraced dam of the triple Group 2 winner Strong Suit.

1495. TELESCOPE (IRE) ♠

b.c. Galileo – Velouette (Darshaan). January 25. Fourth foal. Brother to Circumstances, unplaced in two starts at 2 yrs in Ireland in 2011. The dam is an unraced half-sister to 4 winners including the Group 2 10.5f Dante Stakes and Group 3 10f Select Stakes winner Moon Ballad. The second dam, Velvet Moon (by Shaadi), a very useful Group 2 6f Lowther Stakes and listed 10f winner, is a half-sister to the dual Group 1 winner Central Park. (Highclere Thoroughbred Racing – Wavertree).

1496. WAILA

ch.f. Notnowcato – Crystal Cavern (Be My Guest). February 5. Sister to the fair 2011 2-y-o 7f winner Mr Maynard and half-sister to the useful 2-y-o listed 7f Radley Stakes winner and Group 3 Fred Darling Stakes second Crystal Star, to the fair 2-y-o 1m winner True Dream (both by Mark Of Esteem), the fairly useful 1m and 12f winner The Fonz (by Oasis Dream), the Irish 4-y-o 7f to 8.5f winner of 4 races Christavelli (by Machiavellian), the fair 2-y-o 1m winner True Dream (by Mark Of Esteem), the fair 12f and hurdles winner E Major (by Singspiel) and the French 10f winner Vracca (by Vettori). The dam, a fairly useful 2-y-o 7f winner here and subsequently a dual winner in Canada, is a half-sister to 6 winners including the French 1,000 Guineas winner Rose Gypsy. The second dam, Krisalya (by Kris), a fairly useful 10.4f winner, is a half-sister to 12 winners including the high-class 9.3f Prix d'Ispahan winner Sasuru and the high-class Challenge Stakes and Jersey Stakes winner Sally Rous.

1497. WATCHABLE

ch.c. Pivotal – Irresistible (Cadeaux Genereux). March 23. Sixth foal. Brother to the fair 2011 2-y-o 7f winner New Decade, to the very smart 7f (at 2 yrs) and Group 3 7f Nell Gwyn Stakes winner and Coronation Stakes and Falmouth Stakes second Infallible and the quite useful 2-y-o 7f winner Thrill and closely related to the fairly useful 7f and 1m winner Chilled (by Iceman). The dam was a fairly useful 5f (at 2 yrs) and listed 6f winner and is a half-sister to one winner. The second dam, Polish Romance (by Danzig), a minor 7f winner in the USA, is a sister to the US stakes winner Polish Love. (Cheveley Park Stud).

1498. WEST OF THE MOON

ch.f. Pivotal – Canda (Storm Cat). March 19. Fourth foal. Sister to the fair 2011 2-y-o 7f winner Cantal and half-sister to the 2-y-o Group 3 7f winner Horris Hill Stakes winner and Group 1 St James's Palace Stakes fourth Evasive (by Elusive Quality). The dam is an unraced half-sister to the 2-y-o Group 3 5.5f Prix d'Arenburg winner Moon Driver and the US winner and Grade 2 Californian Stakes second Mojave Moon. The second dam, East Of The Moon (by Private Account), was a high-class winner of the French 1,000 Guineas, the Prix de Diane and the Prix Jacques le Marois and is a half-sister to the top class miler and sire Kingmambo and to the smart Miesque's Son. (Cheveley Park Stud).

1499. UNNAMED

b.c. Oasis Dream – Arrive (Kahyasi). February 27. Brother to the very smart Group 3 6f Princess Margaret Stakes and Group 3 7f Oak Tree Stakes winner Visit and to the quite useful 2-y-o 7f winner Revered and half-brother to the very smart Group 1 10f Pretty Polly Stakes winner Promising Lead (by Danehill). The dam, a very useful 10f (at 2 yrs) and listed 13.8f winner, is a half-sister to the 2-y-o 5f winner (stayed 1m) Hasili (herself dam of the top-class performers Banks Hill, Heat Haze, Cacique, Intercontinental, Champs Elysees and Dansili). The second dam, Kerali (by High Line), a quite useful 7f winner, is a half-sister to the Group 3 6f July Stakes winner Bold Fact and the Group 1 Nunthorpe Stakes winner So Factual. (Khalid Abdulla).

1500. UNNAMED

b.f. Galileo – Butterfly Cove (Storm Cat). April 19. Fifth foal. Sister to the Group 1 Moyglare Stud Stakes, Prix Marcel Boussac, Irish 1,000 Guineas and Pretty Polly Stakes winner Misty For Me and to the promising 2011 2-y-o 7f winner Twirl. The dam is an unraced sister to the Irish 1,000 Guineas Trial winner Kamarinskaya and a half-sister to the champion 2-y-o colt

Fasliyev. The second dam, Mr P's Princess (by Mr Prospector), is an unraced half-sister to the US Grade 1 winners Menifee and Desert Wine.

1501. UNNAMED

b.c. First Defence – Intercontinental (Danehill). February 10. Third foal. Half-brother to the fair triple 9f winner So Wise (by Elusive Quality). The dam, winner of Grade 1 Matriarch Stakes and the Grade 1 Filly & Mare Turf, is a sister to the triple Group/Grade 1 winners Banks Hill and Champs Elysees, the dual Group 1 winner Cacique and the Group 2 winner and good sire Dansili and closely related to the Grade 1 Matriarch Stakes and Grade 1 Beverly D Stakes winner Heat Haze. The second dam, Hasili (by Kahyasi), won over 5f at 2 yrs and stayed a mile. (Khalid Abdulla).

1502. UNNAMED

b.c. Empire Maker – Promising Lead (Danehill). February 12. First foal. The dam, a very smart Group 1 10f Pretty Polly Stakes winner, is a half-sister to the very smart Group 3 6f Princess Margaret Stakes and Group 3 7f Oak Tree Stakes winner Visit. The second dam, Arrive (by Kahyasi), a very useful 10f (at 2 yrs) and listed 13.8f winner, is a half-sister to the 2-y-o 5f winner (stayed 1m) Hasili (herself dam of the top-class performers Banks Hill, Heat Haze, Cacique, Intercontinental, Champs Elysees and Dansili). (Khalid Abdulla).

1503. UNNAMED

b.f. Oasis Dream – Short Dance (Hennessy). January 28. Third foal. The dam, a very useful 6f, listed 7f (both at 2 yrs) and listed 1m winner, is a half-sister to the very useful 2-y-o 7f winner, Group 3 7f Somerville Tattersall Stakes third and Group 1 Criterium International fourth Yankadi. The second dam, Clog Dance (by Pursuit Of Love), a useful maiden, was second in the Group 3 7f Rockfel Stakes and the listed 10f Pretty Polly Stakes and is a half-sister to the smart 14f Ebor Handicap winner Tuning. (Khalid Abdulla).

1504. UNNAMED

b.f. Oasis Dream – Wince (Selkirk). May 6. Sister to the fair 7f to 9f winner Dream Win and half-sister to the Group 1 Yorkshire Oaks winner Quiff, the useful 10f winner and Group

3 Chester Vase second Arabian Gulf and the useful 12f winner and Group 3 placed Total Command (all by Sadler's Wells). The dam won the 1,000 Guineas and the Group 3 Fred Darling Stakes and is a half-sister to 3 winners including the very smart middle-distance winner Ulundi. The second dam, Flit (by Lyphard), is a half-sister to the Grade 1 Washington Lassie Stakes winner Contredance, the listed Roses Stakes winner Old Alliance and the Graded stakes winners Shotiche and Skimble (herself dam of the dual US Grade 1 winner Skimming). (Khalid Abdulla).

LINDA STUBBS

1505. GOLD BEAU (FR) ★★★

b.g. Gold Away – Theorie (Anabaa). March 19. Eighth foal. €10,000Y. Arqana Deauville October. Not sold. Half-brother to the French 2-y-o 6f and 7f winner Theoricienne (by Kendor), to the French winner of 6 races from 2 to 7 yrs Theorique (by Highest Honor) and the minor French winner Talima (by Numerous). The dam, a minor French 3-y-o winner, is a half-sister to 3 other minor winners. The second dam, Timber Nymph (by Woodman), is an unraced half-sister to 6 winners. (D.G Arundale). *"He'll want six furlongs to start with and he'll end up getting seven. A good, strong individual". I have to thank Bill Stubbs for discussing these two-year-olds with me. Bill pointed out to me how well the yard did with their two-year-olds last year with seven wins from just five horses.*

1506. MASTER MOON (IRE) ★★

b.g. Excellent Art – Moon On A Spoon (Dansili). March 6. Second foal. €7,000Y. Goffs Open. BBA (Ire). Half-brother to the minor 2011 French 2-y-o 7f winner Shineside (by Footstepsinthesand). The dam, a fair 10f winner, is a half-sister to 2 winners including the fairly useful 7f to 11.8f winner Pantone. The second dam, Tinashaan (by Darshaan), a useful 12f winner, is a half-sister to 3 winners including the dam of the smart Group 3 May Hill Stakes winner and Group 1 placed Summitville. (P & L Bloodstock). *"He'll need a bit of time and I see him as a seven furlong type 2-y-o. A big horse, he'd be about 16.1 hands now, but he's doing everything right".*

1507. MEGAMUNCH (IRE) ★★★

b.c. Camacho – Liscoa (Foxhound). April 29. Third foal. 15,000Y. Tattersalls October 2. L Stubbs Racing. Half-brother to the 2011 Italian 2-y-o winner Last Child (by Night Shift) and to the fair Irish 5f winner Red Army Blues (by Soviet Star). The dam, a fair Irish 1m and 10f winner, is a half-sister to 4 winners including the useful Irish listed 6f winner Spencers Wood. The second dam, Ascoli (by Skyliner), an Irish, 10f, 12f and hurdles winner, is a half-sister to 3 winners. (P & L Bloodstock). *"An early type and a five furlong 2-y-o, he'll be racing by the end of April or the beginning of May. A strong, sharp colt".*

1508. MIDNIGHT DREAM (FR) ★★★

b.br.g. Country Reel – Tatante (Highest Honor). March 20. Sixth foal. €9,000Y. Arqana Deauville October. Linda Stubbs Racing. Half-brother to the minor French winner Lunix (by Linamix). The dam, a modest 6f placed maiden at 2 and 3 yrs, is a half-sister to 3 winners including the smart Group 2 Prix Hocquart winner Coroner. The second dam, Tamnia (by Green Desert), a useful 2-y-o winner of the listed 7f Milcars Star Stakes, was second in the Group 1 7f Moyglare Stud Stakes and is a half-sister to 7 winners including the very useful Group 2 13.3f Geoffrey Freer Stakes winner Azzilfi and the very useful Group 3 15f Coppa d'Oro di Milano winner Khamaseen. (P. G Shorrock & O. J Williams). *"A nice, classy individual and we think he might be better than the listed winner we had last year. A compact, good-sized 2-y-o and a good-looking horse with plenty of ability, he'll win over five furlongs but he'll want six".* TRAINERS' BARGAIN BUY

JAMES TATE

James, the son of Yorkshire based trainer Tom Tate, has set up his training yard on Newmarket's busy Hamilton Road where he has plenty of other local trainers for neighbours. On my visit to see him in the spring his enthusiasm for his new life as a trainer was palpable. He has a good number of horses to go to war with, including some very decently-bred ones, so he has every right to feel positive and I feel sure he'll be successful in his new career. Let's hope that at least one of these two-year-olds puts his name in the headlines in 2012.

1509. EXCELERATION ★★★★
b.c. Exceed And Excel – Saabiq (Grand Slam). March 25. Third foal. 70,000Y. Tattersalls October Book 2. C McCormack. Half-brother to Saaboog (by Teofilo), unplaced in two starts at 2 yrs in 2011. The dam, a fairly useful 2-y-o 6f winner, was listed-placed over 6f and 7f and is a half-sister to one winner in the USA. The second dam, Lucky Lineage (by Storm Cat), a minor winner at 3 and 5 yrs in the USA, is a half-sister to 6 winners. (S Ali). "You must put this colt in the book! He works extremely well, we're going to wait for the six furlong races and we wouldn't be afraid to take him somewhere nice like the Dante meeting at York in May. Very impressive in his homework, he's a big, strong colt and a fabulous mover. Everything comes easy to him".

1510. EXCEL YOURSELF (IRE) ★★★
b.f. Exceed And Excel – Purple Tiger (Rainbow Quest). March 14. Fifth foal. 28,000Y. Tattersalls October Book 2. Not sold. Sister to the smart 2-y-o 6f winner and Group 2 6f Gimcrack Stakes second Taajub and half-sister to the quite useful 5f and 6f winner Polish Pride (Polish Precedent). The dam is an unraced half-sister to 6 winners including the German Group 2 winner and Italian Group 1 second Notability and the Group 3 Prix La Force winner Simon De Montfort. The second dam, Noble Rose (by Caerleon), won the Group 3 Park Hill Stakes and the listed Galtres Stakes and is a half-sister to 4 winners including Simeon (Group 3 Sandown Classic Trial). (S Ali). "She's got lots of speed and is ready to run. We expect her to run soon and she's an average-sized, strong, fast, five furlong filly".

1511. ROYAL STEPS (IRE) ★★★ ♠
b.f. Royal Applause – Ask Carol (Foxhound). February 21. Third foal. €36,000Y. Goffs Orby. Anthony Stroud. The dam, a fairly useful 5-y-o 7f winner in Ireland, is a half-sister to 6 winners including the very useful Group 3 7f Jersey Stakes winner Sergeyev. The second dam, Escape Path (by Wolver Hollow), placed once over hurdles, is a half-sister to the Group 1 William Hill Futurity Stakes winner Sandy Creek. (S Ali). "A lovely filly that is very straightforward. I wasn't sure how early she'd be because her dam was five before she produced her best run, but the sire gets plenty of precocious horses. She's a fine, good-sized, decent filly that's been working well and she'll debut at Newmarket's Craven meeting. A filly with a lot of speed, I'm looking forward to her".

1512. UNNAMED ★★★
b.c. Exceed And Excel – Darrfonah (Singspiel). March 30. Second foal. The dam, a listed 10f winner and second in the Group 1 1m Prix Marcel Boussac is a half-sister to 8 winners including the very smart Group 1 1m Racing Post Trophy and Group 2 10.4f Dante Stakes winner Dilshaan. The second dam, Avila (by Ajdal), a fair 7f placed maiden, is a half-sister to the smart middle-distance colts Alleging, Monastery and Nomrood. (S Manana). "He's a very nice colt that shows plenty of speed. A nice, strong colt with a good attitude, I'd expect him to start off in May over six furlongs and I like him. A nice, straightforward horse".

1513. UNNAMED ★★
b.c. Manduro – Dust Dancer (Suave Dancer). March 17. Eleventh foal. 38,000Y. Tattersalls October Book 2. Rabbah Bloodstock. Half-brother to the listed 1m and subsequent US Grade 2 winner Spotlight, to the quite useful 2-y-o 7f winner Dusty Moon (both by Dr Fong), the fairly useful dual 7f winner Tyranny (by Machiavellian), the quite useful 2-y-o 7f winner and listed 1m placed Dusty Answer (by Zafonic and herself dam of the Group 1 Phoenix Stakes winner Zoffany) and a minor winner abroad by Dubai Destination. The dam won 4 races including the Group 3 10f Prix de la Nonette and is a half-sister to 6 winners including the Group 3 7.3f Fred Darling Stakes winner Bulaxie (herself dam of the Group 2 winner Claxon). The second dam, Galaxie Dust (by Blushing Groom), a quite useful 2-y-o 6f winner, is a half-sister to 2 minor winners. (S Ali). "Somewhat headstrong, he's a very nice, attractive colt but definitely one for later in the year. He'll start over seven furlongs before we step him up to a mile and I'm looking forward to him".

1514. UNNAMED ★★★
b.f. Exceed And Excel – Fanny's Fancy (Groom Dancer). January 30. Fourth foal. 38,000Y. Tattersalls October Book 3. Rabbah Bloodstock. Half-sister to the unplaced 2011 2-y-o

Calendar King (by Three Valleys) and to the fair 2-y-o 6f winner Jolah (by Oasis Dream). The dam, a fairly useful dual 6f winner, was listed placed. The second dam, Fanny's Choice (by Fairy King), a fairly useful 2-y-o 6f winner, is a half-sister to 3 winners. (S Manana). *"A lovely, strong, powerful filly, she looks like she'll be fast but she's had a couple of niggling issues in the spring which have stopped us knowing how good she is yet, but I'm very much looking forward to her".*

1515. UNNAMED ★★★

b.f. Compton Place – Glimpse (Night Shift). March 29. Tenth living foal. 24,000Y. Tattersalls October Book 2. Rabbah Bloodstock. Half-sister to the useful 5f, 6f (both at 2 yrs) and 7f winner Casual Glimpse (by Compton Place), to the 2-y-o dual 1m winner Shenley Charm (by First Trump), the 2-y-o 6f winner Focus (by First Trump), the 10f winner Raakaan (by Halling) – all quite useful, the Italian 7.5f and 1m winner of 8 races Masazza (by Elmaamul) and two winners abroad by Primo Dominie and Kyllachy. The dam, a fair 2-y-o 6f winner, is a half-sister to 5 minor winners here and abroad. The second dam, Lovers Light (by Grundy), is an unplaced half-sister to 4 winners including the good broodmare Lady Moon (dam of the Group winners Moon Cactus and Shining Steel). (S Manana). *"Shows plenty of speed, she had a tiny setback in early March which held us back a little bit but I'm looking forward to running her over five/six furlongs in May".*

1516. UNNAMED ★★★

b.c. Elusive City – Laheen (Bluebird). April 8. Third foal. 20,000Y. Tattersalls October Book 2. Rabbah Bloodstock. The dam is an unplaced half-sister to 2 winners including the listed-placed New Design. The second dam, Ashirah (by Housebuster), is an unraced half-sister to the US dual Grade 3 winner Mustanfar and the dual listed winner Tadris. (S Manana). *"A typical 2-y-o type, he goes quite well and I can see us getting him out sooner rather than later, over five furlongs, before the good ones come out. He's small, stocky, strong and fairly quick".*

1517. UNNAMED ★★★

br.c. Singspiel – Mexican Hawk (Silver Hawk). March 3. Sixth foal. 30,000Y. Tattersalls October

Book 2. Rabbah Bloodstock. Half-brother to the quite useful 9f and 12f winner Elegant Hawk (by Generous) and to a winner in Greece by Araafa. The dam, a fairly useful 10f winner, is a half-sister to 8 winners. The second dam, Viva Zapata (by Affirmed), won the Group 2 Prix du Gros Chene and is a half-sister to 7 winners. (S Ali). *"One for later in the year, but he's a lovely horse. A beautiful, long-striding colt that goes really well, he won't run until the seven furlong races or maybe even a mile, but he has such a lovely way about him that we're very much looking forward to him".*

1518. UNNAMED ★★★

b.c. Royal Applause – Persian Sea (Dubai Destination). January 25. First foal. 31,000Y. Tattersalls October Book 1. Rabbah Bloodstock. The dam, a fairly useful 6f and 7f winner at 3 yrs, is a half-sister to 7 winners including the very useful 2-y-o listed 7f winner and Group 2 1m May Hill Stakes second Queen Of Poland and the dam of the US dual Grade 2 winner What'sthescript. The second dam, Polska (by Danzig), a useful winner of the 2-y-o listed 6f Blue Seal Stakes, was listed-placed over 7f at 3 yrs and is a half-sister to 7 winners including the useful filly Millstream, a winner of five races over 5f including the Group 3 Ballyogan Stakes and the Group 3 Cornwallis Stakes. (S Manana). *"A nice, strong, straightforward colt. Despite his pedigree he will take a little bit of time to come to himself because he's quite big and he was a bit unfurnished at the beginning of the year. But he's very straightforward to train and I'm looking forward to running him over six furlongs in May/June time".*

1519. UNNAMED ★★★

b.c. Cape Cross – Queen's Best (King's Best). February 28. First foal. 34,000Y. Tattersalls October Book 2. Rabbah Bloodstock. The dam, a smart winner of the Group 3 10f Winter Hill Stakes and the listed 12f Chalice Stakes, was second in the Group 2 Blandford Stakes and is a half-sister to 4 winners including the French 12f winner and Group 3 Prix de Royaumont third Reverie Solitaire. The second dam, Cloud Castle (by In The Wings), won the Group 3 Nell Gwyn Stakes and was placed in the Group 1 Yorkshire Oaks and the Group 1 Prix Vermeille. She is a half-sister to 5 winners including the high-class middle-distance horses and multiple Group 1 winners Warrsan and Luso, and the dam of the Group 3 winners Tastahil, Hattan, Blue Monday and Laaheb. (S Ali). *"A nice horse with a lovely attitude, he's strong, very straightforward and we're looking forward to running him over six/ seven furlongs in mid-season. The pedigree is a blend of speed and stamina but he's a muscular, strong, quite-speedy colt".*

1520. UNNAMED ★★

b.f. *Teofilo – Shimna (Mr Prospector)*. March 4. Eighth foal. Half-sister to the useful 2-y-o 7f winner Santa Fe (by Green Desert), to the useful 1m (at 2 yrs) and 10f winner and Group 3 Derby Trial second Hazeymm (by Marju), the fairly useful dual 10f winner Black Eagle (by Cape Cross), the fairly useful 1m (at 2 yrs) and dual 10f winner Sahrati (by In The Wings) and a winner over hurdles by Shamardal. The dam, placed fourth over 10f in Ireland on her only outing, is a half-sister to the St Leger and Gran Premio del Jockey Club winner Shantou. The second dam, Shaima (by Shareef Dancer), a very useful 7.3f (at 2 yrs) and 9f listed winner here, later won the Grade 2 12f Long Island Handicap and is a half-sister to 6 winners including the Prix Saint Alary winner Rosefinch. (S Manana). *"She's a lovely, easy-moving filly that does need to strengthen up a little, so she'll be the type for seven furlongs or a mile later in the year".*

1521. UNNAMED ★★★ MIRJANE

ch.c. *Sir Percy – String Quartet (Sadler's Wells)*. February 9. Eighth foal. 50,000Y. Tattersalls October Book 1. Rabbah Bloodstock. Half-brother to the Group 2 Park Hill Stakes and Group 3 Lillie Langtry Stakes winner Meeznah (by Dynaformer), to the smart 1m winner (at 2 yrs) and Group 2 12f Princess Of Wales's Stakes second Shahin (by Kingmambo), the fair 10f winner Lady Rosamunde (by Maria's Mon), the moderate 7f winner Lyric Art (by Red Ransom) and a minor winner abroad by Fantastic Light. The dam, a 12.5f listed winner in France and third in the Group 3 Lancashire Oaks, is a sister to the Irish listed 10f winner Casey Tibbs and a half-sister to 4 winners. The second dam, Fleur Royale (by Mill Reef), won the Group 2 Pretty Polly Stakes, was second in the Group 1 Irish Oaks and is a half-sister to 4 winners. (S Ali).

"He's a bit smaller than his half-sister Meeznah, so perhaps that comes from Sir Percy. He has a really good attitude and I imagine we'll start him off over seven furlongs or maybe a stiff six. I like him".

1522. UNNAMED ★★★★

b.f. *Bernardini – Transition Time (Dynaformer)*. May 3. Sixth foal. 40,000Y. Tattersalls October Book 1. Rabbah Bloodstock. Half-sister to the dual listed 10f winner Ticoz (by Cozzene). The dam, a minor stakes winner in the USA, is a half-sister to 7 winners. The second dam, Sharp Tradition (by Sharpen Up), a minor 3-y-o winner in the USA, is a half-sister to 6 winners. (S Ali). *"She's huge and it would be fair to say that her conformation isn't perfect, but she's fabulous. I love her to death and I can't wait to run her over seven furlongs later in the year. I'm holding myself back because she goes really well".*

1523. UNNAMED ★★★

b.f. *New Approach – Wimple (Kingmambo)*. March 6. Sixth foal. Half-sister to the fairly useful 2-y-o 6f winner and listed-placed Sharnberry (by Shamardal), to the quite useful 2-y-o 6f winner Master Rooney (by Cape Cross) and a winner in Russia by Daylami. The dam, a useful 5f and 6f winner at 2 yrs, was listed-placed and is a half-sister to 2 winners. The second dam, Tunicle (by Dixieland Band), won 4 minor races in the USA and is a half-sister to 5 winners. (S Manana). *"A lovely, muscular filly and the dam was a muscular Kingmambo filly herself. She's very attractive, she goes very well and I'm really looking forward to running her over six furlongs in early May".*

JAMES TOLLER
1524. CHESTER ROW ★★★

ch.c. *Compton Place – Sophie's Girl (Bahamian Bounty)*. January 21. First foal. 28,000Y. Tattersalls October Book 2. R Frisby. The dam, a quite useful 2-y-o dual 5f winner, is a half-sister to 9 winners including the listed winner and Group 3 placed Paradise Isle and the dam of the Group placed Sir Reginald and Henrik. The second dam, Merry Rous (by Rousillon), won once at 2 yrs and is a half-sister to 5 winners including the dual Group 3 winning sprinter Tina's Pet. *"A nice, athletic colt, he'll be one of my earlier ones. I'm pleased with him, he's a good, compact, sharp-looking 2-y-o and I would hope he'd be out in May over five furlongs to start with. He's nice, he's got a bit of the sire about him which can't be a bad thing and he's certainly bred to be a sprinter".*

1525. LIVING DESERT ★★★

gr.c. *Oasis Dream – Sell Out (Act One).* February 12. First foal. 100,000Y. Tattersalls October Book 1. R Frisby. The dam, a useful listed 12f winner, was Group 3 placed and is a half-sister to 8 winners including the Group 3 7.3f Fred Darling Stakes winner and Group 2 10f Nassau Stakes third Sueboog (herself dam of the Group 1 Prix d'Ispahan winner Best Of The Bests) and the listed winner Marika. The second dam, Nordica (by Northfields), a useful 6f and 1m winner, is a half-sister to 2 winners. (G.B. Partnership). *"A relatively precocious colt, he's a very nice, strong, athletic-looking horse. I like him, he's got a good pedigree and I would have though he's more likely to be starting at six furlongs".*

1526. SMOKETHATTHUNDERS (IRE) ★★

b.c. *Elusive City – Zinstar (Sinndar).* March 29. Fourth foal. 30,000Y. Tattersalls December. Blandford Bloodstock. Half-sister to the modest 2011 5f fourth placed 2-y-o Mebsuta (by Amadeus Wolf) and to the quite useful dual 7f winner Sinfonico (by Noverre). The dam is an unraced half-sister to 5 winners including the listed 10f winner and Group 2 12f Great Voltigeur Stakes fourth Bustan. The second dam, Dazzlingly Radiant (by Try My Best), a quite useful winner of three races over 6f, is a half-sister to 3 winners including Dance By Night (dam of the French 1,000 Guineas winner Danseuse du Soir). (M. E Wates). *"He took quite a long time to break-in, I quite like him but he's got a touch of sore shins at the moment. He's probably growing but he should make a 2-y-o from July onwards over six furlongs".*

1527. SOHO DANCER ★★★

b.f. *Galileo – River Belle (Lahib).* April 10. Fourth foal. 310,000Y. Tattersalls October Book 1. R Frisby. Half-sister to the fair 2011 2-y-o 1m winner Strathnaver (by Oasis Dream), to the useful 7f (at 2 yrs) and listed 1m UAE 1,000 Guineas winner Siyaadah (by Shamardal)

and the quite useful 2-y-o 7f and 1m winner Bridal Belle (by Dansili). The dam, winner of the Group 3 6f Princess Margaret Stakes and subsequently the US Grade 2 8.5f Mrs Revere Stakes, was Grade 1 placed and is a half-sister to 5 winners including the Italian listed winner and Group 2 Italian 1,000 Guineas third Kiralik. The second dam, Dixie Favor (by Dixieland Band), was a quite useful Irish 6f (at 2 yrs) to 1m winner of 3 races. (G.B. Partnership). *"A very nice, athletic filly for the second half of the year and anything she does this year will be a bonus. A lovely filly and obviously it's exciting for us to have a horse like her. To make her worth the money she cost you'd have to hope she'd be even better than her three half-siblings. One to have two or three runs towards the back-end of the season".*

1528. SUNNY HOLLOW ★★★

b.f. *Beat Hollow – Corndavon (Sheikh Albadou).* May 3. 7,000Y. Tattersalls October Book 3. Henrietta Michael. Half-sister to the smart 2-y-o Group 2 6f July Stakes winner Nevisian Lad (by Royal Applause), to the fairly useful 5f (at 2 yrs) and 6f winner and listed-placed Woodnook and the quite useful dual 7f winner Windermere Island (both by Cadeaux Genereux). The dam, a fairly useful 6f winner of 3 races, is a sister to the listed-placed winner Injaaz and a half-sister to the US sprint winner of 13 races and listed-placed Hardball. The second dam, Ferber's Follies (by Saratoga Six), a winning 2-y-o sprinter, was third in the Grade 2 6f Adirondack Stakes and is a half-sister to 11 winners including the US 2-y-o Grade 2 6f winner Blue Jean Baby. (Mr S A Herbert). *"I like her, she was very small when we bought her but she's grown and done well. She'll make a 2-y-o but I don't know quite when. We bought her thinking she'd need time to grow but she's done that and she's filled out. I had the half-sister Woodnook that won as a 2-y-o and I like this filly, she's a gutsy little thing. I'll let her tell us when she's ready".*

1529. UNNAMED ★★

b.f. *Motivator – Ela's Giant (Giant's Causeway).* March 16. Second foal. 1,000Y. Tattersalls December. Blandford Bloodstock. The dam is an unraced half-sister to the fairly useful 2-y-o 1m winner and listed placed Elas Diamond (by

Danehill Dancer). The second dam, Ela Athena (by Ezzoud), a winner of 3 races including the Group 3 Lancashire Oaks, was placed in 7 Group/Grade 1 events and is a half-sister to 5 winners. (G Wates). *"She was very cheap and I can't understand why – I thought she'd make far more than that. She's got quite a good pedigree and she's a lovely, athletic filly. More of a back-end 2-y-o but I'd keep an eye on her. I like her"*. TRAINERS' BARGAIN BUY

MARK TOMPKINS

1530. ASTROSAPPHIRE ★★

b.f. *Manduro – Astromancer (Silver Hawk).* February 12. Fourth foal. Half-sister to the modest 11f winner Cotton Grass (by Medicean). The dam, a moderate 4-y-o 14f winner, is a half-sister to one winner. The second dam, Colour Dance (by Rainbow Quest), is an unplaced full or half-sister to 4 winners including the very useful French 1m listed winner and Group 1 Prix Morny third Barricade. (Mystic Meg Ltd). *"She's by Manduro who is a sire that seems to be doing well now and this has always been a healthy looking filly, well-grown and strong. She goes well, I wouldn't have a problem with her and she could start off at six furlongs but I reckon she'll want ten furlongs next year. She could be reasonably useful".*

1531. BARBSIZ (IRE) ★★

ch.f. *Elnadim – Bianca Cappello (Glenstal).* April 26. Ninth foal. 8,000Y. Tattersalls October Book 2. Not sold. Half-sister to the modest 2011 7f placed 2-y-o Loved By All (by Elusive City), to the useful 2-y-o Group 3 6.5f Prix Eclipse winner Potaro (by Catrail) and the fair 7f winner Gemini Future (by Flying Spur). The dam is an unplaced half-sister to 4 winners including Idris (a winner of four Group 3 events in Ireland at up to 12f) and the US Grade 3 placed Sweet Mazarine and to the unraced dam of the listed winners Spinning Lucy and Midris. The second dam, Idara (by Top Ville), a very useful winner over 11f and 12f, was third in the Group 2 Prix de Pomone and is a half-sister to 2 winners. (Mr G. J Megson). *"A well-grown filly by a sire I've always liked – I think Elnadim is underrated because he can get a good horse. This filly has always gone well and I think she'll be a mid-season 2-y-o, she has a lovely head on her, a*

great stride and I couldn't be happier with her. A six furlong type and like all mine she'll go on as a 3-y-o".

1532. FREDERICK ALFRED ★★

ch.c. *Halling – Trew Class (Inchinor).* April 8. Fourth foal. Half-brother to Jennifer J (by Motivator), placed fourth once over 7f at 2 yrs in 2011, to the fair 11f and 12f winner Kathleen Frances (by Sakhee) and a bumpers winner by Dubai Destination. The dam, a fairly useful 10f winner of 4 races, was listed-placed and is a half-sister to 2 winners. The second dam, Inimitable (by Saveur), a modest 10f winner, is a half-sister to 3 winners. (Russell Trew Ltd). *"The mare did well for us and her first two foals have won. This is a great, big horse by Halling who is a sire I love. A lovely-moving colt, he won't be out until the back-end but he's a horse for the future and he's typical of the family".*

1533. LIKEITLIKEITLIKEIT ★★

b.f. *Avonbridge – Rutland Water (Hawk Wing).* February 13. First foal. 2,000Y. Tattersalls October Book 3. Not sold. The dam is an unraced half-sister to 2 minor winners. The second dam, Rutledge (by Entrepreneur), is an unraced three-parts sister to the Breeders Cup Turf winner Northern Spur and a half-sister to 5 winners including the Doncaster Cup winners Great Marquess and Kneller. (M H Tompkins). *"I thought she was going to be sharp but she's grown just lately. She has a good temperament and is beginning to show a bit more now, so she could be out in May or June. She was a cheap buy and I think she'll be fine"*. TRAINERS' BARGAIN BUY

1534. MARSH DRAGON ★★★

b.c. *Beat Hollow – Qilin (Second Set).* April 11. Sixth foal. Brother to the fair 1m and 12f winner Drum Dragon and half-brother to the modest 2011 6f placed 2-y-o Shomberg (by Bahamian Bounty). The dam, a fairly useful 6f (including at 2 yrs) and 7f winner, was listed-placed. And is a half-sister to 5 winners The second dam, Usance (by Kronankranich), a German winner and listed-placed, is a half-sister to two German listed winners. (M H Tompkins). *"A lovely filly out of a quick mare. She's showing me plenty and she's a strong, healthy-looking filly with a* good attitude that's doing everything right. I can see her starting off in May or June over six furlongs and then progressing. I like her a lot".

1535. STAR OF MISSOURI ★★★

ch.c. Namid – Missouri (Charnwood Forest). March 28. Half-brother to the quite useful Irish 2011 2-y-o 7f winner Captain Cullen (by Strategic Prince), to the fair 1m (at 2 yrs) and 12f winner Battery Power (by Royal Applause), the modest 9f (at 2 yrs) to 12f and hurdles winner Dee Cee Elle (by Groom Dancer), the modest 10f winner Bella Medici (by Medicean) and the moderate 12f winner Mekong Miss (by Mark Of Esteem). The dam, a quite useful 15f winner, is a half-sister to several winners. The second dam, Medway (by Shernazar), a modest 12f winner at 3 yrs, is a half-sister to 8 winners including the high-class Hong Kong horse Indigenous and the Cesarewitch winner Old Red. (J Benchley). "A great, big, strong horse. All this mare's progeny win and he looks nearly the best of them. I really like him and he'll be running by mid-season. He'll certainly win a race later on and then come into his own next year".

1536. TOPAMICHI ★★★★

b.c. Beat Hollow – Topatori (Topanoora). March 13. Half-brother to the Group 3 10.3f Middleton Stakes winner Topatoo (by Bahamian Bounty), to the quite useful 1m to 14f winner Toparudi (by Rudimentary), the fair dual 1m winner Top Shot (by College Chapel) and the fair 1m winner Top Tiger (by Mtoto). The dam, a quite useful 7f to 11f winner of 4 races, is a half-sister to one winner. The second dam, Partygoer (by Cadeaux Genereux), was unplaced. (Roalco Ltd). "An outstanding horse, I would think he's the best colt I've got at the moment. You would think that being by Beat Hollow he'd want time but he doesn't, he'll be racing in May or June and if he's got an extra gear he could be very good. He looks the part, he's a really nice horse and we'll be aiming him at some nice races".

1537. UNNAMED ★★

ch.f. Haafhd – Sosumi (Be My Chief). March 6. Seventh foal. Half-sister to the modest 2011 2-y-o 5f placed Dine Out (by Piccolo), to the quite useful 7f and 1m winner of 6 races Tevez (by Sakhee), the modest 2-y-o 1m seller

winner Benayoun (by Inchinor) and the modest 11f winner Edward Whymper (by Bahamian Bounty). The dam, a useful 2-y-o dual 5f winner, was fourth in the Group 3 Prix du Calvados. The second dam, Princess Deya (by Be My Guest), ran twice unplaced and is a half-sister to the Eclipse Stakes winner Compton Admiral and the Group 1 1m Queen Elizabeth II Stakes winner Summoner. (Sakal Family). "I've trained nearly all this family and it won't be long before she's out. She goes well, she's strong, not too-big and she'll certainly be OK. I don't know how many gears she's got yet, but she has a good temperament and like all the family she's good-looking".

MARCUS TREGONING

1538. ATALANTA BAY (IRE) ★★★

b.f. Strategic Prince – Wood Sprite (Mister Baileys). February 5. €10,000Y. Tattersalls Ireland. Marcus Tregoning. The dam, a poor maiden, was second once over 14f and is a half-sister to 4 winners including the very smart Group 2 Yorkshire Cup and Group 3 11.8f Lingfield Derby Trial winner Franklins Gardens and the very smart Group 3 7f and Group 3 1m winner Polar Ben. The second dam, Woodbeck (by Terimon), a fairly useful 3-y-o dual 7f winner, is a half-sister to 8 winners including the fairly useful 2-y-o winners Optimistic and Carburton. (Miss S. M Sharp). "A big, scopey filly with a very good temperament. She has a lot of her grandsire Dansili in her I think and she's a nice, easy-moving type for when the seven furlong races come out. She's done nothing wrong and I'd be quite hopeful for her".

1539. CAERWYN ★★

ch.c. Pastoral Pursuits – Preference (Efisio). February 15. Seventh foal. £31,000Y. Doncaster Premier. Peter & Ross Doyle. Half-brother to the fairly useful 5f and 6f winner of 4 races Ice Planet (by Polar Falcon), the modest dual 10f winner Sangar (by Haafhd) and the modest dual 6f winner Maia (by Observatory). The dam is an unraced sister to the Group 3 Beeswing Stakes winner Casteddu and the listed winner Barbaroja and a half-sister to 3 winners. The second dam, Bias (by Royal Prerogative), won 6 races at 2 and 3 yrs. (Mr J. A Tabet). "Yes, I think he's alright, he's one for the middle of *the season and beyond. He's turning out to be quite a big, strong sprinting type and I'm quite pleased with him".*

1540. DELWYN ★★★

b.f. Bahamian Bounty – Acquifer (Oasis Dream). March 18. First foal. £10,000Y. Doncaster Premier. Oliver St Lawrence. The dam, a fair maiden, was third over 6f twice at 2 and 3 yrs and is a half-sister to 6 winners including the Italian Group 3 winner Guest Connections, the listed winner Lady Of the Lake and the smart broodmare Llia. The second dam, Llyn Gwynant (by Persian Bold), won the Group 3 1m Desmond Stakes and the Group 3 1m Matron Stakes and is a half-sister to 2 winners. (Mr J. A Tabet). *"I like this filly, she's short coupled, compact and shows plenty of speed so she'll make a six furlong 2-y-o. Quite a straightforward filly, I'm pleased with her."*

1541. EASY LIFE ★★★

b.f. Sir Percy – Eternelle (Green Desert). April 20. Sixth foal. Half-sister to the moderate 2011 7f placed (from 2 starts) Pearl Frost (by Verglas), to the fair 2-y-o 1m winner Encore Un Annee, the moderate 11f winner Eloise and the Spanish 7.5f winner Sassicaia (all by Hernando). The dam, a quite useful 9.4f winner, is a sister to the useful winner of 11 races at up to 7f Everset and a half-sister to 5 winners including the champion German horse and dual Group 1 middle-distance winner Caitano and to the US Grade 3 1m winner Lady Lodger. The second dam, Eversince (by Foolish Pleasure), won over 5.5f and 1m in France and is a half-sister to the Group 3 Premio Ellington winner and Italian Derby second Artic Envoy. (Miss K Rausing). *"She'll definitely run this year but she's grown a lot and she's quite leggy. She's coming along well and one thing I will say is that the majority of Sir Percy's have very good actions. He sells his foals and yearlings on the way they move and this filly is like that".*

1542. MAREEF (IRE) ★★★

b.c. Oasis Dream – Katayeb (Machiavellian). March 17. Fourth foal. Closely related to the fair 10f winner Tahkeem (by Green Desert) and half-brother to the modest 14f winner Juwireyah (by Nayef). The dam, unplaced on her only start, is a half-sister to the Group 1 12f Italian

Derby winner and King George VI and Queen Elizabeth Stakes second White Muzzle, to the Group 2 German St Leger winner Fair Question and the listed 10f winner Elfaslah (dam of the Dubai World Cup winner Almutawakel). The second dam, Fair of the Furze (by Ela-Mana-Mou), won the Group 2 10f Tattersalls Rogers Gold Cup and is a half-sister to the listed winners Majestic Role, Norman Style and Proconsular. (Hamdan Al Maktoum). *"I quite like him and I trained the dam who wasn't particularly sound but this colt is fine and I think Oasis Dream has injected some quality. He's only been with me for a week, having been in Dubai all winter, but he's a good mover, he seems to have a reasonable temperament and he looks sure to make a 2-y-o".*

1543. MAZAAHER ★★★

b.c. Elnadim – Elutrah (Darshaan). January 30. Sister to the quite useful 2-y-o 1m winner Multames. The dam is an unraced sister to the very useful Group 2 7f Rockfel Stakes winner Sayedah and a half-sister to 4 winners. The second dam, Balaabel (by Sadler's Wells), a quite useful 1m winner, is a half-sister to 3 winners including the US Grade 2 7f winner Kayrawan. (Hamdan Al Maktoum). *"Quite a big horse, he came with a reputation for biting and kicking, but the more I've done with him and the more I've worked closely with him the better he's got. He's a very nice mover, I see him as being one for September/October time and he's a nice type".*

1544. NASHRAH (USA) ★★★

b.f. Jazil – Taleef (Sakhee). February 25. Second foal. The dam is an unraced half-sister to 2 winners. The second dam, Najah (by Nashwan), won the Group 2 Premio Lydia Tesio and is a half-sister to 6 winners out of the 1,000 Guineas Mehthaaf. (Hamdan Al Maktoum). *"She's quite nice, she's good-looking and a nice mover. You'd have to be hopeful for her because I think the sire is pretty useful and this is a medium sized filly with a bit of scope and a very nice temperament".*

1545. NILE KNIGHT ★★★

b.c. Sir Percy – Sahara Belle (Sanglamore). February 7. Seventh foal. 25,000Y. Tattersalls October Book 3. Marcus Tregoning. Half-brother to the fair 9f and 10f winner Strider (by Pivotal), to the modest 7f to 14f winner of 5 races He's A Star (by Mark Of Esteem), the moderate 14f winner Decana (by Doyen) and a 2-y-o winner in Norway by Act One. The dam won twice at 3 yrs in Norway at up to 11.5f and is a half-sister to 8 winners including the Group 3 Lingfield Derby Trial winner and Group 1 Grand Prix de Saint-Cloud second Perfect Sunday. The second dam, Sunday Bazaar (by Nureyev), won over 12f in France and is a half-sister to 8 winners including the US Grade 1 winners Bates Motel and Hatim and the Horris Hill Stakes winner Super Asset. (R. C. C Villers). *"He's a nice type, we didn't pay a huge amount of money for him and he's a lovely mover. He's a colt with a 2-y-o shape, a 2-y-o size and I'll be getting on with him now. He has a good temperament and what I see of him I really like. I'm quite happy with him".*

1546. OBAHA (USA) ★★

b.f. Lemon Drop Kid – Tayibah (Sadler's Wells). Half-sister to the quite useful 1m, 10f and hurdles winner Alsahil (by Diesis) and to the quite useful 12f and hurdles winner Lajidaal (by Dynaformer). The dam, placed second over 11.7f on her only start, is a half-sister to the Group 2 1m Premio Ribot winner Oriental Fashion and to the smart listed 7f winner Makderah. The second dam, Wijdan (by Riverman), a useful 1m and 10.4f winner, is a sister to the 7f (at 2 yrs) and 1m listed winner Sarayir and a half-sister to the brilliant 2,000 Guineas, Derby, Eclipse and King George winner Nashwan and to the high-class middle distance colt Unfuwain. (Hamdan Al Maktoum). *"This is quite a nice-shaped filly, she's only just come in from Dubai so I don't know much about her yet, but she moves well, she seems to have a good temperament and she has a lot of size and scope about her. So hopefully she'll be a back-end type".*

1547. PERDU ★★

b.c. Sir Percy – Misplace (Green Desert). May 10. Seventh foal. 25,000Y. Tattersalls October Book 1. G Howson. Half-brother to the French 1m to 10f winner of 6 races and Group 3 third Mayweather (by Nayef), to the French 1m winner of 3 races (including at 2 yrs) Mistaken Identity (by Vettori) and the minor French 7f winner Milhaarth (by Alhaarth). The dam won once at 3 yrs in France and is a half-sister to 5 winners including the French Group 3 winner Not Just Swing and the French listed winner Minoa and to the unraced dam of the Group 1 1m Falmouth Stakes and Group 2 6f Lowther Stakes winner Nahoodh. The second dam, Misbegotten (by Baillamont), a French listed 1m Prix Finlande winner, was second in the Group 2 Prix de l'Opera and is a half-sister to 4 winners. (Mr & Mrs A. E Pakenham). *"He's a bigger version of the sire and I suspect the mare is throwing some backward types. He's a good mover and has a good temperament but he was a late foal and he looks like taking a bit of time".*

1548. SAINT JEROME (IRE) ★★★

b.c. Jeremy – Eminence Gift (Cadeaux Genereux). March 6. Second foal. £55,000Y. Doncaster Premier. Peter & Ross Doyle. The dam, a moderate dual 10f winner is a sister to the useful 1m and 8.3f winner and listed placed Granted and a half-sister to 3 winners including the Italian listed winner Lucky Chappy. The second dam, Germane (by Distant Relative), a useful winner of the Group 3 7f Rockfel Stakes and placed in 2 listed events, is a half-sister to 9 winners including the very useful German 10f winner Fabriano. (Lady Tennant). *"He's a nice colt and everyone who rides him likes him. He was a Peter Doyle purchase and Peter does like to buy 2-y-o's and I think he's definitely a 2-y-o for the middle of the summer. I like what I see, he's a very active, sound horse and he's showing me a bit of speed so I'm happy with him".*

1549. SWEEPING ROCK (IRE) ★★★★

b.c. Rock Of Gibraltar – Sweeping Story (End Sweep). April 29. Ninth foal. €23,000Y. Tattersalls Ireland. Marcus Tregoning. Half-brother to the useful dual 12f winner and subsequent Australian Group 2 second Bay Story (by Kris S), to the fairly useful 2-y-o 7f winner Bold And Free (by Giant's Causeway) and a minor US 4-y-o winner by Unbridled's Song. The dam, a dual listed winner in the USA and third in the Grade 1 Kentucky Oaks, is a half-sister to 7 winners including Exciting Story (Grade 1 Metropolitan Handicap). The second dam, Appealing Story (by Valid Appeal), is an unraced half-sister to 5 winners including the US Grade 3 winner Cut The Charm. (Mr J Singh). *"This is a nice-looking horse, I think he was a good buy and I'm particularly keen on him. I think the mare must have been pretty sound by the looks of her race record and this colt looks the type to be ready in time for the Haynes Hanson & Clark race. The sire doesn't often get precocious horses but this horse is coming along great and he's a good mover".*

1550. THAKANA ★★

br.f. *Cape Cross – Shohrah (Giant's Causeway).* March 16. Fourth foal. Half-sister to the quite useful 2-y-o 9f winner Shaayeq (by Dubawi). The dam, a useful 2-y-o 6f winner, is a half-sister to 6 winners including the useful 7f winner and 1m listed second Ma-Arif. The second dam, Taqreem (by Nashwan), was second four times over middle-distances and is a half-sister to the high class middle distance colt Ibn Bey, winner of 4 Group 1 events including the Irish St Leger and second in the Breeders Cup Classic and to the very smart Group 1 Yorkshire Oaks winner Roseate Tern. (Hamdan Al Maktoum). *"She's quite nice, we have her 3-y-o half-sister Thawabel who will win this year and she seems to want top of the ground and I think this filly will be the same. She needs to strengthen up but she has a nice temperament, the sire Cape Cross has done a good job there for certain".*

1551. UNNAMED ★★★ *Valais Girl*

b.f. *Holy Roman Emperor – Ellen (Machiavellian).* May 13. Fifth foal. 80,000Y. Tattersalls October Book 1. Oliver St Lawrence. Half-sister to the French 4.5f and 5.5f 2-y-o winner and Group 3 Prix du Bois third Faslen (by Fasliyev) and to the quite useful dual 1m winner Mujrayaat (by Invincible Spirit). The dam is an unraced half-sister to 2 winners including the Group 3 Winter Derby winner Gentleman's Deal. The second dam, Sleepytime (by Royal Academy), won the 1,000 Guineas and is a sister to the Group 1 Sussex Stakes winner Ali Royal and a half-sister to the German and Italian Group 1 winner Taipan. (Mr. C. B Brook). *"We bought her because the sire has done well with his two-year-olds and because we know the family quite well. They tend to be quite big and I was hoping that Holy Roman Emperor might even things out and the filly wouldn't be big and*

backward. I think she's quite nice, she's a good mover and I think we'll see her out from mid-summer onwards, possibly over six furlongs to start with".* made all to win at bf cl 4 mdn Newbury

1552. UNNAMED ★★★★

b.c. *Nayef – Emerald Peace (Green Desert).* February 9. Seventh living foal. 100,000Y. Tattersalls October Book 2. Oliver St Lawrence. Half-brother to the listed 6f winner and Group 3 Princess Margaret Stakes second Vital Statistics (by Indian Ridge), to the quite useful triple 6f winner (including at 2 yrs) Emerald Lodge (by Green Desert), the quite useful 7f winner Carved Emerald (by Pivotal), the fair dual 6f winner Spiritual Peace (by Cadeaux Genereux), the fair dual 6f winner Bahia Emerald and the modest 5f and 6f winner My Meteor (both by Bahamian Bounty). The dam, a useful listed 5f winner of 4 races and second in the Group 2 5f Flying Childers Stakes, is a half-sister to 5 winners. The second dam, Puck's Castle (by Shirley Heights), a fairly useful 2-y-o 1m winner and third in the listed 10f Zetland Stakes, is a half-sister to 6 winners including the champion 2-y-o filly and Cheveley Park Stakes winner Embassy and the Group 2 Pretty Polly Stakes winner Tarfshi. (Mr G. C. B Brook). *"The Nayef 2-y-o's this year are from the strongest book of mares he's had to date. This colt was rather expensive, but I didn't set out to buy a Nayef because I do get them sent to me. I'm always pleased to get them of course because they're very sound like he was. This colt is tough, a very good mover and hopefully he'll be a nice 2-y-o. He could go the Haynes, Hansen and Clark race route and I don't necessarily think he'll go towards the speed side of his pedigree, but at the moment I see him as a seven furlong 2-y-o. A nice horse, very good-looking and plenty of people will notice him when he runs I'm sure".*

1553. UNNAMED ★★★

ch.f. *Sir Percy – Sirena (Tejano).* April 2. Ninth foal. €3,000Y. Tattersalls Ireland. Marcus Tregoning. Half-sister to the fairly useful 10f to 12f and hurdles winner and listed-placed Vinando and to the moderate 12f, 14f and hurdles winner Spanish Conquest (both by Hernando). The dam won 5 races from 3 to 5 yrs in Germany and is a half-sister to 8 winners including the German champion, dual Group

1 winner and sire Silvano and the triple Group 1 winner Sabiango. The second dam, Spirit Of Eagles (by Beau's Eagle), won 11 minor races from 2 to 6 yrs in the USA and is a half-sister to the stakes winners Big Pal and Lovely Habit. *"She's very nice, a good-looking bright chestnut with a beautiful head. I paid very little for her, especially when you consider her dam is a half-sister to two Group One winners! She's nice and I'm very pleased with her"*. TRAINERS' BARGAIN BUY

ROGER VARIAN

1554. AGLAOPHONOS ★★★

ch.c. Dutch Art – Lasting Image (Zilzal). March 7. Second foal. 60,000Y. Tattersalls October Book 2. Roger Varian. The dam is an unplaced half-sister to 4 winners including the Group 3 Curragh Stakes second Janubi. The second dam, Minsden's Image (by Dancer's Image), a modest 3-y-o 2m winner, was a half-sister to 5 winners. (Sir Alex Ferguson & Mr S Hassiakos). *"A nice type that's grown since the sale and he's a good size now with scope. He has a good action, a good attitude and although he's not done any fast work yet I'm happy with the way he moves. A six/seven furlong 2-y-o from July onwards I would think"*.

1555. ARDINGLY (IRE) ★★★

b.f. Danehill Dancer – Asnieres (Spend A Buck). April 8. Twelfth foal. 300,000Y. Tattersalls October Book 1. Hugo Merry. Sister to the smart 7f (at 2 yrs) and 1m winner of 4 races and dual Group 3 placed Forgotten Voice, closely related to the Irish listed-placed 2-y-o and 3-y-o 5f winner Keepers Hill (by Danehill) and half-sister to 6 winners including the 1m (at 2 yrs) and Group 3 10.5f winner Prix de Flore winner Australie and the fairly useful 12f and 14f winner Big Occasion (by Sadler's Wells). The dam, a minor winner in France at 4 yrs, is a half-sister to 9 winners including the Breeders Cup Classic and Prix d'Ispahan winner Arcangues, the Prix de Psyche winner and French 1,000 Guineas second Agathe (dam of the triple Group 1 winner Alexandrie) and the dams of the 1,000 Guineas winner Cape Verdi and the US Grade 1 winner Angara. The second dam, Albertine (by Irish River), a winner of 2 races and third in the Group 2 Prix de l'Opera, was smart at up to 10f and is a half-sister to the

French Group winners Acoma, Ashmore and Art Bleu. (Mrs F H Hay). *"A really sweet filly and a beautiful mover. I quite like her but she's going to need time to strengthen. One for the late summer I think"*.

1556. ASHAADD (IRE) ★★★

b.c. Dansili – Vital Statistics (Indian Ridge). April 5. First foal. 110,000Y. Tattersalls October Book 1. Roger Varian. The dam, a listed 6f winner and second in the Group 3 Princess Margaret Stakes, is a half-sister to 5 winners. The second dam, Emerald Peace (by Green Desert), a useful listed 5f winner of 4 races and second in the Group 2 5f Flying Childers Stakes, is a half-sister to 5 winners. (Sheikh Ahmed Al Maktoum). *"He's out of a family we know quite well. It's not a big family and being a smallish colt he's just the same as the rest of them. A strong fellow that moves well, he could be a May/June runner. He'd be an early runner for the sire but it's a sharp family and he's not the biggest so he probably doesn't want waiting-on too long"*. Bulred up by min winnin

1557. BALLOOR (USA) ★★★

b.f. Pivotal – Nasmatt (Danehill). April 20. Half-sister to the useful 2-y-o 1m and subsequent UAE listed 10f winner Emmrooz (by Red Ransom) and to the fair 1m winner Towbaat (by Halling). The dam, a fairly useful 2-y-o 6f winner, was listed-placed and is closely related to the high-class Group 2 6f Lowther Stakes and Group 3 5f Queen Mary Stakes winner Bint Allayl and to the smart 2-y-o 5f and 6f and 3-y-o Group 3 7f Jersey Stakes winner Kheleyf. The second dam, Society Lady (by Mr Prospector), a fair 6f and 7f placed 2-y-o, is a sister to a minor winner and a half-sister to several others including the useful French 2-y-o 5.5f winner Kentucky Slew. (Sheikh Ahmed Al Maktoum). *"A sweet filly with decent conformation, she moves quite well but she's not going to be particularly forward. One for the late summer or early autumn"*.

1558. BIT OF A GIFT (FR) ★★★★ ♠

b.c. Dark Angel – Dilag (Almutawakel). March 16. Fourth foal. €120,000Y. Arqana Deauville August. Charlie Gordon-Watson. Half-brother to the quite useful 2011 2-y-o 6f winner I'm So Glad (by Clodovil), to the quite useful 5f and 6f winner of 6 races (including at 2 yrs) Living It

[handwritten: Wor 7f mtr Released]

Large (by Bertolini) and the modest 5f winner Pineapple Pete (by Compton Place). The dam, a 3-y-o 7f winner in France, is a half-sister to 4 winners including the US Grade 2 winner Distinct Habit. The second dam, Terracotta Hut (by Habitat), ran once unplaced and is a half-sister to 5 winners. (S Suhail). *"A nice type of horse, he's done well through the winter and he's a strong 2-y-o that moves nicely. He could be a summer 2-y-o and I like him. With his size and pedigree you'd have to hope he could go a bit, once we give him some faster work".*

[handwritten annotation]

1559. CHELWOOD GATE (USA) ★★★

b.c. Aussie Rules – Jusoor (El Prado). February 8. Second living foal. £48,000Y. Doncaster Premier. Hugo Merry. Half-brother to a minor winner abroad by Nayef. The dam is an unraced half-sister to 3 winners including the Group 3 winner Prix Corrida winner Luna Mareza. The second dam, Luna Maya (by Gay Mecene), won once at 3 yrs in France and is a sister to the Group 2 winner Long Mick and a half-sister to the Group 1 winners Luna Wells and Linamix. (Mrs F H Hay). *"A good-moving colt and one of our more forward 2-y-o's, we won't wait on him too long but he just wants to strengthen up a bit more. He'll be a May/June type runner I should think".*

1560. ELKAAYED (USA) ★★

ch.c. Distorted Humor – Habibti (USA) (Tabasco Cat). March 4. Half-brother to the US Grade 2 12f Brooklyn Handicap and dual Grade 3 winner Eldaafer (by A P Indy), to the UAS stakes winner Muhaawara (by Unbridled's Song) and to the minor US winner Jedoum (by Point Given). The dam won the Grade 1 7f Del Mar Debutante Stakes and the Grade 1 8.5f Hollywood Starlet Stakes (both at 2 yrs). The second dam, Miss Sobriety (by Temperence Hill), is an unraced half-sister to the Grade 1 Kentucky Oaks winner Gal In A Ruckus. (Hamdan Al Maktoum). *"Only just arrived from Dubai, he's quite a strong, attractive horse but we don't know much more about him than that at this stage".*

1561. ELSINIAAR ★★★

bl.c. New Approach – Comic (Be My Chief). February 2. Eighth foal. 220,000Y. Tattersalls October Book 1. Shadwell Estate Co. Half-brother to Viva Pataca (by Marju), a winner of

5 races here at 2 yrs from 7f to 9f including a listed event prior to winning the Grade 1 Queen Elizabeth II Cup in Hong Kong and £3.7 million, to the useful 1m and listed 11f winner Laughing (by Dansili), the quite useful 10f to 14f and hurdles winner Comedy Act (by Motivator) and the moderate 15f and hurdles winner Circus Clown (by Vettori). The dam, a quite useful 10f and 11.5f winner, is a half-sister to 4 winners including the 2-y-o Group 3 Solario Stakes and multiple US Grade 2 winner Brave Act. The second dam, Circus Act (by Shirley Heights), is an unraced sister to the listed 10f Lupe Stakes winner Lady Shipley and a half-sister to 6 winners including the listed 10f Upavon Stakes winner Ellie Ardensky and the dam of the Australian triple Group 1 winner Serenade Rose. (Hamdan Al Maktoum). *"A really attractive horse that's very balanced with a good action. I quite like him and he'll be a late summer type 2-y-o".*

1562. EXCEPTIONELLE ★★★

br.f. Exceed And Excel – Turning Leaf (Last Tycoon). February 19. Eighth foal. 85,000Y. Tattersalls October Book 2. Will Edmeades. Half-sister to the German 3-y-o Group 3 1m and listed 11f winner Turning Light (by Fantastic Light and herself dam of the US stakes winner Surrey Star) and to a minor winner in Italy by King's Best. The dam, a German 2-y-o winner and third in the Group 2 German 1,000 Guineas, is a half-sister to the second dam, Tamacana (by Windwurf), a German listed winner of 3 races at 2 and 3 yrs, is a half-sister to 4 winners. (Thurloe Thoroughbreds Ltd XXX). *"A likeable filly, she's strong, well-made and moves very well. She's by a good 2-y-o stallion and she has the strength to match, so she'll be a summer 2-y-o".*

[handwritten: Wor gd 6f mtr Kempton on dbt]

1563. HASHEEN ★★

ch.c. New Approach – Masaafat (Act One). February 17. The dam is an unraced half-sister to the very useful 2-y-o listed 6f winner and Group 1 6f Cheveley Park Stakes second Suez. The second dam, Repeat Warning (by Warning), a fair 8.3f placed 3-y-o, is a half-sister to 9 winners including the Group 2 9.2f Prix de l'Opera winner Bella Colora (dam of the Prince Of Wales's Stakes winner Stagecraft), the Irish Oaks winner Colorspin (dam of the

Group 1 winners Zee Zee Top, Opera House and Kayf Tara) and the Irish Champion Stakes winner Cezanne. (Hamdan Al Maktoum). *"Only been here for less than a week having wintered in Dubai. He's a scopey horse and a likeable model".*

1564. HEKAAYAAT (IRE) ★★★

ch.f. Mr Greeley – Mostaqeleh (Rahy). April 23. Third foal. Half-sister to the quite useful 2011 2-y-o 7f winner Nawwaar (by Distorted Humor). The dam, a very useful 2-y-o 6f and 7f winner, was second in the Group 2 1m Prix de Sandringham and is a half-sister to the very smart listed 7f (at 2 yrs) and listed 10f winner Muqbil. The second dam, Istiqlal (by Diesis), is an unraced half-sister to the Group 1 1m St James's Palace Stakes and Group 1 1m Queen Elizabeth II Stakes winner Bahri and to the high-class 2-y-o Group 2 7f Laurent Perrier Champagne Stakes winner Bahhare. (Hamdan Al Maktoum). *"One of those that wintered in Dubai, she's from a good family and she's a good model".* 2-1 :- gd cls f md 7f l-gr-dl

1565. HAZZAAT (IRE) ★★★

ch.c. Iffraaj – Hurricane Irene (Green Desert). April 10. Third foal. 110,000Y. Tattersalls October Book 2. Roger Varian. The dam is an unraced sister to the quite useful 6f (at 2 yrs) to 10f winner of 4 races and listed-placed Mister Green and a half-sister to the Group 1 Prix Saint-Alary winner Wavering. The second dam, Summertime Legacy (by Darshaan), winner of the Group 3 1m Prix des Reservoirs at 2 yrs and third in the Group 1 Prix Saint-Alary, is a half-sister to 6 winners. (Sheikh Ahmed Al Maktoum). *"He ought to make up into a summer 2-y-o, he's quite likeable and has a good action. Getting stronger all the time, I would think he'd be sharp enough for six furlongs".*

1566. HORSTED KEYNES (FR) ★★★

ch.c. Giant's Causeway – Viking's Cove (Miswaki). February 22. Tenth foal. 145,000Y. Tattersalls October Book 1. Hugo Merry. Half-brother to the French listed 1m winner of 4 races Precious Bunny (by Peintre Celebre) and to the French listed-placed winner of 7 races Flying Blue (by Fly To The Stars). The dam is an unraced half-sister to 6 winners including

the Group 2 Prix du Muguet winner Vetheuil, the Group 3 Prix de l'Opera winner Verveine (herself dam of the Grade 1 winners Vallee Enchantee and Volga) and the dams of the Group 1 winners Maids Causeway and Vespone and the Melbourne Cup second Purple Moon. The second dam, Venise (by Nureyev), is an unraced three-parts sister to the Mill Reef Stakes and Richmond Stakes winner Vacarme and a half-sister to the Prix Jacques le Marois winner Vin de France. (Mrs F H Hay). *"He's quite a nice horse and he's done well since he's been with me. He's thickened out well and grown a little bit. A very easy goer with a good, flat action, he'll not be too forward but by late summer he'll be pulling himself into shape".*

1567. HUFFOOF (IRE) ★★

b.f. Dalakhani – Albahja (Sinndar). March 29. Fourth foal. Half-sister to the unplaced 2011 2-y-o Tazweed (by Dubawi), to the quite useful 2-y-o 7f winner Jaaryah (by Halling) and the fair 10f winner Kronful (by Singspiel). The dam, a useful 12f winner, was second in the Group 3 10f Golden Daffodil Stakes and in the listed 12f Galtres Stakes and is a half-sister to the fair 11f to 14f winner of 4 races Efrhina. The second dam, Eshq Albahr (by Riverman), is an unraced half-sister to the useful 1m to 10f winner Dayflower. (Sheikh Ahmed Al Maktoum). *"She's going to take time to mature but she's not a bad model from one of Sheikh Ahmed's families. I would think she'll be quite a nice filly one day but we'll just have to wait on her a little bit".*

1568. IFFRAAJ PINK ★★★

b.f. Iffraaj – Red Vale (Halling). April 7. Fifth foal. 145,000Y. Tattersalls October Book 1. Stephen Hillen. Half-sister to the 2-y-o Grade 1 8.5f Breeders Cup Juvenile and listed 7f Stardom Stakes winner Vale Of York (by Invincible Spirit). The dam is an unraced half-sister to 6 winners including the fairly useful 10f and subsequent US Grade 3 winner Uraib. The second dam, Hamsaat (by Sadler's Wells), a quite useful winner over 1m at 3 yrs on her only outing, is a sister to 2 winners including the dual Group 2 winner Batshoof and a half-sister to 4 winners. (Mrs F. H. Hay). *"She's quite an attractive filly but she came to me late because she'd been a bit under the weather through the winter.*

So she'll be behind some of the others but I should think she'll catch them up quite quickly. She's quite easy on the eye, she's bred to be a mid-summer 2-y-o and could still make up into one".

1569. IZEM ★★

ch.c. Sir Percy – Bombazine (Generous). May 3. Twelfth foal. 260,000Y. Tattersalls October Book 1. A O Nerses. Closely related to the very useful dual 1m (at 2 yrs) and listed 11f and 12f winner Gravitas (by Mark Of Esteem) and half-brother the Group 2 Prix de Pomone winner Armure (by Dalakhani), the very useful triple listed winner over 7f and 1m Seta (by Pivotal), the French 12f and listed 2m winner Affirmative Action, the fairly useful 10f winner Dubai Venture (both by Rainbow Quest), the fairly useful 1m winner of 4 races Camelot (by Machiavellian) and the moderate 10f winner Big Sur (by Selkirk). The dam, a useful 10f winner, is a half-sister to 7 winners including the Breeders Cup Mile and Irish 2,000 Guineas winner Barathea, the Fillies Mile and Irish 1,000 Guineas winner Gossamer and the US Grade 3 winner Free At Last (herself dam of the US multiple Grade 2 winner Coretta). The second dam, Brocade (by Habitat), a high-class filly at up to 1m, won five races including the Group 1 7f Prix de la Foret and is a half-sister to 7 winners. (Saleh Al Homaizi & Imad Al Sagar). *"Quite a nice individual, but he was a late foal and he's a late maturing colt that needs to grow. He's back at the farm now to give him the chance to do exactly that".*

1570. JALADEE ★★

b.c. Cape Cross – Atamana (Lahib). February 28. Seventh foal. Half-brother to the fair 2011 dual 7f winner Bu Naaji (by Kheleyf), to the Group 3 10.5f Rose Of Lancaster Stakes winner of 6 races Mulaqat, the fair 10f winner Emshabb (both by Singspiel) and the modest 2-y-o 1m and 9f winner Skeleton (by Tobougg). The dam, a quite useful 1m winner, is a half-sister to 6 winners including the Irish 2-y-o 6f winner and Group 3 7f Killavullen Stakes third Dance Clear – subsequently a winner of 4 races and Grade 3 placed in the USA. The second dam, Dance Ahead (by Shareef Dancer), a quite useful 2-y-o 7f winner, is a half-sister to 6 winners. (Sheikh

Ahmed Al Maktoum). *"A really attractive horse but he'll take time and will be an autumn 2-y-o. He's really a 3-y-o model".*

1571. KABBRAAS (IRE) ★★

ch.c. Pivotal – Dorrati (Dubai Millennium). March 24. Fourth foal. Brother to Shaleek, placed second over 6f on both her starts at 2 yrs in 2011 and half-brother to the quite useful 2-y-o 6f winner Dahakaa (by Bertolini). The dam is an unraced half-sister to 4 winners including the 7f (at 2 yrs) and dual listed 1m winner Baharah and the fairly useful 2-y-o winners In Dubai and Naaddey. The second dam, Bahr (Generous), winner of the listed 7f Washington Singer Stakes (at 2 yrs), the Group 3 12f Ribblesdale Stakes and the Group 3 10.4f Musidora Stakes, is a half-sister to numerous winners. (Sheikh Ahmed Al Maktoum). *"He's not a bad individual side-on but he's not very correct head-on. If his conformation withstands the stresses of training then he could be a racehorse one day, but he's not a forward horse".*

1572. KOHLAAN (IRE) ★★★

b.c. Elusive City – Rock Salt (Selkirk). April 16. Fourth foal. 105,000Y. Tattersalls October Book 1. Shadwell Estate Co. Half-brother to the Group 1 7f Moyglare Stud Stakes winner Termagant (by Powerscourt), to the fairly useful 1m (at 2 yrs) to 10f winner of 5 races and listed-placed Splinter Cell (by Johannesburg) and the quite useful 2-y-o 6f winner Planet Waves (by Red Ransom). The dam, placed twice at 3 yrs in France, is a sister to the very smart Group 2 10f Prix Eugene Adam and Group 3 9f Prix de Guiche winner Kirkwall and a half-sister to 4 winners. The second dam, Kamkova (by Northern Dancer), a placed middle-distance stayer, is a half-sister to 10 winners including the top-class US middle-distance colt Vanlandingham and the dams of the Group/Grade 1 winners Distant Music and Funny Moon. (Sheikh Ahmed Al Maktoum). *"A colt that moves nicely, but he's grown a lot since the sales and he's quite a big horse now. We thought he'd be a real summer 2-y-o when we bought him but I think he's going to take a little bit more time".*

1573. LANANSAAK (IRE) ★★★★ ♠

ch.f. Zamindar – Bunood (Sadler's Wells). January 25. Third foal. Half-sister to the fair 7f and 1m winner Bakoura (by Green Desert). The dam, a fairly useful 2-y-o 1m winner, was third in the Group 3 12f Princess Royal Stakes, is a half-sister to 5 winners. The second dam, Azdihaar (by Mr Prospector), a quite useful dual 7f at 3 yrs is a half-sister to the high-class and genuine filly Shadayid, winner of the 1,000 Guineas and the Prix Marcel Boussac and to the very useful listed 7f winner and Jersey Stakes third Dumaani. (Hamdan Al Maktoum). *"She's a really likeable filly with a lot of quality and a lot of scope. She won't be an early type, but in the late summer or early autumn she should be racing and she's a filly that catches the eye".*

1574. MISHAAL (IRE) ★★★

ch.g. Kheleyf – My Dubai (Dubai Millennium). April 12. Closely related to the fair 2011 6f and 7f placed 2-y-o Mizwaaj (by Invincible Spirit) and half-brother to the fair 7f and 9f winner Naddwah (by Pivotal). The dam, placed over 7f on her only start, is a half-sister to 7 winners including the very smart triple Group 2 7f winner Iffraaj, the useful 2-y-o Group 3 7f Prix du Calvados winner Kareymah and the useful dual 1m winner Jathaabeh. The second dam, Pastorale (by Nureyev), a fairly useful 3-y-o 7f winner, ran only twice more including in a walk-over. (Sheikh Ahmed Al Maktoum). *"A racey individual who should make a summer 2-y-o. We had to geld him because he was just a bit too cheeky".*

1575. MORAWIJ ★★★★

ch.c. Exceed And Excel – Sister Moonshine (FR) (Piccolo). February 22. Second foal. 120,000Y. Tattersalls October Book 2. Roger Varian.
The dam won over 5f (at 2 yrs) and 6f in France and was third in the Group 3 5f Prix du Bois and is a half-sister to 2 winners including the French listed winner Mundybash. The second dam, Cootamundra (by Double Bed), won over 1m at 3 yrs in France and is a half-sister to 9 winners including the triple Group 3 winner Big John. (Sheikh Ahmed Al Maktoum). *"He really is a very mature horse for his age – a very strong, thick-bodied colt. He'd be one of the most forward in the yard and he ought to be racing in May".* *Won 6f cl 2n Haydon*

1576. MUTASHADED (USA) ★★

b.c. Raven's Pass – Sortita (Monsun). January 22. First foal. The dam, a quite useful dual 10f winner, is a half-sister to the German Group 1 winners Samum, Schiaparelli and Salve Regina. The second dam, Sacarina (by Old Vic), is an unraced half-sister to 6 winners. (Hamdan Al Maktoum). *"He's only been here a week and he's a big colt that's going to take some time I think. The dam is very well-bred and hopefully the blood will come through, but he's a 3-y-o in the making really".*

1577. ORBISON (IRE) ★★★

b.c. Azamour – Glenmara (Known Fact). April 9. Seventh foal. 70,000Y. Tattersalls October Book 1. A D Spence. Half-brother to the useful 2-y-o 6f winner and Group 3 Flying Five third Leitra (by Danehill Dancer) and to the fair 2-y-o 5f winner Barbieri (by Encosta De Lago). The dam, placed at 3 yrs in France, is a half-sister to 2 minor winners abroad. The second dam, Plentiful (by Lear Fan), is an unraced half-sister to 8 winners including the Super Staff (US Grade 1 Yellow Ribbon Handicap) and Public Purse (Group 2 Prix de Chaudenay, Grade 2 San Marcos Handicap etc) and to the unplaced dam of the Group 2 winning miler Rob Roy. (A. D Spence). *"A very natural-moving, good-bodied horse. He won't be very early but I'm quite happy with the way he moves and he could be a nice horse one day. He's probably sharp enough to be a seven furlong type 2-y-o".*

1578. PUTRA ETON (IRE) ★★★★

b.c. Danehill Dancer – Anna Pallida (Sadler's Wells). March 18. Fourth foal. 400,000Y. Tattersalls October Book 1. Charlie Gordon-Watson. Half-brother to the very useful 2011 2-y-o 5f and listed 7f winner and Group 2 7f Rockfel Stakes second Pimpernel (by Invincible Spirit). The dam, a quite useful 10f winner, is a half-sister to 4 winners including the very smart Group 1 10f Hong Kong Cup, Group 2 1m Beresford Stakes and Group 2 10f Royal Whip Stakes winner Eagle Mountain, the smart 2-y-o Group 1 1m Prix Marcel Boussac winner and triple Group 1 placed Sulk and the smart 1m listed winner Wallace. The second dam, Masskana (by Darshaan), a minor 9f and 10f winner in France, is a half-sister to the Group 2 Gallinule Stakes winner Massyar and the US

Grade 3 Arcadia Handicap winner Madjaristan. (HRH Sultan Ahmad Shah). *"He's a lovely horse with a bit of scope and strength to him. A very attractive, good-bodied colt and a really easy-mover, he cost a lot of money but he hasn't disappointed us yet".*

1579. RIBAAT (IRE) ★★★
b.c. Invincible Spirit – Fonda (Quiet American). March 26. First foal. 280,000Y. Tattersalls October Book 1. Shadwell Estate Co. The dam ran once unplaced and is a half-sister to 3 winners including the Group 3 Sovereign Stakes winner and dual Group 1 placed Layman. The second dam, Laiyl (by Nureyev), won over 10f and is a half-sister to 3 winners including Allurement (Group 3 Prix Cleopatre). (Hamdan Al Maktoum). *"He's been in Dubai and has only just arrived so I can't really comment on him except to say that he's by a top stallion, he cost a few quid and he's quite a good-looking colt".*

Won by cl 5 m\)n H4lcn on debut

1580. ROCKY GROUND (IRE) ★★★ ♠
b.c. Acclamation – Keriyka (Indian Ridge). January 30. First foal. £105,000Y. Doncaster Premier. McKeever Bloodstock. The dam, placed fourth over 7f in Ireland on her only start, is a half-sister to 2 winners. The second dam, Kermiyana (by Green Desert), won the listed Brownstown Stakes and is a half-sister to 3 winners. (Clipper Group Holdings Ltd). *"He's a likeable horse, he's strong and he moves well. I should think he'd make a 2-y-o around June time and he does look a 2-y-o type".*

1581. SAADAAT ★★
b.f. New Approach – Ameerat (Mark Of Esteem). March 20. Half-sister to the quite useful 2011 2-y-o 1m winner Oojooba (by Monsun) to the fairly useful 2-y-o 1m winner Sowaylm (by Tobougg), the quite useful 7f winner Kawssaj (by Dubawi) and the quite useful 7f winner Own Boss (by Seeking The Gold). The dam won the 1,000 Guineas and is a full or half-sister to 3 winners including the smart UAE 1m winner of 11 races Walmooh. The second dam, Walimu (by Top Ville), a quite useful winner of 3 races from 1m to 12f, is a half-sister to 6 winners. (Sheikh Ahmed Al Maktoum). *"Quite a nice model, she's going to take her time because she's not a particularly forward animal. She'll*

be running in the autumn, but she has 3-y-o stamped all over her".

1582. SEVERIANO (USA) ★★★
b.c. Danehill Dancer – Time Control (Sadler's Wells). January 19. The dam, a quite useful 10f winner, is a sister to the Group 2 Prix de Malleret and listed Cheshire Oaks winner Time On. The second dam, Time Away (by Darshaan), won the Group 3 10.4f Musidora Stakes, was third in the Group 1 Prix de Diane and the Group 1 Nassau Stakes and is a half-sister to 6 winners including the 10f winner and Prix de Diane second Time Ahead. (Merry Fox Stud Ltd). *"He's a good model and a good mover and he has an early foaling date, so he'll make a 2-y-o but not until mid-summer at the earliest"*

1583. SHEMAAL (IRE) ★★★
b.c. Monsun – Zahrat Dubai (Unfuwain). March 1. Half-brother to the useful 1m (at 2 yrs) and listed 10f winner Modeyra (by Shamardal) and to the quite useful 2-y-o 1m winner Shariki (by Spectrum). The dam won the Group 1 10f Nassau Stakes and the Group 10.4f Musidora Stakes winner Zahrat Dubai. The second dam, Walesiana (by Star Appeal), won the German 1,000 Guineas and is a half-sister to 8 winners. (Sheikh Ahmed Al Maktoum). *"A nice type, he's a 3-y-o in the making and he'll just have a run or two in the autumn, but he's quite a nice horse".*

1584. SOARING SPIRITS (IRE) ★★★ ♠
ch.c. Tamayuz – Follow My Lead (Night Shift). March 18. Fourth foal. €40,000Y. Goffs Orby. Charlie Gordon-Watson. Half-brother to the fairly useful 2009 2-y-o dual 7f winner Graphic (by Excellent Art), to the quite useful Irish 9f winner Crystal Morning (by Cape Cross) and the modest 7f winner Amity (by Nayef). The dam, a fair 8.3f winner, is a half-sister to 5 winners including the Group 2 Superlative Stakes and Group 2 Bosphorus Cup winner Halicarnassus. The second dam, Launch Time (by Relaunch), is a US placed half-sister to 4 winners including the US Grade 2 winner Palace March and Grade 1 placed Executive Pride. (Mrs G O'Driscoll). *"He's quite a strong horse that moves nicely and he should make a summer 2-y-o over six/seven furlongs".*

1585. STAR PEARL (USA) ★★★★
b.f. Tapit – Lexi Star (Crypto Star). February 9. First foal. $150,000Y. Keeneland September. David Redvers. The dam, a US stakes winner of 12 races, was Grade 2 placed three times and is a half-sister to 3 winners. The second dam, Frozen Lock (by Corridor Key), a US stakes-placed winner of 13 races, is a half-sister to 2 winners. (Pearl Bloodstock Ltd). *"She's a likeable filly and a great model with a bit of size, scope and strength. I'm not that familiar with the stallion, but they're very strong on him in the States. This is a good-moving filly, so hopefully she'll make a nice 2-y-o in the second half of the season".*

1586. TAJHEEZ ★★★
b.c. Raven's Pass – Ghaidaa (Cape Cross). January 14. First foal. The dam, a useful listed placed 10f winner, is closely related to the Group 3 12f Princess Royal Stakes winner Itnab, the very useful 6f winner of 4 races Haafiz and the useful 7f and 1m winner and Irish 1,000 Guineas third Umniyatee and a half-sister to numerous winners including the Group 1 Epsom Oaks winner Eswarah. The second dam, Midway Lady (by Alleged), won the Prix Marcel Boussac, the 1,000 Guineas and the Oaks and is a half-sister to 5 winners including the very useful 11.8f listed winner Capias. (Hamdan Al Maktoum). *"From a good family of Sheikh Hamdan's, this colt carries a bit of quality. He's a good-bodied horse with a good action and although he won't be an early horse there's enough about him to like. I see him starting off at seven furlongs but he'll probably be a mile/ten furlong horse next year".*

1587. TANTSHI ★★★★
b.f. Invincible Spirit – Qasirah (Machiavellian). April 21. Fifth foal. Half-sister to the very useful 2-y-o listed 7f winner Toolain, to the fair 7f winner Kammaan (both by Diktat) and the modest 14f and hurdles winner Harry Hunt (by Bertolini). The dam, a useful 2-y-o 6f winner, was third in the Group 3 8.5f Princess Margaret Stakes is out of the useful 10.5f and 12f winner Altaweelah (by Fairy King), herself a half-sister to 7 winners including the useful 10f to 14f winner Lost Soldier Three. (Sheikh Ahmed Al Maktoum). *"She's a nice, strong, well-made filly that moves nicely. She should*

make a mid-summer 2-y-o and I think she'll be sharp enough to start at six furlongs, after all her half-sister Toolain was a listed 2-y-o winner in July".* Quickened well to win el 4 fillies mdn Newb¹)

1588. TENOR (IRE) ★★★
b.c. Oratorio – Cedar Sea (Persian Bold). February 18. Seventh foal. €85,000Y. Arqana Deauville August. Half-brother to the quite useful 2011 2-y-o 7f winner Holy Roman Warrior (by Holy Roman Emperor) and to the smart 1m (at 2 yrs) and Group 3 13f winner Corsica (by Cape Cross). The dam, a French 1m winner and second in the listed Prix Yacowlef, is a half-sister to 3 winners including the Group 3 6f Coventry Stakes winner CD Europe. The second dam, Woodland Orchid (by Woodman, is an unplaced half-sister to the Group 3 Derrinstown Stud Derby Trial winner Truth Or Dare, the UAE Group 3 winner D'Anjou and the listed winner Sandstone. (Highclere Thoroughbred Racing – John Porter). *"Quite a well-made, good-bodied colt with good conformation. He moves well and although he's not going to be early by any means he should be a 2-y-o in the second half of the season".*

1589. TILAAD ★★★
b.c. Dubawi – Makaaseb (Pulpit). February 11. First foal. The dam, a useful 2-y-o 7f winner and listed-placed over 10f at 3 yrs, is a half-sister to 3 winners including the US stakes winner Sirpa. The second dam, Turn And Sparkle (by Danzatore), a minor US winner of 3 races at 2 and 3 yrs, is a half-sister to numerous winners. (Hamdan Al Maktoum). *"He's only been here a week so it's hard to judge, but he's a really attractive horse by the right stallion – it's nice to have a Dubawi in the yard. We trained the mare but didn't get the full potential out of her".*

1590. TOUCH A MILLION (IRE) ★★
b.c. Green Tune – Janistra (Grand Slam). March 17. First foal. €130,000Y. Arqana Deauville August. Charlie Gordon-Watson. The dam is an unraced half-sister to 4 winners including the US triple Grade 1 winner Exotic Wood. The second dam, J D Flowers (by Dixieland Band), won 3 minor races in the USA at 3 and 4 yrs and is a half-sister to one winner. (S Suhail). *"A nice type of horse that's grown a lot since the*

sale, so he won't be out until the second half of the season".

1591. TUSCAN FUN ★★★

ch.c. Medicean – Elfin Laughter (Alzao). March 25. Twelfth foal. 22,000Y. Tattersalls October Book 2. Roger Varian. Half-brother to the smart listed winner of 6 races from 7f to 1m Smirk (by Selkirk), the very useful dual 6f winner (including at 2 yrs) Stetchworth Prince, the quite useful 1m winner Cartoon (by Danehill Dancer), the UAE 3-y-o winner Joyous Gift (both by Cadeaux Genereux), the UAE dual 6f winner Celtic King (by King's Best), the Italian winner of 8 races Sella del Diavolo (by Barathea) and two minor winners abroad by Vettori and Shamardal. The dam, a fair 2-y-o 7.5f and 1m winner, is a half-sister to 11 winners including the US Grade 2 winner Sign Of Hope. The second dam, Rainbow's End (by My Swallow) was a quite useful 2-y-o 6f winner. (K Allen, R Marchant & G Jarvis). "Quite a likeable horse that'll take a little bit of time, but he moves perfectly fine. There's a racehorse there somewhere, but he's not going to be out until the second half of the summer". TRAINERS' BARGAIN BUY

1592. WILHANA (IRE) ★★

b.f. Singspiel – Jathaabeh (Nashwan). March 28. Eighth foal. Sister to the very useful 1m (including at 2 yrs) and 9f winner Yaddree (by Singspiel) and half-sister to the quite useful 2011 2-y-o 1m winner Mazeydd (by Motivator), the useful 10f winner Mijhaar (by Shirocco) and the quite useful dual 1m winner Sky More (by Xaar). The dam, a useful dual 1m winner, is a half-sister to several winners including the useful 2-y-o Group 3 7f Prix du Calvados winner Kareymah. The second dam, Pastorale (by Nureyev), a fairly useful 3-y-o 7f winner, is a half-sister to the Group 1 Lockinge Stakes winner and high-class sire Cape Cross out of the dual Group 1 winning 2-y-o sire Park Appeal. (Sheikh Ahmed Al Maktoum). "There's not too much wrong with her, but she's on the weak side so we won't see her until the autumn".

1593. YARROOM (IRE) ★★★

b.c. Cape Cross – Aryaamm (Galileo). March 2. Third foal. Half-brother to the 2-y-o Group 2 7f Champagne Stakes winner Saamidd (by Street

Cry). The dam, a quite useful 10f winner, is a half-sister to the French 6f (at 2 yrs) and 7.5f winner and Group 2 1m third Mathematician. The second dam, Zibilene (by Rainbow Quest), a useful 12f winner and listed-placed over 10f, is a half-sister to 7 winners including the Breeders Cup Mile, Irish 2,000 Guineas and Queen Anne Stakes winner Barathea and the Fillies Mile and Irish 1,000 Guineas winner Gossamer. (Sheikh Ahmed Al Maktoum). "He was very small when he arrived but he's done well, he's got stronger and he moves quite naturally, so I think he could be a July/August type of horse".

1594. UNNAMED ★★★

ch.f. Tale Of The Cat – Breathtaking (Mineshaft). January 24. First foal. $120,000Y. Keeneland September. John Black. The dam is an unplaced half-sister to the US winners and Grade 2 placed Pick Six and Conservative. The second dam, Oh What A Windfall (by Seeking The Gold), won the US Grade 1 Matron Stakes and is sister to the champion US 2-y-o and dual Grade 1 winner Heavenly Prize. "She's quite likeable, there's a bit of strength to her and she has a good action. Hopefully she'll pull herself together in time for her to start over seven furlongs in the second half of the summer".

1595. UNNAMED ★★★

ch.c. Giant's Causeway – Danzig's Humor (Lemon Drop Kid). April 23. Second foal. $100,000Y. Keeneland September. John Black. The dam is an unraced half-sister to 6 winners including the US dual Grade 2 winner Distorted Humor. The second dam, Danzig's Beauty (by Danzig), won the Grade 2 Gardenia Stakes in the USA and was second in the Grade 1 Acorn Stakes. (Mrs Gay Jarvis). "A good, honest horse with a good action and a bit of bone and scope. He's not an early 2-y-o but there's a bit of quality there I think".

1596. UNNAMED ★★★

b.f. Danehill Dancer – Dashing (Sadler's Wells). February 19. First foal. The dam is an unraced half-sister to numerous winners including the top-class multiple Group 1 winner Alexander Goldrun and the Group 3 Prix de la Jonchere winner and Group 1 placed Medicis. The second dam, Renashaan (by Darshaan), a listed winner in France, was third in the Group 3 9f

Prix Vanteaux and is a half-sister to 4 minor winners. (Saleh Al Homaizi & Imad Al Sagar). *"She's done well since she's been here, she's grown a bit, got a bit stronger and she moves nicely. Possibly a summer 2-y-o".*

1597. UNNAMED ★★★

b.c. Raven's Pass – Delphinus (Soviet Star). January 29. Sixth foal. 150,000Y. Tattersalls October Book 1. Roger Varian. Half-brother to the Group 3 Cornwallis Stakes and Group 3 Palace House Stakes winner Captain Gerrard (by Oasis Dream), to the Hong Kong Stakes winner and French Group 2 second Saturn, the quite useful Irish triple 1m winner Ballivor (both by Marju), the useful Irish 6f and 7f winner and dual listed-placed Glocca Morra (by Catrail) and the fair Irish 6f and 7f winner Sedna (by Priolo). The dam, a minor winner at 3 yrs in France, is a half-sister to 4 winners including the quite useful 7f (at 2 yrs) and 8.2f winner Deserve. The second dam, Scimitarra (by Kris), a very useful 2-y-o 6f and 7.2f and 3-y-o 10f Lupe Stakes winner, is a half-sister to 6 winners including the top class sprinter Double Form. (A. D Spence). *"Quite a nice type, he's a strong, good-moving horse that should make a 2-y-o by the summer. He's coughing at the moment, which is frustrating me because I'm dying to get on with him and I can't. He's quite a natural mover so I think he'll make a 2-y-o alright".*

1598. UNNAMED ★★★

gr.f. Excellent Art – Divine Grace (Definite Article). March 26. Seventh foal. 125,000Y. Tattersalls October Book 2. Roger Varian. Sister to the useful 2011 2-y-o 6f winner and Group 2 Rockfel Stakes third Gray Pearl and half-sister to the German Group 2 6f Goldene Peitsche winner of 5 races Electric Beat (by Shinko Forest), the fairly useful 2-y-o 7f winner and listed placed Blakey's Boy (by Hawk Wing) and the modest 5.2f winner Divalini (by Bertolini). The dam ran unplaced twice and is a half-sister to 2 winners. The second dam, Grey Patience (by Common Grounds), is an unraced half-sister to 8 winners including the listed winners Cape Town and Regiment. (A. D Spence). *"A sweet filly with a good action, she could be a summer 2-y-o over six/seven furlongs".*

1599. UNNAMED ★★★

b.f. Marju – Much Faster (Fasliyev). April 10. Fifth foal. 180,000Y. Tattersalls October Book 1. A O Nerses. Half-sister to the useful listed 5f winner and Group 3 Flying Five third Sugar Free, to the quite useful 7f (at 2 yrs) and 5f winner Apace (both by Oasis Dream) and the useful 1m (at 2 yrs) and 9f winner High Twelve (by Montjeu). The dam won 4 races including the Group 2 6f Prix Robert Papin and the Group 3 5f Prix du Bois, was second in the Group 1 Prix Morny and is a half-sister to 4 winners. The second dam, Interruption (by Zafonic), is an unraced half-sister to 6 winners including the Grade 2 La Prevoyante Handicap winner Interim (dam of the US Grade 1 winner Midships) and the Group 2 Prix Maurice de Gheest winner Interval (the dam of two stakes winners). (Saleh Al Homaizi & Imad Al Sagar). *"She's done well since she's been here, she's stronger now than when she turned up. It's quite a sharp pedigree and she moves quite well but we haven't done enough with her to get a feel of her yet".*

1600. UNNAMED ★★★

b.c. Green Desert – Thorntoun Piccolo (Groom Dancer). February 25. Third foal. 150,000Y. Tattersalls October Book 2. Blandford Bloodstock. Half-brother to the modest 10f and 12f winner Baoli (by Dansili). The dam, a moderate 6f placed maiden, is a half-sister to 10 winners including the listed Doncaster Mile, listed City Of York Handicap and subsequent Canadian Grade 2 winner Vanderlin. The second dam, Massorah (by Habitat), won the Group 3 5f Premio Omenoni and was second in the Group 3 Prix du Gros Chene and is a half-sister to 4 winners. (Mr P. D Smith). *"A well-made colt, but he was a bit under the weather during the winter so he's a bit behind at this stage. He's got a good action and I'm still hoping he'll become a mid-summer 2-y-o".*

ED VAUGHAN

1601. CLEAR PEARL (USA) ★★★

ch.f. Giant's Causeway – Clear In The West (Gone West). February 14. Fourth foal. $80,000Y. Keeneland September. David Redvers. Half-sister to 2 minor winners in the USA by Touch Gold and Forestry. The dam, a stakes-placed winner of 8 races, is a half-sister to 5 winners including the multiple Grade 3 winners

Bedanken and the Graded stakes-placed Much Obliged, Free Thinking and Get Rich Quick. The second dam, Danka (by Strawberry Road), a winner of 3 races in the USA, is a half-sister to the Graded stakes winners Ganges and Apolda. (Pearl Bloodstock). *"A nice, big, scopey filly that'll probably want seven furlongs. She's had a couple of minor issues but she's fine now and I think we'll see her out in August. It's a good cross and although she isn't a particularly exuberant worker that's typical of the sire".*

1602. UNNAMED ★★

ch.c. Byron – Caldy Dancer (Soviet Star). February 14. Fourth foal. 15,000Y. Tattersalls October Book 3. Not sold. Half-brother to the smart 7f to 9f winner of 5 races and Group 3 placed Dance And Dance (by Royal Applause). The dam, a useful 2-y-o dual 5f winner and second in the Group 3 7f Debutante Stakes, is a half-sister to 3 winners. The second dam, Smile Awhile (by Woodman), ran once unplaced and is a full or half-sister to 3 winners. (Mr M. Rashid). *"He was starting to go well and he's very similar to his half-brother Dance And Dance, but his knees are quite immature so he's one for much later in the season and next year".*

1603. UNNAMED ★★★

ch.c. Mount Nelson – Phoebe Woodstock (Grand Lodge). March 5. Second foal. 29,000Y. Tattersalls October Book 2. Rabbah Bloodstock. The dam, a fair 7f (at 2 yrs) to 14f placed maiden, is a half-sister to 10 winners including the Group 3 Select Stakes winner Leporello, the listed winners Calypso Grant and Poppy Carew and the dam of the US Grade 2 winner Devious Boy. The second dam, Why So Silent (by Mill Reef), is an unraced half-sister to 5 winners including the US Grade 3 winner Supreme Sound. (S. Ali). *"I like him a lot, he's grown quite a bit since he came in but he's a nice type and a very good mover. I've done a couple of little bits with him and I liked what I saw. He'll need quick ground and possibly seven furlongs, but the Danehill cross has worked very well with the dam's side. He should be able to make his mark over seven furlongs or a mile and we'll try and get him out from late May onwards".*

1604. UNNAMED ★★

b.c. Shamardal – Shraayef (Nayef). February 24. First foal. 55,000Y. Tattersalls October Book 1. Not sold. The dam, a moderate 11f winner, is a half-sister to 5 winners including the Group 1 Premio Roma winner of 11 races Imperial Dancer and the useful listed 10.4f winner Lafite. The second dam, Gorgeous Dancer (by Nordico), an Irish 3-y-o 1m winner and third in the listed Irish Oaks Trial, is a half-sister to 3 winners. (Mr S. Misfer). *"A small, very sharp-looking horse, he looks a sprinter-type but actually he's not as precocious as he looks and I'd say he wants seven furlongs. We'll probably start him over six before stepping him up in trip".*

1605. UNNAMED ★★★

ch.c. Starcraft – Shuaily (Shuailaan). February 26. Second foal. 65,000Y. Tattersalls October Book 2. Farrington Bloodstock. The dam won two Grade 1 events in Peru and is a half-sister to 3 winners including the Peruvian Grade 3 winner Precursor. The second dam, Flame (by Farallon P), is an unraced half-sister to 6 winners. (Mr P Anastasiou). *"A nice, big, really good-moving horse. The dam was a multiple Group winning mare in South America and she was very tough. He's more of a 3-y-o type but he's done everything I've asked of him and I like what I've seen so far. I can't see any reason why he shouldn't be running in June and we might start him at six furlongs and then step him up to seven. A really good-looking horse with a great attitude and constitution".*

1606. UNNAMED ★★

b.f. Nayef – Tahirah (Green Desert). March 23. Fifth foal. £3,700Y. Ascot December. Adam Thomas. Sister to Cyrus Sod, unplaced on his only start at 2 yrs in 2011 and half-sister to the quite useful 9f winner Little Rocky (by Cadeaux Genereux). The dam, a useful 3-y-o 7f and 1m winner, was listed-placed over 7f and 1m at 4 yrs and is a sister to one winner and a half-sister to 5 winners. The second dam, Kismah (by Machiavellian), a very useful dual 1m winner, is a half-sister to 10 winners including the dam of the US dual Grade 2 winner Shakis. (C. J. Murfitt). *"I knew the mare who was probably more of a seven furlong type but I think this filly is more like the sire and she'll probably get ten furlongs next year. I've kept her going because she's quite a busy filly, but I'll give her a break now for a few weeks. A nice-moving filly that's very sound, she'll make a 2-y-o over seven furlongs or more".*

DAVID WACHMAN

1607. DREAM INDIA

b.c. Acclamation – Bendis (Danehill). April 25. Seventh foal. 310,000Y. Tattersalls October Book 1. Stephen Hillen. Brother to the quite useful dual 6f (including at 2 yrs) and 7f winner Rubirosa and half-brother to the fairly useful 2-y-o 5f winner and dual listed-placed Walkingonthemoon (by Footstepsinthesand) a winner over hurdles by Golan. The dam, a 7f winner at 3 yrs in Germany, is a half-sister to 6 winners. The second dam, Berenice (by Groom Dancer), a fair 10f winner, was listed-placed and is a half-sister to 3 winners. (Mrs F Hay).

1608. GAME RESERVE

b.c. Oasis Dream – Biriyani (Danehill). April 27. Fourth foal. 360,000Y. Tattersalls October Book 1. Alex Cole. Half-brother to the fair 12f and 13f winner Dynamic Drive (by Motivator). The dam, placed fourth three times over 6f and 1m, is a half-sister to 4 winners including Mister Monet (Group 2 10f Prix Guillaume d'Ornano), Tarascon (Group 1 7f Moyglare Stud Stakes and Irish 1,000 Guineas) and the very useful 5f winner and Moyglare Stud Stakes and Cheveley Park Stakes third Mala Mala. The second dam, Breyani (by Commanche Run), a useful winner at up to 2m, is a half-sister to 4 winners. (Mrs F Hay).

1609. LOVE AND CHERISH (IRE)

b.f. Excellent Art – Party Feet (Noverre). February 4. First foal. 90,000Y. Tattersalls October Book 2. D Wachman. The dam is an unraced half-sister to the Group 2 Sun Chariot Stakes and Group 3 Matron Stakes winner of 4 races Independence (herself dam of the dual Group 1 winner Mount Nelson and the Group 2 winner Monitor Closely). The second dam, Yukon Hope (by Forty Niner), was a fair 6f and 1m placed maiden.

1610. MIRONICA (IRE)

ch.f. Excellent Art – Lisfannon (Bahamian Bounty). April 4. Third foal. €40,000Y. Goffs

Orby. D Wachman. Half-sister to the modest 2011 dual 7f placed 2-y-o Dickens Rules (by Aussie Rules) and to the quite useful 2-y-o 5f winner Dress Up (by Noverre). The dam is a placed half-sister to 3 winners including the listed 5f winner of 5 races Dazed And Amazed. The second dam, Amazed (by Clantime), a modest 5f placed 3-y-o, is a sister to the Group 3 Prix du Petit Couvert winner Bishops Court and a half-sister to 5 winners including the listed winning sprinter Astonished.

1611. MONTJEU MINDER

b.c. Montjeu – Whos Mindin Who (Danehill Dancer). February 23. First foal. 190,000Y. Tattersalls October Book 1. Alex Cole. The dam is an unraced sister to the very smart 2-y-o Group 2 7f Champagne Stakes winner and French 2,000 Guineas and French Derby third Westphalia and a half-sister to 5 winners including the US Grade 3 El Camino Real Derby winner and Grade 2 placed Cliquot and the US stakes winner and Grade 3 placed Stockholder. The second dam, Pharapache (by Lyphard), won over 10f in France and is closely related to the French Group 3 winner Antheus and a half-sister to 7 winners including the French Group 3 winner Alexandrie (herself the dam of 5 stakes winners including the Group 1 10f Criterium de Saint-Cloud winner Poliglote) and to the placed dam of the Group 1 Prix Ganay winner Indian Danehill. (Mrs F Hay).

1612. SEUSSICAL (IRE)

b.br.c. Galileo – Danehill Music (Danehill Dancer). January 31. First foal. The dam, winner of the Group 3 1m Park Express Stakes, is a half-sister to numerous minor winners. The second dam, Tuesday Morning (by Sadler's Wells), is an unraced half-sister to one winner in Germany. (Mrs J Magnier, M Tabor, D Wachman).

1613. SPHEREOFINFLUENCE (IRE)

ch.c. Giant's Causeway – Ashley Hall (Maria's Mon). April 3. Third foal. 55,000Y. Tattersalls October Book 1. John O'Byrne. Half-brother to Mason's Pegasus (by Fusaichi Pegasus), a minor US winner at 2 and 3 yrs. The dam won once at 3 yrs in the USA and is a half-sister to 7 winners including the US Grade 1 and Grade 3 winner Bandini. The second dam, Divine Dixie (by Dixieland Band), a US winner and stakes-placed, is a half-sister to 4 winners including the stakes winner and sire Stormy Atlantic and to the unraced dam of the Group/Grade 2 winners Incanto Dream and Atlando. (J P McManus).

1614. THREE SEA CAPTAINS (IRE)
b.c. Choisir – La Tintoretta (Desert Prince). March 14. Third foal. D Wachman. €30,000Y. Tattersalls Ireland. D Wachman. Brother to the quite useful 2-y-o 5f winner Remotelynx. The dam, an Irish 5f winner, is a half-sister to one winner. The second dam, Lavinia Fontana (by Sharpo), a very smart sprinter and winner of the Group 1 6f Haydock Sprint Cup, the Group 2 6f Premio Umbria, the Group 3 5f Prix du Petit-Couvert and the Group 3 7f Premio Chiusura, is a half-sister to 3 winners.

Won 5f listed Currgy

1615. WELL'S DANCER (IRE)
gr.c. Danehill Dancer – Mystic Mile (Sadler's Wells). January 29. Fourth foal. €220,000Y. Arqana Deauville August. Alex Cole. Half-brother to the fair Irish 2-y-o 7f winner Maundays Bay (by Invincible Spirit) and to the French 10f winners Mystic Joy (by Shamardal) and Angel Of Rain (by Dalakhani). The dam, a fairly useful 10f and 11.6f winner, was listed-placed and is a half-sister to 3 minor winners. The second dam, Delage (by Bellypha), is an unraced half-sister to 5 winners including the Group 2 Prix Maurice de Gheest winner and July Cup second College Chapel. (Mrs J Magnier, Mr M Tabor & Mrs F Hay).

1616. UNNAMED
b.f. Elusive City – Jioconda (Rossini). March 2. Third foal. €100,000Y. Goffs November. Barronstown Stud. Half-sister to the 2011 2-y-o Group 1 6f Cheveley Park Stakes and Group 3 6f Round Tower Stakes winner Lightening Pearl and to the 3-y-o 11f winner and 2-y-o Group 3 Tyros Stakes third Jolie Jioconde (both by Marju). The dam won the listed Silken Glider Stakes and was third in the Group 3 Killavullan Stakes. The second dam, La Joconde (by Vettori), is an unraced half-sister to 4 winners.

1617. UNNAMED
b.f. Danehill Dancer – Mine Excavation (Galileo). March 17. Third foal. 125,000Y. Tattersalls October Book 1. John O'Byrne. The dam is

an unraced three-parts sister to the Group 1 10.5f Prix Lupin and US Grade 2 1m winner Johann Quatz and to the French 10.5f to 13.5f listed winner Walter Willy and a half-sister to 8 winners including the Group 1 Prix du Jockey Club and Group 1 Prix Lupin winner Hernando. The second dam, Whakilyric (by Miswaki), winner the Group 3 7f Prix du Calvados and third in the Prix de la Salamandre and the Prix de la Foret, is a half-sister to 6 winners.

ED WALKER

1618. DARING DRAGON ★★★★♠
gr.c. Intikhab – The Manx Touch (Petardia). April 25. Sixth foal. 90,000Y. Tattersalls October Book 2. Sackville/Donald. Brother to the fairly useful 2011 2-y-o dual 7f winner Frog Hollow and to the fair triple 7f winner Moone's My Name and half-brother to the fairly useful 5f (at 2 yrs) and listed 6f winner and Group 2 Criterium de Maisons-Laffitte second Baby Strange, to the modest 7f, 1m and hurdles winner Mambo Sun (both by Superior Premium) and the modest triple 6f winner Ride A White Swan (by Baryshnikov). The dam, a moderate 7f and 1m winner at 3 yrs, is a half-sister to 2 winners. The second dam, Chapter And Verse (by Dancer's Image), is an unraced half-sister to 4 winners out of the 1,000 Guineas and Oaks winner Altesse Royale. (Mrs A. A. Lau Yap). *"It's a very good family and this is a really nice horse that's grown a lot and he'll be a big, powerful colt one day. He does everything nicely and we like him".*

1619. FAITHFILLY (IRE) ★★★
b.f. Red Clubs – Bauci (Desert King). March 2. Fifth foal. 25,000Y. Tattersalls October Book 2. Sackville/Donald. Half-sister to the Italian 3-y-o winner and listed-placed Lisa's Theme (by Kalanisi) and to the modest dual 6f winner Loves Theme (by Iffraaj). The dam is an unraced half-sister to 7 winners including the Irish listed 10f winner Red Affair (herself the dam of the Group 3 winner Redstone Dancer and the listed winner Red Liason), the smart 7.6f to 10f winner Brilliant Red and the useful 12f to 14f winner and Group 3 2m Queens Vase third Kassab. The second dam, Red Comes Up (by Blushing Groom), was placed 5 times in France and is a sister to Rainbow Quest. (L. A. Bellman). *"She'll probably be my first 2-y-o runner and*

she goes nicely. A small, stocky, robust filly that seems to do everything easily so far".

1620. GLORIOUS PROSPECTOR (IRE) ★★★ ♠

b.c. Azamour – Hasaiyda (Hector Protector). February 22. Fourth foal. 55,000Y. Tattersalls October Book 2. Sackville/Donald. Half-brother to Hassaya (by King's Best), placed fourth once over 7f from 2 starts at 2 yrs in 2011. The dam, a fair 9f and 10f winner, is a half-sister to 5 winners including the dual Irish listed winner Hasanka. The second dam, Hasainiya (by Top Ville), a listed 10f winner in Ireland, is a half-sister to 7 winners. (Mrs A. A. Lau Yap). *"A lovely, scopey Azamour that won't be out until much later in the year. He's an athletic, nice-sized horse but much more of a 3-y-o type".*

1621. GLORIOUS STAR (IRE) ★★★ ♠

ch.c. Soviet Star – Caerlonore (Traditionally). February 20. First foal. 21,000Y. Tattersalls October Book 2. Sackville/Donald. The dam is an unraced half-sister to 7 winners including the Irish 1,000 Guineas third La Nuit Rose. The second dam, Caerlina (by Caerleon), won the Group 1 Prix de Diane and the Group 3 Prix de la Nonette and is a full or half-sister to 8 winners including the dam of the Group 2 winner Sri Putra. (Mrs A. A. Lau Yap). *"He's grown a huge amount since we bought him. I think he was well-bought because he was the first lot in the sale and the auction ring was pretty much empty. He's a lovely individual by a proven stallion and I'd like to think he'd be an August 2-y-o".* TRAINERS' BARGAIN BUY

1622. HARD RUN (USA) ★★

b.c. Cherokee Run – Meniatarra (Zilzal). April 17. Ninth foal. 65,000Y. Tattersalls December. Mark Crossman. Brother to the useful 2-y-o 1m winner and Group 3 1m Autumn Stakes second Menokee and half-brother to the quite useful 1m and 10f winner Gold Hush (by Seeking The Gold), the quite useful 2-y-o 7f winner Magic Doll (by Elusive Quality) and the fair 3-y-o 7f winner Give Him Credit (by Quiet American). The dam, unplaced in one run at 2 yrs, is a sister to the smart 1m to 10f winner Kammtarra and the useful 10f winner Haltarra and a half-sister to 5 winners including the top-class colt Lammtarra (by Nijinsky), winner of the Derby, the King George and the Prix de l'Arc de Triomphe. The second dam, Snow Bride (by Blushing Groom), was awarded the 1989 Oaks on the disqualification of Aliysa and won the Group 3 Musidora Stakes and the Group 3 Princess Royal Stakes and is a half-sister to the useful middle distance filly Habaayib and the US Grade 3 winners Jarraar and Ibn Al Haitham. *"A colt from a slow-maturing family, he's very athletic, good-looking and he's done everything nicely. One for later in the season and next year".*

1623. MEMORIZE (IRE) ★★

b.c. Dark Angel – Cape Cod (Unfuwain). March 23. Fifth foal. 10,000Y. Tattersalls October Book 2. Sackville/Donald. Half-brother to the modest 7f winner Millway Beach (by Diktat) and to the moderate 1m winner Jemiliah (by Dubai Destination). The dam was placed over 6f at 3 yrs and is a sister to 2 winners including the listed-placed Abeyr and a half-sister to 3 winners including the useful 2-y-o 7.3f Radley Stakes winner Boojum. The second dam, Haboobti (by Habitat), is an unplaced half-sister to 6 winners including the US stakes winner and Grade 3 placed Aerturas. (L. A. Bellman). *"A very cheap yearling, he's grown a huge amount and gone very leggy so he's going to take a bit of time. A beautiful-mover, he'll be a late-summer 2-y-o".*

1624. URBICUS ★★

b.c. Holy Roman Emperor – Scottish Heights (Selkirk). April 20. Fourth foal. 22,000Y. Tattersalls October Book 2. Not sold. Half-brother to the modest 7f winner Spirit Of Grace (by Invincible Spirit). The dam ran once unplaced in France and is a half-sister to 6 winners including the listed 7f Oak Tree Stakes winner Maori Moon. The second dam, Dazzling Heights (by Shirley Heights), a useful winner of 4 races from 7f (at 2 yrs) to 11f including a French listed event, is a full or half-sister to 6 winners. (Mr S.A. Stuckey). *"Very athletic, he won't be an early 2-y-o because although he isn't very big he's still a bit weak and is going to take a bit of time. He does everything very nicely, it's a decent family and he'll be a June/July 2-y-o. We may wait for seven furlongs with him".*

1625. YOU'RE THE BOSS ★★★★

b.c. Royal Applause – Trinny (Rainbow Quest). April 6. Fourth foal. £22,000Y. Doncaster Premier. Sackville/Donald. Half-brother to the modest 2011 7f placed 2-y-o Orwellian (by Bahamian Bounty). The dam is an unraced half-sister to one winner. The second dam, Mall Queen (by Sheikh Albadou), won the listed Prix Yacowlef and is a half-sister to 8 winners including two listed winners. (L. A. Bellman). "One of my early types, I really like him. He's strong, he looks physically forward and he has a great attitude in that he's very laid-back. It's so far so good with him and he should be running by the end of April".

1626. UNNAMED ★★★

b.f. Acclamation – Eastern Lily (Eastern Echo). March 28. Third foal. 20,000Y. Tattersalls December. Not sold. The dam, a minor stakes-placed winner of 3 races in the USA, is a half-sister to 10 winners. The second dam, Raawiyeh (by Raja Baba), won 2 minor races in the USA at 4 and 5 yrs and is a full or half-sister to 8 winners including Shaadi (Irish 2,000 Guineas). "She's done really well since we got her at the Sales and she's a nice filly with a good attitude. I expect her to be a June/July 2-y-o. A typical Acclamation, she's strong and well-made. She didn't walk very well at the Sales and hence the relatively cheap price tag but she's very athletic and she's done everything very well".

1627. UNNAMED ★★★

b.c. Exceed And Excel – Ivy League Star (Sadler's Wells). January 8. Fourth living foal. 15,000Y. Tattersalls October Book 2. Rabbah Bloodstock. Half-brother to Hard Road (by Cape Cross), unplaced on both his starts at 2 yrs in 2011 and to a minor 3-y-o winner abroad by Hawk Wing. The dam, a fair 12f winner, is a sister to the fillies Ivrea and Iviza, both 2-y-o 7f winners and both second in the Ribblesdale Stakes and a half-sister to 5 winners including the Group 1 12f Italian Oaks Ivyanna and to the dam of the Group 2 Goodwood Cup winner Distinction. The second dam, Ivy (by Sir Ivor), placed twice at 2 yrs in the USA, is a full or half-sister to 12 winners including the Graded stakes winners An Act, Din and Sarsar and the dam of the Grade 2 winner Herat. (S Manana). "A very well-bred colt, he's big and heavy, growing and changing shape. He's making up into a good-looking horse, I haven't asked any questions of him yet because he's going to take a bit of time, but so far he's doing everything as he should so".

1628. UNNAMED ★★★★

b.c. Soviet Star – Rancho Cucamonga (Raphane). January 31. Third foal. 20,000Y. Tattersalls October Book 2. Rabbah Bloodstock. Half-brother to the quite useful 2011 2-y-o dual 6f winner Heyward Girl (by Bertolini). The dam, a modest 6f winner of 7 races (including at 2 yrs), is a half-sister to 4 winners including the listed-placed Bazroy (by Soviet Star). The second dam, Kunucu (by Bluebird), a fairly useful 5f winner of 4 races (including at 2 yrs), was listed-placed twice and is a half-sister to 7 winners. (S Manana). "A very bonny, athletic little 2-y-o. I expect he'll be out in May, he does everything nicely and has a cracking attitude".

CHRIS WALL

1629. BALLYSHONAGH ★★

b.f. Tiger Hill – Shamara (Spectrum). February 25. Third foal. 27,000Y. Tattersalls October Book 2. Not sold. Half-sister to Ligurian Sea (by Medicean), placed once over 6f from two starts at 2 yrs in 2011 and to the quite useful 2-y-o 6f and 1m winner Rafiqa (by Mujahid). The dam, a fairly useful 10f and 12f winner, was listed-placed and is a half-sister to one winner in Germany. The second dam, Hamara (by Akarad), is an unraced half-sister to one winner. (Lady Juliet Tadgell). "I bred the mare who won twice over middle distances and was listed-placed. This filly is quite nice but she's bred to stay and wants time".

1630. BLESSING BOX ★★★★

b.f. Bahamian Bounty – Bible Box (Bin Ajwaad). February 1. Sixth foal. Sister to the useful dual listed 6f winner of 6 races (including at 2 yrs) Bounty Box and to the French 2-y-o 9f listed-placed Bahamian Box and half-sister to the fairly useful 2-y-o 6f winner and listed-placed Vive Les Rouges (by Acclamation). The dam, a quite useful 7f to 9f winner of 3 races, is out of the 2-y-o 1m seller winner Addie Pray (by Great Commotion), herself a half-sister to 7 winners. (Mr M Sinclair & Mr J Sims). "A full-sister to Bounty Box who was a listed winner for us, this filly was late coming in and we're only just breaking her in now, so if she does anything at two it'll be later in the season like her sister. But she's a nice scopey filly, typical of the family, with a good attitude and a nice way of going. Considering the dam isn't from a particularly blue-blooded family her record is very good, because she's bred three stakes-class horses from her first four foals".

1631. EMERALD SEA ★★★

b.f. Green Desert – Wind Surf (Lil's Lad). February 18. Second foal. The dam, a minor stakes winner in North America, is a half-sister to 2 winners. The second dam, Skirt The Wind (by Red Ransom), won 3 minor races in the USA and is a half-sister to 5 winners. (Lady Juliet Tadgell & Major M. G. Wyatt). "I trained the half-sister called Ride the Wind last year who was desperately unlucky not to win, she got beaten in a photo finish twice. This is a bigger, scopier filly, but that said I could see her making a 2-y-o over six furlongs. She gives a favourable impression and does everything easily".

1632. FIRST PENINSULA ★★★

ch.c. Excellent Art – Sarah's First (Cadeaux Genereux). February 16. First foal. 52,000Y. Tattersalls October Book 1. Chris Wall. The dam is an unplaced half-sister to 7 winners including Applaud (Group 3 6f Cherry Hinton Stakes), the listed 10.2f winner Sauterne and the Group 3 placed Glam Rock. The second dam, Band (by Northern Dancer), is a placed half-sister to 5 winners including the US Grade 3 winner Festive. (Mollers Racing). "A laid-back colt, he's doing a bit of growing at the moment but I'm sure he'll be one for the summer or a bit later and he creates a favourable impression. I should think he'll want a bit of cut in the ground and this year six or seven furlongs will be fine".

1633. MEET ME HALFWAY ★★★

b.f. Exceed And Excel – Pivotal Drive (Pivotal). February 26. First foal. 60,000Y. Tattersalls October Book 1. Chris Wall. The dam is an unraced half-sister to 4 winners including the listed 1m and 10f winner Sublimity and the UAE Group 3 1m winner Marbush. The second dam, Fig Tree Drive (by Miswaki), a fairly useful 2-y-o 6f winner on her only start, is a half-sister

to 4 winners. (Mr D. M. Thurlby). "I suppose we did very well to get anywhere near an Exceed And Excel at the sales because they were all the rage. I think this filly fell through the net a bit because she wasn't overly big, but she's a strong, robust filly and she's grown a bit so she's plenty big enough now. I would have thought she's one you'd start at five furlongs but I can certainly see her getting six. I'll be getting on with her soon with a view to getting her on the track in May or June time. She's a nice enough filly".

1634. NEVER TOO MUCH (IRE) ★★★

b.c. Johannesburg – Muskoka Dawn (Miswaki). March 1. Tenth foal. 46,000Y. Tattersalls October Book 2. Chris Wall. Brother to the fairly useful 2011 Irish 2-y-o 7f winner and listed 1m third Ronan's Bay, closely related to the French 2-y-o 6f and listed 1m winner and Group 2 Prix de Sandringham second Mousse Au Chocolat (by Hennessy) and half-brother to the French 2-y-o 5f winner Melody Dawn (by Tale Of The Cat), the US winner of 3 races and Group 3 Natalma Stakes third Bala (by With Approval) and 2 minor winners in North America by El Prado and Giant's Causeway. The dam, placed once at 3 yrs in the USA, is a half-sister to 6 winners including the multiple US listed winner Sigrun. The second dam, April Dawn Marie (by Baldski), was a minor stakes winner in the USA. (Mr D. S. Lee). "A nice colt, he's not overly-big and he ought to be a 2-y-o. He's a typical Johannesburg in that he just needs to focus on his job a bit more. A horse with a nice stride, most of the family seem to want a bit of cut in the ground, so we'll have to see what the weather's like in the summer".

1635. OH SO SASSY ★★

b.f. Pastoral Pursuits – Almasi (Petorius). January 16. Fifth foal. 5,200Y. Tattersalls October Book 3. Not sold. Sister to the modest dual 6f winner Oh So Spicy and half-sister to the fair 7f and 1m winner Oh So Saucy (by Imperial Ballet). The dam, a fair 7f winner of 8 races, is a half-sister to 2 winners. The second dam, Best Niece (by Vaigly Great), won once at 3 yrs and is a half-sister to 8 winners. (The Eight of Diamonds). "A full-sister to Oh So Spicy who has won twice for us. She didn't come in the yard until late but she's a nice, big, strong filly

– different altogether physically to her sister because she's more robust. A nice filly that's doing everything OK, the dam won as a 2-y-o but none of her daughters have, so perhaps this filly will fall into that category".

1636. PEARL QUEEN (USA) ★★★

b.br.f. Street Sense – Island Queen (Ogygian). January 21. Ninth foal. $125,000Y. Keeneland September. David Redvers. Half-sister to the US Grade 2 and Grade 3 winner and Grade 1 placed Friendly Island (by Crafty Friend) and to the minor US winner of 4 races More Impact (by More Than Ready). The dam won 5 minor races at 3 to 5 yrs in the USA and is a half-sister to 4 winners. The second dam, Regal Peace (by Known Fact), a fairly useful 2-y-o listed 5f winner and third in the Group 3 Phoenix Flying Five, subsequently won in the USA and was stakes placed. She is a half-sister to 4 winners including the Group 1 6f Middle Park Stakes winner Stalker. (Pearl Bloodstock Ltd). "She won't be an early sort but she's a nice filly that's growing at the moment. A filly for the second half of the season, over seven furlongs or possibly a mile".

1637. RUNNINGLIKETHEWIND (IRE) ★★★

b.c. Hurricane Run – Virgin Hawk (Silver Hawk). April 18. 12,000Y. Tattersalls December. C F Wall. Closely related to the 1m (at 2 yrs) and listed 2m winner of 6 races Metaphoric (by Montjeu) and half-brother to the fairly useful triple 1m winner Crown Counsel (by Invincible Spirit), the quite useful 10f winner Meadaaf (by Swain), the minor Irish 7f winner Java Lady (by Mt Livermore) and a minor winner of 4 races in Italy by Spectrum. The dam is a placed half-sister to 6 winners including the US stakes winner and Grade 1 Gamely Handicap second Island Jamboree (herself dam of the US dual Grade 1 winner Fiji). The second dam, Careless Virgin (by Wing Out), is a placed half-sister to the US Grade 1 winners Fabulous Notion (herself dam of the US Grade 1 winner Fabulously Fast) and Cacoethes (placed in the King George and the Derby). (Mr D. M. Thurlby). "I quite like him, he's got a good action and has a good way of going. I'm sure he's not bred to sprint, but I can see him running in mid-summer over six or seven furlongs. He's not overly big but he seems to do

the job well and I'm looking forward to seeing him doing something this year". TRAINERS' BARGAIN BUY

1638. SMART ALICE ★★★

b.f. Soviet Star – Ailincala (Pursuit Of Love). February 24. Fourth foal. 10,000Y. Tattersalls December. C F Wall. Half-sister to the fair dual 12f winner Getabuzz and to the fair 2-y-o 7f winner Take The Micky (both by Beat Hollow). The dam, a fairly useful 1m winner of 5 races, is a half-sister to 4 winners including two over hurdles. The second dam, Diabaig (by Precocious), a fair 1m winner, is a half-sister to 4 minor winners. (Racingeight Partners). "We trained the dam who was a progressive filly. She ran at two but improved with age and was at her best at four. This is a nice filly, not particularly big but very athletic and I can see her making a 2-y-o over six/seven furlongs in mid-summer. She seems to go quite well".

1639. SWITCH ON ★★★

b.c. Oasis Dream – Noodle Soup (Alphabet Soup). March 5. Fourth living foal. 65,000Y. Tattersalls October Book 2. Not sold. Closely related to the moderate 10f and 12f winner Shirataki (by Cape Cross). The dam, a minor French winner of 3 races at 3 yrs, is a half-sister to 9 winners including the French listed winner On A Cloud and the US stakes winners Be Elusive and Vignette (herself dam of the Group 1 St Leger winner Lucarno). The second dam, Be Exclusive (by Be My Guest), won 5 races in France and the USA including the Group 3 Prix Chloe and is a half-sister to 2 winners including the dam of the US Grade 2 winners Lexicon and Cozi Rosie. (Ms A. Fustoq). "He wouldn't be an early sort but I like the way he goes, he does everything OK and he moves well. He's one for seven furlongs or a mile in the second half of the season and he might just want a bit of cut in the ground to be seen at his best. He looks a colt with a future".

1640. TRUCANINI ★★★

b.f. Mount Nelson – Jalissa (Mister Baileys). March 20. Fourth foal. Half-sister to the fair 2011 2-y-o 1m winner Ventura Spirit (by Royal Applause), to the fairly useful 6f (including at 2 yrs) and 7f winner of 4 races Folly Bridge (by Avonbridge) and the fair 2-y-o 6f winner

Bahamian Sunset (by Bahamian Bounty). The dam, a quite useful 6f winner, is a half-sister to 3 winners including the smart 7f (at 2 yrs) to 10f winner of 7 races Vintage Premium. The second dam, Julia Domna (by Dominion), placed fourth over 5f and 1m, is a sister to two winners and a half-sister to the Hungerford Stakes winner Norwich. (Dolly's Dream Syndicate). *"Like a lot of the Mount Nelson's we saw at the sales she's a well-grown, good-sized, robust filly. Early impressions would have been that she needed time but in fact she goes along quite nicely. We won't be rushing to get her out, but she should be able to start in mid-summer over seven furlongs, she has a good attitude to life, she moves nicely and she's the sort you'd be looking forward to doing a bit of work with to see what you've got".*

1641. VANDROSS (IRE) ★★★

b.c. Iffraaj – Mrs Kanning (Distant View). April 20. Sixth foal. 30,000foal. Tattersalls December. RBS. Half-brother to the modest 2-y-o 7f winner Pequeno Dinero (by Iron Mask) and to the modest 2-y-o 7f and hurdles winner Sad Times (by Tendulkar). The dam is an unplaced half-sister to one winner. The second dam, Red Hot Dancer (by Seattle Dancer), is a placed half-sister to 5 winners including the dam of the 1,000 Guineas winner Ta Rib. (Mr D. S. Lee). *"Like a lot by the sire he looks sharp enough, so he should be a six/seven furlong 2-y-o. He could just do with filling out and muscling up a bit more but he moves nicely and looks quite sharp".*

DERMOT WELD

1642. ACTING TALENT (USA) ★★★

b.f. Bernstein – Soaring Emotions (Kingmambo). March 4. First foal. The dam was a quite useful Irish 1m winner. The second dam, Luminous Beauty (by A P Indy), was listed-placed over 1m at 2 yrs in Ireland and is a half-sister to La Nuit Rose, a winner over 7f at 2 yrs and placed in both the French and Irish 1,000 Guineas. (Moyglare Stud Farms Ltd). *"A small, sharp filly that looks a 2-y-o type for six furlongs in May or June".*

1643. AIRMONT (IRE) ★★

ch.f. Duke Of Marmalade – Upperville (Selkirk). March 9. Closely related to the useful dual 7f winner Cannon Hill (by Holy Roman Emperor) and half-sister to the quite useful Irish 9f to 12f winner Blue Ridge Lane (by Indian Ridge) and a winner over hurdles by Verglas. The dam, a fair Irish 12f winner, is a half-sister to 7 winners including the useful Irish listed 12f winner Mutakarrim and the very useful Irish listed 10f winner Nafisah. The second dam, Alyakkh (by Sadler's Wells), a fair 3-y-o 1m winner, is a half-sister to the Champion Stakes and 2,000 Guineas winner Haafhd and to the 1m listed stakes winner and Group 1 Coronation Stakes second Hasbah. (Mr B. R. Firestone). *"The foals from this mare tend to take a bit of time and I see this filly being out over seven furlongs in September/October".*

1644. ALKALI (IRE) ★★

gr.f. Dalakhani – Alambic (Cozzene). February 20. Second foal. Half-sister to Aegean Sky (by Galileo), unplaced in one start at 2 yrs in 2011. The dam, a fairly useful 12f to 14f winner of 6 races, was listed-placed and is a half-sister to 4 winners. The second dam, Alexandrine (by Nashwan), a fair 10f to 13f winner of 4 races, is a half-sister to 7 winners including the Nassau Stakes and Sun Chariot Stakes winner Last Second (dam of the French 2,000 Guineas winner Aussie Rules), the Doncaster Cup winner Alleluia (dam of the Prix Royal-Oak winner Allegretto) and the Moyglare Stud Stakes third Alouette (herself dam of the dual Champion Stakes winner Alborada and the triple German Group 1 winner Albanova) and to the placed dam of the Group 1 winners Yesterday and Quarter Moon. (Lady O'Reilly). *"She's a backward filly and will be a late-season 2-y-o".*

1645. AMBER ROMANCE (IRE) ★★★

ch.f. Bahamian Bounty – Polished Gem (Danehill). April 27. Third foal. Half-sister to the smart 1m, 10f and listed 12f winner Sapphire (by Medicean). The dam, an Irish 2-y-o 7f winner, is a sister to 2 winners including the Grade 1 9f Matriarch Stakes and Group 2 1m Sun Chariot Stakes winner Dress To Thrill and a half-sister to 7 winners. The second dam, Trusted Partner (by Affirmed), was a very useful winner of the Group 3 7f C.L. Weld Park Stakes (at 2 yrs) and the Irish 1,000 Guineas and is a sister to the useful middle distance performers

Easy to Copy and Epicure's Garden and to the useful Irish 7f listed and US Grade 3 winner Low Key Affair. (Moyglare Stud Farms Ltd). *"She's quite a nice filly that looks like making a 2-y-o. I would see her racing by June or July over seven furlongs".*

1646. BIG BREAK ★★★★★

b.f. *Dansili – Fame At Last (Quest For Fame).* April 6. Sister to the very smart Famous Name, a winner of eight Group 3 events in Ireland from 1m to 10f and half-sister to the Irish listed 10f winner Zaminast, the quite useful Irish 1m winner Photo Opportunity, the fair French 1m winner Everlasting Fame (all by Zamindar), the quite useful 6f winner Anchor Date (by Zafonic) and the fair 1m winner Final Esteem (by Lomitas). The dam, a fairly useful 2-y-o 7f winner, is a half-sister to one winner. The second dam, Ranales (by Majestic Light), a minor 2-y-o 1m winner in the USA, is a half-sister to 9 winners including the listed 10f Virginia Stakes winner Rambushka and the Group 2 7f Laurent Perrier Champagne Stakes second Arokat. (Khalid Abdulla). *"Very much a quality filly and one the nicest 2-y-o's I have. Look out for her over seven furlongs in July".*

1647. BOOM TIME ★★★

gr.c. *Empire Maker – Jibboom (Mizzen Mast).* March 15. First foal. The dam, a US dual Grade 3 winner over 7f and 1m, was second in the Grade 1 Santa Monica Handicap and is a half-sister to 2 winners. The second dam, Palisade (by Gone West), a quite useful 2-y-o 7f winner, is a half-sister to the useful 3-y-o 1m winner Emplane and to the useful 2-y-o 1m winner Boatman. (Khalid Abdulla). *"A very nice, big, strong colt that should be racing by August or September".*

1648. BRACING BREEZE ★★

b.f. *Dansili – Nebraska Tornado (Storm Cat).* April 8. The dam won four races including the Group 1 1m Prix du Moulin and the Group 1 10.5f Prix de Diane and is a half-sister to the Group 2 10f Prix Eugene Adam winner Burning Sun and the US Grade 3 winner Mirabilis. The second dam, Media Nox (by Lycius), a useful 2-y-o winner of the Group 3 5f Prix du Bois, is a half-sister to the very useful Bonash, a winner of 4 races in France from 1m to 12f including

the Prix d'Aumale, the Prix Vanteaux and the Prix de Malleret. (Khalid Abdulla). *"A medium-sized filly, she's a little bit immature and I don't think we'll see her out until October".*

1649. COOL METALLIC (IRE) ★★★

b.g. *Medicean – Polite Reply (Be My Guest).* April 21. Half-brother to the fairly useful 2-y-o dual 5f winner Hidden Charm (by Big Shuffle) and to the quite useful dual 7f winners In A Rush (by Hernando) and Flic Flac (by Bahamian Bounty). The dam, a quite useful 7f and 1m winner, is closely related to the Irish winner and listed-placed Dance Pass and a half-sister to 3 winners including the Group 3 Ballyroan Stakes winner Sense Of Purpose. The second dam, Super Gift (by Darshaan), won twice over 1m at 2 yrs and was second in the Group 3 7f C.L. Weld Park Stakes. (Moyglare Stud Farms Ltd). *"He goes alright, he was a bit cheeky so we had him gelded and he'll make a 2-y-o in mid-summer over six/seven furlongs".*

1650. GHAAMER ★★★

b.c. *Hard Spun – Teeba (Seeking The Gold).* April 21. The dam, a fairly useful 3-y-o 1m winner, was listed placed twice and is closely related to 2 winners including the smart 7f (at 2 yrs) and 10f listed winner Imtiyaz and a half-sister to 5 winners including Bint Shadayid, winner of the Group 3 7f Prestige Stakes and placed in the 1,000 Guineas and the Fillies Mile. The second dam, Shadayid (by Shadeed), won the 1,000 Guineas, the Prix Marcel Boussac and the Fred Darling Stakes and was placed in the Oaks, the Coronation Stakes, the Queen Elizabeth II Stakes, the Sussex Stakes and the Haydock Park Sprint Cup. She is a half-sister to several winners including the very useful dual 7f winner and Jersey Stakes third Dumaani. (Hamdan Al Maktoum). *"He's only just arrived from Dubai so I don't know a lot about him, but he looks a 2-y-o and he's a nice colt that should be racing in mid-summer".*

1651. HANDSOME STRANGER (IRE) ★★★

ch.g. *Tamayuz – Just Special (Cadeaux Genereux).* April 1. Sixth foal. €55,000Y. Goffs Orby. Bobby O'Ryan. Half-brother to the French dual 1m winner and listed-placed Best Dating (by King's Best), to the quite useful Irish 7f winner Spesialta (by Indian Ridge) and the fair 1m and hurdles winner Al Qeddaaf (by Alhaarth). The dam, winner of the listed 7f Knockaire Stakes in Ireland and second in the Group 2 Prix d'Astarte, is a half-sister to the listed winner Blue Gold. The second dam, Relatively Special (by Alzao), winner of the Group 3 7f Rockfel Stakes at 2 yrs and third in the Irish 1,000 Guineas, is a half-sister to 8 winners including the Dante Stakes winner Alnasr Alwasheek and the Juddmonte International winner One So Wonderful. (Dr R Lambe). *"A sharp, medium-sized gelding that should be racing over six/seven furlongs in June".*

1652. HAZY GLOW (IRE) ★★★

b.f. Invincible Spirit – Genuine Charm (Sadler's Wells). April 11. Fourth foal. Half-sister to the useful 2-y-o 1m winner Rich Tapestry (by Danehill Dancer) and to the quite useful Irish 1m winner Anywaysmile (by Indian Ridge). The dam is a placed sister to 3 winners including the top-class winner of four Group 1 races from 7f (at 2 yrs) to 10f Refuse To Bend and a half-sister to the Melbourne Cup winner Media Puzzle. The second dam, Market Slide (by Gulch), an Irish 6f (at 2 yrs) and 6.5f winner, is a half-sister to the Breeders Cup Classic second Twilight Agenda. (Moyglare Stud Farms Ltd). *"A nice filly that seems to take after her dam's side, so she'll be a seven furlong 2-y-o in June or July".*

1653. HIGHEST PRAISE ★★★★★

b.f. Acclamation – Yarastar (Cape Cross). February 2. First foal. €165,000Y. Goffs Orby. Bobby O'Ryan. The dam, a French listed 10f winner, is a half-sister to the UAE dual listed 1m winner Emirates Gold and to the Irish 2-y-o 7f and subsequent US stakes-placed winner Yario. The second dam, Yara (by Sri Pekan), was placed second ten times including in the Group 1 5f Heinz 57 Phoenix Stakes. (Lady O'Reilly). *"She's a filly I really like. I don't see her as a five furlong 2-y-o – she's more of a six furlong type and she'll be racing in mid-summer. I'd be disappointed if she's not a good filly. A beautiful mover and full of quality".*

1654. IMPERIAL CONCORDE (IRE) ★★★

b.c. High Chaparral – Irish Style (Mujadil). January 28. Sixth foal. €110,000Y. Goffs Orby.

Bobby O'Ryan. Half-brother to three minor winners abroad by Daylami, Hurricane Run and Sinndar. The dam, a quite useful 7f and 1m winner, is a half-sister to 8 winners including Grey Swallow (Irish Derby, Tattersalls Gold Cup, etc), the Group 3 1m winner Moonlight Dance and the dam of the Group 1 Gran Criterium winner Night Style. The second dam, Style Of Life (by The Minstrel), won over 6f and 7f in Ireland and is a sister to the listed 7f Ballycorus Stakes winner Seasonal Pickup. (Dr R Lambe). *"A very nice colt, he's strong and powerful and a nephew of Grey Swallow who won an Irish Derby for me. I can see him running in June over six/seven furlongs".*

1655. IMPOUND ★★★★

b.c. Oasis Dream – La Coruna (by Deploy). April 16. Fifth foal. The dam, a fairly useful 2-y-o 7f and 7.6f winner, is a half-sister to the useful 2-y-o 6f winner and Group 3 7f placed Cantabria, to the useful 2-y-o 5f and listed 6f winner Deportivo and the useful 2-y-o listed 5f winner Irish Vale. The second dam, Valencia (by Kenmare), placed over 1m at 2 yrs on her only start, is a half-sister to numerous winners including the dual US Grade 1 winner Wandesta, the Group 2 12f winner De Quest and the smart 10f to 15f winner Turners Hill. (Khalid Abdulla). *"He's started coming forward rapidly just recently and I see him as a mid-summer horse over six or seven furlongs".*

1656. JAYED JIDAN (IRE) ★★★

gr.c. Teofilo – Cassandra Go (Indian Ridge). May 20. Eighth foal. €180,000Y. Goffs Orby. Shadwell Estate Co. Half-brother to the 2011 dual 6f placed 2-y-o Tickled Pink (by Invincible Spirit), to the Irish 1,000 Guineas, Nassau Stakes and Sun Chariot Stakes winner Halfway To Heaven (by Pivotal), to the Group 3 6f Summer Stakes winner Theann (by Rock Of Gibraltar), the fairly useful dual 5f winner Neverletme Go and the fair 5f winner Mannikko (both by Green Desert). The dam, a very smart winner of the Group 2 5f Kings Stand Stakes, is a full or half-sister to 8 winners including the smart Group 3 6f Coventry Stakes winner and Irish 2,000 Guineas second Verglas. The second dam, Rahaam (by Secreto), a fairly useful 3-y-o 7f winner, is a half-sister to 8 winners including the French 2,000 Guineas third Glory Forever.

(Hamdan Al Maktoum). *"He's a nice-moving colt that's a little bit immature at the moment. I'd be inclined to think he'd be an August/ September 2-y-o over seven furlongs".*

1657. KHOTHRY (IRE) ★★★★
b.f. *Marju – Esterlina (Highest Honor).* February 16. Sixth foal. 95,000foal. Tattersalls December. Shadwell Estate Co. Half-sister to the useful 2011 2-y-o 6f winner and Group 3 6f Albany Stakes third Illaunglass (by Red Clubs), to the smart 7f (at 2 yrs) and listed 1m Heron Stakes winner and Group 1 1m Criterium International third Redolent (by Redback), the fair 6f winner Hightime Heroine (by Danetime) and the minor French 2-y-o winner Zomorroda (by Chineur). The dam won over 1m at 3 yrs in Ireland and is a half-sister to 3 minor winners in France. The second dam, Shaquick (by Shadeed), won in France and is a half-sister to 8 winners including the dual Group 3 winner and Oaks third Leap Lively (herself dam of the Irish 1,000 Guineas winner Forest Flower). (Hamdan Al Maktoum). *"A lovely, big filly that I see running around July or August. Bethrah was the last Marju filly I had for Sheikh Hamdan and like this filly she was out of a mare by Highest Honor. Bethrah won the Irish 1,000 Guineas, so let's hope that's a good omen".*

1658. LAKE DISTRICT ★★★
b.c. *Raven's Pass – Vista Bella (Diktat).* February 25. Second foal. Brother to Alkadi, a 7f winner on her debut at 3 yrs in 2012. The dam, a very useful listed 1m Masaka Stakes winner, was third in the 1,000 Guineas and is a half-sister to 3 winners. The second dam, Cox Orange (by Trempolino), won 10 races in France and the USA including the Group 3 Prix du Calvados and four US Grade 3 events and is a half-sister to 7 winners including the Group 1 Prix Marcel Boussac winner Amonita. (Sheikh Mohammed). *"A nice colt, I like him well and he's a medium-sized colt for June or July over six/seven furlongs. Raven's Pass is a first season sire of course, and I'd be very hopeful of him being a success at stud".*

1659. LAPIS BLUE (IRE) ★★
b.f. *Invincible Spirit – Triple Try (Sadler's Wells).* March 16. Half-sister to the useful 1m (at 2

yrs) and 10f winner and Group 3 10f Ballysax Stakes third Unwritten Rule (by Dalakhani), to the fairly useful dual 7f winner (including at 2 yrs) Offbeat Fashion (by Rock Of Gibraltar) and the quite useful dual 10f and hurdles winner Absinthe (by King's Best). The dam, a quite useful Irish dual 10f winner, is a sister to the Irish Oaks and Tattersalls Gold Cup winner Dance Design. The second dam, Elegance In Design (by Habitat), a useful Irish listed 6f winner, is a sister to the high-class Coronation Stakes winner Chalon (herself dam of the Prix Ganay winner Creator). (Moyglare Stud Farms Ltd). *"A delicate, backward filly that should be suited by six furlongs in late summer".*

1660. LATE ROSEBUD (IRE) ★★★
b.f. *Jeremy – Nebraas (Green Desert).* May 13. Sixth foal. €85,000Y. Goffs Orby. Skymarc Farm. Sister to the smart 2011 2-y-o 7f winner and Group 2 Debutante Stakes second Yellow Rosebud and half-sister to the fairly useful 6f listed (at 2 yrs) and 10f winner and Group 3 7f third Seeharn (by Pivotal), to the quite useful 7f (at 2 yrs) and 6f winner of 5 races My Kingdom and the quite useful 7f winner Royalist (both by King's Best). The dam is an unraced three-parts sister to the very useful 6f winner (including at 2 yrs) Mutaakkid and a half-sister to 4 winners including the Group 1 Golden Jubilee Stakes winner Malhub. The second dam, Arjuzah (by Ahonoora), a useful winner of the listed 7f Sceptre Stakes, is a half-sister to the Irish listed winner Ormsby. (Lady O'Reilly). *"She was immature but she's doing well now and I could see her running in July or August over seven furlongs".*

1661. MAGNOLIA RIDGE (IRE) ★★★
b.c. *Galileo – Treasure The Lady (Indian Ridge).* April 14. Fifth foal. Half-brother to the quite useful Irish 1m winner Treasure The Cross (by Cape Cross). The dam won once in Ireland at 2 yrs over 7f and was listed-placed and is a half-sister to 7 winners including the Derby winner High Chaparral and the Dante Stakes winner Black Bear Island. The second dam, Kasora (by Darshaan), is an unraced full or half-sister to 8 winners. (Mrs A. M. Coughlan). *"He looks very much like a Galileo and he'll make a 2-y-o over seven furlongs in July or August".*

1662. MANHATTAN SWING (IRE) ★★★

b.c. Invincible Spirit – Bluebell Park (Gulch). April 22. Second foal. €110,000Y. Goffs Orby. Not sold. The dam is an unplaced half-sister to the Group 3 Craven Stakes and US Grade 3 winner King Of Happiness and the dual listed winner Anani. The second dam, Mystery Rays (by Nijinsky), won the Group 3 Prix Fille de l'Air and the Group 3 Prix Minerve and is a half-sister to 6 winners including the Group winners Akraam and Robin des Pins. (Mr Joseph Higgins). *"He'll take a little bit of time but he should be racing over six/seven furlongs in mid-to-late summer".*

1663. MIDNIGHT THOUGHTS (USA) ★★★★

b.f. Henrythenavigator – Irresistible Jewel (Danehill). April 27. Half-sister to the smart Irish Group 3 7f Gladness Stakes winner and multiple Group 1 placed Mad About You (by Indian Ridge) and to the fairly useful 14f winner of 4 races Royal Diamond (by King's Best). The dam won the Group 2 12f Ribblesdale Stakes and the Group 3 10f Blandford Stakes and is a half-sister to numerous winners including the listed 12f winner Diamond Trim and the useful Irish 1m winner Legal Jousting. The second dam, In Anticipation (by Sadler's Wells), won over 12f and 14f in Ireland. (Moyglare Stud Farms Ltd). *"A big, scopey filly, she's very nice and should be racing in July or August over seven furlongs".*

1664. NABAT ALI ★★★★

b.f. Haatef – Laywaan (Fantastic Light). March 8. Second foal. Half-sister to the quite useful 2011 2-y-o 7f winner Madmoonah (by Invincible Spirit). The dam, a fairly useful 1m and 10f winner, is a half-sister to the fairly useful 2-y-o 5f winner Tamasuk. The second dam, Electrostat (by Dynaformer), a minor winner in the USA, is a half-sister to 8 winners including the Grade 1 Beldame Stakes winner Weber City Miss, herself dam of the dual Grade 1 winner Slew City Slew. (Hamdan Al Maktoum). *"A quality filly and I would think she'd make a six furlong 2-y-o in mid-summer".*

1665. PEACE ACCORD ★★

ch.c. Pivotal – Embassy (Cadeaux Genereux). February 22. Brother to the fair dual 7f winner

Gleneagles and half-brother to the useful 2-y-o 7f winner Grosvenor Square (by Dubai Millennium) and half-brother to the fairly useful 6f and 7f winner Felicitous (by King's Best) and the modest 7f winner Diplomatic (by Cape Cross). The dam, a champion 2-y-o filly and winner of the Cheveley Park Stakes, is a half-sister to the smart 7f (at 2 yrs) and Group 2 Pretty Polly Stakes winner Tarfshi and the fairly useful 2-y-o 1m winner Puck's Castle. The second dam, Pass The Peace (by Alzao), won the Cheveley Park Stakes, was second in the French 1,000 Guineas and is a half-sister to 3 winners. (Sheikh Mohammed). *"A strong individual, he's nice but he won't be racing until the autumn".*

1666. RASMEYAA (IRE) ★★★★

ch.f. New Approach – Posterity (Indian Ridge). January 24. Second foal. €350,000Y. Goffs Orby. Shadwell Estate Co. Half-sister to the smart 6f, 7f winner and Group 3 1m Desmond Stakes winner Future Generation (by Hurricane Run). The dam is an unraced half-sister to 7 winners including the very smart French 5.5f (at 2 yrs) and Group 3 6f Prix de Meautry winner Do The Honours and the useful 7f listed Chesham Stakes winner Seba. The second dam, Persian Secret (by Persian Heights), a fairly useful 2-y-o 6f winner here, subsequently won a listed event in France and is a half-sister to 8 winners including the dual Group 2 winning sprinter and smart broodmare Cassandra Go and the Group 3 6f Coventry Stakes winner and Irish 2,000 Guineas second Verglas. (Hamdan Al Maktoum). *"A very nice filly, she's big and has a lot of quality. One for seven furlongs in July/ August and she looks like being a very nice 2-y-o".*

1667. RAWAAQ ★★

b.f. Invincible Spirit – Zaqrah (Silver Hawk). March 25. Fourth foal. The dam, unplaced in two starts, is a half-sister to the very smart listed 7f (at 2 yrs) and listed 10f winner Muqbil and to the very useful Group 2 1m second Mostaqaleh. The second dam, Istiqlal (by Diesis), is an unraced half-sister to the Group 1 1m St James's Palace Stakes and Group 1 1m Queen Elizabeth II Stakes winner Bahri and to the high-class 2-y-o Group 2 7f Laurent Perrier Champagne Stakes winner Bahhare. (Hamdan

Al Maktoum). *"She's what I call a 'tidy' filly, or not very big, and she'll make a 2-y-o in June or July I would say".*

1668. REGAL CONCORDE (IRE) ★★★★

b.c. Lawman – Fernanda (Be My Chief). April 7. Tenth foal. €80,000Y. Goffs Orby. Bobby O'Ryan. Half-brother to the fairly useful 6f, 1m and UAE 10f winner Mubeen (by Barathea), to the fairly useful Irish 7f and 1m winner Favourite Nation (by Cadeaux Genereux), the fairly useful 1m winner Font Of Wisdom (by Montjeu), the minor Irish 12f and hurdles winner Law Officer (by Desert Prince) and a minor winner in the UAE by Giant's Causeway. The dam, a useful 6f (at 2 yrs) and 1m winner, was second in the Group 3 Prestige Stakes and is a half-sister to 5 winners including the listed winner and Group 3 placed Chipaya and to the dam of the Group 2 July Stakes winner Winker Watson. The second dam, Flaming Rose (by Upper Nile), was placed five times in the USA and is a half-sister to 6 winners including the Queen Mary Stakes winner Gwydion (herself dam of the Greenham Stakes winner Enrique). (Dr R Lambe). *"A very nice colt and the sort of horse I'd like to be running in June or July over seven furlongs".*

1669. RESOLUTE RESPONSE (IRE) ★★★★

b.c. Dansili – Lady Luck (Kris). April 5. Half-brother to the very smart 7f (at 2 yrs) and Group 2 10f Leopardstown Derby Trial winner and dual Derby placed Casual Conquest (by Hernando), to the Irish 2-y-o listed 7f winner Elusive Double (by Grand Lodge), the Irish 7f winners A Word Apart (by Desert Style) and Moving Heart (by Anabaa) and the quite useful Irish 9f winner Media Asset (by Polish Precedent). The dam won over 1m in Ireland and is a half-sister to several winners including the Irish Group 3 Boland Stakes winner Social Harmony. The second dam, Latest Chapter (by Ahonoora), is an unraced half-sister to the Grade 1 Belmont Stakes winner Go And Go. (Moyglare Stud Farms Ltd). *"A big colt, he's an excellent mover and a horse I really like for the second part of the year. I would see him running in September/October over seven furlongs and a mile".*

1670. RICH DARK INK (IRE) ★★★

b.br.c. Arch – Society Hostess (Seeking The Gold). March 22. The dam, a US Grade 3 7f and German listed winner, is a half-sister to several winners. The second dam, Touch Of Truth (by Storm Cat), a minor US winner of 2 races at 4 yrs, is a half-sister to 8 winners including the US Grade 1 winner Twilight Agenda and the dams of the Group/Grade 1 winners Refuse To Bend, Media Puzzle and Go And Go. (Moyglare Stud Farms Ltd). *"He's a quality colt and I see him running in June or July over seven furlongs".*

1671. ROSE RANSOM (IRE) ★★★

b.f. Oasis Dream – Rapid Ransom (Red Ransom). February 2. Fifth foal. Sister to the fairly useful Irish 7f (at 2 yrs) and 1m winner and Group 3 7f Debutante Stakes third Rare Ransom, closely related to the fairly useful Irish 10f and 11f winner and listed-placed Ransomed Bride (by Cape Cross) and half-sister to the quite useful Irish 12f winner Rafaello Santi (by Medicean). The dam, a quite useful Irish 10f winner, was Grade 3 placed in the USA and is a half-sister to the Irish 2-y-o listed winner and Group 3 Queen Mary Stakes third Warrior Queen (herself dam of the US Grade 2 winner and Grade 1 placed A P Warrior). The second dam, Call Me Fleet (Afleet), is an unraced half-sister to several winners including Soundings dam of the French Group 1 winners Green Tune and Pas de Reponse. (Lady O'Reilly). *"She's a sharp enough filly and she's strong. I see her running over six/seven furlongs in mid-summer.*

1672. SALHOODA (IRE) ★★★

b.f. Nayef – Alshakr (Bahri). April 29. Eighth foal. Sister to the useful dual 7f (at 2 yrs), 10f and hurdles winner Nafaath and half-sister to the quite useful Irish 14f winner Sufad (by Alhaarth). The dam, a very useful winner of the Group 2 1m Falmouth Stakes, is a half-sister to the dam of the 1,000 Guineas winner Harayir. The second dam, Give Thanks (by Relko), won the Irish Oaks, the Lancashire Oaks and the Musidora Stakes. (Hamdan Al Maktoum). *"Quite a nice filly but one for the second half of the year over seven furlongs".*

1673. SCENT OF ROSES (IRE) ★★★★

b.f. Invincible Spirit – Moy Water (Tirol). April 5. Eleventh foal. €87,000Y. Goffs Orby. Bobby

O'Ryan. Half-sister to the French listed sprint winner Mona Em (by Catrail), to the useful 3-y-o 7f winner and Irish 2,000 Guineas fourth Maumee (by Indian Ridge), the fairly useful 2-y-o 7f winner Watergate (by Verglas), the quite useful 2-y-o 1m winner Kharish (by Desert Prince) and the Irish 3-y-o 8.5f winner Mandhoor (by Flying Spur). The dam, an Irish 1m (at 2 yrs) and 9f winner, is a half-sister to 8 winners including the very useful listed sprint winners Bufalino and Maledetto. The second dam, Croglin Water (by Monsanto), is an unplaced half-sister to 5 winners including the smart sprinter Governor General. (Dr R Lambe). *"A quality filly, she'll be a very nice 2-y-o from June or July onwards over seven furlongs".*

[handwritten: God first run won decent 7f f]

1674. SECRET RECIPE ★★★★ *[handwritten: mdn (maiden)]*
ch.c. Sakhee's Secret – Fudge (Polar Falcon). *[handwritten: Wy]* February 12. Ninth foal. €92,000Y. Goffs Orby. Bobby O'Ryan. Closely related to a winner in Scandinavia by Sakhee and half-brother to the useful 5f (at 2 yrs) to 7f winner of 4 races and Group 3 second Gloved Hand (by Royal Applause), to the fair 10f to 14f winner of 16 races Jackie Kiely (by Vettori), the moderate 7f and 1m winners Rigat (by Dansili) and Magroom (by Compton Place) and a winner abroad by Doyen. The dam is an unraced half-sister to 7 winners including the quite useful 1m to 10f winner Summer Fashion (herself dam of the Group winners Definite Article, Salford City and Salford Express). The second dam, My Candy (by Lorenzaccio), is a placed half-sister to 7 winners including the Ballymoss Stakes and Royal Whip Stakes winner Candy Cane. (Dr R Lambe). *"He's a nice 2-y-o and one I would hope to move along with and have him racing over five furlongs in May or June. A strong, powerful colt".*

1675. SHARP CRISP AIR (IRE) ★★
ch.f. Danehill Dancer – Token Gesture (Alzao). February 2. Eleventh foal. Half-sister to the quite useful 2-y-o 1m winner Hit The Jackpot (by Pivotal), to the 7f (at 2 yrs in Ireland) and Grade 1 Canadian International winner Relaxed Gesture, the useful 10f winner and Group 3 10f Gallinule Stakes third Central Station (both by Indian Ridge), the Irish 1m and subsequent US Grade 2 9.5f American Derby winner Evolving Tactics (by Machiavellian), the fairly useful 7f (at

2 yrs) to 13f winner Braveheart Move (by Cape Cross) and the Irish 1m, 12f and hurdles winner Turn Of Phrase (by Cadeaux Genereux). The dam, a smart winner of the Group 3 7f C L Weld Park Stakes, is a half-sister to the US Grade 2 9f winner Wait Till Monday, to the useful Irish 10f to 12.3f winner Blazing Spectacle and the useful Irish middle-distance stayer and Triumph Hurdle winner Rare Holiday. The second dam, Temporary Lull (by Super Concorde), is an unraced sister to the Nell Gwyn Stakes winner Martha Stevens. (Moyglare Stud Farms Ltd). *"She's a slightly backward filly and one for August or September over seven furlongs".*

1676. SHUNNED ★★
b.f. Three Valleys – Avoidance (Cryptoclearance). February 19. Fifth foal. Half-sister to the fairly useful 2011 Irish 2-y-o 6f winner Swerve, to the fairly useful 6f and 7f winner Brushed Aside and the quite useful Irish 2-y-o 7f winner Broad Meaning (all by Oasis Dream). The dam, a fairly useful 7f and 1m winner at 2 yrs, is a half-sister to several winners including the useful 1m and 10f winner Averted View. The second dam, Averti (by Known Fact), a fairly useful 7f (at 2 yrs) and 6f winner, is a half-sister to the US Grade 1 winner Defensive Play. (Khalid Abdulla). *"A big, rangy filly, she's one for seven furlongs in the autumn".*

1677. SIERRA RED (IRE) ★★
ch.c. Proud Citizen – Burren Rose (Storm Cat). April 6. Third foal. The dam, a useful Irish 1m, 10f and listed 12f winner, is a half-sister to 2 winners. The second dam, Lisieux Rose (by Generous), won the Group 2 11f Blandford Stakes and the US Grade 2 winners Orchid Handicap and the Grade 2 Sheepshead Bay Handicap and is a half-sister to 2 winners. (Moyglare Stud Farms Ltd). *"He's a mid-summer type 2-y-o that will want seven furlongs on 'top of the ground' or the polytrack".*

1678. SLEEPING BEAUTY (IRE) ★★★★
b.f. Oasis Dream – Nightime (Galileo). February 17. Second foal. The dam won 2 races at 3 yrs including the Irish 1,000 Guineas and is a half-sister to 2 winners. The second dam, Caumshinaun (by Indian Ridge), won 5 races from 6f to 1m in Ireland at 3 and 4 yrs including a listed event and is a half-sister to one winner.

(Mrs C. L. Weld). *"A really nice filly that I could see racing in August or September over seven furlongs. A lovely filly".*

1679. THUNDER MOUNTAIN (IRE) ★★★
b.br.c. Elnadim – Dance Clear (Marju). March 15. Eighth foal. Tattersalls Ireland. €50,000Y. Bobby O'Ryan. Half-brother to the useful 2011 2-y-o 7f winner Riviera Poet (by Footstepsinthesand), to the quite useful 2-y-o 7f winner Man Of The Match (by Iffraaj), the fair 14f and 2m winner Twist Again (by Sakhee), the fair 12f and hurdles winner Rosecliff (by Montjeu) and the modest 8.7f winner Dyanita (by Singspiel). The dam, an Irish 2-y-o 6f winner and third in the Group 3 7f Killavullan Stakes, subsequently won 4 races and was Grade 3 placed twice in the USA. She is a half-sister to 7 winners including the dance of the Group 3 winner Mulaqat. The second dam, Dance Ahead (by Shareef Dancer), a quite useful 2-y-o 7f winner, is a half-sister to 6 winners. (Dr R Lambe). *"He looks a 2-y-o type and we'll be moving on with him, so he'll be racing in May or June".* gelled, haened up 7gah Galway

1680. TUSCAN LIGHT ★★★
b.f. Medicean – Bright And Clear (Danehill). February 8. Sixth foal. Half-sister to a minor 10f winner in Qatar by Peintre Celebre and to a bumpers winner by Sakhee. The dam, a very useful 2-y-o 7f winner and Group 1 Italian Oaks second, is a half-sister to 12 winners including the high-class Group 1 1m Ciga Grand Criterium and Group 2 10.4f Dante Stakes winner Tenby, the very useful 1m (at 2 yrs) and 10f winner Bright Water and the very useful 2-y-o 7f winner and Group 1 1m Racing Post Trophy second Bude. The second dam, Shining Water (by Kalaglow), was a very useful winner of the Group 3 7f Solario Stakes and was placed in the Group 2 Park Hill Stakes. (Khalid Abdulla). *"Quite a nice filly and she'll be well capable of running over six/seven furlongs in June or July".*

1681. VIOLET HOUR (USA) ★★
b.f. Elusive Quality – Luminous Beauty (A P Indy). March 5. Fifth foal. Half-sister to the quite useful Irish 1m winner Soaring Emotions (by Kingmambo). The dam was listed-placed over 1m at 2 yrs in Ireland and is a half-sister to La

Nuit Rose, a winner over 7f at 2 yrs and placed in both the French and Irish 1,000 Guineas. The second dam, Caerlina (by Caerleon), won over 5.5f (at 2 yrs), the Group 1 10.5f Prix de Diane and the Group 3 10f Prix de la Nonette and is a sister to the French winner and Group 2 placed Leonila and a half-sister to 6 winners including the French listed winner Swalina. (Moyglare Stud Farms Ltd). *"A lengthy filly, she'll take a little bit of time but she should be out in July or August over seven furlongs".*

1682. UNNAMED ★★★★
b.c. Shirocco – Sharp Point (Royal Academy). May 10. Eleventh living foal. €105,000Y. Goffs Orby. Bobby O'Ryan. Half-brother to the Group 3 9f Prix Chloe and Group 3 1m Premio Sergio Cumani winner Needlecraft (by Mark Of Esteem), to the modest 10f winner Retreat Content (by Dubai Destination), the minor Irish 2-y-o 1m winner Thought (by Zafonic), the minor French 2-y-o winner Mayfield (by Danehill) and a winner over hurdles by Rainbow Quest. The dam, a useful Irish listed 5f winner at 3 yrs, was second in the Group 1 Heinz 57 Phoenix Stakes and is a half-sister to 3 winners including the listed winner High Target. The second dam, Nice Point (by Sharpen Up), is an unraced half-sister to 4 winners including the 2,000 Guineas winner Tirol. (Mr Steven Lo). *"A very nice horse, I trained the dam who was Group 1 placed over six furlongs. I would hope to have him racing in July or August over seven furlongs. He's a really nice colt".*

RICHARD WHITAKER
1683. LICHENANGEL ★★★★
gr.f. Dark Angel – Moss Likely (Clodovil). February 12. First foal. 20,000foal. Tattersalls December. Hellwood Stud Farm. The dam, a quite useful dual 5f winner at 2 yrs, was listed-placed. The second dam, Lichen (by Lycius), a moderate dual 9f winner at 4 yrs in Ireland, is a half-sister to 2 winners. (David Horner & David Walker). *"She's a very forward, very active filly, nicely proportioned and we really like her. She's going really nicely now, just doing half-speeds, so I'd like to see her on a racecourse at the end of April or the beginning of May. We haven't let her off the hook yet but the speed she shows suggests she's very much a five furlong type".*

1684. THREEPENCE ★★★

b.c. Three Valleys – The Jotter (Night Shift). April 18. Tenth foal. £10,000Y. Doncaster November. R Whitaker. Half-brother to the useful 6f (at 2 yrs) and subsequent US stakes-placed winner Final Row (by Indian Ridge), to the quite useful 6f (at 2 yrs) and 7f winner The Jostler (by Dansili), the fair 7f and 1m winner of 12 races Out For A Stroll (by Zamindar), the fair 8.5f winner Ice Prince (by Polar Falcon), the modest dual 10f winner Silken Thoughts (by Tobougg) and the moderate 7f winner Kenswick (by Avonbridge). The dam, a useful 2-y-o 5f and 6.5f winner, was second in three listed events and is closely related to the Group 1 Gran Criterium second Line Dancer and a half-sister to 2 winners. The second dam, Note Book (by Mummy's Pet), a fairly useful 6f winner, is a sister to the Norfolk Stakes winner Colmore Row and a half-sister to 8 winners including the smart miler Long Row. (Nice Day Out Partnership). *"I bought him 'on spec' at the sales because I liked his breeding and in particular his dam. He's not a big horse but there's plenty of him and he'll be racing early doors. I've entered him for the Redcar Two-Year-Old Trophy race in October because he's showing ability now and he's only going to get stronger as the season goes on".* TRAINERS' BARGAIN BUY

1685. TUMBLEWIND ★★★

ch.f. Captain Rio – African Breeze (Atraf). April 11. Fourth foal. £5,000Y. Doncaster November. T Adams. Sister to the moderate triple 5f winner Rio's Girl and half-sister to the fair 2-y-o 5f winner Breezolini (by Bertolini). The dam, a modest 5f (at 2 yrs) and 6f winner, is a half-sister to 3 winners including the useful 2-y-o listed 5f Roses Stakes winner Tabaret. The second dam, Luanshya (by First Trump), a fair 3-y-o 6f winner, is a half-sister to 4 winners. (Nice Day Out Partnership). *"It's a speedy dam-line and although this filly isn't quite as forward as our Dark Angel 2-y-o (Lichenangel) she's going as well as I want her to. Being by Captain Rio you'd think she'd want a bit of juice in the ground, but actually she doesn't have a high knee action, so maybe that won't be the case. A nice, quality filly, she definitely looks a 2-y-o type and she's not too big either".*

1686. WOTALAD ★★★★

b.c. Bertolini – Cosmic Song (Cosmonaut). March 16. Fourth foal. £20,000Y. Doncaster Premier. Peter & Ross Doyle. Brother to the fairly useful 2-y-o triple 6f and subsequent Hong Kong winner Cosmic Art. The dam was a moderate 9f and 11f winner. The second dam, Hotaria (by Sizzling Melody), a fair dual 6f winner at 2 and 3 yrs, is a half-sister to 7 winners. (Mrs J. M. Willows). *"This colt would be the pick of my 2-y-o's. He's bigger, has more scope and looks to have an engine but I won't rush him. A big, strong 2-y-o, he looks a real quality horse and he'll be entered for the Redcar 2-y-o Trophy because I think he'll be a bit better than average. More of a six furlong horse than five I would say".*

Sires Reference

This section deals with the sires that have at least two 2-y-o representatives in the book. Please note the index immediately following this reference.

ACCLAMATION

*2000 Royal Applause – Princess Athena (Ahonoora).*Racing record: Won 6 times, including Diadem Stakes. Also placed in King's Stand and Nunthorpe. Stud record: First crop now six-year-olds, he was an instant hit with his first crop in 2007, notably with his Group 1 winner Dark Angel. His subsequent good winners include the Group 1 King's Stand winner Equiano and in 2011 Harbour Watch (Group 2 Richmond Stakes), Lilbourne Lad (Group 2 Railway Stakes) and Alsindi (Group 3 Oh So Sharp Stakes). Europe's leading sire of two year olds in 2011. Standing at Rathbarry Stud, Ireland. 2012 fee: €35,000.

AD VALOREM

2002 Danzig – Classy Women (Relaunch). Racing Record: Won 4 races including Middle Park Stakes (6f at 2 yrs) & Queen Anne Stakes (1m). Stud record: First runners 2010. Amongst his winners are Pied A Terre (Grade 2 Autumn Stakes at Caulfield), Free Wheeling (Bollinger Champagne Classic at Doomben) and Uate (Group 3 Skyline Stakes at Warwick Farm). Stands at Darley Kelvinside Australia. 2011 fee: $11,000 Aus.

ALHAARTH

1993 Unfuwain – Irish Valley (Irish River). Racing record: Champion 2-y-o of 1995 when the winner of four group races, notably the Dewhurst Stakes. Showed very smart form up to 10f at 3/4 yrs, winning three Group 2 events. Stud record: First runners in 2001. Sire of Awzaan (2009 2-y-o Group 1 6f Middle Park Stakes), Haafhd (2000 Guineas and Champion Stakes), Bandari and Phoenix Reach (Canadian International, Hong Kong Vase and Dubai Sheema Classic) and the smart performers Bouguereau, Dominica, Hoh Buzzard, Maharib, Mourayan and Mutajarred, Morana and Valiyr. Standing at Derrinstown Stud, Ireland. 2012 fee: €4,000.

AMADEUS WOLF

2003 Mozart – Rachelle (Mark of Esteem). Won four races including the 2-y-o Group 1 6f Middle Park Stakes, Group 2 Gimcrack Stakes and Group 2 Duke of York Stakes. Stud record: His first runners appeared in 2011 and amongst his winners of 28 races was the listed winner Caledonian Spring. Standing at Irish National Stud. 2012 fee: €6,000.

ARCH

1995 Kris S – Aurora (Danzig). Racing Record: 5 wins including Super Derby and Fayette Stakes. Stud record: Sire of triple Grade 1 winner Blame, Arravale (Grade 1 Del Mar Oaks), Les Arcs (Golden Jubilee Stakes and July Cup), Pine Island (dual US Grade 1 winner), Overarching (South African Group 1 winner), Prince Arch, Hymn Book & Aracharcharch (all US Grade 1 winners), Montgomery's Arch (Group 2 Richmond Stakes) and the US Grade 2 winners All Star Heart, Lattice and Bauble Queen. Standing at Claiborne Farm, Kentucky, 2012 fee $30,000.

ASSERTIVE

2003 Bold Edge – Tart and a Half (Distant Relative). Racing record: Won the Group 2 6f Duke of York Stakes and second in the Group 1 6f Haydock Park Sprint Cup and the Diadem Stakes. His first two year olds appear in 2012. Standing at Throckmorton Stud. 2012 fee: £2,500.

ASTRONOMER ROYAL

2004 Danzig – Sheepscot (Easy Goer). Racing record: Won the French 2,000 Guineas and Group 3 6f Greenland Stakes, placed in St James's Palace Stakes and July Cup. First two year olds appear in 2012. Standing at Haras de la Reboursier Et De Montaigu. 2012 Fee: €5,000.

AUCTION HOUSE

*1996 Exbourne – Fast Flow (Riverman).*Racing record: Won three races including the Group 2 7f Champagne Stakes. Stud record: His first runners appeared in 2007 and amongst his winners are the useful Bid For Glory, Fratellino and Ghetto. Died 2011.

AUSSIE RULES

2003 Danehill – Last Second (Alzao). Racing Record: Won four races including the Shadwell Turf Mile and the French 2,000 Guineas. Stud record: His first runners arrived in 2010 and among his successes are the dual Group 3 winner Djumame, the Group 3 winner Duck Feet, Group 2 placed Boomerang Bob, the listed winners Cazal, Dinkum Diamond, Staros, Private Jet and Chinese Wall. Standing at Lanwades Stud. 2012 fee: £5,000.

AUTHORIZED

2004 Montjeu – Funsie (Saumarez). Won for races including the Racing Post Trophy, Juddmonte International, Derby Stakes, Dante Stakes. His first runners in 2011 include a number of minor winners like Good Of Luck, Al Saham and Estrela. Standing at Dalham Hall Stud. Fee for 2012: £10,000.

AVONBRIDGE

2000 Averti – Alessia (Caerleon). Racing record: Won the Prix de l'Abbaye and the Palace House Stakes, second in the July Cup. Stud record: First runners in 2009. Best winners to date are Temple Meads (Group 2 Mill Reef Stakes) and the Group 3 winner Iver Bridge Lad. Standing at Whitsbury Manor Stud. 2012 fee: £3,000.

AZAMOUR

2001 Night Shift – Azmara (Lear Fan). Race record: Won St James's Palace Stakes, Irish Champion Stakes, Prince of Wales's Stakes and King George VI and Queen Elizabeth Diamond Stakes. Stud record: His first runners came in 2009 and the best to date are the Group 2 winners Shankardeh, Eleonora Duse and Wade Giles, and five Group 3 winners including the 2,000 Guineas third Native Khan. Standing at Gilltown Stud, Ireland. 2012 fee: €15,000.

BAHAMIAN BOUNTY

1994 Cadeaux Genereux – Clarentia (Ballad Rock). Racing Record: Winner of 3 races at 2 yrs, notably the Prix Morny and the Middle Park Stakes. Stud record: First runners in 2001. Sire of high-class performer Pastoral Pursuits (July Cup), very smart Goodricke (Sprint Cup), Mister Napper Tandy (US Grade 2) and smart performers Fareer, Gallagher, Babodana, Dubaian Gift, Naahy, Paradise Isle, Topatoo and

Bogart (Redcar Two Year Old Trophy). Standing at the National Stud, Newmarket. 2012 fee: £8,500.

BALTIC KING

2000 Danetime – Lindfield Belle (Fairy King). Won 8 races including the Wokingham Handicap. Stud record: His first runners came in 2011 and his best winners include the multiple winners Factory Time and Bella Ophelia. Standing at Tally Ho Stud, Ireland. 2012 fee: €3,000.

BEAT HOLLOW

1997 Sadler's Wells – Wemyss Bight (Dancing Brave). Racing record: Won 7 races including the Grand Prix de Paris, Arlington Million and Woodford Reserve Turf Classic. Stud record: To stud 2003. Sire of 12 stakes winners including Proportional (Group 1 Prix Marcel Boussac), Sea Moon (Great Voltigeur Stakes), Beaten Up (St Simon Stakes), Vagabond Shoes (Prix Messidor), Charlotte O'Fraise (Group 3 Prix du Calvados) and Ted Spread (Group 3 Chester Vase). Standing at Ballylinch Stud, Ireland. 2012 fee: €6,000.

BERNARDINI

2003 A P Indy – Cara Rafaela (Quiet American). Racing Record: Won 5 Grade 1 events in the USA – the 1m Withers Stakes, the 9.5f Preakness Stakes, the 9f Jim Dandy Stakes, the 10f Jockey Club Gold Cup and the 10f Travers Stakes. Sire of Biondetti (Group 1 Premio Grand Criterium), A Z Warrior (Grade 1 Frizette Stakes), Gamilati (Group 2 Cherry Hinton Stakes), Theyskens Theory (Group 3 Prestige Stakes), To Honor and Serve (Grade 1 Cigar Mile), Stay Thirsty (Grade 1 Travers Stakes) and Wilburn (Grade 2 Indiana Derby). Standing at Jonabell Farm, Kentucky. 2012 fee: $150,000.

BERTOLINI

1996 Danzig – Aquilega (Alydar). Racing record: Won 2 races, including July Stakes at 2 yrs, and placed in July Cup, Sprint Cup and Nunthorpe Stakes. Stud record: First runners in 2005. Sire of the Group 1 Cheveley Park Stakes winner Donna Blini, New Zealand Group 1 winner Juice, smart winners Moorhouse Lad and Prime Defender and the useful performers Blades Girl, Bobs Surprise, Come Out Fighting,

Victoire de Lyphar, Mac Gille Eoin, Medic Power (in Hong Kong), Signor Peltro, Suits Me and Tabaret. Standing at Overbury Stud, Gloucestershire. 2012 fee: £3,000.

BYRON

2001 Green Desert – Gay Gallanta (Woodman). Racing Record: Won 3 races including the Group 2 6f Mill Reef Stakes (at 2 yrs) and the Group 2 7f Betfair Cup (Lennox Stakes). Stud record: First runners 2010. Has sired a fair number of winners including fairly useful sprinter Ahtoug. Standing at Woodlands Stud, Ireland. 2012 fee €2,500.

CADEAUX GENEREUX

1985 Young Generation – Smarten Up (Sharpen Up). Racing record: 7 wins, notably the July Cup and William Hill Sprint Championship. Stud record: Best winners include Bijou d'Inde (Group 1 St James's Palace Stakes), Donativum (Grade 1 Breeders Cup Juvenile), Touch of The Blues (Atto Mile in Canada) and numerous other smart performers including Bahamian Bounty (Group 1 Middle Park Stakes), Desert Deer (Group 2 Sandown Mile), Embassy (Group 1 Cheveley Park Stakes), Hoh Magic (Prix Morny), Land Of Dreams (Group 2 Flying Childers Stakes), Major Cadeaux (Group 2 Sandown Mile), Stage Gift (Group 2 York Stakes) and Toylsome (Group 1 Prix de la Foret). Died 2011.

CAMACHO

2002 Danehill – Arabesque (Zafonic). Racing record: Won a listed race over 6f and was second in the Group 3 7f Jersey Stakes. Stud record: Had his first runners in 2009 and his best winners to date are the tough listed winner Star Rover, the Group 3 Fred Darling Stakes winner Puff and the listed winners Humidor and Arctic Feeling. Standing at Morristown Lattin Stud, Ireland. 2012 fee: €4,000.

CAPE CROSS

1994 Green Desert – Park Appeal (Ahonoora). Racing record: Won 4 races, including Lockinge Stakes, Queen Anne Stakes and Celebration Mile. Stud record: First runners in 2003. Sire of the outstanding colt Sea The Stars (2,000 Guineas, Derby, Prix de l'Arc de Triomphe etc,), top-class Ouija Board (7 Group 1 wins

including the Oaks & the Breeders' Cup Filly and Mare Turf), Hong Kong Group 1 winner Able One, Group 1 Grand Prix de Paris winner Behkabad, the 2-y-o Group 1 Gran Criterium winner Nayarra, the New Zealand Group 1 winners Kindacross, Mikki Street and Gaze, and numerous smart performers including Borthwick Girl, Cape Fear, Castleton, Charlie Farnsbarns, Crossing The Line, Crosspeace, Crystal Capella, Halicarnassus, Hatta Fort, Hazyview, Mac Love, Madrid, Mazuna, Musicanna, Privy Seal, Russian Cross, Cape Dollar and I Love Me. Standing at Kildangan Stud, Ireland. 2012 stud fee: €35,000.

CAPTAIN MARVELOUS

2004 Invincible Spirit – Shesasmartlady (Dolphin Street). Racing record: Won the Group 2 6f Criterium de Maisons Laffitte. Stud record: His first crop are two year olds of 2012. Standing at Haras de Fontaines. Stud fee: €2,500.

CAPTAIN RIO

2000 Pivotal – Beloved Visitor (Miswaki). Racing record: Won 4 times, including Criterium de Maisons-Laffitte at 2 yrs. Stud record: From 3 crops racing, sire of the New Zealand Grade 1 winner Il Quello Veloce, Australian Group 1 winner Brazilian Pulse, Group 3 Tetrarch Stakes winner Energizer, Group 3 Select Stakes winner Red Badge, the smart Capt Chaos and Captain Dunne and the Group 3 Sirenia Stakes winner Philario. Standing at Ballyhane Stud, Ireland. 2012 fee: €4,000.

CHINEUR

2001 Fasliyev – Wardara (Sharpo). Race record: Won Kings Stand Stakes and Prix de Saint-Georges. Stud record: His first runners came in 2009 and his best winners so far include the useful colts Roi de Vitesse, Singeur and En Un Clin D'Oeil and the Group 3 placed filly Silver Grey. Standing at Haras Des Granges, France. 2012 fee: €3,000.

CLODOVIL

2001 Danehill – Clodora (Linamix). Racing record: Won 5 races including the French 2,000 Guineas. Stud record: His first crop were two-year-olds in 2007 and from relatively small crops his best winners to date are the Group 1 Falmouth Stakes winner Nahoodh, the very useful Beacon Lodge (Group 3 Horris Hill Stakes), the listed winners Rock My Soul and Coupe De Ville, and the Group 1 Prix de l'Abbaye second Secret Asset. Standing at Rathasker Stud, Ireland. 2012 fee: €6,000.

COCKNEY REBEL
2004 Val Royal – Factice (Known Fact). Racing record: Won 3 races including the 2,000 Guineas and Irish 2,000 Guineas. Stud record: His first runners appeared in 2011 and there were a good number of winners including the useful Rebellious Guest. Stands at the National Stud in Newmarket. 2012 fee: £4,000.

COMPTON PLACE
1994 Indian Ridge – Nosey (Nebbiolo). Racing record: Won 3 races, notably the Group 1 6f July Cup. Stud record: First runners in 2002. Sire of the dual Group 1 Nunthorpe Stakes winner Borderlescott, Group 2 and Group 3 winning sprinter Deacon Blues, the smart Boogie Street and Intrepid Jack, US Grade 2 winner Passified, the Group 2 winners Godfrey Street and Prolific, and numerous useful performers including Compton's Eleven, If Paradise, Judd Street, Hunter Street and Pacific Pride. Standing at Whitsbury Manor Stud, Hampshire. 2012 fee: £6,000.

COUNTRY REEL
2000 Danzig – Country Belle (Seattle Slew). Racing record: Won the Group 2 6f Gimcrack Stakes. Stud record: Sire of the Group 3 winner Absolutely Yes and four listed winners including the French 1,000 Guineas second Baine. Standing at Haras de Logis. 2012 fee: €4,000.

CURLIN
2004 Smart Strike – Sherriff's Deputy (Deputy Minister). Racing record: Won 11 races including 7 Grade One's, notably the Jockey Club Gold Cup (twice), Woodward Stakes, Dubai World Cup, Breeders Cup Classic, Preakness Stakes. Stud record: His first crop of two-year-olds appear in 2012. Standing at Lane's End Farm, Kentucky. 2012 fee: $40,000.

DALAKHANI
2001 Darshaan – Daltawa (Miswaki). Racing record: Won 8 of 9 starts, including the Prix du Jockey Club and the Arc. Stud record: His first crop were two-year-olds in 2007. Sire of the classic winners Conduit (St Leger, Breeders Cup Turf (twice), King George VI & Queen Elizabeth Stakes), Moonstone (Irish Oaks), Reliable Man (Prix du Jockey Club) and Duncan (Irish St Leger). Also worthy of note are the Group 1 Pretty Polly Stakes winner Chinese White, the Group 2 winners Centennial, Armure, Vadamar and Democratie. Standing at Gilltown Stud, Ireland. 2012 fee: €40,000.

DANEHILL DANCER
1993 Danehill – Mira Adonde (Sharpen Up). Racing Record: Winner of 4 races including the Phoenix Stakes and the National Stakes at 2 yrs and the Greenham at 3. Stud record: First runners in 2001. The sire of Choisir (Golden Jubilee Stakes), multiple Group 1 winner Mastercraftsman, Moyglare Stud Stakes & Irish 1,000 Guineas winner Again, the US Grade 1 winners Ave and Alexander Tango, dual Group 1 winner Lillie Langtry, Queen Elizabeth II Stakes winner Where Or When, 1,000 Guineas winner Speciosa, Oaks winner Dancing Rain, Group 1 Prix Ganay winner Planteur, Group 1 Phoenix Stakes winner Alfred Nobel, Australian Group 1 winners Arapaho Miss, Private Steer and Light Fantastic & numerous smart performers including Alexander Tango, Anna Pavlova, Blue Sky Thinking, Contredanse, Express Wish, Fast Company, Ice Queen, Indesatchel, Jeremy, Kissable, Lady Dominatrix, Lizard Island, Medicine Path, Memory, Miss Beatrix, Monsieur Bond and Snaefell. Standing at Coolmore Stud, Ireland. 2012 fee: €60,000.

DANSILI
1996 Danehill – Hasili (Kahyasi). Racing record: Won 5 races in France, and placed in six Group/ Grade 1 events including Sussex Stakes and Breeders' Cup Mile. Stud record: First runners in 2004. Sire of top-class Rail Link (Arc, Grand Prix de Paris), Harbinger (Group 1 King George VI), Passage Of Time (Group 1 Criterium de Saint-Cloud), Zambezi Sun (Group 1 Grand Prix de Paris), Zacinto (Group 2 Celebration Mile), Emulous (Group 1 Matron Stakes), Zoffany (Group 1 Phoenix Stakes) and numerous very smart performers including Aviate, Bated Breath, Dandino, Dansant, Delegator, Dream Peace, Famous Name, Grecian Dancer, Home

Affairs, Illustrious Blue, Passage Of Time, Price Tag (US Grade 1 winner and first past post in Poule d'Essai des Pouliches), Proviso, Requinto, Sense Of Joy, Shaweel (Gimcrack Stakes), Silver Touch, Strategic Prince and Testosterone. Sire of 14 individual Group winners during 2011. Standing at Banstead Manor Stud, Newmarket. 2012 fee: £75,000.

DARK ANGEL

2005 Acclamation – Midnight Angel (Machiavellian). Racing record: Won four races at 2 yrs including the Group 1 6f Middle Park Stakes and the Group 2 6f Mill Reef Stakes. Stud record: His first runners appeared in 2011 and he had an excellent start in terms of number of winners. They included the listed winner Lily's Angel and the Group-placed Tough As Nails and B Fifty Two. Standing at Morristown Lattin Stud, Ireland. 2012 fee: €12,500.

DISTORTED HUMOR

1993 Forty Niner – Danzig's Beauty (Danzig). Racing record: Won 11 races in the USA including the Champagne Stakes, Futurity Stakes, Haskell Invitational and Travers Stakes (all Grade 1). Champion 2-y-o. Stud record: Sire of eleven Grade 1 winners – Any Given Saturday, Awesome Humor, Bit Of Whimsy, Commentator, Drosselmeyer, Flower Alley, Fourty Niner's Son, Funny Cide, Hystericalady, Pathfork and Rinky Dink. Standing at Win Star Farm, Kentucky. 2012 fee: $100,000.

DIXIE UNION

1997 Dixieland Band – She's Tops (Capote). Racing record: Won 7 races including the Haskell Invitational and the Malibu Stakes (both Grade 1 events in the USA). Stud record: Sire of the US Grade 1 winners Dixie Chatter, Union Rags and Hot Dixie Chick, the Group 2 Cherry Hinton Stakes winner Sander Camillo, Group 2 Prix de Sandringham winner Homebound and the US Grade 2 winners Gone Astray, Justwhistledixie, Most Distinguished and Nothing But Fun. Died 2010.

DR FONG

1995 Kris S – Spring Flight (Miswaki). Racing record: Won 5 races, including Group 1 1m St James's Palace Stakes and the Group 2 10f Prix Eugene Adam. Stud record: First runners in

2003. Sire of the US Grade 1 winner Shamdinan, the Premio Lydia Tesio winner Aoife Alainn, the Group 1 Prix Saint-Alary winner Ask For The Moon, the US Grade 2 winner Spotlight, the smart performers Andronikos, Celimene, Doctor Brown, Dubai's Touch, Fong's Thong, Forward Move, Group Captain, Metropolitan Man and Purple Orchid and numerous very useful performers. Standing at Haras Du Thenney, France. 2012 fee: €5,000.

DUBAI DESTINATION

1999 Kingmambo – Mysterial (Alleged). Racing record: Won four races including the Group 1 1m Queen Anne Stakes and the Group 2 7f Champagne Stakes. Stud record: His first crop of two-year-olds in 2007 included the Group 1 winner Ibn Khaldun and the smart gelding Charm School. Subsequently, his best have included the Group 2 Prix Robert Papin winner Family One, the Group 3 Sceptre Stakes winner Alanza, the smart colt Firebet and Italian Group 3 winner Evading Tempete. Standing at Glenview Stud, Ireland. 2012 fee: £2,500.

DUBAWI

2002 Dubai Millennium – Zomaradah (Deploy). Race record: Won the National Stakes at 2 and the Irish 2,000 Guineas and Prix Jacques le Marois at 3. Third in the Derby. Stud record: His first runners appeared in 2009 and he was the leading first-crop sire by number of winners. He has had an outstanding start at stud and his best winners to date include Makfi (2,000 Guineas), Monterosso (Dubai World Cup), the US dual Grade 1 winner Dubawi Heights, the South African dual Group 1 winner Happy Archer, the Group 1 Queen Elizabeth II Stakes winner Poet's Voice, Group 1 Hong Kong Sprint winner Luck Or Design, Group 1 German Derby winner Waldpark, dual Australian Group 1 winner Secret Admirer and the Group 2 winners Dubawi Gold, Irish Field, Prince Bishop, Sand Vixen and Worthadd. Standing at Dalham Hall Stud, Newmarket. 2011 fee: €75,000.

DUKE OF MARMALADE

2004 Danehill –Love Me True (Kingmambo). Racing record: Won 6 races including the Juddmonte International Stakes, King George VI and Queen Elizabeth Stakes, Prince of Wales's Stakes, Tattersalls Gold Cup and Prix

Ganay (all Group 1 events). Stud record: His first two year olds appear in 2012. Standing at Coolmore Stud, Ireland. Stud fee: €20,000.

DUTCH ART

2004 Medicean- Halland Park Lass (Spectrum). Racing record: Won four races at 2 yrs including the Group 1 Prix Morny and the Group 1 Middle Park Stakes. Stud record: His first runners came in 2011 and he was the leading first season sire. With 33 first crop winners (to mid-March 2012), he's had an outstanding start. Those winners include Caspar Netscher (Group 2 Mill Reef Stakes and Group 2 Gimcrack Stakes) and the listed winner Miss Work Of Art. Standing at Cheveley Park Stud, Newmarket. 2012 fee: £12,000.

DYLAN THOMAS

2003 Danehill – Lagrion (Diesis). Racing record: Won 10 races including the Prix de L'Arc de Triomphe & Irish Champion Stakes. Stud record: From a very large first crop of foals he had a fair start with his first runners in 2011 including the winner and Group 2 Beresford Stakes third Athens and the Group 1 fourth Furner's Green. Stud record: Standing at Coolmore Stud, Ireland. 2012 fee: €12,500.

DYNAFORMER

1985 Roberto – Andover Way (His Majesty). Racing record: 7 wins in USA including the Grade 2 Florida Derby and the Grade 2 Discovery Handicap. Stud record: Best winners include the Melbourne Cup winner Americain, the Group 1 St Leger winner Lucarno, the Group 1 Fillies' Mile winner Rainbow View, Blue Bunting (1,000 Guineas, Irish Oaks, Yorkshire Oaks), German dual Group 1 winner Weiner Walzer, the very smart Beat All and (in USA) Grade 1 winners Barbaro, Brilliant Speed, Dynaforce, Film Maker, Perfect Drift, Riskaverse, Star Billing and Starrer, and numerous smart performers including Dynever, Ittasak, Meeznah, Michita, Ocean Silk, Sharp Susan, Spanish John and White Moonstone. Standing at Three Chimneys Farm, Kentucky. 2012 fee: $150,000.

ELNADIM

1994 Danzig – Elle Seule (Exclusive Native). Racing record: Won 5 races, notably the Group 1 6f July Cup and the Diadem Stakes. Stud record: First runners in 2004, first European runners in 2005. Sire of the smart performers Al Qasi (Group 3 Phoenix Stakes), Caldra (Group 3 Autumn Stakes), Culminate (New Zealand Group 1), Elletelle (Group 2 Queen Mary Stakes), Elnawin (Group 3 Sirenia Stakes), Wi Dud (Group 2 Flying Childers Stakes), Soraya (Group 3 Princess Margaret Stakes) and dual listed winner Almass. Standing at Derrinstown Stud, Ireland. 2012 fee: €5,000.

ELUSIVE CITY

2000 Elusive Quality – Star of Paris (Dayjur). Racing record: Won the Group 1 Prix Morny and the Group 2 Richmond Stakes, and also placed in the Group 1 Middle Park Stakes (all at 2 yrs). Stud record: First crop were two-year-olds in 2008. His best winners include Elusive Wave (French 2,000 Guineas), Soul City (Group 3 Prix La Rochette and Goffs Million) and multiple listed winner Nashmiah. Standing at Haras D'Etreham. 2012 fee: €15,000.

ELUSIVE QUALITY

1993 Gone West – Touch of Greatness (Hero's Honor). Racing record: Won 9 races in USA, including Grade 3 events at 7f/1m. Stud record: Sire of top-class Kentucky Derby/Preakness Stakes winner Smarty Jones, Breeders Cup Classic and Queen Elizabeth II Stakes winner Raven's Pass, US triple Grade 1 winner Quality Road, multiple Australian Group 1 winner Sepoy, Prix Morny winner Elusive City, Prix Marcel Boussac winner Elusive Kate and numerous US graded stakes winners including Chimichurri, Elusive Diva, Girl Warrior, Maryfield, Omega Code, Royal Michele and True Quality, the smart dual listed winner Baharah and the Group 3 winning two-year-olds Elusive Pimpernel and Evasive. Standing at Darley Stud Farm Kentucky. 2012 fee: $50,000.

EMPIRE MAKER

2000 Unbridled – Toussaud (El Gran Senor). Racing record: Won the Belmont Stakes, Florida Derby, Wood Memorial Stakes and Jim Dandy Stakes. Stud record: Sire of the US Grade 1 winners Acoma, Battle Plan, Mushka, Icon Project, Country Star, Royal Delta and Pioneerofthe Nile. Standing in Japan. 2012 fee: Private.

EXCEED AND EXCEL

2000 Danehill – Patrona (Lomond). Racing record: Champion sprinter in Australia, won 7 races including the Grade 1 Newmarket H'cap, the Grade 1 Dubai Racing Club Cup and the Grade 2 Todman Stakes. Stud record: First northern hemisphere runners in 2008. His best winners include Infamous Angel (Lowther Stakes), Crown Prosecutor, Excelebration (Group 1 Prix du Moulin), Margot Did (Group 1 Nunthorpe Stakes), Best Terms (Lowther Stakes) and Masamah (Group 2 King George Stakes). His Australasian winners include the Group 1 winners Helmet and Reward For Effort, Group 2 winner Wilander and the Group 3 winners Exceedingly Good, Sugar Babe and Believe 'n' Succeed. The leading sire of juveniles in Britain and Ireland in 2009, with 31 winners. Standing at Dalham Hall Stud, Newmarket. 2011 fee: £22,500.

EXCELLENT ART

2004 Pivotal – Obsessive (Seeking The Gold). Racing record: Won 4 races including the Group 1 1m St James's Palace Stakes and the Group 2 6f Mill Reef Stakes. Stud record: His first runners appeared in 2011 and he had plenty of winners including the Irish Group 3 winner Experience, the listed winners Artistic Jewel & Nimohe and the Group placed Boris Grigoriev and Gray Pearl. Standing at Coolmore Stud in Ireland. 2012 fee: €10,000.

FIREBREAK

1999 Charnwood Forest – Breakaway (Song). Racing record: Won the Godolphin Mile in Dubai (twice), Challenge Stakes and Hong Kong Mile. Stud record: With 3 crops racing his best winners to date are the Group 1 Gran Criterium winner Hearts Of Fire and the listed winners and Group placed Caledonia Lady and Electric Feel. Standing at Bearstone Stud. 2012 fee: £3,500.

FOOTSTEPSINTHESAND

2002 Giant's Causeway – Glatisant (Rainbow Quest). Racing record: Won all 3 of his starts, notably the 2,000 Guineas. Stud record: With 3 crops racing his best winners to date are the Irish Group 3 and subsequent Hong Kong Group 3 winner Steinbeck (renamed Pure Champion), the German Group 2 winner and Group 1 third Shamalgan, the Group 2 Railway Stakes winner Formosina and the Group 3 winners Barefoot Lady, Chachamaidee, Giant Sandman, Sandy's Charm and Sent From Heaven. Standing at Coolmore Stud, Ireland. 2012 fee: €10,000.

GALILEO

1998 Sadler's Wells – Urban Sea (Miswaki). Racing record: Won 6 races, including Derby, Irish Derby and King George VI and Queen Elizabeth Stakes. Stud record: First runners in 2005. Sire of 26 Group 1 winners including champion 2-y-o's Teofilo, Frankel (also champion 3-y-o) and New Approach (subsequent Derby, Champion Stakes and Irish Champion Stakes winner), the triple Group 1 winner Rip Van Winkle, Sixties Icon (St Leger), Red Rocks (Breeders' Cup Turf), Allegretto (Prix Royal-Oak), Lush Lashes (three Group 1 wins), Soldier Of Fortune (Irish Derby & Coronation Cup) and Nightime (Irish 1000 Guineas), Roderic O'Connor (Criterium International, Irish 2,000 Guineas), Cape Blanco (five Group 1 wins), Nathaniel (King George VI & Queen Elizabeth Stakes), Treasure Beach (Irish Derby, Secretariat Stakes), Golden Lilac (French 1,000 Guineas and Prix de Diane), Misty For Me (four Group 1 wins), Maybe (Moyglare Stud Stakes) and Galikova (Prix Vermeille). Standing at Coolmore Stud, Ireland. 2012 fee: Private (was €150,000).

GIANT'S CAUSEWAY

1997 Storm Cat – Mariah's Storm (Rahy). Racing record: Won 9 races, 6 of them Group 1 events, including Prix de la Salamandre, Juddmonte International and Sussex Stakes. Stud record: First runners in 2004. Sire of high-class Shamardal (Dewhurst Stakes, St James's Palace Stakes and Prix du Jockey Club), very smart Footstepsinthesand (2,000 Guineas) and a number of very smart performers including Ghanaati (1,000 Guineas and Coronation Stakes), Aragorn (dual US Grade 1 winner), Heatseeker (Grade 1 Santa Anita Handicap), Maids Causeway (Coronation Stakes), Rite Of Passage (Ascot Gold Cup), Await The Dawn (Hardwicke Stakes), Eishin Apollon (Group 1 in Japan), Eskendereya, My Typhoon, First Samurai & Swift Temper (US Grade 1 winners). Standing at Ashford Stud, Kentucky. 2012 fee: $85,000.

GREEN DESERT

1983 Danzig – Foreign Courier (Sir Ivor). Racing record: 5 wins including July Cup, Vernons Sprint Cup and Flying Childers Stakes. Stud record: High-class sire. Best winners (all very smart or better) include Alkaadhem, Cape Cross (Lockinge Stakes), Desert Lord (Prix de l'Abbaye), Desert Prince (Irish 2000 Guineas, Prix du Moulin, Queen Elizabeth Stakes), Desert Style, Desert Sun, Gabr, Invincible Spirit (Haydock Sprint Cup), Markab (Sprint Cup), Oasis Dream (Middle Park, July Cup, Nunthorpe Stakes), Owington (July Cup), Sheikh Albadou (Nunthorpe Stakes/Haydock Sprint Cup), Tamarisk (Haydock Sprint Cup) and Tropical. Standing at Nunnery Stud, Norfolk. 2012 fee: Private.

HAAFHD

2001 Alhaarth – Al Bahathri (Blushing Groom). Racing record: Won 5 races, notably the 2,000 Guineas and the Champion Stakes. Stud record: First crop were two-year-olds in 2008. His best performers so far include the 2-y-o Group 2 Superlative Stakes winner Silver Grecian, the smart UAE horse Emirates Champion, the listed winners Junoob and Show Rainbow and the very useful Almiqdaad. Standing at Beechwood Grange. 2012 fee: £2,500.

HAATEF

2004 Danzig – Sayedat Alhadh (Mr Prospector). Racing record: Won four races including the Group 2 6f Diadem Stakes. Stud record: His first crop are two year olds of 2012. Standing at Derrinstown Stud, Ireland. 2012 fee: €4,000.

HALLING

1991 Diesis – Dance Machine (Green Dancer). Racing record: Won 12 races including Coral-Eclipse Stakes (twice), Juddmonte International (twice) and Prix d'Ispahan. Stud record: Sire of the Group 1 Grand Prix de Paris winner Cavalryman, the high-class multiple Group 1 placed Norse Dancer, Group 1 Prix Ganay winner Cutlass Bay, Group 2 winners Boscobel, Opinion Poll, Coastal Path, Dandoun, Eastern Aria, Fisich, Franklins Gardens, Giovani Imperatore, Harland, Nordhal, Pinson and Vanderlin, plus numerous other smart performers including Bauer, Chancellor, Foodbroker Fancy, Hala Bek, Hattan, Hero's Journey, Mkuzi, Parasol and

The Geezer. Standing at Dalham Hall Stud, Newmarket. 2012 fee: £10,000.

HARD SPUN

2004 Danzig – Turkish Tryst (Turkoman). Racing record: Won the Group 1 7f King's Bishop Stakes, the Grade 2 9f Kentucky Classic and the Group 2 9f Lane's End Stakes. Stud record: Has made a very good start at stud. Amongst his first crop winners is the Group 2 7f Superlative Stakes winner Red Duke, the North American stakes winners American Wildcat and Hard Not To Like and the Group 3 placed Questing. Standing at Jonabell Farm, Kentucky. 2012 fee: $40,000.

HENRYTHENAVIGATOR

2005 Kingmambo – Sequoyah (Sadler's Wells). Racing record: Won the Sussex Stakes, St James's Palace Stakes, 2000 Guineas and Irish 2,000 Guineas (all Group 1). His first two year olds appear in 2012. Standing at Ashford Stud, Kentucky. 2012 fee: $30,000.

HERNANDO

1990 Niniski – Whakilyric (Miswaki). Racing record: Won 7 races including the Prix Lupin and the Prix du Jockey Club. Stud record: His Group/Grade 1 winners are Look Here (Oaks), Holding Court (Prix du Jockey Club), Sulamani (Prix du Jockey Club, Arlington Million, Turf Classic Invitational, Juddmonte International), Casual Conquest (Tattersalls Gold Cup) and Gitano Hernando (US Goodwood Stakes). Also responsible for the US Grade 2 winners Arvada, Atlando and Herboriste, the multiple German Group winner Alianthus and the very smart performers Asian Heights, Foreign Affairs, Harris Tweed, Mr Combustible, Samando, Songerie and Tau Ceti. Standing at Lanwades Stud, Newmarket. 2012 fee: Private.

HIGH CHAPARRAL

2000 Sadler's Wells – Kasora (Darshaan). Racing record: Won 10 races, including Derby, Irish Champion Stakes and Breeders' Cup Turf (twice). Stud record: First crop were two-year-olds in 2007. Best performers to date include Australian Grade 1 winners So You Think (in Europe winner of the Tattersalls Gold Cup, Eclipse Stakes and Irish Champion Stakes), Descarado, Monaco Consul and Shoot Out,

Grade 1 Northern Dancer Turf Stakes winner Redwood, St Leger runner-up Unsung Heroine, Group 2 Park Hill Stakes winner The Miniver Rose and the Group 3 winners Above Average, Golden Sword, High Heeled, Joanna, Magadan and Senlis. Standing at Coolmore Stud, Ireland. 2012 fee: €25,000.

HOLY ROMAN EMPEROR

(2004) Danehill – L'On Vite (Secretariat). Racing Record: Won four races at 2 yrs including the Group 1 7f Prix Jean-Luc Lagardere, the Group 1 6f Waterford Phoenix Stakes and the Group 2 6f Railway Stakes. Stud record: Stud record: His best winners to date include Banimpire (5 Group wins including Group 2 Royal Whip Stakes and Group 2 Ribblesdale Stakes), Australian Group 2 winner Rollout The Carpet, Italian Group 2 winner Sandslash and numerous listed winners. Standing at Coolmore Stud, Ireland. 2012 fee: €12,500.

HURRICANE RUN

2002 Montjeu – Hold On (Surumu). Racing Record: Won 8 races including the Group 1 12f King George VI & Queen Elizabeth Diamond Stakes, Group 1 10.5f Tattersalls Gold Cup and Group 1 12f Prix de l'Arc de Triomphe. Stud record: First runners appeared in 2010 and his best to date include Future Generation (Desmond Stakes), Kreem (Prix du Lys), Freedom (Diamond Stakes), Ballybacka Lady (1,000 Guineas Trial), Don't Hurry Me (Prix Penelope), listed winners Arizona Run, Barbican, Charleston Lady, Mohedian Lady and Racemate, and the Irish Derby third Memphis Tennessee. Standing at Coolmore Stud, Ireland. 2012 fee: €12,500.

IFFRAAJ

2001 Zafonic – Pastorale (Nureyev). Racing Record: Won 7 races including the Group 2 7f Park Stakes (twice), Group 2 7f Betfair Cup (Lennox Stakes) and the 6f Wokingham Stakes. Stud record: First runners came in 2010 when he had more winners than any first-crop European sire ever. Among his winners are Wootton Bassett (Group 1 Prix Jean-Luc Lagardere), the Group 3 winners Espirita and Stay Alive and two listed winners abroad. Standing at Kildangan Stud, Ireland. 2012 fee: €10,000.

INDESATCHEL

2002 Danehill Dancer – Floria (Petorius). Racing Record: Won 4 races including the Group 3 7f Tetrarch Stakes and the Group 3 7f Greenham Stakes. Stud record: His first runners appeared in 2010 and he's had a decent start with winners such as the listed-placed Galtymore Lad. Standing at Bearstone Stud, Shropshire. 2012 fee: £3,500.

INTIKHAB

1994 Red Ransom – Crafty Example (Crafty Prospector). Racing record: 8 wins including Diomed Stakes and the Queen Anne Stakes. Stud record: First runners in 2003. Sire of Snow Fairy (Queen Elizabeth II Cup in Japan (twice), Oaks, Irish Oaks, Cathay Pacific Hong Kong Cup), Red Evie (Group 1 Lockinge Stakes & Group 1 Matron Stakes), Paita (Group 1 Criterium de Saint-Cloud), the Group 3 winners Ascertain, Glen's Diamond, Hoh Mike, Moon Unit, Toupie and Tell Dad, plus numerous very useful performers including Fine Silver, Leg Spinner, Les Fazzani, Without A Prayer and Tropical Strait. Standing at Derrinstown Stud, Ireland. 2012 fee: £5,500.

INVASOR

2002 Candy Stripes – Quendom (Interprete). Racing record: Ran 12 times and won 11 of them including the Dubai World Cup, the Breeders Cup Classic and the Whitney, Donn and Suburban Handicaps. Stud record: His first runners in 2011 including the listed-placed Midnight Vader. Standing at Shadwell Stud, Kentucky. 2012 fee: $20,000.

INVINCIBLE SPIRIT

1997 Green Desert – Rafha (Kris). Racing record: 7 wins notably the Group 1 Sprint Cup at 5 yrs. Stud record: First runners in 2006. Sire of dual Group 1 winner Lawman (French Derby & Prix Jean Prat), Fleeting Spirit (July Cup, Temple Stakes, Flying Childers Stakes and Molecomb Stakes), Grade 1 Breeders Cup Juvenile winner Vale Of York, Moonlight Cloud (Prix Maurice de Gheest & Prix de Porte Maillot), Yosai (three Group 1 wins in Australia), Group 2 Gimcrack Stakes and Stewards Cup winner Conquest, Group 2 Criterium de Maisons-Lafitte winner Our Jonathan, Group 2 Flying Childers winners Madame Trop Vite and

Zebedee, the smart performers Allied Powers, Campfire Glow, Captain Marvelous and Staying On, and the useful performers Bahama Mama, Hurricane Spirit, Invincible Force and Kingship Spirit. Standing at the Irish National Stud. 2012 fee: €60,000.

ISHIGURU
1998 Danzig – Strategic Maneuver (Cryptoclearance). Race record: Won 3 races including the Group 3 Flying Five at Leopardstown and the listed Belgrave Stakes at the Curragh. Stud record: His best winners are Ferneley (5 wins including the Grade 2 1m Del Mar Handicap), Hellvelyn (5 wins including the Group 2 6f Coventry Stakes) and She's Our Mark (6 wins including the Group 3 10f Meld Stakes, the Group 3 1m Desmond Stakes and two listed events). Died 2009.

JAZIL
2003 Seeking The Gold – Better Than Honour (Deputy Minister). Racing record: Won 2 races including the Belmont Stakes. Stud record: His first runners in 2011 included a handful of winners. Standing at Shadwell Farm, Kentucky. 2012 fee: $7,500.

JEREMY
2003 Danehill Dancer – Glint in Her Eye (Arazi). Racing record: Won 4 races including the Group 2 Betfred Mile at Sandown and the Group 3 7f Jersey Stakes. Stud record: His first runners in 2011 included the winners Yellow Rosebud (second in the Group 2 Keeneland Debutante Stakes at the Curragh) and Princess Sinead (third in the Group 3 C.L Weld Park Stakes). Standing at the Irish National Stud. 2012 fee: €6,000.

JOHANNESBURG
1999 Hennessy – Myth (Ogygian). Racing record: Unbeaten at 2 yrs, when 7 wins included Phoenix Stakes, Prix Morny, Middle Park and Breeders' Cup Juvenile. Stud record: First runners in 2006. Sire of the Group 1 Prix d'Ispahan winner Sageburg, the Group 2 winners Hamoody, Radiohead and Red Jazz, US Grade 1 winner Scat Daddy, US Grade 2 winners Eaton's Gift, Looky Yonder, Phola and Teuflesburg, Australian Group 1 winners Turffontein and Once Were Wild, the Argentine

Group 1 winner Bamba Jane and the smart performers Diamond Tycoon, Jupiter Pluvius, Rabatash and Tombi. Standing in Japan for 2011.

KHELEYF
2001 Green Desert – Society Lady (Mr Prospector). Racing record: Won 3 races including the Group 3 Jersey Stakes. Stud record: Sire of plenty of two-year-old winners. The best of his progeny so far are Sayif (Group 2 Diadem Stakes), Percolator (Group 3 Prix du Bois), the listed winners Captain Ramius, Vladimir (third in Group 1 Prix Morny) and Playfellow and the Group 3 placed Deposer. Standing at Dalham Hall Stud, Newmarket. 2012 fee: £4,000.

KODIAC
2001 Danehill – Rafha (Kris). Racing Record: Won 4 races here and in the UAE over 6f and 7f including the Datel Trophy and Group 3 placed. Stud record: Prolific sire of winners in his first crop of two-year-olds in 2010. Winners include the listed winners Bathwick (Ripon Champion Two Year old Trophy), Kohala (St Hugh's Stakes) and Sweet Cecily and the Group 3 placed Stone Of Folca and Eastern Sun. Standing at Tally Ho Stud, County Westmeath, Ireland. 2012 fee: €7,500.

KYLLACHY
1998 Pivotal – Pretty Poppy (Song). Racing record: Winner of 6 races including the Nunthorpe Stakes at 4 yrs. Stud record: Sire of the Group 1 Nunthorpe Stakes and Group 2 Temple Stakes winner Sole Power, the Group 2 winners Arabian Gleam, Dragon Pulse and Tariq, Hong Kong Group 1 winner Dim Sum and numerous smart performers including Awinnersgame, Befortyfour, Corrybrough, Krypton Factor, Mabait, Mood Music and Penitent. Standing at Cheveley Park Stud, Newmarket. 2012 fee: £10,000.

LAWMAN
(2004) Invincible Spirit – Laramie (Gulch). Racing record: Won 4 races including the Prix du Jockey Club and the Prix Jean Prat. Stud record: His first runners appeared in 2011 and he had an excellent start with winners like Loi (Group 3 Prix de Conde), the Group 1 Dewhurst

Stakes third Most Improved and the Group 3 Acomb Stakes third Fort Bastion. Standing at Ballylinch Stud, Ireland. 2012 fee: €15,000.

LEMON DROP KID

1996 Kingmambo – Charming Lassie (Seattle Slew). Racing record: Won the Belmont Stakes, Whitney Handicap and Woodward Stakes. Stud record: Sire of the US Grade 1 winners Richard's Kid, Christmas Kid, Cittronade, Lemon's Forever and Santa Teresita, and the Group/Grade 2 winners Bronze Cannon, Bear's Kid, Charitable Man, Dreamy Kid, Juniper Pass and Pisco Sour. Standing at Lane's End Farm, Kentucky. 2012 fee: $35,000.

LUCKY STORY

2001 Kris S – Spring Flight (Miswaki). Racing record: Won 4 races including the Group 2 Champagne Stakes and Group 2 Vintage Stakes. Stud record: First crop (bred in Japan) were two-year-olds in 2007. In Europe his winners include the high-class Group 1 Golden Jubilee and Group 2 Coventry Stakes winner Art Connoisseur, the listed Redcar Two-Year-Old Trophy winner Lucky Like and the Group-placed Lucky Rave. Standing at Tweenhills Stud. Died 2010.

MAJESTIC MISSILE

2003 Royal Applause – Tshusick (Dancing Brave). Racing record: Won 6 including the Molecomb Stakes, Cornwallis Stakes and Prix du Petit Couvert (all 5f events). Stud record: First runners appeared in 2010 and include the listed winners Katla, Majestic Myles & New Planet. Standing at Ballyhane Stud, County Carlow, Ireland. 2012 fee: €3,000.

MANDURO

2002 Monsun – Mandellicht (Be My Guest). Racing record: Won 10 races including the Prix Jacques Le Marois, Prince of Wales's Stakes and Prix d'Ispahan. Stud record: First runners appeared in 2011 and he made a good start with Mandaean (Group 1 Criterium de Saint Cloud) and the Group 1 Criterium International third Bonfire. Standing at Kildangan Stud, Ireland. 2012 fee: €10,000.

MARJU

1988 Last Tycoon – Flame of Tara (Artaius). Racing record: 3 wins including St James's Palace Stakes and runner-up in the Derby. Stud record: Sire of the high-class Soviet Song (5 Group 1 wins including the Sussex Stakes), the multiple Hong Kong Group 1 winner Viva Pataca and numerous smart performers including Asset, Brunel, Green Destiny, Marju Snip (Group 1 Australasian Oaks), Naheef, My Emma (Prix Vermeille), Saturn, Sil Sila (Prix de Diane) and Watar. Retired 2011.

MEDAGLIA D'ORO

1999 El Prado – Cappucino Bay (Bailjumper). Racing record: Won the Travers Stakes, Jim Dandy Stakes and San Felipe Stakes. Stud record: Best winners include champion Rachel Alexandra and the Group/Grade 1 winners C. S. Silk, Champagne d'Oro, Gabby's Golden Gal, Passion For Gold, Plum Pretty and Warrior's Reward. Standing at Darley, Kentucky. 2012 fee: $100,000.

MEDICEAN

1997 Machiavellian – Mystic Goddess (Storm Bird). Racing record: 6 wins including the Group 1 Eclipse Stakes and the Lockinge Stakes. Stud record: Sire of Dutch Art (Prix Morny, Middle Park), Nannina (Fillies' Mile, Coronation Stakes), Capponi (Dubai Group 1 winner), Almerita (Group 1 German Oaks), Chevron (Group 1 Raffles International Cup), Bankable (Dubai Group 2 1m winner) and the very smart Abigail Pett, Al Shemali, Cartimandua, Love Academy, Manieree, Mr Medici and Medici Code. Standing at Cheveley Park Stud. 2012 fee: £8,000.

MIZZEN MAST

1998 Cozzene – Kinema (Graustark). Racing record: Won the Grade 1 Malibu Stakes and the Grade 2 Strub Stakes. Stud record: Best winners include Midships (Charles Whittingham Stakes), Mast Track (Hollywood Gold Cup), Jibboom (Buena Vista Handicap), Madeo (Del Mar Derby). Ultimate Eagle (Grade 1 Hollywood Derby and two Grade 2's). Standing at Juddmonte Farms, Kentucky. 2012 fee: $12,500.

MONSUN

1990 Konigsstuhl – Mosella (Surumu). Racing record: 8 wins including 3 Group 1 events over 12f in Germany. Stud record: Sire of the top-class multiple middle-distance Group 1 winners Getaway, Manduro, Samum, Shirocco, Stacelita and Schiaparelli. Standing at Gestut Schlenderhan, Germany. 2012 fee: Private.

MONTJEU
1996 Sadler's Wells – Floripedes (Top Ville). Racing record: Won 11 races, including Prix de l'Arc de Triomphe and King George VI and Queen Elizabeth Diamond Stakes. Stud record: First runners in 2004. A top-class stallion son of Sadler's Wells. Sire of the top-class Hurricane Run (Irish Derby, Prix de l'Arc de Triomphe, Tattersalls Gold Cup and King George), Authorized (Racing Post Trophy, Derby & Juddmonte International), Motivator (Racing Post Trophy and Derby), Pour Moi (Derby), Fame And Glory (Racing Post Trophy, Irish Derby, Ascot Gold Cup), St Nicholas Abbey (Breeders Cup Turf and Coronation Cup), 2011 2-y-o Group 1 Racing Post Trophy winner Camelot, the high-class Alessandro Volta, Frozen Fire, Honolulu, Corre Caminos, Jukebox Jury, Macarthur, Montmartre, Papal Bull, Scorpion and Recital, Masked Marvel, Juke Box Jury, Sarah Lynx and Miss Keller, E P Taylor Stakes. Standing at Coolmore Stud, Ireland. 2012 fee: Private.

MORE THAN READY
1997 Southern Halo – Woodman's Girl (Woodman). Racing record: Won the Grade 1 7f King's Bishop Stakes, the Hutcheson Stakes and the Sanford Stakes. Stud record: Sire of the Australian Group 1 winners Benicio, Sebring, Phelan Ready, Perfectly Ready, More Joyous, Carry On Cutie, Custom For Carlos and Samaready, Canadian Grade 1 winner Regally Ready and US Grade 1 winner Buster's Ready. Standing at Vinery Stud, Kentucky. 2012 fee: $60,000.

MOSS VALE
2001 Shinko Forest – Wolf Cleugh (Last Tycoon). Racing record: Won 8 races including the Group 2 5f Prix Gros Chene, the Group 3 6f Phoenix Sprint Stakes and the Group 3 6f Greenland Stakes. Stud record: His first runners came in 2011 and he had plenty of winners but not much in terms of quality. Standing at Rathbarry Stud, Ireland. 2012 fee: €4,000.

MOTIVATOR
2002 Montjeu – Out West (Gone West). Racing record: Won the Derby, the Racing Post Trophy and the Dante Stakes. Stud record: His first runners came in 2009 and to date his best winners have been Pollenator (Group 2 May Hill Stakes), Skia (Group 3 Prix de Fille de L'Air) and five listed winners including the Group 2 placed Motrice and the Group 3 placed Clinical. Standing at The Royal Studs. 2012 fee: £5,000.

MOUNT NELSON
2004 Rock of Gibraltar – Independence (Selkirk). Racing record: Won the Group 1 1m Criterium International at 2 yrs and the Group 1 10f Eclipse Stakes at 4. Stud record: His first two year olds appear in 2012. Standing at Newsells Park Stud, Herts. 2012 fee: £6,000.

MR GREELEY
1992 Gone West – Long Legend (Reviewer). Racing record: Triple Grade 3 winner in USA and runner-up in the Grade 1 Breeders' Cup Sprint. Stud record: Sire Crusade (2011 2-y-o Group 1 6f Middle Park Stakes), Finsceal Beo (English & Irish 1,000 Guineas), Saoirse Abu (Phoenix Stakes, Moyglare Stud Stakes), Reel Buddy (Sussex Stakes), US Grade 1 winners Aruna, El Corredor, Celtic Melody, Nonsuch Bay, Western Aristocrat and Whywhywhy, the Australian Group 1 winner Miss Kournikova and numerous other Group/Graded stakes winners. Died 2010 (his fee had been $50,000).

MUJADIL
1988 Storm Bird – Vallee Secrete (Secretariat). Racing record: 3 wins (at 2 yrs) including Group 3 Cornwallis Stakes. Stud record: Best winners include Kingsgate Native (Group 1 Nunthorpe Stakes & Group 1 Golden Jubilee Stakes), Bouncing Bowdler (Group 2 Mill Reef Stakes), Galeota (Group 2 Mill Reef Stakes), the Group 3 winners Dancal (in Australia), Daunting Lady, Leggy Lou, Lesson In Humility, Master Plasta, Satri and Show Me The Money and a host of listed winners. Standing at Rathasker Stud, Ireland. 2012 fee: €7,500.

NAMID
1996 Indian Ridge – Dawnsio (Tate Gallery). Racing record: Won 5 races, including the Group 1 5f Prix de l'Abbaye. Stud record:

First runners in 2004. Sire of Total Gallery (Group 1 Prix de l'Abbaye), Pout (Group 2 Ridgewood Pearl Stakes), Redstone Dancer (Group 3 Brownstown Stakes), Blue Dakota (Group 3 Norfolk Stakes), Belle Artiste (Group 2 Leopardstown 1,000 Guineas Trial), the smart Group 1 placed Hamish McGonagall and the smart performers Hogmaneigh and Resplendent Glory and several useful performers including Buachaill Dona, Burning Incense, Damika, Pike Bishop and That's Hot. Standing at Haras Des Faunes, France. 2012 fee: €3,000.

NAYEF

1999 Gulch – Height of Fashion (Bustino). Racing record: Won 9 races including the Champion Stakes and Juddmonte International Stakes. Stud record: His first crop were two-year-olds in 2007. His best winners to date are Tamayuz (dual Group 1 winner in France), Lady Marian (Prix de l'Opera), Spacious (dual Group 2 winner and 1,000 Guineas second), the 2-y-o Group 3 7f Oh So Sharp Stakes winner Tabassum, the very smart Confront (Group 3 1m Joel Stakes), five listed winners and the smart Group 1 German Derby third Top Lock. Standing at Nunnery Stud, Norfolk. 2012 fee: £12,500.

NEW APPROACH

2005 Galileo – Park Express (Ahonoora). Racing record: Won five Group 1's – the National Stakes, Dewhurst Stakes (both at 2 yrs), Derby, Champion Stakes and Irish Champion Stakes. Stud record: First two-year-olds appear in 2012. Standing at Dalham Hall Stud, Newmarket. 2012 fee: £22,500.

NOTNOWCATO

2002 Inchinor – Rambling Rose (Cadeaux Genereux). Racing record: Won the Eclipse Stakes, Juddmonte International and the Tattersalls Gold Cup (all Group 1). Stud record: His first runners appeared in 2011 and he made a decent start with a fair number of winners. Standing at Stanley House Stud, Newmarket. 2012 fee: £5,000.

OASIS DREAM

2001 Green Desert – Hop (Dancing Brave). Racing record: Won 4 races including the

Middle Park Stakes, July Cup and Nunthorpe Stakes (all Group 1 events). Stud record: His first crop were two-year-olds in 2007 and he's built himself an outstanding reputation with the Group 1 winners Aqlaam (Prix du Moulin), Arcano (Prix Morny), Midday (six Group 1 wins), Power (National Stakes), Tuscan Evening (Gamely Stakes), Prohibit (Kings Stand Stakes), Naaqoos (Prix Jean-Luc Lagardere), Lady Jane Digby (in Germany) and Querari (in Italy), along with a large number of Group/Graded stakes winners including Approve, Captain Gerrard, Frozen Power, Main Aim, Misheer, Monitor Closely, Showcasing (Gimcrack Stakes), Sri Putra, Starlit Sands, Visit, Young Pretender and Waiters Dream. Standing at Banstead Manor Stud, Newmarket. 2012 fee: £85,000.

OBSERVATORY

1997 Distant View – Stellaria (Roberto). Racing record: His 6 wins included the Group 1 Queen Elizabeth II Stakes and the Group 1 Prix d'Ispahan. Stud record: First runners in 2005. Sire of the Group 1 Sprint Cup winner African Rose, Twice Over (Champion Stakes (twice), Coral Eclipse Stakes and Juddmonte International Stakes), Violette (2-y-o Group 3 Firth Of Clyde Stakes) and Helleborine (Group 3 Prix d'Aumale) and five listed winners including the Group 3 placed Nidhaal and Sottone. Standing at Banstead Manor Stud, Newmarket. 2012 fee: £5,000.

ORATORIO

2002 Danehill – Mahrah (Vaguely Noble). Racing record: Won the Prix Jean-Luc Lagardere (at 2 yrs), the Eclipse Stakes and Irish Champion Stakes. Stud record: His first crop were two-year-olds in 2009 and they included the first two home in the Group 1 Dewhurst Stakes, Beethoven and Fencing Master. He's also sired the New Zealand Group 1 winners Banchee and Manawanui, Torio's Quest (Group 2 in Australia), Lolly For Dolly (Group 1 Windsor Forest Stakes), King Torus (dual Group 2 2-y-o winner) and Esentepe (Group 3 Nell Gwyn Stakes). Standing at Coolmore Stud, Ireland. 2012 fee: €9,000.

PASTORAL PURSUITS

2001 Bahamian Bounty – Star (Most Welcome). Racing record: Won 6 races including the July

Cup (Group 1 6f), Sirenia Stakes and Park Stakes. Stud record: His first crop appeared in 2009 and his winners to date include the listed winners and Group placed Angel's Pursuit and Rose Blossom, the Royal Ascot listed winner Marine Commando and the very useful Auld Burns and Pastoral Player. Standing at the National Stud. 2012 fee: £6,500.

PEINTRE CELEBRE

1994 Nureyev – Peinture Bleue (Alydar). Racing record: Won 5 races including the Prix du Jockey Club, Grand Prix de Paris and Prix de L'Arc de Triomphe. Stud record: Best winners include Pride (Prix Jean Romanet, Prix Foy, Grand Prix de Saint Cloud, Champion Stakes, Hong Kong Gold Cup), Australian Group 1 winners Bentley's Biscuit, Mr Celebrity and Mr Sandgroper, dual US Grade 1 winner Castledale, dual German Group 1 winner Dai Jin, Italian Group 1 winners Pearl Of Love and Sudan, Vallee Enchantee (Hong Kong Vase), Belle et Celebre (Prix Saint Alary) and Byword (Prince of Wales's Stakes). Standing at Coolmore Stud, Ireland. 2012 fee: €12,500.

PICCOLO

1991 Warning – Woodwind (Whistling Wind). Racing record: 4 wins including Nunthorpe Stakes and Kings Stand Stakes. Stud record: Sire of the Group 1 Nunthorpe Stakes winner La Cucaracha, the Australian Group 1 winner Picaday, the Group 2 winners Ajigolo, Express Air, St Trinians, Winker Watson, Flying Blue (in Hong Kong) and Temple Of Boom (in Australia), plus numerous other smart performers including Aegean Dancer, Bond Boy (Steward's Cup winner), Hoh Hoh Hoh, Hunting Lion, Lipocco, Pan Jammer and Pickle. Standing at Throckmorton Court Stud. 2012 fee: £3,000.

PIVOTAL

1993 Polar Falcon – Fearless Revival (Cozzene). Racing record: 4 wins including the Nunthorpe Stakes and King's Stand Stakes. Stud record: First runners in 2000. An outstanding sire whose best winners include the high-class Excellent Art (St James's Palace Stakes), Falco (French 2,000 Guineas), Halfway To Heaven (Irish 1,00 Guineas, Nassau Stakes and Sun Chariot Stakes, Kyllachy (Nunthorpe Stakes), Sariska (Oaks and Irish Oaks), Immortal Verse

(dual Group 1 winning miler) and Somnus (Sprint Cup, Prix de la Foret, Prix Maurice de Gheest), the very smart Beauty Is Truth (Group 2 Prix du Gros-Chene), Captain Rio (Group 2 Criterium des Maisons-Laffitte), Chorist (Pretty Polly Stakes), Golden Apples (triple US Grade 1 winner), Leo (Group 2 Royal Lodge Stakes), Peeress (Lockinge Stakes, Sun Chariot Stakes), Pivotal Point (Group 2 Diadem Stakes) and Virtual (Lockinge Stakes) and a host of smart performers including Falco (French 2,000 Guineas), Megahertz (2 US Grade 1 events), Regal Parade (Haydock Sprint Cup), Silvester Lady (German Oaks), Siyouni (2-y-o Group 1 Prix Jean-Luc Lagardere) and Saoire (Irish 1000 Guineas). Standing at Cheveley Park Stud, Newmarket. 2012 fee: £45,000.

PROUD CITIZEN

1999 Gone West –Drums Of Freedom (Green Forest). Racing record: Won 3 races including the Grade 3 Lexington Stakes and second the Kentucky Derby. Stud record: His first crop were two-year-olds in 2007. Sire of the US dual Grade 1 winner Proud Spell, the Group 3 Somerville Tattersall Stakes winner River Proud, the US Grade 3 winners Believe You Can, It Happened Again and Motovato and a number of other US stakes winners. Standing at Airdrie Stud, Kentucky. 2012 fee: $7,500.

RAIL LINK

2003 Dansili – Docklands (Theatrical). Racing record: Won 5 races including the Prix de L'Arc de l'Arc de Triomphe, Prix Niel, Grand Prix de Paris and Prix du Lys. Stud record: His first runners in 2011 included a number of winners including Bugie d'Amor (Group 3 Premio Dormello). Standing at Banstead Manor Stud, Newmarket. 2012 fee: £6,000.

RAVEN'S PASS

1995 Elusive Quality – Ascutney (Lord At War). Racing record: 6 wins including the Grade 1 10f Breeders Cup Classic and the Group 1 1m Queen Elizabeth II Stakes. Stud record: First crop are two-year-olds in 2012. Standing at Kildangan Stud, Ireland. 2012 fee: €22,500.

REDBACK

1999 Mark of Esteem – Patsy Western (Precocious). Racing record: Won the Solario

Stakes and the Greenham Stakes (both Group 3 events). Stud record: Winners include the very smart Grade 1 10f E P Taylor Stakes and Group 2 Rockfel Stakes winner Lahaleeb, the Group 2 Queen Mary Stakes winner Gilded and the listed winners Letsgoroundagain, Sonny Red & Redolent (also Group 1 placed). Standing at Haras Du Hoguenet, France. 2012 fee: €3,500.

RED CLUBS

2003 Red Ransom – Two Clubs (First Trump). Racing record: Won 6 races including the Group 1 Sprint Cup, Group 2 Diadem Stakes and Group 3 Greenham Stakes. His first runners appeared in 2011 and he had an excellent start with over 30 individual winners including Group 3 winners Roger Sez and Vedelago (in Italy). Died.

REFUSE TO BEND

2000 Sadler's Wells – Market Slide (Gulch). Racing record: Won 7 races including the National Stakes, 2,000 Guineas, Eclipse Stakes & Queen Anne Stakes (all Group 1). Stud record: His first crop were two-year-olds in 2008 and his best to date include Sarafina (Prix de Diane, Grand Prix de Saint Cloud & Prix Saint Alary – all Group 1), Wavering (Prix Saint-Alary), the Group 3 winners Grace O'Malley, Neon Light and Benny's Buttons (in Australia) and 10 listed winners including the Group 3 placed Croisultan and Fantastico Roberto. Died 2012.

ROYAL APPLAUSE

1993 Waajib – Flying Melody (Auction Ring). Racing record: Winner of 9 races including the Group 1 6f Middle Park at 2 yrs and the Group 1 6f Haydock Park Sprint Cup at 4. Stud record: First runners in 2001. Sire of the US dual Grade 1 winner Ticker Tape, Group/Grade 2 winners Acclamation, Battle Of Hastings, Finjaan, Lovelace, Mister Cosmi, Nevisian Lad, Please Sing and Whatsthescript and numerous very smart performers including Crime Scene, Majestic Missile, Peak To Creek and Prince Siegfried. Standing at The Royal Studs, Norfolk. 2012 fee: £9,000.

SAKHEE

1997 Bahri – Thawakib (Sadler's Wells). Racing record: Won 8 races, including Juddmonte International and Prix de l'Arc de Triomphe, and

runner-up in Derby. Stud record: First runners in 2006. Sire of the Group 1 July Cup winner Sakhee's Secret, Group 1 Hong Kong Queen Elizabeth II Cup and Group 1 Dubai Duty Free winner Presvis, Group 1 French 2,000 Guineas winner Tin Horse, Group 2 Doncaster Cup winner Samuel, Group 3 winner Royal Rock and the Group-placed Salure, Darsha, Sakhee's Song and Sakheart. Standing at Nunnery Stud, Norfolk. 2012 fee: £7,000.

SAKHEE'S SECRET

2004 Sakhee – Palace Street (Secreto). Racing record: Won 5 races including the Group 1 6f July Cup and two listed events. Stud record: His first two year olds appear in 2012. Standing at Whitsbury Manor Stud. 2012 fee: £5,500.

SHAMARDAL

2002 Giant's Causeway – Helsinki (Machiavellian). Racing record: Won Dewhurst Stakes, French 2,000 Guineas, French Derby and St James's Palace Stakes. Stud record: His first European runners appeared in 2009 his best performers to date have been Arctic (Group 3 Round Tower Stakes), Casamento (Racing Post Trophy), Lope de Vega (French 2,000 Guineas and French Derby), Shakespearian (Group 2 Hungerford Stakes), Zazou (Group 1 Premio Roma), Italian Group 2 winner Crackerjack King, the listed UAE 1,000 Guineas winner Siyaadah, Australian Group 1 winners Captain Sonador and Faint Perfume, and eight Group 3 winners including Shamoline Warrior, Dubai Prince and French Navy. Standing at Kildangan Stud, Ireland. 2012 fee: €50,000.

SHIROCCO

2001 Monsun – So Sedulous (The Minstrel). Racing Record: Won 7 races including the German Derby, French Derby, Breeders Cup Turf and Coronation Cup (all Group 1, 12f events). Stud record: First runners 2010. Winners to date include the very smart Group 1 St Leger second Brown Panther, the Group 2 Prix Noailles winner Grand Vent, German Group 2 winner Arrigo and listed winners Wild Coco and Jardina. Standing at Dalham Hall Stud. 2012 fee: £7,000.

SINGSPIEL

1992 In The Wings – Glorious Song (Halo). Racing record: Winner of 9 races notably the Canadian International, Japan Cup (both at 4 yrs), Dubai World Cup, Coronation Cup and Juddmonte International (at 5 yrs). Stud record: Sire of the Group 1 10f Dubai World Cup winner Moon Ballad, US dual Grade 1 winner Lahudood, high-class Lohengrin (in Japan), very smart Asakusa Den'en (Japanese Group 1 winner), Confidential Lady (Prix de Diane), Da Re Mi (Dubai Sheema Classic, Yorkshire Oaks and Pretty Polly Stakes), Eastern Anthem (Dubai Sheema Classic), Hibaayeb (Yellow Ribbon Stakes), Folk Opera (E P Taylor Stakes), Lateral (Gran Criterium), Papineau (Gold Cup), Silkwood (Ribblesdale Stakes), Singhalese (Del Mar Oaks) and numerous other smart performers. Died 2010.

SIR PERCY

2003 Mark of Esteem – Percy's Lass (Blakeney). Racing record: Won 5 races including the Derby and the Dewhurst Stakes. Stud record: He made a good start with his first runners in 2011, including the listed winner Coquet, the Group 1 Fillies' Mile fourth Salford Art and the listed-placed Alla Speranza and Percy Jackson. Standing at Lanwades Stud, Newmarket. 2012 fee: £6,000.

SIXTIES ICON

2003 Galileo – Love Divine (Diesis). Racing record: Won 8 races from 10f to 14f including the Group 1 St Leger, Group 2 Jockey Club Cup and four Group 3 events. Stud record: His first two year olds appear in 2012. Standing at Norman Court Stud, Wilts. 2012 fee: £4,500.

SLEEPING INDIAN

2001 Indian Ridge – Las Flores (Sadler's Wells). Racing Record: Won 6 races including the Group 2, 7f Challenge Stakes, Group 3 7f Hungerford Stakes and three listed events. Stud record: First runners came in 2010 and his best to date is the Group winning sprinter Night Carnation, followed by four listed-placed horses including the useful Morach Music, as well as the winners of over 60 races. Standing at Tweenhills Stud. 2012 fee: £3,000.

SMART STRIKE

1992 Mr Prospector – Classy 'n Smart (Smarten). Racing record: Won 8 races in the USA including the Grade 1 8.5f Philip H Iselin Handicap and the Grade 3 Salvator Mile. Stud record: Best winners include the top-class colt Curlin (Preakness Stakes, Dubai World Cup, Breeders Cup Classic), the US Grade 1 winners English Channel, Fabulous Strike, Furthest Land, Lookin At Lucky, My Miss Aurelia, Never Retreat, Shadow Cast, Soaring Free and Square Eddie, twelve Grade 2 winners and the Japan Cup (dirt) winner Fleetstreet Dancer. Standing at Lane's End Farm. 2012 fee: €85,000.

SOVIET STAR

1984 Nureyev – Veruschka (Venture). Racing record: Winner of the July Cup, Prix Moulin and Trusthouse Forte Mile. Stud record: Best winners include Starcraft (Queen Elizabeth II Stakes, Prix du Moulin), Ashkalani (French 2,000 Guineas, Prix du Moulin), Starborough (Prix Jean Prat, St James's Palace Stakes), Eva's Request (Premio Lydia Tesio), Limpid (Grand Prix de Paris), Pressing (Group 1 winner in Italy and Germany), Soviet Line (Lockinge Stakes, twice), Russian Pearl (Group 1 winner in New Zealand) and six Group 2 winners including Freedom Cry (dual Group 2 & dual Group 3). Standing at Ballylinch Stud Ireland. 2012 fee: Private.

SPEIGHTSTOWN

1998 Gone West – Silken Cat (Storm Cat). Racing record: Won the Breeders Cup Sprint, Churchill Downs Handicap, True North Breeders Cup Handicap & Alfred Vanderbilt Handicap. Stud record: 25 stakes winners in his first four crops. His best performers include Lord Shanakill (Group 1 Prix Jean Prat), Haynesfield (Grade 1 Jockey Club Gold Cup), Jersey Town (Grade 1 Cigar Mile), Mona De Momma (Grade 1 Humana Distaff Stakes), Munnings (three Grade 2 wins, Bapak Chinta (Group 2 Norfolk Stakes) and four Grade 3 winners in North America including the Grade 1 third Gemswick Park. Standing at Winstar Farm, Kentucky. 2012 fee: $50,000.

STORMY ATLANTIC

1994 Storm Cat – Hail Atlantis (Seattle Slew). Racing record: Won two minor stakes events in the USA at 4 yrs over 5.5f and 6f. Stud record: Has sired 8 crops and his winners include Stormello (Grade 1 Hollywood Futurity Stakes, Grade 2 Norfolk Breeders Cup Stakes), Get Stormy (Grade 1 Woodford Reserve Turf Classic, Grade 1 Makers Mark Mile), Canadian Champion 2-y-o and Grade 3 winner Leonnatus Anteas and six Grade 2 winners including My Princess Jess (Grade 2 Lake George Stakes). Standing at Hill N'Dale Farms, Kentucky. 2012 fee: $40,000.

STRATEGIC PRINCE
2004 Dansili – Ausherra (Diesis). Racing record: Won 3 races at 2 yrs including the July Stakes and the Vintage Stakes. Stud record: His first runners appeared in 2011 and he had a very good start with such as La Collina (Group 1 Phoenix Stakes), the US listed stakes winner Tones and the Group 2 Mill Reef Stakes second Redact. Standing at Coolmore Stud in Ireland. 2012 fee: €6,000.

STREET BOSS
2004 Street Cry – Blushing Ogygian (Ogygian). Racing record: Won 7 races including the Grade 1 6f Bing Crosby Handicap and the Grade 1 7f Triple Bend Handicap. Stud record: His first two year olds appear in 2012. Standing at Jonabell Farm, Kentucky. 2012 stud fee: $15,000.

STREET CRY
1998 Machiavellian – Helen Street (Troy). Racing record: 5 wins including the Group 1 10f Dubai World Cup. Stud record: First runners in 2006. Sire of the outstanding multiple Grade 1 winning racemare Zenyatta and the Group/Grade 1 winners Street Sense (Breeders' Cup Juvenile, Kentucky Derby, Travers Stakes), Cry And Catch Me (Oak Leaf Stakes), Majestic Roi (Sun Chariot Stakes), Street Boss (Triple Bend Invitational, Bing Crosby H'cap), Seventh Street (Go For Wand Handicap, Apple Blossom Handicap), Street Hero (Norfolk Stakes), Here Comes Ben (Forego Handicap), Victor's Cry (Shoemaker Mile Handicap), Street Hero (Norfolk Stakes), Zaidan (Hong Kong Classic Cup), Majestic Roi (Sun Chariot Stakes), the Australian Group 1 winners Shocking (Melbourne Cup) and Whobegotyou (Caulfield Guineas and Yalumba Stakes), the Group 2 Dante Stakes winner Carlton House and Group 2 Champagne Stakes winner Saamidd. Standing at Jonabell Stud Farm, Kentucky. 2012 fee: $150,000.

STREET SENSE
2004 Street Cry – Bedazzle (Dixieland Band). Racing record: Won three Grade 1 races in the USA, the Breeders Cup Juvenile, Kentucky Derby and Travers Stakes. Stud record: First runners in 2011 and his winners include the US Grade 3 1m winners Castaway and Motor City, and the 2-y-o Grade 1 third Miss Netta. Standing at Jonabell Farm, Kentucky. 2012 fee: $40,000.

TAGULA
1993 Taufan – Twin Island (Standaan). Racing record: Won 4 races including the Group 1 6f Prix Morny (at 2 yrs) and the Group 3 7f Supreme Stakes. Stud record: Sires plenty of winners, amongst the best being the top-class miler and multiple Group 1 winner Canford Cliffs, the Group 2 Prix du Gros-Chene and triple Group 3 winner Tax Free, the Group 2 Royal Lodge Stakes winner Atlantis Prince, the German Group 2 winner Tagshira, the smart Group 2 placed Beaver Patrol and the listed winners Bakewell Tart, Double Vie, Drawnfromthepast, King Orchisios, Macaroon, Pure Poetry and Red Millennium. Standing at Rathbarry Stud in Ireland. 2012 fee: €4,000.

TAMAYUZ
2005 Nayef – Al Ishq (Nureyev). Racing Record: Won the Group 1 1m Prix Jacques Le Marois and the Group 1 7f Prix Jean Prat. Stud record: His first two year olds appear in 2012. Standing at Derrinstown Stud in Ireland. 2012 fee: €15,000.

TEOFILO
2004 Galileo – Speirbhhean (Danehill). Racing Record: Won 5 races at 2 yrs including the Group 1 Dewhurst Stakes and the Group 1 National St. Stud record: His first runners appeared in 2011 and among the 17 winners were the Group 1 Dewhurst Stakes winner Parish Hall, the Group 3 Tyros Stakes winner Remember Alexander and the listed winners Black Arrow and Teolane. Standing at Kildangan Stud in Ireland. 2011 fee: €25,000.

THOUSAND WORDS
2004 Dansili – Verbose (Storm Bird). Racing Record: Won the Group 3 7f Somerville Tattersall Stakes. Stud record: His first two year olds appear in 2012. Standing at Rathasker

Stud, Ireland. 2012 fee: €4,000.

THREE VALLEYS

2001 Diesis – Skiable (Niniski). Racing Record: Won 5 races here and in the USA including the Group 3 6f Coventry Stakes (at 2 yrs), the Grade 2 1m Del Mar Breeders Cup Handicap and the Grade 3 8.5f Oceanport Stakes. Stud record: His first runners appeared in 2011 and he's made a fair start with the winners of 17 races. Standing at Banstead Manor Stud, Newmarket. 2012 fee: £5,000.

VITA ROSA

2000 Sunday Silence – Rosa Nay (Lyphard). Racing record: Won 6 races from 9f to 13f in Japan including a Group 2 and two Group 3's. Stud record: His first 2-y-o's appear in 2012. Standing in Italy, a son of multiple Japanese champion sire Sunday Silence. 2012 fee: €3,500.

VERGLAS

1994 Highest Honor – Rahaam (Secreto). Racing record: Won 3 races including the Group 3 6f Coventry Stakes. Stud record: Sire of the Group 1 French 2,000 Guineas winner Silver Frost, the Group 1 Prix Jean Prat winner Stormy River, Australian Group 1 10f winner Glass Harmonium, the US dual Grade 2 winner Blackdoun, smart UAE winners Captain Obvious and Leahurst, the Group 3 winners Love Lockdown, Ozone Bere, Spirited One, Tropical Paradise and Wilside, plus numerous listed winners. Died 2011.

WHIPPER

2001 Miesque's Son – Myth To Reality (Sadler's Wells). Racing record: Won the Prix Morny, the Prix Jacques le Marois and the Prix Maurice de Gheest (all Group 1 events). Stud record: His first runners came in 2009 and he's had a decent start to his stud career. His best performers so far have been the Wizz Kid, (Group 2 Prix Gros Chene), Royal Bench (Prix Group 2 Daniel Wildenstein winner and second in Group 1 Cathay Pacific Hong Kong Mile), Group 3 winners Dolled Up and Topeka, four listed winners including the Group 3 placed Whip And Win and the Group 2 Rockfel Stakes second Atasari. Standing at Haras du Mezeray. 2012 fee: €7,500.

WITH APPROVAL

1986 Caro – Passing Mood (Buckpasser). Racing record: Raced in Canada where he won the Triple Crown (Queen's Plate, Breeders Stakes and Prince Of Wales's Stakes). Stud record: His best winners include the US Grade 1 Manhattan Handicap winner Mission Approved, the Group/Grade 2 winners Allende, Dust Me Off, Just Approval, Silverfoot, T H Approval, Talkin Man and Lasting Approval, the US Grade 3 winners OK By Me, Ray's Approval, Tasteyville, Thesaurus, Van Minister and Zanetti and the smart English winners Lonesome Dude and Frosty Welcome. Died 2010.

ZAFEEN

2000 Zafonic – Shy Lady (Kaldoun). Racing record: Won the Group 1 St James's Palace Stakes and the Group 2 Mill Reef Stakes and second in the 2,000 Guineas. Stud record: His first runners appeared in 2009 and although he's had plenty of winners only one of them has been stakes-placed – Zafeen Speed. Standing at Haras Du Petit Tellier. 2012 fee: €4,000.

ZAMINDAR

1994 Gone West – Zaizafon (The Minstrel). Racing record: A full-brother to the champion Zafonic, he was a decent horse himself and won the Group 3 Prix de Cabourg at 2 yrs and was placed in the Prix Morny and the Prix de la Salamandre. Stud record: Has sired a number of very good fillies, notably the outstanding Zarkava (five Group 1 wins including the Prix de l'Arc de Triomphe), Darjina (three Group 1 wins), the Group 1 Prix Saint-Alary winner Coquerelle, the Group 1 French 1,000 Guineas winner Zenda and the Falmouth Stakes winner Timepiece. He also has the Group 2 winners Crossharbour and Modern Look, the Group 3 winner and Group 1 third Zantenda and 10 listed winners. Standing at Banstead Manor Stud, Newmarket. 2012 fee: £10,000.

Sires index

Racing Trends

The following tables focus on those two-year-old races whose winners often train on to win nice races as three-year-olds. In the tables, the figure in the third column indicates the number of wins recorded as a three-year-old, with GW signifying a Group race winner at that age.

The horses listed below are the winners of the featured races in 2011. Anyone looking for horses to follow in the Group and Classic events of this season might well want to bear some of them in mind. Those in bold text are particularly worthy of close scrutiny, I feel.

Best Terms	**Camelot**
Cavaleiro	Chandlery
Crius	**David Livingston**
Dubai Prince	Entifaadha
Fencing	Lightening Pearl
Lyric Of Light	**Mojave**
Nawwaar	**Nephrite**
Parish Hall	**Power**
Red Duke	**Rougemont**
Wading	Wise Venture

Lowther Stakes York, 6 furlongs, August.		
2000	Enthused	0
2001	Queen's Logic	1 GW
2002	Russian Rhythm	3 GW
2003	Carry On Katie	0
2004	Soar	0
2005	Flashy Wings	0
2006	Silk Blossom	0
2007	Nahoodh	1 GW
2008	Infamous Angel	0
2009	Lady of the Desert	1 GW
2010	Hooray	1
2011	Best Terms	

One has to look back to Russian Rhythm for a filly that had a real impact on the following season's Group 1 events, but it remains of race of some importance and Hooray did manage a listed win over seven furlongs last year. Although Best Terms hails from a stamina laden female line tracing back to the to-class Time Charter, she seemingly takes after her sire Exceed And Excel. As such, despite her limitations in terms of size she may well be a force to reckon with over six or maybe seven furlongs this year.

Dewhurst Stakes Newmarket, 7 furlongs, October.		
2000	Tobougg	0
2001	Rock Of Gibraltar	5 GW
2002	Tout Seul	0
2003	Milk It Mick	0
2004	Shamardal	3 GW
2005	Sir Percy	1 GW
2006	Teofilo	NR
2007	New Approach	3 GW
2008	Intense Focus	0
2009	Beethoven	1 GW
2010	Frankel	5GW
2011	Parish Hall	

The Dewhurst Stakes remains our premier race for two-year-old colts. Frankel proved himself a real champion last year and Rock of Gibraltar was a real star in his year too. The other outstanding colts to win this in the last twenty years are Shamardal, Zafonic, Dr Devious, Grand Lodge, Sir Percy and New Approach. Last year's Dewhurst was hardly a vintage renewal and Parish Hall will surprise a few people if he proves to be up to their standard over a mile, but I feel he'll be better suited over ten furlongs plus.

Zetland Stakes Newmarket, 10 furlongs, October/November.		
2000	Worthily	0
2001	Alexandra Three D	2 GW
2002	Forest Magic	NR
2003	Fun And Games	NR
2004	Ayam Zaman	0
2005	Under The Rainbow	0
2006	Empire Day	NR
2007	Twice Over	2 GW
2008	Heliodor	1
2009	Take It To The Max	0
2010	Indigo Way	NR
2011	Mojave	

Previous winners include the St Leger and Coronation Cup winner Silver Patriarch, the good four-year-olds Double Eclipse and Rock Hopper, Bob's Return (also a St Leger hero), the Ascot Gold Cup winner Double Trigger and of course Twice Over who won four Group 1's during his career with Henry Cecil including as a 6-y-o in 2011. So there's clearly an emphasis on winners of the Zetland improving with age. The Dubawi colt, Mojave, is a very interesting prospect this year over middle-distances.

Cheveley Park Stakes Newmarket, 6 furlongs, October.		
2001	Queen's Logic	1 GW
2002	Airwave	1 GW
2003	Carry On Katie	0
2004	Magical Romance	0
2005	Donna Blini	1
2006	Indian Ink	1 GW
2007	Natagora	2 GW
2008	Serious Attitude	1 GW
2009	Special Duty	2GW
2010	Hooray	1
2011	Lightening Pearl	

A number of these fillies have gone on to further Group race success. Indian Ink saved her best day for Royal Ascot having previously been fifth in the 1,000 Guineas. Both Natagora and Special Duty raised the profile of this race even further when winning the 1,000 Guineas and Serious Attitude returned to sprinting for another Group race success. Lightening Pearl may not have won a vintage renewal of this race, but she's bred to get the mile of the 1,000 Guineas and I think she has valid place prospects.

Washington Singer Stakes Newbury, 7 furlongs, August.		
2000	Prizeman	0
2001	Funfair Wane	1
2002	Muqbil	1 GW
2003	Haafhd	3 GW
2004	Kings Quay	0
2005	Innocent Air	1
2006	Dubai's Touch	2
2007	Sharp Nephew	1
2008	Cry of Freedom	0
2009	Azmeel	2 GW
2010	Janood	0
2011	Fencing	

This race can often provide us with Group race or Classic pointers and in that regard the 90's winners Lammtarra and Rodrigo de Triano, plus the more recent winner Haafhd were outstanding. Azmeel trained on to win the Sandown Classic Trial and the Dee Stakes. The very well-bred Fencing (his dam won the French Oaks and is a half-sister to the French Derby winner Lawman) ran third in the Racing Post Trophy after winning this and he can surely win more races.

Veuve Clicquot Vintage Stakes Goodwood, 7 furlongs, July.		
2000	No Excuse Needed	1 GW
2001	Naheef	1 GW
2002	Dublin	1
2003	Lucky Story	0
2004	Shamardal	3 GW
2005	Sir Percy	1 GW
2006	Strategic Prince	0
2007	Rio De La Plata	0
2008	Orizaba	0
2009	Xtension	0
2010	King Torus	2
2011	Chandlery	

All in all this race is very informative in terms of sorting out future stars, with the classic winners Sir Percy, Shamardal, Don't Forget Me, Dr Devious and Mister Baileys and the King George winner Petoski being the standouts of the past twenty years. Aljabr, Central Park, Ekraar and No Excuse Needed were all high-class colts and King Torus won a listed event last year. Chandlery didn't run again last season after winning this race in July, so it will be interesting to see how this useful colt shapes up this season. He'll win more races.

National Stakes, Curragh, 7f, September.		
2000	Beckett	1
2001	Hawk Wing	1 GW
2002	Refuse To Bend	3 GW
2003	One Cool Cat	1 GW
2004	Dubawi	2 GW
2005	George Washington	2 GW
2006	Teofilo	NR
2007	New Approach	3 GW
2008	Mastercraftsman	3 GW
2009	Kingsfort	1

2010	Pathfork	0
2011	Power	

As one can see by the list of recent winners, this race is as important as any for figuring out the following year's top performers. For instance New Approach was outstanding when winning the Derby, the Champion Stakes and the Irish Champion, and Mastercraftsman also managed a couple of Group One wins at 3 yrs. Power, a son of Oasis Dream out of a half-sister to the 2,000 Guineas winner Footstepsinthesand, can win again at the top level.

Racing Post Trophy
Doncaster, 8 furlongs, October.

2000	Dilshaan	1 GW
2001	High Chapparal	5 GW
2002	Brian Boru	1 GW
2003	American Post	3 GW
2004	Motivator	2 GW
2005	Palace Episode	0
2006	Authorized	3 GW
2007	Ibn Khaldun	0
2008	Crowded House	0
2009	St Nicholas Abbey	0
2010	Casamento	1 GW
2011	Camelot	

Some notable performers have won this race, including one of my own favourites the 1995 French Derby winner Celtic Swing, the outstanding colt High Chaparral and the Derby heroes Motivator and Authorized (both by Montjeu – also the sire of St Nicholas Abbey). So impressive was Camelot in this race that it will disappoint a lot of people, not least his trainer, if he doesn't win at least one more Group 1 event. I suspect that any more high quality victories will come at distances of ten and twelve furlongs – quite possibly the Derby.

Haynes, Hanson and Clark Stakes
Newbury, 8 furlongs, September.

2000	Nayef	4 GW
2001	Fight Your Corner	1 GW
2002	Saturn	0
2003	Elshadi	0
2004	Merchant	NR
2005	Winged Cupid	NR
2006	Teslin	2

2007	Centennial	2 GW
2008	Taameer	0
2009	Ameer	0
2010	Moriarty	0
2011	Cavaleiro	

The high-class horses Rainbow Quest, Unfuwain, King's Theatre and Nayef have all won this race and indeed Shergar won it in 1980, but it's been a while since those glory days although Centennial did manage two Group race wins in 2008. The sire of Cavaleiro, Sir Percy, did well with his first crop of runners and Cavaleiro progressed as his 2-y-o season went on. His dam was unplaced in all three of her starts and never ventured beyond a mile, but Cavaleiro should stay at least ten furlongs and he'll win more races.

Fillies' Mile
Ascot, 8 furlongs, September.

2000	Crystal Music	0
2001	Gossamer	1 GW
2002	Soviet Song	0
2003	Red Bloom	1 GW
2004	Playful Act	1 GW
2005	Nannina	1 GW
2006	Simply Perfect	1 GW
2007	Listen	0
2008	Rainbow View	1 GW
2009	Hibaayeb	2 GW
2010	White Moonstone	NR
2011	Lyric of Light	

A very strong race in terms of seeking out future Group winners. Gossamer and Soviet Song are the standouts here, although the latter had to wait until after her 4-y-o career before reaching her full potential. Hibaayib won the Ribblesdale Stakes and then crossed the Atlantic to win the Grade 1 Yellow Ribbon. The well-bred Street Cry filly Lyric Of Light should stay further than a mile as a 3-y-o, but she'll be contesting the top mile races in the Spring before stepping up in trip. It's not difficult to envisage seeing her win another Group 1 event.

Somerville Tattersall Stakes Newmarket, 7 furlongs, September/ October.		
2000	King Charlemagne	3 GW
2001	Where Or When	2 GW
2002	Governor Brown	NR
2003	Milk It Mick	0
2004	Diktatorial	0
2005	Aussie Rules	2 GW
2006	Thousand Words	0
2007	River Proud	1
2008	Ashram	2
2009	Sir Parky	0
2010	Rerouted	0
2011	Crius	

The Group winners speak for themselves but Milk It Mick also went on to win a Grade 1 in America as a five-year-old. Aussie Rules won the French 2,000 Guineas and a Grade 1 event in the America and both River Proud and Ashram won listed races in their 3-y-o season. Crius has already showed that he stays a mile and I suspect that ten furlongs will be within his compass this year. He can win again.

Killavullan Stakes. Leopardstown, 7 furlongs October.		
2000	Perigee Moon	0
2001	Stonemason	0
2002	New South Wales	1
2003	Grey Swallow	2 GW
2004	Footstepsinthesand	1 GW
2005	Frost Giant	1 GW
2006	Confuchias	1 GW
2007	Jupiter Pluvius	0
2008	Rayeni	1
2009	Free Judgement	1 GW
2010	Dubai Prince	1
2011	Nephrite	

The most notable performers here are the Irish Derby winner Grey Swallow and the English 2,000 Guineas winner Footstepsinthesand. Coming from the Ballydoyle yard, Nephrite (who is by the top-class sire Pivotal), may find himself in contention with one or two of his equally highly regarded stable companions in Group races up to a mile this term, but I reckon he'd add to his reputation and win another good prize or two.

Rockfel Stakes, 7 furlongs, Newmarket.		
2000	Sayedah	0
2001	Distant Valley	0
2002	Luvah Girl	1 in USA
2003	Cairns	0
2004	Maids Causeway	1 GW
2005	Speciosa	1 GW
2006	Finsceal Beo	2 GW
2007	Kitty Matcham	0
2008	Lahaleeb	2 GW
2009	Music Show	2 GW
2010	Cape Dollar	0
2011	Wading	

Three Newmarket 1,000 Guineas winners have hailed from the winners of this race since 1999 – Lahan, Speciosa and Finsceal Beo. For good measure Maids Causeway won the Coronation Stakes and Hula Angel won the Irish 1,000 Guineas (a race Finsceal Beo also added to her tally). The Mick Channon trained pair Lahaleeb and Music Show both went on to record Group 1 successes. Wading has the form to win Group One races over a mile this year and the pedigree to do the same over a mile and a half. She looks sure to do well as a 3-y-o.

Beresford Stakes, Curragh, 1m.		
2000	Turnberry Isle	0
2001	Castle Gandolfo	1
2002	Alamshar	3 GW
2003	Azamour	2 GW
2004	Albert Hall	0
2005	Septimus	1 GW
2006	Eagle Mountain	1 GW
2007	Curtain Call	1
2008	Sea The Stars	6 GW
2009	St Nicholas Abbey	0
2010	Casamento	1 GW
2011	David Livingston	

John Oxx must be very fond of this race because he's trained Sea The Stars, Alamshar and Azamour to win it and they've all subsequently hit the headlines as three-year-olds. Among the others, Eagle Mountain also went on to win as a 4-y-o in a Group 1 event (in Hong Kong) and Curtain Call won a Group 3 event at that age. Last year's winner is by Galileo and out of a half-sister to High Chaparral, so further Group race success over ten or twelve furlongs beckons David Livingston – I presume!

Acomb Stakes York, 7 furlongs, August.		
2000	Hemingway	NR
2001	Comfy	NR
2002	Bourbonnais	0
2003	Rule Of Law	2 GW
2004	Elliots World	1
2005	Palace Episode	0
2006	Big Timer	0
2007	Fast Company	0
2008	ABANDONED	
2009	Elusive Pimpernel	1 GW
2010	Waiter's Dream	NR
2011	Entifaadha	

There have been a few disappointing seasons since the victories in the 90's of King's Best (2,000 Guineas) and Bijou d'Inde (St James's Palace Stakes), but Rule Of Law turned things around in 2004 with his St Leger victory and Elusive Pimpernel was successful in the Group 3 Craven Stakes. Entifaadha, a son of Dansili, was subsequently third in the Group 2 Champagne Stakes and he should win another nice race this year.

Horse Index

Dams index

Danzig's Humor 1595
Danzolin 554
Darrfonah 1512
Dashiba 524
Dashing 1596
Date Mate 771
Dawla 1362
Day By Day 864
Dayville 25
Dazzling Dancer 1203
Dear Catch 354
Debonnaire 498
Delisha 373
Delphie Queen 902
Delphinus 1597
Demi Voix 154
Demisemiquaver 382
Desert Classic 1326
Desert Cristal 181
Desert Frolic 581
Desert Gold 466
Desert Sky 1010
Design Perfection 1144
Deveron 967
Dhelaal 1486
Diablerette 77
Diamond Dilemma 800
Diamond Necklace 943
Dibiya 728
Didina 343
Digger Girl 543
Dilag 1558
Dirtybirdie 395
Disco Lights 799
Divine Grace 1598
Dixielake 551
Dodo 533
Dolma 334
Don't Tell Mum 741
Dona Royale 45
Dorrati 1571
Dot C C 1277
Double Eight 743
Downland 670
Drastic Measure 17
Dream Again 679
Dream Day 296
Dreamalot 813
Dresden Doll 595
Dress Uniform 597
Drifting 158
Dubious 394
Dublino 576
Duck Over 357
Dunbrody 861
Dundel 678
Dunya 196

Dust 761
Dust Dancer 1513

Eastern Lily 1626
Easy Option 968
Easy To Love 239
Eccentricity 237
Echelon 1480
Eclaircie 547
Ego 734
Egyptian Queen 1015
Eishin Eleuthera 501
Ejlaal 606
El Morocco 946
Ela Athena 1184
Ela Tina 744
Ela's Giant 1529
Elegant Pride 921
Elegant Ridge 797
Elegant Times 324
Elfin Laughter 1591
Elidore 550
Elitista 1431
Ellanova 1325
Elle Nicole 1220
Ellen 1551
Elutrah 1543
Embassy 1665
Embassy Belle 748
Embers Of Fame 285
Emerald Peace 1552
Emily Blake 716
Eminence Gift 1548
Emirates First 1289
Emma's Star 1382
Emouna 1136
Emperice 686
Enchanted Princess 948
Enchanting Way 920
Encouragement 822
Endis 735
Enforce 58
Enthused 222
Enticing 717
Epiphany 1178
Erne Project 1426
Es Que 496
Esterlina 1657
Eternal Beauty 1185
Eternelle 1541
Eternity Ring 172
Ethaara 689
Etica 316
Etizaan 56
Etizaaz 513
Evanesce 465
Evangeline 762

Ever Rigg 1450
Evil Empire 604
Ewenny 349
Exciting Times 1308
Exhibit One 470
Exorcet 34
Expectation 1140
Extravagance 456
Eyrecourt 1099

Fabuleux Cherie 857
Fabulous Fairy 915
Fabulously Fast 1206
Fading Away 297
Fag End 740
Fairnilee 101
Fairy Of The Night 699
Fall Habit 538
Fame At Last 1646
Fame Game 664
Family 344
Fandangerina 665
Fanny's Fancy 1514
Fantastic Account 1074
Fantastic Santanyi 1106
Fantastic Spring 705
Faraday Light 885
Farbenspiel 906
Farthingale 1455
Fascination Street 671
Fashion Statement 1315
Fashion Trade 634
Fathoming 796
Fawaayid 738
Feather Boa 289
Feet Of Flame 1107
Fen Guest 1089
Fernanda 1668
Fernlawn Hope 895
Ffestiniog 43
Fidelio's Miracle 802
Finlaggan 110
Finnmark 1412
Firebelly 322
First Approval 941
First Fantasy 1035
First Glimmer 849
Flamanda 726
Flames 577
Flamingo Guitar 936
Flash Of Gold 332
Flashing Green 610
Flashy Wings 1302
Flawly 1254
Floppie 14
Flor Y Nata 1386
Fluttering Rose 18

Neat Shilling 637
Nebraas 1660
Nebraska Tornado 1648
Needlecraft 617
Needles And Pins 489
Neutral 1273
Never A Doubt 52
Never Away 869
New Deal 192
New Morning 593
Next 1300
Nice One Clare 781
Nick's Nikita 729
Nidhaal 485 ✓
Night Frolic 1263
Night Gypsy 9
Night Haven 79
Night Of Joy 742 ✓
Night Over Day 299
Night Sphere 1194
Nightime 1678
Nihal 1053
Nitya 388
No Way 1464
Noble Desert 115
Noble One 700
Noble Pearl 919
Noodle Soup 1639
Nordhock 468
Northern Gulch 1228
Northern Mischief 1037
Novellara 219
Now it Begins 969
Noyelles 839
Nubar Lady 1459
Numerus Clausus 139
Nuriva 894

Oatcake 193
Ocean View 387
Oh Hebe 819 ✓
Olaya 882 ✓
Olympia Theatre 790
Ommadawn 452
On The Nile 1465
Onda Nova 683
One So Wonderful 1020
Openness 1456
Opera 81
Opera Babe 352
Ornellaia 562
Ossiana 197
Ouija Board 490
Our Faye 985
Our Little Secret 78
Our Sheila 1112
Out Of Time 1313

Oval Office 1443 ✓
Overruled 660

Pairumani Princess 483
Palace Weekend 1483
Palatine Dancer 48
Palmeraie 1021
Pan Galactic 525
Paquita 131
Paradise Isle 69
Parakopi 711
Paris Glory 1150
Park Acclaim 300
Party Feet 1609
Parvenue 326
Passage Of Time 241
Passarelle 370
Peace Lily 950
Peace Time 638
Peaceful Kingdom 568
Peak Maria's Way 1043
Peeress 1477
Pelican Key 1453
Pelican Waters 998
Penang Pearl 899
Penny Cross 918
Penny Ha'Penny 1404
Peppermint Green 1165
Perdicula 1086
Perfect Partner 301
Perfect Touch 614
Perils Of Joy 1085
Perovskia 130
Persian Sea 1518
Perugia 783
Peshawar 1134
Petite Maxine 15
Petite Spectre 838
Phantom Waters 508 ✓
Phillippa 952
Phoebe Woodstock 1603
Photogenic 1338
Pinacotheque 1409
Pink Sovietstaia 1081
Piquetnol 1215
Pivotal Drive 1633
Pizzicato 579
Play Bouzouki 62 ✓
Playful Act 591
Plenty Of Sugar 888
Pointed Arch 417
Polar Cirlce 218
Poldhu 537
Polished Gem 1645
Polite Reply 1649
Politesse 718
Pompey Girl 393

Pontressina 411
Popolo 311
Poppets Sweetlove 1146
Poppo's Song 293
Poppy Carew 667
Portelet 868
Portmeirion 1174
Portrait Of A Lady 278 ✓
Postage Stampe 1446
Posterity 1666
Poyle Caitlin 1424
Prairie Sun 467
Prayer 491
Precipice 1329 ✓
Precipitous 152
Preference 1539
Pretty Face 100
Pretty Meadow 206
Pride Of My Heart 366
Prima Luce 1022
Primissima 427
Princess Danah 1454
Princess Ellis 6
Princess Georgina 680
Princess Kris 1490
Princess Sabaah 982
Princess Serena 228
Princess Sofia 128
Princess Speedfit 1052
Private Life 1023
Private Whisper 972
Promising Lead 1502
Prowess 88 ✓
Psychic 1113
Pure Gold 353
Purple Tiger 1510
Purring 1175
Puya 204

Qasirah 1587 ✓
Qilin 1534
Quad's Melody 30 ✓
Quadrophenia 559
Quantum 182
Queen Cleopatra 1230
Queen Of Deauville 444
Queen's Best 1519
Queen's Logic 1297
Queen's Pudding 792
Queenie 1356
Queeny's Princess 953
Quenched 625
Query 1405
Questama 1026
Quickstyx 751

Radiancy 1350

Cap o Bales   Al Zaroni   eny winning 1m mdn Kempton
                            won again 1m cl 4 Salisbury

Van der Meer   Hannon   von v.gd 1.5 mdn Yarmouth debut

Hen Duke   E.Burke   hosed up 7f cl 4 mdn Ayr
Mootajan   Botti   easily win Mill Reef
Pace and Status Boiling   won gd   7f cl 4 mdn Newbury